Thomas Wyatt

THOMAS WYATT

The Heart's Forest

SUSAN BRIGDEN

faber and faber

First published in 2012
by Faber and Faber Limited
Bloomsbury House
74–77 Great Russell Street
London WC1B 3DA

Typeset by Faber and Faber Limited
Printed and bound by TJ International Ltd, Padstow, Cornwall

A CIP record for this book
is available from the British Library

ISBN 978–0–571–23584–1

2 4 6 8 10 9 7 5 3 1

To John and David

Contents

CONTENTS

Wyatt's Words

A NOTE ON TRANSCRIPTION

To keep a measure of the distance between then and now, between him and us, his language of heart and mind and ours, in all that follows Thomas Wyatt's words in his letters and his verse are kept very close to the original scribal version, sometimes his own autograph. Grammar, punctuation and spelling were not yet fixed. We will find that, in his travels, even Wyatt's name was mutable – Wiot, Wiat, Wyett, Vugiat, Wyato, Guiett, Huyet. Hoping to come closer to him in his 'lonely strangeness', I have transcribed poems from the manuscripts most closely associated with him. Reading him in his own English, in his spelling, with his punctuation, or lack of it, may be more challenging, but is the way to find him as he was, 'revolutionary and alive'. That is the judgement of one poet upon another, of Alice Oswald upon Wyatt.[1] To hear Wyatt's authentic voice in his poetry we need to listen for the breaks and silences which seem to argue and reply. Each pause and stress has traction. He is best read aloud, as his poems were probably first read among his friends. 'Learn but to sing it,' wrote one of the courtly company.[2] Writing his *Defence*, to save his life, Wyatt insisted that in reporting his speech the change of even a syllable made a great difference. So every transposition may be a traduction. In what follows copies of pages from the manuscripts sometimes face the transcriptions to show the original version, or Wyatt's version into which his contemporary editors intruded. The roughness of Wyatt's translation of *Plutarckes boke of the Quyete of mynde* reveals the urgency of the circumstances of its composition, but also the arrogance of a young man in a hurry. Its preface warns: 'It shall seme harde unto the paraventure, gentyll reder, this translation, what for shorte maner of speche, and what for dyvers straunge names in the storyes.' Nevertheless, there was no concession: anyone who would not persevere, 'I wolde he shulde nat rede this boke. Farewell.'

In this book Wyatt's intransigence is tempered. Any editorial change may compromise the text but may also make it less rebarbative. Contractions and abbreviations have been silently expanded, *ff* becomes *F*, and *i* and *j* and *u* and *v* have been given their modern forms. Wyatt's virgule – / – becomes a comma, and his ampersand – *&* – becomes 'and'. Scribal flourishes are eliminated. Since punctuation imposes certainty where Wyatt often meant ambivalence, I have intruded none, leaving the syntax sometimes uncertain, as he intended. Here the indentation, line breaks and capitalization almost always follow the manuscripts. Wyatt's *The Quyete of mynde*, and his *Declaration* and *Defence*, written at moments of danger, with his heart in press, follow the same rule of modernization as his verse. His diplomatic letters to his king and to Thomas Cromwell, exercises in persuasion, are extensively quoted in later chapters, and although they, too, were written under great pressure, inward and outward, they are modernized here in the interests of some narrative flow. This book is to be read alongside Jason Powell's splendid new edition of Wyatt's prose works, *The Complete Works of Sir Thomas Wyatt the Elder*, vol. i, which is forthcoming. Wyatt's friends and 'back friends', the envious enemies, whose story this is also, are reported in modern English.

List of Illustrations

COLOUR

Forget Not Yet

Thomas Wyatt was the prisoner of memory, the memory that was the territory of guilt and self-judgement. He would be compelled to remember what he tried to forget. In the Tower, twice, suspected of treason to King Henry VIII, he was forced to recall the confusions and terrors which had led him to uncorrectable mistakes. 'God knowethe', he wrote despairingly, 'what restles tormente yt hath byne to me sens my hether commynge to examen my selffe, perusinge all my dedes to my remembraunce.'[1] Possessing secrets that made him vulnerable, he testified, knowing that his testimony was likely to be fatal, either to himself or to his friends. For Wyatt, as for every sinning Christian, sins could not be forgotten when recording them was the way to repentance, confessing them the sign of the 'heart returned' to God. Paraphrasing the Penitential Psalms, perhaps after some great personal dislocation, he followed the Psalmist's painful process of re-membering and forgetting, and wrote divine poetry consonant with the penitent David's singing with his harp, his 'faithful record'. The Psalmist, sleeping, waking, is tormented constantly by 'chastysinges' of sins past, feeling the pain in his heart, the seat of emotion, the organ of compunction:

> filld with offence that new and new begyn
> with thowsand feris the hart to strayne and bynd.[2]

In Wyatt's life, and in poetry which framed the pressures of his time and circumstances, the image recurred of the wound which might heal, while the scar never faded, a biblical image which carried a warning about the danger of secrets betrayed.[3] Horrors not to be told nor ever excised from the mind's eye harrow Wyatt's anguished speaker, recalling what he saw from a grating in the Tower:

1

the bell towre showid me suche syght
that in my hed stekys day and nyght.[4]

The lover, looking back on his former self deluded and captive to love, laughs himself to scorn.[5]

Time past, the distance between 'sometime' and now, a vision of what was once – 'whilom', 'erst', 'quondam' – and what might have been, of loss and mutability haunt Wyatt's love poetry, where his speaker remembers past happiness from present pain. Memory is freighted with disillusion. Moments of bliss, undying promises, pillow talk, are not beyond recall while the faithful lover remembers, even though the faithless beloved forgets.

> Love and fortune and my mynde remembr[er]
> of that that is nowe with that that ben
> *Wyat*   do torment me so.

Here the mind is the re-memberer, reconfigurer of the dismembered, restlessly reminding itself of what is lost. In the staccato, repetitive second line we find a brokenness which mirrors grief.[6] Even the lover's bed may be for him 'remembrer of my wo'.[7] In 'Quondam was I in my Ladys gras' – once in her grace, but no longer – the mordant voice so characteristic of Wyatt appears as the deceived, abandoned lover advises his successor:[8]

> Quondam was I she seyd for ever
> that ever lastyd but a short whyl
> promis mad not to dyssever
> I thoght she laugthe she dyd but smyl   *than quondam was I*
>   W

Imitating Petrarch's sonnet, *Rime* 189, in an extended metaphor, Wyatt compares the plight of the lover steered by his lord and enemy – Love – to a ship storm-tossed in dark, winter seas, veering between rock and rock, on a reckless course. The lover's galley is so laden with love that all else turns to forgetfulness, to oblivion:

> My galy charged with forgetfulnes
>   thorrough sharpe sees in wynter nyghtes doeth pas

	twene Rock and Rock and eke myn ennemy Alas	*also*
	that is my lorde sterith with cruelnes	
Wyat	And every owre a thought in redines	*oar*
	as tho that deth were light in suche a case	
	an endles wynd doeth tere the sayll a pase	
	of forced sightes and trusty ferefulnes	*recte: sighs?*
	A rayn of teris a clowde of derk disdain	
	hath done the wered cordes great hinderaunce	*wearied*
	wretched with error and eke with ignoraunce	
	The starres be hid that led me to this pain	
	drowned is reason that should me confort	
	and I remain dispering of the port	

Wyatt transmutes his source, and tellingly. Where in Petrarch's allegory an endless wind '*di sospir, di speranze et di desio* [of sighs, hopes and desire]' rips the sail, Wyatt imagines an oxymoronic 'trusty ferefulnes'. His guiding lights – the eyes of his beloved – are hidden from Petrarch's lover, who begins to despair of the port. For Wyatt's lover, too, the beloved's eyes are hidden, but they, like sirens, have 'led me to this pain'. Reason, his proper guide, is drowned. With a doubleness quintessentially Wyatt's, the lover either 'remains, despairing', or – more likely – 'remains despairing', condemned to never-ending despair. As so often with Wyatt, the speaker is caught, paralysed and impotent, and the reader suspended between two different meanings.[9] The name *Wyat* in the margin, here and in 'Love and fortune', and 'Quondam was I' with the initial *W* appended, were inscribed by George Blage, the friend of Wyatt's heart, loyal to him when others were not, who determined that Wyatt's name and his poetry should not be forgotten.[10]

In his life Thomas Wyatt fascinated his contemporaries. At his death in 1542 some knew what they had lost. A chorus of epitaphs, elegies, mortuary sonnets and funeral songs – a flood of melodious mourning for a poet, unprecedented in England and not seen again until the death of Philip Sidney – venerated Wyatt's life and the life of poetry. Lamenting Wyatt's loss, they acknowledged not only the example of his life, but that the writing of poetry was a way to honour. In verse

An excellent Epi-
taffe of Syr Thomas Wyat, With two
other compendious dytties, wherin are
touchyd, and set furth the state
of mannes lyfe.

Yat resteth here, that quicke coulde
neuer rest.
whose heuenly gyftes, encreased by
dysdayne
And vertue sanke, the deper in his
brest
Suche profyte he, of enuy could optayne

A Head, where wysdom mysteries dyd frame
Whose hammers beat styll in that lyuely brayne
As on a styth, where some worke of fame
Was dayly wrought, to turn to Brytayns game

A Visage sterne and mylde, where both dyd groo
Vyce to contempne, in vertues to reioyce
                                                        I.t.   Impd

Hans Holbein's woodcut roundel heading the Earl of Surrey's grave epitaph
represents Thomas Wyatt unswayed by the storms of Fortune

4

his friends and fellow poets might keep him in memory and preserve his fame from the ruins of time. Faithful to Wyatt and to their shared vision of poetry, Henry Howard, Earl of Surrey, a noble of princely aspiration, wrote an epitaph of austere and lapidary brilliance, and published it. At the head of this *Excellent Epitaffe* was Hans Holbein's woodcut roundel portraying Wyatt as the noble Roman, victor in life and in death. In thirty-eight lines for the years of Wyatt's life, Surrey laid out a blazon of his body and enumerated the 'heavenly gifts' of the prophet poet who had lived in a time unworthy of him.[11]

Wyat resteth here, that quick could never rest.
Whose heavenly gifts, increased by disdain
And virtue sank, the deeper in his breast
Suche profit he, of envy could obtain

A Head, where wisdom mysteries did frame   *hidden meanings*
Whose hammers beat still in that lively brain   *living*
As on a stithe, where some work of fame   *anvil*
Was daily wrought, to turn to Britain's gain

A Visage stern and mild, where both did grow
Vice to condemn, in virtues to rejoice
Amid great storms, whom grace assured so
To live upright and smile at fortune's choice.

A Hand that taught, what might be said in rhyme
That reft Chaucer, the glory of his wit   *deprived*
A mark, the which (unperfected for time)
Some may approach but never none shall hit:

A Tongue, that served in foreign realms his king
Whose courteous talk, to virtue did inflame
Eache noble heart a worthy guide to bring
Our English youth, by travail unto fame.   *travail; travel*

An Eye, whose judgement, no affect could blind   *affection, passion*
Friends to allure, and foes to reconcile
Whose piercing look, did represent a mind
With virtue fraught, reposed, void of guile.

A Heart, where dread yet never so impressed
To hide the thought that might the truth advance
In neither fortune lift nor so repressed   *lifted*
To swell in wealth, nor yield unto mischance

A valiant Corps, where force and beauty met   *strength*
Happy, alas, too happy but for foes.
Lived and ran the race that nature set
Of manhood's shape, where she the mould did lose

But to the heavens, that simple soul is fled.
Which left with such, as covet Christ to know
Witness of faith that never shall be dead *paraphrase of the Penitential Psalms*
Sent for our wealth, but not received so   *well-being*

Thus for our guilt, this jewel have we lost
The earth his bones, the heaven possess his ghost   *soul*

AMEN.

Surrey celebrated Wyatt in terms which he might have learnt from him and brought a grave posthumous certainty to what had been a tumultuous life. Here the restlessness which was part of Wyatt's nature and the expression of his unease was presented as a response to the humanist call to action. Virtue must be used for the public, and time and occasion seized.[12] Of undaunted virtue, Wyatt could rise above the envy of his enemies, even profit from it: so Plutarch had taught him. The Wyatt of the epitaph was no fool of fortune but, armed within and constant amidst storms, was like the man of 'valyaunt vertue' in his own translation of Plutarch's *The Quyete of mynde*, who lived 'mery and upright as it were with an hevenly grace'.[13] Surrey's Wyatt, whose mind was 'with virtue fraught, reposed, void of guile' and who lived 'Happy, alas, too happy', would instantly remind the classically educated of the virtuous man in the *The Quyete of mynde* who promised 'I wyll nat begyle', and of the farmers of Virgil's *Georgics*, who lived innocently, close to nature and far from the court's furies, happy if only they knew their blessings. (Such guileless labourers toil in the woodcut of the epitaph's initial capital.)[14] The life of Surrey's Wyatt, spent in self-immolating travel and travail in service of his king, would stand as a lasting example to England's

noble youth. Beyond fear or favour, Wyatt had spoken the truth, whatever the consequences. For Surrey, he had taught 'what might be said
in rhyme', and left a poetic legacy surpassing Chaucer's and unsurpass-
able; although 'unperfected for time', for he had died before complet-
ing the poetry he promised. 'That simple soul', 'this jewel', had fled to
Heaven, which deserved him as this world did not, leaving an undying
'witness of faith', his paraphrase of the seven Penitential Psalms.

Surrey's epitaph was laconic and impersonal, befitting its classical form. But he also wrote three mortuary sonnets bewailing Wyatt's
death, recording his own grief. In these Surrey claimed a privileged
intimacy with his fellow 'maker':

> But I that know what harboured in that head,
> What virtues rare were tempered in that breast,
> Honour the place that such a jewel bred,
> And kiss the ground where as thy corpse doth rest.[15]

While now 'in days of truth', Wyatt's friends sorrowed for the loss
of that 'rare wit' and of 'virtues rare' 'employed to our avail /Where
Christ is taught', his envious enemies, who had sought by spite and
'practise' to undermine and destroy him in life, wept crocodile tears
at his death, pretending a grief they did not feel. 'Divers thy death do
diversly bemoan,' wrote Surrey.[16] '*I that know* what harboured in that
head': Wyatt and Surrey had shared an esoteric knowledge and purpose – to create 'some work of fame' for 'Britain's gain'. They were the
'two chieftains' of a 'new company of courtly makers', poets writing
a new poetry for England. 'The two chief lanterns of light to all others that have since employed their pens upon English Poesy', judged
George Puttenham, the Elizabethan theorist of poetry, they were 'the
first reformers and polishers of our vulgar Poesy', 'the most excellent
makers of their time'.[17] In England, as in Spain and France, the enterprise of creating a new poetry would come to be seen as the shared
work of two men: in Spain there were Garcilaso and Boscán; in France,
Ronsard and du Bellay; in England, Sidney and Spenser.[18] But before
the Elizabethan prodigies there had been Wyatt and Surrey, the morning stars of the Renaissance in England.

Other friends mourned and honoured Wyatt. Thomas Chaloner, his servant and one of 'our English youth' whom Wyatt had brought 'by travail unto fame', wrote a Latin epitaph. Praising Wyatt's valour, his wit, his service to his country, his example to youth, Chaloner lamented that Wyatt's thousand virtues could not prevail against the envy of his detractors, but promised that his honour would transcend time. Like Surrey, he regretted a life ended too soon, a work left unfinished:

> *Sed fuit ô utinam semper fore illi Viatus*
> *Foelix, heu nimium foelix, tantum potuisset*
> *Extremam pulchre coeptis superaddere limam.*

> Oh happy as he was, to us so happy might he stay.
> Oh too, too happy so to pass; well (Wyatt) might thou live,
> With thy fair hand to thy fair works fair polishing to give.[19]

The writers of the epitaphs turn and turn again to Wyatt's restlessness in life, to the grace of his person, to what might have been, and to a fame which would live beyond death. For Sir Anthony St Leger, his Kentish neighbour:

> Though he be dead yet doth he quick appear
> by immortal fame that death cannot confound.[20]

In his *Naeniae* – funeral songs, in Latin – John Leland, friend of Wyatt's youth, bade him 'Farewell, beloved Wyatt, a long farewell'. He, too, presented a Wyatt who was indifferent to the promises which the world gave:

Nobleness of Mind

> Despite the ample gifts that Fortune brought,
>   He never swelled with pride, nor set his heart
> Upon the dazzling splendour of the Court,
> Nor on the noise of the great world, nor sought
>   A great man's favour – he chose the better part.

Adducing birds, people, places, divinities, elements to lament Wyatt's loss, Leland showed the Muses mourning:

8

> Though death may take his body,
> The spirit of Wyatt will live on forever.[21]

His friends lauded the Wyatt whom Wyatt had aspired to be. But there was another Wyatt. The restlessness which defined him was partly an effort to confuse himself in the present and confound the passage of time, and it left him 'wearied' – a term which recurs in his life and poetry – and distracted. Restlessness often turned to recklessness and valiant virtue to violence. As Wyatt would admit to his son, 'my foly and unthriftines that hath, as I wel deservid, broght me into a thousand dangers and hazardes, enmyties, hatreds, prisonments, despits and indignations' from which only God's grace had saved him.[22] He was guilty of crimes for which he never legally atoned. Condemned to stay in a marriage destroyed by betrayal, he was bound indissolubly to a wife he was never allowed to forget. This man educated to heroic action and to constancy of mind was led to desperate courses by the exigencies of fortune and by royal command. Wyatt was determined to speak truth to power, but what if that power were despotic and if fearful penalties awaited the messenger of unpalatable truths? In obedience to Henry VIII's terrifying will Wyatt pursued 'crooked diplomacy' and skulduggery, and imperatives of loyalty and survival would turn him into 'such an unscrupulous agent' of his king.[23] Royal service entailed long exile in foreign courts and all the longueurs and indirections of an ambassador's life: the boredom, the fatuities endured, the attempts to please in order to captivate and to influence. 'At other will my long abode my diepe dispaire fulfilles.'[24]

Evasion and dissimulation were part of diplomacy and its darker arts, and if they suited Wyatt's capacity for doubleness and were the politic side of his poetic power of allegory, they came at a price. As ambassador, a 'man sent to lie abroad for his country', Wyatt nevertheless longed to confide the truth, and sometimes appeared with his heart on his sleeve. He could not stay in Castile, he confessed, '*col cor contento perche e scotato* [with a happy heart because he is scalded]'.[25] At whatever cost, he lived through recriminative years with the moral consequences of his choices and of his shifting allegiances. Something of

9

that cost may appear in the Horatian verse epistles he wrote to and for particular friends. At foreign courts, fellow ambassadors described him as a malcontent, and observed this desperate, this *disperatissimo*, orator of the 'tyrant' King of England as he wrestled with fortune. The 'simple soul' and prophet–poet whom Surrey venerated, who pondered deepest questions of God's mercy and justice, was judged by the papal nuncio at the Emperor's court as *un maligno spirito* (an evil spirit), feared by a papal legate as his likely assassin, and investigated by the Holy Office, the Inquisition. And – though Surrey's epitaph hardly admits so – Wyatt, stern paraphraser of the Penitential Psalms, was also the most adept rhymer of courtly verse, effortlessly strumming the 'ditty of pleasure' for the court's delight.

Thomas Wyatt was supremely the poet of love, of 'the hartes unreste . . . / the pain therof, the grief and all the rest'.[26] Not that the love he described was necessarily his own or always heartfelt. At courts, talking endlessly of love, and love, and love again, courtiers wrote poetry as a form of social accomplishment, which might be 'not so much the baring of the soul as a heightened kind of social small talk'.[27] If we seek in Wyatt's poetry the self-conscious 'poet' musing inwardly in some ivy-clad grotto – 'his knee his arme his hand sustenid his chyn'[28] – or the Romantic egotistical sublime, we will be mistaken. He was not the lyric poet, directly expressing his personal thoughts and feelings, but often a 'maker' among 'makers', writing 'balets'[29] within a courtly tradition and convention for performance and iteration. Many of these balets – though how many is unknown – were meant for singing as well as reciting. There is no contemporary musical setting for Wyatt's verse, except for this song, which was already known at court before Wyatt wrote his version:[30]

> A Robyn
> Ioly Robyn
> tell me how thy leman doeth   *sweetheart*
> and thou shall knowe of myn

Mystery surrounds Wyatt the musician. The court looked to him for songs to set to music, yet while it might please us to imagine him as the poet–lover playing upon his lute, 'there is no evidence whatsoever that he had musical ability, as singer, lutenist or composer'.[31] If hearts were mutable, so were words, which were not written and claimed for all time by the autonomous author.[32] 'I lacked discretion/ to fasshion faith to wordes mutable', wrote Wyatt.[33] The coterie who read – or, more likely, listened to – his poems waited eagerly to copy (in a double sense) and transmute them.

Wyatt came to tire of rhyming the old plaints for the court's pleasure, and had far higher aspirations for poetry. For him, 'heroic humanism' was discovered not only in answering the call to action, but also in 'what might be said in rhyme'.[34] He was 'an experimenter', and it was Wyatt who introduced into English the sonnet, the epigram, the Horatian verse epistle, Wyatt who paraphrased the Penitential Psalms in terza rima, who dared to write ottava rima, the heroic verse form of Italy.[35] His fate as 'poet' – as in much else – was to be misunderstood, even traduced, and the misunderstandings of Wyatt's poetic intent began soon after his death. No canon or accepted corpus of Thomas Wyatt's poetry exists, nor is there likely to be an uncontested one. The only treasury of his verse which survives is to be found in the manuscripts which passed among his friends.[36] 'Finis quod Wyatt' [the end, said Wyatt]' – so they would write at the end of a poem which was probably his – but nothing was ended, for they ventured to reply and he might answer their response.[37] The contemporary manuscripts which enshrine Wyatt's verse take us very close to him. In these manuscripts the court's 'makers' and their muses inscribed not only his verse but also the anxieties of their lives, them against the world. In the Devonshire manuscript, a little courtly company who remembered poems which Wyatt may have recited to them, recorded them and answered them.[38] Two of Wyatt's friends and servants, apprentice poets themselves, were guardians of his flame: John Mantell and George Blage (or Blagge) owned a manuscript – usually called the Blage manuscript – where they copied his poetry with faithful intent, for themselves and for posterity.[39] Wyatt carried his personal poetry anthology, the Egerton manuscript, with him even, or especially, in embassy. Reading this manuscript, where Wyatt inscribed '*Tho.*' beside particular poems, and where we find his own hand, writing and rewriting, his own scribe and editor, takes us closest to him.[40] If Alexander placed in a rich ark the works of Homer, who 'sang' of imaginary adventures of 'heathen princes', Surrey asked:

> What holy grave, what worthy sepulture
> To Wyatt's Psalms should Christians then purchase?[41]

To his question Surrey returned no answer. That he chose to publish his epitaph for Wyatt – albeit anonymously – to make Wyatt's fame endure was a remarkable tribute from the proudest of the ancient nobility to a man who, though a 'jewel', a prophet with heavenly gifts, was far beneath him in rank and of tarnished reputation.[42] Surrey may not have imagined Wyatt's poetry forever fixed in print, not least because so much of it was unfinished, 'unperfected for time'. Wyatt himself may not have chosen to be published – perhaps chose not to be published.[43]

Thomas Wyatt wrote for his friends and fellow makers; wrote but also recited, and perhaps even played, and sang. If ever he dreamt of a distant posterity who knew his name, and Surrey's, as 'the first reformers' of English poetry, he would hardly have envisaged his collected verse in a slim, or less than slim, volume, with his the only name on the cover. Over time, editors have brought his verse from the courtly shadows into the light. Each exposure may involve a traduction. Extraordinary difficulties attend the editing of Wyatt's verse – even in knowing which were his poems, and which were not.[44] When the printer Richard Tottel decided, in the reign of Queen Mary, 'to publish to the honour of the English tongue' *Songes and Sonettes* of the most eloquent English 'makers' to rival those of Italy, 'the deep witted Sir Thomas Wyatt the elder's verse' was included and celebrated.[45] In order to aid the 'unlearned', who by reading might 'learn to be more skilful', Tottel decided to inject titles for Wyatt's poems – 'The lover complaineth the unkindness of his love', etc. Creating a romantic narrative for Wyatt's poetic persona, and suppressing any inwardness in the verse which went beyond love, Tottel invented an autobiography which Wyatt never wrote, never intended. Persistently smoothing his rougher rhythms, Tottel brought ease where Wyatt intended dis-ease.[46]

When he quoted and discussed one of Wyatt's sonnets, Puttenham warned 'ye may find a syllable superfluous':

> Like unto these, immeasurable mountains
> So is my painful life the burden of ire:
> For high be they, and high is my desire
> And I of tears, and they are full of fountains.

But, perceptively, Puttenham allowed 'we must think he did it *of purpose*, by the odd syllable to give greater grace to his metre'.[47] Wyatt, who knew the poetic theory of the Italian Renaissance, certainly knew the rhythms of a decasyllabic line, Italian prosodic principles, especially elision, and the rules for placing a caesura in verse in Romance languages. Yet he chose in his own complex rhythms to imitate the cadences of voice and feeling rather than achieve prosodic regularity.[48] When he revised his poems, the revisions were not always towards metrical smoothness, for different patterns accorded with his mood, and through roughness he might achieve the intensity and compression which are poetry's essence. No easy flow or 'riding rhyme' fitted his subject's unease or his purpose to disconcert and unsettle.[49] He lived – and nearly died – by the power of words, knowing the need to use them with absolute and exquisite precision. 'For in some lyttell thynge may apere the truthe', so he wrote in his *Defence*, writing for his life in 1541; altering even a syllable might 'mayke in the conceavinge of the truthe myche matter or error'.[50] With extraordinary originality, he played endlessly on words, turning them, framing them, forging them, filing them. One of Leland's funeral songs acknowledged:

Wyatt's File

> The English tongue was rude, its verses vile;
> Now, skilful Wyatt, it has known your file.[51]

Wyatt's poetry awaits its standard edition. His great nineteenth-century editor Dr George Frederick Nott collected some of the manuscripts and with remarkable erudition discovered the principal sources for the poetry and the lives of Wyatt and Surrey.[52] The edition of

Wyatt's *Collected Poems* (1969) by Professors Muir and Thomson introduced exciting discoveries and brought very many of Wyatt's poems
into view, in original orthography – too many, for they included many
poems which were not Wyatt's.[53] H. A. Mason wrote a whole book –
Editing Wyatt – relentlessly presenting 'the many hundreds of errors'
in their edition. But Mason himself committed the cardinal editorial
sin of rewriting Wyatt, inventing syllables where Wyatt meant none.[54]
Richard Harrier's *The Canon of Sir Thomas Wyatt's Poetry* (1975) prints
the poetry, unadorned, from the principal manuscripts, which he
describes. Professor Rebholz's edition, *Sir Thomas Wyatt: The Complete
Poems* (1978), is invaluable, for it provides a text of the poems most
likely to be Wyatt's, with indispensable notes. Yet here Wyatt's poems
are gathered according to form – rondeaux, sonnets, epigrams, ballades, etc. – in ways which Wyatt himself would not have recognised
and, presented in modern spelling, they are at once seemingly accessible and strangely distant.

This verse, with its shifting refrain, 'Forget not yet', 'Forget not this',
exists in a single version, only in the Devonshire manuscript. Eager editors claim it for Wyatt. 'The critics' – unnamed critics – 'are generally
agreed that this is one of Wyatt's most perfect poems although there is
no direct evidence of his authorship.'[55] So Wyatt's most perfect poem
may not, in fact, be by Wyatt.

> Forget not yet the tryde entent
> of suche a truthe as I have ment
> my gret travayle so gladly spent
>   Forget not yet
>
> Forget not yet when fyrst began
> the wery lyffe ye know syns whan
> the sute the servys none tell can
>   Forgett not yett
>
> Forget not yet the gret assays   *trials*
> the cruell wrong the skornfull ways
> the paynfull pacyence in denays   *denials*
>   Forgett not yet

Forget not yet forget not thys
how long ago hathe ben and ys
the mynd that never ment amys
    Forget not yet

Forget not then thyn owne aprovyd
the whyche so long hathe the so lovyd
whose stedfast faythe yet never movyd
    Forget not thys

Here the speaker of the poem or the singer of the song reminds the beloved – lest she forget – of his long service, his weary life, his patient suit, his plighted 'truthe'; she knows since when, she has 'aprovyd' it. Though time passes, it brings no forgetfulness, to him at least.

Much of what follows is an exercise in retrieving what Wyatt would rather have forgotten – the disappointments and reversals, the times when he was overwhelmed by bewilderment and despair, the sadness, the dismay, the sense of unavailingness and of betrayal – as well as his achievements to be held in memory. So much will stand in the way of finding Wyatt: editors ascribing poems to him which may not have been his, interpolating caesurae where he wanted none and inventing easy rhymes which he had rejected; critics deeming private poems public ones; an historiographical tradition which finds him born where he was not born, educated where he was not educated; the imaginings of a romantic history which may be far from the one he lived; disapproving excisions of scholars shocked by his less than conventional life. We have his very own words, but they may often mislead us. Following him down diplomatic by-ways, reading his letters, we may fail to read between the lines. His poetic selves flee into the silences and obliquities of his verse, and his poetry 'speaks by not saying'.[56]

Wyatt is best found in translation, in the high and creative art of imitation, and he especially discovers himself in his transmutation of Petrarch. Imitating Petrarch, Wyatt was inspired to poetic alchemy, to write poetry of great invention and power. His translated sonnets bring Petrarch's 'original inside, into the distorted topography of the heart'.[57] The constraint and compression of the Petrarchan sonnet form held words in press, and led Wyatt to explore the possibilities of his own language.[58] At some time unknown, a scribe copied into the Egerton manuscript Wyatt's version of Petrarch's *Rime* 140.[59]

The longe love that in my thought doeth harbar   *enduring lodge, encamp*
  and in myn hert doeth kepe his residence
  into my face preseth with bold pretence
  and therin campeth spreding his baner
She that me lerneth to love and suffre   *teaches*
  and will that my trust and lust negligence
  be rayned by reason shame and reverence   *reined; reigned*
  with his hardines taketh displeasur   *audacity*
Wherewithall unto the hertes forrest he fleith
  leving his entreprise with payn and cry
  and ther him hideth and not appereth
What may I do when my maister ferethe
  but in the feld with him to lyve and dye
  for goode is the liff ending faithfully

Here Wyatt is writing 'perfect decasyllabic poetry', finding an English metre to imitate the Italian.[60] Obedient to Petrarch's structure and rhyme scheme – the complex structure and relationship of octave and sestet within fourteen rhymed lines of equal length, the two quatrains within the octave, the *volta*, the turn, which gave new impulsion at the end of the eighth line, the rhyme scheme (except that he ends with a couplet), translating the second quatrain almost literally – Wyatt has nevertheless utterly transformed the mood and inwardness of Petrarch's sonnet.

Amor, che nel penser mio vive et regna
e 'l suo seggio maggior nel mio cor tene,
talor armato ne la fronte vene;
ivi si loca et ivi pon sua insegna.

Quella ch'amare et sofferir ne 'nsegna
e vol che 'l gran desio, l'accesa spene
ragion, vergogna, et reverenza affrene,
di nostro ardir fra se stessa si sdegna.

16

Onde Amor paventoso fugge al core,
lasciando ogni sua impresa, et piange et trema;
ivi s'asconde et non appar più fore.

Che poss'io far, temendo il mio signore,
se non star seco infin a l'ora estrema?
ché bel fin fa chi ben amando more.

Love, who lives and reigns in my thought
and keeps his principal seat in my heart,
sometimes comes forth all in armour into my forehead,
there camps, and there sets up his banner.

She who teaches us to love and to be patient,
and wishes my great desire, my kindled hope,
to be reined in by reason, shame, and reverence,
at our boldness is angry within herself.

Wherefore Love flees terrified to my heart,
abandoning his every enterprise, and weeps and trembles;
there he hides and no more appears outside.

What can I do, when my lord is afraid,
except stay with him until the last hour?
For he makes a good end who dies loving well.[61]

Petrarch's sonnet is an allegory on the theme of unrequited desire, on indiscretion and the danger of incurring the displeasure of the beloved by allowing feelings to show. Love was war, the lover a warrior. Love, a military commander, '*talor* [sometimes]' sallies armed from his redoubt in the lover's heart into the forehead, and there unfurls his banner, ritually proclaiming his devotion. '*Quella* [she]' is Laura, the beloved, whose virtue will never allow her to respond, whose presence is figured in the extremity of '*l'ora estrema* [the last hour]'. Repulsed, routed, the coward Love '*paventoso fugge al core* [flees terrified to the heart]', there to hide, weeping, trembling.

Petrarch wrote an allegory, but Wyatt writes a metaphor, and a metaphor-within-a metaphor.[62] Petrarch's beloved, Laura, loved in life and in death, is known through the devotion of his whole poetic sequence, but Wyatt's sonnet identifies no beloved, which further isolates the lover in his suffering. The love of his lover, too, is a 'longe love', enduringly encamped in his mind, abiding in his heart, but when his lover ventures to declare it 'with bold pretence' and to press his claim, it is not 'sometimes' or 'at times', and this foray, this 'hardines' seems to be Wyatt's lover's last stand. At the turn from the octave to the sestet, the sonnet's reader may expect the unpredictable, and here finds it. In his eleven-syllable ninth line, Wyatt emulates the Italian hendecasyllable and, perhaps playing on the Italian *core* (heart) and *fore* (outside), conjures a remarkable image. His lover flees 'unto the hertes forrest'. The wilderness and hiding place of the forest is brought from the outside inside, into the heart. The forest, though seeming sanctuary, is also a place of bewilderment and danger, to which outlaws flee, to no certain safety. In Wyatt's time, the forest was the preserve of kings, the haunt of huntsmen. For every courtly lover the doubleness of the beleaguered hart/heart – like that of the precious deer/dear – was second nature. 'The hertes forrest', this metaphor of reflexivity and confusion, takes us close to Wyatt.

In Wyatt's 'What no perdye', as so often in his poetry, his lover, steadfast while the lady is inconstant, painfully strives to forget the 'thing' that once was pure.[63]

> [. . .]
> Tho that with payn I do procure
> For to forgett that ons was pure
> Within my [heart] shall styll that thyng
> Unstable unsure and waveryng
> Be in my mynd withowt recure   *remedy*
>
> What no perdye   *by God*
> Fynys quod Wyatt   *the end, said Wyatt*

Here Wyatt plays on the shifting meanings of that word which should, above all others, be constant. Within his lover's heart 'that thyng/ Unstable unsure and waveryng' will stay 'still'. 'Still': always, the quality of abiding, of being quiescent, silent, unperturbed; or having the power to quiet, to subdue, to soothe or relieve pain.[64] Within

his mind there will be no such remedy. Inscribing this poem in the
Devonshire manuscript, replacing the word, the scribe drew a heart
bewildered in a forest of words, and within the heart he hid a face.

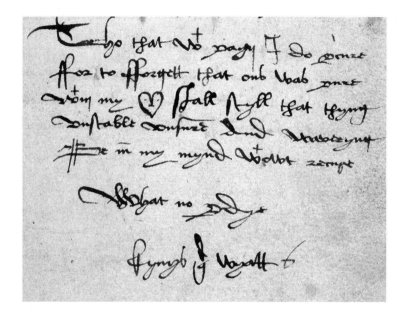

PART I

What Vaileth Trouth?

They fle from me / that sometyme did me seke
with naked fote stalking in my chambre
I have sene theim gentill tame and meke
that nowe are wyld and do not remembre
that sometyme they put theimself in danger
to take bred at my hand & nowe they raunge
besely seking with a continuell chaunge

Thancked be fortune it hath ben othrewise
twenty tymes better but ons in speciall
in thyn arraye after a pleasaunt gyse
when her lose gowne from her shoulders did fall
and she me caught in her armes long & small
therwithall swetely did me kysse
and softely saide dere hert howe like you this

It was no dreme I lay brode waking
but all is torned thorough my gentilnes
into a straunge fasshion of forsaking
and I have leve to goo of her goodenes
and she also to vse new fangilnes
but syns that I so kyndely ame serued
I would fain knowe what she hath deserued

20   18
18   18

2
4

400
18 + 18/18 = 36

400 + 188 = 368

188 = 368 - 400

Wyatt writes his name – *'Tho.'* – beside 'They fle from me'

They Fle from Me

Inscribed in Thomas Wyatt's personal manuscript is this poem, in the margin, his name '*Tho.*' in his handwriting.[1] To read it, perhaps aloud, is to know why all that follows is a quest for Wyatt in his world.

> They fle from me that sometyme did me seke
> with naked fote stalking in my chambr
> I have sene theim gentill tame and meke
> that nowe are wyld and do not remembr
> that sometyme they put theimself in daunger   *subjection; in another's power*
> to take bred at my hand and nowe they raunge
> besely seeking with a continuell chaunge   *busily*
> Thancked be fortune it hath ben othrewise
> twenty tymes better but ons in speciall
> *Tho.*   in thyn arraye after a pleasaunt gyse   *style; fashion*
> When her lose gowne from her shoulders did fall
> and she me caught in her armes long and small
> therewithall swetely did me kysse
> and softely saide dere hert howe like you this
> It was no dreme I lay brode waking
> but all is torned thorough my gentilnes
> into a straunge fasshion of forsaking
> and I have leve to goo of her goodenes
> and she also to use new fangilnes
> but syns that I so kyndely ame served   *according to the law of nature; kindly*
> I would fain knowe what she hath deserved.

This poem seems to speak to us with a colloquial directness. Yet the words hold myriad and mutable meanings. The antiphonic play of Middle English and Romance words tells of a deep preoccupation of a poet caught between two worlds. Old and Middle English 'kyndely', 'tame' and 'meke' might have seemed more stable, more trustworthy than Old French and Latin 'gyse', 'gentill' and 'fortune', with their double meaning and fickleness. Language changes from age to age, words alter their meanings, and the seemingly familiar must be estranged in order to discover the contemporary sense.[2] Even the emotional world the poem presents may now be inaccessible. All is not what it seems.

'They fle from me': who are *they* who flee? Whoever they are, they are also in flight from us, forever fugitive, anonymous in the dark, inner world of the poem, though intensely known to the narrator, and perhaps even recognisable to those for whom it was written, to whom it was first read.[3] Whether the figures are male or female, or male and female in collusion, we never know, but in this erotic venery they are creatures close to an unrefined nature. In the universe of the poem, the narrator's chamber, these figures once stalked, walking softly, stealthily, but with ominous intent. Once kind, gentle and gentled, they dared to approach him, to place themselves at his mercy, in his danger: his was the power, theirs the subjection. 'Gentle', so resonant and multivalent a word, carries ideas of gentle birth and behaviour as well as of tameness, so strangely at odds with the incipient menace of these fleeing figures, now grown 'wild'. 'Wild' – a word with no certain, primary meaning – here implies shy, untamed, unruly, reckless, wayward, but 'wild' resonates, too, with the suggestion of sexual passion.[4] They roam free, altering their attachment, inconstant, disloyal: 'and now they raunge/ besely [busily] seeking with a continuell change'. At this time 'change', like 'novelty', implied not improvement, but subversion and inconstancy.[5] In this mutation, the power and the menace have shifted from the 'I' of the poem to 'them', whoever 'they' are. That their potential to hurt may lie in love and desire may be assumed from the intimacy of their 'stalking' and tentative trust, by the physicality of their 'naked' feet, and by the stanzas which follow. But the body parts, so intimately known, are strangely disembodied – foot, hand, shoulders, arms, and never a face. There is a heart, but a figurative one.

The 'she' of the second stanza is one of 'them', of their fleeing, forsaking kind. But once – 'sometime', one time, 'ons in speciall' – it had been 'othrewise'. 'Thancked be fortune', it had been twenty times better: but better to beware thanking Fortune, the most fickle female of all.

Picture the lady 'in thyn arraye after a pleasaunt gyse', a guise which, to the wary, may also be disguise. A lost moment of intimacy is recalled. We glimpse the loveliness of the mistress and the tenderness of her kiss, overhear her whispered endearment: 'dere hert, howe like you this?' The 'this' which rhymes with kiss makes every reader a voyeur in the tiny everywhere of the chamber, and the desire of the lovers reaches down the centuries, or seems to. Yet the male desire may be a failing, faltering one, his passivity shown in all the passive verbs.[6] The lover's allusion to a dream that 'was no dreme' evokes the erotic dream vision of late medieval lyric, where a poet describes the dream where his lady is 'kind' to him, and his waking disenchantment. Here that vision is evoked, but denied: '*It was no dreme* I lay brode waking'.[7] This stanza presents a different, turning, emotional world, and a 'straunge fasshion of forsaking'. It is the narrator's 'gentilnes' – his kindness, his nobility, his code of honour – that has caused the change. By a covenant of mutual dismissal, he has 'leve to goo of her goodenes', and she to 'use new fangilnes'. Such 'new fangilnes [delusive novelty]' – in love, in faith – will destroy all the old certainties.[8] Though free to leave, he has not left; free to be unfaithful, she may come and go. There is no greater sorrow, of course, than to remember lost happiness in unhappiness. The figures in the poem are poised between 'sometime' and 'nowe', between remembering and forgetting, wildness and tameness, approach and retreat, domination and submission, dreaming and waking, leaving and unleaving. Seeking 'to accorde two contraries' is characteristic of Wyatt the 'maker'.[9]

Behind the narrator's assertion of his lover's 'goodenes' lies the imputation of the contrary. Bitter sarcasm invades to undermine both her 'goodenes' and his 'gentilnes'. These are not the raptures of romantic love. The poem ends with the narrator vengeful, bespeaking his disillusion and pain, and posing a question which is hardly rhetorical: her false faith deserves betrayal in turn.

> but syns that I so kyndely ame served
> I would fain knowe what she hath deserved.

This question takes us to the real world of Henry's court and to Wyatt's companions there, for in an earlier version of the poem, made at some time unknown, a group of noble friends and lovers – and for them 'friend' might be lover, and 'lover' a friend – had read a different ending. In their version the question which the lover directs inward to himself is turned outward:[10] 'What think *you* bye this that she hath deserved?'

The 'you' who might provide the answer were the little company for whom Wyatt first wrote and recited. Perhaps they might have conjectured the distance of the forsaken lover – the 'I' of the poem – from his creator, could have judged the inconstant mistress, construed this 'straunge fasshion of forsaking'. Among the audience there might even have been a real forsaking mistress, to whom a lover–poet had spoken the Rubicon words of love, who would recognise her own 'new fangilnes'. For this audience, the 'they' who fled, who 'sometime', 'once' had sought, were perhaps not beyond knowing. They were the 'company of lovers' at Henry VIII's court, some of them 'makers' themselves.

This poem's concluding play on words – 'serve' and 'deserve' – takes us to the heart of the life at this court, where 'service' was the promise of every courtly lover to his mistress, and of every courtier to his king. 'Serving' and 'deserving' were a constant refrain in this courtly verse, and playing upon words their endless pastime.[11] The 'game of love', in which everyone at least pretended to love and serve, was the fiction whereby they comported and disported themselves, even and especially in the heartland of power and politics.[12] The heart of the 'I' in 'They fle from me' has been broken precisely because he made literal the posture of love, and turned the game into reality. In the conventions of courtly love and service the lover promised to serve his lady faithfully, with no hope of a consummation beyond her chaste grace and favour, while the lady, guarding her honour and chastity as dearer to her than life itself, must be 'pitiful' to the pains of the plaintive lover. In *The Castle of Love*, a chivalric romance dedicated to the 'gentleness' and 'goodness' of a leading lady at Henry's court, when the 'pitious passion' of Princess Laureola 'surmounted her discreet dissimulation' it led to her shame and suffering. Though distancing herself from Leriano's entreaties of love, as honour demanded, Laureola's compassion impelled her pity.[13] In time, in the real life of Henry's court, we will find his pitiful fifth queen interceding to save Wyatt.* At court, women were caught between the domestic and patriarchal imperative of chastity and the adjurations of courtly love to dalliance, to love, even to adultery; they were torn between injunctions to keep distance and silence and pleas for pity and love. They trod the finest line between gracious generosity and dishonour.[14] Wyatt's wife, Elizabeth Brooke, would break the bounds of courtly behaviour.

The life to which the courtly literature belonged was also formed by it. Courtiers grew up reading 'long tales of great delight',[15] and learnt to pattern their own lives and loves upon those of great lovers of the past. Above all, Chaucer – 'I, that God of Love's servants serve' – taught them the art of love and was the master of its language.[16] The tragic love of Troilus and Criseyde, their passion and their despair, resonated in the lives of Chaucer's readers. Writing to her father Sir Thomas More when he was immured in the Tower, Margaret Roper compared herself to Criseyde 'come to Dulcarnon, even at my wit's end'.[17] In the Devonshire manuscript, real lovers struggling to express poetically their own tormented emotions copied Troilus's exhortation to the company of lovers, seeing him, as they saw themselves, in a continuum of those who suffered the pains of love. As they visit his tomb, those happy lovers still favoured by the fickle goddess Fortune will recognise Troilus as their 'fellow' in love:[18]

> O ye lovers, that hygh upon the whele
> ben sette of fortune, in good aventure
> god grawnte that ye fynden aye love of stele
> and longe may yowr lyfe in joye endure
> but whan ye comen by my sepulture
> remember that yowr felowe resteth there
> for I lovyd eke, thowgh I unworthy were.

In the world of the versifiers of the Devonshire manuscript, love was not untouched by power and politics: as in Troy, love might lead to war.

Wyatt's homage to *Troilus and Criseyde* is resonant in the rhyme royale stanzas of 'They fle from me', and also in the language, especially

* For the pitiful queen, see below, pp. 546–7.

where he describes the bliss of the lovers. So his contemporary readers would have recognised.[19] But there had 'sprung up a *new* company of courtly makers' at Henry's court, with Wyatt as one of its 'chieftains'. It was not the existence of the company which was 'new', but the making of these makers.[20] While Chaucer still blazed in their imaginations, this 'new company' looked now to Italy. They paid homage first to Petrarch, as Chaucer had done, for Petrarch taught them how to write of love in their own vernacular. Puttenham described Wyatt and Surrey as 'the first reformers of our English metre and style', 'imitating very naturally and studiously their Master Francis Petrarcha'.[21] They looked also to their own beguiling generation of poets: to Alamanni and Aretino and Ariosto. In her copy of Ariosto's *Orlando Furioso* Mary, Duchess of Richmond, one of the principal lovers and scribes of the Devonshire manuscript, wrote her name and '*de malo en peggio*': from bad to worse, not only for the hapless lovers in this epic romance, but also for herself and her family.[22] For Wyatt's fellow 'chieftain', Henry Howard, Wyatt even transcended Chaucer, 'reft [deprived] Chaucer the glory of his wit'.[23]

Some were growing bored by the old game of love and beginning to question it. Real courtly mistresses might 'disdain' – a baleful word – plaintive lovers and their plaints. In the Devonshire manuscript, in the margin of a conventional love complaint – 'Suffering in sorrow', with its refrain 'to serve and suffer still I must' – one of the heartbreakers at court, Mary Shelton, wrote in her own hand refuting this tedious suit: 'ondesyard sarwes reqwer no hyar [undesired service require no hire]'.[24] Whether she wrote smilingly, teasingly, disdainfully, is hard to tell, but perhaps she responded to the challenge in 'Perdye I saide yt not':

> And as I have deservid
> so graunte me nowe my hire

This canzone was a free imitation of Petrarch, *Rime* 206. Whether it was by Wyatt is uncertain, but Tottel believed so.[25] Courtly love had as its purpose pastime – pass time – to while away the long hours of endless waiting which were the courtier's lot, and to keep chaste their friendships. Yet there was always the danger that the bounds of convention might be broken, that courtly lovers might become pressing and courtly mistresses pitiless; that courtly love might turn to real love, which would bring all romantic passion's malign attendants, jealousy, betrayal, revenge. Even 'grace' might come to imply erotic desire. The 'she' of 'They fle from me', so predatory and faithless, is far from the chaste pity of Princess Laureola.

Wyatt had also been a 'chieftain' of the *old* 'company of makers' at court. No one was more adept at the old game of love, nor rehearsed the typical love plaints more adroitly. It is because he wrote so many of his rhymes in such conformity to the conventions, plundering the same word-hoard and using the same refrains, that often we cannot know what is his, what another maker's. But over time he grew disillusioned with courtly love and its exhausted plaints, excruciatingly aware of its absurdities, tired of 'the sighs, the words and eke the languishment'.[26] And bored. Poetically, he renounced love: 'Farewell Love and all thy lawes for ever . . . goo trouble yonger hertes';

> Me list no more to sing
> of love nor of such thing[27]

Complaining about complaining about love had always been an essential part of the game,[28] but the intensity of Wyatt's cynicism and disillusion and his sardonic rejection of courtly idealism were different in kind. Now he not only mined the stock phrases, but undermined them. Now his imagined lover is forsaken, but with a '*straunge* fasshion of forsaking', and the mistress uses 'new fangilnes'. Wyatt would turn from prodigal, errant ditties of love, to sterner poetic forms and graver subjects.

'The starres be hid that led me to this pain', so the lover complained of his perfidious mistress in 'My galy [galley] charged with forgetfulnes'. Hiddenness and concealment were forced on Wyatt by the conventions in life and art in the courts he inhabited, and were, or became, part of his own nature. Secrecy was paramount for the star-crossed lovers of romance, who must hide or 'wray' their love, and conceal 'secret thoughts of the heart'. Love must be a 'secret glory', shared only by the lovers, or confided to one faithful friend.[29] 'Love . . . oughte

ben secree': so it had been for Troilus and Criseyde, and so for their
real 'fellows in love' at this later court.[30] The first line of the first poem
inscribed in the Devonshire manuscript was 'Take heed betime lest ye
be spied'. This decorum was needed partly to preserve the lady's honour and 'renown' (whether maiden or married), but there was another
imperative. Plainness and openness were not to the courtier's or the
courtly lover's purpose. Those who shared his 'freedom' – in their parlance, not freedom as liberty, but nobility and generosity – had a duty
of discretion, and spoke only to those who could decipher their hidden
meanings. The 'balet' itself was an essential part of this 'covert communication'. Although it might have been a private, inward musing at
the moment of its composition, it was uttered in public performance
among the court coterie: it had, 'or *pretended to have* a secret meaning',
was a confidence which was meant to be overheard.[31] Imagining its
performance is to eavesdrop upon the eavesdroppers.

In very many ways things at court were not as they seemed. So it was
intended, for if it was the purpose of the late medieval courtier to be
'covert', it was even more so for the courtier of the early Renaissance
whose achievement was to cultivate the discrepancy between being and
seeming.[32] The power 'to speak one thing and think another', so that
'our words and our meanings meet not', was the defining ability of the
courtier, to whom subterfuge was second nature and irony his characteristic voice. Mockery, sarcasm, scorn: 'all these be soldiers to the figure' of allegory – the 'Courtly' figure of speech – 'and fight under the
banner of dissimulation'.[33] In everything he did the courtier practised
a certain indirection in order to set himself apart from the 'common
trace'[34] and to communicate directly only with the like-minded, his
familiars. He cultivated obscurity and indeterminacy, a wit which only
fellow wits could decipher.[35] This was a self-defining game for insiders.
The supreme art of the ideal courtier, as taught by the perfect courtier
Baldassare Castiglione in *Il cortegiano* (*The Book of the Courtier*), was to
practise *sprezzatura*: '(to speak a new word) to use in everything a certain
disgracing to cover art withall, and seem whatsoever he doth and saith, to
do it without pain, and (as it were) not minding it'. *Sprezzatura* was not,
strictly speaking, a new word, but a new sense given to an old word,

meaning 'setting no price on'. It also implied the cultivation of sponta-
neity, a studied nonchalance.[36] The courtier was detached from the rest
of society not only by his isolation in the enclave of the court, nor by his
'gentleness' and his 'freedom', but by his 'grace' which sprang from this
very *sprezzatura*. When Sir Thomas Hoby came to translate *Il cortegiano*
into English in 1561 he had trouble finding the right word: 'disgracing'
was one attempt, 'recklessness' another.[37] The verb *sprezzare* meant 'to
despise'.[38] The courtier's seemingly effortless grace was to be compared
to the doltish exertions of dullards; his irony rested on the misunder-
standing of the credulous dupe as well as the sceptic's discernment.[39]
There was a dark edge to Castiglione's courtly perfection.

The courtier was most graceful, most pleasing when he displayed
the art which concealed art, and the gravest faults were to be obvious,
to be tedious. The art of poetry itself was predicated on the poet's
power to hint, to imply, and to 'delay, by indirection, the recognition of
his meanings'.[40] Wyatt himself was the acknowledged master of these
courtly and poetic arts. When Puttenham, later in the century, sought
to illustrate the use of the rhetorical figure *Irmus* in which the sense is
suspended until the very last words, he chose a verse of Wyatt's. Here
Wyatt's speaker is found 'restless', the characteristic state of Wyatt himself, rehearsing the quintessential themes of Wyatt's verse: [41]

> The restfull place Revyver of my smarte
> the labors salve incressyng my sorow
> the bodys ese and trobler off my hart
> quieter of mynd and my unquyet foo   *foe*
> Forgetter of payn Remembryng my woo   *woe*
> the place of slepe wherin I do but wake
> Be sprent with teres *my bed I the forsake*   *sprinkled*

In a verse epistle written for a friend Wyatt presented his courtly
speaker as 'wrapped within my cloak', the cloak itself both the garb of
the Stoic and a metaphor for disguise and concealment.[42] Wyatt, concealment's master, came to suffer from this courtierly art and to despair
of it. His speaker's failure to 'fasshion faith to wordes mutable' is also
Wyatt's own.[43]

Anyone wishing to enter the play world of the 'makers' encounters a further discordance. Amidst an admiring company of his own assumed, assured friends, the 'maker' ventriloquizes the forlorn, forsaken lover, abandoned by friends who 'sometime liked' his 'company'.[44] The plaint of unrequitement and betrayal is made within the 'company of lovers', who will especially feel the pain, whose own 'truth [allegiance]' is called upon. Among the 'company', the claims made upon 'faithful friendship' were so insistent – in art and in life – that they seemed to deny, even defy the possibility of its traduction. It was as though complaining of the forsaking friend might bind the company together, as though their own faithful friendship might be guaranteed by the presentation of its contrary.[45] The idea of faithful friendship preoccupied the 'honest friendly company' who often – as here – wrote anonymously in the Devonshire manuscript. 'What hurt [could] honest friendship bring?' one of the contributors asked, as though the answer must be 'None'. But friends held a terrifying power to hurt, because they shared secrets, because they overheard confidences and might 'bewray [disclose]' them:

> No staring eye nor harkening ear
> Can hurt in this except that she
> have other friends that may not bear
> In her presence: presence of me.[46]

At court it was not only rivalry in love which might sunder friendships, but rivalry in power and politics.

Behind this dissonance of the admired 'maker' singing of forsakenness among his familiars, there was another: that Wyatt, a man with, seemingly, so many friends had so few whom he could trust. His poetry was haunted by the fear of the forsaking friend. Again and again, his narrators present themselves as banished, deserted, unfriended, driven 'from compayne to live alone'.[47] Paraphrasing the Penitential Psalms, who but Wyatt would pun on heavenly 'fere' (companionship) and fear?[48] And in life, Wyatt's friends were less than constant. A friend reported to him, 'I never saw man that had so many friends here, leave so few perfect friends behind him.'[49] Many friends: an oxymoron. At

Wyatt's death, as his sorrowful friends venerated him, one wrote this last envoy:[50]

> When fortune favoureth and setteth a loft
> In high estate man for to reign
> Then all men cometh to him full oft
> And covets with him, for to remain
> His company none will disdain,
> Thus friends he getteth, many a one
> But if he fall, I say certain.
> Of all his friends then hath he none.

Yet perhaps an even greater fear than of the traitor friend was that the times might compel a man, against all faith and honour, to become that traitor friend himself. Wyatt, who prized friendship, also feared it, and betrayed it.

All this secrecy and indirection was part of the life at Henry's court before ever the King changed the rules of the 'game of love'. As at Castiglione's court in Urbino, 'under sundry coverts oftentimes the standers by opened subtly their imaginations unto whom they thought best'.[51] Henry himself had courted secretly, playing the part of his own secretary – bearer of confidences – writing secrets to his mistress: '*Escripte de la main du secretere qui en ceur, corps et volenté este vostre* [written by the hand of the secretary who in heart, body and will is thine]'.[52] In the 'game of love' at his court, Henry had played the lover, leading the revels, disporting himself as 'Cœur Loyal [Loyal Heart]', writing his own ballads which deployed all the conventional phrases and the tried, tired words of love. To the King's love-songs – songs of love written to be sung – his court had amused itself, happily enough, at first.

> O my heart, and O my heart!
> My heart it is so sore,
> Since I must needs from my love depart
> And know no cause wherefore.[53]

The King conducted his own love affairs with the kinds of riddles and love-conceits and playful presents which had always delighted courtly lovers. Sending venison to his lady – 'which is hart flesh for

Henry; prognosticating that hereafter God willing you must enjoy some of mine' – he presented a lumbering emblem which was presciently sanguinary. Anne Boleyn, the mistress whom Henry wooed so intensely, laughed becomingly at his jokes, and sent her own meaningful love tokens. '*Pour le beau diemende et navire, en quy la seulle damoyselle est tormenté* [for the splendid diamond and the ship in which the solitary damsel is tossed about]', he thanked her, but more for '*la belle interpretation et trop humble submission* [the pretty interpretation and too humble submission]'.[54] But in time Anne grew less submissive, and she and her brother George Lord Rochford, a go-between in this royal courtship, would laugh scornfully at the ballads which the King composed. Disdaining his declarations of love was a double and dangerous betrayal, of his art as well as of his heart, 'a great and grievous crime'.[55]

'*Tho.*' posed a riddle:

> **W**hat wourde is that that chaungeth not
> though it be tourned and made in twain
> it is myn aunswer god it wot
> *Tho.*   and eke the causer of my payn
> a love rewardeth with disdain
> yet is it loved what would ye more
> it is my helth eke and my sore   *welfare; safety*

Could the answer be: 'ama' – she or he loves? 'I ama yowrs' promised a doodler in the Devonshire manuscript.[56] However the word is turned, it remains the same. And does the mistress's love remain unchanging, too? Unlikely. Perhaps the answer to '*Tho.*'s riddle was the name of a lady; perhaps it was 'Anna', but which Anna? An answer answerless. These were riddling times for those who lived close to power, because discussing affairs which touched the King rarely allowed straight talking. Wyatt and his friends played endlessly upon words. Wyatt's very name was an anagram: WIAT, a wit.[57] They played on words as though their lives depended on it, even in their deepest despair. Anne Boleyn, hearing that Wyatt had joined her and her brother in an imprisonment that none of them was likely to leave alive, made puns. In her extremity of sorrow, sure that 'my lord my brother will die', she asked who would make their beds now and, playing on 'pallets [beds]' and 'balets', jested that they 'might make balets well now'. In the Tower, they were the most exclusive 'company of makers'.[58]

The 'game of love' at court turned deadly, as the King's domestic and dynastic trials tainted its life. Courtiers found new reasons for indirection. Well versed in Scripture and in the writings of classical antiquity, they remembered the inveterate warnings about the need for secrecy around kings. Learning rhetoric from Quintilian, who wrote in Rome under its tyrant emperors, they knew that if the danger involved in speaking against those in power 'can be avoided by any ambiguity of expression, the speaker's cunning will meet with universal approbation'.[59] Dissimulation became not only a matter of courtierly grace but also a tactic of survival, and plainness became perilous, especially after 1534, after the passage of a new Treason Act – 'the lawe of wordes', as Wyatt called it – by which words alone could incur the terrible penalties for treason.[60] 'It would be a strange world as words were made treason,' mused Lord Montague, yet this was the world in which they now lived, and died.[61]

Wyatt had owed his advancement to his arts of eloquence: his skill as orator determined his success as courtier and ambassador. In the Renaissance the ability to write and speak eloquently was considered powerful in itself. 'Now then who is he, at whom all men wonder . . . and count half a God among men: Even such a one assuredly, that can plainly, distinctly, plentifully and aptly utter both words and matter'.[62] No one was more painfully aware of the infinite and ensnaring power of language than Wyatt. So elusive a writer, who chose to leave his readers uneasily suspended between different meanings – 'twist ernest and game'[63] – was at last endangered by words. At a desperate moment Wyatt, the master of so many tongues, would be described as *'deslenguato'* – 'untongued' and, by extension, insolent.[64] On a distinction between syllables his life would hang in the balance, and in 1541 it seemed that he must suffer under the 'lawe of wordes'. Writing in self-defence in the Tower, he charged his enemies with misconstruing or misremembering his words and, with awful irony, insisted, 'Thiei lye and mysreporte the tale or els that I' – I, Wyatt – 'cane [not] speake Inglyshe.'[65]

The exigencies of love and politics and the tendencies of his own nature led Wyatt to be guarded and obscure. Yet the desire to be known – first to himself, but also to the few he trusted – preoccupied him. In an impassioned verse epistle – 'My mothers maydes when they did sowe and spyn' – Wyatt's speaker insists:

> make playn thyn hert that it be not knotted
> with hope or dred and se thy will be bare
> From all affectes whome vice hath ever spotted   *desires*
> thy self content with that is the assigned
> and use it well that is to the allotted
> Then seke no more owte of thy self to fynde
> the thing that thou haist sought so long before
> for thou shalt fele it sitting in thy mynde[66]

A tension deep within Wyatt himself, between the desire to make plain his heart and the will to concealment, makes the search for him more intriguing and more difficult. He is often fugitive as we attempt to follow, but he left clues enough, if only we could read them. Sometimes there are only shards of evidence and a few marsh lights which seem to lead to him, but at times we hear his authentic voice. His vivid presence and wit are refracted in the memories of his friends and of his enemies. Remembered conversations with him reveal a beguiling charm and confidentiality. His letters from embassy record his service at the courts of foreign princes, though these, too, were works of art, envoys filed and framed to persuade his prince, and these, too, would be edited and rescripted as they were read out to the King.[67] Abroad, his fellow ambassadors reported, fascinated, aghast, the actions of the '*orator d'Inghilterra*', the ambassador of the 'tyrant' King of England, and their letters are discovered in a dozen foreign archives. In the Tower in 1541, in the shadow of death, Wyatt wrote a rhetorical masterpiece, to vindicate himself against charges of treason. Portraits of Wyatt survive – though some are lost – which reveal an intense interest in his self-presentation. We know what stances he chose, what he looked like. A drawing by portraiture's master, Hans Holbein the younger, presents the quintessential Wyatt: eyebrow raised, the look askance, the sidelong glance. Another Holbein portrait presents him as the model of classical fortitude, the man who could 'smile at fortune's choice'.[68] Wyatt's letters of advice to his son, Thomas, remained models for admonitory fathers thereafter. Written with intimations of mortality, they describe a moral sobriety and an honesty to which his son should aspire, and from which he himself all too knowingly, regretfully fell short.[69] At a climacteric of the Reformation, and perhaps of his own life, thinking on the promise that God's mercy is greater than man's despair, Wyatt – doubting Thomas – paraphrased the seven Penitential Psalms. David's sublime poetry had for centuries provided consolation for sinners, but most lucubrations on the Psalms had been written by priests, not courtiers. But Wyatt not only contemplated David's 'deep secrets', but also rhymed them, in terza and ottava rima, 'witness of faith that never shall be dead'.[70]

Wyatt's verse seems saturated in the experience of a life lived so restlessly, so intensely.[71] Yet if we are tempted to believe Wyatt to be simply the 'I', the speaker in his poems, we misjudge him and them, and if we attempt to elide the poetic 'I' with him in his real life we may – as Chaucer and Wyatt might have expressed it – 'pipe in an ivy leaf'.[72] Even if we learn some of the conventions by which he lived, intercept letters, overhear confidences, penetrate the puns and paradoxes, estrange his language so that we read it right, there will still be barriers to entering his emotional world.[73] Yet the themes of 'They fle from me' are recurrent, and a sense of danger pervades Wyatt's most haunting poetry. Often he seems as alert to lurking menace as an animal sensing the soft footfall of a predator. And not every thought and circumstance is beyond recall. Sometimes we will hear the mordant laughter of Wyatt and his friends, or sense the mood and memory captured in his verse. Wyatt's life was not outwardly so different from that of many other courtiers at Henry VIII's court, and the lives and minds of some of them we will explore. Some were 'makers', too. Yet, alone among them, Wyatt was commemorated at his death as a moral and religious exemplar, and as *vates*, the prophet–poet.

At some time now indeterminable – as almost always with Wyatt's poetry – Wyatt wrote a verse epistle for 'Myne owne Jhon poyntz', the friend and mentor of his youth.[74] He ended it with an invitation full of irony:

> but here I am in kent and cristendome
>> among the muses where I do rede and Rime
>> Wher if thow lust my Poyntz for to come
> thow shalt be Judge how I dispende my tyme

Here he was, as so often, writing proverbially. According to proverb, Kent was never converted with the rest of England, was never truly part of Christendom. When Wyatt wrote, Christendom was broken, England was no longer part of it, and he knew that Poyntz might judge him harshly. We accept an invitation never meant for us, and seek Wyatt as he read and rhymed, among his friends in Kent and Christendom. We find him first, with Poyntz and other friends and fellows, at play as knights-errant at a courtly tournament, plotted as upon a tapestry.

2

The Castle of Loyalty

At Christmas 1524 the court was at Greenwich, Henry VIII's palace on the Thames. There the King 'of high courage and noblesse' devised a great feat of arms, one of the most splendid of his reign, and the last of its kind.[1] From early November the Master of the Revels had been planning the building in the tiltyard of a mock castle, twenty foot square and fifty foot high, painted with 'antique work' and defended by deep ditches and ramparts. So daunting was it that some thought it too dangerous to assault, that 'it could not be won by sport, but by earnest'. This was the Castle of Loyalty. Nearby on a mound guarded by a white unicorn, knights' shields and armour hung in a tree of chivalry.[2] On St Thomas's Day, 21 December, Windsor Herald proclaimed in the Queen's Great Chamber that the King had entrusted the Castle of Loyalty to four maidens of his court. Defenceless, the maidens had given its custody to a captain and fifteen gentlemen, who had departed their own 'far countries', drawn by the 'famous renown' of Henry's noble court. As in chivalric romance, these were 'strangers', knights-errant, 'evermore serving ladies' and following their knightly duty to defend the defenceless. Chasteau Blanche, their herald, proclaimed their challenge: they pledged themselves to defend the Castle against 'gentlemen of name and arms'. The unicorn bore shields declaring the four forms of combat: white for the joust, fought on horseback with lances; red for the tourney, fought on horseback with swords; yellow for the barriers, fought on foot with swords; blue for a general assault upon the Castle.[3]

On 28 December, the day following the feast of St John the Evangelist, six challengers appeared from the Castle of Loyalty to await all comers. Suddenly, two ladies mounted on palfreys rode into the tiltyard, leading two 'ancient' silver-bearded knights who petitioned the Queen.

Chasteau Blanche, the herald of the 'stranger' knights, proclaims their
challenge to defend the Castle of Loyalty

Although, they said, their youth was passed, 'courage, desire, and good
will' compelled them to break spears and attempt feats of arms, if she
consented. Queen Katherine of Aragon, the patron of chivalry at this
court, graciously assented. But the 'ancient' knights, like knights of
romance, came incognito; neither were the 'ladies' what they seemed,
but boys disguised. Now the knights discovered themselves – not old,
but in their prime, the pre-eminent champions of so many fantastic
tournaments, the King himself, aged thirty-four, and his brother-in-law
and brother in arms, the Duke of Suffolk.[4] On the first day's festivities
there were splendid feats of arms, but none more splendid than the
King's. As was customary, he carried the day.[5] At that night's celebrations sixteen maskers appeared, including the King, attired in cloth
of gold, tinsel and crimson velvet, 'cut, slit and tied very curiously'.
Scottish ambassadors, who had watched the day's events, marvelled

that Henry and his knights were so 'merry' in wartime, for 'the realm of France is not a realm to sport with, nor to mask with'. They were answered: their king cared not for the French King 'one bean'.[6] Such nonchalance was easier to pretend while the French King, Francis I, faced the troops of his great enemy, the Holy Roman Emperor Charles V. While their armies were encamped in northern Italy outside Pavia, the two rivals were distracted from any enmity towards Henry.

In the following days there were furious assaults upon the Castle of Loyalty. On 2 January 1525 Sir Francis Bryan and Francis Poyntz defended it with pike, target and sword. Sir George Cobham, George Herbert and John Poyntz marched against them, crying 'harr, harr'. 'Fierce was the fight.' The two within fought valiantly but were overmatched and the assaulters gained entry. 'I think', wrote Edward Hall the chronicler, 'there was never battle of pleasure better fought than this was.' Combat continued intermittently until 8 February, when the King tourneyed with Sir Anthony Browne, almost severing Browne's helmet, 'his strokes were so great'.[7]

The tourney between the challengers and defenders at the Castle of Loyalty

The flower of English chivalry came to display their prowess at the Castle of Loyalty. On the King's side rode those closest to him, either by blood or by his choosing, the closest to friends that a king could have.[8] Henry Courtenay, Earl of Devon, was his cousin, brought up with him in the royal household and, as Knight of the Garter, his sworn 'friend of friends and foe of foes'.[9] Then came Henry Pole, Lord Montague, and with him Thomas Manners, Lord Roos, both of Plantagenet royal blood.[10] Five unnamed knights followed. Riding with the nobles of ancient birth were men of the new service nobility: Sir Nicholas Carew, Master of the Horse, Sir Francis Bryan and Henry Norris, the King's Gentlemen of the Privy Chamber.[11] Lord Henry Percy, heir to the earldom of Northumberland, a prince of the north, had been invited to join the assault upon the Castle, to be on the royal team, and for his 'advancement to honour' he burned to take part. Beseeching 'my friends to help me . . . to save mine honour', he tried to borrow £150 to equip himself, an earl's ransom. But, in disgrace because of his 'folly' in pursuing a court lady whom the King desired, he was excluded from the tournament.[12]

If an earl's son longed to advance his honour, so much more did the 'stranger' knights who guarded the Castle. They were a glittering generation. Some of them would hardly be heard of again, but the names of others would burn brightly: Lords Leonard and John Grey, Sir George Cobham, William Carey, Sir John Dudley, Thomas Wyatt, Francis Poyntz, Francis Sidney, Sir Anthony Browne, Sir Edward Seymour, Oliver Manners, Percival Harte, Sebastian Newdigate and Thomas Calen.[13] These men, their friendships and their enmities, which their participation at the Castle of Loyalty helped to form, will be central to all that follows. Most of them were young, born at the turn of the century. In search of glory and favour at court, they came to the Castle of Loyalty with everything to prove. The Castle's very name was resonant to the knightly order, for loyalty – to chivalry itself, to brothers in arms, to their lord, to their sovereign, and to their lady – was their highest duty and aspiration.[14] Loyalty and service to the King was inculcated from childhood. At Henry's tournaments, his knights' banners bore their personal mottoes proclaiming '*loyaulte m'oblige* [Loyalty binds me]', '*loialment je sers* [loyally I serve]', '*loyaulte n'a peur* [Loyalty has no fear]'.[15]

The 'stranger' knights came not from 'far countries' but from the court, from Kent, and the shires around London where, as trusted knights and esquires of the royal household, they ruled under the crown.[16] Some of them, like their captain Lord Leonard Grey, had served in the French wars; some, like Sir Anthony Browne, Sir John Dudley and Sir George Cobham, had been knighted on the battle-field for their 'noble courage'.[17] Many of them still awaited the call to arms and to war for which they were born and for which the tourna-ment prepared them. These men who dazzled in the joust and tourney were trained from childhood to become the leaders of the noble and knightly bands which formed the royal army at war.[18] The right to vio-lence was the defining privilege of the knightly order, yet that military achievement and ability to attract a following made them potentially dangerous, a threat. It was the intent of kings to divert that violence from private quarrels and the pursuit of personal honour and to turn it to the royal service, and the tournament was a means to that end. The play world of the tournament lacked real war's bloody intent, but was its proving ground.

This tournament was a school of arms, fought by the rules, with the sword bated, with the cutting stroke rather than the deadly foin (thrust), yet it had terrors enough. None but the wildly brave, the gallant, the adept could venture to joust. To charge upon a galloping courser, bear the shock of a splintering lance, and still to stay in the saddle, a knight needed all his skill, his strength, his daring, his prowess.[19] In 1517 Nicholas Carew had appeared as the Blue Knight, bearing a lance twelve foot long and nine inches in diameter, the hero of the tilt, and it was in his tilting armour that he chose to be portrayed by Hans Holbein.[20] A knight never appeared more chivalrous than when upon his curvetting, prancing horse. Since the beginning of knighthood the horse was chosen as the beast with nobility and courage equal to the knight's.[21] 'What is a man but when he is on horseback?' Sir Laverock asked his unhorsed brother in Thomas Malory's *Le Morte D'Arthur*.[22] Only the virtue of the true knight could subdue the pride of the horse.

That was the point of the masque played at Windsor in June 1522 to entertain Henry's new ally Emperor Charles V, heir to Burgundian chivalry and, like the English King, proud of his horsemanship. Together they represented Amity. The French King was represented by a proud horse which would not be tamed until Amity sent Prudence and Policy, nor bridled until Amity marshalled Force and Puissance.[23] In the tiltyard was the prospect of honour which outweighed any danger, but the dangers were real. At the Shrove Tuesday joust in 1526, Francis Bryan would lose an eye to a splintered lance, and several times Henry himself lay senseless after a fall, leaving his opponent to contemplate the consequences of injuring his king, even in sport.[24]

Prowess was only one part of chivalry, and this proud violence must be sanctioned, chastened. The true knight understood that he must live not only by the virtues of the body, but by 'the virtues that doth appertain unto knighthood as touching the soul': justice, wisdom, charity, loyalty, truth, humility.[25] From their 'loyalty, courtesy, liberality and pity' derived the honour due to the knight from his social inferiors.[26] When the Earl of Surrey thought of his 'childish' years awaiting knighthood, spent with his 'noble fere [companion]', his sworn brother in arms the Duke of Richmond, he recalled how his 'freedom grew', a nobility and generosity which was acquired and learnt as well as owing to birth. Later, in pain and loss upon Richmond's death, he evoked in 'So cruel prison' the fellowship in chivalry of these boys who had expected to fight and die together:

> The gravelled ground, with sleeves tied on the helm,
>   On foaming horse, with swords and friendly hearts.[27]

Some of those at the Castle of Loyalty were especially charged to teach the duties of chivalry. Bryan and Carew were deputed to 'encourage all youth to seek deeds of arms', and Bryan became Master of the Henchmen, the King's wards and pages.[28] The Duke of Suffolk, the 'ancient knight' of the tournament, gave in condescension to a young knight of the coming generation a manual of chivalry in French. In this manuscript, the knight inscribed: 'This book is myn, George Rocheford'.[29] George Boleyn, Viscount Rochford, had this manual translated into English, and presented it to the King. Perhaps Suffolk and Rochford knew that the work had already been translated and printed by William Caxton, but print may have been a medium too democratic for noble gifts and noble minds.[30]

The work was Ramon Llull's *Order of Chivalry*, the most popular work on chivalry of the Middle Ages. As the work begins, a wise knight, in flight from the world after a life of 'high courage' adventured in war, has retreated to a wood to contemplate last things. Riding to court to attain knighthood, an esquire encounters this 'knight hermit' and seeks to learn from him the rule and conduct of a knight. The hermit knight explains that when charity, loyalty, justice and truth failed in the world, the people elected one in a thousand for his 'noblesse and courage', and that man was 'beloved and doubted [feared]' by the people. 'By the love returned charity . . . and by the fear returned truth and justice.' The office of the knight is to defend the faith and his sovereign lord, and to protect the weak, the widow and the orphan. He will be faithful to God, to his wife, and to his friends. We cannot tell whether George Boleyn was at the Castle of Loyalty, but since he was a Gentleman of the Privy Chamber it is likely. The manuscript copy of 'The Order of Knighthood' which he gave to the King in 1533 was confiscated at his fall, and now lies in the National Archives, the home of the pen rather than of the sword.

The men and women of the court read chronicles of past chivalry to inspire their own. Jean Froissart chronicled the heroism and also the brutality of the knightly order in the Hundred Years War between England and France, and Henry VIII, seeking to revive the conquests of Edward III and the Black Prince, commanded Lord Berners to translate Froissart's *Chronicles*. So he did, knowing 'the great pleasure that my noble countrymen of England take in reading the worthy and knightly deeds of their valiant ancestors'.[31] Eight volumes of Berners' translation were found to be in the possession of his niece, Lady Carew, when an inventory was made of her executed husband's goods.[32] Whether she and Nicholas Carew ever read it is unknown, but one esquire at this tournament knew Froissart's *Chronicles* well. 'Mr John Poyntz told me that Froissart saieth that Chandos died leaving no children,' so John Leland, the poet and antiquary, recalled.[33] Sir John Chandos had fought alongside the Black Prince and was a founding Knight of the Order of the Garter, a hero of English chivalry. In chivalric romance, too, the men and women of the court read tales of knights of renown. Drawing on Arthurian romance for its forms and ideals, they patterned their own lives on the legends of King Arthur and his court, for Arthur and Guinevere and the Knights of the Round Table often seemed to them no less real than English kings and queens of the distant past.[34]

The knight must be adept in letters as well as arms. The perfect gentle knight of medieval chivalry became classically educated at the Renaissance. On the tomb of Francis Poyntz, the fierce defender of the Castle of Loyalty, under his sculpted helm, his grieving widow Joan ordered this inscription to be placed:

M. FRANCISCO. POYNO. SQVIRE.
LITERIS. PRVDENTIA. ARMIS.
FAVORE. SVI. PRINCIPIS. ET
PIETATE. INSIGNI. D. IOANNA.
PIA. ET. AMANS. VXOR. CHARO.
MARITO. POSVIT.

For Francis Poyntz, esquire, distinguished in letters, prudence, and arms, favoured by his prince, of noted piety, Dame Joan, devoted and loving wife to her brilliant husband, places this.

The Roman lettering on Poyntz's tomb adverts to a classical education and to his family's notable cultivation and avant-garde taste.[35] Poyntz's learning and talents were employed in royal service. In 1520 Henry had chosen several of the Poyntz family to attend him at the greatest chivalric pageant of the century, the Field of the Cloth of Gold in France. Francis Poyntz had a special costume made for the jousts, and so distinguished himself that the French King presented him with a gift of gold plate.[36] At the request of his brother Anthony, Francis translated *The table of Cebes*, one of the first classical texts to be printed in English. This was a 'speaking picture', an allegory of a journey toward Stoic wisdom, though Poyntz made the figure of Genius at the heart of this pagan text a good angel.[37] Languages, honed by the arts of eloquence, made Poyntz the perfect orator, and in 1527 his king and queen sent him to the Emperor's court. As 'orator' for his king, Poyntz used his powers of persuasion to mediate for the release of French princes held hostage there; as 'orator' for his queen he had a more secret and urgent mission and her special trust.[38] The Poyntz brothers probably owed their enlightened education to Katherine's patronage, and their loyalty to her marked their lives.[39]

The knights who fought so fiercely at the Castle of Loyalty were intent on proving their prowess not only to each other, but also to their ladies. From the tiltyard gallery at Greenwich, under the towers and turrets of medieval fantasy, the Queen and her ladies in waiting and maids of honour watched the knights disporting themselves below, as ladies had done at the court of King Arthur.[40] As in chivalric romance, maidens might be persuaded to give themselves in marriage to the most valorous, and married women to allow the chaste love and service of the courtly lover. In the knowledge that his lady was looking down, the sighing, aspiring lover might be moved to deeds of valour. Love and prowess, each inspired the other, and love was a great civilizer – or it was meant to be.

> Whoso that will all feats obtain,
> In love he must be without disdain
> For love enforceth all noble kind.[41]

The Queen, above all ladies of her realm, was most deserving of the faithful loyalty and service of true knights. Katherine of Aragon, heir to the crusading blood of Castile, took her chivalric role seriously. While the King fought in France in 1513, she had ridden at the head of her army to war against the Scots, perhaps even in armour.[42] Time was when Henry had jousted in her honour as Cœur Loyal and Sir Edward Howard, the flower of English chivalry, had worn her favour.[43] Now it was as ageing patron rather than as beautiful inspirer of adulation that she presided over the tournament, and though she graciously consented to the 'ancient knights' taking part it was no longer for her favour that they fought.

A view of the towers and tiltyard of Greenwich Palace from
the north bank of the Thames

With the Queen in the gallery at Christmas 1524 were her attendants and favourites. None was named but among them may have been
the wives of the combatants, such as Gertrude, Countess of Devon,
and Lady Carew.[44] The heroines of the festivities were the Four Maidens of the Castle of Loyalty. The names of the Maidens are unknown,
but maybe they were the Queen's maids of honour – maidens indeed,
chosen for their beauty and high birth. 'Angels', 'goddesses', fresh, fair,
virtuous, they were customarily paraded to dazzle foreign visitors by
their loveliness and accomplishment, the sort of maidens to whom any
knight might lose his heart. Yet they were forever unattainable except
in marriage – in theory, at least.[45] Henry Howard would remember the
games in the tiltyard where he and his royal companion, Richmond,
used to linger,

> With eyes cast up unto the maidens' tower,
> And easy sighs, such as folk draw in love.

In the palm play, 'with dazed eyes, oft we by gleams of love/ have
missed the ball' while seeking to attract 'her eyes which kept the leads
above'.[46] Which of Katherine's maids of honour were the Four Maid-

ens in the Castle of Loyalty? Perhaps Anne Browne was one. She was the daughter of Sir Matthew Browne of Betchworth Castle in Surrey, and her half-sisters were married to John and Francis Poyntz.[47] Perhaps another was Jane Parker, who had taken the part of Constancy in the pageant of the assault on the Château Vert in 1522. At Christmas 1524 she was still a maid of honour, but not for much longer, for soon she would marry George Boleyn. They and their marriage would be destroyed in the deadly games of love and beauty played at Henry's court.[48] Was Anne Stanhope one of the four Maidens, or Elizabeth Darrell? Bess Darrell, daughter of Sir Edward Darrell, the Queen's vice-chamberlain, was one of the Queen's maids of honour and she stayed with her until the end.[49] Despite her rank and glamour, Bess would not marry for another two decades, and then disparaged herself by marrying beneath her. Yet she did fall in love, and she became the mistress of the most accomplished man at court, Thomas Wyatt.

Maybe one of the Maidens of the Castle was Anne Boleyn.[50] The part that she would play in shattering the companionships of the court began at about the time of these New Year festivities when the King became mesmerised by her. Kings were, of course, likely to have mistresses, and this King had had mistresses before. There was Elizabeth Blount by whom he had had a son, Henry Fitzroy, Duke of Richmond – still, in 1525, his only surviving son. Mary Boleyn, married off to a complaisant Gentleman of the Privy Chamber, William Carey, was the royal mistress until pregnancy disqualified her, until her sister outshone her.[51] But her sister Anne, who for 'her excellent gesture and behaviour did excel all other', would not be a mistress and looked for a husband worthy her brilliance. In 1522 she returned from a long sojourn in France, a grand court lady, with the power to break hearts.[52] Perhaps it was Lord Henry Percy's desire for Anne which caused the King to thwart his hopes of shining at the Castle of Loyalty. Percy pined for Anne then, and pined still a decade later.[53] By the end of 1525 the King's heart was Anne's, so he promised her. From the New Year of 1527 the 'secret love' between Anne and Henry VIII would derange not only the court but the whole country.[54]

Even if the King's loyalty to his Queen was waning, some of those who fought at the Castle of Loyalty and those who watched owed her special loyalty. Henry Pole, Lord Montague was the Queen's man. Henry Courtenay and his wife Gertrude remained loyal to Katherine while they lived.[55] Thomas Wyatt looked to her as his patron and defended her honour. The Poyntz family were especially close to her. Sir Robert Poyntz, father of the challengers at the Castle, had been vice-chamberlain and then chancellor of her household.[56] In 1511 John Poyntz's wife, Elizabeth, was given the most precious trust when the King and Queen appointed her as wet nurse to the infant Prince Henry, in whom all their dynastic hopes so precariously and so briefly rested. At Prince Henry's christening, Elizabeth received a golden chain from the French King, and after the prince's much lamented death she received a pension.[57] Loyal both to their queen and to the King, soon these men and women would have to choose where their greater loyalty lay. In January 1525, with a sense of foreboding, the Queen was anxious to provide for those who had done her service, before God called her to account. She thought on the remedies of both kinds of fortune, on Petrarch's *De remediis utriusque fortunae*.*[58]

The men and women at the Castle of Loyalty knew well how brittle were the gifts of Fortune. Contemplating the power of the pagan goddess Fortuna, they knew that they were her helpless creatures, and that those who were raised high might soon, in their pride and wealth and happiness in love, be dashed. Anyone might observe how swiftly the wheel of Fortune turned. Wall paintings in churches taught the universal reversal. A thirteenth-century painting in Rochester Abbey showed the tall figure of Fortune standing within her wheel, while two figures climbed upwards among the spokes, and a king at the top was poised to fall. Even a monastic foundation might not stand forever, and soon the monks of Rochester would be evicted.[59] Hapless lovers copied into the Devonshire manuscript Troilus's lament to Fortune as precedent for their own star-crossed love.[60] Fortune – or hap and unhap – held 'Wyatt's world in sway'.[61] Often in his poetry a speaker laments the operations of Fortune, not in the world at large, but in his own life,

* See below, pp. 139–40

causing his happiness and unhappiness. Once, only once, in 'Ons as me thought fortune me kyst', Fortune kept her promise 'in graunting me my moost desire', 'my dere hert', but usually Wyatt's speaker is left to mourn past happiness from present isolation.[62] Fortune's reversals inspire not only poetic lament but also form. In the Egerton manuscript '*Tho.*' acknowledged the following poem which laments a singular unhap never before felt, a predicament not to be uttered. With effortless brilliance he does utter it, writing in chain verse, where the last line of each stanza is repeated in the first line of the next, and the last line returns us to the first, the perfect verse form to suggest the revolving of Fortune's wheel. '*Tho.*' claimed not to be able to write his heart and then discovered it in the writing of it:[63]

Suche happe as I ame happed in
had never man of trueth I wene
at me fortune list to begyn
to shew that never hath ben sene
a new kynde of unhappenes
nor I cannot the thing I mene
my self expres

My self expresse my dedely pain
that can I well if that myght serve
Tho.   but why I have not helpe again
that knowe I not unles I starve
for honger still a myddes my foode
so graunte me that I deserve
to do me good

To do me good what may prevaill
for I deserve and not desir
and still of cold I me bewaill
and raked ame in burning fyer
for tho I have suche is my lott
in hand to helpe that I require
it helpeth not

It helpeth not but to encrese
that that by prouff can be no more
that is the hete that cannot cesse

> and that I have to crave so sore
> what wonder is this gredy lust
> to aske and have and yet therefor
> refrain I must
>   Refrain I must what is the cause
>   sure as they say so hawkes be taught
>   but in my case laieth no suche clause
>   for with such craft I ame not caught
>   wherefore I say and good cause why
>   with haples hand no man hath raught
>   suche happe as I

The hand of Fortune was especially seen in the reversals of the great. Wyatt, drawing on a chorus from Seneca's tragedy *Phaedra*, observed in 'Who lyst his welthe and eas Retayne' that 'the hye montayns ar blastyd oft . . . the Fall ys grevous Frome Aloffte'. Grand families suffered the disasters which blighted any family – childlessness, infidelity, debility, depression, early death. Many in the court were struck down by the virulent sweating sickness in the summer of 1528. Most survived, including Anne Boleyn and her brother, but Francis Poyntz and William Carey, Fortune's darlings, died at the height of their prospects and promise.[64] The decline of noble families came also from the penalties for treason: execution and attainder brought forfeiture and annihilated the right of inheritance.[65] History and experience taught the dangers of trusting in princes' favour, not least because princes themselves were most subject to the arbitrary turning of Fortune's wheel. John Lydgate's *The Fall of Princes* became required reading for some who rejoiced at the Castle of Loyalty but who would later endure a 'fête of sorrow and weeping'.[66] Many at this Christmas tournament had a dangerous inheritance and feared that Fortune would lead them to follow the same course as their ancestors, with the same fatal consequences. Their families had suffered for past allegiances in the long wars between Lancaster and York, now ended but never forgotten. Those at the Castle of Loyalty might bask, for the while, in royal favour, rewarded for their loyalty, but they were tainted by earlier disloyalties. William Carey's Lancastrian grandfather had been beheaded after the battle of Tewkesbury in 1471, and the grandfather of the Browne sisters was executed for his part in the rebellion against Richard III.[67] Lord Montague's grandfather was the 'false, fleeting perjur'd Clarence' who died for treason in 1478. In Richard's reign Henry Norris's grandfather and the Poyntzes' father had sought exile, and returned with the invading army of Henry Tudor. Sir Robert Poyntz had been knighted on the battlefield at Bosworth.[68]

The tyranny of Richard III cast a long shadow. It was followed not only by Henry VII's evanescent gratitude but also by his 'heavy lordship' and minatory policies against his nobility. Henry Courtenay's grandfather was created Earl of Devon at his defection from Richard III, yet Courtenay's early childhood was clouded by his father's imprisonment in Calais, attainted for conspiracy against Henry Tudor. Pole, Courtenay, and Anthony Browne were brought up as royal wards or in the royal household, but this seemingly beneficent surveillance was owing to the King's suspicion of families too close to the throne. Their eminence made them vulnerable, however high they seemed to stand in the royal grace. The succession of Henry VIII in 1509 was celebrated as the end of a tyranny, but soon it appeared to be the beginning of another. His reign began with the politic sacrifice of Edmund Dudley, the father of one of the defenders of the Castle of Loyalty.[69] The association of some of these men with the 'right high and mighty prince', Edward, third Duke of Buckingham, had put them in danger, for in his pride he had 'imagined' the deposition and death of the King and listened to prophecies that he would succeed to the throne.[70] Lord Montague's family connections with the Duke, and his intimacy with him as they played dice for high stakes, invited suspicion and he was imprisoned at the Duke's fall in 1521.[71] As great lord in the west country, Buckingham was overlord of the Poyntzes. They had been his principal estate officers and feasted with him at his castle at Thornbury, but now they made prudential choices. Anthony Poyntz sat on the Bristol jury which found against him. Sir Henry Wyatt, too, sat in judgement against the Duke.[72] The father of Thomas Wyatt, dashing defender of the Castle of Loyalty, Henry Wyatt knew by bitter experience both the dangers and the rewards which came with service to the crown and, seared by their family history, his son and grandson would be forced to choose how to respond to royal power and its abuse. The jousters at the Castle of Loyalty understood how adventitious had been Henry VII's accession, but would learn not to say so openly, for that king's son would claim divine sanction and caesaro-papal powers. In 1541 a knight of Kent, Anthony St Leger (who survived to write an epitaph for Thomas Wyatt), found himself in deep water for his unguarded speech at his table in Kilmainham Castle. Even in Ireland, evasion and indirection might be necessary when discussing Tudor legitimacy. Saying, as he did, that 'the King's father at his first entering into England had but a very slender title to the crown' came perilously close to treason.[73]

At Christmas 1524 the brilliant light of royal favour shone upon those who played at the Castle of Loyalty. The knights were loyal to the ideals of chivalry, to brotherhood in arms, to their ladies, to their sovereign, and to the faith, and these loyalties were, for the moment, unquestioned, untested. But there would be no more tournaments like this one and soon the court would be shadowed by Henry's dangerous policies, by his *dis*loyalty. Remembering a prophecy which foretold that at the beginning of his reign he 'would be as gentle as a lamb, but at the end more fierce than a lion', the King promised that he would prove its truth.[74] The time would come when the loyalties of those at the Castle of Loyalty would be tried and be in conflict, when to be loyal to each other or to be loyal in love might provoke the King, when loyalty to the Queen seemed disloyalty to the King, when loyalty to faith challenged royal authority. Though born and trained to the royal service, some of them who survived began to find that service intolerable.

Family loyalties and the claims of friendship would also be tested. The challengers and defenders at the Castle of Loyalty were united by the claims of blood as well as by brotherhood in arms. The ties that bound them, like all family ties among the gentry and nobility, were close and complex. The Lords Leonard and John Grey were brothers. Francis and John Poyntz were brothers, but also brothers-in-law, for they had married sisters. Nicholas Carew married Francis Bryan's sister, Elizabeth, and Thomas Wyatt married – disastrously married – the sister of George Cobham, who was in turn the brother-in-law of Percival Harte. And so it went on. But family relationship might not bring amity, especially under the new political pressures of Henry's reign. According to the contemporary play of mind, 'cousinage' was deception, and kin might be unkind. In *The History of King Richard III*, which was read by some at the Castle of Loyalty, Thomas More wrote that 'the desire of a kingdom knoweth no kindred'.[75] In time, one of the 'stranger knights' was even accused of fratricide. When Thomas Seymour plotted to usurp his brother Edward's primacy in the reign of Edward VI, Edward Seymour, by then Lord Protector Somerset, pre-sided over the condemnation of this brother. The rivalry between John Dudley and Edward Seymour, who in 1524 had fought – or played – on the same side, would rock the country when they vied for power during King Edward's minority a quarter of a century later.[76] Deepest enmity grew between Thomas Wyatt and the Duke of Suffolk. Politi-cal and religious choices would also estrange many others. The knights at the Castle of Loyalty had professed themselves bound by fidelity in friendship, the fellowship of chivalry – 'the friendship sworn, each promise kept so just'.[77] Friendship was inviolable, Henry Courtenay vowed, or almost so: he 'would never disclose his friend *if it touched not the King*'.[78] But at last Henry VIII would suspect even these friends of his childhood, and would find treason among the families of Cour-tenay and Pole. They would suffer for it, and their nobility would be erased, their arms defaced.[79]

For some at the Castle of Loyalty the favour they enjoyed there was only a beginning. Two knights – Dudley and Seymour – would be cre-ated successively viscount, earl and duke, and would govern the realm during a royal minority. Lord Leonard Grey, captain of the 'stranger' knights, became Lord Deputy of Ireland. But some had known already, and would know again, the chill of exclusion from the royal presence. In 1519 Bryan, Francis Poyntz and Carew had been expelled from the court and exiled to Calais because they were suspected of having too great an influence over the King.[80] Far worse was to be 'sent for' – the command that struck terror into the hearts of Henry's subjects. Bryan would be 'sent for', and Wyatt was twice imprisoned in the Tower of London, whence few returned alive. In time, Seymour, Dudley and Lord Leonard Grey, and others who had jousted with them that Christmas – Courtenay, Montague, Carew and Norris – suffered the dreadful death of traitors. Not many of these men, nor all of the women, died safely in their beds. Translating Seneca in 'Stond who so list upon the Slipper [slippery, unstable] toppe/of courtes estates', Wyatt voiced an aspiration of withdrawal from the perils of court to rural reclusion:[81]

> in hidden place, so lett my dayes forthe passe
> that when my yeares be done withouten noyse
> I may dye aged after the common trace.

But neither he nor many other of his fellows at the Castle of Loyalty sought or found that anonymity, for being yoked to rural life 'after the common trace' held its own horrors of ignominy and boredom. Percival Harte was an exception. Seemingly set for highest honour, he withdrew from court to live on, and on, until his death in 1580, wealthy and safe in his Kentish estates.[82] Wyatt would debate poetically – with John Poyntz, with himself – whether to live at the court or to renounce it, but by then political circumstances had obviated that choice for one of them, who made the great refusal of life around the throne.

The men who fought at the Castle of Loyalty saw themselves as Christian knights in whom piety and prowess were one. 'Without loving and fearing God no man is worthy for to enter into the order of knighthood,' so it was written in George Boleyn's chivalric manual. The knight's sword was in 'similitude of a cross' to signify that just as Christ had vanquished sin and death upon the cross, the knight should 'vanquish and destroy the enemies of the cross by the sword'.[83] In *Le Morte D'Arthur* Sir Percival was saved from sin by the grace of seeing the sign of the crucifix in the pommel of his sword, and Sir Palomedes made knights swear upon the cross of a sword.[84] In real life, as they went to exact terrible justice on rebels in 1549, John Dudley and his captains kissed one another's swords.[85] For the knightly order, piety was a constant ideal which chastened their more brutal tendencies, in love and war. A knight must be 'reverent and faithful to his God'.[86] The esquire received knighthood 'in the intent that in the same he honour and serve our glorious Lord. And if he be clean of sin he should receive his maker', that is, partake of the Mass, 'the sacrament of the altar', without which 'no man can be saved'.[87] No true knight could ever be tainted by heresy. If any Knight of the Order of the Garter – 'as God defend' – were 'attainted of any error against Christian faith Catholic', he must be deprived and degraded.[88] As they fought at the Castle of Loyalty, these men believed that they were part of a chivalric fellowship, serving a king who was the Pope's unswerving champion, and a realm that was a faithful part of Christendom.

In 1521 the Pope had named Henry *Defensor Fidei* (Defender of the Faith) for his defence of the seven sacraments against Martin Luther's challenge. Within a decade, Henry would begin to question the Pope's authority within his realm and make novel claims of supremacy over the Church in England. Then, for Sebastian Newdigate, John Poyntz, Henry Courtenay and his countess, and others at the Castle of Loyalty, Henry became not *Defensor* but *Destructor Fidei*. Newdigate made the supreme refusal of the courtier's life, renouncing the world for the life of a monk in the London Charterhouse.[89] This was the most austere of religious vocations, one which Thomas More had tried and failed. From the Tower in 1535 More would watch Newdigate and other Carthusians as they went to their martyrdom, the lonely, ultimate sacrifice for faith, 'as cheerfully going to their death as bridegrooms to their marriage'.[90] Blessed Sebastian Newdigate died for a new kind of treason – for refusing to swear an oath recognising Henry's supremacy, and for his loyalty to the Pope and the unity of Christendom.[91]

The King abandoned the papal obedience and broke with Rome to become Supreme Head of his own Church just as heresies of an alarming sort were beginning to enter his realm. While he was still in the royal service, in the line of duty, Newdigate had received books impugning the Mass. In conversation with leaders of the Christian Brethren, the advance guard of England's reforming movement, he heard the worst of heresies: 'the sacrament of the altar after the consecration is neither body nor blood but remaineth bread and wine as it did before'. This was a denial of transubstantiation, the most sacred doctrine of the Church. Asking how the King and great lords of the realm regarded the opinions of the Christian Brethren, Newdigate was answered that the King was 'extreme' against them and 'would punish them grievously if he knew it'. The Duke of Suffolk and Henry Courtenay, now Marquess of Exeter, were also 'very extreme' against them. But these reformers and their 'fellows' were defiant: 'They had already two thousand books out against the blessed sacrament in the commons' hands . . . if it were once in the commons' heads they would have no farther care.'[92] It was not long after this that Newdigate entered the Charterhouse and followed the path which led to martyrdom.

The King and Suffolk, Courtenay and Newdigate, and some others who fought and watched at the Castle of Loyalty were fervently opposed to the new religion, but they were wrong if ever they believed that their opposition could make the court safe from it. The evangelical religion was infiltrating secretly. 'Young Karkett', the scrivener who wrote the articles of the challenge of the 'stranger' knights, became one of London's most ardent evangelicals.[93] In about 1522 the sister of the Poyntz brothers, Anne, Lady Walsh, sought a tutor to teach her children and live in her household at Little Sodbury, Gloucestershire. She found William Tyndale, and there he lived 'in good favour'. At the Walshes' table, grand prelates of the neighbourhood debated theology and the works of Luther and Erasmus with Tyndale, who defended his arguments from 'open and manifest Scripture'. Conceiving 'a secret grudge in their hearts' against Tyndale and his opinions, they tried to prevail on Lady Walsh to sack her tutor, and she asked Tyndale why she should believe him rather than 'so great learned and beneficed men'. In response, he translated for her the *Enchiridion militis Christiani* of Erasmus: *The Manual of the Christian Knight*. This work was the manifesto of a reformed Christianity that insisted that Christ be worshipped through inner faith rather than outward works, that Scripture be the rule of faith – the sort of book which transformed lives. For a while, Lady Walsh, who was 'stout [formidable]' and 'wise', sheltered Tyndale.[94] When she could protect him no longer, she sent him to London to her old friend Sir Henry Guildford.[95] The Comptroller of the King's Household, the man behind the festivities of the Castle of Loyalty and patron of several who fought there, including Wyatt and John Poyntz, Guildford came to find life at court unbearable.[96] When Anne Boleyn had returned from France, she brought with her not only courtly graces to ravish the King, but also a spiritual commitment she had learnt there, the Christian humanist imperative to set forth vernacular Scripture and return the Church to true religion. With her came her evangelical friends. The eclipse of Queen Katherine and the rise of Anne Boleyn, and all that followed from Henry's desperate will to secure the succession, compelled stark choices for those who had thought to spend their lives in the royal service.

At the festivities of the Castle of Loyalty, an unclouded time when faith and friendship seemed unchallenged, Thomas Wyatt disported himself with the friends and mentors of his childhood and youth. Soon his world darkened. With these friends, and privately, Wyatt was forced to debate searing choices of allegiance, and friendship itself would be a casualty. His family life, too, was blighted by untoward betrayal. Amidst the restlessness of his life and the court's mutability, he turned to poetry, but even words were fleeting, and steadfastness hardly to be found. Looking back, did he remember with nostalgia the innocence of the make-believe world at the Castle of Loyalty? 'Happy, alas, too happy.'[97]

3

Young Wiat

Soon Thomas Wyatt was in the presence of a greater king at a court far grander than his own. In the spring of 1526 the Pope and the powers of Christendom sent emissaries to France. The French King's catastrophic defeat at the battle of Pavia in February 1525 and his subsequent imprisonment in Castile had left his realm open to his enemies, and there were fears that his great antagonist, Emperor Charles V, would become master of Italy and 'lord of all'. When Francis I, newly released from captivity, returned to his kingdom the Pope and the powers of Italy urged him to head a league to defend *libertas Italiae*.[1] Whether there would be liberty or tyranny in Italy, peace or war in Christendom, seemed to rest on the diplomacy at the French court that spring. Henry VIII, now friend, now enemy, now friend again to Francis, sent 'one of his most secret familiars', Sir Thomas Cheyne, Gentleman of his Privy Chamber, to France in special embassy, as proxy for himself.[2] With him Cheyne took Thomas Wyatt, 'young Wiat'.

Riding hard, Cheyne and Wyatt arrived 'very weary' in Bordeaux on 6 April to await the French King.[3] Three days later, Francis made his royal entry by river, accompanied by a flotilla of boats, each painted the same colour as the livery of the infantry it carried. Bands of artillery lined the river banks, firing volleys of cannon and gunfire. Disembarking, Francis rode in state under a canopy of cloth of gold, between two cardinals. A great noble of France accompanied each foreign ambassador and dignitary: the papal nuncio walked with the Grand Master of Rhodes; the Emperor's ambassador with the Duke of Vendôme; then the English ambassador, then the Portuguese, and lastly, the secretary to the Signory of Venice. Precedence mattered. An unseemly row between the Portuguese and English ambassadors over who should go first marred the solemnity of the procession, and was settled only by the King's ordering the forcible removal of the Portuguese ambassador, 'with shame enough'. As the royal procession entered the cathedral, a *Te Deum* was sung.[4]

That evening Francis summoned Cheyne and Dr John Taylor, the resident ambassador, to an audience in his 'secret chamber'. Embracing Cheyne 'after a very kindly manner', the King told him that 'I like your coming here a great deal better now than I did at your last being with me'. Then Cheyne had brought Henry's menaces of war, now – the 'storms or clouds which had threatened' overblown – he brought declarations of 'great love'. Francis drew them aside to a window – the nearest to privacy that a king could find – and Cheyne delivered Henry's congratulations on Francis's release, but also his 'secret mind' that Francis must not keep the treaty promises made while he was the Emperor's prisoner.[5] Vowing undying friendship to his 'good brother and best friend', Francis divulged poisonous secret evidence of Charles's infidelity to Henry. He joked about the lowly mercantile ambassador of Portugal: 'What a poticary [apothecary] orator . . . Let him to Calicut and there make laws amongst his spiceries.' Cheyne must come 'early and late at his pleasure . . . boldly into his chamber', with the same freedom as he would enter Henry's Privy Chamber. On 10 April the English ambassadors visited the Queen Regent and the King's sister, and the next day delivered letters to the Treasurer and to the Chancellor, who told them how Francis read and re-read letters from the King and from Cardinal Wolsey. Thomas Wolsey, Archbishop of York, Lord Chancellor of England, held such supreme influence in Henry's counsels that he was seen as *alter rex*. Weeping, Francis avowed: 'I were too greatly unkind if I should ever forget the goodness of so great friends as these be.'[6] For some of these visits Wyatt was in attendance, observing, learning.

He witnessed the unusual familiarity of the French King with his courtiers which, in times of amity, extended to his own king and his representatives. Attending his first audience with Francis, Cheyne was grasped in a firm embrace.[7] The exquisite intimacies of the royal Privy Chamber, the decorum of who might hold a candle or pass a towel, told much about princely relations, for by such condescension a prince might express his grace. Finding Francis 'in his night gown', 'ready to

61

the washing of his hands', Cheyne was handed the royal towel by the Grand Master to present to the King, a signal favour.[8] When an English ambassadorial entourage had returned from France 'all French', Henry had copied his 'good brother' Francis in having around him to perform menial services, not lesserlings, but gentlemen of high birth and higher aspirations. Tasks in themselves undignified – washing the royal hands, and worse – were ostensibly dignified by the grandeur of the person for whom they were performed. At the French court Wyatt learnt, even more intently than at his own, the ways in which the intimate, intensely personal relations between princes who rarely or never met were conducted at a distance.[9] He observed the exquisite precision of language, protocol and precedence, the register of voices used in exchanges between kings through the persons of their emissaries. The language of diplomacy was the language of sworn friendship, of *amici amicorum*, 'friends of friends and foes of foes'.[10] Kings who had no equals but each other, nor any true friends but each other, conducted those phantom friendships by proxy. Cheyne's instructions were to deliver his master's message 'well couched' in French, not as an oration, but as a 'familiar, friendly and kind message'. He must discern the French King's response – which would become more difficult once Francis lost his front teeth[11] – and report it acutely. A gulf lay between what an ambassador must say in the royal voice, and what he said in his own, 'as of himself'. As Francis anxiously awaited the arrival of his saviour at Pavia, Charles de Lannoy, Viceroy of Naples, who now came from the Emperor to insist that Francis keep his promises, he thought upon his honour. If the Viceroy himself should speak of Francis's breach of promise, said the King, then he must be challenged by a great noble of France of the same rank. If he said, in the Emperor's name, that the King had broken faith, Francis himself must challenge the Emperor to fight in single combat.[12] On the faithful reporting of ambassadors the friendship or enmity of kings – peace or war – depended.

On 29 April Francis and his court moved to Cognac. That night the King summoned Cheyne and Taylor, who found him discussing the Italian League with the papal nuncio and Venetian ambassador. All decisions waited upon the coming of the Viceroy. When he arrived,

Francis promised that he would only 'feed them forth with fair words', and would delay until he received advice from his 'most trusty friends', Henry and Wolsey. All rested on a despatch being sent to England 'with as speedy diligence as may be' to solicit their answer. This mission was entrusted to Wyatt, as Cheyne explained:

. . . the cause why my companion and I send this bearer Wyatt at this present time, it is for two things: the one for that the matter is of great importance and requireth great haste . . . and the other because he can show your highness the manner and countenance of the noble men and gentlemen to the said Master Taylor and me, for he hath been with us at the court from time to time, and also he can show your grace a part of the commodities belonging to this house.[13]

Leaving the court, Wyatt rode furiously to find a passage for England. On 7 May '*uno zentilhomo anglese*' arrived at the English court. This was Wyatt, with Francis's message for the King.[14] Two days later Wolsey wrote to Henry of letters for France which would be ready, 'God willing', the following morning. 'Young Wiat' would deliver them. After another unsparing ride, Wyatt returned to Cognac on 19 May.[15] The day following, Whitsunday, Cheyne, Taylor and Wyatt went to the Privy Chamber 'secretly', after Francis had received Mass, and found him leaning out of a window, talking to the Grand Master, Anne de Montmorency. Doffing his bonnet, he saluted them 'very lovingly', and when he learnt that the gentleman sent to England at his desire was returned, Francis expressed himself 'joyous' to hear from Henry, 'his most dear and loving brother'. 'Wherupon I presented Wyat who with very good and discreet behaviour' delivered Henry's answer, Cheyne reported.[16] So Wyatt, proxy for his master, and already the perfect linguist, reported Henry's own words to Francis, in French. As youthful emissary between kings at a moment when treaties were reversed and remade, he witnessed the intimacy of diplomacy, the glamour that surrounded princes, and the evanescence of their promises.

Cheyne left France at the end of May. Wyatt probably went with him. This first experience of a successful diplomatic mission was also his last. Francis had sworn an oath of alliance to Henry amidst public ceremonial, and a league was formed for the defence of Italy with Henry as guarantor, the League of Cognac.[17] Cheyne, fluent in French, as Taylor was not, had been 'familiarly admitted in the court . . . and much cherished with all the nobles'.[18] Where Cheyne went, Wyatt was usually in attendance. Most of Wyatt's later missions would be crowned with failure, but for now he could exalt in his success. Why had Cheyne chosen Wyatt to accompany him? He was his Kentish neighbour, but there were other young gentlemen from Kent and the court whom he might have taken, like Harte or Dudley, who had fought at the Castle of Loyalty. Cheyne's letters justifying his trust in Wyatt's carrying a vital despatch provide two reasons: first, 'the matter is of great importance and requireth great haste'. Wyatt would ride recklessly, without sparing himself. Haste, post haste, for his life. Second, he could observe acutely and report: he 'hath as much wit to mark and remember everything he seeth as any young man hath in England'.[19]

Wyatt's wit: Wiat: a wit. Wyatt the traveller: *Viatus viator*. Throughout his life, and after it, people would play upon such anagrams, and recognise his 'rare wit'.[20] Much later, his decorum in speaking, his precision in eloquence, already displayed in that first embassy, were remembered as particular qualities: 'He observed times, persons and circumstances; knowing when to speak and when to hold his peace. His apt and handsome repartees were rather natural than affected: subtle and acute, prompt and easy, yet not careless: never rendering himself contemptible to please others.'[21]

In 1526, as he served on this first mission abroad, Wyatt was already pre-eminently accomplished in the double education of a gentleman: arms and learning. Towards the end of his life, he was recognised as 'apt for the administration of the public weal no less in the perfect knowledge of the diversity of languages, than in the activity of martial affairs'.[22] His reputation was of being 'in wars wise and valiant to repel hostility and in court very courteous'.[23] When, in 1527, Wyatt prepared for a life in service to his king for which all his talents and education equipped him, he praised the man who 'havyng the well of lyfe (I meane wyt and condicions, from whiche commendable dedes do spring) . . . shall bring forth all his dedes, mery and upright as it were with an hevenly grace'.[24]

He might almost have been describing himself, and in almost exactly those terms he would be described at his death.[25]

The date of Thomas Wyatt's birth is known – fittingly enough – through art. An inscription on the frame of a portrait, now lost, fixed his age at twenty-three in 1527.[26] The thirty-eight lines of the Earl of Surrey's epitaph, written at Wyatt's death in 1542, were a blazon of the years of his life.[27] So Wyatt was born in 1504. His father was Henry Wyatt, esquire, his mother, Anne, daughter of John Skinner, esquire, of Reigate in Surrey. The ancestors of Henry Wyatt were, for at least five generations on both his father's and his mother's side, from Yorkshire. Both the Wyatts and the Bailiffs and Skipwiths, Henry Wyatt's maternal forebears, came from South Haugh, a place so tiny that it is hardly to be found unless – as seems likely – it was Southowram, a mile south of Halifax in the West Riding.[28] The Skinners of Reigate were a prominent family of Surrey; a grander Surrey family were the Gaynesfords, Anne Skinner's maternal ancestors.[29] By the time of his marriage to Dame Anne in about 1503, and the birth of his son and heir, Henry Wyatt had moved south. A favoured servant of King Henry VII, he was avidly accruing lands and office under the crown, serving as an active Justice of the Peace in Surrey and Essex, living peaceably in London and in the shires. His life had not always been so peaceful, so secure.

The childhood of Thomas Wyatt is now lost to us. If we choose to read the opening lines of this verse epistle as autobiographical, we may imagine him growing up, as children did, among the female company of his mother's household:

> My mothers maydes when they did sowe and spyn
> they sang sometime a song of the feld mowse.

But that Aesopian fable grew dark, and so Wyatt's childhood darkened. After Thomas, Dame Anne, his mother, bore two further children: Margaret, and Henry, whose name is his only memorial.[30] Henry Wyatt was her tenth and last living child and whether she long outlived him is unknown. Anne had already borne seven children by her first husband, John Wilde of Camberwell, Clerk of the Green Cloth, so when Henry Wyatt married Anne Wilde, the widow of his fellow servant in the royal household, he inherited a family of stepchildren. John Wilde had died in 1502, leaving his widow and John Skinner, his father-in-law, as his executors, and seven children who were not yet of age.[31] 'Young Wiat' had two half-sisters, Edith and Elizabeth, and five half-brothers, Thomas, Harry, John, William and Roger Wilde. With Roger, who became a priest, he remained close throughout his life, keeping him nearby in family benefices. When Wyatt's friends despaired of prevailing on his conscience, they hoped that Wilde might appeal to his better nature, and as Wyatt counselled his son to 'honesty', it was the advice of this 'uncle parson' he wished him to follow.[32] A century later, members of the Wilde family chose Wyatt as a Christian name in memory of this family alliance.[33] The childhood home of the baby Wyatts and their half-brothers and sisters was in Barnes in Surrey, on the south bank of the Thames. There, in the parish church of St Mary, where Henry Wyatt was patron, is a memorial brass to two young sisters who died in 1508, their long, uncovered hair displaying their virgin state. They were Edith and Elizabeth, daughters of 'John Wilde, esquire, and Anne his wife . . . Of whose souls Jesus have mercy.'[34] Here were early intimations of mortality.

Wyatt's was a shadowed inheritance. Every English gentry family was touched by the divisions and dangers of the Wars of the Roses, but the life of Henry Wyatt, a younger son born in around 1460, was turbulent even for the times. In the mythic history of the Wyatts collated by Henry's great-grandson George and his successors, Henry Wyatt's faithful service to the fugitive Henry Tudor, Earl of Richmond, and his heroic suffering – imprisonment, starvation, torture – were revered in family memory.[35] Imprisoned 'often', Henry Wyatt endured 'pains, adventures, courage and sufferance'. Once, according to family legend, 'the tyrant himself', Richard III, interrogated him, wondering at his fidelity: 'Wyat, why are thou such a fool? Thou servest for moonshine in the water a beggarly fugitive. Forsake him and become mine, who can reward thee.' George Wyatt reported his grandfather's answer: 'Sir, if I

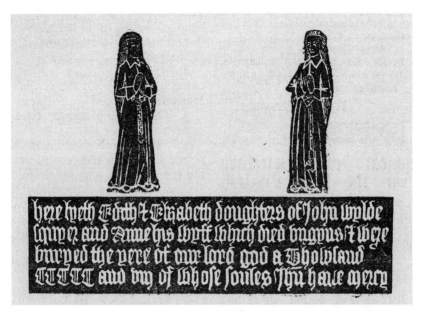

A memorial brass for Wyatt's young half-sisters, Edith and Elizabeth Wilde,
'which died virgyns' in 1508, implores perpetually 'Jesu have mercy'

had first chosen you for my Master, thus faithful would I have been unto
you . . . the Earl, poor and unhappy though he be, is my Master, and
no discouragement or allurement shall ever dissever or draw me from
him . . .' 'At this the tyrant stood amazed', reflecting, 'Oh, how much
more happy is that runaway rogue in his extreme calamity' that he had
such a servant than Richard himself, who 'in this appearing happiness
am unhappy only through the want of this happiness'. A century on,
the family had partly chastened Henry Wyatt's gruesome experience of
torture, presenting it as a story of divine intervention working through
'dumb animals'. The cat which had providentially saved Sir Henry
from starvation in prison was included in a later portrait, honoured in
family memory.[36] But Henry's Wyatt's recollection of his suffering was
more brutal. For his personal emblem – borne on his jousting standard and in tapestry – he chose the barnacle, the instrument of torture
through which mustard and vinegar had been poured into his nostrils.
OVBLIER. NE. PVIS [Forget, I cannot] was his motto, and he would
not allow his son and grandson to forget either.[37]

How Henry Wyatt fell into the hands of Richard, or how he served Henry Tudor on the way to Bosworth and the crown is unknown, but as soon as he seized the throne, Henry VII began to reward Wyatt, 'the King's servant, for services done in England and beyond seas', perhaps services in exile in Brittany.[38] Before September 1486 Henry Wyatt was appointed Clerk of the Jewels. This was a minor post in the royal household, but never unimportant since the royal treasure was partly held in jewellery and plate, nor without its dangers, for the treasure must always be guarded, sometimes transported.[39] The King also entrusted Henry Wyatt with cloak-and-dagger missions and crucial martial commands where his newly gained royal power was most falteringly established – on the embattled borders with Scotland, and in his lordship of Ireland.[40] In Scotland Wyatt was complicit with John Ramsay, Lord Bothwell, Henry's agent there, fighting a dirty war by supporting the rebel lords in the civil war against James III and James IV in 1488–9.[41] In 1491 Wyatt was appointed Captain and Governor of Carlisle, 'the key of these parts', to defend the English west march.[42] Service there was interrupted in 1493 by a mission to Ireland to negotiate with the 'overmighty' Earl of Kildare, to receive his submission, and to administer the Irish revenues. For the next few years Wyatt shuttled between the unforgiving Scottish and Irish marches, sent wherever the emergency was greater.[43] In 1496, as James IV acclaimed Henry's rebel Perkin Warbeck as 'Richard IV' and they prepared to challenge Henry's throne, Wyatt proposed to Bothwell the pre-emptive kidnap of the pretender.[44] At some point during these searing martial years on the borders, he was captured in a raid by some Scottish lord and suffered 'two years and more prisonment in Scotland, in irons and stocks'. Thirty years later southern forces were still fearful of entering the lands of the border reivers of Tynedale and Redesdale where 'they may hap to survey a pair of stocks in Scotland as did Sir Harry Wyatt'.[45] The ransom demanded was so huge that in 1515 Henry VIII renewed his father's annual grant of £20 to help repay it.[46]

Memories of these sufferings, of the consequences of allegiances chosen, of treason and tyranny, hardened Henry Wyatt and shaped the lives of his son and grandson. As he prospered during Thomas's childhood, rewarded as a favoured courtier–administrator, adding office to office, manor to manor, Sir Henry never forgot the perils as well as benefits which came with the duty of service. Years of penury and the burden of the ransom turned him unrelenting, even ruthless in pursuit of his rights, as a series of legal cases pursued down the years reveal. Acquiring lands through many counties, often using the royal treasure he handled as Keeper of the Jewel House and Treasurer of the Chamber, Henry Wyatt exhibited a 'pitiless accumulative streak' as he rapaciously consolidated his landed estate.[47] Even freed from prison, he served still within the terrible fortress of the Tower, becoming Clerk of the Tower Mint, Money and Exchange from 1488, and Comptroller from 1495.[48] During his son's early childhood, Henry Wyatt was still summoned to perform grim martial duties, and Thomas might have witnessed his father ride armed. In March 1506 Henry Wyatt travelled to Calais with a force of sixty soldiers to convey the pretender Edmund de la Pole, Earl of Suffolk, to the Tower, and to certain, though delayed, execution.[49] The traduction of de la Pole had resulted from adventitious, sinister diplomacy. Sailing from Flanders to Castile in January, Philip the Fair of Burgundy and Joanna of Castile had been driven by Channel storms onto the English coast and became the guests – the hostages – of the King. Amidst pageantry and shows of honour and amity, Henry VII prised a concession from Philip: the handing over of de la Pole, who was under his protection, on the false promise that his custody would be 'honourable'.[50] This dishonour was not forgotten – not by the Spanish, not by the English, not by Thomas Wyatt.[51] Thirty years later, when Charles V contemplated sailing from Castile to Flanders, Wyatt doubted that he would risk being shipwrecked on the English coast:

Il suo Re potrebbe justamente dolersi e forse far' di quelle che fece al Re Filippo suo padre quando per passar' in Spagna di Fiandra capito in terre sue non havendo glielo communicato e lo sforzo a dar' nelle man' sue quel parente del suo Re che teniva di Fiandra al qual fece subito mozzar' la testa.

His king would justly complain and perhaps do to him as his own father did to King Philip who, passing from Flanders to Spain, was taken in his lands and forced to give into his hands the kinsman of the King, held in Flanders, who was soon beheaded.[52]

Thomas Wyatt learnt from his father and his example a version of his country's history which was not of glory and pageantry, but of war and of a tyranny past which might come again.

Where and how Thomas Wyatt spent his childhood and youth and the manner of his education are mostly unknown, or known only retro-spectively. In family legend, Wyatt's mother was formidable and for-bidding. If Henry Wyatt was 'shrewdly matched', as he joked, then she was a shrew. Of sternest morals, allegedly she had the Abbot of Boxley watched when she suspected him of 'playing' with her maids, and would have punished Sir Henry, too, if she had found him so of-fending.[53] Were this portrayal true, and had she lived, we might specu-late on her influence on her sons, imagine what it was like to grow up at such a mother's knee. But Thomas presented only his father as a vivid presence in his life. Of his maternal grandparents, John Skinner of Reigate and Jane, the daughter of John Gaynesford of Blockfield in Surrey, nothing is heard, even though his grandfather lived into his grandson's youth. In his wealth and ancestral pride, as well as publicly expressed piety, Skinner built a vestry in 1513 in the parish church of Reigate, in hopes of prayers for his ancestors' souls and all souls. There a brass plaque perpetually beseeches passers by:

Orate pro anima Johannis Skynner generosi qui obiit 8 die mensis Martii anno regni regis Henrici octavi octavo cujus anime propicietur deus. Amen.

Pray for the soul of John Skinner, gentleman, who died on 8 March in the eighth year of the reign of King Henry VIII [1516]. God have mercy on his soul. Amen.[54]

Thomas Wyatt's silence about the Skinners and the Gaynesfords may signify either a familiarity too obvious to be told, or their absence from his life. We will find him at court with Anne Gaynesford later, but to picture him romping with his Gaynesford cousins may be illusory, for he may not have spent much of his childhood and youth with his family.

Since it was the custom of the nobility and gentry to send their sons away to learn what it was to serve and to become a knight, it is possible, even likely, that Thomas left home to serve as page in some great household.[55] His older friend Sir Francis Bryan, whose relations with his own father were clouded, remembered with gratitude the 'great goodness' of the 'special patron' of his youth, Sir Thomas Parr. In his turn, as Master of the Henchmen, Bryan would bring up the King's wards in his household to chivalry and learning.[56] Another friend of Wyatt's, Sir Anthony St Leger, had his 'bringing up' in the household of the Duke of Norfolk and remained, as he wrote, 'bound to love and serve your blood [family]'.[57] Later, Wyatt would gather into his household the children of his sister and of his close friend Thomas Poynings, and it was there that his nephew Henry Lee was brought up from childhood to become a paragon of Elizabethan chivalry, the Queen's champion.[58]

In the childhood home of George Blage, dearest friend of Wyatt's last years, there hung a series of tapestries which depicted the guiding themes in the life of a cultivated gentleman. One showed 'hawking and hunting'; another was of the 'story of shepherds' come in adoration of the infant Christ. Another portrayed 'the story of Rome', telling of a time when virtue was believed to govern public life and men lived not for themselves but for their country.[59] Though seemingly disparate, these tapestry scenes illustrated and inspired the life of a perfect knight, trained to arms, to piety, to virtue, and to service. Every boy of the upper orders learnt the duty of the *vita activa*, the active life of virtue and service and rational freedom. From Cicero they learnt that they must 'consider themselves born for their country'.[60] When Francis I, gritting his remaining teeth, welcomed Charles V to Paris at the New Year of 1540, a pageant scene portrayed the pelican feeding her blood to her young, and beneath it – in French, Latin, Greek and Tuscan – the motto from Cicero: '*non nobis solum nati sumus* [we were not born only for ourselves]'.[61] Men performing some melancholy duty under the crown would remember this truth, dinned into them since childhood.

Enduring the 'doubtful hap' of royal service in Ireland – dear God, not Ireland – William Wise knew that he and his fellow counsellors must 'learn to make virtue of necessity', and remember: '*Nobis nati non sumus*, &c.'[62] In the English shires, gentlemen born to wealth were denied the exercise of working with their hands, for that must be left to labourers. Though they might have spent their time in leisure, they were endlessly taught that doing sweet nothing was no innocent pleasure but dereliction to the commonwealth and the rosy path to sin.

Thomas Wyatt was trained to chivalry, to the brotherhood of arms and to a martial life. The high ideal of Christian knighthood taught fidelity to God and king, and of each knight to another. For any gentleman, the sword was the way of honour, and violence the ultimate sanction. Chivalry, learnt in theory through heraldry, history and romance, and in practice through swordplay, riding, jousting and hunting, was the training for war, for war in a just cause.[63] The touchstone of chivalry was the ability to ride gracefully. 'I will have our Courtier a perfect horseman,' said Count Lodovico in Castiglione's *Book of the Courtier*.[64] Courtiers sometimes rode wretched post horses, driving them, as they drove themselves, to exhaustion, or plodding, hairy-fetlocked plough horses which they disdained, but they were trained to ride the chargers and genets and coursers whose nobility and spirit matched their own, and whose submission was a sign of a rider's virtue as well as of his prowess. The horse was the 'perfect courtier, without flattery'. If an envoy were honoured by being sent some glorious, prancing steed, he must not disgrace himself by falling off. Every journey for a gentleman was on horseback, and the safe delivery of every royal message, the success of every mission, depended on the surefootedness of the horse and the skill, even the daring, of the rider. The principal purpose of riding effortlessly was to be able to fight on horseback, and to urge the horse, against its nature which impelled flight, to charge into the heat of battle. Carlo Cappello, Venetian ambassador to Henry's court, set up a monument for his war horse, with a Latin epitaph.[65] Men trained to chivalry wrote in equestrian metaphors, and even their doodles might be of horses.[66] Equestrian images intruded into Wyatt's love poetry – 'Though I my self be bridilled of my mynde' – and when almost every other subject was barred to him, he would discourse of horses. At the nadir of his fortunes his gravest dishonour would be to walk, rather than ride, to the Tower.*

Hunting and hawking, those country sports, were much more than sport for the gentleman, for they set him apart, on horseback, the owner of the land looking down on those who tilled it. Hunting was the training for war – that most terrible form of hunting – in which he must command. In France Wyatt had witnessed the sport of kings as the French King hunted the hart 'a force', holding it at bay for nine hours.[67] His own king, too, was obsessed by hunting, not least because it allowed him to chase off to seek private diversion, leaving his boring councillors behind. The court would be shocked in July 1531 when Anne Boleyn rode in hunting parties with Henry, with no ladies in attendance.[68] Anyone who sought a prince's favour, to be in his secret counsels, must hunt with him and have covert conversations in coverts, and at dinner talk endlessly of hunting. Wyatt, Francis Bryan, Master of the Toils, and Anthony Browne were masters of the game.[69] Even Wyatt's intimate, John Mason, though scholar and cleric, wrote in hawking metaphor. Wyatt trusted Anthony Lee, his brother-in-law and friend, to protect his prized hunting rights, and Lee, a notable huntsman, would bequeath 'all his horses, greyhounds, spaniels, geldings and mares' to his own son.[70] For all their immersion in the fevered world of the court, Wyatt and his friends lived lives close to nature. The claustrophobia of court compelled them to the freedom of the chase.

In a verse epistle written to John Poyntz, Wyatt describes a country life of hunting, hawking, stalking, riding – metaphors of freedom.† But more often in his poetry images recur of wildness trapped and freedom captive. His tormented speaker in his sonnet 'Unstable dreme', dreaming, waking, ruing the sudden loss of his lady's 'fals fayned grace', compares his mind (or perhaps his bed) to 'this tossing mew' – the mew where the falcon is caged.[71] Thinking on betrayal, Wyatt would find in Lux, 'my faire fawlcon', a fidelity that his friends, with their fashion of forsaking, lacked. With a bitterness far surpassing his usual caustic

* See below, pp. 417, 532.
† 'Myne owne Jhon poyntz'; see below, ch. 9.

humour, Wyatt compared the loyalties of the highest and lowest of creation, according to their kind, in a poem which Tottel entitled:[72]

Of such as had forsaken him

Lux, my faire fawlcon, and thy felowes all:
How wel pleasant it were your libertie:
Ye not forsake me, that faire mought you fall.
But they that sometime liked my company:
Like lice away from dead bodies they crall.
Loe, what a proufe in light adversitie?
But ye my birdes, I sweare by all your belles,
Ye be my frendes, and very few elles.

That abiding sense of fidelity and fidelity's betrayal returns in a story told in Wyatt's family. 'He brought up at Alington Castle a lion's whelp, and an Irish greyhound in which he took much delight.' They would await his return and greet him rapturously, until one day, when the lion grew to maturity, 'it ran roaring upon him', and would have killed him but for the greyhound's courage and Wyatt's. He 'drew forth his rapier, and ran it into the rebel's heart'.[73] Cock-fighting, the game which was so fatal for the birds, elicited from Wyatt a paean to their courage: seeing how 'fervently these little animals seek for victory at the expense of their own lives' will inspire any man to fight and die for 'the honour and salvation of his country'.[74]

In Wyatt's boyhood, his father served as 'captain in the King's wars'. In June 1513 when the royal army sailed for France to assert Henry's claim to his lost kingdom and revive the glories of Henry V, Henry Wyatt was in the middle ward, leading a retinue of a hundred men.[75] Warfare was his son's inheritance, as it was for every boy of knightly rank. A knight would bequeath to his heir his weapons and armour, so that he would be 'ready to serve his prince in time of need'.[76] George Zouche, Wyatt's ally, bequeathed to his son 'all my harness and other my habiliments of war'. Sir Edward Darrell, whose eldest son died a death of careless valour in the French wars, left a 'white cuirass [body armour]' to his heir, and maintained a store of arms at Littlecote for defence and for war.[77] These families were inured to war and their sons

were trained to fight, even to die, in battle. Thomas Becon's *The new pollecye of warre* (1542), which he dedicated to Sir Thomas Wyatt, knight,
commended the 'governors of the public weal' who instilled 'goodly
sweet sentences . . . into the breasts of their younglings even from the
cradle . . . *Dulce & decorum est pro patria mori* [it is sweet and right to die
for one's country]'.[78] One such was Wyatt's younger friend, Charles
Blount, Lord Mountjoy, who, composing his epitaph and will when he
went to fight in the French wars in 1544, hoped that his sons might
'keep them selves worthy of so much honour as to be called to die for
their master and country'.[79] The knightly orders hoped that the battles
they fought would be glorious, and that the King's enemies would be
found abroad, rather than at home. But the gentry, even in the shires
around London, might need their martial skills simply to keep order,
not only over lesserlings but among themselves.

The manor of Barnes in Surrey, where Henry Wyatt's young family
lived, was only a short journey, by river or by land, to Westminster and
London. Though so close to the centre of power, Surrey's peace was
broken by the chronic rivalries and violence of its leading families who
fought and perverted the course of justice.[80] By marrying Anne Wilde
and aligning himself with the Skinners and the Gaynesfords, Henry
Wyatt, this migrant from Yorkshire, thrust himself into the midst of the
county's feuding. The feud between the Brownes of Betchworth Castle
allied with the Scotts of Camberwell, and the Howards of Lambeth in
alliance with the Leghs of Stockwell, never slept even during Thomas
Wyatt's life, and would play a part in it later. Henry Wyatt's alliance
through marriage with the Skinners might have aligned him with the
Browne–Scott camp against the Howard–Legh faction – for the Scotts
and Skinners were interminably engaged in litigation with the Leghs
– but Sir Matthew Browne was so wildly refractory that Wyatt kept his
distance.[81] Royal intervention in local politics might exacerbate as well
as ease the tensions. Richard III's purges of the Justices of the Peace on
the Surrey bench at his accession and after the Duke of Buckingham's

failed rebellion of 1483 had left lasting enmities which intermittently threatened violence.

In 1503 Henry Wyatt was appointed to the Surrey commission of the peace. By appointing an outsider, the King's man, the hope was to disrupt and curb the factional rivalries between the county's traditional rulers. As an active JP in Surrey for two decades, Wyatt tried to be above the fray, to keep the peace and dispense equal justice.[82] But by May 1519, when he presided at the Reigate quarter-sessions, Surrey's legal system was in chaos. Sir Matthew Browne appeared menacingly with a retinue of up to a hundred servants, friends and tenants, to intimidate witnesses and the jury. He 'spake many hasty words, insomuch that Sir Henry Wyatt . . . desired him to keep silence and hold his peace, or else he would rise from the bench and go his way'. Unrepentant, Browne said that 'he was sorry that he had done no more than he did'.[83] The very model of the old kind of 'overmighty' subject, Browne was also the father-in-law of John and Francis Poyntz, who had received a humanist education.

The lord of the manor of Barnes was not Sir Henry Wyatt – however much property he acquired there[84] – but John Bourchier, Lord Berners. A soldier and ambassador, Berners was a figure worthy of admiration and emulation, even if he had not also been the translator of Froissart's *Chronicles* and of chivalric prose romances, but whether Thomas Wyatt knew him we cannot tell.[85] At some point in Thomas's childhood the Wyatt family moved from Barnes. In a list of 'noblemen and others', Henry Wyatt was still named as 'of Surrey' in 1520, but by then his pride of place, and his aggrandizing ambitions, lay elsewhere.[86] In January 1507 the heralds had granted a difference in arms to Henry Wyatt, esquire, councillor to the King, and he was now described as of Alington in Kent.[87] Alington Castle, the new seat of the aspirant Wyatts, already had a long history.[88] Once the stronghold of Norman conquerors, of the Longchamps, of Stephen of Penchester, and of the Cobhams of Rundale, Alington had been one of the great castles of Kent, but its recent history in the Wars of the Roses had been of disarray and disgrace. It had descended from the heiress Eleanor Cobham to her daughter Joan Moresby and her husband, John Gaynesford. The Gaynesfords were ringleaders in the October 1483 rebellion against Richard III, and when John Gaynesford of Alington and his father Nicholas suffered attainder for their treason Alington was forfeit to the crown. Although pardoned his life, John Gaynesford had died by 1486.[89] His widow remarried, to Robert Brent, a Kentish gentleman, but by 1492 they were both dead, leaving as heir to Alington sixteen-year-old Robert Gaynesford.[90] In 1491 Brent had bequeathed a missal and vestment to the church of Alington in the pious hope that the rector there would pray for his soul. To his widow Joan Brent he left five hundred marks for alms deeds for the health of her husbands' souls, her soul and all Christian souls, and died in the hope that her son, Robert, would be 'set . . . to school and learning in such wise as it may be to his worship [honour]', until he came of age.[91]

Whether Robert Gaynesford became learned is unknown, but he expressed his 'worship' through arms and allegiance to the old order in Kent. By 1503, now of age, Gaynesford of Alington was a leader of the huge, illegal retinue of George Neville, Lord Bergavenny, lord of nearby Birling Castle. Bergavenny became ever more 'overmighty' as his power and lordship in Kent were challenged by his enemy Sir Richard Guildford. In April 1503, allegedly, Robert Gaynesford led a heavily armed gang of more than thirty men which 'riotously . . . after the manner of war' invaded the manor court of Aylesford, where George Guildford was 'keeping the law-day', and assaulted him. Gaynesford counter-claimed that as he rode peaceably to attend the law-day at the Carmelite friary outside Aylesford he was set upon by Guildford and his retinue.

In 1505 Bergavenny's Maidstone tenants again disrupted the Aylesford court and its justice. Since Bergavenny was unwilling or unable to restrain his vast retinue, huge penalties were imposed in King's Bench in Michaelmas 1507.[92] Robert Gaynesford's conception of 'worship', and his turbulence in proving it, provided opportunity for the coming family of the Wyatts. Henry Wyatt, primed to restore order under the crown, related to the Gaynesfords by marriage, and watching Alington fall from hand to hand and into ruin, seized his chance. By 1511 Wyatt – once the northern outsider – was described as 'of Barnes, Surrey, alias of Alington, Kent'.[93]

Alington Castle, the newly acquired ancestral home of the Wyatts

If Henry Wyatt gained possession of Alington Castle in the first decade of the sixteenth century, it was not until the next that he moved there and established his power base in Kent. The castle, after years of ruin and neglect, was restored to receive its new lord.[94] In 1514 Wyatt exercised for the first time his patronage at Alington church, instituting a monk of Boxley Abbey to the benefice.[95] Four years later, he was granted free warren on his demesne lands in the manors of Alington, Boxley, Ovenall, Rundall, Okington and Milton.[96] Free warren, the right to hunt hare, fox, badger – lesser game – was not the noble privilege of hunting deer, but still a right strenuously to defend. Henry Wyatt did defend it, down to the last rabbit. Around this time we find the hapless Thomas Elson before Wyatt, confessing to having poached eighteen 'conies' from Wyatt's grounds on two occasions before Christmas.[97] By 1520–2, when Henry Wyatt drew up an account of all his possessions at Alington, in pride of ownership, he had departed Surrey for Kent, and by 1522 he was on the Sheriff roll there.[98] Despite this new allegiance, he sought to distance himself from the traditional Kentish custom of tenure and partible inheritance – gavelkind, 'a common law in Kent' – and in the Parliament of 1523 introduced a private bill to disgavel his lands, converting all his holding to standard common-law tenures. This would allow him to pass them on intact to his descendants. His son and heir, and Thomas Wyatt's son and heir in turn, would inherit by primogeniture. In time, Henry Wyatt might regret the change.[99]

Between the newly arrived families in Kent – the Wyatts, the Guildfords, the Boleyns – and the old families who were the 'natural rulers' of the county, such as the Nevilles and the Cobhams, intermittent antagonism simmered. In 1516 the unsleeping feud between the Nevilles and Guildfords again flared into violence, and a Neville retinue was accused of terrorising Cranbrook hundred. Bergavenny's alliance with a greater Kent magnate, the third Duke of Buckingham, made him complicit, or suspect of complicity, in the Duke's treason, and after a year's imprisonment in the Tower in 1521–2 he was forced to sell Birling to the crown.[100] At Buckingham's demise, Kentish families fell on his estates and divided them among themselves.[101] Perhaps significantly, it was at this time that the Wyatts took up residence at Alington. Tensions existed, too, among lower social orders as the new families intruded themselves into the county and disrupted the old loyalties and tenures. Poaching deer in noble parks revealed animosity and subversion as well as a desire for illicit game. In 1538 – a generation after Thomas Boleyn had settled at Hever in Kent, after he had become Earl of Wiltshire, and the father of a queen – a servant of Sir Edward Neville's would justify poaching expeditions in Postern Park, held by the Boleyns after Buckingham's fall. Because 'my lord of Wiltshire was not beloved in the country', he was 'gladder to go hurt his parks'. Another servant agreed: 'they were the more willing to make these huntings because my Lord of Wiltshire was so extreme a man amongst them . . . and he had no love of the country neither'.[102] [By their 'country', they meant their county]. The exchanges between the new families also were complex and intense, and the friendships which Thomas Wyatt made in his youth, with the Guildfords, with Guildford's ward, John Dudley, and with the Boleyns, would mark his life.

John Leland the antiquary, who knew Kent and Thomas Wyatt very well, wrote that Alington was 'sometime the Grays' castle', and 'since the Saviles' and the Wyatts".[103] Maybe Leland was wrong about the Saviles' possession of Alington, but he was right to make the connection between the Wyatts and the Saviles – the Saviles of Thornhill and the Saviles of Lupset, leading families of West Yorkshire. Leaving Yorkshire, Henry Wyatt had not left his connections or his lands and duties there. He was steward of the honour of Tickhill, steward of the lordship of Hatfield and Thorne, and from 1487 he shared with Sir John Savile the office of bailiff of the great castle of Conisbrough.[104] Anne Wyatt, daughter of William Wyatt of Essex, married John Savile of Lupset, keeper of Sandal Castle.[105] In 1521 Henry Wyatt was in close contact with the Saviles, and still at his death adjured his son to look after Henry Savile.[106] In 1545, John Savell (Savile) of Lupset, first Henry Wyatt's servant then Thomas's, lived and died at Alington.[107] But if there were Yorkshire alliances, there were also rivalries, for Yorkshire – no less than Kent and Surrey – was rent by family feuding. Alignment with one family brought enmity with another. The Wyatts' allegiance to the Saviles

brought them into contention with the Tempests of Bracewell and Bowling, for a vendetta flourished between Sir Henry Savile of Thornhill and
Sir Richard Tempest.[108] Sir Anthony Browne, who would play a malign
role in Thomas Wyatt's life, was also connected with Conisbrough and
Tickhill. His mother Lucy, the widow of Sir Thomas Fitzwilliam, built
a magnificent Renaissance tomb for her first husband in Tickhill parish
church. In 1518, when Browne was made master of hunting for the
royal lordships of Hatfield, Thorne and Conisbrough, we may doubt
that the Wyatts rejoiced at his good fortune.[109]

It was in Yorkshire – not at court, nor in Kent – that the name of
Thomas Wyatt first appears in the public record.[110] Henry Wyatt's sister, Joan, married into the Yorkshire family of Drax, but with these
relations Henry Wyatt was hardly 'in charity'. He caused Thomas
Drax, Doctor of Divinity, seventh Rector of Lincoln College, Oxford,
and vicar of Derfield, to be arrested for a £10 debt and sent to the
Marshalsea prison, but Drax absconded and returned to Yorkshire.[111]
Wyatt turned to private distraint to enforce the obligation, or so Drax
alleged as he petitioned Cardinal Wolsey in Star Chamber. His plea
was that in July 1517 Sir Henry Wyatt had sent Thomas Kendall of
Conisbrough with another dozen of his servants, armed and at mid-
night, to drive off Drax's cattle from his lands at Woodhall. The cattle
were impounded at Tickhill Castle, and there starved. Again at Wyatt's
command, Roger Rockley, esquire, of Worsborough, with Thomas
Wyatt, Thomas Drax the younger, Thomas Kendall and eighteen
others, forcibly seized Drax's land in June 1519. Denying the charge,
Henry Wyatt insisted that the land was his: he, and others, including
John Savile, and Thomas Wyatt, his son and heir, were invested with
the lands in June 1517.[112] Maybe the Thomas Wyatt who took part in
the raid was Henry Wyatt's brother, rather than his son, but youth was
no deterrent to distraining. Thomas Drax the younger was only twelve
at the time of this raid, and these sons of the gentry were trained to
arms to defend what was theirs – or what they claimed was theirs: the
lands upon which their wealth and honour depended.

At the manorial court at Conisbrough on 5 October 1519, as Sir
Henry Wyatt was elected reeve of Conisbrough and Bracewell, Thomas

Wyatt, gentleman, appeared in person. He was sworn to the tourn, which dealt with infringements of manorial custom, and levied fines upon those who had offended against the local community. In March 1523 he appeared again, with Thomas Kendall whom his father had sent to raid Tickhill.[113] The Wyatt family had long held office in Conisbrough and taken part in local government in the West Riding. In 1481 William Wiott had been elected and sworn to office at the session of the Conisbrough manorial court, and in the first years of the sixteenth century Sir Henry's brother Thomas had annually been sworn to the tourn.[114] Regularly through the 1520s Thomas Wyatt, son and heir of Sir Henry, also presented himself to be sworn to the tourn, absent only when serving more glamorously elsewhere.[115] Deputing for his father in the lordship of Conisbrough was part of his apprenticeship, preparing him for the time when he would take over his father's lands and offices.

Late in 1523 Thomas Wyatt went on his first mission in the royal service, sent for the 'King's affairs in the North'. England was at war with Scotland, and royal treasure was needed in the marches to pay for the garrison. Henry Wyatt, Treasurer of the Chamber, entrusted his son with transporting the vast sum of £2,000 in gold. During what Lord Dacre called 'this hollow time of winter', on 26 October and 20 November Thomas made two journeys of great difficulty and danger, riding armed and guarded, brave enough to defend the King's treasure to the uttermost.[116] Picture him meeting Lord Dacre, a great lord of the north, who could marshal hundreds of men and whose battle cry was 'A Dacre, a Dacre'. Later, Wyatt would contemplate the challenge that Lord Dacre's power posed to the crown, and how Henry countered it. This mission to the marches was essential, dangerous and, as any royal service, honourable, yet it carried none of the glory of the battlefields of France, where Wyatt's contemporaries were fighting and dying. *Sir* Anthony Browne and *Sir* John Dudley had already been knighted for their valiant service there. Wyatt's inheritance seemed, instead, to be to follow his father in a life of self-immolating service to the crown, in the royal counting houses. With that deliberate intent, in October 1524 Henry Wyatt vacated one of his lesser offices to his son, the Clerkship of the Jewel House. It has been well observed of Thomas Wyatt that 'it would be hard to think of anybody less temperamentally suited to accountancy as a career'.[117]

Somewhere, somehow, Thomas Wyatt received an education which distanced him from the kind of life his father had lived. Evidence of his learning comes later in his life, in his application of it, and it would be remembered long afterwards. William Camden would describe him as *splendide doctus* (brilliantly learned).[118] Sir Robert Lee, whose son married Wyatt's sister Margaret, willed that his youngest son 'be brought up in virtue and learning as a knight ought to be'.[119] Perhaps this was Sir Henry Wyatt's aspiration for Thomas – an education that he had not received himself. Even a fervent admirer of Henry Wyatt would judge his written style 'uncouth'. A letter written from Carlisle in 1496 had the urgency and intonation of his rough Border command, the diction of a soldier rather than a courtier.[120] Later, his letters – even the most desperate, personal ones – would be written by a secretary. But when Thomas Wyatt expressed himself roughly, avoiding 'the delicacy of sayeng, and the piked [flowery] delight of spech', his was a roughness of artistry, learnt from classical theorists and chosen when more golden diction was rejected. When he 'rappe[d] owte an othe in erneste tawlke', or wrote proverbially, this expressed a literary and a moral stance.[121] We will discover his ambivalence about the arts of eloquence, but it was the ambivalence of a man who was rhetoric's master, an orator of marvellous gifts. He acquired a classical education, and exquisite proficiency and fluency in Latin to be written, spoken, and used in the service of his king.

Henry Wyatt was soldier, not scholar, but two of his brothers were priests. One, John Wyatt, lived obscure, away from the bright light of court and from business, until and unless summoned by Henry to act as signatory to some contract or deed or other. In his will he named himself vicar of Cley on the farthest coast of Norfolk, and his bequests to his church – to the Rood light, to the young men's light, to Jesus Mass, to the gild of St Margaret – and of 4d to every household in his parish, suggest how settled he was in that little, remote community.[122] Their brother Richard had grander ambitions and rose in the Church just as Henry rose in royal service. Richard Wyatt collected benefices and became prebendary of Southwell in 1507, of Lichfield in 1509, and precentor of York by 1519.[123] Numerous business dealings with his brother Henry reveal his worldliness as well as their continuing connection.[124] When Richard Wyatt made his will in July 1522 he bequeathed £100 toward the marriage of his niece Margaret, and entrusted Henry and his heirs – that is, Thomas – with the maintenance of a priest to 'sing for me and my father and my mother' at Southwell Minster.[125] John and Roger Wilde, Thomas Wyatt's half-brothers, were also priests and notably well educated. John attended the University of Oxford, where he was Junior Proctor in 1521–2, and Roger was admitted BA in the University of Cambridge in 1519–20 and incorporated at Oxford in 1522. That first John, then Roger, were presented to the parish of Milton by Gravesend, where Henry Wyatt was patron, suggests that their education received the blessing and perhaps the munificence of their stepfather.[126] The stepsons, bound for the priesthood, needed a university education. What of the son and heir? Thomas Wyatt may have been sent first to learn what could not be learnt at the universities: the common law of England.

On 19 May 1517 'Wyot' was admitted to the Middle Temple.[127] Knowledge of the common law was necessary not only for those who would practise it – the black-gowned lawyers at Westminster – but also for the gentry with landed interests to extend and protect. Thomas Wyatt's grandfather John Skinner had been admitted to Lincoln's Inn in 1487, and Henry Wyatt was associated with that Inn.[128] If 'Wyot' was Thomas Wyatt, his admission at thirteen was precocious, but perhaps not extraordinarily so, not for a youth of his 'wit' and connections. His friend George Blage was admitted to Gray's Inn at the age of sixteen, George Carew at fifteen.[129] We might speculate about Wyatt's legal learning, imagine him struggling with rebarbative law French, attending readings and poring over books of cases and precedents, but since he was quick to lose what his father had so relentlessly gained we may doubt the seriousness of his engagement. He would need some law when – as a gentleman must – he served briefly as Justice of the Peace and sheriff, but if he proceeded further in his common law studies than Littleton's *New Tenures*, the most basic primer of land law, it leaves no trace.[130] But time spent at the Inns of Court could never be wasted. Anyone of any status and ambition studied for a while there, as a staging post on the way to power.

The Inns of Court were a liminal place on the journey to the royal court, where young men on their way to rule might engage in misrule. Here they sharpened their wits, and used their ingenuity in plays and poetry as well as in more dismal studies. During the traditional Christmas revels a Lord of Liberty reigned and turned the world upside down. Cardinal Wolsey was splendidly mocked in the Gray's Inn Christmas play of 1526.[131] At the Middle Temple Parliament held at the feast of All Souls in 1518 'Wyat' was chosen for 'the office of Master of the Revels for the feast of Christmas next coming'. Three of his fellows – Darkenall, Molyneux and Cutte – did occupy the office, but of Wyatt's part nothing is known. In February 1520 'Master Wyat' was pardoned from exercising all offices in the Temple on payment of a fine of forty shillings.[132] What Wyatt learnt of the common law is unknown, but much later, his life might depend on some knowledge of it, and of civil law.[133] Towards the end of his life, we find him debating the nature of law and of sovereignty and, for dark reasons, thinking upon the new law of treason. In audience with the Emperor he protested that he could not dispute regarding matters of law: '"Sir", quod I, "I know not the law." "Yes, mary, do ye," replied the Emperor, and he laughed.'[134]

Down river from the Inns of Court, only a few hundred yards away, was the precinct of Blackfriars which contained places of learning of another kind. Within this walled enclosure of about five acres were not only the Dominican priory but also the London lodgings of many leading courtiers. The priory had a great hold over the spiritual imagination of many of the nobility and gentry, who wished to be buried there by the 'friars preachers' and requested prayers for their souls. An anchoress lived immured within its walls. But since Blackfriars was adjacent to the royal palace of Bridewell many secular events took place in the precinct, including the Parliaments of 1523 and 1529.[135] In 1522 Sir Henry Wyatt lived in Blackfriars and still did in 1526, at least in the winter, returning to Alington for the summers. Among his Blackfriars neighbours were families who would play crucial parts in the life of his

Blackfriars precinct, where the Wyatts and their friends
had their London lodgings

son. Here were the households of Lord Zouche, Lord Cobham, Sir William Kingston, Sir William Parr, Sir Thomas Cheyne, and Dame Jane [or Joan] Lady Guildford.[136] These families were bound by marriage and kinship in patterns unusually convoluted, even for the gentry and nobility. Sir Richard Guildford, who had died in pilgrimage to Jerusalem in 1506 and was buried in the priory of Blackfriars, had married Jane, the sister of Nicholas Lord Vaux of Harrowden, whose son Thomas married the daughter of Sir Thomas Cheyne, another Blackfriars resident. Thomas Lord Vaux became Wyatt's friend and a fellow 'maker'.[137] George Zouche, who was Wyatt's ally in business, married Wyatt's cousin, Anne Gaynesford. We can tell as little of the making of friendship as we can tell of falling in love, but some of these friendships lasted for life.

Thomas Wyatt found friends in the little world of Blackfriars who were notably cultivated and like-minded. The household of Lady Parr, the mother of a future queen, was a school for the nobility where a boy or girl 'might learn with her . . . as well nurture, as French and other language'.[138] Lady Guildford's lodgings played a pivotal role in life and learning at the Blackfriars. In Guînes, Robert Wotton recorded that 'my daughter Margaret was married at the Blackfriars in London in mine old Lady Guildford's lodging . . . unto the Marquis Dorset. 30 May 1513'.[139] As governess to the royal princesses, the King's sisters, Lady Guildford had travelled with Princess Mary to France, and perhaps a sustained interest in the language remained, for she bequeathed 'my book of French' to her nephew Thomas Vaux.[140] Early in her widowhood Lady Guildford seems to have lived with the already-married Sir Thomas Brandon. Making his will in 1509, he left her extensive property, thanked her servants for 'their kind labour about me in time of my sickness', and her son Henry Guildford was witness. Thirty years later she would ask for prayers for Brandon's soul. This old intimacy between the Guildfords and the Brandons had consequences, for Charles Brandon and Henry Guildford would find a common cause in which they would enrol Wyatt.[141] When Lady Guildford finally remarried, to Anthony Poyntz, they continued to lodge in the Blackfriars for part of each year. At his

country seat at Iron Acton, Poyntz did his duty as a country gentleman, and at sea he served as admiral in the French wars, but he also
thought on Stoic philosophy and urged his brother Francis to translate *The table of Cebes*.[142] Sir Henry Guildford, Lady Jane's only son,
was Master of the Henchmen, trusted to educate the royal wards to
prowess and virtue, a post given to 'one well mannered and having
the French tongue'. This post passed to Guildford's brother-in-law,
Sir Francis Bryan, who probably also spent time in the Blackfriars.[143]
Writing to Henry Guildford in 1519, Erasmus sent a greeting which
was more than conventional: 'warmest good wishes to the noble lady,
your mother, whose acquaintance I owe to several conversations'.[144]
These Blackfriars neighbours – Brandon, Guildford and Bryan, Vaux
and Poyntz – will return and return in the story of Thomas Wyatt as
formative influences in his life. And among the noble families of the
Blackfriars he would find his wife.

At Wyatt's death, a friend of his youth wrote mourning songs,
lamenting his passing and remembering a lost time spent together:

> By lovely Granta I was joined to you
> In friendship, Granta, the glory and renown
> And ornament of the Muses. Shall grim death
> Sever our minds? O let it not be so!
> Farewell, beloved Wyatt, a long farewell.[145]

The friend was John Leland, antiquary and neo-Latin poet. Leland
was an undergraduate at Christ's College, Cambridge, by about 1519,
and there still in 1522: 'I was one who took pains in the liberal arts at
Cambridge, in the College dedicated to Christ's name.'[146] Tradition
places Wyatt at St John's College – but tradition alone. If he did study
in Cambridge, he was more likely to have been at Christ's, with Leland.
His uncle, Richard Wyatt, Master of Arts and Doctor of Divinity, had
been the second Master of Christ's College between 1507 and 1510.
John Wyatt, from another branch of the family, was Fellow of Christ's
between 1519 and 1540.[147] As at St John's, preference in the election
of fellows at Christ's was given to northerners. If, though not formally
matriculated, Thomas Wyatt was at Christ's for a time, the allegiance

was important, because of those who studied with him, and because of the college's intellectual stance.

Christ's, refounded in 1506 from the decayed Godshouse by Lady Margaret Beaufort, at the instigation of John Fisher, was dedicated to teaching (among other things) 'the works of poets and orators'. Scholars there received a more thorough grounding in grammar and rhetoric than those at other colleges, and the emphasis was on the exposition of divinity, with the clear purpose of producing an improved clergy.[148] To be in Cambridge at this time was to witness the new teaching of Greek, and to experience the impetus to scriptural piety and spiritual reform. An old guard disapproved of the displacement of speculative grammar by Plautus and Quintilian, but for young scholars like Leland, who watched, or like Thomas Wriothesley and William Paget, who took part in the production of Plautus' *Miles gloriosus* (*The Swaggering Soldier*) in 1522 the excitement was remembered long afterwards.[149] For Erasmus, the centres of the new studies and the heart of reform were Fisher's colleges, Christ's, St John's, and Queens'. Scholars of Christ's and St John's became the most stalwart defenders of the Church against royal ambitions and against those who would introduce heresy along with humanism.[150] From the tiny generation who studied at Christ's around 1520 would come a martyr for papal primacy and the unity of Christendom – William Exmewe of the London Charterhouse – and Dr Nicholas Wilson, who was imprisoned in the Tower for refusing the Oath of Supremacy, as well as a martyr for the new faith – Thomas Dusgate, alias Benet.[151]

Reformed learning and reformed spirituality reached from Cambridge to Kent. John Fisher, the enlightened founder of St John's and Christ's, was Bishop of Rochester, and there he favoured Cambridge scholars, finding them Kentish livings.[152] Around 1525 St John's presented its fellow Henry Gold, University preacher, to the college living of Ospringe in Kent. At the visitation of a monastery in Kent, Gold preached a sermon of remarkable power. Comparing those living under religious vows to the children of Israel persecuted by the tyrant Pharaoh, he warned that unless they provided 'holy examples of living' as 'lanterns of light', the sacrilege of those who oppressed them could be easily excused, just as Pharaoh had justified the dispossession of the children of Israel because of their 'sinful living'. Now, in Gold's time, some proposed to 'destroy religious places', to put their possessions to 'better uses'. Lamenting the 'common proverbum' of men 'of great authority' and 'all manner of men' that 'true religion is wonderfully decayed from her old state of perfection', Gold might almost have been describing the conversations of Wyatt and his friends: 'where shall a man find envy, pride and gluttony . . . but in the cloister?' Writing cynically, proverbially, to Francis Bryan in the verse epistle 'A spending hand that always powreth owte', Wyatt would echo the 'proverbum' of a religious life fallen from its perfection:

> So sackes of durt be filled up in the cloyster
> that servis for lesse then do thes fatted swyne.

Gold's warning that God permitted the oppression of His people by tyrants – by Nebuchadnezzar, by Pharaoh – when they forsook His laws, and ignored His promise of deliverance from the wilderness to those who repented and reformed, was prophetic.[153] In 1525, around the time of Gold's sermon, Thomas Cromwell was in Kent on Wolsey's service to supervise the suppression of some lesser monasteries.[154] Henry Gold and Wyatt were perhaps at Cambridge at the same time and they lived only a few miles apart in Kent, yet if they met, their lives far diverged. When Nicholas Darington, '*amicus non vulgaris* [no common friend]', wrote to Henry Gold from Louvain in July 1522, sending greetings to mutual friends, it was not Wyatt he remembered, but Dudley.[155]

Where Wyatt's religious sympathies lay as Gold preached in Ospringe is unknown. His deepest meditations on the Psalms, on 'inward Sion' and 'hertes Hierusalem',[156] even if they began earlier, were not committed to paper until he composed his paraphrases on the Penitential Psalms much later in his life.* If during his youth in Kent and Christendom he was pondering the secret workings of God's providence, or thinking on the nature of salvation, or meditating on his soul's health, no trace remains; if he questioned how divine mercy and justice were

---

* See below, ch. 15.

imparted – or inferred, or imputed – to the sinner, we do not know. He may have followed his father's traditional counsels to penance and the confessional. The first expression of his religious truth that is known to us did not come until 1537, and then it was remarkable for what it omitted: he made no mention of the Church or its sacraments, wrote nothing of the religious observance which marked the 'worship' of a gentleman, nothing of confession to a priest nor of any examination save self-examination.* An exploration of traditional religious life in Kent – of houseling and singing bread, of obits and anniversary Masses, candles and lights and bells, of the invocation of saints and the intercession for souls, of shrines and painted windows in churches, of monks and nuns and chantry priests[157] – would be revealing of his background, but might not take us very close to the faith of young Wyatt.

Henry Wyatt, who would choose to be portrayed by Holbein grimly clutching a pectoral cross, the sign of salvation, inscribed with the traditional initials INRI ('Jesus of Nazareth, King of the Jews'), expressed his religious beliefs more self-consciously.[158] In April 1524, thinking anxiously on the passage of his soul in the next life, he founded a perpetual chantry for two priests to sing for his soul, for the souls of his ancestors and his heirs, for the souls of the faithful departed, forever. This chantry – 'Sir Henry Wyatt's' – was founded in the dissolved hospital in the old Chapel of St Mary in Milton Church by Gravesend. The two chaplains were to be a body corporate and to have a common seal.[159] One of the first chaplains of Wyatt's chantry was Sir William Broadbent, who had been the curate of the parish of Hoo where Nicholas Metcalfe, Bishop Fisher's right-hand man, was rector. Living on until 1562 while his world changed around him, Broadbent bequeathed his soul in the old way, to 'our blessed Lady St Mary and the holy company of heaven to pray for me', and he lamented his unpaid pension. Another priest of Milton, Sir Robert Tuttisham, made his will in June 1541 in confident expectation 'of the money I shall receive of Sir Thomas Wyatt', and left his soul only to God. The rectors of Milton by Gravesend, where Sir

* See below, pp. 299–302, 459–60.

Henry was patron, were his stepsons: first John, then Roger Wilde.[160] Henry Wyatt had provided for a perpetual chantry, for priests to sing endlessly for his soul and all souls suffering their penitential stay in the fires of Purgatory. Nothing lasts forever.

Marriage might be the friend or enemy of promise. For Thomas Wyatt it was both. To mark his entry into county society Henry Wyatt staged the classic coup of the arriviste by marrying his son and heir to the daughter of one of the leading magnates of Kent. Sometime before 1521, Thomas married Elizabeth, daughter of Thomas Brooke, Lord Cobham of Cobham.[161] In the chantry college at Cobham a spectacular collection of memorial brasses commemorates the lineage and piety of the Cobhams, and there Elizabeth's grandfather, John Brooke, seventh Baron Cobham, lies buried.[162] The placing of his brass in the chapel asserted the Brooke claim to be the legitimate successors of the Cobhams, whose family had become extinct in the senior line, and it made its own claim. John Brooke chose to be commemorated, forever, with his second wife Margaret, the daughter of Edward Neville, first Lord Bergavenny. The Nevilles quartered their arms with their own grand Beauchamp, Clare, Despenser, Fitzalan and Warenne ancestors.[163] Elizabeth's father, Thomas, eighth Lord Brooke, married three times. With his first wife, Dorothy Heydon, he had seven sons and six daughters, among them Elizabeth. Her portrayal as a weeper on his tomb – mourning her loss, but also looking to the future of the family – is her only known memorial.[164]

Thomas Wyatt's marriage to Elizabeth Brooke was strategic. Perhaps a dynastic merger to shore up the Brooke fortunes and to dignify the Wyatt family was forced on unwilling partners. But perhaps they also *chose* each other; perhaps they had long known each other; perhaps they fell in love, the kind of love which promises to last forever, to overcome all. We cannot tell. Two children survived from this union: Thomas, born in about 1521, and a daughter, Frances.[165] Otherwise, all that we know of this marriage is of its desolation and demise, and the extremity of Wyatt's subsequent aversion to his wife. By 1526 Wyatt, the knight-errant who fought for the honour of maidens at the Castle of Loyalty, had suffered a personal cataclysm. The marriage on which the future of his family and his own honour depended was destroyed, apparently by infidelity, her infidelity. Marriage is a secret place, where only the couple know the inwardness, but in the disaster of its breakdown the Wyatt marriage, and the affair which ostensibly broke it, became wider – shamingly wider – knowledge. Fifteen years later, the story at court was that '*laquelle il avoit chassee de la maison pour lavoir deprehendee en adultere* [he had chased her from his house on account of her being caught in adultery]'. The identity of Elizabeth's forbidden lover – perhaps an open secret at court – is lost. A wife might learn to bear a husband's adultery, but only the rarest husband could countenance his wife's. If there did exist a complaisant husband, content to allow his wife a lover, it was not Wyatt. It was said that he defamed her.[166]

'Adulterous embraces', as the Church called them, were common enough at court, where the King had taken mistresses, and openly favoured his natural son, Henry Fitzroy. Yet marriage was a sacra-ment, a divine institution and indissoluble, and the breach of vows was believed to call down divine retribution as well as the penalties of the Church. If adultery among the upper orders was tacitly condoned in practice, it was utterly condemned in canon law, and to argue that adultery should not be a capital crime was controversial. A popular handbook for clergy, *The Commendations of Matrimony*, upheld the death penalty for male adultery.[167] 1526 was a particularly inopportune time to capsize a marriage, just as the King doubted the validity of his own, and the Queen and her friends called on Erasmus and Juan Luis Vives to write in defence of Christian matrimony.[168] Soon the wives of Eng-land would be summoned by the prophesying widow of Wyatt's col-league Robert Amadas, Master of the Jewel House, to rise as a single woman in defence of Queen Katherine and the institution of mar-riage.[169] When the King attempted to extricate himself from a mar-riage he saw as damned, not only England but all Christendom would be rocked. For the Wyatts there could be no divorce. Where death, not divorce, was the quietus of a marriage, the unhappily married were condemned to stay together until one of them by dying allowed the other to remarry. Other couples might have found some way to continue cohabiting in the same great household. But Wyatt cast out his wife, did not maintain her, would not see her.

The lady's betrayal brought not only pain but dishonour. In a poem of the Earl of Surrey a friend lamented his fellow knight's shadowed 'freedom [nobility]':

> Where thou hast loved so long with heart and all thy power,
> I see thee fed with feigned words, thy freedom to devour.
> I know, though she say nay and would it well withstand,
> When in her grace thou held thee most, she bare thee but in hand.
> I see her pleasant cheer in chiefest of thy suit:
> When thou art gone I see him come, that gathers up the fruit.
> And eke in thy respect I see the base degree
> Of him to whom she gave the heart that promised was to thee.[170]

The dishonour of betrayal by a lady was great; greater still was betrayal by a wife. Any man who could not order a wife could hardly order others over whom he had rule. 'The order of knighthood' owned by Lord Rochford taught that 'gentleness and honour of knighthood doth accord in a knight and in a lady by virtue of marriage, and the contrary is destruction of knighthood', and that the lady's infidelity, especially with a 'man of low estate', 'doth destroy . . . the noble confraternity and the noble lineage of the knight'.[171] Enraptured by the great love of Sir Lancelot and Queen Guinevere, Henry's courtiers may have believed that Lancelot's chivalry lessened the dishonour to King Arthur. Such a romance was less fatal in art than in life, as they would discover.

Much later, Thomas Wyatt would describe to his son an ideal of companionship in marriage:

Love wel and agre with your wife, for where is noyse and debate in the hous, ther is unquiet dwelling – and mitch more wher it is in one bed. Frame wel your self to love, and rule wel and honestly your wife as your felow, and she shal love and reverens you as her hed. Such as you are unto her such shal she be to you.

94

Such charity and reciprocity had been lacking in his marriage, damaged by his own failings, he admitted, but more by those of his estranged, all unforgiven wife. More than a decade later in 1537 he
could not recollect his marriage in tranquillity, nor attribute equal
blame: 'And the blissing of god for good agrement betwen the wife
and husband is fruyt of many children, which I for the like thinge
doe lack, and the faulte is both in your mother and me, *but chiefelye in
her.*'[172] In the same way, 'They fle from me' ends 'I would fain knowe
what *she* hath deserved'.[173] Perhaps George Brooke blamed his sister,
for he remained an intimate of Wyatt's. Elizabeth weeps eternally on
the tomb of her father, but in his will of 1529 Lord Cobham made
no mention of her, as though he had disowned her.[174] Shamed and
exiled, Elizabeth was sent to live in any household but her husband's
– where she went, with whom she lived, now unknown. According
to her grandson, George, she and her friends kept a close eye on her
lost husband.[175] Wyatt and Elizabeth never saw each other again, until
a reunion was forced upon them in 1541, in extraordinary circumstances. Their hapless children, casualties of this vitiated marriage,
were brought up somehow, somewhere: Thomas probably lived at
Alington, in the vigilant care of his grandfather; Frances may have
stayed with her mother, thereby losing her father.*

Maybe the women of the Cobham family were particularly desirable, famously alluring. In the next generation, Elizabeth Brooke, niece
and namesake of Wyatt's wife, would be a court beauty. A century earlier, Eleanor Cobham of the Surrey branch of the family had been
mistress, then wife of Humphrey, Duke of Gloucester.[176] Mary Brooke
– not Elizabeth's sister Mary, but perhaps a cousin – had a romantic
history scandalous and grand. Shortly before January 1530 Lord Bergavenny married as his fourth wife 'Mary Brooke, otherwise called
Mary Cobham'. Once his servant, Mary had been his mistress before
being his wife, or so his will hints: 'and so I did accept her service that
she hath served unto me by such love and favour as I have born to her
to have taken her my bedfellow in marriage'. The animosity of Mary's

---

* See below, pp. 290, 496–7, 547–8.

stepchildren towards her appears from Bergavenny's warning to his heirs not to evict Mary and her unborn child if they wished for 'the grace of good fortune in this life with my blessing and the blessing of Our Lord in heaven'. The romantic histories of the Cobham women threatened to compromise their family honour.[177] Elizabeth would marry again, but not for a long time, not until after Wyatt's death.

And Wyatt: married but separated, bound forever to a woman who had betrayed him, forbidden to marry again, was he left to live alone? At a dark moment, he would make the laconic confession, revealing in its compression and fierce reticence: 'I graunte I do not professe chastite, but yet I use not abhomination.'[178] This is his only direct – unpoetic – statement of the affairs of his heart. Much later, we will learn of '*deux quil a ayme*', of *two* women he had loved, apart from his wife.[179] One of these two we will meet, but the identity of the other we can only guess. Searching in the verse of Wyatt the 'courtly maker' for self-expression, we will seem to find evidence enough of grief, of joylessness, of heartbreak, of the sullen reverberations of failed romance. Yet complaint of the forsaking, faithless lady is the characteristic pose of the courtier–poet and none was more convincing than Wyatt in expressing the conventions of pain, disillusion, loss, none more bitter in his singing. If, reading his poetry, we look directly for his particular experience and pain we may be deceived, for it is the alchemy of the poet constantly to make his own life unreal and to transmute it into form, to turn real experience, perhaps long afterwards, and imagined experience into art. True, Wyatt's poetry gives little hope of believing in unclouded, untroubled love which lasts forever, but it was refracted through more than his own disillusion. He wrote in a long tradition, and for readers of Chaucer the tragedy of the fickleness of Criseyde was that of many another woman.

fynys qd Wyatt —

The end, said Wyatt. In the Devonshire manuscript, the plaything that turned tragic for some of the leaders in the court's game of love, this song appears within a section where many poems end with Wyatt having said (not written) that they are finished:[180]

ys yt possyble
that so hye debate
so sharpe so sore and off suche rate
shuld end so sone and was begone so late
   is it possyble

ys yt possyble
so cruell intent
so hasty hete and so sone spent
From love to hate and thens for to Relent
   is it possyble

ys yt possyble
that eny may fynde
within on hert so dyverse mynd
to change or torne as wether and wynd
   is it possyble

is it possyble
to spye yt in an yIe   *eye*
that tornys as oft as chance on dy   *dice*
the trothe wheroff can eny try
   is it possyble

it is possyble
For to torne so oft
to bryng that lowyste that wasse most Alofft
and to fall hyest yet to lyght sofft
   it is possyble

All ys possyble
Who so lyst beleve   *desires*
trust therfore fyrst and after preve   *prove*
as men wedd ladyes by lycence and leve
   All ys possyble
    fynys qd Wyatt

Is it possible? Eight times the 'maker' asks, aghast to discover how soon love turns to hate, how 'dyverse mynd' is found in one 'hert', how 'trothe' – fidelity and truth – spins like a dice, how soon highest hopes are dashed. In this hymn to disenchantment he turns to answer with the sarcasm of one who was duped, who should have known: it *is* possible, *all* is possible.[181] Mutability – the turning of words, the random changing of hearts and minds, reversal of truth and 'trothe' 'as wether and wynd' – is a returning theme of Wyatt's. Applying the tested proverb about friendship – 'he who trusts before he knows doth hurt himself and please his foe' – to marriage, where custom will not allow prior proving, he warns 'All ys possible/Who so lyst beleve'. As 'ladyes' may prove not to be 'ladyes', men swear vows they do not keep: 'As men wedd ladyes by lycence and leve'. 'Who so lyst' believe him: nothing can be trusted to last forever, or even for long.

If we read the following sonnet in Wyatt's personal manuscript, claimed by '*Tho.*' and annotated in Wyatt's hand, we might surmise that he, like his speaker, learnt to love again:[182]

	If waker care if sodayne pale Coulor	*wakeful, vigilant*
	if many sighes with little speche to playne	
	now joy, now woo, if they my chere distayne	*stain my face (blushing and*
	for hope of small if muche to fere therfor	*growing pale)*
	To hast to slake my passe lesse or more	
	by signe of love then do I love agayne.	
Tho.	if thow aske whome, sure sins I did refrayne	
	brunet that set my welth in suche a rore	*well-being tumult*
	Thunfayned chere of phillis hath the place	
	that brunet had she hath and ever shal	
	she from my self now hath me in her grace	
	She hath in hand my witt my will and all	
	my hert alone wel worthie she doth staye	
	without whose helpe skant do I live a daye	

Rewriting his first thought in line 8 – 'her that did set our contrey in a rore' – he makes his speaker claim his former love only to disclaim her: 'I did refrayne/brunet that set my welth in suche a rore', and gives his heart, 'my witt my will and all' to 'Phillis'. Imagining Wyatt himself to be the lover has invited the happy game of guessing the identities of 'Brunet' and 'Phillis', of invoking a cast of courtly 'ladyes' waiting in the wings with whom to pair him. To generous Phillis the sighing lover has abandoned himself, 'from my self', and in her grace – her sexual grace –

98

may rest his desire, 'and all . . .'[183] The 'contrey' the abandoned Brunet set in uproar may be England, yet when the speaker's friends thought of their 'country', they meant their county. We will save the game of find-the-lady in Wyatt's poetry until later, and find him instead thinking on Petrarch and playing brilliantly with rhetorical technique. Puttenham chose this 'Sonnet of *Petrarca . . .* thus Englished' by Wyatt to illustrate *Irmus*, the figure he called 'the *long loose*', where 'all the whole sense of the ditty is suspended till ye come to the last three words, *then do I love again*'.[184]

In a manuscript containing two medieval French poems – 'Les Lamentations de Matheolus' and 'Le Livre de Leesce' – was inscribed:

> thys boke is myn
> George Boleyn 1526

'Les Lamentations' by Matheolus of Boulogne were satires on women and the torments of marriage. Women's natural treachery, viciousness, cruelty, infidelity, jealousy, etc., as Matheolus described them, made marriage hell on earth – for men. Bathsheba's destruction of Uriah and Dalila's of Samson provided persuasive examples of the wives of nightmare. While 'Les Lamentations' described the martyrdom of marriage, 'Le Livre de Leesce' refuted Matheolus' arguments. Since 1526 was the year of George Boleyn's marriage to Jane Parker, these were unhappy portents for newly-weds, and may even have been a subversive wedding gift from a cynical friend.[185] A name for the donor may spring to mind when, at the end of the manuscript, we find Wyatt's handwriting and signatures – 'Wyot' writing in French, and 'Wyato' in Italian. In Italian, 'Wyato' wrote:

> *Auditori mei notate questo argumento*
> *che il novo cassa il vechio pensamento.*
>
> My listeners, note well this point,
> that the new quashes the old way of thought.

In French, 'Wyot' copied a popular proverb:

> *Qui asne est et cerff cuyde bien estre*
> *a sallir une fosse on le puyt bien cognestre.*

That same proverb appeared, in English, in another contemporary manuscript. For the scornful courtier, the spectacle of the felled upstart held particular delight:

> He that is an ass, and hart himself doth ween
> at leaping over the ditch, the truth is easily seen.[186]

Here was Wyatt, displaying the sardonic mockery of the courtier intent upon teasing and pleasing his friends. Since 1526 was also the time of Wyatt's own marital catastrophe these interjections can be read in the light of his experience, by those who would see it so. Written beside the initials 'JP' – Jane Parker? – was the motto: '*presto para servir* [ready to serve]'.[187] Here 'VVyat' wrote sarcastically '*forse* [perhaps]'. And, more doubtful than hopeful, he wrote in Latin: 'LAVDA: FINEM [praise the end]'. Written below was the elliptical, existential motto, '*Rien que detre* [only to be]'. Only to be what? That was the question.

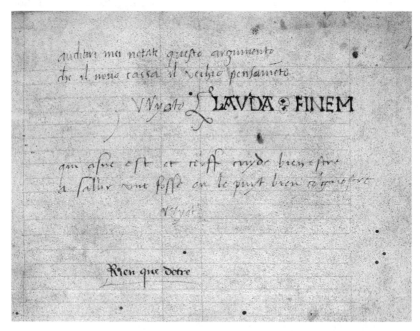

Wyatt's messages for his friends, inscribed in George Boleyn's manuscript

Dramatis Personae

The French Court

Francis I, King of France
Marguerite d'Angoulême, Duchess of Alençon, sister of Francis I
Anne de Montmorency, Grand Master of France
Dr John Taylor, Henry VIII's resident ambassador
Sir Thomas Cheyne, Henry VIII's special ambassador
Thomas Wyatt
John Corbett, Taylor's secretary, and 'Martin Luther scholar'

The Papal Court

Guilio de' Medici, Pope Clement VII
Giovan Matteo (Gianmatteo) Giberti, papal datary (the officer
    charged with the duty of registering all the bulls and other
    documents issued by the Pope)
Paolo Giovio, historian
Matteo Casella, the Duke of Ferrara's ambassador
Cavaliere Gregorio Casali, Henry VIII's resident ambassador
Sir John Russell, Henry VIII's special ambassador

The Imperial Army

Charles III, Duke of Bourbon, Constable of France
Alfonso d'Avalos d'Aquino, Marquess of Vasto
Philibert of Châlon, Prince of Orange
Ferrante Gonzaga, general, brother of Federico II Gonzaga,
    Marquess of Mantua
Georg von Frundsberg, captain of the German landsknechts
Charles de Lannoy, Viceroy of Naples
Cesare Ferramosca, envoy of the Viceroy

The League Army

Francesco Guicciardini, Lieutenant General of the papal army

Niccolò Machiavelli, sent by the Otto di Pratica ['Eight of Affairs'] of Florence

Francesco Maria I della Rovere, Duke of Urbino, Captain General of the League army

Andrea Doria, Admiral of the League (until his change of allegiance in 1528)

Venice

Andrea Gritti, Doge

Altobello Averoldi, Bishop of Pola, papal nuncio

Ercole Gonzaga, brother of Federico II Gonzaga, Marquess of Mantua

Prothonotary Giambattista Casali, Henry VIII's ambassador

Ferrara

Alfonso I d'Este, Duke of Ferrara

4

Viatvs Viator: Wyatt the Traveller

Restless Wyatt, 'that quick could never rest', now looked to leave England for the while, in search of adventure and escape.* At the New Year of 1527 he encountered Sir John Russell travelling down the Thames, and hearing that Russell was on his way to Rome, in embassy to Pope Clement VII, Wyatt offered his services: 'And I . . . if you please, will ask leave, get money and go with you.' 'No man more welcome.' Thus the story passed down in Wyatt's family, as Wyatt's grandson began a history which Wyatt himself left 'some helps thereto'.[1] The serendipity of this encounter accords with the effortlessness a courtier cultivated, but it was more likely that Wyatt was commanded to accompany Russell. Like Russell, he was 'well languaged' and proven in the dangerous enterprise of guarding the royal treasure, and in the embassy to France the previous year Wyatt had done credit to himself and his patrons. As Esquire and as Knight of the Body, Wyatt and Russell were the King's natural emissaries and orators.[2] Russell already knew Italy and its tormented politics well; Wyatt did not, but perhaps he knew enough of the language to be *italianizzato*, and he had the sensibility and imagination to be drawn to the glories of Italy. Fatefully, he was 'desirous to see the country'.[3]

In France, in May 1526 Wyatt had been present as a league was made for the defence of Italy, the League of Cognac. The French King, the Pope, the Most Serene Republic of Venice, and Francesco Maria Sforza, recently deposed Duke of Milan, were signatories, and Henry VIII was guarantor.[4] Telling the 'unfortunate and pitiable' history of

* Jonathan Woolfson and I have told this story before: 'Thomas Wyatt in Italy', *Renaissance Quarterly*, 58 (© 2005 by the Renaissance Society of America), pp. 464–511. I am grateful to the editors of *Renaissance Quarterly*, but especially to Dr Woolfson, for their kind permission to retell it in a modified version. The original discoveries which began the quest for Wyatt in Italy were all Jonathan Woolfson's, and in this chapter his was the research in the Italian archives.

the League, Luigi Guicciardini, who was Standard-Bearer of Justice in Florence in 1527, believed that it 'ought to inspire terror in anyone who would attempt serious actions without considering the luck, strength and courage of his enemy, with overconfidence in his own forces', and with unrealistic goals.[5] The League for defence turned to war, and by the late autumn of 1526 the campaign was going disastrously for its forces.[6] In the margin of one of his *Ricordi* (*Maxims and Reflections*) – 'Those who would finish a war too quickly often lengthen it' – Francesco Guicciardini, Lieutenant General of the papal army and famous historian of these wars, wrote: 'our fate at Cremona'.[7] Writing from the field early in October, Niccolò Machiavelli gave a lapidary explanation of the 'mistakes that have deprived us of victory', and which had allowed the 'disorders in Rome'.[8] On 20 September the Colonna faction had raided papal Rome, with Imperial connivance, and relations between Charles V and the Pope were at such a nadir that the Emperor threatened to withdraw his allegiance.[9] In Lombardy Imperial troops were massing. Italians waited in anguish as German landsknechts (foot soldiers) under their captain, Georg von Frundsberg, threatened to join the Imperial troops led by Charles, Duke of Bourbon, and to march south, into the Papal States, into Tuscany, and finally to Rome itself. By the end of November, the landsknechts had crossed the Po, and seemed to be advancing on Modena.[10] A sonnet by Giovanni Guidiccioni expressed the despair of those who witnessed the unforgettable descent of Frundsberg's troops on '*l'Italia, misera, dolente* [wretched, sorrowful]':[11]

> *Ecco che move horribilmente il piede*
> *e scende, quasi un rapido torrente,*
> *dagli alti monti nova ingorda gente*
> *per far di noi più dolorose prede*
> [. . .]

> Here comes, with terrifying step,
> descending like a rapid torrent from
> the high mountains, a fresh and greedy horde,
> to turn us into still more pitiful prey
> [. . .]

An Imperial fleet under Charles de Lannoy, Viceroy of Naples, had sailed from Spain, and the long-feared defection from the League of Alfonso I d'Este, Duke of Ferrara, was a grave blow. 'The King of England should act,' implored the Venetian Senate.[12]

By the end of the year Henry and Wolsey were at last convinced that the plight of the League was so desperate and the Pope in such danger that it was in the King's interest to make real his promise to be guarantor of the League – Defender of the Faith indeed. If the Pope, in his extremity, were forced to make a separate peace with the Emperor, his League allies would be abandoned to fight the war alone.[13] Henry finally sent aid: as special ambassador, Sir John Russell was charged to convey twenty-five thousand ducats to Rome to support the papal forces, to travel to Ferrara to persuade Duke Alfonso to an armistice, and then into the Kingdom of Naples to protest to the Viceroy about his campaign against the Pope and the Church.[14] Wyatt went with him to grace and defend Russell's embassy. Together, they set out for France. Arriving in Poissy on 8 January 1527, they found the King hunting, as usual. The story in diplomatic circles was that Russell dared tell Francis to leave 'his hunting and ceaseless pleasures' and attend to the war, 'so that the enterprise may not be endangered, as the loss and dishonour would be his alone'.[15] On 11 January Francis duly sent an envoy to the Pope.[16] Departing Paris for Lyon, Russell and his retinue travelled from Lyon to Chambéry in the territory of the Duke of Savoy.[17] The Duke offered a safe-conduct to defend them from the danger of arrest or attack, and sent them on their way with his herald and a messenger as protectors and guides. As they journeyed through the mountains, they received warning that unless they hurried they would be stopped by Imperial forces, so Russell left his entourage – 'my folks' – to follow, and rode on alone with Wyatt. Riding furiously, day and night, they reached Savona on 28 January. There Pedro Navarro, an admiral of the League fleet, promised them sea passage to Rome.[18]

Sailing from Savona, they reached Civitavecchia on 4 February, where the great Admiral Andrea Doria met them and gave them armed escort to Rome. Clement sent 'Turkey horses' – the epitome of glamour and grace – for Russell and Wyatt to ride, and his datary,

Gianmatteo Giberti, and other gentlemen, came to greet the English ambassadors and accompany them into the city. This was a welcome to honour the King whom they represented, and a mark of Clement's gratitude for Henry's aid in his hour of need.[19] Declining the offer of lodging in the papal palace, they chose to stay with Cavaliere Gregorio Casali, Henry's resident ambassador and Russell's '*bon amy* [good friend]'.[20] Doubtless they wished to be briefed on the confused and changing situation in Italy. On 7 February Giberti took Russell for a first audience with Clement, who declared himself as 'bound' to Henry as 'ever pope was to any prince'. Russell marvelled at the honour of his treatment: the datary 'keepeth me company and rideth about the town with me for recreation'. 'Where I lie in the palace I am marvellously well entreated, and all at the Pope's cost, and gentlemen sent to keep me company daily.'[21] Since an ambassador needed gallants in attendance, Wyatt probably enjoyed these courtesies along with Russell. Throughout Rome the English King was celebrated as true Defender of the Faith, and his ambassadors' arrival caused a stir. '*C'è maestro Rosello e maestro Guiet ambassatori anglesi galanti omini* [Here are Master Russell and Master Guiet, English ambassadors and true gentlemen],' wrote the historian Paolo Giovio.[22] True, Giovio described the French King's ambassador in the superlative, '*galantissimo*', and could not spell Wyatt's name – no Italian ever could – but this notice marked the presence of a young man from Kent in the heart of Christendom, and his glittering encounter with papal Rome.[23]

Rome has the power to dazzle any visitor. Wyatt now saw the Eternal City for the first time, walked amidst the numinous remains of a civilization in which – so he had been taught – virtue had governed public life, witnessed the splendours of Christendom's capital, and conversed in the Latin of which he was master. Beyond all this was the excitement of being a close observer at a climacteric of Renaissance diplomacy, and of having a part to play, however small, at the moment when the Pope and the Emperor seemed poised to raise spiritual and temporal swords against each other. Clement was oscillating between peace and war. 'In great danger' as the Viceroy and his army advanced on Rome at the end of January, the Pope had acceded to terms he found intolerable, and agreed a truce: '*volemo zozo le arme* [we have chosen to sheathe the sword]'.[24] But Russell's arrival, and the unlikely victory of the papal army against the Viceroy at Frosinone on 2 February, changed the balance in the peace negotiations. Clement – newly, fleetingly confident – urged Russell not to go yet to negotiate with the Viceroy or with the Dukes of Ferrara and Bourbon, but to 'tarry a while'.[25]

In these tremulous days Russell and Casali – and perhaps Wyatt with them – met envoys from other princes. With Matteo Casella, the Duke of Ferrara's ambassador, they spoke '*molte e molte parole*' – not in Latin, but partly in English, partly in French, partly in a kind of Italian.[26] With the Duke of Bourbon's envoy they played for time. Now Wyatt witnessed again the play of friendship in diplomacy, for Bourbon claimed Russell as 'one of his great friends'. Russell had twice been emissary to Bourbon, had been encamped with his army at Marseilles and Milan, had had his trust, and certainly was a partisan of Bourbon's and not of the Viceroy, Bourbon's rival. Russell agreed to use that trust and mediate between Bourbon and the Pope, on condition that Bourbon's army attempt 'no new enterprise'. 'By fair words', Russell hoped to play for time, to delay the Imperial army which was marching inexorably south.[27]

Having determined only days before to prosecute 'the wars to the uttermost of his power', Clement quailed. On 13 February he sent Russell with the General of the Franciscan Order to the Viceroy's camp to negotiate a truce, 'to protest and bluster'. The Viceroy, 'with whom was all the great princes of Naples', came to Ceprano, mid-way between Naples and Rome, to parley. Wyatt may have been there to observe this encounter with the great princes of the Empire. After a week the papal emissaries returned to Rome, to find Clement havering between peace and war. Bankrupt, terrified of the sack of his native Florence, torn by conflicting counsels, Clement was being persuaded in almost hourly audiences – by the Imperial emissaries and the Florentines, to peace; by Russell and Casali to war. 'By many great arguments' the English ambassadors convinced him that he must not make the peace treaty alone nor abandon the League.[28] Playing for time, Russell offered to consult the other League ally: La Serenissima, the Most

Serene Republic of Venice. Acute observers understood that his real intention was not to persuade the Venetians to an armistice, but to argue against it, to convince them that while the papal army was victorious it must fight on. Now, abandoning the caution which haunted the military and political thinking of the Republic, they must give this vital aid. From Venice, Russell would ride to Ferrara to win over the Duke to the League.[29]

Russell and Wyatt left Rome on 24 February, on a mission to secure either universal peace or effective war. Knowing the dangers of the road and the likelihood of capture, Russell had tried to avoid so hazardous a journey: he 'durst not' visit their masters, so he had told the ambassadors of Bourbon and Duke Alfonso.[30] Not capture, but the hazard which is ever present when riding horses brought calamity. Russell broke his leg when his horse fell and was forced to return to Rome, ignominiously in a litter.[31] Wyatt went on alone, riding furiously in post, with a mission crucial for all Christendom. He had orders to present his commission to Prothonotary Giambattista Casali (Gregorio's brother), the English agent in Venice, a man of great cultivation, the friend of leading humanists, but unfortunately 'very incapable and inexperienced in statesmanship'.[32] Arriving in Venice on 1 March, Wyatt probably stayed at Casali's lodgings on San Giorgio Maggiore.[33] We might imagine him there, by the great Benedictine abbey of San Giorgio, gazing across to the Ducal Palace and the Basilica di San Marco, then and now wonders of the world. Unfortunately, it was raining torrentially.

On the following day Wyatt went with Casali to the Ducal Palace to make their proposal before the College of Venice. This was Wyatt's moment of glory, but observers noted only 'an Englishman named . . .' An unknown Englishman.[34] Ambassadors would climb the Scala d'Oro and wait in the Sala dell'Anticollegio until summoned into the Sala di Collegio, where they were received. If that was the path which Wyatt took, what he saw is not what is seen now, for the decorations of that time were lost in the fire of 1574, but the Gothic splendours of the Ducal Palace were glorious enough. The College was the executive body of the Most Serene Republic, responsible for making unserene decisions about peace and war.[35] We cannot tell whether Wyatt had the

chance to display his powers of eloquence before men who appreciated an ambassador who could play '*un Marco Tullio*' and address them
in '*le belle parole . . . in Latino*', in elegant Latin.[36] Revealing the terms of
the truce which Clement, in his terror, proposed to accept, Casali and
Wyatt urged the Venetians either to accept it also, or else 'not to make
provision for war so tepidly'.[37] On 3 March, Casali and Wyatt, together
with the papal nuncio in Venice, Altobello Averoldi, and the Florentine
ambassador, had audience with Doge Andrea Gritti. The Doge was, he
told them, waiting for letters from Rome to know whether the Pope, on
hearing from the French King, had changed his mind. Two days later,
Casali announced to the College his intention to go to Alfonso d'Este
in Ferrara.[38] Learning of this mission, Francesco Guicciardini was dismissive, as he had been dismissive of the whole English intervention:
to those who lived 'in the midst of danger' it offered words instead of
action, empty reassurance rather than military resolution.[39]

Wyatt and Casali left Venice on the evening of 6 March, travelling
by barge through the lagoon, along the coast to the Po delta, and down
by river to Ferrara.[40] The Ferrara they saw as they arrived can now
only be imagined, but this was the capital of a great Renaissance *signore*.
Encircled by great walls, newly constructed by Alfonso, filled with palaces and churches, this was a city built to awe. Here the magnificence
and the piety of the Este Dukes were displayed, and their utter dominance. Their splendour and wealth appeared in the Ducal Palace; their
terrible military power in the great moated fortress, the Castel Vecchio,
a place of safety but also of intimidation, in whose dungeons Duke
Alfonso's brothers were immured for life for their conspiracy, a perpetual reminder that a despot is never secure.[41] Just as Wyatt and Casali
reached Ferrara, the son of Girolamo Morone, the High Chancellor
of Milan, was being held hostage there, in fear of his life.[42] Famine
gripped the city, and plague was beginning to spread.[43] In the military
emergency of early March, Ferrara was poised for war and the piazza
thronged with the Duke's gentlemen, ready to ride.[44] Casali and Wyatt
had arrived too late. On 5 March, as Casali announced his mission to
the Doge, Alfonso had ridden to Finale near Modena, for a council
of war with the Imperial generals: Bourbon, the Prince of Orange,

the Count of Egmont and the Marquess of Vasto.[45] Alfonso d'Este, renowned as an artillery captain, had already given ordnance, artillery, ammunition, pioneers and provisions to the Imperial army, and now promised further aid. On 7 March he returned to Ferrara to raise money from its bankers for Bourbon's troops.[46] Receiving the English emissaries, he definitively rejected the League's offers: though he wished to be a 'good Italian', he must keep his promises to the Emperor. When Casali returned to Venice on the 11th with this dismal news, he returned alone.[47]

Never were the peace and liberty of Italy so endangered. Bourbon's army, with its vast train, was advancing south by forced marches, the desperate, unpaid troops sustained only by hope, and a promise – that the sack of Florence would recompense their suffering.[48] The council of generals at Finale had resolved that the army should march on Florence to pacify the troops – according to what he called '*la loi de Mahomet*' – and to force the Pope to terms. On 8 March Bourbon's army reached the fortress of San Giovanni, ten miles outside Bologna, and finally joined forces with von Frundsberg's landsknechts who had been bivouacked there, drenched and wretched, since late November. The two armies shared grievances and mutual jealousy. On the evening of the 13 March some Spanish infantry incited the German troops to mutiny. When one landsknecht cried '*Gheltan, Gheltan* [pay, pay]', everyone joined in, the Spanish infantry also demanding '*Paga, Paga* [pay, pay]'. Bourbon fled in disguise before the mutinous troops, seeking refuge in the Prince of Orange's camp. Storming Bourbon's quarters, the mutineers ransacked them, stealing, looting, burning. The 'mutation' lasted all night, with the soldiers firing guns, until the Spanish troops were finally appeased with the promise of a ducat a man, and the Germans with half a month's pay. But on the 16th they mutinied again. Only von Frundsberg might have restrained the landsknechts, but even he could control them no longer. In shock at the mutiny, he suffered a stroke and now lay paralysed and close to death. By the 17th the starving soldiers were crying '*Pane, pane* [bread, bread]' because there was none, and the snow was knee-deep and still falling.[49] Desperate soldiers, ranging and marauding, skirmishing with anyone they encountered, beyond any control of their captains, threatened desertion unless they had money, from whatever source. When Cesare Ferramosca, the envoy sent from the Viceroy of Naples, arrived at Bourbon's camp around 21 March with news of the truce and money from the Pope to keep the army at bay, he found the soldiers '*furieux comme de lions* [savage as lions]'.[50] And there, at the fortress of San Giovanni, Spanish soldiers, at the end of their patience, were holding a hostage: Thomas Wyatt.

Wyatt had left Ferrara on about 10 March. 'Desirous to see the country', this fortuitous tourist proposed to travel to Rome by way of Bologna and Florence.[51] Even for Wyatt, the gallant and swordsman, such a journey at this moment seemed wildly reckless. Yet his proposed venture was a cover for a mission to carry vital diplomatic despatches. And he should have been protected, for he travelled with a safe-conduct from Alfonso d'Este, who had given him his own courier as guide. The safe-conduct was an almost sacred pledge: the person who carried it was under the protection of the person who gave it, and in his safety. To violate it was to invite retribution. Upon the granting of safe-conducts the whole diplomatic system depended.[52] As he reached the gates of Bologna, '*un gentil hombre ingles*' – Wyatt – encountered a company of Spanish light horse. Did he spur his horse to outrun them, did he draw his sword? Outnumbered, he was captured. 'The King of England's man, coming from Ferrara, has been taken,' wrote Guicciardini to Giberti on 13 March, and by that night the Duke of Ferrara knew 'what had befallen that English gentleman'.[53] Wyatt's despatches – letters from the Florentine ambassador in Venice, and from Casali – were seized and, save for the parts in cipher, copied to the Emperor so that he might see the League's arguments to win over Alfonso, and how he resisted them.[54] Wyatt's ransom was set at three thousand ducats – a vast sum, nearly an eighth of the treasure which Henry had sent to relieve the League – for the soldiers knew the value of their captive. Even if the ransom were paid, the soldiers might not keep their part of the bargain. Recently, Imperial forces who had taken Girolamo Morone prisoner in Milan had freed him upon payment of a ransom, only to recapture him. They were 'ready to have stricken off his head' unless he paid the same sum again, and his son was being held hostage in Ferrara's Castel Vecchio.[55] In the

Imperial camp Wyatt was alone, unable to speak the languages of his captors, and suffering their privations. He had witnessed the mutinies of the previous days, heard the soldiers' demands, saw their desperation. Alone, he now waited on the soldiers' decision about his fate and hoped, against hope, that there would be diplomatic efforts to free him.

Dishonour to the King's 'beloved familiar' was dishonour to the King. Although Wyatt was not an accredited ambassador, *in extremis* he had acted in place of one. An ambassador was universally recognised as being safe – even in war, even in the midst of armies – for without that immunity there could hardly be diplomacy.* Everywhere the ambassador was protected, everywhere, except in Bourbon's camp. News of Wyatt's capture was not at first believed in the College of Venice. When Giambattista Casali heard of it, he warned that although the King of England had no intention of breaking with the Emperor, he might well do so once he heard that his servant was captive and abducted, especially since this servant's '*barba* [uncle: in fact, father]' was the King's Treasurer.[56] Once he discovered the capture of this 'gentleman of his chamber', he would be incensed against the Emperor.[57] Russell and Gregorio Casali kept news of Wyatt's disaster secret from the King – matters were difficult enough already without this diplomatic outrage. While peace or war in Christendom hung in the balance, offending Henry threatened grave diplomatic repercussions.

Every effort was now made to extricate, to ransom Wyatt. In Rome Russell wrote to his 'great friend' Bourbon soliciting Wyatt's release, and he persuaded the Pope to urge Giberti to write to him also.[58] From the camp of the League army in Bologna on 21 March Guicciardini wrote assuring Giberti that he had sent Bourbon 'the letters on behalf of the young Englishman', and that Ferramosca would try personally to secure his release: '*quanto potrà*'.[59] 'As much as he will be able' – perhaps hardly at all. Ferramosca had arrived at Bourbon's camp on about 21 March, where he learnt of the mutinies and, in an audience with Bourbon, was told '*des choses diaboliques* [devilish things]'. Fleeing for his life, Ferramosca sought refuge with Ferrante Gonzaga.[60] Who could,

* See below, pp. 332–4, 392–3, 434–7.

or would rescue Wyatt? All hopes now rested with Alfonso d'Este. The capture touched him personally, for it was his safe-conduct that was disregarded, his protection and his word dishonoured. The plight of the young Englishman offered the Duke the chance to prove his magnanimity. But even for Alfonso, finding ways to penetrate Bourbon's camp and the means to pay the ransom was not so easy.

Enter Ercole and Ferrante Gonzaga, Gonzaga princes, sons of Alfonso's famous sister Isabella d'Este, and brothers of Federico Gonzaga, Marquess of Mantua.[61] In the summer of 1527 there would be a revealing exchange of letters between Henry VIII and Ercole Gonzaga. Henry thanked Ercole for his 'recent humanity' towards 'our beloved familiar, Thomas Wyatt', which he would never forget.[62] Ercole, acknowledging the service with the easy grace of the great nobleman, disclaimed it as 'paltry and really nothing'.[63] Ercole had the means to pay Wyatt's ransom or could raise the money, for his family was fabulously rich: he also had the ways, for his brother Ferrante was one of Bourbon's captains. If anyone could free Wyatt from the anarchy of Bourbon's camp, it was this Imperial commander. Ferrante had little personal interest in serving the English King, beyond sustaining Henry's ties with the princely house of Gonzaga, which was important enough, but Ercole hoped that by binding himself closer to the King and Wolsey he could gain what he most desired: the Gonzaga birthright, a cardinal's hat.[64] Early in May 1527 Clement would reluctantly, in his financial extremity, be forced to grant – to sell – him one.[65] Later that summer, Ercole acknowledged his gratitude to Wolsey, for he knew that he had been created cardinal at Wolsey's request.[66] A favour returned for Ercole's favour to the King.

Maybe Wyatt had met Ercole Gonzaga. At the end of February Gonzaga had arrived in Venice, where he disported himself at the carnival masques 'all day and a good part of the night'.[67] Giambattista Casali may have been among his companions, for he and Ercole Gonzaga had been brought up together since their youth, had studied together at Bologna in 1524–5, and 'loved each other like brothers'.[68] Casali might easily have appealed to him to help ransom Wyatt. Early in March Ercole was in Venice, pawning his possessions and raising loans, and was apprised of Casali's diplomatic initiatives.[69] Wyatt's friends now looked to the power and resources of Alfonso d'Este. Protesting against the capture of an emissary who was owed diplomatic immunity, Casali warned of Henry's likely fury, of the risk of his severing relations with the Emperor once he heard that his man was thus '*spogliato* [ill treated]', and he sent a servant to the Duke.[70] A report of Alfonso's sending three thousand ducats to the Imperial camp on 16 March to free Morone may even have mistaken that ransom for one sent for Wyatt.[71] By 24 March Wyatt was released. 'It was laborious and difficult', so Casali acknowledged, 'to wrest him from the hands of rapacious soldiers, who wished to mulct the man by all means, as the Duke of Ferrara wrote to me.'[72] Wyatt escaped in the nick of time. At a council of war on 25 March Bourbon and his captains agreed to retreat. Yet they could no longer command their troops. On the following day the mutinous companies of Spanish light horse and men-at-arms sent a fateful message: they were preparing to march on unpaid, rather than go back.[73]

Ransomed and free, Wyatt now made for the camp of the papal army at Bologna. There Guicciardini and Machiavelli contemplated the implosion of the League and the disaster for Italy.[74] Machiavelli reported on 27 March the confusion – their wavering between peace and war and truce – and their impotence: '*ma i cieli quando vogliono colorire I disegni loro, conducono gli uomini in termine, che non possono pigliare alcun partito sicuro* [but the heavens, when they wish to disguise their designs, lead men to a point, where they can take no safe resolution]'.[75] In a letter to Giberti so despairing that it was crossed through and never sent, Guicciardini reported passingly on the 28th: '*hanno lasciato lo Inghilese et stasera è venuto qua* [they have released the Englishman and this evening he came here]'. For Guicciardini, always scornful of English meddling in the 'miseries of Italy', Wyatt's arrival was another irritation in the midst of the uncertainty and desolation. '*Io vi confesserò liberamente che io non so stasera dove io mi sono, vedendoci in tanto chaos* [I will confess to you freely that this evening I do not know where I am, seeing us in so great chaos].'[76] To be in Bologna at that moment was to be 'in Purgatory . . . in the Devil's house', such was the poverty, confusion and fear.[77] Not Stoic indifference to fortune was needed now, but Machiavellian *virtù*: skill, energy, courage, prowess. In *The Prince*, preparatory to his last chapter, the 'exhortation to

liberate Italy from the barbarian yoke', Machiavelli had urged impetu-
osity rather than caution, 'because Fortune is a woman, and if you wish
to control her, it is necessary to treat her roughly'.[78] On 29 March, as
Bourbon capitulated to the will of his troops and declared his intention
to breach the truce and to march forward, Guicciardini wrote again
to Giberti. As he saw it, three paths remained open to the Pope and
his advisers: to accede to everything by a new treaty, to take flight, or
to defend themselves to the death: '*Dio vi illumini* [May God enlighten
you].' '*Siamo di animo, potendo farlo*', wrote Guicciardini, '*di tentare la fortuna*
[We intend, since we can, to attempt fortune].'[79]

Wyatt, too, contended with fortune. Somehow he left Bologna, perhaps in these exigent last days of March, but he is lost from sight. Only
at night and in greatest danger could anyone leave the camp. Horsemen who sallied out of the city by daylight were captured by Imperial
troops.[80] Bourbon's army was poised to leave San Giovanni and march
towards Bologna, thinking to find the Romagna open to plunder. Only
'the strangest weather' prevented its moving on the night of the 29th.
Finally, the army marched two days later, but whether on Tuscany or
the Romagna was still unknown.[81] '*La trista nostra sorte* [our unhappy
fate]', wrote Machiavelli, was that it was impossible to know how best
to act, though they knew that on their decision rested potential ruin
for the '*bene publico*'. Guicciardini now 'lives in great anguish'.[82] From
Rome on 1 April Casali received news – from Giberti, who received
it from Guicciardini – of Wyatt's escape and his arrival at Bologna.
The English ambassadors reported that 'Guicciardino writeth that the
Duke of Urbino with the Venetians' army were retired and repassed
the Po . . . contrary to their promise' – a terrible betrayal.[83] Through
waiting months the League army of nearly thirty thousand, composed
mainly of Venetian mercenaries, under the command of Francesco
Maria I della Rovere, Duke of Urbino, had been shadowing the Imperial forces, but never engaging with them.[84] Abandoned by the Pope's
Venetian and French allies, bound still by a truce which no longer
bound the enemy, Guicciardini was forced to watch as Bourbon's army
marched on.[85] This was an army, some said, no longer led by Bourbon
but leading him, a virtual prisoner; others said that Bourbon had been

suborned. The Spanish troops marched south in unison with the land-sknechts, 'in beautiful order', by forced marches of fifteen and twenty miles a day, their intentions dreaded, though still unknown.[86]

Picture Wyatt, riding furiously for Rome ahead of Bourbon's advancing army. That he returned to Rome we learn only at his leaving of it, for Russell and Casali's reports never referred to him. In England, all Henry's emissaries in Italy were under a cloud: Gregorio Casali for some past failing; Russell for handing over the King's money to the Pope even as Clement abandoned his League allies and the war, and for exceeding his charge.[87] Wyatt's adventures had brought embarrassment: his capture had threatened to rupture the King's relations with the Emperor, and his ransom had placed Henry under obligation to other princes. Maybe his English masters believed that Wyatt's going to Venice instead of Russell had sunk the League cause. If Russell had been able to go to Venice himself to argue for outright war, would it have made a difference? Cesare Ferramosca believed so: Russell 'sent his kinsman [Wyatt] to Venice; and owing to this, nothing was signed'.[88]

The failures of this accidental ambassador hardly caused the loss of *libertas Italiae*. Observers blamed Italy's fatal disunity on a failure of leadership, especially the Pope's. Had Clement only waited for the French and Venetians' unequivocal commitment to fight, the war – so Russell believed – might have been won. Even as Clement made a truce with the Imperialists in March, Russell remonstrated with him: 'he is causer of that there shall be more wars in Italy than ever there was'.[89] As the papal forces disbanded by land and sea, according to the terms of the truce, many saw this as 'the beginning of the greatest misfortunes' for Rome and Italy, and to the League ambassadors the Pope could only answer, in the words of Pilate: '*quid scripsi scripsi* [what I have written, I have written]'.[90] Soon he would understand, wrote Guicciardini, that '*li accordi non sono el remedio ma la ruina sua* [the agreements are not the remedy but his ruin]'.[91] On 25 April Russell and Casali, orators of 'the Most Serene King of England', were witnesses when Clement, finally understanding the danger, rejoined the League, too late, far too late, to save it. Was Wyatt in attendance, in the papal presence?[92]

The Pope, this failing prince of Rome and fainéant leader of the

League, was also, of course, the spiritual head of Christendom. As Easter approached and Rome prepared for the splendid, solemn liturgies of Holy Week, Russell and Wyatt were still there, awaiting their recall. The Eternal City became not only a city of ambassadors but a city of pilgrims, who congregated to receive the papal blessing and to see displayed the most sacred relics of the Church: Christ's shroud, the Veronica, and a fragment of the lance which pierced His side.[93] For most of Holy Week the Pope kept within his private apartments, attending the celebrations of the principal rites within the Sistine Chapel, but on Easter Sunday – which fell on 21 April in 1527 – he appeared before the faithful, and was carried in procession to the Basilica of St Peter where he celebrated High Mass. Ambassadors were honoured by administering the water to wash His Holiness's hands. After Mass, the Pope ascended to his balcony to pronounce a public blessing. The English ambassadors were likely to have attended the Easter rites, and the ceremony for the presentation of the Papal Rose to the Venetian ambassadors two days later.[94]

While the timeless ceremonies were celebrated that Easter, news was reaching Rome of Bourbon's advance. On Easter Day Guicciardini wrote that all was uncertain, but that Bourbon's army could easily change its course from Florence, and turn to march on Rome: it was well to think the unthinkable. '*Però è bene cominciare a pensare.*'[95] If they came, there was reason for terror. 'These men work more cruelly than Turks.' Fevered stories spread of their sacrilege; of their burning houses of religion, forcing 'nuns and friars to lie together', 'thrusting into a priest's brain a crucifix [they] burnt both the priest and it'. At Easter, 'when men should have received their maker', Bourbon's troops 'finding many hosts [Mass wafers], cast them into the water'. So Russell and Casali reported in horror on 26 April.[96] The League forces, powerless to stop them, followed at a distance: 'where the Imperials dine, they [the League] sup'. At their last audience on 30 April, the Pope sent Russell to plead with the French and English Kings to aid him in his 'extreme necessity'. Departing instantly, Russell and Wyatt reached Civitavecchia the same night, but 'by reason of evil weather' the galley could not sail.[97] There, kicking their heels, they awaited the news from Rome. A sleepless Gregorio Casali wrote, still hoping that Bourbon might divert to Naples. But as the Imperial army reached Viterbo on 2 May it was finally understood that it would march on Rome.[98] By the 10th Russell's galley had been driven 'by tempest' to harbour at Porto Venere on the Ligurian coast, and by the following day they had reached Savona, only 'danger of . . . Turks and . . . tempest' delaying their vital mission.[99] Although they could not yet know it, no English or French aid would now save the Pope or the liberty of Italy. On 6 May Bourbon's army began its sack, and made of Rome 'Rome's grave'.[100]

Wyatt's thoughts on leaving Rome are unknown. But George Wyatt's history (owing much to his Protestant sensibilities) recorded his grandfather's experience of *la dolce vita* and his response to Rome's voluptuary pleasures. On their arrival in Rome, a 'chief favourite of his Holiness' came to entertain Russell and Wyatt at their lodgings. As 'special tokens of compliment', the Pope sent two of the 'most choice of courtesans . . . to refresh them withall after their long journey and absence from their wives, with a plenary dispensation verbal for that should be done by them'. Knowing the customs of the papal court, Russell found the offer 'not impertinent', 'so after laughing together, and some secret conferences', and some wine shared, he sent them away with a few crowns and excuses 'for the other courtesy' because of their weariness.[101] This story of the 'courtesies of courtesans' is not incredible, for the courtesans of Rome, famously cultivated and alluring, did entertain ambassadors and procure information, as well as inspiring poets and breaking hearts.[102] Wyatt would encounter again their power in love and politics.* A later poem denouncing Popish practices told a revealing story of Sir Francis Bryan. In search of intelligence, he had selflessly slept with a cardinal's courtesan at the papal court:

> She lying a night with Sir Francis Bryan
> disclosed to him the whole matter
> which when he perceived the cardinal's treason
> thought to procure her the letter to obtain.[103]

From Paris in December 1530, Bryan wrote to the English ambassador in Rome: 'I pray you recommend me most heartily to Signora Angela,

* See below, pp. 355–6.

and desire her to send me a pair of sweet perfumed gloves.' Maybe 'Signora Angela' was Angela Greca, one of the most famous and astute courtesans of her age.[104] Unlike Bryan, Wyatt was far from embracing courtesans or Roman customs. According to his grandson, he construed the 'courtesies of courtesans' as an 'Italian scorn and a kind of prognostic of the evil of their success'.[105] A disdain for Rome's decadence remained.

Wyatt's vision of Rome appears in another story which entered mythic family history. George Wyatt had it from two sources: 'One a gentleman, a follower then of Sir Thomas. Another, a kinsman of his name.' Riding from Rome in post, Wyatt and Russell stopped at an inn to change horses. On the wall of his chamber Wyatt drew a 'Maze and in it a Minotaur with a triple crown on his head, both as it were falling'. Around the maze lay a ball of thread and broken shackles and chains, and above it this inscription: 'LAQVEVS CONTRITVS EST ET NOS LIBERATI SVMVS [The snare is broken and we are freed].' A circular painting of a falling papal minotaur within a maze portraying exactly this story

The papal minotaur, with his triple crown, in the midst of a maze

is found on the reverse of a portrait of Wyatt which passed down to his descendants. This *impresa*, so George Wyatt believed, was drawn from Plutarch's *Life* of Theseus and recalled Theseus' adventures in the labyrinth of the Minotaur. Yet the superscription was not classical, but scriptural, from Psalm 124:7. Petrarch had also associated the papal captivity at Avignon with the labyrinth. For Wyatt's grandson, the meaning of the *impresa* was pellucid: it 'fitted to the affairs of the king with the Bishop of Rome', and his determination to deliver himself and his people 'from the servitude of the Romish Minos and Minotaur Clement the 7th'.[106]

The Italian journey of the '*giovane Inglese*' marked his life. Sent by hazard on a crucial mission in the heart of Christendom, he had failed, was bound to fail. 'A great feare leste anye thynge shulde quayle throughe my fawte' would haunt him thereafter. As he admitted later to his son, through his own 'foly and unthriftnes', he had suffered 'a thousand dangers and hazardes'.[107] Many of these dangers befell him in Italy. Sailing to outrun Turkish corsairs in the Mediterranean, riding recklessly in dread of capture, had been terrifying. Worse was the captivity itself. In the freezing misery of Bourbon's camp, at the mercy of mutineers, Wyatt could not know, but only hope, that rescue would come. Yet he had had the chance to marvel at the glories of Italy. Imagine Wyatt: in Venice, crossing the lagoon from San Giorgio to Piazza San Marco, like the English ambassador in Carpaccio's painting; or in Rome, entering the Vatican Palace, or St Peter's, walking amidst the ancient ruins of the capital of the Roman Empire.

In Italy, Wyatt learnt to love its language and its poetry, and to become 'a good Italian', an Englishman *italianizzato*.[108] With whom could he share tales of his Italian adventures? Perhaps with Thomas Cromwell. Cromwell, who would become Wyatt's great friend and patron, had also sought refuge in travel. In his 'ruffian' youth, he had journeyed to Italy, and fought with the French at the battle of Garigliano in 1503. In Rome in 1510 he delighted the Pope with his English part-songs – the 'threemans song' – and jellies, and four years later he returned to Rome where he stayed at the English hospital. The story of 'Cremuello', the indigent *oltramarino* (foreigner) among Florentine merchants, fascinated

Matteo Bandello, who dedicated a novella – one of the very first examples of a new literary form – to this Italianate Englishman who, becoming great, returned the favours received in his youth.[109] In England, those who wished to know Italy looked to Cromwell as their guide. In April 1530 Edmund Bonner asked that Cromwell, who wished to make him a 'good Italian', lend him copies of Petrarch's *I trionfi* (*Triumphs*) and, if he had it, Castiglione's *Il cortegiano*.[110] Castiglione's book of the ideal courtier, which he reluctantly published in 1528, had been written in deepest pessimism about the delinquency of Italy's rulers and the decadence of its political life.[111] In this spirit, Cromwell hung in his London house a painted cloth depicting the 'eversion of Italy'. In 1531 his servant Stephen Vaughan remembered this painting and the verses painted on it:

> *Et sola et mediis haerens in fluctibus, ecce*
> *Me miseram, quantis undique pressa malis.*

> Alone, caught in the midst of waves, here I am
> in my distress; how great the evils that oppress me
> on all sides.[112]

Wyatt also contemplated the tragedy of Italy. Through waiting months he witnessed at close hand its fatal divisions which had invited and been deepened by foreign invasion, and observed the failed leadership which had led to its loss of liberty. He had watched the gathering crisis and the conflict between Pope and Emperor, the great antagonists who should have been allies, which culminated apocalyptically in the Sack of Rome. He had seen foreign armies circling Florence, Bologna and Ferrara, threatening their stability and autonomy. When news came of the 'Friday tumult' in Florence on 26 April, he was in Rome to hear it. The names of those who opposed the Medici and defended Florentine liberty – including Luigi Alamanni and Filippo Strozzi – would recur in his life.[113] The swathe which the Imperial army cut through Italy left the Emperor, as so many had warned, 'lord of all'. To be in Italy at this time was inescapably to think of liberty and of tyranny. In the camp of the papal army, in the shadow of Italy's ruin, Machiavelli and Guicciardini had lived with the imagination of Italy's calamity and anatomised the causes. Wyatt had been fleetingly in the camp with them at Bologna – though if they had met him, he was only an unwelcome distraction in the midst of the chaos and their despair. In the tradition of classical and humanist historiography, Guicciardini described Italy's tragedy in terms of personal interests and prejudices, follies and weaknesses, which drove historical action. To understand the working of history in this way was to place greater emphasis on character than upon policy or strategy in the shaping of events. So, for Guicciardini in the *Storia d'Italia*, as well as in the letters he wrote as he watched the disaster unfold, it was the craven delays of the Duke of Urbino and the vacillations of Clement VII which delivered Italy to its ruin. Yet even if men had acted prudently and followed reason rather than their ambitions and desires, the working of fortune made them impotent to control events.[114] Did Wyatt, too, think in these terms?

Later, Wyatt condemned papal power and its abuse. He may have done so already in Rome in 1527 as he saw the part the Pope played in Italy's ruin. There was the tyranny of rulers who flouted the law and oppressed their people, and there was the tyranny of weak rulers who left their people ungoverned. Clement's tyranny was of the latter kind, with terrible consequences. Ludovico Ariosto, the author of *Orlando Furioso*, blamed the papacy for Italy's misfortunes. He saw Italy given in prey, just as Guidiccioni remembered the descent of the German troops to make '*di noi più dolorose prede* [of us more pitiful prey]'.* In his *satira* II Ariosto depicted a generic Pope, who

> *trionferà, del crestian sangue sozzo.*
> *Darà l'Italia in preda a Francia o Spagna,*
> *che sozzopra voltandola, una parte*
> *al suo bastarda sangue ne rimanga.*

> he will triumph, drenched in Christian blood.
> He will give Italy in prey to France or Spain,
> so that, after she is turned upside down, one part
> will remain for his bastard blood.[115]

* For Guidiccioni's sonnet, see above, p. 104.

Luigi Alamanni may have thought of Ariosto's *satire* as he wrote his own condemnation of papal Rome in his *satira* X:

> *Non in Germania ove 'l mangiare e 'l bere*
> *M'habbia a tor l'intelletto, et darlo in preda*
> *Al senso, in guisa di selvagge fere.*
> *Non sono in Roma, ove chi 'n Christo creda,*
> *Et non sappia falsar, nè far veneni*
> *Convien ch'a casa sospirando rieda.*

> Not in Germany, where eating and drinking
>   would take away my brains and make them prey
>   of the senses, in the manner of wild beasts;
> I am not in Rome, where he who believes in Christ
>   and does not know how to cheat or poison
>   should suffering go home.[116]

In one of his verse epistles addressed to 'Myne owne Jhon poyntz', Wyatt followed Alamanni, but his deeper vituperation may owe something to Ariosto also.[117]

> Nor am I wher Christ is geven in praye
>   For mony poyson and treason at Rome,
>   a common practice used night and daye.

Ariosto served the most anti-papal of princes, Alfonso d'Este. Since the Duke liked to summon Ferrara's famous poet to impress foreign visitors, there is a chance, the slightest chance, that Wyatt may even have met Ariosto.[118] When Wyatt arrived in Ferrara early in March, the Duke's mind was turned not to hospitality but to war, but he may have used his chance to display his princely condescension to the envoy of the English King, and to show Wyatt treasures of which his king could hardly dream. The Ducal Palace, as splendid as any in Italy, was joined by a corridor, the Via Coperta, to the massive Castel Vecchio.[119] Within the Via Coperta were the Duke's private apartments. Here in Alfonso's *studiolo*, the *camerino d'alabastro*, Titian had recreated an ancient picture gallery, for the Duke's private delight, and to show to honoured guests.[120]

From his succession in 1505 Alfonso, who was both a feudatory of the Church and an Imperial vassal, had been in dispute with successive Popes over claims to lands which bordered his own great territory and the lands of the Church.[121] Alfonso's persistent disobedience had led to his excommunication and to proceedings against him as a contumacious vassal.[122] By 1527 his enmity to the papacy and allegiance to the Emperor had been so disastrous to the Church that, in an unlikely comparison, he was said to be to the Holy See as Helen was to Troy.[123] The Duke continued his feud with the papacy in his patronage of art. He chose to have himself portrayed by Titian and by Dosso Dossi leaning upon a cannon, perhaps his personal cannon, 'la Giulia', allegedly forged from the melted bronze of a bust of his enemy, Pope Julius II.[124] On his coin Alfonso had had depicted the figures of Christ and the Pharisee, inscribed with Christ's words 'QVE. SVNT. DEI. DEO'. To God what is God's: a transparent political allegory of papal usurpation and abuse of secular power, as well as a statement of what was due to the ruler.[125]

The same image was transcendently portrayed by Titian in a work specially commissioned by Alfonso in 1516, *The Tribute Money*. In an intimate exchange, Christ gazes at the Pharisee, who tempts Him to deny the legality of paying tribute to Caesar. Shown a gold coin, Christ asks: 'Whose is this image and the superscription? They said unto him: Caesar's. Then said he unto them: Give therefore to Caesar, that which is Caesar's: and give unto God, that which is God's' (Matthew 22:20–1). According to Vasari, Titian's panel was in the door of a cabinet. Seemingly, tellingly, this cabinet contained Alfonso's collection of ancient coins and medals, and Titian's sublime painting acted to protect the contents and to remind all who needed reminding of the power that Christ attributed to the Emperors of Rome, and to rulers in general.[126] Despite its location in an inner room, and this prosaic, ironic function, this picture, so original and beautiful, became 'very famous'. We cannot know whether the Duke honoured the 'young Englishman' in March 1527 by showing him his *camerino*, whether Wyatt saw *The Tribute Money*. But this biblical passage, 'Render unto Caesar', resonated in his imagination and in his poetry.*[127] The vision of 'lordly looks', of *terribilità*, and of the belligerence of a secular lord towards his Holiness may have stayed with Wyatt as he returned to the English court and stood in the presence of his king.

Before returning to England, Wyatt and Russell visited the court of the French King, who was in Paris in mid-May, awaiting Russell and his message from the Pope.[128] Of their mission no record remains. As yet unaware of Rome's catastrophe, they could only report the Pope's desperation and the imminence of Bourbon's advance. In Paris, the household of Thomas Winter, Cardinal Wolsey's illicit and favoured son, was a way-station for English visitors and and a quasi-official centre for English scholars. On their outward journey to Rome in January Wyatt and Russell had visited Winter. 'He is in the face of the world', wrote Russell, telling Wolsey what he wanted to hear, 'and many learned and worshipful men resort unto him, besides the English.'[129] Winter's tutor was the Scottish humanist Florens Volusenus (Florence Wilson), who became a close observer of the English court, and thought on the quiet of mind.[130] Since Winter resisted the best efforts of leading humanists to educate him, these scholars turned to discuss matters of intellectual and political moment amongst themselves.[131] John Leland, Wyatt's friend from Cambridge, was in Paris in 1527, and the encomia he wrote and dedicated to English friends and mentors give a vivid picture of intellectual life and aspirations.[132] Among the other scholars in Paris then were William Paget and Thomas Lupset. Perhaps Richard Pate and Anthony Barker, who had been studying with Juan Luis Vives in Bruges, were there also.[133] In May, as Wyatt passed through, Francis Poyntz was waiting in Paris.†[134] All these men received encomia from Leland and had parts to play in Wyatt's life.[135]

In Paris, these men thought on Christianity and the classics, studying the texts of Scripture along with those of ancient Greece and Rome, and mused on philosophy. They also thought of poetry. Acknowledging all that Cambridge had taught him, Leland credited Paris with teaching him what Cambridge had not – poetry:

* See below, pp. 161–2.
† For Poyntz and his mission, see below, pp. 136–7.

Most famous Cambridge taught me the seven arts
And the school which takes its famous name from the Isis.
But it was Paris that taught me to honour the Muses:
And henceforth I sang songs composed in varying metres.[136]

Most promising of all the young scholars in Paris was Francis Dinham. Leland praised him as Apollo's disciple:

> You are sipping the learned poetry of war-sounding Homer, sucking the Attic honey with your lips. Proceed with a brave spirit: sometime in the future beautiful Apollo will give full success to your bold beginnings . . . Meanwhile, Francis, may you enjoy days of good fortune: for without literature the fleeing hour dies.[137]

In Dinham all virtues and talents met. 'A personage of goodly fashions [handsome]', he was 'marvellously well learned both in Latin and Greek . . . right excellent in musical instruments'. And he was a poet.[138] Dinham, who was not yet nineteen, had studied at Cambridge and at the Middle Temple, where he was admitted in 1524. In Cambridge, his tutor was Henry Gold of St John's, who was warned not to allow him to go astray, but to drive him and make him translate Lucian from Greek into Latin.[139] But Dinham did go astray: he began ardently to be drawn to the evangelical religion. Thomas Lupset, another scholar who had been studying in Paris, warned his students of 'the foolish dreams of these young clerks' who speculated too far in Scripture, claiming to 'know God's will', for young minds were susceptible and 'foolish meddlers be daily sore punished'.[140] In the company of leading evangelicals in London and in Cambridge – Simon Fish, George Constantine, Thomas Bilney and William Gonnell – Dinham had studied the formative texts of the new religion, including Luther's *De servo arbitrio* (*On the Bondage of the Will*) and *De captivitate Babylonica* (*On the Babylonian Captivity of the Church*). So he confessed.[141]

Dinham, with powers to charm and persuade, was 'infecting' others with the new theology. In 1525 Philip Smith, a priest of Calais, meeting Dinham at the house of the Merchant Staplers, had talked with him of poetry and of Luther. That they had debated a quintessential doctrine of the Reformation – the bondage of the will – is suggested by Smith's ownership of Luther's *De servo arbitrio* of 1526, which Dinham had sold him, and Erasmus's answer: *Hyperaspistes* (*The Protector*). Their debate continued by letter.[142] Dinham had also been writing to John Corbett, secretary to the English ambassador at the French court, John Taylor. 'Companions and favourites', Corbett and Dinham were both 'well learned *grece et Latine*', and had studied at the Inns of Court.[143] In June 1528 the fateful discovery of a letter of Corbett's in Dinham's possession threatened to bring a swift end to this youthful promise. With heavy hearts, the English ambassadors sent Dinham, aged only nineteen, and Corbett towards Calais and England to face heresy charges. Dinham died of the sweating sickness that summer.[144]

Exalting in their studies of evangelical religion and of poetry, these brilliant young 'Martin Luther's scholars' had the power to persuade and to convert. Dinham studied Homer along with Scripture, as did John Frith, the evangelical theologian and future martyr, who knew by heart 'Homer's verses out of his first book of the Iliad'.[145] For the community of scholars in Paris in the late 1520s, poetry might remain a common inspiration, but religion would soon divide them. Confessional rifts appeared as they avowed different beliefs about the nature of salvation, about what a sinner could *do* – if anything – to be saved, and as the King challenged the universal Church. These great transformations would involve the hardest choices. Wyatt knew some of these young men, at Cambridge, in Paris, and in embassy. In the tiny world of the English embassy in France in 1526, they had all lived at closest quarters, because there were no lodgings; 'we have been compelled to be together all the time that we have been at Cognac'. There Wyatt was thrown into the company of John Corbett, the ambassador's secretary and 'Martin Luther scholar'.[146] But there were other companions with quite different faiths and allegiances, and there would be nothing simple about Wyatt's own choices.

Wyatt returned to the English court to explain his mission and his ransom. By 18 May the King, learning that 'a gentleman of his chamber had lately been taken prisoner in Italy', threatened reciprocal dishonour to the Emperor by officially demanding a safe-conduct for an ambassador travelling to the Spanish kingdoms: the mark of distrust.[147] Back in England, Wyatt perhaps took up his duties at the Jewel House, perhaps attended to the stewardship of his father's scattered estates. On 2 October 1527 Thomas Wyatt, gentleman, was sworn to the tourn at Conisbrough – a far cry from Ferrara.[148] He also returned to Paris that autumn. In a lost account book kept for an embassy to France between May and November 1527, Wyatt's name appears. The fleeting record of an expenses payment indicates that Wyatt was, at least for a time, serving in France with Sir Anthony Browne: 'to Osborne, Wyatt and Browne for money paid by them to priests singing mass before my M[aster]. Thursday, Friday and Saturday, ixs [nine shillings].'[149] In May 1527 Sir Thomas Boleyn and Browne had been sent as special ambassadors to the French King.[150] In October, the French court was at Compiègne, observing the ceremonies of the Order of St Michel at Michaelmas, before moving to Senlis and to Paris. Browne, who knew more of venery than of eloquence, was Wyatt's exact contemporary from Surrey and Yorkshire, a fellow knight-errant at the Castle of Loyalty, and he was, or would become, one of the malevolent 'they' who willed Wyatt harm.[151] Browne's vanity and jealousy made him a man to guard against. Later judgements by Wyatt's friends – Browne's enemies – are revealing. In 1538, as Browne damaged diplomatic relations with France which he was charged to further, Thomas Cromwell called him *'glorieux coquart* [a swaggering coxcomb]'. A decade later, Russell judged him 'a man most unreasonable, and one whose words and deeds do not agree together . . . one that will blame every man for that fault and yet will do worse himself'.[152]

A lost portrait showed Wyatt in 1527. In the possession of the third Earl of Stafford in the eighteenth century, this profile of a head was said to have been painted in Italy. 'Round on the Frame. old writing – is thus ANNO Æta SU. XXIII D.M.DXXVII [in the year of his age 23. 1527]'. George Vertue believed this to be a portrait of Wyatt's son Thomas, but the inscription fits only Wyatt himself, the traveller to Italy, aged twenty-three in 1527.[153] And we have a portrait of him of a different kind in this year. John Leland addressed an encomium to his friend: '*Viate*', Wyatt the traveller. The verse speaks of a moment when Wyatt, the traveller, was no longer *viator*, but back in England, planning a project. It was brought home to England from Paris by Sir John Dudley, the mutual friend of Wyatt and Leland.

> *Dudlegas patrias suum hinc in oras*
> *Ornaturus iter, monebat ut te*
> *Et notum & veterem mihi sodalem*
> *Impetirem aliqua memor salute.*
> *Feci quod voluit, lubensque certe.*
> *Illum nam studiis tuis sciebam*
> *Vinclis mirifici quibusdam amoris*
> *Coniunctum: ac etiam addo litterarum*
> *Fautorem & niveum quidem mearum.*
> *Tu nunc fac animum rogo Viate*
> *Nostrum, non Veneres style fluentis*
> *Expendas propius nitentiores.*
> *Quas sic Castalia tibi puella*
> *Consensu facili simul dederunt,*
> *Ut vel montibus Aonis in ipsis*
> *Te natum chorus aestimet virorum*
> *Doctorum niveus fuisse plane.*
> *Tu nunc officium vides amici*
> *Qualecunque tui, probe & valete.*

Dudley, about to arrange a journey from here to his native shores, advised that I should remember to present you, my familiar and old companion, with a greeting. I have done what he wanted, and certainly with pleasure. For I knew that he was bound to your studies by the chains of a wonderful love – and also, I add, a supporter (snow-white) of my own letters. Now, Wyatt, I ask, make your spirit ours; do not weigh up at close hand the more gleaming charms of a flowing style. The Castalian girls, with easy agreement, all gave you them so that the snowy chorus of learned men should think that you had clearly been born even in the very mountains of Boetia. Now look to your responsibility (such as it is) to your friend, my good man, and fare well.[154]

Historical precision was never the purpose of such verse. It was written to honour the virtue of the subject, for his immortality and the poet's. Yet these verse epistles addressed to friends were often written for particular occasions and serve as miniature portraits.[155] Dudley was Wyatt's contemporary and friend from their youth in Kent and Christendom. Their fathers had been fellow counsellors of Henry VII, but while Edmund Dudley had been sacrificed by Henry VIII on the altar of popularity, Sir Henry Wyatt had survived to serve him. John Dudley was brought up by Sir Edward Guildford of Hallden, while Wyatt's patron was Sir Henry Guildford of Leeds Castle. By the early 1520s, Dudley was a soldier, knighted for his feats on the battlefield, but he also had intellectual interests, attested by his patronage of Leland, and – or so it seems – by his connections with the circle of St John's men who were beneficed in Kent. In July 1522 Nicholas Darington, writing from Louvain to Henry Gold in Rochester, sent greetings to Dudley.[156] The precise occasion of Leland's verse was Dudley's journey, along with other court gallants, in the great entourage which Cardinal Wolsey took with him to France in the summer of 1527.[157] Dudley was now *viator*; Wyatt had returned home, perhaps to read and rhyme among the Muses.

5

Depe Witted Wiat

Thomas Wyatt was contemplating some literary enterprise. John Leland's admonition to him – 'Make your spirit ours: do not weigh up the more gleaming charms of a flowing style' – is now opaque, but perhaps he was encouraging Wyatt to allow inspiration from the Muses, rather than deliberately ponder prosody. Leland himself, composing in Latin hendecasyllables, was one of the chorus of humanist neo-Latin poets who applied their formal knowledge of metre and rhythm in the universal language of the learned, Latin. But Wyatt did not join them, nor make his spirit theirs. Learned in Latin, and trained to compose in it, maybe he chose not to do so. If Wyatt wrote Latin poetry, we know of none. Instead, his Muses inspired him to write in English and to become one of the first of the 'new company of courtly makers' who turned England into a sanctuary of the Muses, a new Helicon. Perhaps, like Count Lodovico in the *Book of the Courtier*, he believed that 'writing is nothing else, but a manner of speech, that remaineth still after a man hath spoken, or . . . an image, or rather the life of the words', and chose his literary language accordingly.[1] To Wyatt's language, his experiments in verse, and his rhetorical skills, we will turn and return. 'Now look to your responsibility,' so Leland adjured him. Poetic gifts imposed duties, and could be used to sublime purpose. Poets could work wonders, and the times had need of them.[2]

As Wyatt returned to England in the winter of 1527, he devoted himself, in public at least, not to poetry, but to prose; not to write in Latin, but in English, and in an English style he thought fitting for an essay of sober moral philosophy. This work he proudly proclaimed as his own, and he published it. The frontispiece declares:

Tho. Wyatis translatyon
of Plutarckes boke/of
the Quyete of
mynde

♦ ♦

♦

The Quyete of mynde was almost certainly Wyatt's only work to be published in his lifetime, the only work whose date of composition is certainly known, one of the very few which bears an unequivocal dedication and which can be located to a certain time and place. 'At Alyngton the last day of Decembre. M.D.xxvii.' He dedicated it to his queen, her 'most humble subject and slave, Tho. Wyat'.[3]

Wyatt presented his 'symple labour' to Katherine 'for the good lucke of this newe yere . . . and with as moch quiete of mynde as this boke pretendeth, alwayes prayeng god to sende you thonorable desyre of your vertuous hert'.[4] Yet the theme of his work is precisely that the constant, the wise, dependent upon nothing outside the self, will not need good luck. 'Knowing our selfes of unvyncible minde, fortrusting to our selfes', we will be guarded against 'thinges to come'.[5] Thus armed, we will be indifferent to what fortune gives, or takes away, free 'assuredly and unferfully thus to say to fortun, if thou gyve it I shalbe right glad, if thou take it agayn, I shalbe indifferent'.[6] Plutarch's is a work more of the rational mind than of the 'vertuous hert', and Wyatt's prayer for the Queen is perhaps the last reference in the work to his God, for Plutarch's wisdom is that of the pagan sage, and Wyatt, faithful to his text, introduces no good angel.

This gift of *The Quyete of mynde* to the Queen for the New Year of 1528 had a particular inwardness and timeliness. Katherine was already vaunted as the Stoic – the Christian Stoic – princess. In her exile from the Spanish kingdoms, she was especially consoled by the company of her compatriot Juan Luis Vives.[7] At Christmas 1523, travelling by river from the Bridgettine house at Syon towards Richmond, she and Vives had had a conversation which Vives remembered often. Thinking upon adversity and prosperity in this life, the Queen had reflected:

If I could choose between the two, I would prefer an equal share of both, neither complete adversity nor total success. And if I had to choose between extreme sorrow and extreme well-being, I think I would prefer the former to the latter, for people in disgrace need only some consolation while those who are successful frequently lose their minds.

The following summer, Vives recalled that conversation for Princess Mary as an exemplar of constancy.[8] Understanding that Christian fortitude might be especially demanded in marriage, the Queen commissioned scholars to write works on Christian matrimony.[9] Early in 1525 Vives began work on a new moral treatise on the duties of marriage: *De officio mariti* (*The Office of a Husband*). By the time that he published it four years later, and dedicated it with deliberate intent to the Queen – 'that woman, possessed of such great and steadfast manliness of spirit in the midst of such adversity and sadness' – her theoretical choice between 'extreme sorrow and extreme well-being' had become cruel reality.

Those men whom noble antiquity commended to the memory of posterity for their bravery and strength of spirit never endured such fierce onslaughts of fortune as she nor were they able to regulate its blandishments with such self-control and such invincible and unshakable integrity. If such incredible virtue had occurred in those times when honour was awarded for great distinctions, this woman . . . would be adored in temples like some supernatural power descended from heaven.[10]

Katherine's constancy to the ideals of marriage and fortitude in adversity were tested to the uttermost. The summer of 1527 saw the beginning of her ordeal.

Early in July 1527 Cardinal Wolsey set off for France to woo a French princess for his master, if Henry should become free to remarry. Passing through Kent, moving from gentry household to gentry household, Wolsey discussed with William Warham, the Archbishop of Canterbury, and with Bishop Fisher the gravest matter of state: the *quietus* of the royal marriage.[11] Ostensibly, the Cardinal's mission to France was to affirm the league between the French and English Kings, to consider the calamity of the Church and the plight of Italy. But even as this 'English Idol' set out on his quasi-regal legation, hostile observers suspected darker motives. Who would act as vicar to the captive Pope, and perhaps even claim the papal tiara for himself: who but Wolsey?[12] With that office he might settle an English matrimonial matter of incendiary potential. All the while he was in France Wolsey was 'daily and hourly musing' upon the King's 'great and secret affair', this 'great matter' that was no longer secret: 'the divorce to be had between Your Highness and the Queen'.[13] 'Our matter', as Henry and Anne Boleyn called it in their love letters.[14] Wolsey believed – had been led to believe – that his new queen would be French, but the wooing of a French princess was a fool's errand. Soon he understood, in horror, that his king was determined to marry Anne Boleyn.[15]

Thirty years later, George Cavendish, Wolsey's gentleman usher, wrote an account of the French embassy, in all its outward show and its inwardness. Although he muddled the order of events, Cavendish did not mistake the transformation in his master's mood from consternation to desperation as Wolsey understood the threat to his policies and his own position. To Cavendish it seemed that the Cardinal had been sent away so that Anne Boleyn and her friends could scheme in his absence. If that was not the first cause of the mission, it was certainly its consequence.[16] While Wolsey feasted and parleyed with the French King and his great nobles, seemingly at the height of his power, that power was being lost at home as Henry and his councillors, led by Anne's uncle and her father, schemed to take the 'Great Matter' out of his hands.[17] At Compiègne on 5 September, Wolsey learnt of the decision to send Dr William Knight, the royal secretary, to Rome to seek papal dispensation for Henry's remarriage even while Queen Katherine lived. He wrote despairingly, unavailingly, to dissuade Henry, and now hastened home.[18] Cavendish recorded that Wolsey's reunion with the King was 'at Sir Harry Wyatt's house in Kent'.[19] It seems that Cavendish was mistaken, for it was at Richmond that the King and Cardinal had their unhappy first audience.[20] Yet perhaps Wolsey did stop briefly at Alington before he went to the King. Soon thereafter, Sir Henry Wyatt retired as Treasurer of the Chamber – retired because he was old, but also perhaps because he had lost heart for service in the royal household, now so divided by the 'Great Matter'. Thereafter, Sir Henry's services would be given in Kent, at the local assizes.[21] As the King determined to marry Anne, by whatever means and at whatever cost, the Queen began to rally support at home and abroad. Consciences and allegiances were tested. Soon one gallant in Wolsey's service and in his entourage – John Legh of Stockwell, whom we will meet again – chose exile.[22] The Queen's friends lived in dread. On 1 October, Vives wrote of the Cardinal's return to England (disguising Wolsey's name in Greek letters for safety): '*Nos hic inter spem et metum pendemus* [we here hang between hope and fear].'[23]

The Queen to whom Wyatt dedicated *The Quyete of mynde* had often thought how to withstand fortune, but at the moment of the dedication, the New Year of 1528, she was no longer the Stoic princess, indifferent to what fortune gave or took away. Wyatt's translation of Plutarch for the Queen conformed exactly to the educational programme of the humanists she patronized, and Plutarch's *Moralia* was the *vade mecum* of her supporters. Plutarch already had a following in England. Thomas More's Utopians were 'very fond of the works of Plutarch', and perhaps their creator was also.[24] In 1510 and 1513 William Latimer and John Stokesley had borrowed a copy of Plutarch's *Moralia* from the Vatican library.[25] In Rome Richard Pace had translated moral essays by Plutarch from Greek into Latin, and published them.[26] Composing his *De fructu qui ex doctrina percipitur* (*The Benefit of a Liberal Education*) in the desolation of his diplomatic life in 1517, Pace counselled his schoolboy readers: 'I'll mention just one thing about Plutarch alone: never let him out of your hands . . . it seems to me that he alone is enough to make a man learned.'[27]

In his immensely popular *Introductio ad sapientiam* (*Introduction to Wisdom*) and his collection of spiritual mottoes and devices for Princess Mary, *Satellitium animi* (*Escort of the Soul*), both composed in England, Vives had written on the themes of tranquillity of mind and of the moderation of the wise, which guarded 'with an iron curtain' against the convulsions of fortune.[28] In his educational tracts, he proposed the reading of Plutarch, particularly Budé's translations of 'some small works of Plutarch'.[29] Guillaume Budé, prince among humanists, was a close friend of Vives, who lauded him for always having 'fortune in his power'. In about 1520 Budé wrote *De contemptu rerum fortuitarum* (*On Contempt of Fortuitous Events*) which echoed the themes of his translation of *De tranquillitate animi* (*On Tranquillity of Mind*) from Plutarch's Greek.[30] It was Budé's Latin translation of 1505, made during the longueurs of an embassy to Rome, which inspired and enabled Wyatt's translation of the work into English: indeed, without a Latin translation there could have been no *Quyete of mynde*, for – so far as we can tell – Wyatt did not know Greek.[31] When Wyatt translated Budé's *De tranquillitate animi*, it was almost as if it was at Vives's prompting. Yet whether the paths of Wyatt and Vives ever crossed is unknown. At the end of June 1527, just as Wyatt had returned to England, Vives left; as Vives returned for his fifth visit on 1 October, Wyatt was probably in Yorkshire and shortly afterwards in France.[32] Maybe they saw each other, as Budé put it, 'out of a grating'. Some of Wyatt's closest friends and associates later had been Vives's pupils in Oxford or in Louvain: John Mason, Anthony Barker, and Richard Pate. John Leland wrote an encomium for Vives.[33] When Wyatt, the Queen's 'slave', dedicated his tract to Katherine – a manifesto of his intent as a moralist – Vives was living at court in fear of his life, convinced that 'the swords are ready for action' against him.[34]

To dedicate Plutarch's meditation upon the quiet of mind to the Queen at the New Year of 1528 was to declare a particular and daring allegiance. The progress of the 'Great Matter' and the Queen's tribulation as her marriage and even her queenly title were threatened drew her friends to her defence – indeed, she summoned them. Yet to choose between Juno and Jove – the names which humanists covertly gave them[35] – was now a political act and had dangerous consequences. In May 1527, just as the judicial proceedings for the royal divorce began, Francis Poyntz was sent to the Emperor.[36] He was the King's ambassador but also the Queen's devoted servant. Katherine wrote to her nephew Charles, requesting him to credit anything 'Francisco Poynes' said in her name, 'Poynes being a person whom I entirely trust, and to whom I bear much good-will, and am besides under great obligation, on account of his many virtues'.[37] While Poyntz waited in Paris in May for safe passage to Spain, and Wyatt arrived there on his way home from Italy, did they meet and discuss the plight of the Queen, and Stoic consolation in the travails of a diplomatic life?[38] We cannot know, but at some point Poyntz translated *The table of Cebes* with its theme of withstanding the blows and seductions of fortune. It is more than coincidence that Wyatt's *The Quyete of mynde* and Poyntz's *The table of Cebes* were among the very first English versions of Greek authors ever to be printed.[39]

Some of Plutarch's followers were in trouble in the winter of 1527–8 because they were also the Queen's. Returning from embassy in 1525, Richard Pace, Dean of St Paul's, had withdrawn to the cloister of Syon to recover his perfect mind, and there found consolation in the Psalms and in biblical exegesis. In July 1527 he was still at Syon, engaged in scholarly work which 'will make him immortal'.[40] Disputing with John Fisher the doctrine of the inspiration of the Septuagint, Pace had, in the course of their discussions, been convinced of the validity of the royal marriage, and turned from the King's supporter in the 'Great Matter' to become the Queen's.[41] Back in residence at St Paul's, Pace became aware of popular support for Katherine, and began to engage again in politics, however reluctantly. He spoke to the King 'touching this matter of the Queen and the government of the Cardinal, express-ing himself like a good and loyal subject', so Don Iñigo de Mendoza, the Imperial ambassador, heard: that is, Pace had dared to support the royal marriage and criticize Wolsey. Late in October he and some of his servants were sent to the Tower. In Pace's disaster Mendoza was impli-cated. A fortnight earlier, Pace had sent a message promising Mendoza that 'His Imperial Majesty's interests might be served'. Mendoza sent a servant, Juanin Corchiero, who returned with a request from Pace that Mendoza meet him in St Paul's, deemed the least suspicious place for their assignation. Believing the Cardinal's spies to be everywhere, Mendoza presciently declined, yet spies were already planted in Pace's household, and they reported Corchiero's visit and Pace's possession of the ambassador's cipher.[42] Behind this cloak-and-dagger diplomacy lay a conspiracy among the Queen and her friends to urge her cause to the Emperor and, by means of the Emperor, to the Pope.

Vives had returned to England on 1 October. He came to teach Princess Mary Latin and 'such precepts of wisdom as would arm her against any adverse fortune'. But the Queen, in her distress, drew her countryman to her cause. The Christian consolation he offered – her pain was sent by God 'to the increase of highest virtues' – did not suffice: she demanded his practical help, asking him to act as her intermediary to Mendoza. On 26 October, forwarding a letter from Katherine, Mendoza wrote to the Emperor: if he 'really has the Queen's honour and peace of mind at heart', he should send to Rome for a 'trusty messenger to bring us the Pope's decision'.[43] By January 1528 Vives knew that he was closely watched and he feared for his life. Soon he was interrogated by Wolsey.[44] Vives protested: his conversations with the Queen were private, her loyalty to the King was beyond reproach, and anything she confided was so faithful that it might be posted on church doors.[45] Yet even the Queen's fidelity came in doubt once she was known to be in secret communication with the Emperor, who became Henry's declared enemy at the end of January 1528, and once she demanded the partisanship of the King's subjects. The private matter of their doomed marriage became inescapably public. 'The divorce is more talked of than ever', so Mendoza had written the previous autumn. 'The people are greatly aggrieved at the arrest of . . . [Pace]; they say openly that he has been imprisoned for speaking the truth.'[46] Early in 1528 not only Vives and Francisco Felipe, Katherine's messenger, were arrested, but Mendoza also. On 10 February he was taken from his residence in St Swithun's Lane, and held 'in free custody'.[47] As war threatened, the Emperor sequestered the French and English ambassadors and Henry and Francis retaliated. Diplomatic immunity was withdrawn, and one prince's ambassadors were seized and held hostage for the security of another's. While Vives and Mendoza were detained in London, Francis Poyntz and Edward Lee, along with the French ambassadors, were immured in the great Spanish fortress at Posa, all at the menacing pleasure of their princes.[48] Vives had written a treatise on diplomacy, and now learnt by experience what happened when *ius gentium* (the law of nations) was broken.[49] Ambassadors were the pawns of princes and always vulnerable.

It was in these circumstances, as war with the Emperor lowered, as public opinion was so inflamed, as the Queen's partisans rallied to her defence, and despite all the dangers, that Wyatt not only wrote *The Quyete of mynde*, and dedicated it to his Queen, but published it. Perhaps someone had chosen Wyatt, of all the young men at court, to write on Katherine's behalf; perhaps she had sought him.

Wyatt's translation was at the Queen's request, her wish, his command. Yet he had disobeyed her. The work for which she had asked was not Plutarch's moral essay, but 'The boke of Fraunces Petrarch, of the remedy of yll fortune'. *De remediis utriusque fortunae* (*Of the Remedy of Both Kinds of Fortune*) was Petrarch's most popular work in England up to that time, though known in manuscript, not in print.[50] Dutifully, Wyatt had turned to his task: 'I assayd, as my power wolde serve me, to make into our englyssh'. After translating nine or ten dialogues, he gave up. His excuse: 'the labour began to seme tedious'. It is true that Petrarch's work is exhaustive, and exhausting. In two books, and 254 dialogues, Petrarch counsels indifference alike to the delusiveness of good fortune and the blows of ill fortune, an exhortation to contempt of this world. With 244 dialogues still to go, Wyatt abandoned an endeavour which he found pointless and for which he did not have time. The 'frutes of the advertysmentes' – the lessons – of Plutarch's essay, so he assured the Queen, were the same as Petrarch's.[51] Although shorter, it was 'nerawhyt erryng' from Petrarch's purposes. Commending himself and his 'lytell boke' to Katherine's protection, he made this promise:

. . . if it may please your hyghnesse to accept it, it shall nat onely be a defence for the symplenesse of the boke, agaynst over busy serchers of other mennes actes, whan the good wyll shall have the alowance of so vertuous a jugement, but also corage to the symple endevour of this hande, towarde better enterprises.

This 'symple' author – using the rhetorical figure *litotes* and denying the contrary – ventured the opinion that the 'sentence', the message, of the work 'paraventure shall nat be moche unacceptable' to his queen.[52]

His reluctance to translate Petrarch's *De remediis* lay not only in his restlessness, but in the potential of his own language, for it lacked the diversity and copiousness of Latin:

The labour began to seme tedious, by superfluous often rehersyng of one thyng. Which tho peraventure in the latyn shalbe laudable, by plentuous diversite of the spekyng of it . . . yet for lacke of suche diversyte in our tong, it shulde want a great dele of the grace.[53]

For Wyatt, the perfect courtier, tediousness was a cardinal sin, and the 'tedium of explicitness' always to be avoided.[54] He sought an English style consonant with the style of the work he translated.[55] The preface to his 'gentyll reder' – most likely written by Wyatt himself rather than by Richard Pynson, the printer – expressed Wyatt's manifesto for a new English style fitting the subject matter, and the ardour of a young man in a hurry:

It shall seme harde unto the paraventure gentyll reder, this translation, what for shorte maner of speche, and what for dyvers straunge names in the storyes. As for the shortnesse advyse it wele and it shalbe the plesaunter, whan thou understandest it. As for the straunge names stycke nat in them, for who that can take no frute in it, without he knowe clerely every tale that is here touched, I wolde he shulde nat rede this boke.

Farewell[56]

The language might seem rebarbative, the proliferation of Greek names confusing. Wyatt did not care. Those who could not persevere with the language or profit from the work's truths did not deserve to read it. Like the friend, Paccius, for whom Plutarch wrote his essay, Wyatt sought 'nat the delicacy of sayeng, and the piked [flowery] delight of spech'. The essence of eloquence for which Wyatt – following Budé following Plutarch – strove was naturalness, that art which concealed art.[57] Through a plain, unornamented style, the use of earthy proverbs and of a determinedly English rather than Latinate vocabulary, Wyatt sought the natural diction of everyday life to express moral teachings which spoke not only to a queen but to her subjects. Whether he succeeded will be clear from the passages which will follow. Too often, in following Budé's Latin phrase by phrase, he produced a distorted, involuted English of shaky syntax. But that the clauses jostle and clash may be part of his desired effect, for he spurned orotundity and smoothness. Roughness and obscure brevity, proverbs and metaphor, were ways to estrange language and unsettle readers' expectations, and by such literary *virtù* the author might capture his audience.[58]

Plutarch had written his essay in reply to his friend Paccius's request for a 'more exquisite declaration' of Plato's *Timaeus*.[59] His response was a practical, empirical 'doctryne, to be as helpe for the lyfe to be ordred';[60] no exposition of Platonic truths, but closer to the 'Stoyik philosophers' whom he sometimes quotes, sometimes mocks. The doctrine which Plutarch expounded was for someone who lived in the world, someone like Paccius, who had 'great privalte [intimacy] with princes'. Unusually, Paccius 'dasyst [gazes, bedazzled] nat folysshly at the fawnyng of glory', remembered that 'sore toos [toes] are nat esed with gorgious showes [shoes], nor the whithlowe with a ring, nor the hedach with a crowne', and understood that money provided no cure for sickness of mind. Nor did 'glorie, or among courtiers apparence' assure the 'easy and sure passage of lyfe'.[61] Plutarch's essay was for anyone seeking calm of mind amidst tribulation, but especially for those at court where the temptations to flattery and to contention, and the spinning of fortune were the greater, because everything rested on the will of the ruler which might be as unpredictable as Nature. Those in public life especially must learn to apply reason and forethought and 'nat to suffre to stray the apasionate parte of the mynde'.[62] That there might be 'affections of the mynde' as well as mental powers Wyatt and his contemporaries allowed.[63]

Retreat and inactivity were not the way to the quiet of mind, nor 'faynt hert forsaker of frendes, kyn, and countrey'.[64] Indeed, 'what if that same, nothyng to do, hath troubled many from the ryght order of the mynde? As sayth Homere by Achylles', who sat idle by his ships.[65] Ambition was futile: had not Alexander himself wept when he learnt that 'there be infynite worldes, and we are nat yet lorde of one'?[66] Knowing 'the well of surete of the minde, springing in our self', we must meet 'foren thinges and chaunceable' by 'suffring with gret uprightnesse of the mynde'.[67] The wise man made virtue of necessity. Zenon, the Stoic, when his ship went down with all hands, responded: 'Fortune . . . thou doest very wel with me, that drives me to myn old cloke, and to the porche of philosophy'.[68] If troubled by 'backbityng, . . . envy, or nouhhty sclaundre', the wise man will seek remedy 'with the muses, or in som place of lernyng', as did Plato. If a man's particular anguish was 'thy wife be nat chast', 'knowest thou nat thepygram of Agys in Delphos?'[69] The constant man must learn to count his blessings, to be grateful for what he has rather than to repine for what he has not. Yet the natural condition is to wish for more: even 'the goddes . . . it irketh also of their godheed, outcept [except] they myght have power of thunder and lightning'.[70] We must consider the lot of others and be grateful for our own; 'that among porters and berers, we wery us nat with burdens, nor like flatterers, are constrained to be as parasites to princes'.[71] This last tribulation was one which Wyatt dreaded and which he contemplated with his friend John Poyntz.

Plutarch teaches that the constant person will be able to distinguish between enduring truths and fleeting appearances. It is a particular folly to look to those who seem to be 'very blessed, and (as they say) in Jovis lap', for things are not as they seem: 'but the curten and the fayr travers [screen] drawen, lettyng passe their glory and utter [outward] apparence, if aswell thou loke with in them, thou shalt truly fynde many inwardes, sower and troblous'.[72] This difference between appearance and reality, between outwardly seeming and inwardly being, will recur in Wyatt's thought and writings. Self-knowledge is essential: 'So al thinges is nat for every man, but he that wyll obey the poesy of Appollo must first knowe him self, and so take advyse of his owne nature.'[73]

Self-love and lack of self-knowledge lead always to disappointment and instability, for which 'we accuse wicked fortune and our desteny'. Instead, we should blame our own folly, for it is as pointless to blame fortune as to 'shote an arowe with a plou[gh], or hunt an hare with an oxe', as do those fools who protest that 'some cruell god shulde be agaynst them, that with vayn indevour, hunt an hart with a dragge net'.[74] Wyatt will be haunted by these images, and wearied by this kind of 'vain travail'. The fool will never recognise good things, even while he has them, but his 'thoughtes gape gredily after thynges to come'.[75] These images recur in 'My mothers maydes', a verse epistle to John Poyntz, where Wyatt's speaker counsels not to 'let present passe and gape on tyme to com'.[76] The person who has attained self-knowledge, who has learnt to distinguish between things within his control and things beyond it, and to subdue his passionate nature by the exercise of reason, will be constant and will not live in fear of future uncertainty and loss.

Surely we may stay forthwith ech misfortun, I knew I had slypery riches, nat nayled with sixe peny nayl . . . I knew well inough that they that gave me power, myght also take it from me. I knew that my wyfe was wyse, but that she was also a woman . . . I knew that my frende was a man . . . a lyvely thyng redy of nature to be depraved.[77]

The student of Plutarch's wisdom, who could follow his precepts, would be able 'with valyaunt vertue' to overcome fortune, and to say 'I may go, I may go my way . . . with the good leve of god . . . I have prevented the, o fortune'.[78] Wyatt praised the constant man who 'havyng the well of lyfe (I mean wyt and condicions, from whiche commendable dedes do spring) clere and untroubled, shall bring forth all his dedes, mery and upright as it were with an hevenly grace'.[79] In almost Wyatt's own words, Henry Howard would praise him for his Christian constancy:

> Amid great storms, whom grace assured so
> To live upright and smile at fortune's choice.[80]

Yet if Wyatt ever achieved that constancy, we may doubt that he had done so by 1527.

Thomas Wyatt was the Queen's man, and his *Quyete of mynde* was a public declaration of allegiance made at the moment when she had greatest need of friends, even young, untested ones. How and when he became her man, and why Katherine gave him her patronage, are less clear. Certainly, Henry Wyatt's position had brought his son into the orbit of the court, and the office of Clerk of the Jewels which Thomas had held since October 1524 entrusted him with conveyance of royal jewels and treasure. But it was not as factotum that Wyatt won the Queen's trust, but as a young man of rare talent, a talent that might have come to her notice in various ways. The Queen was a noted and enlightened patron of learning, 'remarkably learned', according to Erasmus.[81] She gathered scholars and patrons of scholars in her household, among them the Poyntz brothers. Leland, Wyatt's 'familiar and old companion', had experienced Katherine's beneficence.[82] She exercised her patronage at both universities. Visiting Oxford in 1518, she was received as though she were Juno or Minerva, and in 1523 she visited again, attended by a crowd of courtiers. In 1521 she went to Cambridge.[83] The chamberlain of her household was William Blount, Lord Mountjoy, the Maecenas of Erasmus and father of Charles Blount, to whom Vives dedicated part of *De ratione studii*. Mountjoy's mastership of the mint placed him close to Henry Wyatt, and perhaps also to Thomas Wyatt in the Jewel House. Much later, Charles Blount, fifth Lord Mountjoy, would guard the memory of Thomas Wyatt and treasure his verse.[84]

In the account book of the Queen's receiver general, the names of various Wyatts recur in the service of the Queen, alongside those of the Poyntzes and the Darrells, her closest English servants. In the Queen's lands in Essex, Henry Wyatt was keeper of Great Baddow, and farmer of the manor of Bretts.[85] On the coast of Essex, on the edge of England, Katherine's interests and those of the Wyatts converged. The Essex Wyatts leased the manor of Bradwell-next-the-sea from the Queen, and William Wyatt, Thomas's cousin, became her ward.[86] From 1530 Thomas Abell, one of Katherine's most devoted advocates, whose path soon converged with Thomas Wyatt's, held the benefice of Bradwell by her patronage.[87] Wyatt took into his service John Savile, the husband of his Essex cousin, Anne.* Such connections are shadowy, and conclusive evidence of Wyatt's association with

* See above, p. 80.

Katherine's closest allies will come a little later. Even in this account book, secrecy is enjoined among the Queen's servants. One of them scribbled a note 'faithfully declaring unto you as my very friend . . . as shall here my secret letter specify'.[88]

At about the time that Henry determined finally, fatally, to marry Anne Boleyn, perhaps shortly before *The Quyete of mynde* was dedicated to the Queen, Thomas Wyatt may have done something extraordinary, something so audacious and so extreme that many have not credited it. The story came from Nicholas Harpsfield, the Catholic apologist, who heard it from the merchant Antonio Bonvisi, who learnt it 'of them very likely to know the truth thereof'.[89] Harpsfield's conversations with Bonvisi took place during their exile for their faith in Louvain, twenty years after the putative event, yet Bonvisi's undying friendship with Thomas More takes us close to the heart of power and to Katherine's friends.[90] This was the story. When he understood that the King meant to marry Anne, Wyatt went to him and made a remarkable confession:

Sir, I pray your grace, pardon me, both of my offence and my boldness. I am come to your grace of myself to discover and utter my own shame; but yet my most bounden duty and loyalty that I owe to your grace, and the careful tendering of your honour more than my own honesty forceth me to do this.

As here related, Wyatt's 'shame' – and Anne's – was that they had been lovers. Bonvisi judged that Wyatt warned the King lest Henry marry her not knowing that she had an amorous history:

. . . I beseech your grace to be well advised what you do, for she is not meet to be coupled with your grace, her conversation hath been so loose and base; which thing I know not so much by hear-say as by my own experience as one that have had my carnal pleasure with her.

Another, more fevered story circulated in Catholic circles. Nicholas Sander, 'the Romish fable framer' who alleged even that Anne was the King's daughter, and – only half correctly – that Henry had slept with both her mother and her sister,[91] reported a perfervid account of Wyatt's confession. Allegedly, Wyatt had gone to the council, 'for his conscience accused him grievously . . . and confessed that he had sinned with Anne Boleyn, not imagining that the King would ever make her his wife'. Stunned by Wyatt's bombshell, Henry was silent for a while, then spoke. 'These stories were the inventions of wicked men', and Anne was 'of the purest life', of untainted virtue. Wyatt, dishonoured by the King's refusal to believe him, now proposed a plan which seemed to have come from Chaucer: 'to put it in the king's power to see with his own eyes the truth of his story, if he would but consent to test it, for Anne Boleyn was passionately in love with Wyatt'. The messenger brave enough and close enough to the King to broach the scheme was his brother-in-law, Charles Brandon, Duke of Suffolk. Henry was appalled: 'Wyatt was a bold villain, not to be trusted'. 'Why should I go on?' asked Sander.[92]

There was a further story of Wyatt's revelation to the King of his own intimacy with Anne. 'Entertaining talk' with Anne as she was 'earnest at work', Wyatt seized a little jewel, a tablet, which was hanging by a lace out of her pocket, and refusing to return it, he wore it about his neck as a pledge of her favour. The King, meanwhile, was wearing a ring of Anne's on his little finger. A few days after these dalliances, playing a game of bowls with his courtiers, including the Duke of Suffolk, Sir Francis Bryan and Wyatt, Henry disputed a cast. Gazing meaningfully at Anne's ring on his finger, and then looking up at Wyatt, the King said: '"Wiat, I tell thee it is mine," smiling upon him withall.' Wyatt, replying, "And if it may like your majesty to give me leave to measure it, I hope it will be mine," took her jewel from around his neck and stooped to measure the length of the cast with its lace. Recognising the jewel as Anne's, Henry 'spurned away the bowl, and said, "It may be so, but then I am deceived"; and so broke up the game'.[93] The story of this game of bowls and its inwardness – so intimate, so secret that it could not have been known to many – was told to George Wyatt from those very close to the participants. He heard it from 'a lady that first attended on her [Anne] both afore and after she was Queen, with whose house and mine there was then kindred and

. . . alliance'. This lady was Anne Gaynesford, Thomas Wyatt's cousin. Her betrothal to George Zouche, who was also in Anne's service and acted as messenger between her and the King, took her closer still to Wyatt, for Zouche was his neighbour and friend.[94] The other source for the story was a 'lady of noble birth living in those times, and well acquainted with the persons that this most concerneth, from whom I am myself descended'. There is a chance that this lady was Elizabeth, Wyatt's bitterly estranged wife, for she did not die until 1560, when her grandson George Wyatt was sixteen, but the more likely informant was his aunt Margaret, Lady Lee.[95]

A decade later, as he and Anne faced disaster, Wyatt would adduce as proof of his undaunted loyalty his confession to the King. 'I have not wronged him even in thought. The King well knows what I told him before he was married.'[96] This admission was recorded by the fanciful, anonymous Spanish chronicler. Since his vision of the times was usually as unreliable as it was vivid, his account might be discounted altogether, *except* that he had a source very close to the Wyatt family. What might have led Wyatt to reveal to the King a love affair with Anne Boleyn? For those who did not doubt their forbidden love, Wyatt's motive was self-protection, his fear 'if the King discovered afterwards how shameless Anne's life had been that his own life might be imperilled'.[97] It was true that Henry's fury, should he discover after his marriage Anne's loss of virtue, might be even greater than if he discovered it before. Since Wyatt knew that at court there was no secrecy in matters of the heart, he might have revealed the liaison before his 'back friends' there could do so. To confess might be to save the royal honour, and his. If Wyatt were indeed involved in so hazardous a plan, he is unlikely to have acted alone or, as he said, 'come to your grace *of myself*'.[98] George Wyatt dated the game of bowls to shortly before the Cardinal's return from France in October 1527.[99] In the late summer, Anne's friends had been colluding to advance her cause and scotch a proposed marriage to a French princess.[100] Katherine's friends, too, in horrified realization of the King's dishonourable intentions, turned in desperate times to desperate measures. That autumn 'there were practices discovered on all sides under sundry arts, on the parts of Spain, from Rome and that faction, and from the queen herself, and specially some with the king'. All these plots were directed 'to break or stay' the marriage.[101]

The presence of Charles Brandon, Duke of Suffolk, in two of the stories – the game of bowls and the surreal scheme to make the King voyeur – is revealing. Suffolk and his wife Mary – the King's sister, Katherine's sister-in-law – were bitter opponents of the divorce. In all the known attempts to dissuade Henry from marrying Anne, Suffolk was at the forefront. At some time unknown, he became 'most heavy adversary' to Wyatt, who would accuse him later of 'olde undeservyd evyll will'.*[102] The origin of that enmity is shadowy, but George Wyatt speculated that it began at the time of the game of bowls; 'it was as old as this'. Allegedly, the Duke, seeing the exchange between the King and Wyatt, saw his chance 'to dissuade the marriage' and, Iago-like, insinuated that Wyatt's possession of Anne's jewel was proof of their liaison. But once Henry was persuaded that Wyatt had the jewel 'without her dishonour', he and Anne remained angry with Suffolk for this false accusation, and Suffolk turned 'his heavy displeasure to the knight [Wyatt] ever after'.[103]

Were the stories of the plot to dishonour Anne the fevered imaginings of the 'Romish fable-framer', 'the Roman legender' Sander, and completely incredible? George Wyatt believed them, but thought they concerned, not Wyatt and Anne, but Francis Bryan (who was believed capable of any outrage) and another court lady.[104] He believed, too, the story of the game of bowls, but was convinced – as Henry was convinced – that Wyatt's possession of Anne's jewel was innocent. Allowing that there were plots abroad to discredit her and prevent the marriage, George Wyatt told of a book of prophecy shown to Anne, where figures representing A, K and H were taken to foretell 'certain destruction if she married the king'.[105] Yet his intent was to write the life of 'the excellent the LADY ANNE BOLEIGNE, whose so royal parts of mind and spirits did so precell, as . . . seemed to be breathed some such heavenly thing as might well show her an elect instrument of the Heavens', and to proclaim her providential part in England's

* See below, pp. 280, 532.

148

history as the mother of Queen Elizabeth.[106] He doubted the existence of Wyatt's plot because he could never believe the existence of the love affair that lay behind it.

George Wyatt listed the compelling reasons to doubt that Wyatt and Anne had ever been lovers. Firstly, there was the unfortunate, insurmountable matter of Wyatt's marriage. 'That princely lady, she living in court where were so many brave gallants at that time unmarried, she was not like to cast her eye upon one that had been then married ten years.' Her parents, resident at court, were sure to keep a watchful eye over her honour. 'The King's eye also was a guard upon her.' 'Those that pleased the King in recounting the adventures of love happening in court' were likely to bring him news of any romantic attachment of this lady. Was it likely that 'she that held out against such a king where was hope of marriage' would succumb 'to the knight, where his own lady and her friends' were so vigilant? Even more tellingly, 'And for the knight, if he had enjoyed her, was he so far desperately wicked and a monster in love', that he would vaunt the 'spoil of a maid of so good friends'? Surely not. The knowledge that the King was more likely to believe Anne than Wyatt, and the fear of their likely fury and 'heavy displeasure . . . upon himself ever after', would be enough to dissuade him from so dishonourable, so perilous a plan.[107] All these were indeed convincing reasons why Anne and Wyatt *should* never have been lovers.

Yet perhaps Wyatt, the Queen's man, prevailed upon by her friends and his, at a desperate moment, *did* take the risk – the terrible, incalculable risk – of confessing a forbidden love in order to prevent the marriage. Certainly he warned the King later about the tainted reputation of a foreign princess.[108] And in the midst of all the alleged revelations of romance, there lay the human possibility that Anne and Wyatt *had* once been in love, that Anne '*amava ardentemente il Vuiet* [ardently loved Wyatt]',[109] that Wyatt, adrift after the shipwreck of his marriage, might have been, at least, the courtly lover and Anne the courtly mistress. Behind all the rumours lay the imagined romantic imperative that the most brilliant man at court and the most brilliant woman should fall for each other. Friends and enemies alike testified to their powers of enchantment. Among Henry's courtiers, Wyatt had claims to pre-eminence in personal grace and accomplishment, and throughout his life his charm and talent drew the admiration of men who sought his friendship, and of women also. For the Spanish chronicler, 'This Master Wyatt was a very gallant gentleman, and there was no prettier man at court than he was.'[110] For George Wyatt, writing to glorify Wyatt and Anne, but also informed by those close to them, his grandfather was equalled only by the King: 'these two were observed to be of principal mark: one TW; the other, the King himself'. Wyatt was – so George was told – 'a man of his person of right goodly shape and presence, for gifts of mind accomplished with singular graces of nature and learning'. Those gifts were nobly employed in 'great affairs': in wars he was 'wise and valiant', in court 'very courteous and of firm fidelity to get and keep friends'.[111]

We might imagine Thomas Wyatt and Anne Boleyn as childhood sweethearts, romping in the Kent countryside. But not so. True, their fathers, both servants in the royal household, had long been connected, but Sir Thomas Boleyn had grand designs for his daughters. Anne Boleyn had been sent away to foreign courts to become a great court lady: first, to be maid of honour to Archduchess Margaret of Austria, then to join the household of Claude, Queen of France. Anne did not return to England until the winter of 1521–2, and then she arrived more cultivated, more accomplished, more ambitious than even her father could have imagined, and also more sexy, more provocative. In March 1522 'Mistress Anne Boleyn' made her debut at the court's Shrovetide festivities, prophetically taking the part of Perseverance. Her sister Mary, already the King's mistress, aptly played Kindness. Anne began to turn heads and break hearts.[112] It was as Anne came to court that she and Wyatt encountered each other, in all their brilliance and promise.

Upon the 'sudden appearance of this new beauty' at court, Wyatt was smitten. So George Wyatt heard. 'His heart seemed to say "I could gladly yield to be tied forever with the knot of her love".' As for Anne: knowing that Wyatt was married, 'and in the knot to have been tied then x years', she rejected 'all speech of love'. And yet, she did not altogether discourage him, for she saw that the 'general favour and good will' in which he was held might 'occasion others to turn their looks to that which a man of his worth was brought to gaze at in her, as indeed after it happened'.[113] As Anne shone in the reflected glory of Wyatt's admiration, the bright light of his attention added to her glamour. A court obsessed by the cult of courtly love constantly watched for any real romance. Where the King's heart was touched, the romance was of consuming interest. Lancelot's warning to Guinevere held for Henry's court also: 'Also, madam, wit ye well, that there be many men speaken of our love in this court, and have you and me greatly in a-wait.'[114] The court's rumours and speculation about a liaison between Anne and Wyatt provide evidence for its reality, and to the glimmering evidence of a fleeting romance, we will turn, to find a picture in a flame.

To the question why we should care whether Anne and Wyatt were in love, nearly five hundred years ago, three answers might be returned. Firstly, Anne Boleyn became Henry's queen, and the mother of a greater one. Secondly, though few were so prescient as to see the consequences for Christendom of Henry's repudiation of Katherine and disobedience to the Pope, some already foresaw the 'tragedy which began with a marriage',[115] and fought to prevent it. Lastly, from his own time until now, proof of that love affair has been sought in Wyatt's poetry.

'Depe witted Wiat', the sober moralist who translated *The Quyete of mynde*, who had been teaching himself to retreat to the redoubt of his mind and to 'smile at fortune's choice', was still the ardent player of the 'game of love' at court and composer of its verse. Though for Wyatt to love was potentially adulterous, he might heroically play the lover. Who was more exquisitely able to promise undying love and service by singing and rhyming? So much of Wyatt's verse testifies to his superlative engagement in that fiction. Here is one of the many paradoxes of his life. Like Vives a follower of Plutarch and ardent defender of Queen Katherine, Wyatt was nevertheless the most accomplished 'maker' of the poetry to which the court was addicted and which Vives deplored and warned against. Concerns about the seductiveness of poetry were ancient. Homer had been banished from Plato's *Republic*. That the harmony of poetry might correspond to the 'melody of the human soul', Vives admitted: 'the words proper to poetry . . . are lofty, sublime, brilliant', but with 'these so charming virtues, very fatal faults are mixed', and 'disgraceful subjects' treated. Danger lay in poetry if the 'verses gain a lodgement in the listener's mind, unconsciously through the sweetness of the verse'. Plutarch had wisely given 'precepts whereby the study of poetry may be made less harmful', but this was only like a poisonous mushroom being counteracted by an antidote.[116]

'Depe witted Wiat' might waste his wit devising dainty devices, turning pleasing ditties. While at New Year 1528 he presented *The Quyete of mynde* as a gift for a Stoic queen, at another New Year – or perhaps even the same – '*Tho.*' gave quite another gift to another lady: a poem in which he dedicated his heart to her, perhaps accompanied by an emblem, even a jewelled heart. Even so did lovers woo their ladies.[117]

	To seke eche where where man doeth lyve	
	the See the land the Rocke the clyve	*cliff*
	Fraunce Spayne and Ind and every where	*India*
	is none a greater gift to gyve	
	lesse sett by oft and is so lyff and dere	*precious*
Tho.	dare I well say, than that I gyve to yere	*this year*
	I cannot gyve browches nor Ringes	
	these goldsmythes work and goodly thinges	
	piery nor perle oryente and clere	*gems*
	but for all that is no man bringes	
	leffer juell unto his lady dere	*more precious*
	dare I well say then that I gyve to yere	
	[. . .]	
	To the therefore the same retain	
	the like of the to have again	
	Fraunce would I gyve if myn it were	
	is none alyve in whome doeth rayne	
	lesser disdaine frely therefore lo here	
	dare I well gyve I say my hert to yer	

Wyatt was trying to serve at the same time his Stoic queen and the courtly mistress who threatened his queen. We may glimpse what that conflict of allegiance cost him.

But Wyatt's profound belief, his hope, lay in poetry's ethical purpose.[118] Plutarch had taught that 'the maxims of the moral poets should be opposed to the immoral teachings of the others'.[119] The times demanded poets. Towards the end of 1523 Martin Luther had written to his friend Georg Spalatin: 'Everywhere we are looking for poets.' His hope was 'that the Word of God even by means of song may live among the people'.[120] Phillip Melanchthon wrote over five hundred poems, but they were in Latin and Greek, and could serve no popular evangelical purpose.[121] Reginald Pole, the King's scholar and theologian, who like Wyatt would not 'allow himself to be understood', and who would become so important in Wyatt's life, was also devoted, too devoted to literature. Pole's sternest critic, Gian Pietro Carafa, the future Pope Paul IV, wondered whether he distinguished sharply enough between secular and sacred literature.[122] In time, 'Wiat wrote of wondrous things', and would turn at last to write divine poetry, to be the kind of poet whom Luther had sought.[123] For the while he was writing verse for the court's delight, but alongside that poetry of higher aspiration, to please and test himself.

6

Who So List to Hounte

Wyatt was reading Petrarch. Petrarch's *Rime sparse*, the great sequence of poems almost all written of his love for Laura, in life and in death, was the greatest single inspiration for poets writing of love in their own language. In these 'scattered rhymes' Petrarch celebrated a lifetime of passionate sustained devotion to a single mistress which lived beyond her death. This was a love of *lontananza*, of exile and longing, a love never to be returned, for any reciprocal desire would be dishonour to her and death to the poet. Abandoned to pensiveness and loneliness, in wildest place or most deserted shore, the poet imagines Laura vividly present to him in the landscape, as his thought 'shadows her forth': in clear water, on the green grass, in a white cloud. Above all, he *feels* her where the breeze – *l'aura* – stirs through the fragrant laurel – *lauro*. In Petrarch's canzone '*Di pensier in pensier, di monte in monte* [From thought to thought, from mountain to mountain]', Love guides this man who is burning with love, his state uncertain.

Di pensier in pensier, di monte in monte	From thought to thought, from mountain to
mi guida Amor, ch'ogni segnato calle	mountain Love guides me; for I find every
provo contrario a la tranquilla vita.	trodden path to be contrary to a tranquil life.

Only the forgetting of himself in the vision of his beloved can calm his troubled soul.

Ma mentre tener fiso	But as long as I can hold my yearning mind
posso al primo pensier la mente vaga,	fixed on that first thought,
et mirar lei et obliar me stesso,	and look at her and forget myself,
sento Amor sì da presso	I feel Love so close by
che del suo proprio error l'alma s'appaga;	that my soul is satisfied by its own deception;
in tante parti et sì bella la veggio	in so many places and so beautiful I see her,
che se l'error durasse, altro non cheggio.	that, if the deception should last, I ask for
	no more.

When the truth dispels that '*dolce error* [sweet deception]', he is left '*in guisa d'uom che pensi et pianga et scriva*', the man who thinks and weeps and writes. The suffering of the lover turns him into a poet, and through passion for Laura he may claim the poetical laurel.[1]

A fragment exists of Wyatt's translation of this famous canzone: in his handwriting, in his manuscript he begins to write, but stops:[2]

> Ffrom thowght to thowght, from hill to hill Love dothe me lede
> Clene contrary from restfull lyff, thes common pathes I trede.

Elsewhere Wyatt does not falter. Entered earlier in the manuscript, and ascribed to '*VVyat*' by his friend George Blage, is a sonnet – a verse form almost unknown in English and now transformed – a new kind of love poetry for England. This sonnet is Wyatt's 'Who so list to hounte', his homage to Petrarch's '*Una candida cerva*':

Una candida cerva sopra l'erba	A white doe on the green grass
verde m'apparve con duo corna d'oro,	appeared to me, with two golden horns,
fra due riviere all'ombra d'un alloro,	between two rivers, in the shade of a laurel,
levando 'l sole a la stagione acerba.	when the sun was rising in the unripe season.
Era sua vista sì dolce superba	Her look was so sweet and proud
ch' i' lasciai per seguirla ogni lavoro,	that to follow her I left every task,
come l'avaro che 'n cercar tesoro	like the miser who as he seeks treasure
con diletto l'affanno disacerba.	sweetens his trouble with delight.
'Nessun mi tocchi,' al bel collo d'intorno	'Let no one touch me,' she bore written with
scritto avea di diamante et di topazi.	diamonds and topazes around her lovely neck.
'Libera farmi al mio Cesare parve.'	'It has pleased my Caesar to make me free.'
Et era 'l sol già vòlto al mezzo giorno,	And the sun had already turned at midday;
gli occhi miei stanchi di mirar, non sazi,	my eyes were tired by looking but not sated,
quand' io caddi ne l'acqua et ella sparve.	when I fell into the water, and she disappeared.[3]

Brilliant in its compression and ellipsis, Wyatt's sonnet imitates Petrarch's, yet its mood is strangely, utterly changed.[4]

> Who so list to hounte I knowe where is an hynde   *likes, pleases*
> but as for me helas I may no more
> the vayne travaill hath weried me so sore   *effort, labour*

VVyat   I ame of them that forthest cometh behinde

yet may I by no meanes my weried mynde

drawe from the Diere but as she fleeth afore

faynting I folowe. I leve of therefor

sethens in a nett I seke to hold the wynde   *since*

Who list her hount I put him owte of dowbte

as well as I may spend his tyme in vain

and graven with Diamondes in letters plain

There is written her faier neck rounde abowte

noli me tangere for Cesars I ame

and wylde for to hold though I seme tame.

Petrarch's transcendental vision of a white doe in green pastures evokes his beloved Laura, and her heavenly enfranchisement. Her lord, her God has made her free in death, and her very whiteness is emblematic of her purity, her sublimity. Like Narcissus, the lover gazes with longing at a fleeting reflection in water, but here it is the doe's vanishing reflection, not his own, which he seeks and destroys, as he falls into the water.[5] Here is a beautiful alloy of love and death. In Wyatt's sonnet we find a radical, remarkable transmutation. The dream vision is debased to an elemental hunt: enamelled spring is become high summer. There is no white, no green. It is open season on the 'hynde', the 'Diere' who is so 'dear', beloved and costly, prey to nameless, numberless huntsmen. Flagging, faltering in futile chase, the exhausted speaker in the poem watches others chase past him. If there may be rest for the body, there is none for his 'weried mynde' which cannot stay its obsession and impels him still faintingly to follow. Seeking to catch the wind in a net expresses proverbially the futility of the chase but also calls to mind the inglorious sport of hunting into toils, where the fleeing deer must be caught inexorably in a waiting net, there to be cut down by hunters and hounds. When he assures his hapless rival that he 'may spend his tyme in vain', his mordant irony appears in the doubleness of 'as well as I'. Perhaps the rival will hunt alongside him, perhaps as effectively as he: he too will waste his time, be humiliated. Be my guest. Where Petrarch imagined Laura forever free, Wyatt thinks of the wild hind in this parodic hunt as kept and chained, bodily restrained, yet tantalizingly alive.

Here we find Wyatt engaged – imaginatively, inventively engaged – in the high and creative art of imitation.[6] Renaissance poets in an ancient tradition – following Petrarch, who followed Seneca, following Horace and Lucian – imagined their poetic endeavour to be like the bee making honey.[7] As the bee flies from flower to flower, taking nectar from each blossom in order to make its mysterious, mellifluous conversion, so the poet should, according to Seneca, 'blend those several flavours into one delicious compound that, even though it betrays its origin, yet it nevertheless is clearly a different thing from that whence it came'.[8] This metamorphosis was the essence of the poet's purpose and achievement. 'Take care', warned Petrarch, 'that the nectar does not remain in you in the same state as when you gathered it; bees would have no credit unless they transformed it into something different and better'.[9] The resemblance will remain, but from the poet's engagement with the text which inspires imitation and a process of discovery and self-discovery will come something rare and strange. The reader, discerning and subtle, will read behind the surface text an antecedent text, and behind that another, and another. Echoing and echoing through the poet's mind and through the verse are remembered images and allusions, perhaps even pictorial as well as verbal. Anyone reading a sonnet and finding the dazzling light of the poet's imagination playing on latent, antecedent texts will recognise resonances and shadows. Maybe some of them will be accidental. The poem is a palimpsest, with every fleeting subtext helping the poet in his alchemical, mysterious *translatio*.

We can never tell how deliberate Wyatt's allusiveness was; whether he intended his readers to read between the lines and, knowing the texts to which his adverted, to bring them to mind, placing themselves in a literary continuum from classical and biblical times to their own. John Leland saw an affinity between Wyatt and Catullus, and in Wyatt's wearied lover – wearied by travel, wearied by emotional turmoil – we may find shades of Catullus' lover in his *Carmina*.[10] Maybe a 'good Italian' at court sensed a fleeting presence of Ariosto's *Orlando Furioso*, where

> *come segue la lepre il cacciatore*
> *al freddo al caldo, ala montagna, al lito*
> *ne più l'estima poi, che presa vede*
> *e sol dietro a chi fugge affretta il piede*

so the hunter follows the hare, in cold and heat, on the mountain and along the shore; but once he has caught it, he cares no more for it, he only chases what flies from him.[11]

– and echoing behind Ariosto, even Horace?

> *'leporem venator ut alta in nive sectetur, positum sic tangere nolit',*
> *cantat et apponit 'meus est amor huic similis; nam transvolat in medio*
> *posita et fugientia captat'.*

The gallant sings how 'the huntsman pursues the hare mid the deep snow, but declines to touch it, when thus outstretched', and adds: 'My love is like unto this, for it passes over what is served to all, and chases flying game'.[12]

We know that in 'Who so list to hounte' Wyatt composed a version of Petrarch so free as to be 'rebellious'. How did Wyatt read his Petrarch? To imagine him keeping in his doublet a cherished copy of the *Rime sparse*, a souvenir of his Italian journey, and using that alone to translate, to imitate Petrarch may be – as with most imaginings of him – far too simple. He drew deeply on a long Petrarchan tradition in England, but also on the commentary that gathered around the *Canzoniere* in Italy.[13] The vernacular songs and sonnets of Petrarch were first published in 1470. Very soon, in subsequent editions, his verse began to be annotated and interpreted by successive commentators. In August 1525 *Le volgari opere del Petrarcha con la espositione di Alessandro Vellutello* (*The Vernacular Works of Petrarch with the Exposition of Alessandro Vellutello*) appeared, in which Vellutello re-ordered the sequence of the poems in the *Rime sparse*, disrupting Petrarch's 'scattering' to frame a narrative different from the passage of time which Petrarch had left his readers to supply. That September, Pietro Bembo published in Venice his *Prose . . . della volgar lingua* (*On Prose Written in the Vernacular*), which celebrated Petrarch's style. In 'At last withdrawe youre cruelltie' Wyatt imitated a canzonetta from Book I of Bembo's *Gli Asolani* (*The Asolans*), but whether he also knew the

Prose we cannot tell.[14] In 1533 *Il Petrarcha colla spositione di Misser Giouanni Andrea Gesualdo* appeared, in which Gesualdo subjected Petrarch's *Rime* and *Trionfi* to rhetorical analysis. Explaining Petrarch's eloquence, his masterly use of figures of speech, Gesualdo understood that all was not what it seemed, that the name of Laura represented Petrarch's ardent love of poetry as well as her historical reality.[15]

In sonnet 190, so Vellutello explained, '*Volse il Poeta* [the poet turned]' to give a brief account of his love for Laura from its beginning to her death, telling of the place, the time, and the season of his love's beginning, and the age she was when she died, leaving him continually to lament. The golden horns represent her golden tresses, the shade of the laurel, her name. According to Solinus and other Roman writers, after Caesar's death white stags were found with collars inscribed: '*Noli me tangere, quia Caesaris sum*', so that no one would ever violate them.[16] Like these stags of Caesar who were set free, Madonna Laura – not stag, but doe – was freed by her Caesar, Almighty God. Laura's collar testified to the triumph of her constancy and chastity over any lascivious impulse. The midday sun signified that she died in the middle of her life.[17] In Gesualdo's exposition, Il Poeta is in hot pursuit of Laura: '*il Poeta descrive l'amorosa caccia prendendo la metaphora da cacciatori* [the Poet describes the amorous chase, taking the metaphor of huntsmen]'. This amorous hunt takes us close to Wyatt's version of Petrarch. It was the Latin motto found in the commentators – not in Petrarch – which provided Wyatt's translation: 'noli me tangere, for Cesars I ame'.[18]

No courtly reader could mistake the sacred text with which the profane venery is so tellingly counterpoised. Around her lovely neck Wyatt's hind wears a collar: 'graven with Diamondes in letters plain' there is written 'noli me tangere'. 'Touch me not': the words of Christ to Mary Magdalen in the garden. Every reader is transported to the Gospel of St John 20:11–17, to one of the most numinous scenes of the New Testament. Mary Magdalen, in her beauty and despair, stands at the empty sepulchre of the crucified Christ, weeping: 'For they have taken away my Lord, and I wot not where they have laid him.' Still unknowing, she turns to encounter the risen Christ. 'Jesus said unto her: Mary.' Answering 'Rabboni, which is to say master', she reaches out to him, but 'Jesus said unto her, touch me not, for I am not yet ascended to my Father'. The Magdalen was the first witness of Christ's triumph over death and – after the Blessed Virgin Mary – the first redeemed member of the human race. She was also a woman who had 'loved much' (Luke 7:47). Remembering her pity and her penitence, Wyatt's contemporaries did not forget what it was she had repented. When the Venetian ambassador archly made a petition on the feast of St Mary Magdalen – 'who found forgiveness for her sin, with much more reason' – Wolsey rebuked him. '*Domine, orator!* St Mary Magdalen did intreat remission of Christ, but ere doing so, she repented her of her errors, and departed from her wickedness. Do you the like'.[19] Presenting a gift to the King in 1532, Lord Rochford implored him to account not the gift but the will of the giver 'as God did unto Mary Magdalen that was a sinner'.[20]

In his sonnet Wyatt has rejected the pictorialism of Petrarch, discarded and debased the bright vernal images of an idealised nature, but by evoking Christ's words to the Magdalen he called an image to every mind's eye. Mary Magdalen's beauty and her penitent tears, her humanity as a woman who had 'loved much', her ardent love of Christ, gave her a powerful spiritual but also a sensual charge. Renaissance artists often portrayed her, and her image might be at once devotional and voluptuous, spiritual and amorous.[21] Real women were portrayed as the Magdalen, and there was a long tradition of believing that courtesans posed as this saint, their special patron.[22] Images or portraits of Mary Magdalen began to be collected in England precisely at this time, and by men whom Wyatt knew.[23] Thomas Cromwell possessed a gold brooch depicting her, and her image was embroidered on vestments in the Marquess of Exeter's chapel. At Littlecote, the home of the Darrells, was a painted cloth depicting the Magdalen. Painted on the ceiling of the house of Richard Fermor, a great merchant who plied his trade in Calais and in Spain, were two 'tables'; one of Lucrece, the other of Mary Magdalen.[24] For a medallion – real or imaginary – Hans Holbein drew three tiny sketches of the penitent Mary Magdalen, alone and weeping in the wilderness.[25]

The King, above all, wished to look upon her.[26] In Henry Wyatt's indenture of royal possessions of 1527 was an 'image of St Mary Magdalen with a box', and 'a table with the picture of Our Lord

appearing to Mary Magdalen' was listed in the royal inventory of
1542.[27] It was probably during his first visit to the English court that
Holbein painted his dramatic, sublime *Noli me tangere*. In the garden at
first light, Mary Magdalen encounters her Saviour. As she reaches out
to Him, incredulous, imploring, He draws back. Dressed in all the finery
of her former profession, she carries a casket, a box. Uncertainty surrounds this work, but there is reason to believe that Holbein painted it
in 1526–8, the time when Henry Wyatt and Henry Guildford were his
patrons, when he painted Guildford's portrait and also John Poyntz's.*[28]
Imagining Thomas Wyatt looking on such depictions of the Magdalen
– at the English court, or at the court of Ferrara, where the paintings of
the *Noli me tangere* by Il Garofalo and Dosso Dossi may have hung – or
having them in his mind's eye may not be to imagine too far.

In the sonnet there has been a remarkable, radical transposition. It
is not Christ who is untouchable, but the chased, chaste deer, the metaphor for the woman so costly to pursue. In Petrarch's sonnet the deer is
beyond any mortal reach because she is Laura, impossibly desired and
forever chaste, but also because of her sublime and absolute freedom
in death, her immortality. In Wyatt's she is unattainable because of a
secular proscription, subject not of divine power but human. Aligned
with the sacred text *Noli me tangere* is an intimation of another. On her
collar – 'graven with Diamondes', the symbol of adamantine chastity –
is also the legend: 'Caesar's I am'. This implies Christ's admonition to
the Pharisees in St Matthew's Gospel 22:21: 'Give therefore to Caesar,
that which is Caesar's: and give unto God, that which is God's.' Princes
read this text as validation of their ineffable possession. Alfonso d'Este,
in his struggle with the papacy, made this text his own, inscribing on
his coins DEI: DEO, and it was his absolutist visual jest to place on the
door of his coin cupboard Titian's transcendent *The Tribute Money*.† In
England, Christ's injunction that tribute be paid to Caesar became the
proof text for the royal supremacy.[29] But others read this text otherwise,
as Christ, whose kingdom is not of this world, intended: to Caesar the

---

* For John Poyntz and his portrait, see below, pp. 246–7, 622n.5.
† See above, p. 124.

things of this world, evanescent, corruptible; to God those of the heart and soul, pure and perdurable. The text in the sonnet also bears less sacred interpretation. Just as Caesar had held stags captive, so in the world of Wyatt and his readers deer were not only chased but caught, kept as pets by the nobility whom it pleased to make wild things tame. Lord Leonard Grey, captain of the knights-errant at the Castle of Loyalty, had kept two tame harts with bells around their necks, until his vindictive enemies killed them by night 'in great despite' and set their severed heads upon stakes.[30] In 1531 a servant was rewarded with forty shillings 'for bringing a tame deer' to the King who also held wild deer captive.[31]

At court, at least one reader of this sonnet found a not so secret message encrypted. Later, George Wyatt recalled Anne Boleyn's absolute determination to 'have the King whole, or none', and he found her 'conceit and resolute purpose . . . ingeniously expressed in those two verses whose invention taken out of Petrarch was applied to her by some noble spirit in her times:

> Let none touch me Caesars I am
> Wild to be taken though I seem tame'.[32]

The King who played on 'hart' and 'heart' would take the deer as his 'dear' into his protective possession, at such great cost to his kingdom. 'Some noble spirit in her times' was not named, but who he was might be guessed. Critics thereafter have believed that they know who and 'where is an hynde'. The hunt in the sonnet for Anne Boleyn as the hind, for the King as Caesar, and the hapless Wyatt as the 'I', and the search for evidence of real love and fated desire, has been relentless.[33] Yet anyone attempting to date the sonnet based on historical evidence 'plowithe in water and sowith in sande', and we should not suppose that poetic expression is synchronous with real experience of love or pain. Literary evidence is more likely to provide a date. If Wyatt did read Gesualdo's edition, then he wrote his sonnet after 1533. Perhaps only a lifetime of poetic endeavour enabled the sinuousness and ellipsis and compression of 'Who so list to hounte'.[34] What would it have meant for Wyatt to associate – through the complex processes of transfer –

the dear deer/woman who was Anne Boleyn with Mary Magdalen, the sanctified woman who had loved much, especially since Anne was committed to a scriptural piety and knew her New Testament so well? In Heaven, Mary Magdalen had given her special patronage to Queen Katherine's friends, so they believed. An angel brought Elizabeth Barton, the visionary Nun of Kent, a miraculous illuminated 'letter of Mary Magdalen'.[35]

'And wylde for to hold though I seme tame': the last line of Wyatt's sonnet – so utterly changed from Petrarch's – conjures the besetting emotions and language of 'They fle from me', with its insistent antithesis and paradox. 'Wylde' is a word which is mutable: wild as unrestrained, wild as restive, shy or wayward, wild as dissolute. It implies danger. The preoccupations of the sonnet – impotence deeper than frustrated desire, flight and loss, following and withdrawing, seeming and being, wildness and tameness – are quintessential themes of Wyatt's art, and of his life also. Some of his contemporaries did contemplate the real human predicament of loving a woman whom the King claimed, and believed that Wyatt had suffered because he had been close, too close to Anne Boleyn. We turn first to the smoke which billows from the flame of romance which supposedly burned between Wyatt and Anne.

In May 1530 a story percolated from the rumour mill at court of the mysterious exile of the Duke of Suffolk and of an unnamed gentleman. 'Some say' that Suffolk was banished from court 'for a while' for revealing to the King that

the Lady [Anne] was found in compromising circumstances with a gentleman of the court, who was previously banished on suspicion, and this last time he was expelled at the instance of the said Lady who pretended to be very angry with him; but at last the King interceded with her in order that the gentleman might return to court.

What lay behind these episodes – the exile of Suffolk, the double banishment of the gentleman, the Lady's pretence – is dark. Suffolk's disgrace and the royal anger followed by grace revert to the story of the game of bowls, to real plots to 'dissuade the marriage', and to Wyatt.[36] The gentleman's first banishment – 'on suspicion' of intimacy with Anne – was probably at Henry's command in the autumn or winter of 1527. 'This last time' he was sent away at Anne's insistence, and allowed to return only by the King's pleas, seemingly in the spring of 1530. The story of the banished gentleman fits none so well as Wyatt, and seems almost to confirm the account of the fantasist Spanish chronicler, who tells of Wyatt's later confession that 'Your Majesty angrily ordered me to quit your presence for two years' for saying that Anne 'was a bad woman'.[37]

If not at court, where was Wyatt? On the last day of 1527 he had been at Alington, where he dedicated *The Quyete of mynde* to Queen Katherine. Throughout 1528 and for several years afterwards, Wyatt's career is shadowy. Only a few glimmering marsh lights lead to his restless, sometimes clandestine life. He continued to hold appointments in the royal household – Esquire of the Body, Clerk of the Jewels – but often in absence. The fixed points of the turning years of 1528 and 1529 were his dutiful appearances in Yorkshire, to be sworn to the tourn at the manor court of Conisbrough, on 21 April 1528 and 7 April 1529.[39] But he was missing in October 1528, because late in that autumn or in the winter he was sent to Calais as high marshal.[39] Service in the Calais garrison was part of the way of honour for favoured southern gentry and nobility, and posts there were highly sought after. Yet Calais was also a place of exile. In *The Obedience of a Christian Man* of 1528, William Tyndale alleged that 'if any faithful servant be in all the court . . . he shall be cast out of the court, or, as the saying is, conveyed to Calais, and made a captain or an ambassador; he shall be kept far enough from the King's presence'.[40] If the court's story is to be believed, Thomas Wyatt left England under a cloud.

Calais was a fortress and a colony.[41] As the King's last bridgehead on the continent, 'key and principal entrance' to English dominions, it was of vital strategic importance. Were the English ever to lose it, they would be cut off from the continent and international commerce, dependent on other sovereigns for free access to ports, denied the passage across the Channel from Dover which was 'so easy, so short and so secure'. Worse, they would be without a redoubt for defence or for waging foreign war. The town was heavily fortified, garrisoned by a standing retinue, surrounded by massive walls, entered only by guarded gates, and defended by the sea: 'an impregnable fortress'. Yet, wrote a Venetian ambassador presciently, some who knew the arts of fortification doubted that it would be so impregnable, if put to the test.[42] And worse, Calais was always vulnerable to betrayal from within. '*Judas non dormit* [Judas does not sleep]', so Thomas Wriothesley would write at the moment of England's greatest danger, fearing that 'somewhat may be attempted'.[43] The King's enemies – the Pope's friends – did conspire to undermine Calais from within, for they understood how vital this 'principal treasure of the realm' was to his kingship.*

Within the walls of Calais lived a civilian population of some four thousand, plus the military establishment: the Retinue. Beyond the town, the English Pale – remnant of the Angevin and Lancastrian inheritance – stretched for eighteen miles along the coast from Gravelines in Flanders to near Wissant in Picardy, extending inland for some eight to ten miles. Divided by the River Hammes, the forested high country lay to the east and the marshy low country to the west. Though the English frontiers with Flanders and France were indistinct and disputed, border warfare was rare in the first decades of the century. After the early 1520s when Sir John Wallop, Marshal of Calais, led devastating attacks on the French from the Pale, there followed years of peace, a peace which had consequences for Calais and its Retinue.[44] The soldiers, no longer kept in a state of war-readiness, had grown soft and almost indistinguishable from civilian society. As the wool trade slumped and they were deprived of regular wages, they turned to domesticity and trade. The martial character of the garrison was undermined not only by the lack of outward threat but also by the King's successive appointment to lucrative office there of his servants and clients, who were often absentee.[45]

As high marshal of Calais, the third-ranking officer in the colony, Wyatt had a personal retinue of sixteen soldiers, five paid at eight

* See below, pp. 511–14.

pence a day, eleven at six pence.[46] Trained to a martial life, he now had
soldiers to command, a garrison to ward and watch. In this post he followed such seasoned soldiers as Sir John Dudley, Sir Edward Guildford
and Sir John Wallop. But perhaps Wyatt was that kind of courtier–
soldier who neglected the numbing daily round of drilling and over-
seeing the watch. A grim military figure – Sir Edward Ringley – was
deliberately appointed as his successor, and soon after Wyatt's time in
Calais the Retinue was remilitarized, and the marshal sternly charged
with the watch of the walls from Milkgate to the Dublin tower in the
south-east, and round to the Prince's tower.[47] As marshal, Wyatt may
hardly have been martial, hardly even resident. Whenever we find him
in Calais, he is always on the point of departure or return.

Arriving in Calais in late autumn or winter of 1528, he discovered
the town and garrison in a state of disrepair, which was cause and
consequence of a failure of morale. The England he left was also in
the grip of dearth and facing incipient rebellion, because the collapse
in the wool trade affected Kent as well as Calais, yet the complaints
of the Calais governors were so insistent, so perennial that they suggest a chronic malaise.[48] The town's fortifications were in ruins and
many of its houses desolate. Symptom of this general dereliction was
the absence from their benefices of half the clergy of Calais and the
Pale.[49] Throughout the 1520s its governors lamented the colony's
plight, and passing through on his way to France in 1527, Wolsey had
been shocked by its state.[50] 'If the town be not succoured soon', so its
deputy Sir Robert Wingfield wrote in January 1529, he 'wishes he had
never seen it'. The soldiers, for months unpaid, could get no credit, buy
no victuals, and Wingfield feared 'for the weal and safety of the town,
for hunger often forceth the wolf to leap out of the wood'.[51]

Wyatt's companions in the little world of the Calais colony were,
for the most part, an elderly generation: men like Wingfield, Sir Richard Whetehill[52] and Sir Christopher Garneys. Not all were military
diehards. Wingfield knew Erasmus. He had written an account of
the Council of Constance. Having travelled 'into the holy land' and
become a Knight of the Holy Sepulchre of Jerusalem, he wished for his
tomb in St Nicholas in Calais to be engraved with the cross of Jerusa-

lem. Among his bequests were 'all such books as be in my library or in any other place'. One of these was perhaps his illuminated manuscript book of hours, inscribed '*Posse et nolle nobile* [to be able to do, and not to want to do, is noble]'. Wingfield was married to Joan, the sister or half-sister of Wyatt's great friend Thomas Poynings.[53] With a man like this Wyatt might have conversed, from him he might learn. Another soldier arriving in Calais at the same time as Wyatt became his friend and shared some of his beliefs and dangers. They would later be found together in a sterner fortress than Calais, the Tower. This was Thomas Palmer.

An 'impecunious, raffish, old soldier of fortune', Palmer was also a courtier who found consolation in books. Veteran of Henry's French wars and of the tiltyard, he was Sewer of the Chamber and gentleman usher in the court, where Wyatt may already have met him.[54] In July 1528 Palmer was granted the captainship of Newnham Bridge in the Pale, and in August came to claim it.[55] A decade later, Wyatt sent greetings to Calais, to Palmer – now 'Master Porter' – 'with all the rest of my friends': a show of friendship for which Palmer had need.[56] Like Wyatt, Palmer lived life on the edge, and they may have sought similar recourse in dark moments. In the autumn of 1537 Palmer had been 'ramplied [*rempli*, filled]' with deepest despair which derived not only from his own nature but the times. On 3 November, writing to Lord Lisle, Wingfield's successor as deputy, Palmer sent him a book 'which hath much matter against melancholy, and counsels me to take patience, which I have much to do, I ensure you'. The book proved that what 'is good for the body is nought for the soul'. 'I think that if I had not met with my book I had been stark mad ere this time.' Though the book was not named, Palmer's account of his restoration – 'Captain Reason hath subdued melancholy and all is at rest' – suggests some classical counsel of Stoic fortitude and quiet of mind, rather than a work of Christian consolation.[57] If it was a religious work, maybe it had a confessional stance. When Palmer and Wyatt first came to Calais any divisions within the colony were mostly the perennial ones over patronage and place. Yet Francis Dinham had already been proselytizing the new faith there, and by November 1537 as Palmer struggled with melancholy, divisions deeper by far, over the nature of faith and of authority in the Church, rent it. '*Silencium in claustro* [silence in the cloister]', so Palmer warned Lisle: 'everybody is not of your fashion'. He must share the book only with his wife, 'no other, for there is more than my friends at Calais'.[58]

To be in Calais was to be so near, yet so far from England and the court. Calais was not exile exactly but, in the way of exiles, its colonists thought more often of the court than those at court thought of them. But if the tides were right and the Channel pacific, the passage to Dover was relatively quick and easy. In Calais they were constantly informed of events at court; so, too, news from Calais soon reached the court. If a proclamation was made in Calais on Saturday, the King knew of it by Monday morning.[59] 'You must keep all things secreter than you have used', so Sir Francis Bryan warned his friend Lisle, for in Calais 'there is nothing done nor spoken but it is with speed known in the court'.[60] Calais office-holders were closely linked to the royal household in England, and not only shared the political concerns of those at court but at times had a part to play in its struggles.[61] A stream of ambassadors and envoys passed through the town, bringing news and secrets. Calais was a place of transit, for holding and waiting: waiting for tides, for ships, for horses, waiting for news, for safe-conducts to travel, for the arrival of important visitors, for messengers. There gallants and swordsmen kicked their heels.

In November 1528 there was unusual coming and going, more than usual anguished waiting. Calais was preparing for war. Earlier that year warfare between French and Imperial armies and their incursions into the Pale led the King to raise reinforcements from among the royal affinity for the defence of the fortress of Guînes.[62] Through the summer the English colony trembled as 'inconstant fortune of war . . . somewhat turned her wheel'. The Calais garrison was still unpaid, and Guînes 'in ruins'.[63] As spies returned from Flanders and Dunkirk in late November reporting impending war with the Emperor, urgent attempts were made to fortify and provision the garrisons.[64] The arrival of a flurry of ambassadors was ominous. On the 27th Jehan Joachin de Passano, Sieur de Vaulx, ambassador of the French King, came from

England, and within days Silvester Darius, Henry's envoy, returned from the Emperor via Calais. Early in December the new Venetian ambassador to the English court was in Calais also.[65]

Agents for the latest, last-ditch manoeuvres in the King's 'Great Matter' also passed through. Two 'great clerks', jurists from Flanders, arrived with Juan Luis Vives in mid-November on their way to advise the Queen in her defence of her marriage.[66] Francis Bryan, too, came to Calais by late November – not travelling to England, but leaving it, not working for the Queen's cause, but against it. He was bound for Rome, in embassy to the Pope. In all the comings and goings, Wyatt was leaving. John Cheyney, deputy to the Captain of Guînes, reported that he was sending a letter to his master in England; he had asked 'Master Wiat . . . to see it conveyed unto you with dilig[ence]'. But Wyatt's departure was delayed. There was no passage to Dover on Sunday 29th, and none in the following days.[67] The Channel storms in that autumn and winter were the worst in memory: 'the seas here seem to have in them such cruelty as hath not been oft seen'. Bryan had sailed to Calais in a gale so fierce that one of his party vomited blood.[68] A Channel crossing in such weather would be ventured only for the most desperate mission.

War was imminent. Wingfield told Cheyney that there would be 'war between the Emperor and the [King] our master', and that 'Master Bryan should say the F[rench] King would take part with the King our master'.[69] Defence of Calais was vital, and Wingfield at his wits' end. The very stones of the castles of Guînes and Hammes, if 'they could speak, they would cry out [upon] the King and his council' for delaying the fortifying and repairs. And he prayed the 'Prince of Steadfastness' to 'establish the hearts of princes in perfect peace'.[70] In these circumstances Wyatt was returning to England – either sent back by the Calais governors or summoned home by a command from the court brought by Bryan. War and peace were only the public, outward reasons for Bryan's embassy to the Pope. Whether he revealed to Wyatt the deeper, deadly secret purpose of his mission we cannot know. Bryan went to Rome in search of a document: to find it, and put it where it might never be found again. This document was the mysterious 'Spanish brief'.

In England in mid-November, the Queen had shown the papal legate, Cardinal Campeggio, a document which could wreck the King's long-revolved arguments for the annulment of their marriage: the transcript of a brief which had – so she claimed – been given to her six months before by the Spanish ambassador.[71] Hitherto unknown in England, this brief supplemented and clarified the bull of Pope Julius II which dispensed Henry and Katherine from the impediment of affinity which would have existed if the Queen's first marriage to the King's brother had been consummated.[72] The King was 'taken by surprise and exceedingly displeased', his advisers suspicious of the brief's provenance, doubtful whether it were genuine, but fearful of it.[73] Possession of the original copy of the brief was of infinite importance to the King, and no less to the Queen. Summoning Mendoza to come to her 'in disguise and with the greatest possible secrecy', Katherine told him: 'all the strength of her case now lies with that document'. She lived in terror of it 'falling into the hands of her enemies'.[74] The Queen and her friends suspected – with reason – that Francis Bryan was sent to bribe the papal datary, Gianmatteo Giberti. By purloining the register containing the brief, they might conceal it where 'it might not be found' or else so falsify it that it could 'have no force'.[75] Bryan's instructions were to investigate the brief 'with great and high policy', 'secretly'; to 'make use of some trusty person among the scribes, writers [of the] registers, making sure of him either by ready money or continual entertainment'. Here was Bryan, the intelligencer of legendarily dubious method, an unlikely researcher in the Vatican Secret Archive.[76] By the end of January 1529 he reported that 'we have searched all the registers, and can find no brief'.[77]

The sole copy of the brief was in Castile, with the Emperor. A race began between the Queen's agents and the King's to procure it. Late in November Henry contemplated sending a special ambassador to Charles, who 'by fair words' and 'show of friendship' would get hold of the original copy of the brief, in order to lose it.[78] The Emperor might send the brief to Katherine, but never to Henry, so the King forced the Queen to swear 'a most solemn oath' and to write begging Charles to send the original brief. Her letter was sent overland through France with her messenger, Francisco Felipe, and the King's. On leaving, Felipe was sworn to take no private letter for the Queen, and in fear of being spied on and searched, he could not disobey. Instead, he committed to memory a verbal message: that the Queen wrote under compulsion and her enemies conspired to destroy the brief. On Christmas Day the French King granted a safe-conduct to the Queen's servant, but this could not protect Felipe from an accident, a suspiciously convenient accident. 'Running in post . . . the horse fell down with me, where my right arm was broken and out of joint.' The King's servant, John Curson, rode on alone. But since the Queen 'placed no trust' in him, he did not carry her secret message.[79]

New messengers were sent urgently to Spain. Sometime between 9 and 16 January 1529 Juan de Montoya, Katherine's servant, and her chaplain, Thomas Abell, left England, carrying the Queen's secret message. Travelling by sea in order to be safe from spies and footpads, if not from winter gales in the Bay of Biscay, they sailed to Fuenterrabía on the Basque coast, where they met Curson, who had ridden through France.[80] At the border, Curson was detained by the Emperor's men, forced to 'tarry somewhat behind', in order to allow Abell to speed 'afore'. In Toledo, Abell delivered Katherine's plea to Charles to intercede with the Pope.[81] As for the brief: Charles would never hand over the original, for it touched 'the validity of the dispensation and the authority of the Holy See'. At first, Henry's ambassadors did not realize just how comprehensively they had been outmanoeuvred by the Queen's envoy.[82] The Spanish chronicler, with his unique ability to marry truth with fantasy, with contacts with the Queen's household and with the Wyatts, told the story of Montoya who 'was so diligent, that within twenty days he went to Spain and brought back the dispensation'.[83]

And Wyatt? He had left Calais to cross a stormy Channel for England, probably in the first days of December. When we next discover him, it is not at court, but in the far south-west of England, in strange circumstances. On 8 February 1529 a 'Thomas Wyatt' was riding peacefully near Bloffleming when he was set upon by a Cornish tanner, William Bonsall, and some unknown companions, who robbed him of nearly £50 and so severely wounded him with knives and cudgels that his life was in danger.[84] If this was our Wyatt it is odd that he is not styled 'esquire', but it would be even stranger if an unknown Wyatt carried so much money. Not the least of the puzzles is why Bonsall was pardoned nearly two years later. A beating by yokels – as humiliating as painful for a courtier – may have been another of the 'thousand despites and dangers' of Wyatt's life. Bloffleming is on no modern map, but Botusfleming lies just outside Plymouth. Why would Wyatt have travelled there? If he was on a progress to the farther reaches of his father's landed empire, midwinter was no time to travel, except through necessity.[85] The reason for a gentleman of the court and Calais to journey to distant Devon was to take ship. Plymouth was the port of embarkation for Spain. It seems that Wyatt was about to embark on a sea voyage, or to return from one, or was escorting those who were to sail. To suppose that the Spanish chronicler deviated to accuracy when he wrote of Juan de Montoya's voyage to Spain and his return within three weeks may be to suppose too far, yet if he were correct, Montoya's return might be dated to the first week in February, the very time of Wyatt's unfortunate journey. On such fleeting and mysterious evidence rests the suspicion that Wyatt had been sent to escort and guard Abell and Montoya as they returned from the Emperor's court, with or without the brief. Far more certain is the evidence of Wyatt's continuing and deep attachment to the Queen's friends.

Wyatt had returned to England and the court as the King and Queen had begun to live apart. So great was their mutual suspicion that Wolsey and Henry accused Katherine's agents of plans to assassinate them, while Katherine and her friends believed that it was she who was the target of assassins. In Rome, Henry's ambassadors admitted that 'faithful servants would not have been wanting to do his pleasure' had he wished to remove the Queen. Katherine was obdurately, inconveniently refusing to get herself to a nunnery.[86] Instead, the politic Queen was courting the adoration of the Londoners. In November, when she and the King passed through a gallery from Bridewell Palace to the convent of the Black Friars, Katherine was acclaimed by great crowds 'who publicly wished her victory over her enemies'. The incensed King tried to ban public entry to Blackfriars precinct, but he could not curb Katherine's popularity among the citizens, especially among their wives.[87] Despite all the evidence to the contrary, Henry proposed to send a letter to Rome attesting to popular support in England for the annulment, with the intent of persuading the Pope to make speedy determination. 'Principal men of the kingdom' were called on in December to sign it.[88] That winter the King, in his frustration and suspicion, dispersed his displeasure generally. Back at court after his misadventure, Wyatt felt the royal wrath.

At a royal audience, probably in the second half of February 1529, Wyatt received a tirade intended for the governors of Calais. Departing the court, 'Master Marshal' asked the King 'if he would command him any service'. Henry's reply was scorching: 'Nothing'. The deputy and council had performed their duty 'right shrewdly [badly]' and had allowed 'all things there [to] go to ruin'.[89] Wyatt returned to Calais, only to depart again. Leaving and returning had become the pattern of his life. In April 1529 he was sworn to the tourn in Conisbrough.[90] Though reappointed as marshal in June 1530, in November he was replaced.[91] His patrons called him home. Life in the colony was parochial, confining, boring for men like Wyatt, but it offered quiet, and some quotidian certainties never found at court. From the purgatory of court, Thomas Palmer would pray 'God for His Passion' to be 'well rid'.[92] If in Calais Wyatt pined for the court, returning to court, he soon longed to leave it. It was ever thus: Horace and his readers observed the paradox, and soon we will find Wyatt discussing it with his friends: 'At Rome you long for the country; in the country, you extol to the stars the distant town.'[93] Thereafter Wyatt would remember the little world of Calais as a haven, and dream of returning there. Late in 1535 he resolved to be high marshal again, and later he schemed to become deputy.[*]

When we discover Thomas Wyatt again he is among the patrons and mentors of his youth, men who were the most resolute of the Queen's defenders, at a time of personal sorrow and loss, and a shattering

---

[*] See below, pp. 214, 511.

moment for Christendom. On 18 May 1532 Sir Henry Guildford, 'sick in body but whole of mind', made his last will and testament. Close to death, he gathered around him men who were tied to him by blood or marriage, service or friendship. A priest was present, and perhaps a doctor. Guildford had all the outward shows of wealth displayed in his great oil portrait by Holbein but, as a younger son, none of the substance. His will was short, though his inventory was very long: there were no lands, no heirs, and his goods were forfeit to the crown to repay his debts. His soul he bequeathed to 'Almighty God, my maker and redeemer, to the most glorious Virgin Our Lady Saint Mary and to all the holy company of heaven and saints in heaven', and his body to be buried in the Blackfriars, 'where already I have ordained my tomb'. He requested the Black Friars to bury him, to 'remember my soul with their devout prayers' and to sing for 'one whole year next ensuing my departure out of this world one mass for my soul and the souls of my father, my wife [his first wife, Margaret Bryan] and all Christian souls'. His witnesses were his half-brother Edward Guildford, John and Anthony Poyntz, Edward Wotton, Dr Nicholas Wilson, and Thomas Wyatt.[94] Two of these men – John Poyntz and Edward Guildford – he had already chosen as his feoffees, a mark of special trust.[95] But these witnesses were also tied to Guildford by their shared allegiance to the Queen and their horror at the direction royal policy was taking. This was a *salon des refusés*. When last we found Wyatt and the Poyntz brothers together they were celebrating the festivities at the Castle of Loyalty, before the court divided. Now the names of Wyatt and John Poyntz are inscribed side by side in Henry Guildford's will; also in his voluminous inventory, where they were among the first of his debtors.[96] On 18 May Wyatt and John Poyntz were at the deathbed of their patron, lamenting not only his passing, but the passing of the world they had known.

Guildford had been the *beau idéal* of chivalry, the champion of so many fantastic tournaments. He had fought the Saracens in Spain, and been knighted by Ferdinand of Aragon. At home, he was Knight of the Garter, royal standard-bearer, Master of the horse and Comptroller of the Royal Household, the most trusted of royal servants.

Harry Guldeford Knight.

Hans Holbein's drawing of Sir Henry Guildford, Comptroller of the Royal
Household, Wyatt's patron and creditor

While Master of the Henchmen he had held particular influence over the noble youths of the court.[97] A fierce critic of clerical exactions, in 1530 he had signed the parliamentary petition to the Pope, as the King desired.[98] Yet Guildford was a man who had made – or tried to make – a great refusal. Increasingly, he had found the 'Great Matter' and Anne's dominance intolerable. In the summer of 1531 he had been, all unwillingly, part of the King's deputation to Queen Katherine, sent to induce her to consent to the removal of the matrimonial cause from Rome to England. Thus far, and no further: as she refused, utterly refused, Guildford was heard to protest: 'It would be a very good thing if all the doctors who had been the inventors and abettors of the plan could be tied together in a cart and sent to Rome, there to dispute and maintain their opinions, and meet with confusion and defeat as they deserved.' A vengeful Anne threatened Guildford 'most furiously', vowing that once queen she would have him punished and deprived of his office. His response: she need not bother – he would resign. Reporting 'the Lady's threats', he surrendered his seals of office on the plea of ill health, though the King told him not 'to mind women's talk' and tried to dissuade him. Guildford retreated to the country, to Leeds Castle, in Kent and Christendom.[99]

Two of the deathbed witnesses – John and Anthony Poyntz – were closely aligned to Guildford by marriage and friendship. Anthony was Guildford's stepfather, and they had long known each other, perhaps from a Kentish childhood, certainly since the days of Prince Arthur's court. Guildford's half-sister, Frideswide, was the mother-in-law of both John and Francis Poyntz.[100] Beyond such tangled relationships was the enduring loyalty of the Poyntz family to Katherine of Aragon, which reached back to her first arrival in England as infanta of Castile, the bride of Prince Arthur. Sir Robert Poyntz was successively vice-chamberlain and chancellor of her household.[101] Sending 'Francisco Poynes' with a vital message, Katherine requested the Emperor that 'he be credited in whatever he may say in my name'.[102] When Francis Poyntz died in 1528, he left his brothers to defend her cause. The fidelity of John Poyntz to the Queen marked his life. By 1520, he was her sewer – an intimate attendant in her chamber, superintendent of arrangements at her table, the seating of guests, the tasting and serving of food. At the Field of the Cloth of Gold, he attended in the Queen's train, together with her devoted servant Francisco Felipe.[103] As deputy to Katherine's receiver general, Griffith Richards, he served her in various routine ways.[104] But once the King determined to end the royal marriage, far greater demands were made upon his allegiance.

While the Queen suffered 'the pains of Purgatory on earth'[105] as her place with the King was usurped by Anne, so her friends began to be excluded, exiled or self-exiled from a court where Anne and her party gained ascendancy. In June 1530 the Marquess of Exeter had gone down on his knees before the King, imploring him not to provoke the people by marrying Anne without the definitive judgement of the Church. The Marchioness of Exeter and two others of the Queen's most devoted ladies in waiting were sent away, and in the summer of 1530 there were rumours that officers of the royal household would be dismissed 'to please the Lady'.[106] It was around this time that the unnamed gentleman who had been too close to Anne was banished from court: if it was Wyatt, he was also compromisingly close to Katherine, by association. By the autumn of 1530 the gentlemen who used to visit the Queen were forbidden to attend upon her.[107] The following summer saw further moves against the Queen's friends.[108]

The court was no longer a forum in which to defend the Queen. Parliament was. In November 1529 a Parliament had been summoned to meet at Blackfriars. Since the Pope refused to allow the matter of the royal marriage to be settled within England, the King's advisers planned a démarche in the course of this Parliament, a 'statutory coup'.[109] But the calling of Parliament had offered an opportunity also to the Queen's allies. On 8 November Katherine sent 'two of her secretaries, members of her Council', to Mendoza, the Imperial ambassador, with a copy of a paper written in her defence (perhaps one of the many tracts by John Fisher). 'Mr Griffithe' – Griffith Richards with whom Poyntz worked so closely – 'practised with the bishops and doctors of her council and with the Emperor's ambassador'.[110] John Poyntz was never named among the 'practisers', but his service to the Queen continued as she suffered her 'fête of sorrow and weeping'.[111] John Poyntz sat as the member for Devizes, the Queen's man. This seat was part of the jointure of queens consort, and the parliamentary patronage was exercised that time by her vice-chamberlain, Sir Edward Darrell of Littlecote, whose daughter Elizabeth was the Queen's devoted attendant.[112] It is not certain that Poyntz was part of the shadowy group of the Queen's friends who not only sympathized with her, grieved for her, but were prepared to act for her, yet there are reasons to think so. Many of the Queen's adherents had been angry with the Pope for failing sufficiently to support her – 'those who are on the Queen's side accuse his Holiness of having encouraged the King in the first instance', believed Mendoza. Yet there was a natural association between defending the Queen and defending the papacy, especially since there had been fears, as early as 1530, that 'some bill will be voted to exempt this kingdom from Papal rule'.[113]

The spring of 1532 was a time of great uncertainty and danger, as the Queen's party grew more daring in her defence. At Greenwich on Easter Day, William Peto, provincial of the Friars Observant, preached before the court, warning the King of the danger to his soul if he insisted upon the divorce, telling him that 'the ruin of kingdoms always proceeds from the evil counsels of flatterers'.[114] In Westminster sanctuary a murder was committed when the rival retinues of the Dukes of Suffolk and Norfolk fought, and to avenge his slaughtered kinsman Suffolk threatened to breach sanctuary again. This went far beyond a private, local quarrel, for the Duchess of Suffolk was the King's sister, and she had insulted Anne Boleyn.[115] In April two members of the Commons dared to propose that the King be petitioned to return to his queen, otherwise feuding would 'destroy and subvert the whole kingdom'.[116] Opposition to royal policy was mobilizing in Westminster and in London, and like-minded members of the Commons dined together frequently at the Queen's Head tavern by the gates of the Temple, there to lament the King's moves against the Church and to conceive ways of resistance.

In the second week of May 1532 the Queen's most fervent defenders came into the open and opposed the King directly. They now rallied not only to her but also to the Holy Church. On 10 May Henry demanded that the clergy should renounce all authority to make laws without royal licence. Three days later Sir Thomas More challenged the King at last. On the 16th the Submission of the Clergy was signed. That day, faced with this traumatic assault on the liberties of the Church, More resigned as chancellor, vowing never more 'to study or meddle with any matter of the world', but to 'contemplate his soul'.[117] In shock, the people construed the fourteen suicides which followed in London in the next few days and the stranding of two whales in the Thames as 'a prodigy foreboding future evil'.[118] At this providential moment, Henry Guildford was dying. On the 18th, just days after this rupture in Christendom, he gathered his friends about him to witness his will. By the end of May he was dead and interred, where his father was buried, in the Blackfriars. As his friends attended his obsequies on the 29th they knew that they would face tests of conscience which Guildford, by his death, was spared.[119]

The testimony of Sir George Throckmorton reveals the crisis of allegiance faced by the defenders of the Queen and the Pope and takes us close to Guildford and his allies.[120] Claims of family and friendship bound Guildford and the Throckmortons. George Throckmorton married Sir Nicholas Vaux's daughter (Henry Guildford's cousin), and in 1521 Throckmorton and Guildford acted as executors for Vaux's will. 'Master Throckmorton' – maybe George, maybe a brother – lodged in Guildford's London house.[121] In the spring of 1532 George Throckmorton was among the MPs dining at the Queen's Head tavern and debating how to act in Parliament, when the Queen's allies summoned him to her defence. In his prison cell at Lambeth, Friar Peto adjured him to defend the Queen's right when Parliament met, 'as I would have my soul saved'. Sir Thomas More also counselled him. Leaning on an altar in an anteroom to the Parliament chamber, commending Throckmorton for being 'so good a catholic man as ye be', More promised that 'if ye do continue in the same way that ye began and be not afraid to say your conscience, ye shall deserve great reward of God and thanks of the King's grace at length'. Racked by doubt, Throckmorton consulted Bishop Fisher, who advised him to speak to Dr Nicholas Wilson. 'Divers times' Throckmorton went to Wilson's house in the parish of St Thomas the Apostle to discuss the justice of the Queen's cause and his matter of conscience. If he should consent to royal policy 'for fear of any earthly power or punishment', would he be damned? Wilson showed him 'divers books noted with his own hand to prove that he said to be true', and offered the same counsel as Fisher about whether to intervene in the Commons debates: 'if I did think in my conscience that my speaking could do no good, that then I might hold my peace and not offend'.[122] When the time came to make a stand for conscience Throckmorton chose to defy 'earthly power'. On a list of members drawn up early in 1533 the name of Throckmorton appears, together with that of John Poyntz and of others opposed, in conscience, to the passage of the bill in restraint of appeals to Rome.[123]

The priest who Henry Guildford chose to have at his deathbed as his confessor was Nicholas Wilson, counsellor to the conscience-stricken. Wilson was also chaplain and confessor to the King. Once of Christ's College, Cambridge, he was conspicuously learned and had used that learning to defend the Church against heresy. He wrote a preface for Richard Pace's translation of John Fisher's sermon preached at the burning of Luther's books in 1521, and became an inquisitor of heretics and their books. But Wilson, the King's chaplain, was also the Queen's almoner, and when the 'Great Matter' forced him to choose between his royal patrons, he wrote against the divorce.[124] When the consequences of Henry's moves to destroy his marriage and challenge the papacy loomed more clearly, Wilson sought to avoid his duty to give court sermons, so he told his friend and patron Anthony Poyntz in November 1531.[125] Wilson knew another of Guildford's witnesses, Edward Wotton. Perhaps it was his brother-in-law and neighbour of that name whom Guildford called to his deathbed, but he might have summoned another Edward Wotton, the physician. In 1525 Dr Edward Wotton had studied in Padua with Wilson and with Reginald Pole and, returning to England, became Pole's agent as well as his friend. Hearing that Thomas Abell had written *Invicta veritas* (*Unconquered Truth*) to defend the Queen's cause, Wotton wrote to Pole in June 1532: 'I would get one and send it . . . but it is not commonly abroad, nor I dare not be so curious about getting it'.[126] Wotton remained in close touch with Michael Throckmorton, Sir George's brother, who was Pole's agent.[127]

Another friend of Wotton's was John Leland, who congratulated him at his return from Italy. Leland also wrote an encomium for Wilson, whom he had known at Christ's in Cambridge, which was a nursery of resistance to the royal supremacy. And Nicholas Wilson might even have known Wyatt there, before Henry Guildford brought them together at his deathbed. [128]

Following the flickering lights that seemed to lead toward Thomas Wyatt, sometimes we may have been led astray. But amidst so many uncertainties, we have found Wyatt among men whose consciences and allegiance were tested, the most ardent defenders of the Queen and Pope, most resolute opponents of the King. Some of them would make the great refusal: one, Thomas Abell, would die for that faith and allegiance. In his head, though perhaps no longer in person, Wyatt conducted an intense and tortured conversation with Poyntz, when their paths divided, as his verse epistles prove. Poyntz left the court – left it forever, as it happened – while Wyatt was described as 'Master Wyatt of the court'. Wyatt would be the Queen's man still, but now he would serve a different queen. Soon we will hear Queen Anne and Wyatt laughing together.

Sometimes we hear the scathing laughter of Wyatt and his friends echoing in his verse, the laughter of scorn and derision, laughter that is the salve of disappointment and confusion. In his personal manuscript, Wyatt revised an epigram, both 'maker' and his own reader. His speaker – 'I' – recovering from a searing passion, turns to 'he' who can deride his former self for his absurd captivity to love:[129]

> Some tyme I fled the fyre that me brent
> by see by land by water and by wynd
> and now I folow the coles that be quent — *quenched*
> *Tho*   from Dovor to Calais against my mynde
> Lo how desire is boeth sprong and spent
> and he may se that whilome was so blynd — *once*
> and all his labor now he laugh to scorne
> mashed in the breers that erst was all to torne — *briars once*

But although 'he' laughs himself 'to scorne', it is against his mind that the lover leaves Dover for Calais. We have seen some – not all – of

Wyatt's Channel crossings, but his 'partings from the fire' are harder
to discover. Some, seeking certainty – a precise journey, a real woman
– have found Wyatt himself fleeing the fire that 'brent' him at a particular moment. They have found him – as I have not, in any known
list – in the train of King Henry and Anne Boleyn, now triumphantly
Marchioness of Pembroke, as they left for France in October 1532 and
a long-awaited consummation.[130]

7

Imprisoned in Liberties

It may be good like it who list   *pleases*
but I do dowbt who can me blame
for oft assured yet have I myst
and now again I fere the same
The wyndy wordes the Ies quaynt game   *changeable eyes'*
of soden chaunge maketh me agast
for dred to fall I stond not fast
Alas I tred an endles maze
that seketh to accorde two contraries
and hope still and nothing hase   *hazard?*
imprisoned in libertes
as oon unhard and still that cries
alwaies thursty and yet nothing I tast
for dred to fall I stond not fast
Assured I dowbt I be not sure
and should I trust to suche suretie
that oft hath put the prouff in ure   *to the test*
and never hath founde it trusty
nay sir In faith it were great foly
and yet my liff thus I do wast
for dred to fall I stond not fast

'Assured I dowbt I be not sure': certainty dissolves within a word, and assurance collapses at every broken line. Though the eyes' 'quaynt game' leads us to think of love – or sex – and Tottel entitles the poem 'the lover, taught, mistrusteth allurements', the lover has learnt nothing so certain, and the failures of trust may go beyond those of love. In a series of paradoxes and antitheses, the lover, fearfully sure of 'soden chaunge', describes the agony of trying to resolve 'two contraries'. He wastes his life as he teeters, impossibly poised between standing and falling.[1] He is freedom's prisoner. There are many worlds for our different choices, and we will find Wyatt, too, inhabiting different worlds and contrasting thoughts at a court where 'all ys possible'.

'The Lady said . . . that she was as sure as she was of her own death that she should be very soon married to the King,' so the Imperial ambassador reported early in February 1533.[2] Anne Boleyn was given to dark prophecies, but this one was already fulfilled, for a clandestine marriage had taken place between her and Henry VIII.[3] In October 1532 the King had taken her with him, as his consort, to a conference with the French King. '*Vanitas vanitatum et omnia vanitas* [vanity of vanities, all is vanity]', so a contemporary wrote on a copy of the tract published in celebration.[4] In Calais, so it was alleged, God revealed His anger in a eucharistic vision. As Henry prepared to receive the host at Mass, an angel took it out of the priest's hands and gave it to a miraculous apparition of the Nun of Kent, Elizabeth Barton.[5] Returning to England after a stormy crossing, Henry made an offering to Our Lady in the rock at Dover on 14 November, and perhaps even that day – the day of St Erkenwald – he and Anne 'married privily . . . which marriage was kept so secret that very few knew it'.[6] On a slow honeymoon journey through Kent the secretly married, bigamous King amused himself with his new wife and favoured courtiers. In glorious contempt, they played 'Pope Julius' game' at cards, with the King – in this at least – the loser.[7] If Wyatt was part of the royal retinue to Calais, or was summoned to celebrate with them on their journey through Kent, we cannot tell. A more formal marriage took place soon afterwards at York Place, early in the morning of 25 January 1533, without the Pope's knowledge or consent. Whether in Kent or in Calais, Anne, certain that she would be queen, had slept with the King, and by the end of the year was pregnant with the heir whose necessity had compelled the 'Great Matter' from the beginning.

The marriage was a secret, even at court, but the unborn child required its disclosure. Preparing the way, the court's Lenten sermons of 1533 concerned the penitential matter of the King's first marriage: all the time that Henry had lived with Katherine he had lived in adultery and sin. Loyal subjects must pray to God to forgive him and 'enlighten' him soon to marry again. 'No wonder then', urged the preacher, if the King were to take a wife whose 'virtues and secret merits' outweighed her low rank: had not Kings David and Saul done the same?[8] For Katherine, this sermon was the sign that her cause was irretrievably lost.

Anne herself – the King's wife, though not yet his queen – could not wait to tell her secret. On 22 February she appeared from her private apartments to join a throng of courtiers, and made a startling declaration to one of them. Three days earlier, she said, she had had a violent, unaccountable craving for apples. The King had assured her that this was the sign of her pregnancy, though she denied it. Laughing wildly, she withdrew to her chamber, leaving the court 'ashamed and abashed'. The courtier in whom she confided was *'ung quelle ayme bien et le quel le Roy a autreffois chasse de la court pour jalousie* [one whom she loved well and whom the King had, through jealousy, banished from the court previously]'.[9] Was Wyatt this courtier whom she loved? He had returned to court and become sewer extraordinary in the royal household, sworn to the King to attend in his chamber, to superintend his table, to taste his food.[10] His transformation to 'Master Wyatt of the court', the perfect, complaisant courtier, seemed complete. Though his admirers claimed that he 'by freedom of nature and inclination of will, [was] most far from the custom of flattery incident to court', he had learnt the need to 'grynne when he laugheth that beres all the swaye'. Wyatt was almost alone in making the transition from Katherine's 'side' to Anne's. Reading his verse epistles to John Poyntz, we may begin to imagine what this reversal of allegiance cost him.[11]

On 29 May 1533 Anne Boleyn, Marchioness of Pembroke, came by water in Queen Katherine's barge from Greenwich to the Tower of London.[12] There the King met and embraced her. Honoured as foreign and royal princesses of the past, she was taken from the Tower to be received by the City of London and taken to Westminster for her coronation.[13] She processed through London, dressed all in white, in an open litter drawn by two white palfreys caparisoned in white damask. Allegorical and mythical pageants designed by Holbein and scripted by Nicholas Udall and John Leland lined the route. At Westminster on

Whitsunday Anne was crowned with the crown of St Edward, received
the sacrament, and after Mass went behind the high altar to offer at the
Confessor's shrine. At her coronation feast, Thomas Wyatt was chief
ewerer. The following day there were jousts at the tiltyard at Whitehall.[14] The Queen's coronation was as 'honourably passed as ever was,
if all old and ancient men say true', wrote her vice-chamberlain to
her brother, Lord Rochford.[15] Honour was satisfied, though dishonour
had been feared. The City fathers had been consulted about whether
London's clergy should even attend, for their allegiance lay with Katherine.[16] Sir Thomas More stayed away, in silent disapproval, and Sir
Henry Wyatt's ceding to his son the office of chief ewerer may have
revealed his distaste for the new regime. Friends of the old Queen,
who were compelled by their rank to play a seemingly loyal part in the
festivities, inwardly repined. At midsummer the Marchioness of Exeter,
fearing that her unborn child might die, summoned the Nun of Kent
to ask for her prayers, and told her that she 'much lamented her husband's sickness at the time of the Queen's coronation . . . though her
person was there, her heart was at home with her husband'.[17]

Prophecies circulated, and were believed, a measure of the persistent uncertainty. Haunted by sinister forebodings, Queen Anne lived in
fear that her seeming triumph was evanescent. Before she was queen,
she read in an old prophecy her own destruction. Calling her lady in
waiting, '"Come hither, Nan", said she, "see here . . . this the king, this
the queen"', mourning, weeping and wringing her hands, '"and this is
myself with my head off."' 'Nan' – Wyatt's cousin, Anne Gaynesford –
nervously dismissed her alarms.[18] At Alington, William Glover, a servant 'dwelling with Sir Henry Wyatt', was visited by a ghostly messenger,
an apparition no one dismissed as imaginary. This 'messenger of Christ'
visited Glover several times in the spring of 1533, and Glover was 'sore
afraid', believing that the messenger was his 'ghostly enemy', until he
'showed himself angel like'. After Anne's coronation, the messenger
required Glover to tell her that she was 'with child, as Christ would
have it', with a 'woman [child wh]ich should be [prin]cess of the land',
who would be born at Greenwich. Learning that Glover passed the
message not to Anne but to her chaplain, and to her almoner Nicholas

Shaxton, the messenger warned: 'William Glover, [give] the message' to the Queen in person 'or else . . . Master Christ would strike'.[19] Here was evidence of a fevered anxiety in the Wyatt household. Anne herself had violent thoughts, imagining her own death and that of others. The King's daughter Mary was the gravest threat to her well-being and that of the prophesied princess: 'she is my death, and I am hers', said Anne.[20]

'May God permit' that Anne content herself with the 'barge, the jewels, and the husband' of Queen Katherine, 'without attempting' anything against the lives of the Queen and Princess. So Eustace Chapuys, the Imperial ambassador, wrote, more in hope than expectation.[21] Their existence was a constant threat to Queen Anne and the King's longed-for heirs. Since it was never consonant 'with the law of God nor man nor with the King's honour to have two Queens',[22] on 10 May 1533 Thomas Cranmer, the new Archbishop of Canterbury, opened a court at Dunstable to try the 'King's great matter'. The trial began badly when Katherine – predictably – would not attend, and nor did the 'looked-for witnesses', Sir Francis Bryan, the Duchess of Norfolk and Jane Lady Guildford.[23] But on 23 May the sentence of divorce was finally pronounced.[24] The King claimed 'the notable consent' of England's divines to the justice of his cause – 'unless it be such as apply their minds to the maintenance of worldly affections'.[25] He meant the Queen's friends, a declining band, but some faithful still.

In the first days of June Katherine's principal household officers were sent to her to persuade her no longer to call herself, or be called, queen. To refuse and provoke the King might be the cause not only of her own 'utter grief [and] sorrow . . . but also the undoing' of her whole household. She must think of the sacrifices that they had already made for her and the threat that they would be 'utterly abject and destroyed'. A month later, she answered defiantly: as for the marriage to Anne, 'all the world knoweth by what authority it was done, much more by power, than by justice'; as for her servants – and here she turned to those present – 'she would not hinder her own cause, nor put her soul in danger for them'.[26] The household which stayed with her, despite all the deprivations and dangers, had been counselled in conscience.

By October 1533 the King knew that some serving the 'Lady Princess Dowager' still called her 'Queen'. Ominously, he asked for their names. Some, broken by threats, had conformed, but Thomas Abell and another chaplain, Barker, could not 'call her Princess, they being sworn to her as Queen; and of that mind were also the gentlewomen, aswell of the Privy Chamber as other'.[27] When, in December, the Duke of Suffolk came to Buckden to force her household to swear an oath no longer to call Katherine their queen, some complied. Others were obdurate: having sworn an oath to her as queen, they could not swear a second oath without committing perjury. Under duress, they confessed that her chaplains had counselled them and shown 'what was their conscience'. Abell went to the Tower, and finally to a traitor's death.[28] The Queen's female attendants, in an act of consummate loyalty and bravery, refused to swear.

Elizabeth Darrell, Elizabeth Fiennes, Elizabeth and Margery Otwell, Elizabeth Laurence, Emma Browne, Dorothy Wheler and Blanche Twyford were gentlewomen. Some of them had been brought up in the Queen's household.[29] The name of Elizabeth Darrell will appear and reappear in the life of Thomas Wyatt. When all her protectors were gone – father, brother, her queen, the Marquess of Exeter – Wyatt would take her into his protection. At the end of his life she was his acknowledged mistress, the mother of his child, the châtelaine of Alington; at his death, he provided for her. Never his wife, never his widow, she was his lady, his lover, and perhaps the inspiration of his poetry. Elizabeth was the daughter of Sir Edward Darrell of Littlecote, Wiltshire, who was by 1517 vice-chamberlain in the household of Queen Katherine.[30] In his summer progress in August 1520 the King had stayed at 'Mr Darrell's place'. This had been a cloudless time: 'there is no other news here, but goodly pastimes and continual hunting'.[31]

Darrell – whose banner bore the motto SI IE PVYS IE LE FERAY (If I can, I will do it) – had grand ambitions for his children.[32] At Michaelmas 1521 his accounts for apparel show him purchasing glamorous crimson velvet and black damask for £4 8s 4d for 'Mistress Elizabeth' – court finery fit to wear to serve a queen or to charm the grandest suitor. Two years later, £13 10s was owed for black and crimson velvet and black and yellow satin for 'Master John'.[33] By then John Darrell, the flower of chivalry, was dead, having 'cast himself away' in a reckless venture in the French wars. With only six in his company he set upon two hundred French horsemen and – unsurprisingly – was killed.[34] When his proud, bereft father made his will in July 1528, he asked for a brass memorial of the time and manner of John Darrell's death to be placed on John's grave at Calais. To his daughter Elizabeth Sir Edward bequeathed three hundred marks 'towards and for the preferment of her marriage', in hope and expectation of the noble alliance which she would never make.[35]

Darrell wrote his will before the lists were finally drawn between the Queen's friends and the King's, but his allegiance was clear. The feoffees he chose to guard his heir's inheritance included Lord Mountjoy, Sir William Essex and William Newdigate, his son-in-law. Essex's name would appear in the list of those opposed to the King's moves against the Church, beside that of John Poyntz, who became MP through Darrell's patronage. William Newdigate's brother was Sebastian, who abandoned the world for the London Charterhouse, and their sister was a nun.[36] In religion, Darrell's allegiance – naturally enough, for one of his generation – was to the traditional faith. Beseeching the intercession of the Virgin and of Saints George, Katherine, Barbara and Anthony, he willed that for three years after his death a priest should sing mass daily in the Lady Chapel at Ramsbury – the Darrell chapel – with the Psalm *De profundis*, and pray for his soul and the souls of his late wives, Jane and Mary, of his father and mother, 'all other my friends' souls' and all Christian souls. Darrell's mother, the grandmother of Elizabeth, was Joan, daughter of William Haute (or Hawte) of Bishopsbourne,* who had owned cherished religious relics, including the stone on which Archangel Gabriel stood at the Annunciation.[37] All the hangings and tapestries at Littlecote Sir Edward bequeathed to his heir. Hanging on the walls of Littlecote in Elizabeth Darrell's childhood were tapestries depicting dauntless biblical heroines. In the chamber next to the great bedchamber was

* For the Hautes, see below, pp. 249, 290, 321.

a painted cloth of Mary Magdalen. 'A little painted cloth of the story of Judith' celebrated the heroine of her apocryphal book of the Old Testament. A divine instrument to save the people of Israel, Judith, in her beauty and chastity, went into the camp of the Assyrians and killed their general, Holofernes.[38]

In March 1530 Darrell died at Littlecote and was buried with the splendour due to a knight.[39] He left Elizabeth in the protection of a queen who was soon unable to protect herself. At the end of 1531 Katherine's household was still two hundred strong, with thirty maids of honour in attendance, but once princess dowager, her 'family' shrank and dispersed.[40] By July 1534 she counted only five or six servants as truly her own, the rest as guards and spies. Sequestered at Buckden, Katherine's maids of honour who had once gazed down from the maidens' tower of chivalric romance hoping for rescue by knights-errant, were sometimes glimpsed looking down from a real tower. When the retinue of the Imperial ambassador visited Kimbolton in the high summer of 1534 the Queen's ladies 'spoke to them from the battlements and windows'.[41] In devotion to their desolate mistress, these maidens lived in a kind of secular nunnery, but Katherine remembered that otherworldly seclusion had not been their first reason for serving her. At the end of her life she petitioned the King to safeguard the marriage portions of her maids, 'they being but three', and in her will Katherine's first and largest bequest was to 'Mistress Darrell': £200 towards her marriage.[42]

Thomas Wyatt and Bess Darrell may have known each other, loved each other from their youth, but it was not until much later that she would become his mistress. He would, he could never marry her – or anyone else – since he was married already, with a wife living determinedly on. 'I graunte I do not professe chastite', so he would confess, but nor would he allow any imputation of promiscuity.[43] At the end of his life, at a tragic parting, it was claimed that there were '*deux quil a aymé*', two women whom he had loved. One was Bess: the other was not his wife. Who she was – this other woman whom Wyatt loved – is now a mystery. Whether circumstances forced him to live in an amatory twilight, or whether his first mistress was openly acknowledged, is unknown. Since she still lived in 1541, it was not death which separated them.[44] If Wyatt was deserted, or deserting, or how he suffered in this personal abyss, leaves no trace. Except in his poetry.

In the febrile world of courtly romance men offered to serve ladies, and these ladies might choose to scorn or to favour them, or pretend one thing, while doing another. In the 'game of love', courtly lovers made promises and built castles of love in the air. In his poetry, Wyatt – most accomplished poet-as-lover, or lover-as-poet – left clues of real women whom he might have served, and tireless editors have found some where perhaps he meant none.[45] Tottel's title for the poem – or song – 'Marvell no more' was 'The lovers sorowful state maketh him write sorowful songs, but *Souche* his love may change the same'. Here 'Souche', and all the repetitions of 'shuche' and 'suche' that follow, may even refer to a real lady of the court: Mary Zouche or, more likely, Anne Zouche: 'Nan', Queen Anne's lady in waiting. Born Anne Gaynesford, she had married Wyatt's friend, George Zouche:[46]

> But yet perchance sum chance
> may chance to change my tune
> and when shuche chance dothe chance
> then shall I thank fortune
> and if suche chance do chawnce
> perchance ere yt be long
> For suche a pleasawnt chance
> to syng sum plesawnt song

> Fynys quod M Wyatt

In 'Accusyd thoo I be without desert', each successive line begins with the initials of a court lady whom the wheel of fortune raised high: A N N E S T A N H O P E. When she married in 1535 her name changed to S E Y M O U R.[47] Her husband was one of the knights of the Castle of Loyalty, Sir Edward Seymour. An acrostic message in another poem names one of the scribes in the Devonshire manuscript. Sometimes attributed to Wyatt, this poem is almost certainly not his, but the world of the poem is, and the woman who inspired it was muse of the 'makers' at court. This poem which names her, she acknowledges, she judges worthy, and she signs:[48]

fforget

thys

[Lady Margaret Douglas's hand]

yt ys worthy

[Mary Shelton's hand]

Sufferyng in sorow in hope to attayn
desyryng in fere and dare not complayn
trew of beleffe in whome ys all my trust
do thow apply to ease me off my payn
els thus to serve and suffer styll I must

Hope ys my hold, yet in dyspayre to speke
I dryve from tyme to tyme and dothe not Reke   *hurry*
how long to lyve thus after loves lust
in studye styll of that I dare not Breke
wherefore to serve and suffer styll I must

Encrease of care I fynd bothe day and nyght
I hate that was sumtyme all my delyght
the cawse theroff ye know I have distrust
and yet to reffrayn yt passyth my myght
wherfor to serve and suffer styll I must

Love who so lyst at lengthe he shall well so
to love and lyve in fere yt ys no play
Record that knowythe and yf thys be not just
that where as love dothe lede there ys non [trust]
but serve and suffer ever styll he must

Then for to leve with losse of lybertye
at last perchawnce shall be hys Remedye
and for hys trewthe Requit with fals mystrust
who wold not rew to se how wrongfullye
thus for to serve and suffer styll he must

Untrew be trust oftymes hathe me betrayd
mysusyng my hope styll to be delayd
fortune allways I have ye found unjust
and to with lyke rewarde now am I payd
that ys to serve and suffer styll I must

Never to cesse nor yet lyke to attayn
as long as I in fere dare not complayn
trew of beleff hathe always ben my trust
and tyll she knowythe the cawse of all my payn

content to serve and suffer styll I must

Fynys

ondesyard sarwes	*undesired service*
reqwer no hyar	*require no hire*

mary mary Shelton

Maybe Mary was responding to the lover's claim in 'Perdye I saide yt not':

And as I have deservid
so graunte me nowe my hire.[49]

Maybe she was answering the last stanza of 'Ons as me thought fortune me kyst':[50]

For fortune hath kept her promes
in graunting me my moost desir
of my sufferaunce I have redres
and I content me with my hiere

Disdainfully, as a courtly mistress must, Mary rejected the lover's suit, but she judged his balet 'worthy'.

Mary Shelton's signature appears on the first page of the Devonshire manuscript, and her hand represents her presence witnessing and perhaps inspiring the rhyming and romance.[51] Mary was foremost among the ladies who incited the court's game of love while Anne, her cousin, was queen. The story at court in the autumn and winter of 1534–5 was that the King had revived an old flame, and that a 'very beautiful maid of honour' had become his mistress, to the distress of her cousin the Queen.[52] Henry's ardour for Mary Shelton may have meant no more than conventional courtly service, but a later rumour, during a vacancy between royal wives, that she might even be the King's next 'make [mate]' suggests her beauty and allure.[53] In December 1537 the resemblance between 'Mistress Sheltun that sometime waited in court upon Queen Anne' and Christina, Duchess of Milan, was noticed. When the Duchess 'chanceth to smile', delicious dimples appeared, and so perhaps with Mary Shelton.[54] To Mary Shelton, the court's lovers confided. In time, 'many secrets . . . passed' between her and the

The Lady Heneghom.

Mary Shelton, muse of the 'makers', drawn by Hans Holbein the younger. The inscription names her as 'Lady Heneghem', recognising her later marriage

Earl of Surrey. In a beautiful epitaph for his squire, Thomas Clere, Surrey would celebrate her as Clere's betrothed:

> Shelton for love, Surrey for Lord thou chose:
> Ay me, while life did last that league was tender.[55]

Only the Devonshire manuscript certainly connects Mary Shelton with Wyatt, but maybe she was the muse of Wyatt and Surrey, and their confidante. Like Bess Darrell, Mary Shelton was intended for some dazzling marriage, but would not find a husband until much later, and then married some dullard country gentleman. At the end of his life, Wyatt, sometime knight-errant at the Castle of Loyalty and defender of its maidens, would take Bess Darrell into his protection. But for the while, he was among the galaxy of courtly lovers who served the court's new mistress of the games of love, Queen Anne.

'Master Wyatt of the court with many divers gentlemen' was entertained by Queen Anne's chaplains. On 12 or 13 May 1534 Thomas Goodrich invited the courtiers to his house in Canon Row by the Thames, where they dined on fish – ling, stockfish, salmon, pike, plaice, flounder – and two hundred eggs, and drank a gallon of wine.[56] Goodrich was a canon of Westminster and Bishop-elect of Ely, and another guest, Nicholas Shaxton, Anne's almoner, soon became Bishop of Salisbury: '*my* bishops', so Anne proudly claimed them. Also at Goodrich's table was the court physician Dr William Butts, who had saved Princess Mary not only in illness but also from suspected plots against her life. Like Goodrich, Shaxton and the Queen, Butts's religious allegiance was evangelical, and he acted as Anne's intermediary, discovering the brightest young reformist scholars for her service.[57] Why did Goodrich invite Wyatt to dinner?

At Queen Anne's court evangelical divines freely consorted with courtiers. While she was ascendant the Gospel was ascendant also. Through all the time of her power and influence over the King, Anne used that power to advance the Bible and to promote evangelical schemes

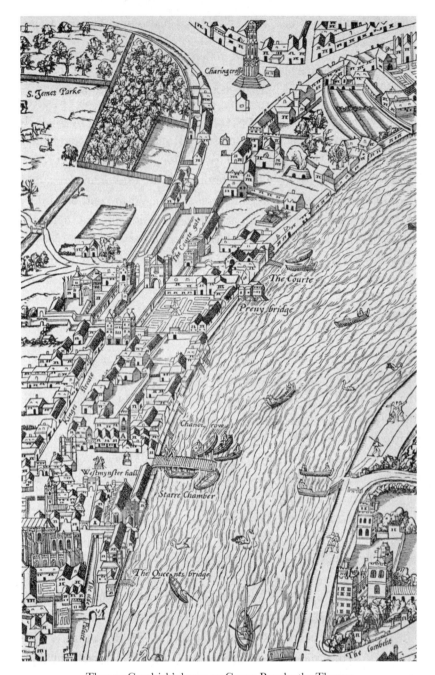

Thomas Goodrich's house on Canon Row by the Thames

for the reform of the commonwealth.[58] Much later, the reformer Alexander Alesius proclaimed to Anne's daughter Queen Elizabeth that 'true religion in England had its commencement and its end with your mother'.[59] 'True religion' meant absolute conviction in the truth of Scripture and a life lived in accordance with its precepts. Anne read the Bible assiduously, in the vernacular – not only in English, but in French, the language of her girlhood. Her chaplain, William Latymer, remembered her 'exercising her self continually in reading the French bible and other French books of like effect and [she] conceived great pleasure in the same'.[60] Several of her French books survive, and they reveal the springs of Anne's evangelical piety. Her copy of 'the Epistles and Gospels for the LII Sundays in the year' is part copy, part English translation of a work written by Jacques Lefèvre d'Étaples and his disciples. It was a digest of the evangelical doctrine propounded within the Christian humanist circle of Meaux in the 1520s, and expressed the belief that Scripture should be freely given to the people and that the tradition of the Church was always secondary to Christ, His example and His commandments. *The Ecclesiaste*, too, was a paean of evangelical faith, testament to the aspirations to a Christian life of the Queen and of its donor. Both these works were translated and presented as beautiful illuminated manuscripts to Anne while she was still Marchioness of Pembroke. They came from one bound to her by the closest tie, 'the perpetual bond of blood' – from 'her most loving and friendly brother', George Lord Rochford.[61] At the end of his life, at the scaffold, beyond any evasion of the truth, he would avow that 'I was a great reader and a mighty debater of the Word of God and one of those who most favoured the gospel of Jesus Christ ... Truly and diligently did I read the Gospel of Christ Jesus.'[62] Not only did Rochford read Scripture himself but he also ardently pressed for the free publication of 'the Word of God among the people'.[63] Yet the vernacular Scripture was then forbidden, and those who disseminated it, or procured its dissemination, did so under penalty.

Even before she became queen, Anne protected those who were persecuted for the Gospel's sake. When an evangelical book-running operation was discovered in London in 1528, she interceded with Cardinal Wolsey: 'I beseech your grace with all mine heart to remember the parson of Honey Lane for my sake shortly'.[64] Somehow she knew how to contact Simon Fish, the author of the virulently anticlerical *Supplicacyon for the Beggers*, in his hiding place among the City's gospellers, and an evangelical merchant procured the Gospels and Epistles for her from 'beyond sea'.[65] On the day after Goodrich's dinner, 14 May, Anne wrote pleading for one who had set forth the New Testament in English to be restored to his 'pristine freedom, liberty and fellowship'. But two years later, her enemies would accuse her of far less pristine conduct on that same day: they claimed that she had 'allured Mark Smeaton', a court musician, to violate her.[66]

Presenting the 'rude translation of a well-willer' of the 'Epistles and Gospels' to his sister, knowing it 'perfectly to reign with you more' than 'jewels or gold, whereof you have plenty', Rochford half-recognised the seeming paradox of a worldly, glittering queen advocating a life of Christian charity and sobriety.[67] While the court offered the broad pathway to sin and hell, Anne sought in Scripture the 'true and narrow way to all virtues'.[68] At Anne's court Scripture and pastime coincided, though increasingly uneasily. Her chaplain, Robert Singleton, a passionate evangelical, wrote an audacious preface in 'Troilus' verse' to a miscellany of courtly lyrics, *The Courte of Venus*, in which he identified the Pope as Antichrist and expounded his view of true religion. Preaching at Paul's Cross in 1535 he denounced the doctrine of Purgatory and claimed that monastic wealth was acquired by deception. Singleton's religious fervour went beyond the 'little tittling' he admitted, and to an extremity which led to his recantation of heresy and finally to his execution for treason in 1544. In this Queen's household, chaplains might be poets as well as religious zealots.[69] Even Anne's fool had been on pilgrimage to Jerusalem.[70]

Anne, who had allowed her ladies to triumph at her coronation with 'dancing and pastime', began to expect their modesty and restraint once she was Queen. Having played a dazzling part in the games of courtly love and won the King's heart, she now ordered her maids of honour not to 'consume the [time] in vain toys and poetical fancies as in elder time they wonted were'. Anne, who had once inscribed promises of love in a prayer book, now castigated her maid of honour Mary

Shelton for writing 'certain idle poesies' in her book of prayer. Summoning this 'pensive gentlewoman', the Queen 'wonderfully rebuked her that she would permit such wanton toys' in her book of devotion: it should have been a 'glass wherein she might learn to address her wandering thoughts'.[71] If Mary Shelton was indeed the courtly mistress the King served, this story has a bitter inwardness. Any queen might envy her maids an amorous freedom which she was forever denied, and watch wistfully as they inspired dalliance in rhyme, and as the most desirable courtly lovers really fell in love with them. Within Anne, the tensions between the imperative to champion reform and the need to preside over the fevered game of love at court became unbearable.

Her brother George Rochford, who had once mocked women and the institution of marriage with Wyatt, had thought to be a 'maker' among makers. He wrote poetry which was admired by his contemporaries, but now is lost. Once he was credited with writing this song which almost certainly belongs to Wyatt, but the confusion may itself testify to their perceived association.[72]

> My lute awake perfourme the last
> labor that thou and I shall wast
> and end that I have now begon
> for when this song is song and past
> my lute be still for I have done
> As to be herd where ere is none
> as lede to grave in marbill stone
> my song may perse her hert as sone
> should we then sigh or syng or mone
> no no my lute for I have done
>
> *Tho*   . . .

The song 'Blame not my lute' has also usually been accepted as Wyatt's.[73] It became so popular as a love complaint – popular way beyond the courtly circle for whom it was written – and so closely identified with courtly excess that in the next generation a moralist chose to parody it: 'Blame not my lute though it do sound the rebuke of your wicked sin'.[74] In time, an extraordinary transmutation would make 'Awake my lute' holy, for it resonated in George Herbert's sublime 'Easter'. Borrowing the ardour of secular love poetry to express human love for the divine, Herbert played on the universal awareness of this lament:

> Awake, my lute, and struggle for thy part
> With all thy art.

Rochford and Wyatt had continued to 'make balets well', to play and sing the old songs of love, even while Rochford studied Scripture. Rochford the 'maker' came to speak 'the language of Zion' and became so fervent an evangelical that the Imperial ambassador dreaded his gospelling diatribes at dinner.[75]

In *Pasquil the Playne* (1533) Thomas Elyot explicitly satirized the supposed doubleness of the evangelical gallants. In art, Elyot derided the hypocrisy of the flatterer Gnato, although in life he probably envied the smooth rise of such courtiers.[76] Enter Gnato, 'strangely disguised'. Sporting a courtier's bonnet trimmed with aiglets and ostrich feathers, he also wears the long gown of a divine, stolen from 'some worshipful doctor', and ostentatiously carries a New Testament. Pasquil, the plain speaker, who believed Gnato 'skilled of nothing but only of flattery', doubts that he is worthy its message. In Gnato's bosom is concealed every courtier's pillow book: Chaucer's *Troilus and Criseyde*. 'Lord, what discord is between these two books,' protests Pasquil. He taunts Gnato for carrying the New Testament 'as solemnly with thee, as thou shouldst read a privy lesson', as if he were on his way to a Bible reading among the brethren of the secret evangelical underworld of London – 'Hem, I had almost told where openly.' Gnato advises caution: Pasquil should beware 'what, and to whom, and where thou speakest': 'in words opportunity and time always do depend on the affection and appetite of him that heareth them'.[77] Yet to believe inwardly something different from that asserted outwardly was a vice particularly condemned. Hypocrisy was held to damn the soul, even though it might salve social divisions and save the hypocrite from worldly penalty. A woodcut in William Marshall's *Goodly Prymer in Englyshe* of 1535 showed the evil, winged figure of Hypocrisy, but Truth, the daughter of Time, emerging. Inscribed underneath was this text from St Matthew's Gospel 10:26.

> Nothing is covered that shall not be discovered,
> And nothing is hid that shall not be revealed.[78]

The Devil, who walked unseen through the mortal world, was the arch-hypocrite.

In the real world of the court, there were open and there were covert evangelicals. Asked who 'in Mass do use to clap their finger on their lips and say never a word?' Dr Rowland Phillips – the model for the missionary preacher in *Utopia* – named no one, but he knew that 'some great men in Court did so'.[79] Some believed Wyatt to be this kind of evangelical gallant or gallant evangelical. Yet if Wyatt imbibed the spirit of evangelical reform at Anne's court, it left no trace in his words or actions until much later. 'Truth' – an evangelical watchword – will suffuse his letters to his son in 1537, yet it was not a reformed belief in salvation which lay behind his understanding of truth then, for he expressed a vision of the sinner's relation to God which no true evangelical would countenance.* We will examine later Wyatt's faith, his understanding of truth – the truth implied in *troth*, the faithfulness to a vow, the truth that meant integrity and virtue – but even asserting his truth, he might question its possibility.† In the following rondeau all the metrical variation and shifts and counter-rhythms hold the refrain – 'What vaileth [use is] trouth' – in extraordinary tension. This poet–lover understands that his 'trouth' will be rewarded by the contrary:[80]

> W hat vaileth trouth or by it to take payn
> to stryve by stedfastnes for to attayne
> to be juste and true and flee from dowblenes
> sythens all alike where rueleth craftines   *since*
> rewarded is boeth fals and plain
> sonest he spedeth that moost can fain   *pretend*

---

* See below, pp. 301–2, 460.
† For 'truth' in Wyatt, see below, p. 300.

true meanyng hert is had in disdayn
against deceipt and dowblenes
    What vaileth trouth

Deceved is he by crafty trayn   *trick*
that meaneth no gile and doeth remayn
within the trapp withoute redresse
but for to love lo suche a maisteres
whose crueltie nothing can refrayn
    What vaileth trouth

It was the doubleness of the courtly game that Wyatt hated. The perfect courtier, he possessed consummate powers of eloquence, and could 'gloze [pretend]' as well as Gnato, if he chose. Yet he had a particular horror of the flatterer, the 'gnatomical elbow hanger' who could turn his words according to time and place and person. The kind of courtly feigning and pastime of which Wyatt was past master became morally repugnant to him even while it was increasingly demanded of him. Doubtless, he could pretend an unwillingness to sing, and perform with seeming reluctance the balets which the friendly company expected. Singing this song, he may have been singing the truth, heart-felt:[81]

Me list no more to sing
of love nor of suche thing
howe sore that yt me wring
for what I song or spake
men dede my songis mistake
my songes ware to defuse
theye made folke to muse
[. . .]

Again and again, Wyatt denounced a discordance between being and seeming, insisting on making his words and deeds accord. In 'Myne owne Jhon poyntz' his speaker utterly refuses to play the hypocrite at court:

I cannot speake with loke ryght as a saynt . . .
    . . . I could never yet
hang on their sleves that waye . . .

Here the condemnation of flattery and hypocrisy may take us close to Thomas Goodrich and his invitation of Wyatt to dinner, for the most complete contemporary version of 'Myne owne Jhon poyntz' is found in the commonplace book of Bishop Cox of Ely, to whom Goodrich had been chaplain. There the name of Wyatt recurs.[82] Goodrich may have invited Wyatt through admiration of his wit, for his talent, for his favour at court, as much as for any known religious allegiance.

What did the courtiers and the Queen's chaplains talk about at dinner in May 1534? Never were events more controversial or dangerous to discuss than those that spring. On 20 April – the day that Sir Nicholas Carew and Sir Francis Bryan dined with Goodrich – the Nun of Kent and her adherents were drawn from the Tower to Tyburn to die the terrible, public death of traitors, though they had conjured no rebellion, raised no army.[83] They were the first to suffer the penalties of the new Treason Act – the 'law of words' – which punished not for express act against the King, or even for conspiracy, but for calling him heretic, schismatic, tyrant, infidel or usurper.[84] On the same day the Bishops of Durham, York and Winchester were 'sent for'. An oath of compliance to the new succession – not to Queen Katherine's heirs, but to Queen Anne's – was demanded of the people: the first time that a spiritual instrument of commitment had been used as a political test.[85] On the day of the execution of the 'traitor' nun, every citizen of London was summoned to swear the oath in his gild, and the sight of her quartered body might have encouraged compliance.[86] Between 17 and 20 April all the City's friars were called to swear the Oath of Supremacy – not only to declare their obedience to the King and his new queen, but also to repudiate papal supremacy and to acknowledge Henry as Supreme Head of the Church in England.[87]

Time was when silence – even if concealing inward resistance – might have been interpreted as consent and not interrogated. 'In silence is surety,' promised Harpocrates. This priestly figure of hypocrisy in *Pasquil the Playne* was portrayed 'holding his finger at his mouth, betokening silence'.[88] The King was making a revolution in Parliament. The allegiance of the English clergy and people was transferred from the Pope as sovereign of Catholic Christendom to Henry as Supreme

Head. This transformation in authority, which had begun with the Submission of the Clergy in May 1532, continued with the Act in Restraint of Appeals in March 1533 (forbidding appeals from Canterbury to Rome) and was accompanied by the exclusion of Princess (now Lady) Mary in the Succession Act, could not be entirely secured by silent, seeming acquiescence. The English people had to be persuaded of the royal usurpation of papal supremacy and of Anne's usurpation of the queenly title, and if not persuaded, punished.[89] Although many – even most – saw the changes as a tragedy which began with a marriage and bore 'the crossed keys close within their hearts',[90] every submission, even if only outward, every silence instead of protest, was a victory in the making of the royal supremacy, religious schism and political revolution.

'*Cor Regis in manu Domini* [the heart of a king is in God's hand]', so Thomas More wrote in his letters from the Tower.[91] Upon resigning as chancellor, he had vowed withdrawal from the world, and silence: 'I would never meddle in the world again, to have the world given me'.[92] But his silence was eloquent, for it signalled a conscience opposed to the King's proceedings. On 13 April 1534 he was summoned to swear a special oath to acknowledge both supremacy and succession.[93] For reasons 'secret in mine own conscience' he could not swear it, but neither would he openly speak against it: 'in the saving of my body should stand the loss of my soul'.[94] From a Lambeth garden he watched as the City clergy 'played their pageant' and acknowledged the royal supremacy. All swore, save Dr Nicholas Wilson, the priest who had been with Wyatt at the deathbed of Sir Henry Guildford. He joined More and Fisher in the Tower. Having once counselled the conscience-stricken, Wilson now sought advice which More refused to give, because he could not know his own resolve until the test came: 'whether I shall have finally the grace to do according to mine own conscience or not hangeth in God's goodness and not in mine': '*Cor Regis in manu Domini*'.[95] Shadowy alignments of those opposed to the King's proceedings emerged. Christ's College, Cambridge paid 'Master Doctor Wilson's servant to deliver letters to my Lord Montague', and other alumni of Christ's began to signal their resistance.[96] To be in London at this time was to face a test of conscience and to fear a reign of terror. Lamenting the news of the arrests, Vives wrote: 'We pass through difficult times in which one can neither speak, nor keep silent, without danger.'[97]

At this moment of acute tension and uncertainty, subject to unknown, untold pressures, Thomas Wyatt, our swooning poet–lover, turned to violence. He committed murder.

On Wednesday 13 May – the day of his dinner with Goodrich, or the day following – 'there was a great fray between Master Wyatt and the serjeants of London, where one of the serjeants was slain, and divers of them hurt'. So John Rokewood reported to Lord Lisle in Calais. 'Master Wyatt is committed to the Fleet'.[98] That Wyatt was resisting arrest seems likely. Many young blades were involved in such affrays, including Wyatt's friends and 'back friends', but their fury was usually turned against each other, and plebeian officers became involved only when they tried to break up disturbances. Unless Wyatt single-handedly killed one man and wounded several – which is possible – he did not act alone, but no one else was named. Whatever the circumstances of the affray, nothing diminishes its violence and extremity. In their pride and arrogance, gallants shed blood carelessly, thinking themselves exempt from laws that bound lesser men – until they were taught otherwise.[99] Men trained in war and the mock war of the tournament, thrilled by their skills as swordsmen, too easily turned that prowess to private violence.

Fighting at royal courts – the English King's or the Emperor's – was punishable by maiming, so aristocratic 'frays' often took place in the streets of the capital. There, courtiers, followers of rival noble houses or opposing political factions, armed retainers of foreign ambassadors, were quick to take arms for the sake of honour, of love, of faith, or simply through pride and temper and lack of self-control. Swaggering, cloaked, through the streets, their hands hovering over their sword hilts, they were poised to throw aside their cloaks, to draw their swords at the least hint of slighted honour. Proud recklessness probably occasioned the repeated sword fights of John Mantell.*[100] Yet though Wyatt, and friends and servants like Mantell and George Blage, were rash and intemperate, they were also exquisitely learned and of poetic sensibility. So, too, were the Earl of Surrey, who 'rashly adventured' himself 'in revenge of mine own quarrel', and Edmund Knyvet and John Legh.[101] Richard Southwell – one of the most violent of them all, whose ferocity is suggested by the scar on his neck lividly portrayed by Holbein – was chosen for his 'prudent wisdom' by Thomas Cromwell as tutor for his son in 1535. During a summer 'consecrated to Apollo and the Muses', Southwell tried to teach Gregory the finer points of 'etymology and native signification of such words as we have borrowed of the Latin or Frenchmen'.[102] For men like these the life of poetry was no cloistered or etiolated one.

The 'rakehell [thoughtless] life' and 'reckless youth' explain much of the violence, but not all.[103] With the traumatic political and religious changes had come division, and with division came discord, fury and revenge. The urgency of the evangelical mission meant that contention was to be expected, even necessary, in a greater cause. Bishop Latimer counselled his fellow reformers: 'where as is quietness . . . there is not the truth'.[104] When in April 1532 the rival retinues of the Dukes of Suffolk and Norfolk had fought in the sanctuary at Westminster and murdered Sir William Pennington, the quarrel was partly over primacy in East Anglia, but also caused by the dishonour done to Anne Boleyn by the Duchess of Suffolk. Suffolk's servants vowed eternal vengeance on Norfolk's client Richard Southwell, but he would live to sequestrate Wyatt's household and become the Earl of Surrey's nemesis. Southwell, so violent and learned, expressed a private piety by wearing around his neck a cross of gold which he bequeathed at last to the son of the man he had betrayed.†[105] In 1542 the Earl of Surrey would challenge John Legh to a duel. In the Fleet prison in consequence, Surrey pleaded 'the fury of reckless youth' as excuse and offered to curb his 'heady will', but matters of faith and conscience lay behind their quarrel, and the circumstances of the duel may take us close to Wyatt.[106] When Wyatt's

* See below, pp. 320–1, 549.
† See below, pp. 533–4.

friend George Blage challenged Surrey to a duel in 1546, religion was at the heart of their quarrel.[107] Wyatt's murderous affray in May 1534 happened in days of anguish for defenders of the old faith, at the moment of capitulation for all those who lacked the supreme courage for resistance, and as deep resentment swelled. The timing may – or may not – be purest coincidence, for whether honour or conscience lay behind his violence is mysterious, and this is one of the most unfathomable moments of his life.

Wyatt, who contemplated 'the quyete of mynde' and sought to be indifferent to the reversals of fortune, was nevertheless addicted to the spin of the dice and the placing of wagers. The language of the gambler intruded even as he attempted to offer counsel to his son – 'I dare lay ten to one, ye shal perisch in the adventur' – and at his darkest moment, he would lay odds on his life. Gambling among 'rakehell' companions, he overreached himself. The court's gamblers bet heroically and often lost. A story was told of William Pickering playing dice one Christmas. His luck was out – 'as Fortune now and then will be hostile' – and when the King sympathized, Francis Bryan pointed out frankly that sympathy might come better from those who could offer no help. So Henry bankrolled Pickering in his misfortune.[108] Reckless gamblers were often wild in other ways. George Cornwall, reprobate heir to a disputed fortune, was dismissed from the Duke of Suffolk's retinue at the end of 1532 for his 'assaults and affrays'.[109] The following February he killed the Sergeant of the Mace of London in a sword fight, and with his companion fled into Westminster sanctuary.[110] By May 1534, Cornwall was pardoned and had succeeded to his inheritance. Around this time, at 'Cornwall's house', among the high-rolling gambling fraternity of the court, we find Wyatt.[111] In Edward Seymour's accounts of sums won and lost at the gaming tables Wyatt's name recurs. Seymour had lost to Wyatt in 'my chamber at Cornwall's house' and at Windsor. At York Place he had lost to Domingo – Domenico Lomellino, who ran an aristocratic gambling den. He lost to William Pickering at Crane's house in Greenwich, to Sir John Russell in 'the King's chamber', and to 'my lord of Rochford' at Hampton Court and Greenwich. Seymour's luck was in as he played 'at the King's Privy Chamber door' at

Bridewell, at the house of the Earl of Northumberland, and at 'my lady Cobham's house'. He won £10 from the Earl of Cumberland at Westminster, £65 from Pickering at Cornwall's house and 'at Domingo's', £20 from Sir John Wallop. Gambling with Seymour, Northumberland and Thomas Palmer – who pawned a gold chain to pay his debt – were the losers.[112] According to John Skelton,

> Domingo Lomelyn
> . . . was wont to win
> Much money of the King
> At the cards and hazarding.

The King lost hundreds of pounds to him at dice and 'gaming'. Courtiers named Domingo in their wills as friend and creditor, and several Chancery suits attest that he grew rich on their losses.[113] How could Wyatt afford to play in such prodigal, profligate company? Well, he could not. At Henry Guildford's death, Wyatt had been first among his debtors, and by 1532 his debt to the crown was listed among 'desperate bills', ones which could not be repaid.[114]

Wyatt was not alone among his friends at court to live desperately while hoping for grace. It was one of the paradoxes of his life that on the same day that he dined with Anne's chaplains he committed murder. Later, he would confess his extremity in 'the most of my rage', 'my foly and unthriftnes', and the disasters which, 'as I wel deservid', had followed.[115] If the horror of this escapade stayed with him and he repented it, he got away with it, in this life. The only account of the murder or of Wyatt's imprisonment was Rokewood's. Confirming evidence lies not in any indictment so far discovered, nor in any pardon, but in Wyatt's regret, and in his father's actions. Within the year Sir Henry Wyatt moved to protect not his son's inheritance, but his grandson's. Advanced age made settlement urgent, but so did his son's wildness which raised the spectre of an early death, a minority, even forfeiture. Henry Wyatt had earlier procured an act for his estate to be changed from gavelkind to feudal tenure, but now regretted its vulnerability to the claims of a feudal overlord – the King – especially if his likely heir was not his son Thomas, but his grandson, a minor.

His fear was that the King would exact the royal rights of wardship in the younger Thomas's minority. On 20 March 1535 Henry Wyatt granted all his manors and estates in Kent to feoffees of the uses of his will.[116] The use was the way for a landowner to divest himself of the legal estate in his property in favour of a group of feoffees – trustees – who could fulfil his wishes for him. It gave the grantor some insurance against the consequences of personal or political calamity – Fortune – and made it possible to avoid the burdens of feudal tenure. 'Fear and Fraud', claimed Sir Edward Coke, the famous common lawyer, were 'the two Inventors of Uses'. 1535 was a particularly necessary but dangerous time to enfeoff lands, just as the crown was rigorously asserting its feudal rights and determined to outlaw uses, and as the King and his lawyers proceeded in a test case against the feoffees of Lord Dacre of the south for just such evasion of feudal rights, especially of wardship. As he made his will in 1535 George Neville, Lord Bergavenny, anxiously consulted about uses.[117] Henry Wyatt not only shared the collective anxiety of landowners about the extension of royal power, but feared intensely that his estate, so ruthlessly acquired, would be threatened by his son's recklessness.

For Thomas Wyatt, the month of May was full of romantic and tragic portent. Like the imagined gallant who cherished his copy of *Troilus and Criseyde*, he knew how its second book began: 'In May, that mother is of months glad', as 'Pandarus for all his wise speech/Felt ek his part of love's shoots keen' and contrived to bring together the fated lovers.[118] Chaucer's salutes to May echo in a sonnet '*Tho*' claimed, urging others – 'Yow that in love finde lucke and habundance' – to celebrate the season of May, while he lies 'dreming in mischaunce', remembering 'the happs most unhappy/ that me betide in may'. Here the speaker is dreaming of 'mischaunce' in love. 'Sephame saide true that my nativitie/mischaunced was with the ruler of the may' – Venus – and that 'mischaunce' has governed his whole existence – 'my welth [well-being, happiness] and eke my liff'. That the poem referred to Sephame, an astrologer around the court, may take us closer to a real time and place.[119] At Henry's court life often imitated art, particularly Malory's art, where May and May Day celebrations recur 'as metaphor as well as event'.[120] In *Le Morte D'Arthur* the tragic consequences of May are prophesied from the beginning, 'for Merlin told King Arthur that he that should destroy him should be born in May-day'. It was in May that romance especially flourished, and from such romance – at King Henry's court as well as King Arthur's – followed malign as well as happy consequences.[121]

'Master Wyatt is committed to the Fleet.'[122] If Wyatt was flung into the Fleet prison in May 1534, he was soon released, soon favoured. His martial energies were to be turned to the public good. In June he was granted for life the 'conduct and command of all men able for war in the liberty of the seven hundreds of the weald, in the parishes of Tenterden, Goudhurst and Staplehurst, and in the Isle of Oxney', and licensed to retain twenty men in his livery.[123] This was the beginning of his personal advancement in Kent, and the sign that he had a powerful new patron. Henry Guildford's death in May 1532 had left Wyatt without a friend at court or in the county. Though Sir Thomas Cheyne and Sir John Russell might have forwarded him, their bitter private quarrel and their antipathy to Anne Boleyn exiled them from royal favour.[124] In Kent, the deaths of Henry and Edward Guildford ended the family's domination and brought the disintegration of the royal affinity which they had led since the accession of Henry VII.[125] After decades of struggle for control of county politics, finally 'the house of Bergavenny had subverted the house of Guildford'. Lord Bergavenny – so Lord Montague dreamt – might have raised 'a great number of men in Kent and Sussex', perhaps ten thousand. He was the most powerful man in Kent, but Wyatt could not look to him for protection, for the old enmity between Bergavenny and Guildford probably extended to him, not least because Bergavenny had married 'Mary Brooke, otherwise called Mary Cobham', of the family of Wyatt's abandoned wife.* In June 1535 Bergavenny died, leaving the old patterns of power unsettled.[126]

---

* See above, p. 95.

Sir Edward Guildford had died at Leeds Castle in June 1534 – shockingly, without confession, without the sacraments, without a will. His death led to a division of spoils and a land dispute which revealed new alignments in Kent politics juxtaposed with those at court.[127] Viscount Rochford now became Warden of the Cinque Ports and Constable of Dover Castle, marking the local as well as national ascendancy of the Boleyns.[128] John Guildford, the nephew, was supported by Sir John Gage, a bitter opponent of the royal marriage and the religious changes, who had withdrawn from court, 'the water standing in his eyes'.[129] His rival was Edward Guildford's ward and son-in-law, John Dudley, who was Wyatt's friend in Kent and perhaps from Cambridge. A man of fervent ambition, with an eye for the main chance, Dudley sought support from the King's pre-eminent counsellor. Both Wyatt and Dudley looked to Thomas Cromwell as their patron.[130]

Thomas Cromwell, a common lawyer, had been Cardinal Wolsey's most loyal servant. At Wolsey's fall he had feared his own overthrow also and made his will. But seizing the moment with a bravura resolution – 'a natural heroical audacity' – that would be typical of his political interventions, he determined 'to ride to London and so to the court, where I will either make or mar or I come again. I will put myself in the press to see what any man is able to lay to my charge.'[131] His enemies saw such opportunism, such 'pragmatical dexterity', as Machiavellian. They charged him with forging a pact with Henry to make him the most wealthy and powerful king that England had yet known; royal power would grow at the clergy's expense and the wealth of the Church would finance reform of the common weal. Cromwell was only the King's servant, of course, an agent of the royal will, acting at his master's command. But what if the King did not know how or when to act? It was true that Cromwell led Henry out of an impasse and found the way legally and politically to break with Rome and to achieve the royal supremacy; to use Parliament to make laws to enshrine the supremacy and national sovereignty with the assent of the King's subjects or, at least, the illusion of it.[132] When the King appointed him royal vicegerent or vicar general in spiritual matters in January 1535, Cromwell effectively eclipsed Archbishop Cranmer as principal minister of the Supreme Head's spiritual jurisdiction.[133] By the end of that year Chapuys reported that Cromwell stood above everybody except 'the Lady', Queen Anne.[134]

Cromwell was a rising man in Kent as well as a power in the King's counsels. As he made his will in 1529 he was already a landowner in north-east Kent, and was soon accumulating more land in the county.[135] His aspiration to marry his children into Kent's grandest magnate family, the Nevilles, reveals the trajectory of his ambition, and by the autumn of 1537 the story circulated that he would be Earl of Kent.[136] The leaders of Kent society looked to him to defend their interests. 'My very trust is in you above all the world,' wrote Dudley.[137] Among the prizes most intensely fought for were stewardships of monastic houses. Early in 1535 five contenders presented themselves for the high stewardship of the Benedictine abbey of Malling. Among them, Wyatt. All five looked to Cromwell to advance their claims, and the Abbess appealed to him when the claimants alleged prior promises and exerted huge pressure on her.[138] Edward Wotton, the Abbess's brother-in-law, admitted threatening her. But Wotton knew that Cromwell's 'very great displeasure' and the King's would extend to him, 'unless he gave the office to Mr Wyatt'. The King intervened in Wyatt's favour, and the stewardship of Malling became his.[139] There were special reasons for favouring Wyatt, so Wotton sourly acknowledged: although Cromwell had Wotton's 'unfeigned heart and good will . . . as ever you had Mr Wyatt's', yet 'I be not able to do *such and so many pleasures* as Mr Wyatt is'.[140] Pleasures: Wyatt's charm and wit had powers to allure.

Thomas Cromwell was a man of immense intellectual range and curiosity, a patron of scholars and artists, the host of convivial dinners for the like-minded. Youthful travels in Italy had made him an Englishman *italianizzato* to whom other Englishmen turned to make them 'good Italians', and he spoke and read Italian and French fluently. Revelling in his own language, he would speak 'with all the eloquence he was master of (and certainly he was master of the best)'.[141] Among Cromwell's welter of papers were tracts which reveal something of his literary tastes pursued even in the press of business.[142] There was a parchment-covered book *Of Desire in forma Juvenis* (*Youth*) beginning

'Amongst all flowers the Rose doth excell', and a short interlude 'Of Pleasure and Disport'. There was a collection of verses in Italian, a dialogue between the speaking statues of Rome 'Pasquillus and Maforius', and a book about the most anticlerical of states, 'Of the Venetians' life and of their prelates and curates'. The 'Jests of Skelton' were in his collection. More obscure tracts hint at the alchemical world of Cornelius Agrippa, by which Cromwell was intrigued: 'an argument between Raphael the Archangel and a certain gentleman of England', and 'an old bill how Abraham taught the seven sciences'. Formally, however, Cromwell was of 'small learning', and the feline Stephen Gardiner – his sometime, supposed friend – adverted to his less than perfect knowledge of Latin. Having perused letters of Cromwell's in Latin, he returned them 'corrected in [a] few places where I thought it requisite. And thus fare ye heartily well.'[143] Yet Cromwell's fluency in Italian and facility in Latin were assumed by his agents who even added tags in Greek when they wrote to him. Certainly he read vernacular literature. 'I send you a book of Our Lady's miracles, well able to match the Canterbury tales', wrote Richard Layton, Cromwell's agent in the suppression of the monasteries.[144] Anticlerical jokes were the common currency of the court, but no one enjoyed the teasing of sanctimonious clerics more than Cromwell, and his servants sent jests about the 'puffing pride' of prelates to amuse the harassed minister.[145] Such a man, with such a mind, might well admire the eloquence and mordant wit of Wyatt, and hope for his plain speaking. Such men might be friends.

The friendship between Cromwell and Wyatt was noticed, but not as a force for good: 'Sir Thomas Wyatt's being at that time highly in favour with Thomas Cromwell . . . which was a man of great power and might all England over and he bearing . . . great affection zeal and love unto Wyatt'.[146] In such language of power and favour, how a man was 'befriended' implied force and intimidation. Friendship had meant affinity and armed retinues in an older world of 'bastard', degenerate feudalism which was passing. 'We should do more', promised Sir Geoffrey Pole, 'when the time should come, what with power and friendship.'[147] In Chancery, a Kentish neighbour, Alexander Frognall, accused Wyatt and Cromwell of collusion and menace. In 1531 or

1532 Alexander Frognall's son Thomas had fled into sanctuary. There 'for fear of death and safeguard of his life', he bargained away his inheritance to Wyatt. Cromwell 'sent for' – dread words – Thomas Frognall, threatening that unless he kept his bargain with Wyatt he would be hanged 'by the neck and that no sanctuary should hold him'. The sale of the manor of Frogenhale in Kent to Wyatt was duly recorded.[148] In March 1535 Alexander Frognall sought Cromwell's 'answer concerning this matter between Master Wyatt and me', and did not receive the one he had wanted.[149] The forced disinheritance reveals not only the alleged collusion of Wyatt and Cromwell but also the gains and losses of the new order. The Frognalls were old-established gentry in Kent, a sometime power in the county, but their choices and allegiances in the 1530s fatally undermined them. Alexander Frognall had been and remained Queen Katherine's man. He had attended her as her carver at her coronation, and was with her at the Field of the Cloth of Gold, alongside John Poyntz and Francisco Felipe. He was with her still at Kimbolton, her last refuge. Writing to Cromwell in 1535, he dutifully called her 'my Lady Princess Dowager', but his constancy to her suggests that he thought of her always as his queen.[150]

We have discovered Wyatt in his different worlds, making his different choices. Waiting to be called to some service, he had not been summoned yet. Usually hidden from us, though perhaps more often in Kent than at the court, perhaps reading and rhyming, he was 'geven to a more pleasaunt kynde of lyf'. Yet late in 1535 he was bidding to leave England, to return to Calais and his old post of high marshal.[151] The only other surviving traces of him that year are his signature, his land transactions in pursuit of his family's ambition to buy up Kent, field by field, farm by farm, until they reached the sea, and his involvement in a northern feud.[152] In July 1535 Wyatt was granted Erringden Park in West Yorkshire, which had long ago been enclosed as a deer park: a grant which came to him because of his Yorkshire antecedents, but also now as southern courtier and carpetbagger. When his retainers from Alington, Servacius Franke and Peter Lloyd, rode north in the autumn to enter this new property and claim rent, they were met by two hundred of Sir Richard Tempest's tenants and servants, 'in riotous manner arrayed' with swords, bucklers, bows and arrows, shouting 'after the manner of war'. Wyatt's servants prudently withdrew. This encounter was part of the unsleeping feud between the Wyatt allies – the Saviles – and the Tempests.[153]

There was also friendship. One document is a testament to friendship reaching back into Wyatt's childhood and youth. On 10 March 1535 Wyatt with Thomas Poynings witnessed the signature of Thomas Vaux, Lord Harrowden, acknowledging the sale for £280 of his manor of Newington Lucy in Kent.[154] Poynings, the illegitimate son of Sir Edward Poynings, was from Westenhanger, Kent. A soldier and a courtier, he was 'honoured' by Wyatt 'for his generous heart', and Wyatt would trust him to guard his interests and protect his household. Vaux and Wyatt may have known each other from the Blackfriars, where their families lodged, and from their close association with the Guildfords. At court they were part of an even more exclusive company, the 'new company' of 'courtly makers'.[155] Perhaps these were unshadowed boyhood friendships, but as they witnessed this document they were boys no longer, and Fortune's wheel turned. Hap and unhap. The Wyatts were gaining land, while Vaux was losing his, and the friendship of prosperity might not survive adversity, so they had been taught. In his youth and promise, Vaux was drawn at court by Hans Holbein in the early 1530s, but soon afterwards Vaux withdrew to his country estate in Northamptonshire, rather than abide in a court where Queen Anne presided with her evangelical friends.[156] Time was when religion had not divided friends, and even as the King assumed power over the English Church confessional lines were not yet sharply drawn, but soon friends like Vaux and Wyatt were forced to decide their allegiances, and might make different choices. The times were not made for friendship or trust:

> Assured I dowbt I be not sure
> and should I trust to suche suretie
> that oft hath put the prouff in ure
> and never hath founde it trusty
> nay sir In faith it were great foly
> and yet my liff thus I do wast
> for dred to fall I stond not fast

8

Friendship

Growing up in Kent and Christendom Wyatt and his friends learnt the claims and duties of friendship. In the Renaissance, friendship was a shining ideal of mutual obligation and honour, of love and virtue.[1] John Donne would call it his second religion.[2] The idea of the friend as another self – another I – was commonplace even as Plato and Aristotle contemplated it. 'Among friends all is in common' was an ideal advocated by Pythagoras millennia before it was explicated by Erasmus in his *Adages* (1515) and realized for him by his friend Thomas More in his imaginary commonwealth of Utopia.[3] From classical texts the Renaissance learnt about friendship as a public matter as well as private, rational as well as emotional. Men – for friendship was prevailingly a male subject – versed in the classics knew the rules and patterns of perfect friendship; brought up in chivalry, they revered the sworn brotherhood of arms and vowed the fidelity of knighthood. In Scripture there were the greatest friendships of all the world: in the Old Testament, 'the soul of Jonathan was knit with the soul of David', perfect friends; in the New, there was the friendship of Christ and His disciples.

When Christ came to earth and became man, He needed friends, and there was never greater friendship than His. At the Last Supper, He told His disciples: 'This is my commandment, that ye love together as I have loved you. Greater love than this hath no man, than that a man bestow his life for his friends' (John 15:13). Christ's sacrifice to save mankind from sin and death was the greatest ever 'proof of friendship', and made the highest form of friendship sacramental. Explaining the central Reformation doctrine of imputed righteousness, Melanchthon used an analogy of friendship: just as a person might pay the debt of a friend, though it was not his own, so the believer may be reckoned righteous on account of the alien merit of Christ.[4] On the cross Christ commended the care of His mother to St John the Evangelist, the disciple whom He loved, whose image would be found beside that of Christ crucified in every church, in sublime remembrance of that friendship. But the New Testament also witnessed the greatest betrayal. As Judas kissed Him, Christ asked ironically, 'Friend, wherefore art thou come?' (Matthew 26:50).[5] A quintessentially Renaissance subject was also, inescapably, a Reformation one. On the eve of his martyrdom, Bartlet Green, a young lawyer in the Inner Temple, would write to his friends, quoting Horace on the impossibility of their separation by death: '*Caelum, non animum, mutant qui trans mare currunt* [Those who rush across the sea, change the sky, not their mind].' Then he corrected himself: 'What speak I of Horace? saith not St Paul the same thing?'[6]

Every schoolboy learnt the rules and patterns of friendship. They knew that true friends swore friendship so profound that they were bondsmen forever. They read that friends come in pairs, and remembered the heroic friendships of Orestes and Pylades, Titus and Gesippus, Scipio and Laelius, Achilles and Patroclus, etc. Thomas Elyot, teaching the ideal of friendship to the political orders in his *Boke Named the Governor*, told the story of Damon and Pythias, faithful friends to the end, even under the tyrant Demetrius.[7] In the boredom of waiting on Cardinal Wolsey, when even gazing at the wonderful tapestries palled, Thomas Lupset, the friend of Nicholas Wilson and John Leland, wrote *An Exhortation to Yonge Men* in 'true friendship'. He advised young men who sought to 'know them that be worthy to be your friends, and by what means and what way friends be both gotten and also kept, ye shall best learn in Cicero's little book *De amicitia*'.[8]

Cicero's *De amicitia* (*Of Friendship*), the most famous work on friendship of all, was one of the very first classical texts to be translated into English and printed. So from 1481 less studious schoolboys even had a crib. In the Tower in 1549 John Harington 'tried prisonment of the body, to be the liberty of spirit: adversity of fortune: the touchstone of friendship', and he translated *The Booke of Freendeship of Marcus Tullie Cicero*.[9] Renaissance readers found guides to friendship pithily summarized in collections of *sententiae*, and in turn copied these moral sayings into their own commonplace books.[10] So yawningly obvious did these nostrums about the true, the perfect friend become that later in the century they would be gently mocked by Philip Sidney in his *Old Arcadia* and by Cervantes in *Don Quixote*.[11]

The theme of undying friendship was pervasive in the chivalric romances which were beginning to be printed. In *The History of Oliver of Castile* (1518) Henry Watson, 'apprentice of London', regaled his fellows with the story of 'Oliver of Castile and Arthur of Algarbe his loyal fellow', their 'great adversities and marvellous fortunes', their 'fidelity and promise'.[12] Here were fevered accounts of Oliver slaying his children 'for love of his fellow' so that Arthur might drink their blood to save his life. At a dark moment of mistrust Oliver threw Arthur from his horse, believing falsely that Arthur 'had lain with his wife'. All was well that ended well because surely – surely – no true friend would so betray his sworn brother. The fellowship in arms of knights was a distant prospect of impossible glamour and glory for City boys avidly reading of it in print, but in the lives of some 'childish' knights in waiting at Henry's court it was a lived ideal. After the death of the Duke of Richmond, Henry Howard, Earl of Surrey, remembered in pain and loss perfect times spent with his 'noble fere [companion]', an irrecoverable 'friendship sworn, each promise kept so just'.[13] What no schoolboy or 'child' knight could know was whether, when the test came, they would behave heroically: whether when overwhelmed by passion they would sleep with the wife of a friend, whether they would be brave enough to protect a friend in the midst of battle, whether when threatened by a tyrant they would act as nobly as Damon and Pythias. The sceptical wondered whether perfect friendship could ever now be found. In Castiglione's *Book of the Courtier* the character Pietro Bembo lamented: 'Neither do I believe that there are any more in the world, those Pylades and Orestes, Theseus and Perithous, nor Scipio and Laelius.'[14] And Castiglione wrote before the trials of faith and friendship which would come with the Reformation.

Thomas Wyatt's power 'friends to allure'[15] was noted even by his rivals. Wyatt and his circle thought on the nature of friendship, pondered the possibility of true friendship, and wrote self-consciously in the language of friendship. What they sought was not the casual companionship which came easily to anyone of charm and wit and influence, nor the utilitarian reciprocity of mutual service, but a sterner, graver bond: a friendship which made moral claims. 'If he may be your friend that willeth you no harm, forsake me not,' wrote Stephen Vaughan to Thomas Cromwell, but friendship was nothing so passive, so anodyne.[16] That the verbs used for making friends – proving, trying, forging – were the same as those applied to metal-working was natural, for true friendship was perdurable. Adamantine, it transcended the frailties of human nature and imitated the divine. It was found in adversity, not prosperity. So these men learnt in the verities imbibed in childhood and never forgotten, but also – excruciatingly – in practice, as they 'put the prouff in ure [to the test]'. The ideal of friendship to which they aspired was one based on reason and virtue, a friendship for constant men in inconstant times, a refuge of calm in the midst of chaos, and a bulwark in a sea of troubles. John Harington would call a faithful friend 'a strong garrison'.[17]

Wyatt often wrote of friendship in his poetry. Beside the conventional verse for the courtly company, we find him addressing two verse epistles to his friend John Poyntz – 'Myne owne Jhon poyntz' – and another to Francis Bryan. Verse epistle is especially resonant of friendship; familiar conversation continued under a different form. These personal letters – the only surviving personal letters of Wyatt, save those to his son – anticipate a response, a judgement, and take us to the heart of their amity. To Bryan he also dedicated an epigram, and he composed a double sonnet for an unnamed 'friend so dear', who – if he ever read it – should have been impressed by the very novelty of its form as well as its content. These works of Wyatt's imagination might alone invite a pursuit of his own quest for a friendship which might be trusted. Beyond that, the inculcation of friendship and the musings upon its gains and losses by Wyatt and his closest friends lead us to consider not only how friendship was professed, but also how it was lived. These were not unclouded friendships for the calm of country reclusion, for lives lived remote from power and politics, but friendships for harder times, bonds to sustain them in the turning world of the court. Their writings were haunted by the vision of the false friend: not just the fleeting, forsaking friend, but the traitor friend. The times began to place an impossible premium and pressure upon friendship, and circumstances beyond any individual control might turn a man into a traitor friend himself. Yet that friendship was so hard to find, especially at court, made it more, not less, an ardent aspiration among men who sought its sanctuary.

In a manuscript treatise written as a 'mirror of princes', 'Ion Poyngz', the friend of Wyatt's youth, wrote his signature, a Greek inscription 'ΤΕΛΟΣ [the end]', and a question: '*et quoy donc* [what then]?'[18] An unknown reader underlined crucial passages and drew a pointing hand, a manicule, in the margins of the text. Perhaps that admonitory reader was John Poyntz himself, perhaps not, but the places where the underlining is thickest, where the pointing hand appears most often, take us close to his ethics. In the treatise's first and second books concerning the dignity of the royal estate and the duties of a Christian king, the pointing hand is almost absent, but once the treatise discusses the duties of counsellors and provides classical and scriptural truths about friendship it becomes insistent. Here the reader learns from Solomon that 'better are the wounds of a friend than the kisses of an enemy', that the faithful friend is a sure protector and whoever finds such a friend finds treasure. Cicero teaches that friendship can only be between good men. Only the wise man can be a true friend, so Seneca advises. A true friend is above gold and silver. From Proverbs came the truth that 'he that is a friend loves at all times'. From Boethius he learns that friendship is the noblest kind of riches. What the good man, the wise man sought was the perfect friend.

In this text, as so often, the advice upon friendship turned not to what a friend was but to what he was not. Friendship might spin to its obverse, and the friend become the flatterer, the feigned friend, the friendly foe. With the admonitions to faithful friendship came stern warnings of its contrary. Seeming friends might be enemies, as Judas was to Christ. The rules of friendship, for finding the true friend, lay primarily in avoiding the false one. Again, pagan and Christian wisdom was plundered for these teachings. Beware of the man who, under colour of friendship, wishes harm. Never trust to friendship without first testing it. Time will prove whether a friendship is a true one. A friend cannot be known in prosperity, and an enemy cannot be hidden in adversity. We must despair of the man who closes his ears to the truth and will not hear the truth from his friend. Whoever reveals the secrets of a friend will be lost. Be wary – always, especially – of false friendship at court. The principal anxiety was that – although opposed – flattery and friendship might be hard to distinguish. The flatterer was the enemy of all virtue, and flattery a honeyed poison. St Jerome gave a warning to flee flatterers like the plague. When it was that John Poyntz read these maxims we cannot know – perhaps in his childhood – but that he learnt them, and tried to live by them, appears from the course of his life and the depth of his allegiances.*

Another friend and mentor of Wyatt's youth took friendship seriously, and meditated on the truths which had enlightened Poyntz. If friendship could be – as Cicero insisted – only between good men, then Sir Francis Bryan might seem an unlikely friend and counsellor. So often we find Bryan at the gaming table, or in some courtesan's chamber, or drinking immoderately, as became Henry's libertine companion, his notorious 'Vicar of Hell'.[19] His speech was noted to be pungent: '*Non, diavolo, non* [No, devil take it]'.[20] When Bryan wrote to his friends it was not always according to Cicero's stern conception of an amity based on virtue. To cheer Lord Lisle, his 'loving brother of old', in his honourable exile as Deputy of Calais, Bryan wrote smutty, anticlerical letters which spoke of their easy companionship as well as Bryan's gleeful disrespect for conventional pieties. Writing in October 1533 from Marseilles, where the French court was awaiting the Pope, Bryan desired Lisle 'to make more ready for me a soft bed than a hard harlot'. Teasingly thanking Lisle for the provision of Calais 'courtezans to furnish and accomplish my desires', he protested that he had had 'absolution of the Pope' for 'the misliving that ye . . . hath brought me to'.[21] As if. Yet he wrote, too, in the classical terms of friendship, describing Lord and Lady Lisle as 'but one soul though ye be two bodies'. Telling Lisle hard truths, he assured him that 'amity bindeth me

---

* For John Poyntz's life, see above pp. 50, 176–8, and below, ch. 9.

to do it'.²² And while Lisle was marooned in Calais Bryan acted as his friend at court, urging secrecy – 'you must keep all things secreter than you have used', 'I pray you keep this secret' – and warning him to remember that 'the minds of princes sometime change'.²³

The King kept Francis Bryan, his favoured courtier, always close to him. At court Bryan was Cupbearer and Gentleman of the Privy Chamber, in the chase he was Henry's constant companion, and for most of the reign he was Master of the Toils (the nets into which the wretched deer were chased). He was sent in embassy as the King's own proxy and self. Succeeding his brother-in law Henry Guildford, Bryan became Master of the Henchmen, entrusted with bringing up the royal pages and wards in chivalry, virtue and learning. Bryan himself was peerless in chivalry. He had fought in France and Scotland and was knighted on the battlefield for his 'noble courage'. A hero of the joust like his other brother-in-law Nicholas Carew, he had performed gloriously in the court's tournaments. No one was better fitted than Bryan to teach chivalry and the chase to the 'childish' knights of the court, not only how to ride and fight, but also the knight's duty of fidelity to the brotherhood of arms. His qualifications for inculcating virtue and learning were less obvious. He admitted little 'knowledge of the [h]istories, which I do profess is hard for to understand for one of no greater literature than I profess me to be', and less Latin.²⁴ Yet although no scholar himself, he took very seriously his duty of educating the young.

Bryan's uncle Lord Berners – lord of the manor of Barnes, Wyatt's childhood home – translated chivalric romances which might chasten the more ardent desires of young knights and their ladies. Confident that it would encourage 'strong hardy warriors . . . promptly to go in hand with great and hardy perils in defence of their country', he also translated Froissart's *Chronicles*, a work which inspired John Poyntz.²⁵ 'At the instant desire of his nephew Sir Francis Bryan knight', who had been staying with him in Calais, Berners translated from a French version *The Golden Boke of Marcvs Avrelivs*, finishing it on 10 March 1532.²⁶ Here Berners promised 'marvellous devises against the encumbrance of fortune'. The chapter teaching 'How the emperor would have them of his court to live' – especially 'the little young folks that are here', given by their fathers to the Emperor 'for to nourish you in my palace' – is revealing of Bryan's advice for his own young charges. In this work of Stoic ethics they would learn how to avoid vice, especially idleness (one vice of which Bryan was guiltless), and also 'whereby they ought to live and resist each disfavour and falls of fortune'. Before they could govern others or counsel governors they must be able to govern themselves. 'The universal school of all the world is the person, the house, and court of a prince.'[27]

The truths which John Poyntz had learnt in French and Latin in the 'mirror of princes' text were increasingly proverbial, and printed in English, by the time that Francis Bryan composed a long poem on how to live a moral life at the courts of the great. Sometime after 1534 Bryan paraphrased – wrote alongside – Thomas Elyot's *Bankette of Sapience*, a compendium of moral sentences drawn from the same Christian and pagan wisdom studied by Poyntz.[28] Bryan's ottava rima stanzas testify to his poetic ambition and desire to be a 'maker' among 'makers': not that he did it well, but that he did it at all. At the heart of the poem is the concern of all those in high places who contemplated how to remain constant – 'philosophical' – when assailed by the blasts of Fortune, the same concern which led Wyatt to translate Plutarch:

> Needs must he that is valiant be of great constancy;
> Whom Fortune high riseth, she listeth to let fall[29]

The wise man – of course – eschews vice, excess, corruption, vainglory and falsehood, and aspires to patience, beneficence, obedience to the sovereign, and true faith in and emulation of Christ.

> Our Lord will reward every man according to justice;
> We that believe Christ, let us follow his living[30]

Throughout the poem one vice is particularly abhorred, a vice which especially perverts life at court where envy and pride are rife, a vice which threatens both friendship and true counsel. That vice is flattery. Admonitions to beware the flatterer crowd in: 'In truth, which showeth openly there is no flattery'; 'Separate from thee that craftily doth flatter'; 'The feat of a flatterer is his own cause to advance'; 'nothing is more feigned/Than to promise faith; and to be brittle as glass'; 'A flatterer can make a false tale for to seem fair'.[31] The friend makes an appearance in the poem only fleetingly:

> In things displeasant an enemy is spied,
> And in adversity a friend is tried[32]

Praise for the true friend's fortitude is less necessary than warnings of the feigned friend.

Bryan claimed so many vices as his own, but flattery he shunned. In that lay his honour and his truth to his king; in that, too, lay his truth to his God. While other knights and courtiers around the King chose mottoes promising loyalty to their secular lord – like Guildford's '*Loial.mant. ie. sers* [Loyally I serve]' – Bryan's was '*Ia. tens. grace* [I hope for, I wait for salvation]'.[33] To Bryan's religious faith we will return, but at court his saving grace consisted in his fearless plain speaking to the King, his insistence – as Wyatt expresses it in his verse epistle 'A spending hand that always powreth owte' – 'with fre tong what the myslikes to blame', and his desire 'next godly thinges to have an honest name'. Again and again, Bryan's audacious freedom of speech was commended. Lord Darcy looked to him, because he 'dare and will speak to the King the truth' – a rare virtue at court – and Bryan's friend the Abbot of Woburn said admiringly that 'Sir Francis dare boldly speak to the King's grace the plainness of his mind . . . and his grace doth well accept the same'.[34] Not only Bryan's lack of formal education prevented him using aureate diction, full of Latin-derived words, for he distrusted its polished delusiveness and preferred the seeming truth of homely, proverbial speech. A natural orator, a dazzling talker, he would use those powers in the King's service, to persuade others, but not to tell Henry what he wished to hear.

Thomas Cromwell adjured Wyatt in 1537: 'your part shall be now like a good orator'; 'Mr Wyatt, now is the time . . . for you to play your part of a good servant'.[35] Playing the orator at a foreign court, Wyatt was to cajole another prince in his own prince's name, but in Cromwell's service and as Cromwell's friend, he must speak plainly. Playing, telling truth: this was a perilous double game. The masters of rhetoric, men practised in the arts of eloquence, had been taught to *move* their hearers towards virtue, to persuade them to the good. But such men, playing freely with language, could flatter without seeming to do so, or could criticise and tell the truth even while seeming to flatter.[36] Consummate actors, they played their roles exquisitely, but could use their sinuous arts for devious purposes. Irony – the art of saying one thing and meaning another – was their characteristic device. The sceptical, disdainful courtier would discern one meaning, and the dupe another. Irony could not be entirely a dark art, since Christ had used it, but anxiety attended it. The wary, the subtle would suspect extravagant praise as concealed mockery. Erasmus recalled John Colet wondering whether his praise of Aquinas was in earnest, or ironic. Erasmus himself was averse to extravagant praise, believing it better suited to a tyrant than a friend. Vanity and insecurity, as well as stupidity, might make a man vulnerable to flattery. Thraso, the braggart soldier in Terence's play *The Eunuch*, was not forgotten by the classically educated. Insistently flattered by the parasite Gnatho, Thraso took the adulation at face value, while all the other characters sniggered at Gnatho's irony.[37] In courts there were men who would 'lick the crumbs' from a great man's beard.[38] But Wyatt was not one of them. According to his grandson, he was no 'favourite', for he dared to disagree with the King 'in particular opinion of things', because he was by nature and will 'most far from the custom of flattery incident to court'.[39]

With friendship, as so much else at court, all was not what it seemed. The most ardent professors of friendship might instead be feigning. The problem was an ancient one, and particularly exercised those with power, men who became great, around whom flatterers swarmed. Erasmus translated from Greek into Latin Plutarch's *How to Tell a Friend from a Flatterer*, and sent it to Henry, who fondly believed that he learnt its lessons.[40] Yet Henry's failure to listen, when time was, to those he should have trusted as his best friends – Fisher, More and Reginald Pole – had tragic consequences for England and Christendom. So Pole believed. Bereft of true friends, Henry was at the mercy of flatterers and self-servers among his counsellors.[41] Thomas Cromwell understood the language of friendship before ever he wielded the influence which drew a host of suitors to besiege him with claims of remembered friendship. In 1522, borrowing from Cicero and using the language of friendship as a means to favour, a friend wrote to him:

Carissimo quanto homo in questo mondo [the dearest man in this world], the great amicitia that hath been between us cannot out of my memory, the affection was so perfect . . . my love toward you resteth in no less vigour than it did at our last being together. My [hear]t mourneth for your company . . . as ever it did for men.[42]

To this letter came Cromwell's guarded reply: 'I assure you, if it were in my little power, I could be well contented to prefer [you] as far as any one man living.'[43] Imposing obligation was part of friendship, but it made friendship, supposedly between equals, unequal.[44] 'The name of a friend, friendship and love which are names of familiarity commonly used among men of like condition' were soon applied to the very different relationship of 'mastership and service'.[45] The nature of the friendship which was possible between masters and servants was considered seriously in the Renaissance. Giovanni della Casa wrote a treatise on the friendship between great and rich men and those who served them, and in 1543 Wyatt's former servant Thomas Chaloner would translate and publish Gilbert Cousin's *Of the Office of Servauntes*.[46]

Great men had to look harder for true friends. Seneca, who had been Nero's tutor, believed that such men might have 'chief friends, ordinary friends, never true friends'.[47] For Cromwell this problem became acute as he grew powerful and greater demands were made on his friendship. He advised his old friend and client Stephen Vaughan 'not overmuch to press your friend for friendship'.[48] Vaughan, setting himself and his own good will towards his master against the place-seekers and flatterers, wrote a treatise on plain speaking. Larded with references to Ovid's *Metamorphoses*, the treatise described the fatal envy which overcame 'our lodesman [pilot] Reason'. 'With flaming eyes and wrinkly faces ever pining and macerate [wasting], we never cease the rage', as we see those advanced 'whom willingly we would tread underfoot'. 'I know myself by speaking truth to have poisoned a great many hearts.'[49] The more adept seekers of patronage learnt to disavow flattery when they wrote to Cromwell, but the protests of friendship came thick and threefold. 'I give you my heart, the greatest jewel I have,' wrote Anthony St Leger, the Kentish friend and neighbour of Cromwell and Wyatt.[50] Cromwell was a man to whom friendship mattered, and was remembered for his loyalty to his friends. John Foxe, who had spoken to some of them, headed one chapter of his life of Cromwell: 'The Lord Cromwell: Not forgetting his Old Friends and Benefactors'. Cromwell's client Richard Morison, who needed to believe it, wrote: 'My lord, your joy and comfort may be great that you, almost alone of all men that ever were in your place, have never forgotten your old [friends].'[51]

Wyatt and his friends read meditations upon friendship in Seneca's *De beneficiis* (*Of Benefits*), and thought on the Stoic ethics which commended friendship between good men, and constant friendship as a refuge in troubled times. True friendship and true counsel were synonymous, and the duties of friends to each other and to the King were analogous: telling the truth and constancy. In his verse epistle to Francis Bryan – 'A spending hand' – Wyatt insisted on that duty of friendly counsel:

> Brian to the who knows how great a grace
> In writing is to cownsell man the right

Friendship and plain speaking would be the preservative against tyranny.[52] Virtuous counsellors must learn to speak persuasive truth while avoiding flattery. At Henry's court, as in imperial Rome, groups around the prince might see themselves as his friends, while their enemies saw them as a faction. What was faction but friendship, at least to those within the faction? Guiding the King was the part of the loyal counsellor, but to challenge the royal will or overrule it was conspiracy, even treason. This was the problem for courtiers who opposed royal policy; they must work by devious means. In such circumstances faction, with all its malign consequences, flourished. What the factions, the 'friends', sought was to win the ear of the King and gain his favour and patronage, and to use it to advance themselves and oust their rivals.[53] Yet now men and women at court began to fight not for power alone, but for a cause: to further or to extinguish the new religion. In a regime which turned to persecution, factions could use religion as the means to bring down their rivals, but that very rivalry often arose from divergent beliefs about what was true religion. In the aleatory world of the court, friends spun to become 'back friends' with the power to harm, and the mutual jealousies between sometime friends turned enemies became fatal. Wyatt and his friends profoundly understood this, and we will find supposed friends circling each other distrustfully, as friendship was subverted.

True friendship might be expressed in words which were only words, sustained by none of the constancy which was perfect friendship's essence. Here is a rhapsody on friendship sent to Thomas Wriothesley, promising friendship 'so strongly rooted in the ground of your gentle heart that it cannot be plucked up or overcast by no stormy nor windy weather'. This benevolence was

not hidden in heart and mind . . . but appeareth outwardly in every part of your body: your forehead which maketh plain all wrinkles when I come, your eyes that looketh so friendly, your tongue which comforteth so lovingly, counselleth so providently . . .

[. . .]

It is not fortune which hath worked this friendship. She hath place in other things which are easy to be changed, but this I reckon very fatal and of God and therefore I trust perpetual.[54]

If someone as subtle as Wyatt had received this letter he might have read it ironically. Wriothesley was subtle, too, superbly trained in the arts of eloquence – even though he promised 'I will speak plainly after my country fashion'[55] – yet he was also insecure, vain and jealous, weaknesses which made him susceptible to cringing flattery.

Wriothesley: writhesly: *nomen omen*. The son and grandson of heralds, Thomas Wriothesley received a perfect humanist education at St Paul's School and Trinity Hall, Cambridge, and rose inexorably in the royal service, by the pen rather than the sword. His was a career which could not be 'matched outside the church before 1529'.[56] At Cambridge, his tutor in the civil law was Dr Stephen Gardiner, and when Gardiner became royal secretary, Wriothesley was appointed

Clerk to the Signet. Here his official career began. But Wriothesley was in Cromwell's service also, and as Cromwell's private secretary was deep in all the secrets of policy.[57] The man who read and drafted so much correspondence, ciphered so many letters knew all the *arcana imperii*. With Cromwell's advancement, Wriothesley was promoted too, and by 1537 was more than secretary, in a position of independence and influence. The doubleness of his service to both Gardiner and Cromwell would become an undertow in the currents of court politics thereafter. Wriothesley's ability was undoubted, but with that ability and ambition came unquietness. Richard Morison wrote, after Wriothesley's death, that 'he was an earnest follower of whatsoever he took in hand, and very seldom did miss where either wit or travail were able to bring his purpose to pass'. 'I was afraid of a tempest all the while Wriothesley was able to raise one . . .'[58]

Wriothesley was an actor. At Cambridge in 1522 – Leland's contemporary, and perhaps Wyatt's – he had, rather aptly, played the part of the artful slave Palaestrio in Plautus' comedy *Miles gloriosus* (*The Swaggering Soldier*), with William Paget, his school friend, taking the role of the maid Milphidippa, his accomplice.[59] At court, Wriothesley remained an actor. Some observed him 'playing his part in that play', and he would describe himself thus to Wyatt: 'I have played the honest man with you'; 'I played the jolly courtier, faith!'[60] The jolly courtier: trained among black-gowned lawyers, Wriothesley longed for the glamour and grace of a courtier – that is, to be like Wyatt. By the mid-1540s, his gentlemen servants, always in attendance, were liveried in velvet and wore gold chains. Cattily, Gardiner remarked upon Wriothesley receiving a letter in Italian, the language of the would-be courtier.[61] Whether Wriothesley was ever let in to the 'company of makers' and allowed to read Wyatt's poetry we may doubt. Like Wyatt, handsome, a 'favourite of Apollo', Wriothesley was portrayed by Holbein. Like Wyatt, he chose horses of mettle. But, unlike Wyatt, he needed to have them already 'bitted' and broken in.[62] During his failed embassy to the Netherlands Wriothesley would be disparaged as 'a man of no estimation, a secretary', because he lacked the grace and skills of the orator which Wyatt supremely possessed.[63] Yet he was adept enough in some courtly skills. 'As for Mr Wriothesley's promise', so Lord Lisle's agent wrote in October 1538, 'fair hests [vows] and promises of the court are holy water', sprinkled randomly.[64] Wriothesley was well able to play the friend, but he learnt painfully the most savage lesson of courts: 'Spare no man when the time shall come, but be thine own friend and thine own executor.'[65] As the friendship between Wriothesley and Wyatt became clouded by jealousy and suspicion, they held each other in mutual danger. Some equivocal friendships will unsettle and darken all that follows.

The rhetoric of friendship was not inimical to the truth. But it might be. Stephen Gardiner knew the pull of friendship. He had written letters verging on the erotic to Thomas Arundel, who served with him in Wolsey's household: 'though I depart from you in body, I depart not in mind and soul . . . during my life wheresoever this body shall fortune to wander . . . Entirely your own.'[66] Gardiner thought so naturally in the conventions of friendship that he could compare the amity between Thomas Smith and John Cheke – perhaps ironically – to the 'famous friendship' of Damon and Pythias.[67] Once, Gardiner and Cromwell had both served Cardinal Wolsey and written to each other in the pure language of friendship, yet their friendship was never proclaimed more constantly than at the losing of it.[68] From their failing friendship there grew a rivalry, then an enmity, which in time would poison the political life which they dominated. Yet even at the most desperate moment, with all former friendship forsaken, these accomplished courtiers – by now a bishop and a principal counsellor – could recall their forgotten friendship and feign what they did not feel. As Gardiner dined with Cromwell in the fateful spring of 1540 they 'opened their hearts, and so concluded that, and there be truth or honesty in them, not only all displeasures be forgotten, but also in their hearts be now perfect entire friends'.[69]

It has been well said that 'the ethics of friendship were a response to the potential for a peaceful life'.[70] With the advent of religious reform and with the King's assault upon the universal Church the potential for a peaceful life and for friendship was undermined. In circumstances of great stress, indifference was unthinkable, and every opinion, even every relationship might become political. Friendship according to classical definitions – 'a perfect agreement with good will and true love in all kind of good things and godly'[71] – was the more cherished as the unity of Christendom was broken, and those who held to the old faith clung to each other. In the Tower, facing the 'indignation of my Prince, of me no less loved than feared', Thomas More wrote in the most beautiful language of friendship to Antonio Bonvisi, his friend of forty years, 'the apple of mine eye'. He thanked him for an amity which 'seemeth . . . to counterpeise [counterweight] this unfortunate shipwreck of mine'.

But if I should reckon the possession of so constant friendship . . . amongst the brittle gifts of fortune, then were I mad. For the felicity of so faithful and constant friendship in the storms of fortune (which is seldom seen) is doubtless a high and noble gift proceeding of a certain singular benignity of God.

More looked beyond their friendship in this world to an unthreatened one 'where shall need no letters, where no wall shall dissever us, where no porter shall keep us from talking together': Heaven.[72] For More and Fisher, Heaven would be a haven of perfect friendship, and Hell defined by friendship's absence.[73]

Among the evangelical 'brethren', the advance guard of the new faith, extraordinary friendships were sustained under persecution. Through all the time of his political eminence, Cromwell protected his friends among the 'brethren'. That he was acquainted with evangelicals in the Inns of Court, in the merchant community of the City and among English merchants abroad, is not by itself proof of his sympathy with their convictions, for no man is his friend's keeper, but his protection of them might be. He kept secret the networks of reform of which he had been part, and thereby put himself in danger, partly for reasons of faith, and partly also – we might surmise – for reasons of friendship.[74] For Cromwell, as for many others, religious convictions evolved in the company of friends, and conversion was both the cause and consequence of friendship. Remembering the process of his conversion from the darkness of papistry into 'this world which is lightened . . . with the pure . . . truth of the word of God', an anonymous correspondent recalled his first conversation with Cromwell in 'your law parlour in your old house' at the Austin Friars. Only 'a stony heart and a blockish wit' would resist 'such colloquy' as was had at Cromwell's table, and he had returned home with 'my English Bible'. 'I found always the conclusions which you maintained at your board to be consonant with the holy word of God'.[75]

Religious faith which strengthened friendship might also destroy it. Friendship which, by Cicero's definition, rested on 'perfect agreement . . . in all kind of good things and godly' became more difficult and sometimes impossible as friends conceived different paths to salvation and confessional rifts began to appear. In 1534 Thomas Elyot disavowed his former religious allegiance. He had 'often wished a reformation; which brought him into contention with certain persons . . . they could not persuade him to approve that which faith and reason condemned, nor could he dissuade them; which caused a separation between them'.[76] In the first generation of reform, everyone from whom 'the veil of Moses was lifted', who was 'born again' in the new faith, was won away from the old, a convert. Such conversions were not made without pain and loss, and friendship might be a casualty. Nowhere was the breach in friendships which came with religious conversion deeper than in the household of Francis Bryan, where exegesis of Scripture led to bitter confessional divisions among young scholars there. Writing in Greek – to vaunt his scholarship, and to conceal the letter's contents – one lambasted the other's learning, but lamented their lost friendship: 'and what you call heretical, I have acquired with no less pains than you have acquired your hypocritical show of knowledge . . . You seemed to be a friend. I sang your praises on all occasions . . . [but] the friend stopped . . .' Common faith, for them, had become the test of friendship. Though their friendship was broken, their faith was proved, proved in fire, for one would die a martyr's death.[77] Friendship had the power to enable people to live in peace across their divisions, but it also had the power to intensify those divisions. At the Reformation, we witness that 'equivocal capacity' of friendship in acute form.[78] Faith became a bond or solvent of friendship, as religious change, and life under a persecuting regime, imposed hard choices and friendships were made which were tested. Would friendship transcend religious division, and might a friend love the man, not his religious error? Sometimes, but friendship became harder to sustain in the trials of the Reformation. If there was friendship, there was also betrayal.[79]

In the new world of power – as the King claimed supremacy over the English church, as criticism of royal policy became potentially treasonable, and as religious oaths were commanded to prove political loyalty – new demands were made on conscience and on friendship. In the Tower, Thomas More thanked Nicholas Wilson for not showing him the book he had written against the 'Great Matter' and published in Paris, for by his 'secret manner' Wilson had spared More a dangerous knowledge. But now, as Wilson was deprived of 'liberty . . . and comfort of . . . friends' company', tormented by 'doubts falling in your mind, that diversely to and fro toss and trouble your conscience', he compromised More by seeking his counsel.[80] Wilson made some accommodation with his conscience and with the King, and left the Tower, at least for a while, but More could not. On the eve of his execution, he wrote a last letter to his daughter: 'tomorrow long I to go to God'. That day would be the octave of the feast of St Peter, 'a day very meet and convenient for me'.[81] More thought on St Peter, not only because Peter was prince of the Church to whom Christ had given primacy and from whom all popes succeeded, but because Peter, in his human frailty, had faltered in faith and in friendship by denying Christ. More, fearful of his own frailty, had prayed 'Our Lord for his tender passion' to keep him from swearing and forswearing as Peter had done, but if he had to 'play St Peter', to 'cast upon me his tender piteous eye, as he did upon St Peter, and make me stand up again and confess the truth of my conscience afresh'.[82]

John Mason, More's protégé, who became Wyatt's secretary and close friend, also thought on Peter's example. What Mason read and thought mattered in the life of Wyatt, for 'in all his facts and doings' Wyatt came to trust him as 'a God almighty'.[83] In the library of All Souls College, Oxford, where Mason was a Fellow, is his copy of Erasmus's paraphrase of the New Testament, printed in Basle in 1535.[84] At points in the text we find Mason's hand annotating and underlining, and nowhere more than in the eighteenth chapter of the Gospel of St John. Here Judas turns from Christ's friend to His betrayer, and Peter who had promised never to forsake Christ, forswears Him three times. The Evangelist, recounting Christ's trial before Caiaphas and Pilate, taught how the Christian must confront injustice, and that Christ's kingdom is not of this world.[85] Paraphrasing the Gospel accounts of Peter's denial of Christ, Erasmus described Peter becoming 'a true courtier', and wrote that the first requisite for 'those who wish to attach themselves to the courts of princes' was 'to deny Christ, that is, to deny the truth'.[86] Once destined for a starry career in the Church – which would bring its own worldly compromises – Mason was plucked from Oxford in 1527 and recruited instead for the royal service by More. Years of study in Paris and Padua gave Mason the perfect humanist education to use to guide a prince's will, but he learnt from experience that princes may be resistant to good counsel and counsellors complicit in policies they deplore. In his copy of Erasmus's paraphrase of John he wrote beside Christ's saying 'My kingdom is not the kind that Caesar's is': '*Regnum meum non est de hoc mundo*'.[87]

In Paris with Mason in 1529–30 was the humanist Thomas Starkey, who was there with Reginald Pole, serving as his secretary.[88] Mason and Starkey became friends. While in Paris, Starkey began to compose his astonishing 'Dialogue between Pole and Lupset'. This unpublished tract analysed the social and political degeneration of the English commonwealth and proposed a startling remedy for the realm's discontents. Hopes for reform lay in the abridgement of royal power: Starkey proposed no less than an elective monarchy, with the king counselled by properly educated nobles.[89] Whether Mason and Starkey debated the nature of royal power and its abuse, we cannot know, but Mason's confidences to Starkey and his acquaintance with Pole would come to endanger him. Mason's entry into royal service was in the English embassy in Spain. When Wyatt came to serve there, Mason was his secretary. The post of secretary was one of such intimacy and trust that St John the Evangelist was described as Christ's secretary in the court of Heaven.[90] A secretary is, first, a keeper of secrets. Yet in June and July 1534 Mason was writing extremely indiscreetly from

Valladolid to his 'sure friend', his 'assured friend', Starkey in Padua. Reporting freely on the news from England – that those refusing to swear the oaths were sent to the Tower – he lamented 'what end this tragedy will come to, God wot'. 'If that may be called a tragedy *quae inceperit a nuptiis* [which began with a marriage].' For Mason, Queen Anne – 'Gallina [the Hen]' – 'hath been the cause of all'. Absence from England spared Mason any imminent crisis of conscience, any taking of oaths, any facing of music, but his sympathy plainly lay with More in the Tower. 'I could write you many things but I must remember mine office,' he wrote, as if this letter had been sufficiently guarded.[91] Yet it was preserved for sinister reasons, to be examined for evidence once Mason's loyalty became suspect. If Mason's allegiance was doubted, then so was Wyatt's: and if Wyatt's, then also Mason's. Critics of the King now learnt that 'the keeping of letters m[ight turn a man]'s friend to hurt'.[92]

To make a friend was to give a hostage to fortune. The particular risk lay in the sharing of secrets, which is what friends do, and lies at the heart of friendship. Yet to entrust secrets to another was to place oneself in his power, a kind of voluntary servitude.[93] In *The Book of the Courtier* the figure of Pietro Bembo admitted that he had been 'deceived of him whom I loved best, and of whom I hoped I was beloved above any other person', and had secretly wondered whether it were better

never to put a man's trust in any person in the world, nor to give him self so for a prey to friend how dear and loving so ever he were, that without stop a man should make him partaker of all his thoughts, as he would his own self: because there are in our minds so many dens and corners, that it is unpossible for the wit of man to know the dissimulations that lie lurking in them.[94]

Trust might be betrayed, and betrayal by friends is not only the most painful, but the most dangerous enmity, because they know more. At the Reformation, friends naturally discussed religion and politics, but this might be to run into the danger of the 'law of words', the Treason Act. Thomas Elyot included this counsel from Ecclesiasticus in *The Bankette of Sapience*: 'Among thy friends, detract not the king, nor in the most secret place of thy chamber report none evil of a great man:

for the birds of heaven will bear about thy voice, and they that have feathers will tell thine opinion.' In turn, men around the court copied this into their commonplace books.[95] The pointing hand in Poyntz's manuscript marked the danger of the perilous, perfidious friend who revealed his friend's *arcana* (secrets). Wyatt and his intimates, reading the maxims about the risks of friendship, learnt these truths also by bitter experience and sent warnings of the consequences of betrayal.*[96] They knew that friendship might turn to enmity, that bosom friends might turn secret enemies. The maxim of Lord Thomas Howard was 'as the deepest hate is that which springs from violent love, so the greatest discourtesies oft arise from the largest favours', and his brother, the Earl of Surrey, wrote bitterly: 'Such as in folded arms we did embrace, we hate.' Thinking in anguish of the enemy within, the traitor friend, they turned to the Psalmist whose agonies prefigured their own. Betrayed, accused of treason, Surrey paraphrased Psalm 55:

> It was a friendly foe, by shadow of good will,
> Mine old fere and dear friend, my guide, that trapped me;   *companion*
> Where I was wont to fetch the cure of all my care,
> And in his bosom hid my secret zeal to God.[97]

What would happen if ever the claims of friendship and obedience to a prince clashed? Was a higher duty owed to a friend or to the state? The question was an old one before it was posed acutely at the court of Henry VIII. Famously, in Cicero's *De amicitia* Gaius Blosius insisted that he would have set fire to the Capitol had his friend Tiberius Gracchus asked him to do so. Laelius repudiated this choice.[98] Thomas Elyot – prudentially, self-servingly – distanced himself from Thomas More. He asked Cromwell to forget the former friendship between him and More, telling him that it 'was but *usque ad aras*, as is the proverb, considering that I was never so much addict unto him as I was unto truth and fidelity toward my sovereign lord'.[99] *Usque ad aras*: 'I am your friend as far as the altar'. Erasmus had considered this proverb in his *Adages*. It was the reply of Pericles to a friend's request to help him in a law suit

---

* See below, p. 285.

by lying for him: certainly he had a duty to his friend, but only so far as it did not trespass against the deity.[100]

Early in 1539 John Beckinsaw wrote to John Mason: 'I desired you to continue your friendship to me so long as I do not offend grievously nor my maker nor my prince.' Behind his protestation lay the understanding that their shared loyalty to the old order was disloyalty to their prince, and that their friendship as well as their allegiances threatened them. That letter survives because they were already under suspicion, and Mason had just survived – though who knew for how long? – inquisition into his beliefs and associations.[101] The friendship between Richard Morison and Cardinal Pole could not survive their different choices. Once Pole's treason was known, Morison, who had become a propagandist for the King, wrote, 'all they, whom friendship and affinity had in time past knit unto thee, wish for no traitor's death so much as they do for thine'. 'He is much more thy friend, that wished thee dead than alive.'[102] Reading this renunciation of friendship from a man he had once sheltered in his house as a brother, Pole could not help but smile.[103] The classically educated had believed that friendship and true counsel might be a preservative against tyranny, but they might have reflected, too, on Aristotle's claim that in perverted constitutions there can be no friendship, where there is no justice.[104]

For the 'friends' and 'lovers' who disported themselves by writing in the Devonshire manuscript, friendship was their *raison d'être*. Though we find them singing of forsaking lovers, and imagining flight 'from company to live alone', this was part of the game, for it was pleasing to imagine abandonment while enjoying the companionship of – surely – assured friends.[105] Yet their amusement was attended by anxiety. One wrote '*mentire non est meum* [I am not given to lie]' and 'deceit deserveth death'.[106] If deception was their enemy, they hoped, they were sure, that it would not be found within *their* 'company', for treachery among them was unthinkable. But the fear of infidelity echoes through the insistent call for 'all ye lovers' to remember that friends might revert and lovers prove untrue. A poem claimed by Anthony Lee, Wyatt's brother-in-law, urged that in love the best way was 'first to prove and after trust'.[107] '*TH*' – Lord Thomas Howard – wrote a lover's hymn to the 'friendship of a faithful friend', hoping not for 'raging love most amorously' but for 'honest friendly company'.[108] In the world of these versifiers, betrayal was the more feared because for them love was not untouched by royal power and will. Howard's love and life ended in pain in the Tower, where he was sent for secretly marrying Lady Margaret Douglas.[109] In the anonymous, mysterious 'Greeting to you both in hearty wise' lies a warning: 'Mark well my words', says the unknown speaker, though words are not to be trusted.[110]

> [. . .]
> beware hardily ere ye have any need
> and to friends reconciled trust not greatly
> for they that once with hasty speed
> exiled themselves out of your company
> though they turn again and speak sweetly
> feigning themselves to be your friends fast
> beware of them for they will deceive you at last.
> [. . .]
> Written lifeless at the manor place
> of him that hath no chave nor nowhere doth dwell   *chaff?*
> but wandering in the wild world wanting that he has
> and neither hopes nor fears heaven nor hell
> but liveth at adventure ye know him full well
> the twenty day of March he wrote it in his house
> and hath him recommended to the cat and the mouse.

This poem is epistolary, though both the speaker and the recipient remain deliberately 'unknown', and it resonates with proverbial wisdom. It may, therefore, seem to have something in common with Wyatt's verse epistles. It has the nature of a riddle which the reader – the listener – may unlock. Who is the 'unknown' speaker: 'ye know him full well'? He may be you yourself? If so, the dialogue is between the soul and the body: it is within.[111]

In friendship, as in so much else, Wyatt was elusive. Writing his verse epistle to Francis Bryan – 'A spending hand that always powreth owte' – he referred to that easy kind of instrumental friendship found everywhere:[112]

> thou knowest well first who so can seke to plese
> shall pourchase frendes where trowght shall but offend.   *truth*

Wyatt himself had all the grace to amuse and please, to win friends, if it suited him. Even his rivals admitted his graceful ability 'to do such and so many pleasures', and that 'witty he is, and pleasant amongst company'. Victims of their collusion, however, saw the 'great affection zeal and love' between Cromwell and Wyatt as a friendship exercised for extortion. We have heard Wyatt's derision as he and the gilded youths of court laughed lesserlings to scorn. Like Bryan, he was found with his companions in gambling dens, though not in courtesans' chambers. For the amusement of the 'company' '*Tho*' penned 'Ye old mule that thinck yorself so fayre', a poem demeaning women, or perhaps one particular woman.[113] Yet such locker-room companionship was far from the true friendship to which he aspired. Writing his verse epistle to Bryan, Wyatt adjured him to keep his own counsel, to forget friendship – even as he hoped for his cynicism to be confounded: 'be nexte thyself, for frendshipp beres no prise'.

When Wyatt wrote of friendship it was usually with anxiety and doubt, and dread that human nature and the press of circumstance must vitiate it. In *The Quyete of mynde*, translating Plutarch, he held up as an example of true constancy the man who could withstand even the 'faynt hert forsaker of frendes', and who lived equably with the knowledge that his 'frende was a man, that is to say, a lyvely thyng redy of nature to be depraved'.[114] In his poetry the theme of friendship – or friendship's loss – recurs. The proverbial admonition to try before trusting appears in the following epigram, where the anxiety may be about love or about politics: not that the two were ever far separated at this court.[115]

> Dryven bye desire I dede this dede
> to daunger my self without cause whye
> to truste the untrue not like to spede   *prosper, be successful*
> to speke and promise faithefullie

but nowe the proof dothe verifie
that whoso trustithe or he kno
Dothe hurte him self and please his Foo.

Haunted by the fear that his friend might, in the end, prove to be his enemy, Wyatt wrote not only of the forsaking friend but also of the 'friendly foe', the enemy within. '*Tho*' claimed a poem which breathes the proverbial wisdom of Wyatt's conversations with Bryan:[116]

Ryght true it is and said full yore agoo *a very long time ago*
take hede of him that by thy back the claweth
Tho. for none is wourse then is a frendely Foo
though they seme good all thing that the deliteth
yet knowe it well that in thy bosom crepeth
for many a man such fier oft kyndeleth
that with the blase his berd syngeth. *beard*

Wyatt, of course, inhabits many voices, and if we read this as the confessional voice of Wyatt, himself the victim of a 'frendely Foo', we may be failing to discern a more bitter possibility. The greatest fear was that the times would turn a man into the traitor friend himself. At the thought of friendship did pain sweep over Wyatt, did he flinch as he remembered betrayals, some of them by him?

A man might look within, and even there find betrayal. Paraphrasing the Penitential Psalms, Wyatt would contemplate friendship. His David, in the depths of sin and despair, encircled by enemies, finds something worse: that there are traitors within, 'my frendes most sure wherein I sett most trust', and he names these forsaking friends as 'my own vertus': 'reson and witt unjust', 'kyn unkynd'. Here Wyatt was following no known source.[117] As he paraphrased the sixth Penitential Psalm, thinking on the most sublime company of friends, the company of Heaven, even here he played on 'fere' – companionship – and fear of God:

the gretest confort that I can pretend
is that the childerne off thy servantes dere
that in thy word ar gott, shall withowt end
byfore thy face be stabisht all in fere[118] *established*

Yet for all the warnings about trusting friends, who could you trust but them? At times in his life Wyatt's friends, or seeming friends, would be his last chance, his last illusion. He must hope, too, that he himself would be a friend to be trusted. By the late 1530s Wyatt had chosen for his seal a *V* on an ivy leaf: *V* for *Viatus*. The ivy was worn in the poet's crown, but in heraldry, the ivy leaf – evergreen, clinging tenaciously – signifies strong and lasting friendship.[119] The verse epistles he addressed to Poyntz and to Bryan were, in part, meditations on the nature of friendship and whether it might survive at court.

Myne owne Jhon poyntz sins ye delite to know
    the causes why that homeward I me drawe
    and flee the presse off courtes where so I goo   *throng; tribulation*
Rather then to lyve thrall under the awe
    of lordly lookes, wrapped within my cloke
    to wyll and lust lernyng to set a lawe
It is not bycawse I scorne or mocke
    the power of them to whome fortune hath lent
    charge over us, of ryght to strik the stroke   *with the right to punish*
but trew it is that I have allwaies ment
    lesse to esteme them then the Commune sorte
    of owtwarde thinges that juge in their intent   *way of thought*
withowt regard that dothe inwarde resort   *withdraw; retire*
    I graunt somtyme that of glorye the fyer
    dothe touche my harte and me lust not repent   *wish*
blame by honour and honor to desier
    but howe may I this honour now attayne
    that cannot dye the colour of blak a lyer
My poyntz I cannot frame my tonge to fayne   *feign*
    to cloke the trewthe for prayse without desert
    Of them that lust all vices to retayne
I Cannot honour them that sett their part
    wythe venus and bacchus all their lyfe longe
    nor holde my peace off them althoughe I smart
I cannot crouche nor knele nor do suche wrong
    to wurchippe them like God on erthe alone
    that are like wolfes thes sely Lambes among   *helpless; innocent*
I cannot with my worde complayne and mone
    and suffer nought, nor smart wythout complaynt
    Nor torne the worde that from my mouthe is gone
I cannot speake with loke ryght as a saynt
    use wyles for wytt and use deceyt a pleasure
    And call craft counsall for profit still to paynt
I cannot wrest the lawe to fyll the cofer
    with innocent blode to fede my selfe fatte
    and do most hurte where moste helpe I offer
I am not he that can allowe the state   *praise*

Hans Holbein the younger, *Thomas Wyatt*

Katherine of Aragon, sixteenth century, English School
Anne Boleyn, 1534, English School

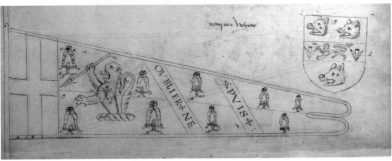

Hans Holbein the younger, *Sir Henry Wyatt, c.*1536
Sir Henry Wyatt's standard, with his motto 'OVBLIER.NE.PVIS [Forget
I cannot]'. Crest: on a wreath argent and azure, a demy lyon rampant sable,
holding an unplumed arrow or and charged with a pheon of the last. Sprinkled
with nine barnacles barry of silver and gold, fastened with blue cords

François Clouet (and workshop), *Francis I on Horseback*
Titian (Tiziano Vecellio), *Charles V, Holy Roman Emperor, with His Dog*, 1533

Sebastiano del Piombo, *Andrea Doria*

An image of *terribilità*. Dosso Dossi, *Alfonso I d'Este, Duke of Ferrara*

Hans Holbein the younger, *Noli me tangere*, 1526–8?
Titian (Tiziano Vecellio), *The Tribute Money*, 1516

Plan of the Harbour and Road of Calais, drawn *c.*1535–40

Hans Holbein the younger, *Thomas Cromwell*
Hans Holbein the younger, *Thomas Wriothesley, c.*1535

off him Caesar and deme Cato to dy *condemn*
   that by his deathe dide escape out off the gate

40 from caesars hand if livye did not lye *Livy*
   And wold not lyve wher libertye was lost
   So did his hart the comon welthe applye *devote himself*
I ame not he suche eloquence to bost
   to marke the singing crowe as the swanne
   nor call the lyon off coward bestes the most
that cannot take a mouse as the catt can
   and he that diethe for hungar off gold
   Call him Alexander and saye that pann *Pan*
passeth Apollo in musike many a fold

50   prayes Sir thopas for a noble tale *Chaucer's travesty of a courtly romance*
   and scorne the storye that the knight tolld
prayse him for counsall that is dronke off Ale
   Grynne when he laugheth that beres all the swaye
   frowne when he frowneth and grone when he is pale
On others lust to hang bothe night and daye *will; desire*
   non off thes poyntz wyll ever frame wyth me *courses; Poyntz suit*
   My witt is nought I cannot lerne the waye
And moche the lesse off thinges that greater be
   that asken helpe off colours off devise *clever tricks; rhetorical figures*

60   to joyne the meane with eche extremitie
with the nerest vertu to cloke alwey the vice
   And as to purpose like wyse may fall
   to presse the vertu that it may not ryse
As dronkynnes good felowschippe to call
   the frendly foo with his double face
   Say this is gentle and curteis therwithall *courteous*
and say that favell hathe a goodly grace *image of flattery*
   In eloquence, And crueltye to name
   zeale off justice and change in tyme and place

70 And he that suffreth offence without blame
   call him pityfull And him trewe and playne
   that rayleth recheles to every mannes shame *heedless*
Say he is rude that cannot lye and fayne
   the lecher a lover, And tyrannye

to be the ryght off a princes rayne
I cannot I no no it wyll not be
　　this is the cause I could never yet
　　hang on their sleves that waye as thow mayst see
A chippe of chaunce more then a pownde of wytt
　　this maketh me at home to hunt and hauke
　　and in the fowle wether at my book to sytt
In frost and snow then with my bowe to stalke
　　no man dothe marke wher to I ryde or goo
　　in lusty lees at libertie I walke
and off thes newes I fele nor well ne woo
　　save of a clogg that yet doth hang at my heele
　　no fors for that for it is ordred soo
that I may leppe bothe hedge and diche full weelle
　　I am not now in france to juge the wyne
　　Wyth savory sawces thes dilicates to feele　　　　*dainties*
Nor yet in Spayne wher one must him enclyne
　　rather then to be owtwardly to seeme
　　I medle not with wyttes that be so Fyne
nor flaunders chere letteth not my wyt to deme　　　*judge*
　　off black and whyght, nor takes my wyttes a waye
　　which bestlines those beastes do esteme
Nor am I wher Christ is geven in praye
　　For mony poyson and treason at Rome
　　a common practice used night and daye
but here I am in kent and cristendome
　　among the muses where I do rede and Rime
　　Wher if thow lust my Poyntz for to come
thow shalt be Judge how I dispende my tyme

　　　　　　　　　　T.W.

80

90

100

9

Myne Owne Jhon Poyntz

At some time and in some place unknown Thomas Wyatt addressed two verse epistles to his 'owne Jhon poyntz', 'my poyngz': 'My mothers maydes when they did sowe and spyn' and 'Myne owne Jhon poyntz sins ye delite to know'.[1] Verse epistle is a literary form particularly expressive of friendship, a continuation of conversation by another means. The friends are apart, and the poet speaks through distance and absence to share thoughts that only the two of them will understand, and contemplates his own life under the gaze of his attentive friend.[2] Reading these poetic epistles, we observe an intimate exchange: between the confiding, protesting Wyatt, or his poetic persona, speaking insistently in the first person, and the silent, listening Poyntz. These epistles are written only to, only for Poyntz who, Wyatt knows, will read between the lines. The play on his name – 'non off thes *poyntz* wyll ever frame with me – is only the most obvious expression of an esoteric meaning. What Wyatt read, Poyntz may have read before him; what Wyatt had learnt, Poyntz might have taught him. In these verse epistles, writing of fleeing the press of courts, of searching for 'the thing that thou haist sought so long', and finding it within, Wyatt, who so often contemplated Chaucer, might have remembered the 'Balade de Bon Conseyl':

> Flee fro the prees and dwelle with sothfastnesse;
> Suffyce unto thy thing, though it be smal.[3]

Wyatt chose to share his mordant reflections on life at court, and his secrets, with John Poyntz in these verse epistles. Beyond Poyntz himself – to whom he may never have sent them – lay the imagined audience of friends who would transcribe the poetic letters in the Devonshire manuscript, and perhaps a coterie of like-minded courtiers. Beyond

Wyatt's 'owne Jhon poyntz'

them, no one. 'Myne owne Jhon poyntz' was in part, we may suppose, a private musing written in search of self-knowledge, but it also contemplated – in hope, or dread – some response, a judgement: 'thow shalt be Judge how I dispende my tyme'. Since 'dispende' implies wasting time as well as merely passing time, Wyatt seems to await Poyntz's just disapproval. This verse epistle evokes the maxim that true friends must, unflinchingly, tell each other the truth. Why choose John Poyntz as judge and entrust him with secrets? The principal evidence of the friendship between Wyatt and Poyntz is found in the world of imagination, in the verse epistles themselves, but in ways and at times which cast light on the poetry their real lives converged. We first found Wyatt jousting with John and Francis Poyntz at the Castle of Loyalty at Christmas 1524, but they may have known each other long before.

The 'I' of the epistle is elusive. Though the speaker in a verse epistle comes closer to the poet than the 'I' of other literary forms, he is not Wyatt, nor necessarily Wyatt's alter ego. 'My Poyntz' is elusive also. Yet to know John Poyntz is to enter the world of the poem, to understand why Wyatt chose to confide in him, and to know more about Wyatt himself. There were two contemporary John Poyntzes, with far different allegiances, who made radically different choices. John Poyntz, esquire, of North Ockenden, Essex, was William Tyndale's patron and, for so long as it was possible, his protector. He was receiver for Anne Boleyn's estates. That John Poyntz was not, could not have been, Wyatt's 'owne Jhon poyntz'.[4] His John Poyntz was from Alderley in Gloucestershire. Drawn by Hans Holbein the younger, perhaps around 1527, Poyntz's stance is unusual, his upward glance reminiscent of a donor in a religious painting.[5] We might easily imagine him listening, quizzical. At the time that Holbein drew his portrait Poyntz had not yet experienced fully the doubts and dangers which the verse epistle evoked. Yet his family had intensely known the reverses of what they called fortune. Poyntz would soon learn searingly, from life as well as literature, the impossibility for the servant of a prince to retain his freedom and integrity while all around were losing theirs, the unlikelihood of remaining steadfast where the will of the prince was as mutable and irresistible as the weather.

John Poyntz was born around 1485, the child of a new reign. His inheritance was of political loyalism – often on the losing side – of chivalry, of learning, and of piety. His father, Robert Poyntz of Iron Acton in Gloucestershire, was a household knight of Edward IV; his mother, Margaret, was the illegitimate daughter of Anthony Wydeville, Earl Rivers, and the niece of Edward IV's queen.[6] Wydeville, the soldier and chivalric hero of the tournament, was also a crusader, a pilgrim and a scholar. He was appointed tutor and governor to Edward, Prince of Wales, one of the tragic princes in the Tower, 'that he may be virtuously, cunningly and knightly brought up'. Wydeville translated *The Dictes and sayings of the philosophers* and *The book named Cordyal* (a meditation on the four last things). In his last days he wrote verse upon the fickleness of fortune. For his disloyalty to Richard III and for standing too close to the throne he was executed in June 1483.[7] In the aftermath of Buckingham's failed rebellion which Wydeville kin and clients had led, Robert Poyntz went into exile in Brittany with Henry, Earl of Richmond.[8] His eldest son Anthony was born in Kent in 1479 and probably stayed with his mother there, where the manors of their Wydeville and Haute cousins lay, rather than enduring the deprivations of exile.[9] John, the second son, was born after his father's return with Richmond's triumphant expeditionary force, and Francis, the third son, was born around 1487. Anthony Poyntz had served Prince Arthur, until Arthur's much lamented death, and was present at his fated marriage to Katherine of Aragon.[10] His life was spent at court, or at sea, or at Iron Acton which he inherited in 1520. When Anthony Poyntz married Jane, Sir Richard Guildford's widow, he allied his family to another which had rebelled against Richard III. Marrying the daughters of Sir Matthew Browne and his wife Frideswide (Richard Guildford's daughter), John and Francis Poyntz also aligned themselves with families which had suffered at the hands of a tyrant.[11] These close family associations matter in the story of the Poyntzes and of the Wyatts, shaping their allegiances and marking their lives.

The Poyntz inheritance was not only of shadowed political experience but also of intense religious devotion and remarkable literary and cultural taste. In the tight-knit community of Kent, certain families were united by shared sensibilities and reading.[12] 'Elyanor Guldeford' owned and read intently the *Merlin*, an Arthurian prose romance.[13] Sir Richard Haute of Bishopsbourne was one of the Wydeville faction. Surviving his capture during Richard of Gloucester's *coup d'état*, he lived under the tyrant in quiet obscurity. He owned an English translation of Christine de Pisan's *Livre du corps de policie* (*Book of the Body of Policy*) – a manual of chivalry and of advice for princes – perhaps by his friend and cousin Anthony Wydeville. 'Thys boke ys myne dame Alyanor Haute', so Sir Richard's wife wrote in her copy of the French romance of the 'Saint Graal' which was bequeathed to her by her uncle, the poet Sir Richard Roos.[14] Duke Humfrey of Gloucester passed to her father a manuscript of a mirror-of-princes text. '*Ce livre de linformacion des princes est a moy, Robert Roos, chivaler* [this book for the instruction of princes is mine, Robert Roos, knight]'. That manuscript passed in turn to John Poyntz, and in it he inscribed his motto: '*Felix qui poterit*'. In the margin a pointing hand indicated maxims which mirror the concerns in the verse epistles: how to live virtuously at court where virtue is subsumed by vice and friendship turns to flattery.[15]

The advanced education of the Poyntz brothers is revealed in their patronage and avant-garde taste. The astronomer Nicolaus Kratzer designed a polyhedral sundial for Iron Acton in 1520, when Anthony Poyntz inherited the estate.[16] Erasmus and his works were known in the circle of Haute and Poyntz and Guildford. In May 1519 Erasmus remembered himself to Jane, Lady Guildford, Anthony Poyntz's wife, recalling his conversations with her.[17] Henry Haute, a young priest in royal service, copied excerpts from Erasmus's *Enchiridion militis Christiani* (*The Manual of a Christian Knight*), the work which William Tyndale translated while he was tutor in the household of the Poyntzes' sister, Anne.[18] Anthony Poyntz persuaded his brother Francis to translate a remarkable text of classical philosophy. *The table of Cebes* is a 'speaking picture', an allegory of a journey towards wisdom.[19] The story begins as the narrator and his friends visit the Temple of Saturn and find a bewildering picture portraying neither a 'city nor a fortress' but a landscape divided into concentric circles. At the entrance to the first circle is a gate guarded by an old man, Genius – 'our good Angel', explains a marginal note[20] – where a crowd of people waits. Following a winding path, the people continue towards True Learning. But True Learning is discovered only via Untrue Learning's circuit. In a meadow, the 'habitation of blessed folk', a beautiful woman stands upon a square stone. This is Learning, and with her are her daughters Truth and Persuasion. At last the pilgrim, now 'lord over himself', reaches their mother, Felicity. This adept has learnt not 'to trust nor hope of his felicity in other things than in himself', the only true happiness. Genius adjures him never to trust Fortune, nor 'be affectionate to Fortune's gifts', 'neither to rejoice when she giveth . . . nor to be sorry when she taketh away'; rather, to trust Learning's gifts. The philosopher who devised the Table was said to be a follower of Pythagoras or Parmenides, but the teaching is closer to that of the Stoics. The adoption by the Poyntz brothers of a classical philosophical stance, taught by a 'good Angel', which fused Christian and Stoic ethics, was precocious, but it would become the rage for the world-weary in public life later in the century.[21] Few in England would follow them yet, but Wyatt did, and his search for constancy and for the ability to bear and forbear inspired not only *The Quyete of mynde* and his translation from Boethius, but also 'My mothers maydes'.*

For his personal motto Francis Poyntz had chosen a different definition of the happy man. In a book of hours belonging to a grand court lady he wrote '*Felix quem faciunt aliena periculum cautum* [happy is he who learns caution from the perils of others]'. John Poyntz's name is signed beside that of his brother, with his motto: '*Felix qui poterit*'. For this unknown lady, Henry VII and his queen inscribed pious autographs, and on the same page as the Poyntz brothers' autographs, Thomas Manners, Lord Roos wrote:

> Madam, when you are disposed to pray
> Remember your assured servant alway.
>   T Roos[22]

Another queen, Katherine of Aragon, also wrote in this book:

* See above, pp. 141–3, and below, pp. 553–4.

I think the prayers of a friend be most acceptable unto God and because I take you for one of my assured I pray you to remember me in yours.

Katherine the queen[23]

But now only her Christian name appears, for an unknown hand obliterated her queenly title. These inscriptions belonged to a period before the life of the Queen whom all these men served was shadowed by tragedy. With the loss of her royal title came the loss of many of her friends, but never John and Francis Poyntz. In 1527 Katherine gave a secret message for the Emperor to 'Francisco Poynes . . . whom I entirely trust'. By the following summer Francis was dead, lamented by his grieving widow, and by John Leland whose encomium recognised the loss.[24] But John Poyntz lived on to face the tests which the 'Great Matter' and the King's assaults upon the Church would pose to his fidelity and religious faith.

We last discovered Thomas Wyatt with John Poyntz at the deathbed of Sir Henry Guildford in May 1532, as the court divided and England broke from Christendom. While Wyatt found new friends, new patrons, and transferred his service to a new queen, John and Anthony Poyntz retreated to Gloucestershire and their country estates. Soon afterwards Anthony died, and on Christmas Eve 1532 his brother John oversaw the inventory of his goods. Tapestries of the Passion, altar cloths, vestments, and a pax testified to the family's celebration of Mass and their piety; a tapestry of the joust recalled happier times.[25] In the Commons in the following spring John Poyntz opposed, in conscience, the Act in Restraint of Appeals to Rome. By the end of 1533, as Katherine's household suffered humiliation and harassment, Poyntz may have been threatened also. On 18 November Cromwell 'sent for' Katherine's chancellor and her receiver to recover the keys to the room in Westminster where the title deeds and documents relating to the Queen's domain and dower were kept, and though Cromwell swore that he did not know the King's purpose, plainly sequestration was intended. Poyntz was not named, but he was one of Katherine's key estate officials.[26] Testament to his undaunted loyalty to her, his refusal ever to accept the legality of the royal divorce, is found in the secluded, fan-vaulted 'Chapel of Jesus' in Gaunt's Hospital in Bristol. This Poyntz chantry chapel was founded by Sir Robert and completed by John Poyntz. Once decorated with wall paintings, it bears the arms of Henry and Katherine in its roof and, defiantly inscribed in the east window, the date '1536' – three years after Henry's repudiation of his queen, and the year of her death.[27] Though Poyntz was defiant, his cause seemed lost. At Queen Katherine's death in January 1536 Henry rejoiced and there was dancing at court. Their royal daughter Mary was demoted in title from Princess to Lady and by the Act of Succession was implicitly a bastard. But in England and in Christendom Katherine's supporters, mourning her deeply and revering her memory, hoped for her daughter's restoration to the succession and to her due honour.

John Poyntz removed himself to Gloucestershire, but here he was forced to watch the progress of the King and Queen to his family home, Iron Acton, in 1535. He had made the great refusal of the court, but even in the country that world intruded. In the traditional way he still headed his letters 'Jhs' – *Jesu hominum salvator*, Jesus, saviour of men.[28] Finding consolation in reading of England's past glories in the wars in France in the chronicles of Froissart and Enguerrand de Monstrelet, he discussed chivalry with John Leland and with his lawyer friend Thomas Matston.[29] Poyntz fought in the French wars of the 1540s – though old by then – once again serving his king. Since his son and heir 'Harry' was somehow debilitated – 'not able by reason of his weakness to govern himself' – some of the usual family strategies were pointless.[30] The Poyntz inheritance became one of recusancy and witness for the Catholic faith. The faith of John Poyntz's younger son Robert (born around 1535) suggests the intense and traditional piety of his upbringing. Robert Poyntz chose exile for religion. In Louvain he wrote *Testimonies for the Real Presence of Christes body and blood in the blessed Sacrament of the aultar* (1566), and planned a pilgrimage to Jerusalem.[31] Living in country retreat, John Poyntz made destiny his choice. With himself, and with his friends, he had long debated how and where virtuous freedom and the happy life was to be found.

John Poyntz's choice of personal motto is revealing. In two manuscripts he wrote beside his name: '*Felix qui poterit* [Happy the man who will be able]'.[32] Perhaps he meant '*Felix qui poterit mundum contempnere* [happy the man who will be able to disdain the world]'?[33] But '*Felix qui poterit*' might be completed thus by those who knew: '*Felix qui poterit causas cognoscere rerum* [happy is he who will be able to know the causes of things]'. In his motto, written before his own world shattered, Poyntz had adapted a very famous assertion about the past – '*Felix, qui potuit* [happy the man who *has been* able]' – into a confident stance about the future.[34] His motto is taken from a climacteric in Book 2 of Virgil's *Georgics*, where the poet echoes Lucretius' *De rerum natura.*[35] 'Happy the man who has been able to discover the causes of things, to trample underfoot every fear and implacable fate, and the din of greedy Acheron. Fortunate too is he who knows the rustic gods, Pan and old Silvanus and the sister nymphs'. Here Virgil, having described the life of the countryman, nature's adept, who lives in harmony with the '*iustissima tellus* [just earth]' which freely gives its bounty, but also repays with fertility his wonder-working, watchful care, and ceaseless labours – planting, grafting, layering, pruning – turns to images of violence and destruction, to 'the strife that pits brother against disloyal brother', to the 'affairs of Rome and kingdoms doomed to fall'. The 'untroubled peace' of the countryman is opposed to the frenzy and violence of those who 'press within the courts and doors of princes', who exchange the delights of hearth and home for exile and 'a new country seek beneath an alien sun'. This passage follows one which recurred in the poetry and lives of Wyatt and his friends:

O fortunatos nimium, sua si bona norint, agricolas! . . . at secura quies et nescia fallere vita . . .

O farmers, happy beyond measure, could they but know their blessings! . . . they have sleep free from anxiety, a life that is innocent of guile and rich with untold treasures.

'Happy, alas, too happy'.*[36] Here is the ideal of withdrawal from life at court to find self-knowledge and mental tranquillity. Like Wyatt, Poyntz

* See, for example, above, pp. 6, 8.

preferred to imply, to allow those possessed of arcane knowledge to infer something of his moral stance and cast of mind.

This, then, was the John Poyntz to whom Wyatt wrote. *Why* he might have invoked Poyntz becomes clearer, for so many of the themes of the epistles were resonant in their lives. Yet even though the verse epistle seems confessional, and to touch experience, still it is separate from it. A work of art and imagination implies also detachment, in which the poet invents the 'I' and distances himself from his speaker.[37] Here, in art, Poyntz is the imagined passive listener to the speaker's overheard soliloquy. And Wyatt writes in search of self-knowledge, needing less to persuade Poyntz – who, we may imagine, is persuaded already – than himself. For Wyatt there are choices still to be made – though some have already been forced on him – but his 'owne' Poyntz has irrevocably chosen.

Imagining Wyatt in Kent as he fled the press of courts, perhaps after some great dislocation, we may be mistaken. *When* and *where* the satires were written is unknown. Since the opening and closing lines of a verse epistle sustain the fiction of a real letter, written in a real time and place, Wyatt's speaker seems to tell Poyntz where he is, and he issues an invitation:

> Myne owne Jhon poyntz sins ye delite to know
> the causes why that homeward I me drawe
> and flee the presse off courtes where so I goo
> [. . .]
> but here I am in kent and cristendome
> among the muses where I do rede and Rime
> Wher if thow lust my Poyntz for to come
> thow shalt be Judge how I dispende my tyme

Some, reading these lines literally, have elided Wyatt and his poetic persona, and have sought to place the poetic invitation at some historical moment when Wyatt was at home at Alington, fugitive from the court's fury.[38] Perhaps. Yet pressures of form and literary convention as well as personal circumstance spurred the poet. Inviting a friend to the country was the way in which classical poets and their Renaissance imitators framed their verse epistles. Supremely the poetry of distance and exile, such verse letters are written when friends are apart. From his desolation in the Garfagnana Ludovico Ariosto wrote his *satire* to the friends he missed, and Luigi Alamanni wrote in anguished exile from Florence; so too, Giovanni Guidiccioni, Francesco Berni, Clément Marot and, of course, Horace himself. It is a real winter world in the countryside that Wyatt evokes for Poyntz, of stalking in the frost and snow, or snuggling indoors 'in the fowle wether at my book to sytt'. But it may be the winter of memory.

Literary evidence provides some answers about the time and place of writing. 'Myne owne Jhon poyntz' was certainly written *after* Wyatt had read Luigi Alamanni's *satira* X addressed to Tommaso Sertini, for he creatively imitated it. As a literary form, verse epistle has a long history. Horace, the poet of Augustan Rome, was its master. Here, writing to Poyntz, Wyatt was imitating Horace. Rather, he was imitating Alamanni imitating Horace, or perhaps even imitating Alamanni imitating Ariosto imitating Horace.[39] Between 1524 and 1527 Alamanni wrote thirteen *satire* in terza rima, and in 1532 he published them in his *Opere toscane*. From 1529 Alamanni was in close touch with Florentines in London, advocating that an ambassador be sent to the English King to stir him to aid Florence's tottering republic, and it is just possible that his works reached England in manuscript.[40] But it is much more likely that Wyatt read the *satire* in the *Opere toscane*, after 1532.

There was one man in London who surely had an early copy of Alamanni's *satire*. Carlo Cappello, ambassador of Venice, was a fervent advocate of Florentine liberty. After Alamanni's conspiracy against the Medici in 1522 Cappello had sheltered him in exile. Exquisitely educated, Carlo Cappello was also a poet, writing sonnets and Latin epigrams (though it was his brother Bernardo who was the poet of renown).[41] While ambassador in London between August 1531 and February 1535 Cappello attended Queen Anne's coronation and the court's festivities, and 'had not failed to give banquets, and to live grandly and nobly, for the honour' of Venice. That John Leland addressed an encomium to '*Carolum Cappellum, oratorem Venetum*' suggests the ambassador's acqaintance with English literary circles.[42] Cappello knew the English court well; knew it, but profoundly disapproved of it.

Forced into Thomas Cromwell's company, Cappello despised his origins and his purposes, and lamented how 'marvellous' it was that a king with such gifts had 'fallen into so many errors and false tenets'.[43] On his return to Italy, he wrote in 1537 – *De iusta Dei contra nos indignatione et ira* (*Of God's Just Indignation and Anger against Us*) – calling for moral reform and an interior religion, and hoping for the summoning of a General Council of the Church to restore a broken Christendom. He was, so an evangelical English scholar in Padua found, 'much devoted to the Pope's authority, and . . . very vehement against these most Christian and good reformations in England'.[44] This ambassador's allegiances were John Poyntz's, but in these years at court and among English poets he might have found himself in the company of Wyatt.

When and where Wyatt wrote his verse epistles for Poyntz lies hidden in the complex story of the transcription and transmission of his poetry. In the Devonshire manuscript, at some time unknown, his friends copied the verse epistles.[45] Wyatt's personal poetry manuscript – the Egerton manuscript – contains important clues. Both verse epistles for Poyntz, and the epistle for Francis Bryan, were inscribed there with 'leisurely elegance' by the copyist whose secretary hand is known as 'hand *A*'. Poems copied in this hand appear through the initial stages of the composition of this volume, where fair copies were made, and survive in a greyish-black hue. The colour of the ink is highly significant. Later in the manuscript, Wyatt copied and composed in his own hand, and there the ink is faded to a light brown. As Wyatt took the Egerton manuscript with him on his travels, it became a working manuscript in which he wrote in the dry ink which he found convenient to use while travelling; ink which then faded. The parts of the manuscript where faded ink appears coincide with the inclusion of poems which seem to have been written during Wyatt's embassy to Spain in 1537–9. The three verse epistles were all fair copies made by the first amanuensis – hand *A* – in grey-black ink, and are likely to have been inscribed in the manuscript before Wyatt took it with him to Spain in the spring of 1537, or during his embassy.[46]

Wyatt's were the first Horatian epistles known to be composed in English. When he turned to compose them, he was imitating not only Horace, but also the most innovative poets of his own time. Verse epistle was an ancient form, a form ardently emulated by Renaissance poets, who now addressed them to friends in their vernacular languages. From Ferrara and the Garfagnana Ariosto composed seven verse epistles between 1517 and 1525.[47] Alamanni followed him. Clément Marot, in exile from the French court, composed his epistle to Monsieur Bouchaut in 1526.[48] A year later Giovanni Guidiccioni wrote a verse epistle for Girolamo Campo.[49] The first verse epistle in Castilian was written in 1534 by Garcilaso de la Vega for Juan Boscán, who soon responded in kind.[50] Diego Hurtado de Mendoza composed two verse epistles for his friend Don Luis de Zúñiga y Ávila, a fellow courtier and poet. Mendoza's library included copies of the *satire* of Alamanni and Ariosto, and Manutius' 1527 edition of Horace.[51] In time, Wyatt's path – and not only his poetic path – would cross with those of some of these poets. Whether he met Marot in Paris or Ariosto in Ferrara is a matter of surmise, but he was certainly at the Imperial court at the same time as Guidiccioni in the summer of 1537, and we will find him, at a grim moment, in conversation with Mendoza.[52]

These poets composed in terza rima in their own inflected Romance languages. To attempt this metre in English and to achieve the chain of rhymes was more brilliant and daring by far. Chaucer was the first to master this metre in English, but few would venture to follow Chaucer, or Wyatt.[53] Terza rima – these rhyme-linked tercets – was the metre Wyatt chose for his deepest meditations upon the Psalms, and here in the verse epistles, as he sought to know himself. For Poyntz, he attempted 'the taming of some private feeling into a public poem that in its own way *sings*' – 'singing prose' – and wrote both verse epistles to him in terza rima.[54] Whether Poyntz ever read Wyatt's verse epistles, or appreciated the poetic achievement and the tribute, we can only guess.

In 'Myne owne Jhon poyntz' Wyatt chose to imitate the more Horatian of Alamanni's *satire*, more intimate and reflective in style than those owing more to Juvenal which are bitter, vituperative, savage.[55] Even so, it is an unremittingly dark view of political authority and life at the courts of princes which Wyatt presents: a world of unrelieved despotism and deception, of tyrants who desire to use their coercive power to attain their private good, at the expense of those they rule. They – for

257

they are always plural – are 'like wolfes thes sely Lambes among'. He seeks to explain 'the causes why that homeward I me drawe/and flee the presse off courtes'. It is not that he disputes 'the power of them to whome fortune hath lent/charge over us', or that he is without ambition. 'Somtyme', he admits, 'of glorye the fyer/dothe touche my harte'. Yet, desiring honour, he cannot creep in order to rise.

> I cannot crouche nor knele nor do suche wrong
> to wurchippe them like God on erthe alone
> that are like wolfes thes sely Lambes among

Here is the quintessential image of cruelty and deception – the wolf in the fold – taken from Scripture and from Aesop's fables.

Wyatt is anxious about the power of words, and his own power to use them, the very power that fitted a courtier to speak at courts in the first place. In this epistle, telling 'My poyntz I cannot *frame* my tonge to fayne', he chooses a verb with 'a bewildering number of meanings'. It might mean to perform, or to be of service, or to prosper, or fashion or contrive, or – as Thomas More used it – to adapt oneself or conform.[56] When Wyatt writes of the inability to 'torne the worde that from my mouthe is gone', he implies instead an infinite facility to apply the seemingly simple verb 'turn' in many senses: to turn or form a word as on a lathe; to turn or *frame* a word as a compliment; to turn back on a word and so break a promise; to deflect or pervert its course; to convert it. He cannot recall a word already sent forth. Here is the power of two words to mislead and beguile.[57] The speaker is speech's master, an orator trained in rhetoric to move and persuade, to *turn* his audience. But he has become suspicious of that power to align powerful reasoning with powerful speech which is the adept courtier's first tool. His insistent 'I cannot I, no no' – where the repeated 'I' sounds like 'Aye', the contrary of 'no' – tells not of his lack of rhetorical skills but his moral revulsion at using them for delusive purposes. The danger was always that the courtier's arts of eloquence became the flatterer's dark arts of deception.

In the Renaissance there was a growing disquiet about the moral ambiguity latent in that power to move which was at the heart of the art of eloquence. The doubt and difficulty concerned particularly the description of human actions, where the orator sought to redescribe a given action or situation in order to extenuate or augment its moral significance. This was rhetorical redescription: the figure *paradiastole*, or, as George Puttenham, the Elizabethan theorist of poetry called it, 'the curry favell', for it was the particular tool of the flatterer.[58] Such rhetorical redescription was made possible because the vices and virtues might border each other, with a virtue standing as a mean between two vices. So, courage stood midway between timidity and recklessness. That recklessness imitated courage allowed a gifted orator to disguise a vicious action by cloaking it in the name of a contingent virtue. Conversely, he might denigrate a virtuous act by imposing upon it the name of a neighbouring vice. The Roman poets, and Renaissance poets following them, insisted on the disquieting possibility of masking or cloaking vices under the cover of goodness.[59] Following Alamanni, Wyatt repudiated the facility to cloak a vice with the adjacent virtue.[60] As always in creative imitation, the moments when the poet diverges from his source – omitting, emending, adding – may be the most revealing. These lines, where Wyatt invokes Poyntz, are found nowhere in Alamanni's *satira*:

> non off thes poyntz wyll ever frame wyth me
> My witt is nought I cannot lerne the waye
> And moche the lesse off thinges that greater be
> that asken helpe off colours off devise
> to joyne the meane with eche extremitie
> with the nerest vertu to cloke alwey the vice

Who knows which voices, besides Alamanni's, echoed in Wyatt's head? Perhaps he remembered Count Ludovico's account: 'And thus doth every man praise or dispraise according to his fancy, always covering a vice with the name of the next virtue to it; and a virtue with the name of the next vice: as in calling him that is saucy, bold . . .'[61] The idea that vices could be made to take on the character of virtues was known to everyone with rhetorical training around Henry's court, and had been played on before. Magnificence, the prince in the eponymous satire by John Skelton of around 1520–2, forgets the virtue of moderation – 'measure is treasure' – and succumbs to flattery:[62]

> *Magnificence*: Thy words and my mind oddly well accord.
> *Abusion*: What should ye else? Are you not a lord?
> Let your lust and liking stand for a law.

In the play each vice acts according to his name: Folly is foolish, Counterfeit Countenance forges a letter for Crafty Conveyance to carry. Collusion, bearing 'two faces in a hood covertly', boasts that 'Falsehood-in-Fellowship is my sworn brother' and that with a 'tongue with favel forked and tined' 'I move them, I maze them'. He would be the perfect orator, except that his purpose is malignant. Conspiring to deceive their prince, they *cloak* themselves as the nearest virtue: Cloaked Collusion became Sober Sadness; Counterfeit Countenance, Good Demeanance; Courtly Abusion, Lusty Pleasure. If this play was a satire on the expulsion of Henry's favourites from court in 1519, then it specially touched Poyntz, whose brother Francis – along with Henry Guildford and Francis Bryan – had been exiled to Calais.[63] Whether John Poyntz or Wyatt saw *Magnificence* we cannot tell, nor whether they knew Tyndale's translation of Erasmus's *Enchiridion militis Christiani* which Tyndale made while living in the household of Poyntz's sister. It contains this warning: 'we must beware of this only that we cloak not the vice or nature with the name of virtue, calling heaviness of mind gravity, cruelty justice, envy zeal, filthy niggishness thrift, flattering good fellowship, knavery or ribaldry urbanity or merry speaking'.[64]

Beyond the orator's power 'with the nerest vertu to cloke alwey the vice', lay the equally disturbing but opposite capacity to redescribe virtues as vices: 'to presse the vertu that it may not ryse'. So, the adept courtier knew not only how to disguise princely excess: he could use the very same device to discredit honesty, or to disparage forbearance as weakness.[65]

> And he that suffreth offence without blame
>   call hym pityfull And him trewe and playne
>   that rayleth recheles to every mannes shame
> Say he is rude that cannot lye and fayne
>   the lecher a lover, And tyrannye
>   to be the ryght off a princes rayne

Soon we will discover courtiers in the real world of the court using these same malevolent arts to discredit Queen Anne. In words which might almost have come from his grandfather, George Wyatt told how 'fawning flattery put in ure [into practice] the foul skill of construing her virtues to vices, the likeliest colour of evil laying upon the truth of good, the better to shadow it'.[66]

Renaissance anxiety about 'coloured doubleness' in words and deeds turned to Reformation dread. Believing one thing inwardly, and seeming something different outwardly, was not only dissimulation – the vice of tyrants' courts – but hypocrisy, and damnable, for it was the Devil's own vice. Thomas More accused a reformer of being one 'that bear two faces in one hood': a heretic while among heretics, but dissembling traditional belief while among churchmen. Anyone who believed 'that if they say one thing and think the while the contrary, God more regardeth their heart than their tongue' was far deceived.[67] Wyatt had come to hate the courtly game of which he was past master. Wyatt – the 'courtly maker' – abandoned his old verse forms in favour of terza rima as he rhymed for Poyntz, and described the man who utterly refused to play the sycophant: 'I cannot speake with loke ryght as a saynt', 'I could never yet/hang on their sleves that waye'. Unlike 'the frendly foo with his double face', his 'I' could never flatter and 'say that favell hathe a goodly grace/In eloquence'. Here Wyatt chose the late medieval image of currying favour, grooming Fauvel, the horse whose name was spelt by the initials of the vices Flatérie, Avarice, Vilanie, Variété, Envie and Lascheté.[68]

Wyatt's preoccupation with what was inward – passing show – and outward, recurs in this epistle for Poyntz. His poetic persona lives 'wrapped within my cloke' – an image both for dissembling and for the Stoic philosopher. The copyist hesitates between 'I' and 'ye', as the speaker insists that he, unlike ordinary people, judges the great not by outward appearances but by what abides inside:

> but trew it is that I [*ye*] have allwaies ment
>   lesse to esteme them then the Commune sorte
>   of owtwarde thinges that juge in their intent
> withowt regard that dothe inwarde resort

It would be impossible to live

> . . . in Spayne wher one must him enclyne
> rather then to be owtwardly to seeme
> I medle not with wyttes that be so Fyne

Decades later, the musician Thomas Whythorne remembered and cited this passage in order to make the point that 'seeming to do a thing is rather not to do the thing than to do it'; 'as Sir Thomas Wyatt the Elder saith in one of his sonnets [*sic*] (writing to one named John Poynz, a friend of his)'.[69]

Telling his story, Wyatt assumed Poyntz's knowledge of classical history and his application of it to his own time. Like Alamanni, Wyatt takes his reader to the Roman republic at the moment of its passing, but where Alamanni could not condemn Brutus by praising the tyrants Caesar and Sulla, he found another hero.

> I am not he that can allowe the state
> off him Caesar and deme Cato to dy
> that by his deathe dide escape out off the gate
> from caesars hand if livye did not lye
> And wold not lyve wher libertye was lost
> So did his hart the comon welthe applye

Marcus Brutus and his fellow conspirators had assassinated the tyrant in defence of republican liberty. Forever after, they were either damned as rebels and tyrannicides or praised as champions of freedom and models of classical virtue. Wyatt adduced instead the figure of Cato of Utica, the uncle of Brutus, who fought Caesar at the battle of Thapsus and, defeated, chose suicide rather than either lift his hand against or live in thrall to the tyrant. Cato the younger was Livy's hero, and Plutarch's, and Horace's, but also the hero of some in the Renaissance who sought the mean between openly resisting the tyrant and living 'wher libertye was lost'. 'This man was truly a pattern', Montaigne would write, 'whom nature chose to show how far human virtue may reach, and man's constancy attain unto.'[70] Although for the noble Christian – unlike the noble Roman – self-slaughter was forbidden, Cato's example was powerful.

In 1537, Filippo Strozzi,* a champion of Florentine liberty, conspired against the tyrant Alessandro de' Medici, and for his suspected collusion in the assassination was immured and tortured in the terrible Fortezza da Basso. For months, news of Strozzi's heroic resistance to tyranny and his fortitude haunted many of Wyatt's companions at the Imperial court, and perhaps Wyatt also. In December 1538, choosing death rather than dishonour, to end his life rather than betray his friends, '*Philippus Strozzi, jamjam moriturus* [even now dying]' wrote a last letter, claiming Cato as his inspiration. Alamanni wrote a sonnet on Strozzi's death: '*Partendo dal mortal carcel terreno* [leaving the mortal earthly prison]'.[71] Why Wyatt substituted Cato's stoical non-resistance for Brutus's tyrannicide, Poyntz might have known, though we cannot. Given their sometime shared allegiances, there were politic reasons for Wyatt's obliquity.

'Myne owne Jhon poyntz' offers no hope that a wise counsellor might persuade a prince to virtue, no hope that truth and honesty could prevail over flattery and deceit. The only recourse seems to be withdrawal from the 'presse off courtes' to live 'unknown', like Virgil's farmers and Plutarch's constant man whose examples had inspired Poyntz and Wyatt: 'O happy and blessed that ferre out of danger, unnoble, and unglorious, have passed their lyves.'[72] Yet even life in the countryside might offer not the '*pace vera* [true peace]' of Alamanni's exile in Provence, but relentless country sports pursued with restless energy: 'at home to hunt and hauke'; 'with my bowe to stalke'; to 'leppe bothe hedge and diche'. Only 'in the fowle wether' is there any time 'at my book to sytt'. Yet here, if anywhere, was seeming freedom – 'in lusty lees at libertie I walke'.

We may imagine that Wyatt and Poyntz were apart, as Wyatt wrote. Yet whether Wyatt was really in Kent, or in England, whether living this ideal life, or exiled from it, we cannot know. His speaker hears news that does not touch him, and his freedom is constrained:

> and off thes newes I fele nor well ne woo
> save of a clogg that yet doth hang at my heele
> no fors for that for it is ordred soo

* See below, pp. 355–6, 373–4.

The 'clogg that yet doth hang at my heele' has been interpreted as an image only quasi-metaphorical: of a hobbled, rusticated Wyatt, living in his father's estate under paternal house arrest after some disastrous dislocation.[73] Maybe so, but the image has classical origins. For Seneca, the man on the road to virtue, still struggling in the toils of human affairs, drags a loosened chain. So, too, in his fifth satire on the Stoic theme of freedom, Persius paints a graphic picture of the bitch who, breaking free after a long struggle, trails a broken chain. For Wyatt, who had read Persius and Seneca, the inspiration was literary as well as personal, but the clog that weighs the shackle hangs heavy.[74]

Once, Poyntz had felt at home in Kent where his family had connections, and where he still owned land in some of the same manors as Wyatt.[75] But events had made him an exile in his own land. And when Wyatt placed himself 'among the muses', reading and rhyming, 'in kent and cristendome', he was playing on an ambivalent proverbial truth. Since Canterbury was the metropolis, Kent should have been the heartland of all English Christianity. Yet Kent was not, was never, *in* Christendom. According to proverb, most of the English people had been converted to Christianity and christened in the reign of King Ethelbert, but the people of Kent had not.[76] For Poyntz, the ideal of Christendom was resonant – even tragic – as England was wantonly severed from it, and the King's opponents sacrificed themselves for the principle of the universality of the Church. Wyatt's summons to Kent and Christendom pressed this fracture upon Poyntz. This was a lament for a world which was lost.

From the epistle's ending, we return to its beginning. What can it have meant for Wyatt to imagine that his 'owne Jhon poyntz' will '*delite* to knowe/the causes why that homeward I me drawe'? Conversing with Poyntz in his head, remembering past conversations in a Kent and Christendom now dismembered, did Wyatt contemplate with clouded conscience Poyntz's likely judgement on the path he had taken? This verse epistle does not celebrate the symmetry of equal friendship, of shared choices of two friends, them against the world, for Poyntz, staunch in his old loyalties, had abandoned the life at court which Wyatt continued ardently to pursue. In retreat to his study, to his country estates, and to the redoubt of his mind, Poyntz was living – so it seems – according to the Christian Stoic principles which he and his brothers might once have taught Wyatt. If Poyntz was the mentor of Wyatt's youth and had tried to direct his talents toward virtue and service, Wyatt's life among the hell-raisers and self-seekers of the court, and his allegiance to Anne Boleyn and Cromwell, probably appalled him. Whether, at some shipwreck of Wyatt's fortune, Poyntz did 'delite' to know of his flight from court we are left to guess, but Wyatt, maybe imagining so, wrote with unquiet mind, knowing Poyntz's disappointment and wincing at his judgement. With their old intimacy broken and betrayed, as Wyatt turned from the friends and principles of his youth, writing verse epistle, perhaps at some unspecified moment of undoing, may have been his last way of communicating with Poyntz, and with his former self. Yet we need not suppose that these verse letters were ever sent.

My mothers maydes when they did sowe and spyn		
they sang sometyme a song of the feld mowse		
that forbicause her lyvelood was but thyn	*livelihood*	
Would nedes goo seke her townyssh systers howse		
she thought her self endured to much pain		
the stormy blastes her cave so sore did sowse		
That when the forowse swymmed with the rain	*furrows*	
she must lye cold and whete in sorry plight		
and wours then that, bare meet ther did remain		

10   To comfort her when she her howse had dight   *wiped clean and dry [north country dialect]*
        sometyme a barly corn sometyme a bene
        for which she laboured hard boeth daye and nyght
    In harvest tyme whilest she myght goo and glyne   *glean*
        and wher stoore was stroyed with the flodd
        then well awaye for she undone was clene   *alas*
    Then was she fayne to take in stede of fode   *forced*
        slepe if she myght her hounger to begile
        my syster quoth she, hath a lyving good
    And hens from me she dwelleth not a myle
20   in cold and storme she lieth warme and dry
        in bed of downe the dyrt doeth not defile

Her tender fote she laboureth not as I
   richely she fedeth and at the richemans cost
   and for her meet she nydes not crave nor cry
By se by land of the delicates the moost   *dainties*
   her Cater sekes and spareth for no perell   *buyer of provisions*
   she fedeth on boyled bacon meet and roost
And hath therof neither charge nor travaill
   and when she list, the licor of the grape
30   doeth glad her hert till that her belly swell
And at this Jorney she maketh but a Jape   *jest; trifle*
   so fourth she goeth trusting of all this welth
   with her syster, her part so for to shape
That if she myght kepe her self in helth
   to lyve a Lady while her liff doeth last
   and to the dore now is she com by stelth
And with her foote anon she scrapeth full fast
   thothre for fere durst not well scarse appere
   of every noyse so was the wretche agast
40   At last she asked softly who was there
   and in her langage as well as she cowld
   pepe quoth the othre syster I ame here
Peace quoth the townysshe mowse why spekest thou so lowde
   and by the hand she toke her fayer and well
   welcom quoth she my sister by the Roode   *by Christ's cross*
She fested her that Joy it was to tell
   the faer they had they drancke the wyne so clere
   and as to pourpose now and then it fell
She chered her with how syster what chiere
50   amyddes this Joye befell a sorry chaunce
   that well awaye the straunger bought full dere   *alas*
The fare she had for as she loke a scaunce
   under a stole she spied two stemyng Ise   *gleaming eyes*
   in a rownde hed with sherp erys, in fraunce
Was never mowse so ferd for tho
   had not I sene suche a beest before
   yet had nature taught her after her gyse
To knowe her Foo and dred him evermore

the towney mowse fled : she knowe whether to goo
60   thothre had no shift but wonders sore
Ferd of her liff, at home she wyshed her tho
     and to the dore alas as she did skipp
     thevyn it would lo and eke her chaunce was so
At the threshold her sely fote did tripp   *pitiful, helpless*
     and ere she myght recover it again
     the traytor Catt had caught her by the hipp
And made her there against her will remain
     that had forgotten her poure suretie and rest
     for semyng welth wherin she thought to rayne
70 Alas my poyngz how men do seke the best
     and fynde the wourst by error as they stray
     and no marvaill: when sight is so opprest
And blynde the gyde anon owte of the way
     goeth gyde and all in seeking quyete liff
     o wretched myndes there is no gold that may
Graunt that ye seke no warr no peace no stryff
     no: no: all tho thy hed were howpt with gold   *hooped*
     Sergeaunt with mace hawbert sword nor knyff   *halberd*
Cannot repulse the care that folowe should
80   eche kynd of lyff hath with hym his disease
     lyve in delight evyn as thy lust would   *desire*
And thou shalt fynde when lust doeth moost the please   *pleasure*
     it irketh straite and by it self doth fade
     a small thing it is: that may thy mynde apese
Non of ye all there is that is so madde
     to seke grapes upon brambles or breers
     nor none I trow that hath his witt so badd
To set his hay for Conys over Ryvers   *rabbits*
     no ye se not a dragg net for an hare
90   and yet the thing that moost is yor desire
Ye do mysseke with more travaill and care
     make playn thyn hert that it be not knotted
     with hope or dred and se thy will be bare
From all affectes whome vice hath ever spotted   *desires*
     thy self content with that is the assigned

and use it well that is to the allotted
  Then seke no more owte of thy self to fynde
    the thing that thou haist sought so long before
    for thou shalt fele it sitting in thy mynde
100   Madde if ye list to continue your sore   *pain, grief*
    let present passe and gape on tyme to com
    and diepe yorself in travaill more and more
  Hens fourth my poyngz this shalbe all and some
    these wretched fooles shall have nought els of me
    but to the great god and to his high dome   *doom*
  None othre pain pray I for theim to be
    but when the rage doeth led them from the right
    that lowking backward vertue they may se
  Evyn as she is so goodly fayre and bright
110   and whilst they claspe their lustes in armes a crosse
    graunt theim goode lorde: as thou maist of thy myght
    to frete inward for losing suche a losse.

Wyatt addressed another verse epistle satire to Poyntz – a darker one – 'Alas my poyngz'. 'My mothers maydes' is also composed in terza rima, and as before, the date and place of writing are unknown. Here he tells the story of the 'feld mowse' and her 'townyssh syster'. Aesop's fable of the two mice (or two rats) was printed – by Caxton and Pynson in English – and Wyatt probably knew it in various versions, in various languages. Aesop's fables, a staple of the humanist grammar-school curriculum, were widely known and their wisdom was applied in the world of power. Seeking to describe the political scene in Italy, Richard Pate, Henry's ambassador with the Emperor, found an analogy in the 'wise fable of Aesop'.[77] If Wyatt read Robert Henryson's wise and wonderful tale in Lowland Scots –

> Esope, myne authour, makis mentioun
> Of twa myis, and thay wer sisteris deir –

he read it in manuscript.[78] In his fable, too, the mice are sisters, though not always 'dear' ones. Wyatt tells us that 'My mothers maydes when they did sowe and spyn/ they sang sometyme a song of the feld mowse', as though we are to imagine a listening boy sitting at their feet, as if we should sympathize with the lot of maids who, like the country mouse, 'laboured hard boeth daye and nyght', and who might yearn, like her, to 'lyve a Lady while her liff doeth last'. Perhaps, but Wyatt and Poyntz had also read of the two mice in Horace, *Sermones* 2.6. The fable was part of a folk wisdom and oral culture so pervasive that it was common to both maids who sang it and to knights who grew up reading Horace and Aesop. Wyatt and Poyntz knew – as did that other Kentish knight Philip Sidney – that animals may teach truths to poor humans: 'whereof Aesop's tales give good proof: whose pretty allegories, stealing under the formal tales of beasts, make many, more beastly than beasts, begin to hear the sound of virtue from these dumb speakers'.[79] Things may be said in mouse language, and horror stories told of traitor cats, that may not be said or written in the courts of princes, especially not at the courts of tyrants, and particularly not under a 'law of words'.

Wyatt's own philosophy appears not only in the long moralising ending but also where his telling of the fable diverts from other known versions. Here there is no visit from the town mouse to the country, no paean of rustic freedom. Poyntz, who had taken his motto from the *Georgics*, needed no convincing of the integrity of rural life. Nature has given no easy living to Wyatt's country mouse, who 'endured to much pain', lying drenched, freezing, starving in her cave. Her harvest store – gleaned with so much labour – swept away by the flood, only sleep might 'begile' her hunger pangs. Enticed by a vision of her sister who 'lieth warme and dry/in bed of downe', living without labour 'at the richemans cost', dining on 'boyled bacon meet and roost' and drinking wine 'till that her belly swell', the country mouse determines to leave her wretched cave, and so becomes the author of her own destruction. Her 'towney' sister's welcome is muted by a dim dread, her mousey timidity is turned to preternatural terror, and mouse speech becomes a chastened whisper. '[O]f every noyse so was the wretche agast', and so fearful was she that she dared not come to the door. 'In her langage' – a rustic mouse squeak – her sister pipes her password: 'pepe . . . I ame here'. '"Peace" quoth the townysshe mowse "why spekest thou so lowde?"'

The country mouse's dream of the sisters' joyful reunion and mousey banquet soon turns to nightmare. 'Askance' she 'spied', lurking under a stool, 'two stemyng Ise/in a rownde hed with sherp erys': a nameless thing, instinctively known as her natural enemy. In terror, 'the towney mowse fled', streetwise, to a place of safety: 'she knowe whether to goo', unlike her bumpkin sister. Abandoned, thinking longingly of home, the country mouse trips in her flight and the 'traytor Catt had caught her by the hipp'. Why 'traitor' when it is in his feline nature to catch and torment mice, just as it is theirs to run from him? Perhaps the cat puts her swiftly out of her misery. We hope so. The moral of the fable is clear: if only the mouse had been content with her small blessings while she enjoyed them, but she 'had forgotten her poure suretie and rest/for semyng welth'. Her country life, unlike that of Virgil's farmers, has been brutal, but Wyatt, like Poyntz, might have remembered 'O farmers, happy beyond measure, could they but know their blessings!'[80] In this telling of the tale even sisterhood fails: in terror, it is every mouse for herself.

From the fable, Wyatt turns abruptly to preach a sermon on self-knowledge to Poyntz, who might once have preached it to him.

> Alas my poyngz how men do seke the best
> and fynde the wourst by error as they stray.

As he points the way to quiet of mind and insists that no search outside oneself – no gold, no war, no peace, no strife – can bring content, his own restlessness appears in the tumbling images, and in pronouns of address which veer from singular to plural to singular, from 'my Poyngz' to the 'wretched minds' who were Poyntz's antithesis. 'Eche kynd of lyff hath with hym his disease', he insists, implying not only morbidity but dis-ease, discomfort. Wyatt's philosophical stance is taken, in part, from his *The Quyete of mynde*, and some of the images also. These images of perversity, of acting against nature, are drawn from Scripture, too, and perhaps from Boethius, but the very words of his own translation echo through the epistle:[81]

We accuse wicked fortune and our desteny, whan rather we shulde dam our selfes of foly, as it were to be angry with fortune, that thou canst nat shote an arowe with a plou[gh], or hunt an hare with an oxe, and that some cruell god shulde be agaynst them, that with vayn indevour, hunt an hart with a dragge net[82]

In the shadows behind Wyatt's making of *The Quyete of mynde* had been the Queen's friends, the classically educated Poyntz brothers. Francis Poyntz's *The table of Cebes* also teaches that things received from Fortune are neither good nor bad until false desire makes them so.

Early adherents of Christian Stoicism in the English Renaissance, the Poyntzes had sought the rational freedom which indifference gave, and in this epistle Wyatt paid tribute to their philosophy. Since what lay beyond any individual's control was neither to be desired nor feared, the future was not worth worrying about. Learning this from Plutarch, 'for foles let good thynges passe tho they be present, and regarde them nat whan they perisshe, so moche doth their thoughtes gape gredily after thynges to come',[83] Wyatt reminds Poyntz:

> Madde if ye list to continue your sore
> let present passe and gape on tyme to com.

The insistence that the mind is its own place, that only there is true contentment found, resonates through Horace, as through Wyatt's epistle: '*quod petis hic est, / est Ulubris, animus si te non defecit aequus* [what you seek is here, it is Ulubria, if you do not lack a contented mind]'.[84] Hope and dread and restless longings are delusive, as is anything outside oneself. The 'thing' that has been sought for so long can only be found within.[85] Only the mind is redoubt and refuge, and self-knowledge is the path to self-control which makes a man constant, indifferent.

> make playn thyn hert that it be not knotted
> with hope or dred and se thy will be bare
> From all affectes whome vice hath ever spotted
> thy self content with that is the assigned
> and use it well that is to the allotted
> Then seke no more owte of thy self to fynde
> the thing that thou haist sought so long before
> for thou shalt fele it sitting in thy mynde

271

That Wyatt himself is not yet that constant man seems clear from the crepuscular pessimism of the epistle's ending. Here he turns from Horace to borrow from Persius, a satirist more savage by far, and utters an excoriating curse.[86]

> Hens fourth my poyngz this shalbe all and some
>> these wretched fooles shall have nought els of me
>> but to the great god and to his high dome
> None othre pain pray I for theim to be
>> but when the rage doeth led them from the right
>> that lowking backward vertue they may se
> Evyn as she is so goodly fayre and bright
>> and whilst they claspe their lustes in armes a crosse
>> graunt theim goode lorde: as thou maist of thy myght
>> to frete inward for losing suche a losse.

As in all Wyatt's most tantalising poetry, we never know who 'they' are. If 'these wretched fooles' had a real existence, it is fugitive now. They lurk nameless, like the beast with steaming eyes. But to Wyatt and his friends they were known, more than instinctively known. When Thomas Wriothesley died in failure and despair in July 1549, perhaps even by his own hand, it was believed that 'he killed himself with sorrow in so much as he said he would not live in such misery'. George Blage, the friend of Wyatt's heart, wrote a poem rejoicing at his death: 'From vile estate, of base and low degree'.[87] And he chose the same image of the traitor cat:

> Picture of pride, of papistry the plat
> in whom treason, as in a throne did sit
> with ireful eye, aye glearing like a cat   *casting cunning glances; sly*

We may imagine that Wyatt wrote this verse epistle to Poyntz after his world darkened, when it was better to live away from court, watchful and silent.

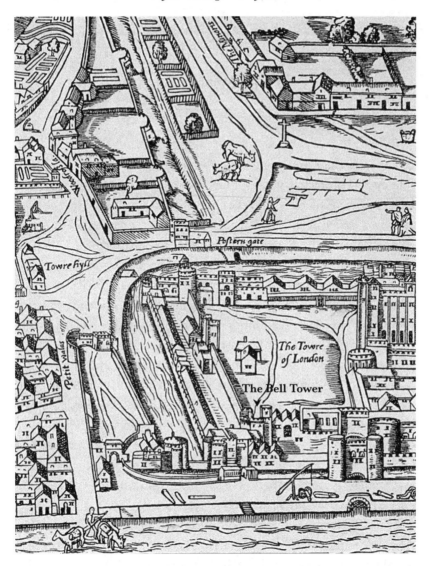

The Bell Tower of the Tower of London

273

10

Circa Regna Tonat

In a manuscript belonging to Wyatt's friends his name – '*Viat*' – is surrounded by protective virtues – innocence, truth and faith – guarding against circling enemies.[1] The last line of the inscription, '*circumdederunt me inimici mei*', is from Psalm 17:8–9 where the Psalmist prays for divine protection: 'Keep me as the apple of thy eye, hide me under the shadow of thy wings . . . from my deadly enemies, who compass me about'. Whoever wrote this inscription, or the poem itself, associated Wyatt's plight with the Psalmist's. But the poem's source is classical. *Circa Regna tonat* ('around thrones it thunders'). It: the bolt of Jove high-thundering. This poem is based on the concluding judgement of the chorus in Seneca's *Phaedra*, where the self-knowledge and peace of the countryman are compared to the great upheavals and dangers for those who pass their lives at court.[2] Seneca's tragedies – the only complete Latin tragedies to survive – were read by the cultivated and educated in the Renaissance.[3] Known to Wyatt, they were almost certainly also known to his friends John Mantell and George Blage – the owners of this manuscript and keepers of his flame – who would in time experience their own theatre of blood.*

The narrator recalls a moment of almost unspeakable horror. The reference to the Bell Tower takes us to a real place, and perhaps even to a real time: a place and a time which seared Wyatt. For a few terrifying days in May 1536 he was imprisoned in the Tower of London, most likely in the Bell Tower. Here, at the corner of the inner curtain wall, next to the lodgings of the Lieutenant of the Tower, important political prisoners were detained. Here Bishop Fisher had been held until his execution in the previous year.[4] From its iron-barred windows prisoners

---

* See below, pp. 463–4, 549.

. *V. Innocencia.*
Veritas Viat ffides
circumdederunt me inimici mei
W

Who lyst his welthe and eas Retayne   *desires*
  hym selffe let hym unknowne contayne
  presse not to Fast in at that gatte
  wher the Retorne standis by desdayne   *is in the hands of*
  for sure, circa Regna tonat

the hye montayns ar blastyd oft
  when the lowe vaylye ys myld and soft
  Fortune with helthe stondis at debate *safety; well-being at variance*
  the Fall ys grevous Frome Aloffte
  and sure, circa Regna tonat

these blodye Dayes have brokyn my hart
  my lust my youth dyd thenc departe   *joy youthfulness*
  And blynd desyre of astate   *office; rank; status*
  who hastis to clyme sekes to reverte   *fall back*
  of truthe, circa Regna tonat

the bell towre showid me suche syght
  that in my hed stekys day and nyght
  ther dyd I lerne out of A grate
  For all vavore glory or myght   *favour*
  that yet circa Regna tonat

by proffe I say the[r] dyd I lerne,
  wyt helpythe not deffence to yerne   *earn*
  of innocencie to pled or prate
  ber low therffor geve god the sterne   *be humble*
  For sure circa Regna tonat

could not, in fact, look north over the walls and ditch, to Tower Hill beyond and its tragic scaffold. But in their imaginations they might. The 'bloody days' which broke the heart of the narrator, the sight he saw from a 'grate' which stuck in his head 'day and nyght', advert, it seems, to the most romantic tragedy in English political history and a most cynical coup. On 30 April Mark Smeaton – Queen Anne's musician and alleged lover – was taken to Thomas Cromwell's house in Stepney. Within three weeks, Smeaton, the Queen, her brother Viscount Rochford, Francis Weston, William Brereton and Henry Norris were tried, condemned and executed. Henry's queen and his companions of the Privy Chamber – the closest to friends that a king could have – died: falsely condemned, many believed. They died as traitors, under the new law of treason. Sir John Spelman reported that 'the justices murmured at this judgment against the Queen':

... she procured the said lord her brother and the other four to defile her and have carnal knowledge of her, and that they did so; and that they conspired the King's death, for she said that the King should never have her heart and she said to each of the four by himself that she loved him more than the others, and this slandered the issue which was begotten between her and the King.[5]

The story, often told, is soon told, but at its heart remains mysterious.[6] Late in April, as though all were well, the King and Queen were preparing to travel through Kent to Calais, the scenes of the heady first days of their doomed marriage. Before they left a 'solemn joust', a tournament, was held at Greenwich on May Day.[7] This was a day resonant with meaning for courtiers steeped in chivalric romance, the day that Queen Guinevere was kidnapped outside Westminster while Maying with her knights, the day that marked the beginning of the end for the fellowship of the Round Table.[8] It was a day fateful for this queen and her knights. At the jousts, Rochford was the challenger, curvetting on his horse, breaking lances, and 'Master Wyatt did better than anybody'.[9] There were already signs of disquiet, for those who could read them. Sensing what must soon befall his master, the horse of Henry Norris refused. All day long, while Henry pretended good humour he dissembled, for he was revolving in his mind the very recent, secret revelations of his queen's adultery, his courtiers' treason.[10] Suddenly, shockingly, he departed the tournament, accompanied by only a very few of his closest companions, among them Norris and Rochford. 'Of this sudden departing many men mused, but most chiefly the Queen.'[11]

Riding from Greenwich to Westminster, interrogating Norris all the way, Henry promised him pardon if he would admit the truth. Norris's servant George Constantine heard two contrary accounts: that Norris would not confess to the King, and that – deceived by Sir William Fitzwilliam – he did.[12] 'For not having revealed the matter' Norris was sent to the Tower the following morning. On 2 May Rochford was arrested at York Place and conveyed to the Tower. A few hours later Anne was examined at Greenwich, and conducted 'in full daylight' to the Tower by her uncle, the Duke of Norfolk. Soon after, Weston and Brereton followed. It was 'wonderful', reflected the Imperial ambassador, 'to think of the sudden change from yesterday to today, and the manner of the departure from Greenwich'.[13] Once in the Tower, the prisoners and every observer knew that they were 'like to suffer, all the more is the pity'. As William Brereton told his old school friend Constantine, who visited him in the Tower, 'there was no way but one'.[14] Returning to the Tower where she had last stayed in triumph on the eve of her coronation, the Queen asked the Constable, 'Master Kingston, shall I go into a dungeon?' 'No, madam, y[ou] shall go into your lodging that you lay in at your coronation'. 'It is too good for me . . . Jesu, have mercy on me.' She knelt down, weeping, and 'in the same sorrow fell into a great laughing, and she hath done [so] many times since'.[15]

Beyond recording Anne's febrile, labile state, Kingston's letters from the Tower witnessed the Queen's closeness to her brother – 'O [where is] my sweet brother?' – the intimacy of her friendships, and the indiscretion of her conversations: the supposed misconduct which had brought her there in the first place.[16] The fall of Anne Boleyn was, in its inwardness, a story of friendship. Her friendships with the Gentlemen of the King's Privy Chamber and the women of her chamber, their shared confidences and jokes, allowed her enemies to destroy her. 'The Queen's abhomination' was so outrageous that the ladies of her privy chamber 'could not contain it within their breasts', so Cromwell reported.[17] 'The first accusers [were] the Lady Worcester, and Nan Cobham, with one maid more,' so John Husee informed the Lisles: 'my Lady Worcester beareth name to be principal'.[18] If Margery Horsman was the maid, it was the more dangerous for Anne, because there had been 'great friendship between the Q[ueen and] her of late'.[19] Lady Wingfield, too, had been a crucial witness, though we may or may not believe the Spanish chronicler's account of her earlier testimony that she had 'never even seen' Wyatt speak to the Queen privately, 'but always openly'.[20] What Nan Cobham may have revealed about Wyatt, whose errant wife was her sister-in-law, we do not know.

From the moment of her arrest Anne understood that she 'should be accused with three men' and that nothing could save her. '[O Nor]ris, hast thou accused me, thou art in the Tower with me, and [thou and I shal]l die together: And, Mark, thou art here too. O my mother, [thou wilt die] for sorrow.' On the eve of their arrest, Norris had – ominously – promised her almoner John Skip that he would avow that 'she was a good woman'.[21] *Qui s'excuse, s'accuse.* The Queen's confessions in the Tower, weeping, laughing, weeping, though meant to prove her innocence, revealed instead that she and her friends had said enough to condemn them, under the law which made words treason. Her conversation with Henry Norris at Greenwich during the weekend before the May Day tournament proved fatal for them both. Asked by Anne why he delayed his marriage, Norris answered that he would 'tarry'. She replied: '[you] look for dead men's shoes', for if anything should happen to the King, 'you would look to have me'. Not so: rather 'he would his head were off', replied Norris, presciently. 'And therewith they fell out.'[22] Anne's retort about dead men's shoes could be, and would be, construed as compassing the King's death. This row between his queen and his chief gentleman, before witnesses, was revealed to the King. It became the catalyst for their arrests and the cataclysm which followed.[23] Anne also confessed a similar conversation with Francis Weston. Charged by the Queen with loving her kinswoman Mary Shelton, and not his wife, he told her that he 'loved one in her house better than them both': 'it is yourself'. Although 'she defied him', these conversations, once the King knew of them, were treasonable, and damning.[24]

The news that soon spread in London and in the country – the official story – was not only of the 'Queen's abhomination' but also of the terrible danger that her lovers posed to the King. 'There brake out a certain conspiracy of the King's death' – so Cromwell wrote to the ambassadors in France – 'which extended so far that all we that had the examination of it quaked at the danger his grace was in'.[25] From Alington on 7 May Sir Henry Wyatt wrote to his son. Too old, too ill, to ride 'in this dangerous time' in defence of his king threatened by 'false and untrue traitors', Sir Henry told Thomas: 'I trust that ye have so declared yourself that ye are found true.' He charged him – 'upon my blessing' – to give 'due attendance night and day'. Here Henry Wyatt expressed not only his own 'love, faith, and troth' to the King, but also a hint of doubt about his son's, and of fear that Thomas's closeness to the Queen and her secrets put him in danger.[26] At nine o'clock in the morning of 8 May Thomas Wyatt was taken to the Tower.[27]

In her imprisonment, the Queen contemplated Wyatt's, and thought on happier times and on mutability. 'He had . . . on his fist the other day . . .' What did Wyatt carry on his fist: perhaps a falcon, perhaps a favour, at the May Day tournament? Playing on words – words too intimate for safety – Anne asked Lady Kingston 'whether anybody makes their beds . . . ?' 'Nay, I warrant you.' Anne replied: '[The]y might make balets well now.' Beds: pallets: balets. Making beds, 'making balets'. Puns for the courtly makers, who might while away their durance by rhyming, and find pastime with good company, had they the heart for it. 'There is none bet[ter than Rochfor]d that can do it.' 'Yes', answered Lady Kingston, 'Master Wyatt.' Through the charred fragments of the manuscript, the Queen's desperation speaks still. 'My lord my brother will die.'[28]

With the Queen and leading courtiers in prison, compelling charges must be found against them, otherwise 'it should much touch the King's honour'. Sir Edward Baynton – Anne's vice-chamberlain, who had been complicit in the pastime in her chamber – wrote anxiously to Sir William Fitzwilliam: 'no man will confess anything against her, but all only Mark, of any actual thing'. (And Smeaton confessed only under torture.) Baynton suspected collusion, that 'the one keepeth the other's counsel'.[29] In search of further evidence 'in most secret sort certain persons of the Privy Chamber and others of her side' were now examined.[30] Sir Francis Bryan – Anne's cousin, but no longer of 'her side' – was 'sent for', 'a marvellous and peremptory command-ment', 'charging him upon his allegiance to come . . . wheresoever he was within this realm'. Later, Bryan claimed a quiet of mind which he can hardly have felt at the time: 'I was suddenly sent for, marvelling thereof and debated the matter in my mind why this should be. At the last I considered and knew myself true and clear in conscience unto my prince, with all speed without fear, lighted and sped me forward.' Going first to Cromwell, then to the King, he was soon restored to the royal grace and favour.[31] It was in these circumstances that Wyatt, together with Sir Richard Page, was arrested.

We have seen Wyatt's long acquaintance with Queen Anne and with her brother and his painful progress to her 'side'. If there was ever any truth in the old story of his revelation to the King of Anne's dishon-our before their marriage, or of his banishment for being too close to Anne, then Wyatt became a prime witness in May 1536, and acutely vulnerable.*[32] It seems that his interrogation did turn on his old inti-macy with Anne and his exile, for Wyatt blamed his arrest on the Duke of Suffolk. In the early days of the 'Great Matter', when Katherine's friends were seeking to discredit Anne, Wyatt and Suffolk had been allies. From allies, they turned enemies, and that enmity did not fade. Later, charged with blaming the King for putting him in the Tower, Wyatt insisted: 'I never imputed to the kyngis hyghenes my impryson-mente. And herof can Mr Levetenant . . . testifie to whom I dyd ever impute yt. Ye, and farther, my lord of Suffolke hym selffe cane tell that I imputed yt to hym.'[33]

By 12 May – the day of the arraignment of Norris, Brereton, Wes-ton and Smeaton – the news at court was that Wyatt and Page were in the Tower 'without danger of death, but Mr Page is banished the King's presence and court for ever'.[34] On the following day the Lisles'

* See above, pp. 145–6, 163–4.

agent reported: 'here are so many tales I cannot well tell which to write'. Some said that 'young Weston', 'for whose life importunate suit is made', would escape. 'Some other say that Wyatt and Mr Page are as like to suffer as the others.'[35] On the 19th Wyatt and Page remained in the Tower: 'What shall become of them, God best knoweth.'[36] Soon they were freed. 'I am long ago at liberty,' so Page wrote on 18 July, though no longer aspiring to be a 'daily courtier', and 'more meet for the country than the court'. In the following summer Page was still in the country, entertaining the King's daughter, the Lady Mary.[37]

The story told in the Wyatt family was that Sir Henry, reading the letter which told of his son's being 'clapped' in the Tower, said: 'if he be a true man, as I trust he is, his truth will him deliver'. Then he went straight back to sleep.[38] Such Stoic indifference seems unlikely. Whatever Sir Henry did or said, the terror that his son would be executed (and the Wyatt inheritance lost) was short-lived. Already by 10 May Henry Wyatt had received a letter from Cromwell to his 'great comfort', assuring him of Thomas's safety. Yet the disgrace remained. Never doubting that Cromwell – friend in his son's adversity as well as prosperity – was responsible for saving him, Henry Wyatt besought him: 'show him that this punishment that he hath for this matter is more for the displeasure that he hath done to God otherwise. Wherein I beseech you to advertise him to fly vice and serve God better than he hath done.'[39]

Though promised immunity from prosecution, Wyatt may not have known that yet, as he waited in the Tower. On 17 May Norris, Rochford, Brereton, Weston and Smeaton were beheaded on Tower Hill. At the scaffold, conscious of a greater judgement to come, they confessed past sins, warned against the flatterers of the court, but none of them – not one – confessed to misconduct with the Queen. She looked on as they were led to execution, waiting her turn.[40] The legend in London, as well as in poetic tradition, was that Wyatt witnessed the deaths. Ascribed to Wyatt – though perhaps not by him – was 'In mornyng wyse', a ballad lamenting the deaths of each of the men in turn.[41]

> In mornyng wyse syns daylye I increas,   *mourning*
> Thus shuld I cloke the cause of all my greffe;

So pensyve mynd with tong to hold his pease,
My reasone sayethe ther can be no relyeffe:
Wherffor geve ere, I umble you requyre,   *humbly*
The affectes to know that thus dothe mak me mone.
The cause ys great of all my dolffull chere,
Ffor those that were, and now be ded and gonne.
[. . .]

In the Tower, Anne had looked to her friends to intercede for her. 'I w[ould God I had m]y bishops for they would all go to the King for me.'[42] Anne's bishops, who owed their promotion to her marriage and to her patronage as well as to their evangelical faith, now contemplated not only her destruction but that of their cause. 'And I am in such perplexity', Cranmer wrote to the King on 3 May. 'And if it be true . . .' He could hardly believe her guilty, but surely the King would never have proceeded against her if she were not. 'Next unto your grace, I was most bound unto her of all creatures living . . . I loved her not a little for the love which I judged her to bear toward God and His gospel.' If she were guilty, everyone who favoured the Gospel must now hate her.[43] Nicholas Shaxton, too, renounced her: 'she hath exceedingly deceived me'.[44] But John Skip, her almoner, remained with her. Kingston reported that 'the Queen hath much desired to have here in the closet the sacraments, and also her almoner, whom she supposeth to be devout'. And if her friends could not intercede for her, or save her, then Anne's last hope was that they might be with her for her consolation, until the end. Even this she was denied, the only 'unkindness' of which she accused the King. 'I think [much unkindness in the] King to put such about me as I have never loved . . . I would have had [of mine own privy chamber], which I favour most.'[45]

In her despair, Anne thought in anguish of her friends. She 'much lamented my lady of Worcester', fearful that the 'sorrow she took for me' would threaten her unborn child.[46] Lady Worcester's grief was perhaps partly due to her own, all unintended, part in the Queen's fall. During an argument with her brother, Sir Anthony Browne, in which he accused her of '*amour deshonneste* [illicit love]', she had defended her own lesser impropriety by claiming that Anne's was greater:

> *Mais vous, messieurs, jugez les coulombeaulx,*
> *Et pardonnez aux infames corbeaulx*

> But you, sirs, blame doves
> And pardon infamous crows

Anne: 'the night crow'. And Lady Worcester named names – not only Mark Smeaton, but also the Queen's brother.

> *C'est que son frere souvent a avec elle*
> *Dedans son lict acointance charnelle*

> That her brother often has carnal knowledge
> of her in her bed

This story comes from a French romance about Anne, a tragedy of pride's fall and the relentless turn of fortune.[47] Anthony Browne and his half-brother Fitzwilliam, Treasurer of the household, were prime movers in the destruction of Anne and her friends.[48] Browne was linked with the Duke of Suffolk by marriage, and by old antagonism to Anne and to Wyatt. Between Browne and Wyatt, who lived parallel lives – in Surrey and in Yorkshire, in the tiltyard, at court, in embassy – was a closeness which was no friendship.* Abandoning Queen Katherine for Queen Anne, Wyatt had left enemies behind who waited for their chance to undo him. Their lurking presence surfaces in his darkly ironic references to 'some of my good friends', to 'they', with the power to harm him.†

Wyatt lived to tell the tale. But what was the price of his freedom? In part, it was his confession. Yet more may have been needed to save him. The price of Wyatt's freedom was perhaps the freedom of Francis Bryan. Once of Anne's 'side', Bryan had quarrelled with George Rochford at the end of 1534 and realigned himself with Nicholas Carew, his brother-in-law. Carew was Anne's sworn enemy, a loyal supporter of the late Queen Katherine and of her daughter. In the May debacle Cromwell 'sent for' Bryan. Bryan may have been offered immunity, and handed over to Carew and his allies, in exchange for

---

* See above, p. 128.
† See below, pp. 400, 408, 532.

Wyatt's release.[49] Soon Bryan was restored to favour and rewarded. If Cromwell intervened to save Wyatt, he took a great risk for friendship; if he did intervene, it was at the moment of the King's greatest volatility and menace. In the Spanish chronicler's fanciful account, Cromwell sent his nephew, Richard Cromwell, to fetch Wyatt for examination. Here Cromwell was accorded the proper response to a friend whose allegiance was in doubt: 'Master Wyatt, you well know the great love I have always borne you, and I must tell you that it would cut me to the heart if you were guilty in the matter of which I wish to speak.' And Wyatt protested his innocence: "I have not wronged him even in thought. The King well knows what I told him before he was married . . .' Taking him to the Tower, Richard Cromwell ordered: "'Sir Captain . . . do all honour to Master Wyatt." So the captain put him into a chamber over the door.'[50] Cromwell's friendship was 'usque ad aras [as far as the altar]', constrained by his truth and fidelity to the King. Of course: it could hardly have been otherwise. Wyatt's freedom depended essentially on the King's favour: for no favour or disfavour from anyone else much mattered.

The cost of Wyatt's freedom was also his willingness to depose against his friends.[51] His dangerous intimacy with Anne Boleyn before her marriage had fascinated the court, and even as queen she had shared secrets with him. Wyatt's friendship with Rochford, his fellow 'maker', is inscribed in his withering comments on the vanity of human wishes in the misogynist manuscript which was perhaps his wedding gift. We have found them among the gambling fraternity at court, and might imagine them riding together in royal hunting expeditions or, privately, in their parks in Kent. Wyatt may have been among the company who were thrilled, or bored, by the gospelling at Rochford's table. In Rochford's manuscript, thinking on the joys and otherwise of marriage, 'Wyato' had written bleakly: 'LAVDA: FINEM [praise the end]'. There was an end far darker than Wyatt could have foreseen.*

Wyatt was forced to live on with the knowledge that his testimony

* See above, p. 100.

had helped to secure the condemnation of his friends. Yet in the Tower, suspect and witness, under interrogation, he had had little choice. How could fidelity to friendship stand against the uncertainty, the danger, the terror? Although perfect friendship was proved in adversity, few could endure such horrors. Wyatt never forgot the risk of friends revealing secrets, the danger of their testifying, perhaps under torture, the agony of thinking of 'familier frendes examined in holde and aperte'.[52] At some time unknown, never recollecting in tranquillity, Wyatt wrote this epigram for Francis Bryan:[53]

Tho. W. to Bryan

Syghes ar my foode drynke are my teares
Clynkinge of fetters suche musycke wolde crave
stynke and close ayer away my lyf wears
Innocencie is all the hope I have
Rayne wynde, or wether I judge by myne eares
mallice assaulted that rightiousnes should have
Sure I am Brian this wounde shall heale agayne
but yet alas the scarre shall styll remayne

The nourishing sighs of its opening recall the first lines of Petrarch's *Rime sparse*:

Voi ch'ascoltate in rime sparse il suono	You who hear in scattered rhymes the sound
di quei sospiri ond'io nudriva 'l core	of those sighs with which I nourished my heart
in sul mio primo giovenile errore	during my first youthful error. [54]

But its ending is from Scripture: a message, a warning for Bryan, calling upon the duties of friendship. Certain of Bryan's knowledge of scriptural *sententiae*, Wyatt reminded him of the image of the unfading scar from the Book of Ecclesiasticus (or Book of Sirach), 27:25:[55] 'As for wounds, they may be bound up again, and an evil word may be reconciled; but who so bewrayeth [discloses] the secret of a friend, there is no more hope to be had unto him.'

The events of May 1536 proved – if proof were needed – that the times were not fitted for trust, that innocence was not enough to save you. Surviving once did not ensure survival in the future. If *Viat* had been protectively surrounded by his virtues –

.*V. Innocencia*
Veritas Viat ffides

– his enemies still circled. The imagined sight from the Bell Tower, which 'in my hed stekys day and nyght', was unforgettable, unforgotten. Wyatt would live to see other friends at the scaffold.

In the French court, where Anne had been brought up to glory, to be 'the Most Happy', her death was lamented. Étienne Dolet wrote an epitaph for 'the Queen of Utopia' – happy place, no place – falsely condemned for adultery and destroyed by a tyrant.[56] But it was reports from the French court which had made her quietus necessary. In the shadows, behind the destruction of the Queen and her friends, lay a conspiracy. An account of 'the history, or tragedy' of Anne Boleyn was written a quarter of a century later, in piety, for her royal daughter.[57] Alexander Alesius, who was attending Cromwell in 1536, remembered letters from Bishop Gardiner to friends at court who were opposed to Anne and to the course in religion. While ambassador to the French King, Gardiner was exiled from the English court but – involved at a distance through intermediaries – 'not altogether asleep'.[58] Alesius recalled the revelation of 'certain reports' circulating in the French court, and the discovery there of 'certain letters' accusing Anne of adultery. Gardiner sent these incendiary letters first to his old pupil, Thomas Wriothesley, whom he 'had placed in the Court to watch over his interests'. Wriothesley passed them to Cromwell, 'the King's ear and mind'. Both Cromwell and Wriothesley hated the Queen 'because she sharply rebuked them and threatened to inform the King that under the guise of the Gospel and religion they were advancing their own interests, that they had put everything up for sale.' Fearing her, 'these spies' watched the Queen's private apartments day and night, and saw her dancing with the Gentlemen of the Privy Chamber and kissing her brother. Now the King summoned them to tell what they knew. Skilled in the dark arts of which Wyatt wrote to Poyntz, they used all their lethal powers of insinuation to bring down the Queen, even rhetorical redescription. 'And now fawning flattery put in ure [practice] the foul skill of construing her virtues to vices,' wrote George Wyatt. 'Her study of Christianity they said was woman's curiosity and desire of meddling in matters of state.'[59]

Alexander Alesius wrote his account 'as admonished from heaven as a vision or dream', and he wrote with hindsight, yet his claims convince. It was true that Cromwell and the Queen, once allies, were now bitterly opposed. On Passion Sunday, 2 April, Anne's almoner John Skip had preached a court sermon, almost certainly at her behest, in which he accused Cromwell of spectacular self-enrichment as the monasteries were dissolved.[60] And it was true that letters from France did arrive at the English court on Friday 28 April, just before the Queen's fateful row with Norris. Those letters were in cipher. Thomas Wriothesley, Clerk to the Signet, was the decipherer, and Cromwell's response to Gardiner – sent on Sunday 30th – was in Wriothesley's hand.[61] Fevered stories had been circulating at the French court that spring: of 'that woman' – Anne – pretending to miscarry a male child, with her sister abetting her in the pretence. Mary Boleyn's romantic adventures were notorious, even in France, where King Francis remembered her with great disapproval as scandalously promiscuous: '*una grandissima ribalda*'.[62] On 30 April, the day of Mark Smeaton's arrest, memoranda in Wriothesley's hand noted that letters from the King and Cromwell were sent to Gardiner and Sir John Wallop in France, letters bringing news of the Queen's disaster.[63] If Henry did discover from Gardiner that his marriage – already scandalous throughout Christendom – was vitiated by rumours at the French court of Anne's adultery with his closest servants, then his own dishonour, his shame, his fury, could only be assuaged by her death. No foreigner was admitted to witness her execution, none except the French ambassador.[64]

The King was writing a tragedy. While Anne waited to die, Henry diverted himself, feasting with ladies of the court and finding a new queen. One night, dining with the Bishop of Carlisle, he showed '*une joye desespere* [an extravagant joy]' and admitted that he had long expected this turn of events. Accordingly, he had composed 'a tragedy' which he just happened to carry with him, and 'drew from his bosom a little book written in his own hand'. Although the bishop – fending off the royal bore – did not read it, the Imperial ambassador surmised that it contained 'certain ballads' which Anne and Rochford had mocked 'as foolish things'. Their laughter was a *'grand et grief cryme* [a great and lamentable crime]'.[65] The too-ardent games of the 'makers' were fatal at last.

On 19 May Anne was exquisitely beheaded. An expert executioner had been commissioned from Calais to 'handle that matter'.[66] The Queen's death brought renewed hope for all at the court and in the country who blamed her – not entirely wrongly – for the progress of evangelical reform, and for the disgrace of Queen Katherine and her daughter. Conspiracy did not end with Anne's death, and those who had engineered her fall now planned to restore the world they had known before her ascendancy. Anthony Browne denied knowledge of 'any conventicle devised by any one for the advancement of the lady Mary', yet there was one, and he was part of it.[67] Crucial in the coup against Anne had been the provision of a new queen for a king who never found a queen for himself, and who had expeditiously been divorced from Anne between her attainder and her death.[68] Jane Seymour was presented to Henry by the Marchioness of Exeter and Nicholas Carew, who saw in her a way to restore the Princess Mary (as they called her still) as heir to the throne, and to halt religious reform.[69] On 19 May it was Francis Bryan whom the King 'sent in all haste' to Jane with the happy news of Anne's execution.[70] Jane and Henry were betrothed on the following day, and by 2 June they were married.[71] Jane – not quite the demure and docile consort Henry had desired – determined to use her new influence to effect reconciliation between the King and his daughter. Yet Mary's hopes early in June that her father would forgive her, would withdraw 'his displeasure long time conceived against her', were futile while she refused 'to obey his pleasure and laws in all things'. 'Sinister counsels', Cromwell warned her, 'have brought you to the point of undoing.'[72]

Not only Mary was threatened, but also her supporters. The expulsion of the Marquess of Exeter and of Sir William Fitzwilliam from the Council, Lady Hussey's imprisonment in the Tower in June 1536 for insisting on calling Mary 'Princess', and the interrogations of Anthony Browne and Francis Bryan presaged worse to come. Nicholas Carew wrote to Mary urging her to yield. Lady Carew, Bryan's sister, and in happier times inspirer of chivalric romance at court, sent a desperate message: 'for the Passion of Christ, in all things to follow the King's pleasure, otherwise she was utterly undone'.[73] To save her friends as well as herself, Mary now bore the unbearable, and acknowledged not only the supremacy, but also the illegality of Queen Katherine's marriage, her own bastardy. From the Pope she sought secret absolution. At the court of the Emperor they watched the intimidation and humiliation of the Princess with a potent fury, not yet unleashed.[74]

In the wings waited another whose prospects and hopes were all blighted. Enter Elizabeth Darrell. Questioned on 14 June about his part in the 'conventicle' to restore Mary, Francis Bryan confessed a conversation with Bess Darrell. She had 'desired him to be her friend in such su[its] as she had to make'. The first was to 'move' Cromwell to help her to get the three hundred marks which Queen Katherine had bequeathed 'towards her marriage'. But the King, who repudiated Katherine as his wife, claimed her property as her widower, and though Cromwell made a note of 'Besse Darell' in his memoranda he could do little to help.[75] Neither her bequest nor a marriage was forthcoming. Secondly, 'seeing she saw no hope in Mary', she besought Bryan that 'he would help her to be with the Queen'. '"Why", quoth he, "what mean to say ye see no hope in the lady Mary?" "I think and hear say she will not [be] obedient to the King."' But Bryan did not ask or know what Bess had heard of Mary's disobedience.[76] Probably Bess was too far compromised by her closeness to Queen Katherine for Queen Jane to take her into her service. Instead, Bess turned once more to those whose allegiance she shared, but whose disobedience had alarmed her: to Lady Mary and the Marchioness of Exeter. In January 1537, and again in 1538, Mary made payments to 'Mistress Elizabeth Dorrell', in gratitude for her loyalty to her mother, and to sustain her in her distress.[77]

On 14 June, the day of the inquest into the 'conventicle', Thomas Wyatt was at Alington, sheltering from the storms at court and enduring the just reproaches and Christian admonitions of a heavy father. On that day Henry Wyatt wrote to Cromwell, thanking him for letters 'declaring unto me the King's pleasure':

After I had considered to my great comfort with myself the King's great goodness toward my son with his so favourable warnings to address him better than his wit can consider, I straight called unto me my said son, and as I have done oft not only commanded him his obedience in all points to the King's pleasure, but also the leaving of such slanderous fashion, as hath engendered unto him both the displeasure of God and of his master, and as I suppose I found it not now to do in him, but already done . . . On my blessing I have charged him not only to follow your commandments from time to time, but also in every point to take and repute you as me, and if whilst he liveth he have not this for sure printed in his heart that I refuse him to be my son . . .

I pray God send you as well to fare, mine own good Master Secretary, as I would mine own heart, and I shall daily pray for you. At Alington.[78]

'On my blessing': a threat and a promise. As the King made his delayed progress to Kent, he and Queen Jane favoured the forgiven Wyatts with a visit, and on 31 July the royal party was entertained at Alington.[79]

Works of art made by Hans Holbein at this time celebrated the fortunes of the Wyatts, this family who were his constant patrons. Designs were commissioned for a metalwork cover for a prayer book. Against a background of arabesques are the linked initials I:W:T to commemorate a marriage.[80] In the autumn or winter of 1536 young Thomas Wyatt married Jane Haute, the daughter of Sir William Haute of Bishopsbourne. This was an alliance with one of the principal gentry families of Kent – a family into which the Wyatts of Essex were already married – which further linked the Wyatts with the Guildfords, the St Legers, the Culpeppers and Mantells.[81] By this marriage Henry Wyatt hoped to secure stability for his grandson after his own death. A casualty of his parents' disastrous marriage, young Thomas seems to have been brought up at Alington by Sir Henry, who was determined that he should not follow 'such slanderous fashion' as his errant father, which had earned him 'the displeasure of God' and the King. In this he failed, for young Thomas would turn at last to desperate, disastrous courses – to treason and rebellion.

In the midst of all these celebrations and hopes of settling worldly fortunes, Henry Wyatt was thinking on last things, on divine as well as royal favour. At about this time – certainly after 1535 – he was portrayed by Holbein. Ancient, with cheeks sunken on toothless jaws, nevertheless he appears formidably substantial, encircled by a massive gold chain. In one hand he holds a letter, in the other he clutches a pectoral cross – symbolizing perhaps his petitions to earthly and heavenly lords.[82] At the very end of his life he wrote a last letter to the King, thanking him for his grace toward his prodigal son and for sending him home for Sir Henry's 'recomfort', and praying for divine favour to bless the King with an heir, a 'young master':

In most humble wise I thank your Highness that it hath pleased you in chastising my son to have used no extremity . . . it may please you to accept my prayer for nothing else is left to me but my . . . will and my son to supply my room [position]. In whom is my most comfort next God only for your service whose troth toward your grace if I thought anything spotted the loss of him should not be only no discomfort but my desire to see him perish afore my face. And I beseech your grace to be good lord unto him, as the last suit that I think to trouble your grace withall. And I am greatly deceived if ye find him not trusty and faithful and with good will to do you service . . . Amen.

Your old true subject
Henry Wiat[83]

Making his will, Henry Wyatt bequeathed his soul, in the old way, to 'Almighty God my Saviour and Redeemer, and to our blessed Lady Saint Mary, and to all the holy company of heaven'. He wished his body to be buried beside his wife Dame Anne in the church of St Peter and St Paul at Milton by Gravesend, where his funeral was to be conducted with 'no pomp or vainglory'. Years earlier, he had founded a chantry there to sing perpetually for souls, and now he adjured Thomas to ensure its permanent endowment. He also trusted him to look after his servants. 'For a small and poor remembrance' he bequeathed a cup to Cromwell. Henry Wyatt had enfeoffed his lands in order, he hoped, to secure them for his heirs, but even his residual estate did not pass straightforwardly to his heir. Still in 1559, Thomas Wyatt's ungrieving widow Elizabeth and her second husband, Sir Edward Warner, were petitioning for the administration of Henry Wyatt's goods, and even by 1576 the estate was not finally settled, for George Wyatt, Sir Henry's great-grandson, was petitioning for the same.*[84] This will was testament to mutability and to the vanity of human wishes. Even as Sir Henry died, requesting infinite prayers for his soul, in sure hope of passage through Purgatory, the doctrine was fatally undermined in official policy, while its pains remained terribly vivid in the popular imagination. By early November 1536 Henry Wyatt was dead, unable to rule his son or grandson from beyond the grave.

At around this time Holbein drew an unknown lady. Written in the corner of the drawing is 'Anna Bollein Queen', but the portrait is unlikely to be of her. This lady – golden blonde and double-chinned – is demurely dressed in cap and tightly-laced collar. Holbein's sketch on the reverse of the drawing associated the lady with the Wyatt family, for there he roughed out a Wyatt coat of arms. Is it possible that she is the so long disgraced and abandoned wife, Elizabeth?[85] All is possible. More likely, she is Jane Haute, drawn to celebrate her marriage.[86] The coat of arms was not drawn for the unknown lady, or any lady, for it had the shield and crests proper to a man. Heraldry – so mystifying, so remote from more democratic times – was the esoteric and defining language and preoccupation of the gentry in the sixteenth century, and the most exact of sciences. The Wyatt crest of the demi-lion rampant sable holding in his dexter paw a spear argent appears in the drawing's bottom right corner; in the bottom left corner, he holds an arrow. In the centre is a heraldic shield. The charge in the first and fourth quarters is per fesse azure and gules, a horse barnacle ringed argent. The barnacle, a vicious curb to subdue a horse, was an instrument of torture for men also, though it had failed to subdue Henry Wyatt. The second quarter was of the arms of the Wyatts of Essex: gules, on a fesse or, between three boar's heads couped argent, three lions rampant sable. The third quartering – the arms of the Bayliffes of Yorkshire – was argent, on a bend gules, a martlet between two cinquefoils or, a bordure

* See below, p. 317.

engrailed azure bezantée.[87] This coat of arms was symbol and signal of Thomas Wyatt's restored, resurgent fortune, perhaps drawn to recognise his knighthood. When he became a knight is unknown, but maybe the King dubbed him privately, preparatory to some special service: *Sir Thomas Wyatt* at last.

'Ber low therffor, geve god the sterne'. Be humble, allow God to steer the ship, so the speaker in 'Who lyst his welthe and eas Retayne' adjured. Perhaps Wyatt, too, the nonchalant courtier, was chastened and contrite during a waiting summer at Alington. Kicking his heels in enforced country retreat, under the disapproving gaze of his father, he was left out of the court's hunting parties. Maybe now he found time to practise terza rima and to write to John Poyntz. If he was looking for his chance to prove the 'troth', 'faithfulness', 'service' which his father had promised on his behalf, soon it came. In November 1536 the King pricked Thomas Wyatt as Sheriff of Kent, 'for a speciall confidence in suche a busy tyme'.[88] 'A busy tyme': the people of the north, dismayed by the continuing influence of the evangelicals in the court and counsels of the King, appalled by the assault upon the old religion and the imminent dissolution of the monasteries, fearing the destruction of the old ways, and worse to come, rose in protest. From early in October tens of thousands were in revolt, and the gentry and nobility of the north could not, or would not, stop them. Inchoate protest turned into a Pilgrimage of Grace for the commonwealth. Here were rebel forces so vast that no royal army could suppress or withstand them, if it came to battle.[89]

Royal orders came early in October for the southern nobility, gentry and great clergy to summon their retinues. Men who had been shadowed by suspicion in May and June were now called upon to prove their allegiance, to ride against the rebels – among them, the Marquess of Exeter, Carew, Bryan, Browne, Page and Wyatt. Some prepared to fight those whose beliefs they shared but whose rebellion they hated. Wyatt was first called to raise 150 men, then a further fifty.[90] He recalled his readiness: 'In the commotion tyme . . . I was appoynted to go agaynste the kynges rebels, and dyd untyll I was countermaunded, as speddylie and as well furnysshed as I was well able'.[91] Most of the southern troops who rode to the musters at Ampthill were turned away, for in London no one yet understood the extent of the revolt. By 12 October letters were sent to countermand the summons to arms.[92] But the happy belief that the Lincolnshire rebellion was subdued was premature, and soon Yorkshire also rose. Although attempts were made to countermand the countermand, troops once dismissed could only with great difficulty be raised again.[93] 'This matter hangeth yet like a fever, one day good, another bad,' so Thomas Wriothesley wrote to Cromwell on 15 October. Within days forty thousand were in revolt, their captains 'the worship of the whole shires' from Doncaster to Newcastle.[94]

Wyatt, by origin a Yorkshireman, was now seen as the sort of courtier whose intrusion in the north had been a catalyst of the rising. One of the Pilgrim captains feared that 'if the traitor [Cromwell] live . . . we shall lose our lives, goods, or lands so that his frympyll frampylles [favourites] shall be promoted thereby'.[95] On 1 September Wyatt, jointly with Sir Arthur Darcy, had been granted in survivorship – that is, on the current holder's death – the offices of bailiff and steward of the lordship of Conisbrough and of constable of the castle.[96] Wyatt could hardly have come into his office at a worse time. On 9 November, at the height of rebellion, Sir Brian Hastings, who had been deputy to the recently demised Henry Wyatt – 'whose soul God pardon' – in the honour of Tickhill and Conisbrough, complained to the Duke of Suffolk: 'Sir Arthur Darcy saith he now hath the rule by young Master Wyatt by reason whereof the King is unserved.'[97] So Wyatt's absence and ignorance of his duty now imperilled order in the West Riding. Arthur Darcy visited Tickhill during the course of the rebellion, to put his men in readiness, but did not stay to defend the castle.[98] The royal paymaster stationed himself with the royal treasure at Tickhill Castle for a while, as though a place of safety, and on 22 November ordnance and gunners and a hundred troops led by a 'substantial gentleman' were ordered to Tickhill's defence. Even though the rebel armies massed at Doncaster, only five miles away, and the commons seem to have called upon the friars of Tickhill for support,[99] Tickhill and Conisbrough stayed loyal and were not attacked. This was fortunate, for in the aftermath of revolt, a survey discovered Tickhill and Conisbrough castles dilapidated and indefensible, with fallen gates and drawbridges, and lacking ordnance.[100]

Wyatt's friends and 'back friends' played crucial roles in the rebellion – loyal to the King, or to the Pilgrims, or acting as intermediaries between them. In the undying feud between Sir Richard Tempest and Sir Henry Savile the Wyatts, as friends of the Saviles, were implicated. Even during the rebellion the feud flared, for Tempest and Savile could never make common cause. Savile mustered his tenantry 'on pain of death' against the rebels, while Tempest sympathies lay with the Pilgrims. As Savile broke the truce made at Doncaster, the Pilgrim leaders plotted his capture by Sir Richard Tempest.[101] After the revolt, Nicholas Tempest was executed at Tyburn, and his brother Sir Richard died in the Fleet in August 1537.[102] Sir Anthony Browne, with all to prove after colluding to restore the Lady Mary, determined to vindicate himself. He rode at the head of 560 horsemen (after asking for two thousand). 'I marvel that Sir Anthony Browne should have so many . . . I am apt to think that some desire great company more for glory than necessity,' wrote Norfolk: a judgement which Thomas Wriothesley snidely repeated to Cromwell.[103] Wriothesley had also been given a great chance, first by the fall of Queen Anne in which he played his part, and now by the Pilgrimage. In constant attendance on the King, privy to all his correspondence, making his way by the pen rather than the sword, he glided to power.

Sir John Russell and Sir Francis Bryan – 'God never died for a better couple' – had led the vanguard of the scratch royal forces sent north against the rebels. By the end of November they were based at Newark with a garrison of seven hundred men, a tiny force if ever it was ventured against the rebel armies. 'God and St George be our foreman.'[104] As the King's forces and the Pilgrims drew back from the terrible possibility of battle, the Grand Captain, Robert Aske, wrote to Bryan to warn of 'serious commotions'.[105] At this dark moment, the one-eyed Bryan wrote jokingly to the King of the one-eyed Aske – 'I know him not nor he me, but I am true and he a false wretch, yet we two have but two eyes' – and his wisdom was still proverbial. 'The proverb is true "that when one false knave apechys [accuses] another, true men shall come to their goods".'[106] At an even darker moment, Bryan and Russell – 'for they dare tell the King the truth' – were trusted by the Dukes of Suffolk and Norfolk to bring Henry warning that if the armies engaged the royal forces would be overwhelmed. Even then he did not listen.[107] Some had foreseen from the beginning of the revolt that 'the common people of all the North are so confederated that they will not be stayed without great policy'.[108]

In the end, it was royal 'policy' and 'practises', and the Pilgrims' fundamental loyalty to the crown, that ended this great rebellion. The Pilgrimage of Grace never came south of the Trent, but in London and Kent many sympathized with their cause, and some even hoped that the Pilgrims would prevail. The judgement of Sir Marmaduke Neville was acute: 'Ye Southern men thought as much as we . . . but if it came to battle you would have fought faintly.'[109] When the King mustered troops from Kent in early October, there were rumours – not without foundation – that he countermanded them through fear that 'they will turn their coats like the others', because they 'wish to live like their ancestors, defend the abbeys and churches, be quit of taxes'.[110] Murmurings of sympathy for the Pilgrimage were heard at the musters at Faversham and Strood on 11 and 12 October.[111] The Pilgrims' heroism emboldened those who shared their beliefs to speak out in their support and to denounce the evangelicals. Religious divisions ran deep in Kent. Rivalries and resentment between adherents of the old faith and the new were close to the surface in the autumn and winter of 1536, and alarming evidence of resistance began to emerge. During the rebellion, John Drury of Ashford encountered a priest, Sir Davy. When Sir Davy asked whose part he would take, Drury answered that he would be loyal to the King. 'No', replied Sir Davy, 'a tyrant more cruel than Nero; for Nero destroyed but a part of Rome, but this tyrant destroyeth the whole realm' and persecuted the Holy Church. A murderous fight followed. More alarming was the collusion of the Commissary of Maidstone, a principal ecclesiastical officer, who gave Sir Davy a gown and gold, 'commanding him to flee'.[112] The vicar of Mersham also took the Pilgrims' side.[113] As sheriff, Wyatt was charged with discovering resistance and treason, with preventing confessional divisions from turning violent, with keeping Kent quiet, if not loyal.

In Kent, so close to the Continent, so near yet now so far from Christendom, people looked across the Channel, either hoping for deliverance from Pope and Emperor, or fearing it. In April 1537 the priest and schoolmaster of Wyatt's neighbourhood of West Malling played cards for a pot of ale. A row developed which revealed wider divisions. When Adam Lewes, the schoolmaster, asked a man riding to London to buy him a copy of the New Testament (the 'Matthew's Bible', in John Rogers' new translation), the priest, James Fredewell, expostulated that he wished every copy burnt. Lewes was outraged: 'What [would] ye burn the gospel of Christ and the word of God?' (Lewes had been a priest himself, but decided to marry: a sure sign of evangelical conviction.) Later, in John Doomewright's shop, the conversation turned treasonous. Doomewright proclaimed, loyally enough, that the King 'hath overrun his enemies of the north for they hang at their own doors'. Fredewell replied: 'What then? . . . there is another bird a breeding . . . which will come forth before midsummer' to threaten the King as never before. This mysterious prophecy concerned some new alignment of forces between the Emperor and the French and the Scottish Kings, and Fredewell believed that the Emperor had given Flanders to Henry. 'God forbid that that bird should be known,' replied Lewes; 'if we be true within ourselves they both can do us little hurt.'[114] His confidence was misplaced.

Those who feared for the faith in England had prophesied that, in the end, only the sword might save it. Bishop Fisher, Queen Katherine's unswerving champion, had called on Pope and Emperor to lead a crusade which would be 'a work as agreeable to God as going against the Turk'.[115] In 1531 Reginald Pole, the King's cousin, had pondered how he might be stopped, and asked: 'And what if he [Charles V] will thereto draw his sword, wherin is so much power . . . ?'[116] In 1529 some at Charles's court counselled that he 'could very easily, with the assistance of the English themselves, have their King dethroned', 'the very English would help . . . in dethroning their King'. 'Your Majesty might make a new king of England.'[117] In June 1535 Pole wrote to Charles of England's spiritual danger and called for his aid. By the same messenger Cardinal Contarini also lamented that Henry had 'rent the mystical body of Christ which is His Church', and summoned the Emperor to act.[118] 'Prince and prophet', Pole composed, in anguish, a private letter to Henry VIII which turned into a political tract for other princes of Church and state.[119] The *De unitate*, written between September 1535 and March 1536, denounced Henry for breaking the unity of the Church, and foretold his destruction. Calling prophetically upon the Catholic monarchs, especially the Emperor, to invade England, Pole promised 'whole legions, lurking in England', a fifth column.[120]

The Pilgrimage was the great rising in England for which Pole and the papacy had prayed, and they saw its failure as Christendom's loss. In 1535 Paul III had prepared a sentence of excommunication against the English King; prepared it, but not proclaimed it.[121] As news reached the French court that Henry had been unable to disarm the rebels, Montmorency, the Grand Master, believed that the censures could be published, and that the English people 'will in the end kill the King if he persist in his errors'.[122] The Pope now created Pole a cardinal and prepared to make him his legate, and the new English cardinal sent Michael Throckmorton as his emissary to England.[123] The Pilgrimage of Grace had failed, but the ardent hope remained – in the Curia at least – that the English people would rise again, and that when they did their King – now in thrall to the 'Enemy of mankind' – would be overthrown. Soon a crusading indulgence was offered to justify the English rising to return their king to 'the way of truth', promising full remission of sin. Cardinal Pole prepared to bring it to England.[124] In Kent in December 1538 men still talked sadly of the failure of the Pilgrimage, but hoped for Cromwell 'to flee the land' and for 'England to shine as bright as St George'.[125]

Henry faced an immeasurable threat from the forces of the great Catholic powers: immeasurable because he could never know how many 'secret papists' – 'hollow hearts', 'wounded myndes' – there were in England who might find a higher allegiance to the Pope than to their king, and turn to aid the crusade against Henry.[126] Even the loyalty of some royal servants, even of his ambassadors, was in doubt. In November 1536, as the Pilgrims rose, Henry's resident ambassador in Rome, Cavaliere Gregorio Casali, offered sanctuary to Richard Pate, the ambassador to the Emperor.[127] As Casali wrote, Pate was with Charles V in Genoa, entertaining men exiled from England for faith and conscience. At Pate's table – with Montmorency among the guests – Thomas Dingley, a Knight of the Order of St John, spoke openly, and treasonably: 'if anything should fortune to the king otherwise than good in this insurrection then Lady Mary the King's daughter might marry with the Marquess of Exeter's son and so they to enjoy the realm'. That conversation was remembered by another guest, the exiled Robert Branceter, who would have a fateful role in the life of Thomas Wyatt.*[128] Later, Wyatt would write bitterly that he wished his king would send in embassy 'suche as he trustethe or truste suche as he sendythe'.[129] But as Henry contemplated sending his so trusted Wyatt in embassy to France and sent him to Spain instead, Wyatt's confidence in the King's confidence in him was unclouded. On 12 March 1537, 'knowing the wisdom, learning, and fidelity of his trusty and well-beloved servant, Thomas Wyatt, Esquire', the King appointed him 'ambassador resident' in the Emperor's court. Wyatt confessed later: he had 'divers tymes bosted therof and taken yt for a great declaration of my truthe, for all my puttinge in the tower'.[130]

The chaos of Wyatt's life was resolving into some sort of domestic order at just the moment when he must disrupt it by leaving. The death of Henry Wyatt ('whose soul God pardon') allowed Thomas Wyatt at last to play the father to his son. Looking back on Sir Henry's life and example – in unhappy contrast to his own – Wyatt had been revolving a paternal letter of advice.[131] He wrote partly to console himself for the loss of his father whom he had endlessly disappointed, but more to comfort his bereft son. Belatedly, uneasily, taking the role of heavy father, Wyatt's language bore traces of the gambler and huntsman he still was: 'I dare lay ten to one, ye shal perisch in the adventur'; 'shote at

* For Branceter and Dingley, see below, pp. 378–80, 406, 493, 501–4, 507–9.

the mark'. His intent was to counsel his son, as 'you should gather within your self sume frame of honestye'. By 'honesty' Wyatt meant not mere reputation – the 'honest name' which he deployed in his verse epistle to Bryan – but that honesty that Sir Henry would rather have left him than all his lands: 'that was wisdome, gentlenes, sobrenes, disire to do good, frendlines to get the love of manye, and trough above all the rest'.

'Truth', 'honesty' – the meaning of these words was shifting.[132] 'Honesty' was a romance word which underwent a sea-change as it crossed the Channel. 'Honest' meant 'deserving and receiving social honour', having a decent reputation, but also carried a general slang sense of praise among friends, of hearty good fellowship. 'Trust me', wrote Wyatt, 'that honist man is as comen a name as the name of a good felow . . . a dronkerd, a taverne haunter, a riotter, a gamer, a waster': this was far from the honesty he meant. As he insisted to John Poyntz, he could not call drunkenness good fellowship.[133] It was the promise-keeping, truth-telling 'honesty' to which Wyatt adjured his son. But in 'truth' there was doubleness.[134] In the time of chivalry, in Wyatt's time, the sense of 'troth' as faithfulness and the loyalty of the sworn vow was not lost, and 'troth' meant belief in God, a solemn creed. Ethically, 'truth' meant virtue and integrity, the righteousness of the gathered self which Wyatt intended as he told his son 'to *gather within* your self sume frame of honestye'. Philosophically, it meant concordance with reality. The meaning of 'truth' which was supreme for Wyatt in this first letter is that used by William Tyndale in his version of St John 3:21: 'He that doeth the truth': truth as conduct consonant with the divine standard, spirituality in life and behaviour. 'The dread and Reverens of God', reiterates Wyatt, is 'the chiefest and infallible ground'. 'I say the only dred and reverens of god that seeth al things is the defens of the creping in of al thes mischiefs into you': 'ignorans, unkindnes, Raschnes, desire of harme', 'unquiet enmytie, hatred, manye and craftye falshed'. 'I had rather have you liveles then subject to these vices.'

Here is the first known statement of Wyatt's religious and moral credo, remarkable for what it says and does not say. Here is ethical advice offered from bitter personal experience of following its contrary. 'Think and ymagine always that you are in presens of some honist man that you know' – Sir John Russell, Sir William Haute, 'your unkle parson' (Roger Wilde, Wyatt's half-brother) – for the shame of their displeasure will be deterrent to wrongdoing. 'The pleasure of a noughty deed' is fleeting, the shame everlasting, and shame is the greatest of worldly punishments, 'ye, greater then death'. But above all, his son must always remember that 'ye are alwaye in the presens and sight of god . . . he seeth and is not seen'. God's punishment is to abandon the sinner:

first the withdrawing of his favour and grace and in leving his hand to rule the sterne, to let the ship runne without guyde to your owne distruction, and suffreth so the man that he forsaketh to runne hedlong as subject to al mishaps, and at last with shameful end to evirlasting shame and deth.

The confusion of pronouns signifies a deeper confusion and anxiety, as Wyatt contemplated how 'god hath of his goodnes chastizid me and not cast me cleane out of his favour'. 'Ber low therffor, geve god the sterne', so his narrator had warned in 'Who lyst his welthe and eas Retayne', as though the sinner's will could affect whether God took the stern or not.

From reverence of God, Wyatt turned to reverence of his own father. A Christian example, in life and in death, Henry Wyatt had had 'a great reverens of god and good opinion of godly things . . . ther was no man more piteful, no man more trew of his word, no man faster to his frend'. Such virtues, 'specially the grase of god that the feare of god alway kept with him', saved him from the 'chansis of thes troublesome worlds', from the hands of the tyrant. Finally, 'welbelovid of many, hatid of none, in his fair age and good reputation, godly and Christenly, he went to him that lovid him'. This vision of a sainted Sir Henry may not accord with the known facts of his life, but his son intended it in stark contrast to his own 'foly and unthriftnes'. That God had chosen to 'chastize' him, and 'not cast me cleane out of his favour', he imputed to the residual 'fear that I had of god in the most of my rage', but much more to the 'goodnes of my good father, that I dare wel say purchasid with continual request of god his grase towards me'. *Purchased*: any belief that God's infinite mercy or His infinite justice might be altered by any act of human will, that one Christian could prevail on God for the salvation of another, that human prayers could affect divine judgement, was regarded with horror by reformers as a kind of Pelagianism, the kind of false belief that had required reformation. Humbly, Thomas Wyatt counselled his son not to count on 'my wisch or desire of god for you . . . we ar not all acceptid of him'.

In his paean to his father's influence with the Almighty, Wyatt's religious advice was deeply traditional. In other ways, it was not. The letter was remarkable for what it omitted. Nowhere was there any mention of the Church or its sacraments, nothing of the public worship which marked the 'honesty' of a gentleman, no confession to a priest nor any examination save self-examination, no penance save penitence. The advice of his 'unkle parson' was perhaps commended more because he was uncle than because he was a parson. Of outward shows of faith and traditional pietistic practice, Wyatt was silent. Rather he adjured his son to 'have god in your sleve', to an inward faith, living conscious of being always in the divine sight and presence. That consciousness will keep him from unkindness: 'god is Justiser of that alone'. If, when he wrote to his son, the Church was markedly absent from Wyatt's religious thinking, there was also little explicit reference to the Bible. Yet so obvious was it that young Thomas should trust Scripture that he wrote, 'Of them of god ther is no question.' Soon we will have evidence of Thomas Wyatt's deepest contemplation of God's Word.

Wyatt's letter to his newly married son concluded with uneasy reflections on the state of marriage:

Love wel and agre with your wife, for where is noyse and debate in the hous ther is unquiet dwelling. And mitch more wher it is in one bed. Frame wel your self to love and rule wel and honestly your wife as your felow and she shal love and reverens you as her hed.[135]

Uneasy, because Wyatt's relations with his estranged wife had nothing mellowed during their long separation. As he left for his uncertain exile, his friends tried to prevail on him to provide for her. Desperately seeking aid for his 'poor sister Wyatt', 'she being now destitute of help', George Cobham sent Sir John Russell, Sir William Haute, the Wilde half-brothers – the very men whose disapproval Wyatt had appointed to shame his son to good behaviour – to persuade him. Wyatt was obdurate: 'nothing will be granted'. At last, Cobham turned to Cromwell – 'I have now none other refuge of trust' – to write to Wyatt before he sailed, and 'my poor sister' would be his 'continual orator'.[136] But Elizabeth Wyatt, dependent on charity from her family whose reputation her banishment tainted, remained in the wilderness.

Bess Darrell was in the wilderness also, but because of her fidelity. Queen Katherine's death in January 1536 had left Bess bereft of her mistress, of the fortune promised toward her marriage, and of prospects. Vulnerable herself, Lady Mary sent her gifts to tide her over.[137] Bess chose to join the great household of Katherine's loyal friend, Gertrude, Marchioness of Exeter, at Horsley in Surrey. As Wyatt left for Spain, he left his heart with her. How can we tell? The evidence comes later, at Wyatt's brief return to England, and when a new catastrophe for Katherine's friends left Bess Darrell again in need of protection. Writing letters to her from France, he confided secrets too secret to share. And it seems that she wrote to him. Part of the evidence gathered at a terrible moment was 'letters . . . written or by Mistress Darell or by the Lady Marquess of Exeter'.[138] Maybe Bess and Wyatt had always loved each other; maybe she had turned down suitor after suitor because she pined for Thomas Wyatt. Maybe. Brought up with the myth of romantic love, historians have imagined Wyatt in love, with Bess as his muse. But Wyatt's status – married, but without marriage's consolations – meant that he was forbidden to any woman of virtue. Bess had been the devoted servant of a devout queen, and her loyalty was all to the old order. Clinging to the wreckage of the old world, even at the end of her life it would be to friends of Queen Katherine – by then favoured by her daughter Queen Mary – to whom she would turn for help.* In her desperation, as fortune – through the agency of the King – destroyed her protectors, one by one, she would seek sanctuary with Wyatt at Alington, become his mistress, and be safe for a while. 'In Spayne', his thoughts may have turned and turned again to Bess, and he may have written all his poetry of love and yearning for her. Leaving England was a sustained farewell.

* See below, p. 553.

PART II

In Kent and Christendom

Dramatis Personae

The Papal Court

Alessandro Farnese, Pope Paul III

Alessandro Farnese, Cardinal, Vice-Chancellor of the Roman
   Church, grandson of Pope Paul III

Marcello Cervini, secretary to Cardinal Farnese, later Pope Marcellus II

Ambrogio Ricalcati, papal secretary

Juan Fernandez Manrique, Marqués de Aguilar, Imperial ambassador

Ottavio Farnese, Prefect of Rome, later Duke of Camerino

The French Court

Francis I, Most Christian King of France

Eleanor of Portugal, Queen of France

Henri, Dauphin of France

Marguerite d'Angoulême, Queen of Navarre, sister of Francis I

Charles, Duke of Orléans

Anne de Montmorency, Grand Master and Constable of France

Charles de Cossé, Count of Brissac, Marshal of France

Philippe Chabot, Seigneur de Brion, Admiral of France

Ippolito d'Este, Archbishop of Milan, Cardinal, friend of Sir Francis
   Bryan

Luigi Alamanni, Florentine exile, secretary to Ippolito d'Este

Jean de Guise, Cardinal of Lorraine

François de Tournon, Archbishop of Bourges, Cardinal

Jean du Bellay, Bishop of Paris, Cardinal

Ambassadors

Rodolfo Pio da Carpi, Bishop of Faenza, Cardinal, papal nuncio
Filiberto Ferrerio, Bishop of Ivrea, papal nuncio
Reginald Pole, Cardinal, papal legate *a latere*, 1537
Gianmatteo Giberti, Bishop of Verona
Latino Giovenale Manetti, papal legate *a latere*
Jean Statilio, Bishop of Alba Julia, ambassador of the King of Hungary
Alberto Turco, ambassador of Ercole II d'Este, Duke of Ferrara
Francesco Giustiniani, ambassador of the Republic of Venice

The English Embassy

Stephen Gardiner, Bishop of Winchester, resident ambassador, October 1535–September 1538
Sir John Wallop, resident ambassador, intermittently, September 1532–February 1537, February 1540–March 1541
Sir Francis Bryan, special ambassador, April 1537, April–August 1538
Peter Mewtas, gentleman of the Privy Chamber
Edmund Bonner, Bishop of Hereford, resident ambassador, September 1538–February 1540
Sir Anthony Browne, special ambassador, September–October 1538
Germain Gardiner, nephew and secretary of Bishop Gardiner
Michael Throckmorton, agent of Reginald Pole

The Imperial Court

Emperor Charles V, Holy Roman Emperor, Most Catholic King of the Spanish kingdoms, etc.
Empress Isabella of Portugal
Nicolás Perronet, Sieur de Granvelle
Francisco de los Cobos, High Commander of Leon in the Order of Santiago, principal secretary
Alfonso de Idiáquez, clerk of the Emperor's privy council
Diego Escudero, councillor
Jean de Hainin, Sieur de Bossu, Master of the Horse

Pedro de la Cueva, Chamberlain, High Commander of Alcántara

Luis de Zúñiga y Ávila, Knight Commander of Santiago, councillor
    of state

Diego Hurtado de Mendoza, ambassador to England, 1537–8

Antonio Manrique de Lara, Duke of Nájera

Beltran de la Cueva, third Duke of Albuquerque

Gonzalo Pérez, secretary

Jean d'Andalot, equerry

Francesco d'Este, brother of the Duke of Ferrara

Anne de Peloux, falconer

Robert Branceter, English exile

Clergy

Juan Pardo de Tavera, Cardinal Archbishop of Toledo, Inquisitor
    General

García de Loaysa, Cardinal of Sigüenza, General of the Dominicans,
    Inquisitor of Toledo, confessor of Charles V

Juan Yanés, Inquisitor of Toledo

Ambassadors

Domenico Jacobazzi, Bishop of Luceria, Cardinal, papal legate *a latere*

Reginald Pole, Cardinal, papal legate *a latere*

Giovanni Guidiccioni, Bishop of Fossombrone, papal nuncio

Giovanni Poggio, papal nuncio

Giorgio Palleano, secretary to the nuncio

Claude Dodieu, Sieur de Velly, envoy from the Queen of France

Charles de Cossé-Brissac, Marshal of France, ambassador of Francis I

Antoine de Castelnau, Bishop of Tarbes, ambassador of Francis I

Martín de Salinas, agent to Ferdinand of Austria, King of the Romans

Cristóbal Castillejo, secretary of Ferdinand of Austria

Averardo Serristori, ambassador of Duke Cosimo I de' Medici of
    Florence

Lorenzo Pagni, secretary of Averardo Serristori

Giovanni Bandino, agent of Duke Alessandro I de' Medici of Florence

Giovanni Antonio Venier, ambassador of the Venetian Republic,
 1535–8

Pietro Mocenigo, ambassador of the Venetian Republic, 1538–40

Alfonso Rossetto, ambassador of Ercole II d'Este, Duke of Ferrara

Bernardo Tasso, secretary of Ferrante Sanseverino, Prince of Salerno,
 agent of the Strozzi

Giovanni Agnelli, ambassador of Federico II Gonzaga, Duke of
 Mantua

Ottaviano Vivaldini, ambassador of Federico II Gonzaga, Duke of
 Mantua

Felice Tiranni, special ambassador of Guidobaldo II della Rovere,
 Duke of Urbino

Captain Giovanmaria [Giannettino] Doria, nephew and envoy of
 Andrea Doria, Prince of Melfi, Admiral of the Imperial fleet

The English Embassy

Dr Richard Pate, resident ambassador, November 1533–June 1537

Sir Thomas Wyatt, resident ambassador, June 1537–June 1539, November 1539–April 1540

Sir John Dudley, special ambassador, October–November 1537

Dr Edmund Bonner, special ambassador, April–July 1538

Dr Simon Heynes, special ambassador, April–July 1538

Philip Hoby, special ambassador, October–December 1538

John Mason, secretary to the embassy

Ambassador's household

Edmund Baker, servant of Thomas Wriothesley

Anthony Barker

George Blage

John Brereton

Thomas Chamberlain

Thomas Chaloner

Henry Knollys

Roger Le Strange

John Mantell
Peter Rede, secretary
Robert Rudston
William Wolfe, steward
John Morris
George Rowse
Bartholomew Butler, Rouge Croix pursuivant
Francis [Francisco] Pitcher, King's messenger

For a full reconstruction of the court and government of Charles V, see
La Corte de Carlos V, dir. J. Martínez Millán, 5 vols (Madrid, 2000), vols
1–2 *Corte y gobierno*; 3 *Los consejos y los conseyeres de Carlos V.*

Ambassador

God's blood! was not that a pretty sending of me ambassador to the Emperor, first to put me into the Tower, and then forthwith to send me hither? . . . By God's precious blood, I had rather the king should set me in Newgate than so do.[1]

So Wyatt's enemies ventriloquized his continual complaint, putting oaths and words into his mouth. Yet to serve as resident ambassador at the court of Charles V, Holy Roman Emperor, Most Catholic King of the kingdoms of Spain, ruler of the Low Countries, master of Italy, Lord of the New World, paladin of Catholic Christendom, 'lord of all', was a great, an unsurpassed honour – surely?[2] Any ambassador was privileged to represent his prince at the court of another, not only to act for him, but also to *act* him, to *perform* as his proxy. The intensely personal relations between princes – with no equals but each other, thus no true friends but each other – were conducted in their absence, at a distance, by the ambassadors they chose to speak their words, to personify them, the ambassador's every move 'a shadow gesture of his prince's intent'.[3] Like herald angels, ambassadors acted as messengers for higher powers, though the higher powers they served were far from divine. It was well said that only the perfect prince had the perfect ambassador. Delivering messages between quarrelling princes, an ambassador might need to dissemble to the foreign prince while, seemingly, always telling truth to his own. For if an ambassador were only to report faithfully what he had been told, what would be the point of his essential virtues, eloquence and prudence? Discerning what seemed to be the advantage of his prince, he must respond with acutest sensitivity.[4]

The ambassador was, first, an orator. Ambassador: orator: the names were interchangeable. The perfect rhetorician, he must be able to move and *turn* the mind of the prince. Étienne Dolet, who served in the embassy of the Bishop of Langeac in Venice in 1529–30, described an ambassador's necessary eloquence: he must know

how to employ a careful manner of speech, well polished and adorned by wise opinions and weighty words; and how to be at times brief, at times lengthy, sometimes forceful, sometimes calm and gentle, sometimes exalted, sometimes lowly and commonplace. In short, he should possess such ability as speaker as to be able to turn, lead, draw, and compel the minds of those with whom he may be dealing in any matter in whatever direction he wishes and the situation demands.[5]

It went without saying that he must have 'learning and divers languages', and be fluent in Latin above all – but this alone would not make him an orator. Later in the century, Francis Thynn would insist that a man 'is not sufficient to play the ambassador, unless he be able in like sort rhetorically by persuading eloquence, in apt words, ready tongue, sweet voice, and speedy deliverance to discharge his message; for such is the force of words, as it often worketh strange miracles'.[6] 'Play the ambassador': exactly in these terms Cromwell adjured Wyatt in October 1537: 'Your part shall be now like a good orator . . . to set forth the princely nature . . . with all dexterity.'[7] Wyatt would need all his arts – even dark arts – of eloquence to *play* his prince and set forth 'the princely nature', now jovial, now menacing.

King Henry himself once said that 'the discretion or indiscretion of ambassadors is often the cause of the enmities and quarrels of princes as it is also the cause of their friendships and alliances'.[8] No wonder that Wyatt had a 'great zeale that the kynge myght be well served by me, a great feare leste anye thynge shulde quayle throughe my fawte'.[9] The ambassador must be constantly alert, observing the slightest fleeting nod or frown: there was 'nothing, even to a look', which Sir Francis Bryan did not report to the King.[10] To learn the exquisite precision of language and protocol, the register of voices used in exchanges between kings, even this was not enough. The ambassador–orator, speaking for his prince, could dishonour him by a word out of place. But since he was not the prince, he also acted as scapegoat, taking the blame for the words his prince had placed in his mouth, if they were ill received. The hapless ambassador was also charged to speak '*as of himself*', to relay in his own words orders coming from his prince, who could then disavow them.[11]

The language of peaceful diplomacy was the language of friendship. Princes were '*amici amicorum* [friends of friends]' and foes of foes. At the Field of the Cloth of Gold in 1520, the decorations of the banqueting hall celebrated friendship – '*Fidelis amicus protectio fortis* [a faithful friend is a strong protector]', '*Amicus fidelis est alter ego* [a true friend is another self]' – and a chapel was dedicated to Our Lady of Friendship. Meeting Henry in person, at last, the French King swore: '*Mon frère* . . . although I have been very deeply in love . . . I have never had so strong a wish and desire to gratify any of my appetites as that of seeing and embracing you.'[12]

We have seen Wyatt in France in 1526, as Sir Thomas Cheyne played the role of King Henry at the court of his fleetingly ardent friend, Francis. Diplomacy was the 'weaver' of friendship: the ambassador 'should always strive for peace and tranquillity', wrote Dolet, and had a role as peacemaker.[13] As King Francis said, when he fell out with his '*frère*' in 1540, 'Great princes sometimes speak words suddenly, whereof after they be sorry, and the part of a good ambassador is to make the best of princes' words spoken to them.'[14] But diplomacy might not succeed; friendship might fail. Honoured as the prince himself, the ambassador would be dishonoured when princely friendship faltered. As the prince's representative, the ambassador suffered – at the least – the snubs of exquisitely calculated condescension calibrated to the cadences of the princes' relations, and lived in fear of worse. In time of war, as diplomacy collapsed and ambassadors were withdrawn in disgrace, they might be held hostage for the safety of the ambassadors of their prince's enemy. No one in England forgot the incarceration of Francis Poyntz in the great fortress at Posa, nor in Spain the dishonour to the Imperial ambassador in England, when Henry and Charles had last been at war.*

In happy times, as their princes promised undying friendship, ambassadors basked in a double royal favour and trust, laughing 'when

* See above, p. 138.

he laugheth that beres all the swaye', frowning 'when he frowneth', honoured at banquets and ceremonies in tapestried halls, dining on 'delicates', dressed in velvet and silk, wearing golden chains, prancing on elegant steeds.[15] However, when courtiers and councillors contemplated the prospect of diplomatic service, especially in Spain, it was often with horror. Returning to Spain years after serving with Wyatt's embassy, Thomas Chaloner despaired: 'Spain, quoth he? Nay, rather pain.' 'Hispania, *vallis miseriae, fons superbiae* [vale of misery, well of pride].'[16] Thomas More, perhaps while in embassy in Flanders, wrote mockingly of vainglorious ambassadors visiting Utopia, and dreaded becoming one himself. Seeking 'revengement' on More, Wolsey painted his gleaming qualities to the King as none better to serve as ambassador in Spain, 'knowing right well that . . . he should send him into his grave'.[17] Naturally enough, some ambassadors did die in Spain. Sir Richard Wingfield spent long years in embassy to the Emperor, 'having the pilgrim's fortune to change many lodgings and find few friends'. He died in Toledo in the heat of high summer in 1525, finally called to his rest in 'a strange country': that is, in Heaven.[18] In Aragon in January 1534 Nicholas Hawkins died – poisoned, claimed Anne Boleyn.[19] A litany of complaints about the miseries of embassy in Spain fills the diplomatic correspondence. There was the nightmare of the journey – the endless riding on broken-down horses, the ghastly food and grim lodgings, the heat, the cold, the stink, the safe-conducts which were not safe, the perennial danger. During a fearful crossing of the Bay of Biscay in 1523, Sir Thomas Boleyn promised to go in pilgrimage, if he lived. Such promises – as Wyatt would point out – are easier made than kept, but Boleyn did become a pilgrim to St James.[20] With their stipends and expenses unpaid, diddled in the exchanges, the ambassadors often lived wretchedly, subsidising the monarch they were so honoured to represent.[21]

Worse than these quotidian miseries was the growing awareness that the English were anathematised in Spain. When Henry cast off Katherine of Aragon he was dishonouring the Infanta of Castile, the daughter of Spain, and his marital adventures caused outrage. 'A great Marquess of Spain' remonstrated with an English ambassador in 1532: 'I marvel not a little why the King dallieth so with the Emperor's aunt.' Charles 'would not suffer such injury to be done to his blood and lineage . . . If a poor varlet had so long served a prince, what heart could then have rejected him?' After Katherine's death, the Emperor acknowledged his duty to avenge the dishonour '*al sangue suo* [to his blood]'.[22] Anna Bolena was – is – a pariah in Toledo, her wooden image still carried annually in procession, a figure of obloquy.[23] Charles had never thought that that marriage would last, 'never looked for good end therof'.[24] Henry's persecution of his daughter Mary was taken as further proof of his unnaturalness, his tyranny.[25] In 1537, when Wyatt went to the Imperial court, Henry had broken the mystical unity of the Church, but still claimed to be orthodox in everything except the matter of authority. He had not yet introduced any new form of worship in his nascent national Church; there was no new English Prayer Book which would institute a reformed liturgy. But throughout Christendom the English King was accounted schismatic and heretic. Especially in the Spanish kingdoms, where fevered reports spread of Henry's apostasy, tyranny and adultery, and every Englishman was tainted with the reputation of being '*Luterano* [Lutheran]'.[26] The prospect of further religious change in England was a ticking time bomb in the midst of Wyatt's embassy.

With his appointment to this grand embassy, Wyatt's chance to serve had come at last. And dread overwhelmed him: rather 'I had byne at the ploughe'. He never sought the office, tried to excuse himself, would have refused it but for his obedience to his master, so he insisted later: 'I wishte a meter man then my selffe in the Rowme [office].' Anyone would confirm this: ask the lords of the Council, ask his companions in embassy, ask anybody: 'I knewe my owne unhabilite whearby I shulde [be] wonderously accombred [encumbered] for that I was geven to a more pleasaunt kynde of lyf.'[27] Life in the country must be abandoned for the while, and even the compromised life of courtier would be transposed to another court with different duties and dangers. Taking up the honourable post of ambassador, he knew that he would not be untainted by the dishonourable words and actions necessary to an ambassador's success. Wyatt went away in the knowledge that his enemies – 'some of my good frendes', so he called them, with deepest irony[28] – would be scheming in his absence, disparaging him to the King to whom access was now impossible. His interests would be safeguarded by those he was forced to trust. He would miss the consolations of family and of friends, and suffer the aching lack of female company. All the while ambassadors were away, they pined for home and the lives they had left behind. Humanist diplomats, like Stephen Gardiner, would refract their expression of the pains of exile through the prism of Ovid: '*Nescio qua natale solum dulcedine cunctos/Attrahit* . . . [Our native land charms us with inexpressible sweetness and never allows us to forget that we belong to it]'.[29] Not Wyatt. 'In Spayne', he mused on Petrarch and wrote his own poetry of *lontananza* and longing.

Wyatt was broke, as usual, and there was little time for him to put his chaotic affairs in order. In January 1537 he borrowed £100 from Cromwell, with his friend Thomas Poynings acting as guarantor of the bond, and by 1540 his brother-in-law Anthony Lee had lent him 250 marks.[30] When on 1 February 1537 Wyatt was granted the livery of his father's lands – 'all the lands that he did leave me' – he became lord of Alington and of the estate that his father had so remorselessly acquired. But he may have inherited the lands without his father's goods, or the wealth required to run the estate and sustain him and his household. In 1559, and even by 1576, the inheritance of Sir Henry Wyatt's goods was still unsettled.[31] Within three weeks of inheriting the lands, Wyatt alienated some of them, making an exchange with George Zouche, witnessed by City plutocrats, and granting lands to John Savile, formerly his father's servant and now his own.[32] From now until his death, land sale followed land sale, as he dispersed the family estate.[33] Years of generosity with what was not his to give, of reckless expenditure, of heroic gambling, had left debts, and the time would come for Wyatt to repay what he had borrowed and wasted. Still the 'King's debtor of no small sum', Wyatt not only refused to pay that debt before he left, but also extracted some extra expenses, 'more than his warrant'. Cromwell 'much marvelled' that Wyatt had – unprecedentedly – left 'the charge of your interests' to be paid by the King.[34] But for Henry's ambassador to be cashiered would have been worse than shocking. Control of his foundering finances Wyatt left in the less than capable hands of Sir William Haute (whose daughter had married Wyatt's son), and the estate management of Alington to various of his father's old servants, overseen by Poynings and Anthony Lee. While in England, Wyatt had been inept in the management of his affairs, and in his absence, his friends were as inept, or negligent. Even the most loyal of servants, the most conscientious of friends, could not help him, in worldly ways, beyond the grave. Servacius Franke, his father's right-hand man, died before February 1537 and Haute was dead by June 1539.[35] While in embassy, almost the first letter Wyatt received from Cromwell concerned the waywardness of his servants.[36] Anxiety about his financial affairs distracted Wyatt as he left and all the time that he was away.

A novice ambassador had few guides to prepare him for embassy. A few years later, there would be handbooks for the fledgling diplomat. In 1557 William Pickering owned and studied a copy of Memmo's *L'oratore*, printed in Venice in 1545.[37] Such texts were unavailable to Wyatt. His apprenticeship had been his chequered experience atttending Cheyne and Russell in 1526–7, and perhaps in later missions of which we have little clue. Certainly he lacked the formal learning of his recent predecessors as ambassadors to the Imperial court. They had mostly been clerics, learned in canon or civil law – Richard Sampson, Edward Lee, Nicholas Hawkins, Thomas Cranmer, Richard Pate. In Italy, Richard Pace had encouraged ambassadors to study European codes of law.[38] To Wyatt's intense mortification, learned doctors were soon sent to lend weight to his embassy and, whether he knew it or not, a papal legate would describe him as '*molto leggiero*', as frivolous, a lightweight, a 'puppy'.* Before leaving, he read the correspondence of Richard Pate as a melancholy guide to recent exchanges at the Emperor's court. Wyatt was sent off with instructions, letters of credence, 'muniments and escripts' and a letter from the Lady Mary to the Emperor. He was also entrusted with vital ciphers which

---

* See below, pp. 364, 370.

would keep his correspondence secret and safe – if he bothered to use them.[39] We will find him in trouble for sending letters 'open': that is, failing to cipher them. Crucially, unwisely, he would rely for advice on the secretary to the embassy, John Mason.

That spring Wyatt urgently gathered a company of men to take with him to Spain, to serve him as secretaries and spies, stewards and swordsmen: his 'family'. He chose men of rank and education, gallants and blades who could attend him with grace, and force if need be. He *chose* them, for it was the ambassador's privilege to take his own famil-iars. His household would be a nursery to bring 'our English youth, by travail unto fame', for young men to observe and learn the ways of foreign courts, in expectation of becoming ambassadors themselves, in time.[40] Among Wyatt's entourage were gilded youths, born to privilege and honour; others were lower-born, with their way to make in the world. Now that Wyatt was in a position to offer patronage as well as seek it, the anxious petitions of friends and relatives lay behind these appointments – not least because England had grown too hot for some of these young men, who needed to leave the country for a while.

George Blage was a friend of Wyatt's heart. Like Wyatt, he was from Kent, and like him, exquisitely educated. Wyatt 'took delight in Blage's subtle mind', wrote John Leland.[41] Aged twenty-four as he rode gal-lantly to Spain, George was the son of Sir Robert Blage, Baron of the Exchequer, and of his second wife Mary Brooke, daughter of the seventh Lord Cobham. Robert Blage had died in 1522, leaving his soul to the blessed company of Heaven – especially to Saints John the Baptist, Jerome, Francis and Mary Magdalen – and trusting his widow to 'do for my soul as her good mind shall serve her'. George's mother, a woman of some determination and wealth, was the aunt of Elizabeth, Wyatt's disgraced wife, so Wyatt and George Blage were related. In the cultivated household of Blage's stepfather, John Barret, tapestries and carpets from 'beyond sea' decorated the walls, and an 'image of Our Lady of Assumption' presided.[42] We have no portrait of George Blage; we hardly need one. The King called him 'my pig', and we may imag-ine Blage plumply squeezed into his velvet doublet, and merry. Nick-named 'Tom Trubbe' for his wantonness, he wrote lubricious rhymes as well as perfervid spiritual verse, and would jest about even the most sacred matters. Later, a sarcastic sacramentary, he would even describe the efficacy of the eucharist in hunting metaphor: 'belike for a gentleman when he rideth a hunting to keep his horse from stumbling'.[43]

Blage's elegant italic handwriting signals his humanist education. '*Humanissimo viro Domino Georgio Blaag*', so a friend addressed him, recognising his learning in humane studies. Like Wyatt, Blage was educated at the Inns of Court, trained to royal service and chosen in youth to grace embassies. He had been among the throng of youths serving in Bishop Gardiner's suite in France, but by the dangerous spring of 1536 had returned to the English court. Writing from France, a friend asked Blage to commend him to '*Dominus Wiotus . . . summo amore, summaque observantia* [with greatest love and respect]', and to '*Dominus Brianus*', and to burn this letter which was too compromising to keep.[44] Like Wyatt, Blage was a gallant, ready to defend his truth by the sword. We will find him riding headlong, but also an exquisite courtier, honourably received at the French court.*[45] And soon we will discover Blage's graceful handwriting in Wyatt's poetry manuscript, as he gamely accepted Wyatt's poetic challenge. During Wyatt's life, and beyond, Blage would be his friend of friends and foe of foes, the guardian of his fame.

Another gilded youth in Wyatt's retinue was Henry Knollys, then aged about sixteen. His mother, Lettice, had been brought up, 'nourished together', with Francis Bryan and remained Bryan's 'great friend'. Since she was also the stepmother of Wyatt's brother-in-law and friend Anthony Lee, her son had claims to join his company. Educated perhaps at Oxford, certainly later at Padua, Knollys would own books in Latin, Greek and, very unusually, in Hebrew, and his mastery of French, Italian and Spanish was admired by his contemporaries.[46]

Elegant and reckless, a hero of the tiltyard, John Mantell, a young Kentish neighbour, had urgent reasons for leaving England as he joined Wyatt's embassy. Weeks earlier – on 15 February, a traditional time for misrule – Mantell was swaggering through Lombard Street in the com-

* See below, pp. 342, 365, 428.

pany of his page and eight or nine servants, when they encountered a City sergeant. Casting aside his cloak and looking to his companions, Mantell drew his sword, taunting the officers: 'Ye whoreson catchpoll knaves, well met. Ye shall drink or ye go.' 'Art thou a sergeant? Let me see thy mace.' He fought furiously until his sword broke – 'God's wounds, what fortune have I?' – and fleeing down Abchurch Lane, was arrested in the house of George Cornwall, the aristocratic bravo who was Wyatt's gambling companion.[47] Saving Mantell from the consequences of his pride and violence – at least for the while – Wyatt took him into his service, partly because he might need a swordsman, even a scapegrace, partly perhaps because he had been rescued from a similar catastrophe himself, but also as a favour to Mantell's mother. The widowed Lady Mantell, marrying Sir William Haute, brought up her children in Bishopsbourne in Kent.[48] And there was another reason to take him. Although Mantell was violent and flawed – and service with Wyatt did little to moderate him – he was 'as witty and toward a gentlemen as any was in the realm'. Well educated, and versed in the literary traditions of the Haute household, he wrote the humanist hand we will find copying Wyatt's poetry.[49]

John Brereton, too, was Wyatt's poetic scribe. A member of the ramified family of Brereton in Cheshire, he was another for whom exile from England appealed, for his family had recently been tainted by the disgrace and death of Sir William Brereton.[50] Robert Rudston also had reasons to leave, for he was the ward of Sir Robert Constable of Flamborough, whose loyalty to the Pilgrimage of Grace brought him to the Tower, and finally to the block in the summer of 1537. Rudston's mother and his stepfather, Sir Edward Wotton of Boughton Malherbe, were other Kentish neighbours who prevailed on Wyatt to take their son into his service.[51] Roger le Strange of Hunstanton in Norfolk was the son of Anne Vaux, and the nephew of Wyatt's friend Thomas Lord Vaux. Le Strange's family packed him off to Spain with Wyatt with £3 in expenses, and forwarded some shoes for him and his lackey. Within the year he seems to have been extricated from Calais by his elder brother Nicholas.[52] Others, too, would come and go, sometimes sent back to England with urgent messages.

Wyatt's embassy was a school for ambassadors. Later recollections of Thomas Chamberlain and Thomas Chaloner record their formative experience with Wyatt in Spain, and their letters inscribe the friendships which sustained them long before, and their lasting affection for their former master. In time, they suffered the purgatory of returning to Spain. The penitential miseries of the journey, the attentions of 'inquisitive inquisitors', the poverty, the pointlessness, were all familiar, even as they were honoured to be sent by Queen Elizabeth to the court of Philip II.[53] From Madrid in 1562 the new ambassador, Chaloner, wrote asking John Mason why he was there – 'if he serves but to stop a hole' – in letters which reveal a friendship founded on shared endurance. Gnomically, Chaloner recalled Mason's danger in England in 1538, far greater than any discomfort in Spain, when he suffered the consequences of the King's suspicion: 'Remember how your own well meaning authorized by such setters on was not so well taken in King Henry's time.' These former servants of Wyatt's would do favours for each other, in mutual gratitude, and in his memory. It is likely that Chaloner also learnt poetry and a religious stance from Wyatt.[54]

William Wolfe was the steward of the embassy, charged with the provisioning and running of the household. Unless an ambassador lived honourably, entertained liberally, not only his own dignity but that of his prince suffered. So, his horse should be 'a genet with gylt harnes', on which he could prance. Unlike the ambassadorial limousine of latter days, the horse symbolised prowess, for only the noble rider could master the noble horse. An ambassador's apparel must be elegant and fashionable, his beard the requisite length. And his table must be munificent. Wolfe's duties were to keep a 'well ordered' and 'honourable' household – and much more.[55] Though 'the news of the street corners was not good for an ambassador to seek' – so Montmorency, Grand Master of France, judged[56] – such intelligence was vital, even if the ambassador did not search for it himself: 'an ambassador should have among his servants some one man who is cautious and versatile, who will wander about the city, joining in conversations and courting familiarity with a large number of persons, to gather every breath of rumour'.[57] Wolfe was such a man in Wyatt's *familia*. Later, still serving in the English embassy at the Imperial court, he was found 'walking toward the Emperor's palace to harken some news (as his custom was often to do)'. Exploiting his 'familiar acquaintance' with a merchant in order to gain information, 'he granted him friendship'. Chaloner remembered walking up and down in a piazza in Regensburg with Wolfe, when Ludovico, a banker, 'saluted Wolfe: and they two . . . fell in talk of matters of exchange'. Wolfe's acquaintance with 'divers strangers of the Emperor's court' and his 'soothing talk ministered' to them in Italian led to the discovery of devastating evidence of treason.[58] Whether he was handy with a sword like his brother, Edward, a servant of Edward Seymour, Earl of Hertford, who fought and killed a fencing master in London and fled into sanctuary, we can only guess.[59] With servants like Wolfe – ingratiating and discreet – Wyatt might gather the intelligence which would allow him to command events.

Vital to the ambassador and his embassy were his secretaries. Wyatt composed his diplomatic letters on paper and corrected the text himself, rather than dictating them. Of his thirty-two letters from embassy, twenty-five survive in his own hand. Yet he relied on his secretaries to make fair copies. In a despairing moment, he lamented, 'My secretary is sick, and is scant able to write.' At the least, the secretary was amanuensis: 'these are servants with whom we cannot dispense unless we are willing to write everything with our own hands', wrote Dolet. Their discretion and confidentiality were paramount, and they were trusted to 'keep faithfully the scrolls, ciphers, and other papers of importance'.[60] Even the lesser-ranking secretary in Wyatt's embassy was far more than scribe and record-keeper. Sending the King 'reliable intelligence' in a crisis, Wyatt entrusted a secretary to ride post haste to France with a message, and the Emperor also gave him letters. That hard-riding secretary was Peter Rede who, Gardiner allowed, 'can skill of running'.[61] If Rede once imagined a secretary's life as one of sedentary taking of dictation, he was deceived. Sailing with the Emperor's crusading fleet to Tunis, assailed by 'an infinite number of enemies' – 160,000 Moors and Turks – Rede had 'wished myself in Calais', even if he were whipped, 'with my back full of stripes'. The refractory Rede had served already in Pate's embassy – a service which proved as dangerous to him as the Turk – and Wyatt inherited him when he came to Spain.[62]

Wyatt specially trusted and revered John Mason. 'In all his facts and doings he useth Mason as a God almighty,' complained a man who distrusted that trust and friendship.[63] The essence of the role of secretary was the sharing and keeping of secrets, which is what friends do, and the perfect secretary, in whom his master confided, was especially close to him. St John the Evangelist was imagined not only as Christ's friend, but as His secretary.[64] Allowing his secretaries freedom to polish his language and imitate his style, Cardinal Pole compared the duty of secretary to that of the painter: 'to express in words his lord's inner meaning, just as the painter paints the exterior figure of the body'.[65] In the Renaissance the intimacy of master and secretary was celebrated in double portraits. In 1536–9 Titian portrayed Georges d'Armagnac, Bishop of Rodez, French ambassador to Venice, with his secretary, Guillaume Philandrier, a scholar of Quintilian. The ambassador, in remote profile, gazes leftward into the distance, while his secretary – so near, yet so far – looks up devotedly: he is taking dictation and hanging on his master's every word.[66] Wyatt and Mason were far more intimate than this: they were friends.

Although the secretary and the ambassador, of separate status, could not quite be equal friends, the secretary's learning raised him to a different social plane. At Renaissance courts, in Renaissance diplomacy, the role of the humanist secretary acquired crucial significance.[67] The most brilliant of the time served as secretaries. Pietro Bembo, Guillaume Budé, Étienne Dolet, Clément Marot, Niccolò Machiavelli, Luigi Alamanni, Mario Equicola, Bernardo Tasso, Johannes Secundus were all secretaries. At the courts of princes, scholars chose to become secretaries in order to use their learning to give their masters the education they lacked the time to acquire, and to guide their wills to the good. Mason aspired to be this kind of secretary. Less altruistically, such a path would allow this son of an Abingdon cowherd to ascend to high office, even to evade the clerical career marked out for him.[68]

Describing a triumvirate of special friends, Leland recalled that Wyatt 'valued Mason for his radiant learning'.[69] Mason's brilliance had won him a fellowship at All Souls, the patronage of Thomas More, and the King's scholarship to study at the Sorbonne. Fluency in French and Latin, and almost certainly in Italian and Spanish, allowed him to converse universally, yet experience would teach Mason silence. Edmund Bonner would remember him in the summer of 1538 'sitting as quiet as one at a sermon'.[70] Mason's taciturnity and circumspection, for which he became known, were learnt the hard way. In 1534, while serving as secretary in Richard Pate's embassy, he had written unguardedly to his 'assured friend' Thomas Starkey, describing the royal supremacy as 'a tragedy *quae inceperit a nuptiis* [which began with a marriage]'. Starkey and Mason had become friends in 1529–30 in Paris, where Starkey was serving as secretary to Reginald Pole. This letter of Mason's reveals another reason why Wyatt treasured him. It was full of caustic humour. Proud of his own lapidary learning, Mason was supercilious when others lacked it, especially the clergy. All was going to ruin in England, he wrote. 'They have played as the ignorant priest . . . which would not suffer the name of Satan in the mass book, but struck it out and put God in the place of it, and so made "*Abrenuncio deo et omnibus operibus eius* [I renounce God and all his works]"'.[71] Roger Ascham remembered Mason later, debating at dinner 'after his manner . . . very merry with both parties, pleasantly playing both'.[72] Here was a man who might amuse Wyatt during the boredom and anxiety of his exile.

In the winter of 1535, Mason had been plying between England and the peripatetic Imperial court. News of his travels, of the 'passage of an Englishman . . . redoubled the Pope's fear' of Henry and the Emperor 'joining to attack him'. Charles, triumphant after his great victory at Tunis, was travelling to meet Paul III, who imagined in anguish that the Emperor planned to 'make himself lord of Rome'.[73] Journeying through France and Piedmont, Mason sailed from Genoa, but was driven back by terrifying Mediterranean mistrals. From Florence, he rode to Rome, where he languished with tertian fever. Recounting his adventures to Starkey, Mason told of following in the footsteps of Aeneas, visiting the ruins of ancient Greece and Rome, wondering at Vulcania, an island volcano. Finally, joining the Emperor's suite at Palermo, he travelled with it through Sicily and Calabria. At Messina, he met Reginald Pole's agent. He did not say – though probably knew – that this agent brought a letter from Pole urging the Emperor to action to save England from schism. By mid-December 1535 Mason had arrived in Naples – a 'city I think in this world peerless' – marvelling at beauties in 'the streets and churches . . . more like heavenly things than women'.[74] So Wyatt and Mason had both had picaresque adventures in Italy.

In April 1536 Mason was in the heart of Christendom. In Rome, he witnessed in sympathy Richard Pate writing to implore the King – '*cum lacrimis rogo et supplex peto* [with tears I beseech, on bended knee, I plead]' – to restore Princess Mary to the succession and reconcile himself with the Pope: 'all in the court of Rome desireth to have your love again'. Between the lines trembled Pate's own fervent hope of reconciliation.[75] Returning to the English court just in time to witness Queen Anne's catastrophe, Mason was sent to the King, who was in dangerous mood, with alarming advice from Cromwell 'to speak out freely', disregarding 'any signs of approbation or disapprobation in the King's countenance'.[76] Long intended for the life of a priest, Mason now sought dispensation to postpone taking holy orders. Self-knowledge, aversion to celibacy, and a desire for life in the midst of courts might have dissuaded him from the priesthood, but his decision was also politic: if not a priest, he need not swear the Oath of Supremacy. For a while he immersed himself in the politics of All Souls, before joining Wyatt's suite in the spring of 1537.[77]

Well versed in the customs of Spain and of the Emperor's court, fluent in languages, Mason was ostensibly the perfect secretary for Wyatt's embassy. Trusted beyond all others, he shared all the secrets of Wyatt's mission, was the first person consulted, the first to be sent as go-between and proxy. A secretary could go where his ambassador could not, speak to those whom his master could not countenance, and his actions were deniable, just as the ambassador's might be disowned by the prince. At one point, Mason became not only the ambassador's secretary, but 'Master Mason . . . his Majesty's secretary', with his own commission, and Wyatt 'bade' him 'speak boldly'.[78] This double role presented its own difficulties: Wyatt relied on Mason's counsel, but Mason was the

King's secretary too. The sharing of secrets was mutual, and Wyatt's knowledge of Mason's allegiances posed a danger to him, just as his secrets and commissions endangered Mason. At last, Wyatt would live in fear of the secrets of their friendship.

Coming and going between the English court and the embassy were messengers. Their arrival was keenly awaited for they brought vital instructions. Very often an ambassador waited anxiously for instructions about how to act – 'in following and executing them lies the whole duty of an ambassador', wrote Dolet.[79] Very often the instructions did not arrive in time. Riding furiously, couriers carried messages prophesying peace or war:

> In haste
>> post
>>> haste
>>> *Cito cito*

Cito: quickly. The life of the King's courier, Francis Pitcher – 'Francisco' or 'Fraunces' – spent endlessly travelling, is exhausting to contemplate.[80] Bartholomew Butler, Rouge Croix pursuivant, was a trusted envoy, and as a herald he should have been allowed to ride freely. But in this uneasy world even heralds might not be safe.[81] With the arrival of each messenger from some distant court the balance of politics and possibilities would change. In his uncertainty – and boredom – every ambassador lived in hope or dread of news: news of the outbreak of peace or war, the outcome of a battle, of the death of a prince, the birth of an heir, the arrival of ships bearing gold from the New World to finance some new venture. Life in embassy was spent waiting; not waiting which allowed some purposeful activity, but waiting of anguish and distraction.

Travelling with Wyatt, some of his servants were seeking escape from troubles in England; others, restless like their master, sought new experience. With this little band Wyatt's life was now entwined. During long months following the Emperor's court he would depend on these men for company, for counsel, for intelligence, for amusement, for defence, and for his honour. An ambassador's reputation rested on the behaviour of his servants, who were believed to pattern their lives on his example: any disorder among them, any behaviour which shocked Spanish sensibilities, would compromise him. Wyatt must especially keep these youths, used to the easier ways of the English court, away from cloistered Spanish women. If they offended against the laws and customs of the country, he might be unable to protect them. The theory of immunity for an ambassador was still unsettled, the practice uncertain: far more so was the question of the immunity for his suite. If one of them committed a crime, who would judge and punish it? If one of them was a heretic, could he speak freely in the sanctuary of the embassy? What would happen when the ambassador of the schismatic Supreme Head of the new Church of England came to the court of the Most Catholic King of Spain: was he still protected? Diplomacy at the Reformation, in the age of Luther, must differ from more politic diplomacy in the Renaissance, 'diplomacy in the age of Machiavelli'.[82] Wyatt and his retinue would test all these yet untested questions. As they set out for Spain the precedents were not encouraging. For importing 'a foolish book against the Pope' two English merchants had been arrested in Valladolid in the summer of 1534, and 'their bodies in danger of burning if we had not made for them great friends and entreatance', wrote Mason.[83] As Spanish hatred of English apostasy grew, and Henry's envoys were instructed to disparage the Bishop of Rome, the English embassy became vulnerable. Clinging to the rockface in emergencies they could not have imagined, these men were bound to each other. The time would come when they wished themselves back in England.

Sailing from Dover for France on about 7 April, Wyatt and his train – Mason, Blage, Mantell, Knollys and 'Chambers [Chamberlain?]' – landed to receive disturbing news.[84] On 10 April Wyatt sent a messenger post haste to England 'with the tidings of Mr Pole'. Cardinal Pole, papal legate *a latere*, the highest class of legate, had made his solemn entry into Paris on that day, honoured as a papal ambassador must be.[85]

But also dishonoured, for almost at the 'doors of the court' the most Christian King refused him audience. 'Nobody has the right to call us . . . traitors or rebels, when our causes are good,' Pole thundered, but Francis argued that he could never harbour a traitor to 'the best brother and friend he has in the world', the English King.[86] Francis Bryan also came to France, at the same time as Wyatt, sent on an extraordinary, an unprecedented mission.[87] Pole reported in outrage Bryan's orders to insist that 'friendship demanded that the Most Christian King should lay hands upon an ambassador and legate of the vicar of Christ . . . and deliver him bound to a hostile king'. In violation of the laws of nations, the Cardinal was no longer protected, and was forced to leave the realm.[88] So deep was the enmity of the Emperor and the French King that it seemed there could never be peace between them. In Rome, in the previous spring Charles had offered to fight Francis in single combat, and when Francis declined, there had been war, devastating campaigns in Provence and Picardy, which had humiliated Charles, but settled nothing. While their honours were engaged, neither could retreat from war.[89] Thus neither of them could afford to alienate Henry, 'that impious King', however deeply they deplored his actions. 'Never before was Christianity in such turmoil as today,' judged Gianmatteo Giberti, Pole's companion in his mission: 'the King of England now triumphs in his ruin.'[90] Pole had always known that his red hat would have crimson consequences. He thought often of Thomas Becket.[91]

Leaving Paris, Cardinal Pole was travelling '*pian piano* [very slowly]' northwards towards Cambrai, a free city of the Empire which seemed to offer sanctuary.[92] The papal nuncio in France expected Pole to reach there on 15 April, but on that day he reported the arrival of agents in Amiens whose presence was ominous for the Legate. 'Brian has come from England, and another gentleman . . . going to Spain as ambassador': Wyatt.[93] The paths of Bryan and Wyatt so often converged in embassy, and now travelling to France they encountered each other along the way. Sent on a sinister and secret mission, Bryan confided it to Wyatt. Bryan – the King's 'mignon', his '*favorito*' – was set on a last-ditch attempt to seize the Cardinal and take him to England to join the 'catalogue of martyrs'. This was the news at the French court by the

21st. Bryan was allegedly 'very desperate', boasting that 'if he found Pole in the middle of France, he would kill him with his own hand' – a threat not only of assassination but also of the violation of the laws of nations.[94] Yet in these public threats there was doubleness, for even as he proclaimed his loyalty to his King, Bryan was forewarning Pole of the plot against his life. In England, Henry waited, suspicious of his envoys. On 15 April he had written in fury on receiving 'the tidings of Mr Pole', the news of his honourable reception and safe departure. He 'wondered' that Bryan had not 'quickened' the French King against Pole, was 'surprised' by his 'pompous receiving', and demanded that they have 'good spial' on him.[95] Some – at the French court and the English – knew why it was politic for Bryan to prove his allegiance, why the King was right to be suspicious. On the 16th the royal agent Peter Mewtas wrote confiding his doubts about the fidelity of Bishop Gardiner and of Bryan, who shared a hatred of the evangelicals and the reforms in religion.[96]

Openly, the English ambassadors in France could not, would not, countenance meeting Pole themselves, nor receive letters from him, for any contact with the Pope's messenger, the King's enemy, was treason. Secretly, perilously, they might communicate by way of intermediaries, by their secretaries, acting as their proxies. Outwardly, Bryan and Gardiner treated Pole as 'devils' would. They declined to meet Giberti themselves, but sent Germain Gardiner to him at Abbeville to learn more of Pole's legation.[97] Germain was Stephen Gardiner's nephew as well as his secretary; he also happened to be Thomas Wriothesley's brother-in-law. Trusted by the English ambassadors, Germain was also trusted by the papal envoys, because his sympathies were with Rome. Gardiner and Bryan had known Giberti before, during their embassies to the papal court, and they regretted not having the 'pleasure of seeing and embracing me', so Giberti wrote. 'Their messenger . . . seemed inclined to the Cardinal [Pole], speaking most gently of him.' 'With sighs, as of one unwillingly doing a wicked duty', Germain Gardiner brought messages urging Pole to write to the King.[98]

By 16 April Pole had reached the outskirts of Cambrai. He knew already that Bryan and Mewtas had been sent to kill him.[99] Pole's friends in England had received news from France, and were fearful. 'The King had sent Peter Mewtas into France to kill the Cardinal Pole.' 'How?' 'With a handgun.' This was the confession of none other than Elizabeth Darrell.[100] Sir Geoffrey Pole, the Cardinal's brother, told her, she recalled. He remembered quite otherwise: 'Mistress Darrell showed him that there was one of the privy chamber with the French King very familiar with Sir Francis Bryan which gave the Cardinal Pole warning that it was intended to slay him'.[101] By implicating Sir Geoffrey, she was shielding Wyatt, who had been close – very close – to the plot and the plotters. In Lord Montague's garden in England there was a revealing conversation between Pole's brothers: 'What news?' asked Montague. 'Marry . . . I hear that our brother beyond the sea shall be slain,' replied Sir Geoffrey. 'No . . . he is escaped. I have letters,' so Montague assured him. These letters came from either the Marchioness of Exeter, or her intimate, Mistress Darrell.[102] If we ask who entrusted such secrets to Bess Darrell, Wyatt's name hovers.

In the shadows we glimpse exchanges between Wyatt's agents and Pole's. At Saint-Denis, just north of Paris, Wyatt sent John Mason to Pole. So Edmund Bonner alleged: 'Upon the coming of Pole in his ungodly legation to France and being at St-Denis by Paris . . . Mr Wyatt would not receive wine sent by the said Pole nor yet speak with him. This Mason went and spake with him a great space . . .' Perhaps Mason had this treasonable meeting 'by the advice and counsel of Mr Wyatt', perhaps 'they did it upon good and faithful considerations', perhaps they had reported it at the time. Perhaps, but Bonner doubted it.[103] Desperate to contact the King, Pole made a last attempt to suborn an English envoy. In Saint-Denis Michael Throckmorton came to Wyatt from Pole, bringing letters wrapped round a present of a bottle of wine. Throckmorton was playing a brilliant double game. Though Cromwell believed that he had turned Throckmorton and was running him as a double agent, Throckmorton was still, and always, Pole's devoted servant.[104] Later, charged to remember whether he had ever spoken with a traitor, Wyatt admitted that he had: 'to Throckmorton at S. Davis [Saint-Denis], that wolde have brought me a present of wyne from Pole'. As for Pole, 'yf I ever spake worde to hym beyonde the see . . .'

– Wyatt left the possibility hanging – 'and yet to my remembrauns but ons a this syde', in England.[105] Pole probably knew Mason already – they had studied in Paris at the same time – and in the spring of 1539 he would claim that he had known Wyatt 'before'. Whether this was in 1537, as his legation failed, or in some more distant time, when Pole was still honoured by the King, we cannot tell. It is likely that Wyatt knew Throckmorton already through their shared associations with the families of Guildford and Vaux. In this *sub rosa* world, did Wyatt believe that he was meeting Throckmorton, Cromwell's double agent, or Throckmorton, Pole's man?

Kings rarely give open orders for assassination. But on 25 April, in his rage, Henry made his desire plain: 'we will that you Sir Francis Bryan shall secretly appoint such fellows for the enterprise of his [Pole's] apprehension': 'by some mean' have him 'trussed up and conveyed to Calais'.[106] 'Such fellows' now lay in wait for Pole in Cambrai, among them, Wyatt's friend Thomas Palmer. 'The man you wot of doth not come out of his lodging nor intends not,' Palmer confided on 16 May to Lord Lisle, who secretly hoped for Pole's safety.[107] Henry now offered a ransom for Pole, alive or dead. As Cromwell told Throckmorton, 'ways enough may be found in Italy to rid a traitorous subject'.[108]

In theory, ambassadors were sacrosanct. In the sanctuary of the laws of nations, they enjoyed immunity and were protected, even in the midst of armies, even though their masters were at war, not for their own sake nor for their master's, but because without them there would 'never be an end of hostility, nor any peace after wars'.[109] If the laws of nations gave immunity to secular ambassadors, then the legate of Holy Church must be inviolable – surely. As Pole protested: 'he was coming not merely as ambassador but as Legate – the highest embassy used among Christian princes'. That one Christian prince desired another to 'betray thine ambassador, betray the Legate, and give him into my ambassador's hands' was to violate 'both God's law and man's'.[110] Henry disagreed: although the 'privilege of a Legate is sacrosanctum and inviolable, wheresoever they be (*de jure gentium*)', the privilege did not extend to a 'traitor fugitive and a forsaker of the commonwealth'.[111] Neither theory nor precedent provided for the case of a king's ambassador who threatened, or even killed, a pope's ambassador. In 1539, believing Bryan again to be plotting Pole's assassination, the nuncio in France warned that this would be a cause of war.*[112] But by then the threat to Pole came not from Bryan but from Wyatt, who knew his duty regarding troublesome priests.

While Pole sought sanctuary in Cambrai, Wyatt and his train were travelling south through France. Their safety as they passed through the realm of the King of France toward the Emperor, that king's enemy, was uncertain, and Wyatt knew from bitterest experience that there might be nothing safe about safe-conducts. 'Men who did not wish to obey natural law and God's law would hardly obey the laws of men,' wrote Bernardo Tasso, who travelled fearfully to Aragon in the autumn of 1537.[113] Passing through Lyon and Avignon, towards the coast of the Mediterranean, Wyatt and his band reached the border fortress of Salses, just north of Perpignan. It was the 'strongest castle . . . in the world', so John Brereton reported to Wriothesley.[114] Mighty armies were mobilizing at the borders of France and Spain, and there were fears that Francis, in league with the Turk, was about to attack the frontier of Catalonia. The fortifications at Perpignan were being strengthened, and soon the passes into the Spanish kingdoms were stopped.[115] There could hardly have been a more dangerous time to travel.

At the height of this emergency, Don Francés de Beaumont, captain general of the Imperial forces in Roussillon, received an unwelcome visitor. Early on 18 May the English ambassador, 'a man of rank with a large and honourable retinue, and a train of thirty-five horses and eight mules', appeared without warning in Perpignan and lodged at an inn. Beaumont invited Wyatt to 'favour' him by staying at his house for a few days, a courtesy which couched a threat. When Wyatt declined, Beaumont 'continued to insist' – so he told the Archbishop of Zaragoza, Viceroy of Catalonia. Delaying his 'guests' until he received instructions – without 'it appearing clearly as a form of detention' – Beaumont listened with alarm to Wyatt's news of the great army Francis was marshalling at the border, and Wyatt fretted. 'It would not have

* See below, p. 434.

been appropriate to stop him,' agreed the Emperor. Just as Wyatt came to the Imperial court, Charles was sending Don Diego Hurtado de Mendoza as his special ambassador to the King of England, and if Wyatt were harmed so might Mendoza be. In diplomacy, one monarch's bad turn would deserve another. Freed to continue their journey, Wyatt and his company were expected to reach Figueras in Catalonia on Whitsunday, 20 May.[116]

From Barcelona the English party turned inland. Crossing the border between Catalonia and the kingdom of Aragon at Zaragoza, they were stopped again – stopped, stripped, searched, humiliated by the 'spitefullest people in the world'. 'Extremely handled as though we had been Jews', wrote Brereton, who may not have known – yet, though soon he learnt – how Jews might be handled in Spain. Forced to pay import duties, Wyatt protested that 'he would pay no custom, for . . . every ambassador should go and come free in all places christened'. The response: 'if Christ or St Francis came with all their flock, they should not escape'. Even the Empress's messenger was searched. Wyatt threatened to ride in post to the Emperor to tell him, 'he being an ambassador after what sort he was handled'. In his new pride as ambassador he forgot the irony of pleading his own immunity under the law of nations just as Pole was being denied it. On 4 June Wyatt rode fast from Zaragoza with one companion, leaving his train to follow. John Brereton – who may have been Wriothesley's mole in Wyatt's retinue – reported with relief: 'My master with all the rest of his company have passed a long and a painful journey in safety without any perishing of horse or man, thanks be to God.'[117]

The little band would endure many long and painful journeys. Wyatt was responsible for these men who looked to him for command, but who had not all been amenable to discipline. Stoical acceptance must be the condition of his task and of his travels, but these youthful companions might lighten the sombre service. As they crossed from one Spanish kingdom to another, arriving in unknown towns, they tried new lodgings and new food, discovered local languages and different customs, all foreign to them. The dazzle of the landscape and the spur of danger led them on as they wound through high passes toward the

Spanish court, vividly imagined and yet unknown. Riding through high hills, they knew that with the least slip of their horse they might plunge into the valley below, and that in the barren emptiness they were vulnerable to ambush, beyond any ready help. 'Hye hilles' became a metaphor for the force of love and the inspiration of poetry. Wyatt himself inscribed this poem – a *strambotto* composed in ottava rima – into his poetry manuscript, in the pale ink he used while travelling. His companion John Mantell retained it in memory:[118]

> From thes hye hilles as when a spryng dothe fall
> it tryllythe downe with still and suttyll corse
> off this and that it gaders ay and shall
> tyll it have just off flowd the streme and forse
Tho   then at the fote it ragithe over all
> so farythe love when he hathe tan a sorse   *taken*
> his rayne is rage resistans vaylyth none
> the first estew is remedy alone   *avoidance (of danger)*

Even here Wyatt is alert to danger. This is the first such use of the noun 'eschew' known in English.

After the horrors of the previous year, his memories a prison, Wyatt was a man without illusions, but not without curiosity, which was now revived by the prospect of arrival and the uncertainties of what awaited him. Even amidst the companionship of his retinue, he was reserved and apart. As ambassador, he must prepare to exchange ordinary friendship for deference. If a sudden loneliness assailed him now, as he rode towards the Emperor's court, there may also have been the satisfaction of self-possession, and excitement, as he took on the office for which all his education and experience had prepared him, or not prepared him.

In the golden early summer in Valladolid, the Emperor was expecting the new ambassador from England. The court waited with suspicion, for few knew why he came, and Wyatt's arrival on 9 or 10 June was at first kept secret, even – or especially – from the papal nuncio.[119] 'Tommaso Vuiat' made his entry into Valladolid on 14 June, and was honoured with the 'fairest lodging' in the city. Grandees welcomed and fêted him. At the same time Henry was celebrating the arrival of the Emperor's ambassador, Mendoza, sending fifty nobles to greet him, and lodging him and his train in his own palace.[120] So far: so reciprocal. Yet the Imperial court was greater by far than Henry's, the grandees far grander than English nobles. The Duke of Alva was so wealthy that he could entertain for four days the four thousand people who composed the Emperor's court – as John Mason had recorded in amazement – and send generous provisions to the English embassy.[121] While ambassador at the court of Ferdinand of Aragon in 1512–13, Francesco Guicciardini had reported distrustfully the customs of the court: 'They are of infinite ceremony, which they perform with great humility in words and titles, with kissing of hands. Everyone is their lord, anyone can command them: but, in fact, this comes to nothing.'[122]

Amidst the Gothic splendours of Valladolid, great spectacles and celebrations were now prepared to honour the English ambassador – head-turning for the man from Kent.[123] On 22 June the Emperor granted Wyatt his first audience and, introduced by the Chamberlain, Don Pedro de la Cueva, High Commander of Alcántara, Wyatt offered his letters of credence and represented 'the princely nature' of his king.[124]

Charles 'gently entertained' Wyatt, 'not with pomp and setting forth of himself, but with sober and discreet words like a wise man'.[125] The Emperor was of grave demeanour and few words, and his first words to Wyatt were almost certainly French. Whenever Wyatt reported his conversations with Charles, they were always speaking French together: 'I will tell you, *Monsieur l'ambassadour* . . .' Famously, Charles believed that Italian was the language for friendship, French to be spoken to women, German to horses, and Spanish to God. He 'loved to read only three books', so it was said, and two of these were in Italian – Castiglione's *Il cortegiano*, Machiavelli's *Discorsi* and the history of Polybius. (Maybe he also read *Il cortegiano* in Juan Boscán's Castilian translation of 1534).[126] Though Holy *Roman* Emperor, by Charles's own admission his Latin was poor.[127] As for Wyatt, *The Quyete of mynde* shows his accomplishment in Latin, and he spoke it. His French, practised in embassy to France and service in Calais, was also fluent. As a special grace, Charles might deign to speak Italian, so perhaps sometimes Wyatt and he conversed in Italian.[128] But probably never in Castilian. After decades in Spain Nicolás Perronet, Sieur de Granvelle, did not know how to write it, so he admitted to Charles's other principal counsellor, Francisco de los Cobos. French was their *lingua franca*.[129]

At this first encounter with the Imperial court, Wyatt witnessed both its grave clericalism and its chivalry. Present at his first audience was Juan Tavera, Cardinal Archbishop of Toledo, a great prince of the Church. Ranking second to the crown in power and wealth, he would be entrusted with the regency during Charles's absence from his Spanish kingdoms. Later, as Inquisitor General, Tavera would take a special – and terrifying – interest in the English ambassador and his household.*[130] Among the celebrations in Valladolid were games of canes and a bull-fight in which courtiers showed their prowess. When his favourite, Don Luis de Zúñiga y Ávila, was badly gored, Charles himself despatched the bull with a 'skilful lance-thrust'.[131]

On 28 June Richard Pate took his leave. Wyatt was now resident ambassador. The Emperor gave Pate a parting gift of three gold cups worth three thousand ducats as a sign of his favour. Pate lacked such favour from his own king, who now regarded him as inept and disloyal – not without reason.[132] One of Wyatt's principal qualifications for this embassy was not being his predecessor. The papal nuncio had been cultivating Pate, '*il quale è veramente uomo da bene e piange del continuo l'errore del suo Re* [who is truly a man of good will, and laments continually the error of his king]'.[133] Charles, too, used powers of persuasion to win over English emissaries: it was noticed that envoys who 'go to the Emperor return better Imperial from him'. Successive ambassadors – Sir Nicholas Carew, Dr Richard Sampson, Sir Thomas Elyot, Dr William Bennet –had lamented the divorce in secret audience.[134] It was politic, of course, not openly to approve Henry's challenge to the Holy

* See below, pp. 418–25.

See at the courts of Catholic princes, but in the Curia they hoped that some of Henry's ambassadors would move him to reconciliation. Why else would letters be sent directly from Rome to Gardiner and Wallop in March 1537?[135] In Spain, a papal nuncio even had hopes – though not for long – that Wyatt was on the side of the angels.

Rome's emissaries watched with alarm a renewed amity between the English King and the Emperor in the spring and summer of 1537. The death of *la regina vera*, 'the true queen', the year before had removed a principal obstacle to alliance, and the terrible escalation of Habsburg–Valois hostilities made it necessary. Henry, whom it pleased sometimes to play the peacemaker, pursued the idea of acting as arbiter between Francis and Charles, while wishing for their continued rivalry and discord, in which lay his own security and his chance to influence events.[136] Gianmatteo Giberti, observing with bewilderment the rapprochement of the Holy Roman Emperor with the schismatic King, could only think that '*le necessità delli stati*' – reason of state – drove him to it. The pledge of this alliance would be the marriage between Henry's daughter Mary and Dom Luis, Infante of Portugal, who would jointly be invested with Milan.[137] Charles was once told that 'in time of war the English make use of their Princess as of an owl, with which to lure birds'. Not understanding the simile, he enquired what was meant by the 'owl', and when it was explained, 'he laughed heartily'. For him to laugh was '*cosa rara* [a rare thing]'.[138] But Wyatt arrived at a low moment of this princely friendship. Henry's last letter to Pate complained of Charles's 'ingratitude', a word that would toll percussively through his instructions to Wyatt. Typically, Henry – claiming the Emperor as his nephew – resented that nephew's just defence of the aunt whom he repudiated. Resentment festered. 'He who has offended once will never forgive', said a Spanish proverb.[139]

Wyatt's mission was to mediate between these friendly enemies. Tentatively proffering Henry's friendship – so tentatively that his offer could not be slighted – he must add '*as of himself* that he trusteth, before his return again, to see . . . a renovation of the old amity'. If the Emperor imputed 'any unkindness or sinister proceeding' to his king, Wyatt was to retaliate: Henry 'was as evil handled in the discourse as ever was

prince of honour'. Should Charles dispute the declaration of illegitimacy of 'my Lady Mary', Wyatt must insist that even if she was conceived in good faith, 'where the prohibition is of the law of God, there
cannot be alleged *bona fides*'. And he was instructed to deliver a letter
from the wretched, persecuted Mary in which 'she doth repent herself'.
Only if Henry were to die without issue would she have any claim to
the succession. In this world of shadows and appearances, Wyatt was to
show the French ambassador, too, 'a *countenance* of great friendship', but
with 'such a *temperance*' that the ambassador would know that a '*correspondence* of like gratitude and kindness' was expected.[140] By answering
becks and bows, by smiles and frowns, each speaker should so mirror the other that no unguarded gesture or misread sign could dishonour his master. Carrying out these instructions would need all Wyatt's
'dexterity', all his power of allurement to make men 'take bread at
his hand'. Beyond the written instructions – what to say on his king's
behalf, what to say 'as of himself' – there were parting monitions from
the King, hidden then and now. Official and half-official letters followed from Cromwell, and half-private letters from Wyatt's 'own Wriothesley', entrusted to messengers who also brought private missives
and secret messages. Wyatt waited on the uncertain arrival of orders,
which usually came too late. The interplay of personal relations and
the succession of events would impel him to more independent action,
to the real diplomacy to which an ambassador must turn when instructions from home bear little relation to reality.

His was a mission impossible. Charged to arrange the marriage of
a princess who was no longer princess, Wyatt could only make the
lame claim: 'though not lawful, yet a King's daughter'.[141] But the really
impossible ground of his diplomacy was Henry's insistence that by
their alliance – 'friends of friends' – Charles must now be the enemy
of Henry's enemy, the Pope. 'In more than haste' Wriothesley wrote
in June, telling Wyatt to 'travail', to 'labour' to persuade the Emperor
'to aid no man directly or indirectly against the King; whether the
Bishop of Rome, or any other'. 'Any other'? – Cardinal Pole. In case
of the invasion of England, the Emperor must aid the King 'against
the Bishop' – the Bishop of Rome: the Pope – 'and all others'. 'Stick

you upon the Emperor's joining against the Bishop.'[142] But how could any ambassador make the *Holy* Roman Emperor challenge the Pope? Not even 'reason of state' could justify so malign an Imperial course. In March 1537 Charles had insisted to the nuncio – and continued to insist – that he would make Henry humble himself and return to the true path. But, he said, because of his own enmity to the Turk and the French King, he could not afford to make an enemy of Henry also.[143] There was also the small matter that Henry was lending him money. At least – so Charles promised at the end of July – he would make sure that Henry became no worse. This was a promise he could not keep.[144]

Charles's perennial political ploy was temporizing, delaying, waiting to see, kicking matters into the long grass. Despairing complaints of this cunctatory Emperor fill the letters of the ambassadors. Yet he could hardly act otherwise when constantly beset by intractable problems of uncertain priority. Obsessed – as were all kings – with honour and reputation, his first passion was war. He was also deeply pious and conscious of his duty to secure lasting peace in Christendom and to launch a crusade against the Turk.[145] The Great Turk posed an immanent, an imminent threat, the spectre of absolute power. Khair-ad-Din Barbarossa – no longer simply chief corsair of the Barbary coast, but Kapudan Pasha, the Sultan's admiral of the sea – menaced the entire western Mediterranean. At Tunis in July 1535 the Emperor had led a crusading armada to a great victory; a victory which left him contemplating leading a campaign against the Turk to his 'eternal fame', and Sultan Süleyman determined to avenge the defeat.[146] While the Emperor and the French King remained at war, seemingly irreconcilable, there was no counter to Ottoman power, and the alliance of the French King with the Sultan, his enemy's enemy, made the danger to Christendom even greater.[147] There was also an enemy within Christendom: the heretic. Which should be vanquished first: the enemy within, or the enemy without: the heretic or the infidel? These were the great questions which Charles pondered, and the reasons why he was forced to consider alliance with England's schismatic king and to countenance his ambassador.

As Charles left Valladolid on 10 July to ride north, Wyatt endured the purgatory of following the court. A month later, the Emperor opened the Cortes of Aragon. There at Monzón, this 'doghole', 'the barrenest country in the world', and in surrounding villages, the Imperial court would be stranded through three weary months.[148] Worse than endless riding through the blazing high summer heat, the desolation of the landscape, the bare lodgings along the way, the lack of any comfort, were the longings for home and the uncertainties of his mission.[149] Persuading others, persuading himself, Wyatt pretended outwardly a confidence he could not feel. We find him now, as often afterwards, 'piping in an ivy leaf', boasting of Charles's amity toward his king. Early in August Alfonso Rossetto, the Ferrarese envoy, wrote from Zaragoza: '*lo oratore di Inghilterra* [the English ambassador]' was letting it be known that an alliance between the Emperor and his king was close to conclusion: they proposed to marry the English Princess to the Infante, with Milan as dowry.[150] But the opinion at court was that no alliance was likely any time soon. Martín de Salinas, the agent of Ferdinand, King of the Romans, reported not the imminence of alliance, but the impediments in its way: first, Henry's insistence that his friendship with the Emperor should be 'perfect' and 'protect him from his enemy the Pope'; second, his condition that Mary relinquish all claims to the throne.[151] The Pope need never fear: no alliance between the Emperor and the King of England could ever harm the Holy See, so Granvelle had promised the nuncio at Calatayud at the end of July.[152]

How was Wyatt to fan the flames of fraternal amity between King and Emperor? One way was to blur the distinction between the shows of love which came from his king and those he offered 'as of himself'. At the Spanish court, as at the English, he would be witty and winning, be handsome, and exploit his lethal charm. Though in his verse epistle to Poyntz, Wyatt denounced the dark arts of flattery, in life he would pay compliments of exquisite eloquence. 'Hoyet' said 'such splendid things of me that I now judge myself much wiser than ever I thought', reported the French ambassador.[153] Friendship and confidentiality became the touchstones of Wyatt's diplomacy. His way as ambassador was to speak '*come amico et fratello* [as friend and brother]', '*amichevolmente* [friendlily]', '*con protestatione de secretezza appresso noi* [with protestation of secrecy between us]', *'pensan' farmi piacere* [thinking to please me]'.[154] His charm had a way with the Emperor, for a while, even as Charles's relations with Henry collapsed. Passing through the French court early in 1538, an English gentleman – probably George Blage – declared that the Emperor *'faceva ogni dì ad esso oratore le maggior carezze che si potessero desiderar* [made daily to that ambassador the greatest shows of love that could be desired]'.[155] Charles described to his sister Wyatt's talking to him *'par manière de bonne affection envers moi, et en grand secret, en jurant que c'est de lui mesmes* [with show of good affection towards me, in great secret, swearing that he acts as of himself]'.[156] A suspicion lingers that Wyatt, who prized honesty, who dared to tell the truth, even or especially to princes, sometimes told the Emperor what the Emperor wanted to hear. The fiction of friendship was an essential part of diplomacy, and behind this not wholly delusive front, the real diplomacy was conducted. Yet by the summer of 1538 Henry came to believe that Wyatt was more Charles's ambassador than his own, that he had 'gone native'.

To sustain the fictive friendship Wyatt must sometimes suppress overtures from his king which he knew would anger Charles. So, he did not present the penitent letters extorted from the Lady Mary; did not present them, even though this was part of his initial instructions. 'It is much marvelled', wrote Cromwell on 10 October, that Wyatt had 'very negligently' ignored this order. 'Do it now,' urged Wriothesley (who, with Cromwell, had covered up for Wyatt), write 'as though you had none advertisement from hence that we think of it'. Whether Wyatt ever did bring himself to outrage Charles and dishonour the Princess by delivering her letters is unknown. Wriothesley's assurance that 'my Lady Mary's grace is merry and in very good health' may merely have been conventional, but maybe it marked their allegiance to her.[157] At Monzón at the end of September Wyatt went to confide in Alfonso Rossetto, the Ferrarese ambassador. It was a long time since he had received letters from England, he said, many days since he had had audience, but he believed that the negotiations between Charles and his king would go well. Disturbed, however, by the robbing of English merchants by 'Biscaglini [Biscayans]' which went unpunished, he also feared for the consequences for his diplomacy: 'I will be forced to complain sharply to the Emperor, but then I will not be able to speak to him of other things . . . and I do not wish to go to speak to him of this annoying matter.'[158] Through these months we have no letters from Wyatt – only responses from home to his reports on his successes, only descriptions from the court in Aragon of the English ambassador and his faltering embassy.

Already we find Wyatt in search of intimates, in search of intelligence, offering confidences in order to win them in return. Later, he recalled insistent instructions from England – 'Vuse [use] now all your pollicy, vuse nowe all yor frendes, vuse now all yor dexterite.' It was in exactly these terms that Cromwell wrote to him: 'Your part shall be now like a good orator'; 'with all dexterity' 'fish out the bottom of his [the Emperor's] stomach'; 'continue vigilant now of the ensearching out of things meet to be known'; 'Gentle Master Wiat, now use all your wisdom.'[159] Bishop Gardiner advised Edmund Bonner how to gain intelligence. 'Princes' ambassadors be reckoned to have the most intelligence of the state of things . . . for commonly they be chosen men of experience.' 'Wise they be, and without great familiarity they will go about to know what they can, and say themselves as little as they may.' The way to knowledge was through friendship: 'by all ways and means to insinuate yourself into their friendship, and by conformity of manners to attain their amity'. This intimacy would come, as in all friendship, by trust: 'not pretending to search tidings at their hands, for then they will avoid you'. 'Certainty' would be rare, 'for one thing the world laboureth now chiefly in, to make by secrecy all things uncertain'.[160] Machiavelli had given the same advice to Raffaello Girolami when Girolami went as ambassador to the Emperor in 1522: 'the best way of gaining information is to give it'.[161] Germain Gardiner's counsel to novice ambassadors was that 'till they knew the court well, they should believe no man . . . a newcomen man shall wondrously beguile himself'.[162] But without trust there would be no intelligence. Wyatt – like Gardiner, like Bryan – founded his diplomacy on 'especial' friends. With so much uncertain, in the end friendship might be all that was left.

Casting around for allies, Henry had begun to align himself with the German Protestant League of Schmalkalden. Accordingly, Wyatt found affinity with League envoys at the Imperial court. Later, in grim days in Toledo he came to trust 'Hulrik thalmayne [Ulrich the German]' – Dr Udalricus of Strasbourg – and gave him a horse. Recalling Wyatt's kindness to them in Spain, German envoys promised to favour 'all the King's servants for Wyatt's sake'. Hans Bockle, a young German, hoped that the friendship he formed with Wyatt in Spain would be perpetual.[163] But Wyatt's – Tomasso Viato's – closest allies in the little world of the resident embassies were the ambassadors to the Italian powers. On them his quixotic diplomacy and his vision of England's safety came to depend. Through waiting months, so often in the dark, they consulted and colluded, making mutual promises which, in time, portended peace or war. Remembering that the man without history is forever a child, ambassadors recorded history for present purposes, reminding princes of earlier periods of concord and the ancient friendships which bound their houses.[164] With the ambassadors from Ferrara and Mantua, Alfonso Rossetto and Ottaviano Vivaldini, Wyatt recalled '*la benivolenza che anticamente è stata e perseverata*', the ancient amity between their princes and his king, and spoke of '*la amicitia che particolarmente è fra noi* [the friendship which is particularly between us]'.[165] Maybe Wyatt recalled the ransom and rescue of the '*giovane Inglese*' in 1527, and expressed his gratitude to the princes of Mantua and Ferrara to whom he owed his life.

Wyatt spoke to these envoys in Italian – even colloquially, as he did in English. Their language and culture drew him, and the possibility hangs beguilingly that they passed among themselves the latest *rime* from Italy. Among the *nunzi* at the Emperor's court was a poet, a friend of poets. Giovanni Guidiccioni had addressed to his friends political *rime* expressing fears of Charles's threat to Italian liberty and hopes for peace, lamenting the Sack of Rome and the miseries of Italy. He wrote Petrarchan sonnets of love and death, of *lontananza*. One of the first *novelle* was his: a romance of Francesco who killed his friend for love of a lady. To his friend Girolamo Campo he wrote a verse epistle. Here was a kindred spirit for Viato, seemingly. But Guidiccioni had also written a sonnet sequence on the triumph of chastity; he was also the papal

nuncio.[166] Maybe he tried to cultivate Wyatt, to insist on England's reconciliation with Rome, as once he had 'worked' on Richard Pate. At the
end of August 1537 Guidiccioni left Spain, to be replaced as nuncio by
a man he despised, a man of no political skill and less sensitivity, whose
burning ambition was to be a cardinal and whose imagination was all
directed to the heretical threat to the Church: Giovanni Poggio.[167]

At the courts of Christendom the nuncios pursued the diplomacy of
the papal monarch in ways not so different from those of the ambassadors of other monarchs. Yet they were not like other ambassadors, for
all princes must defer to the Holy Father, the arbiter of international
law and of all treaties. The nuncios held authority within the Church
of the country to which they were accredited, and in Spain, where
they even intervened in the affairs of the Inquisition, their jurisdiction
came to be seen as a threat to Spanish liberties. Their duty was missionary and evangelical: to defend and restore the unity of Christendom, to uphold the universal authority and primacy of the Holy See.[168]
In 1528, when Alfonso de Valdés composed the anti-papal dialogue
Lactantio, the nuncio Baldassare Castiglione had virulently attacked
him, claiming that Valdés had Jewish ancestry.[169] At the court of the
Holy Roman Emperor the papal nuncio had greater access to him than
other envoys – especially if they met coming from Mass – and was held
apart from the rest of the diplomatic community. Writing to the Cardinal Secretary of State Alessandro Farnese, Poggio reported with satisfaction that the new emissary from Urbino '*mostrò temer di me* [showed
fear of me]'.[170]

The best way for Wyatt to conciliate the Emperor would be to show
himself a loyal son of the Church. Given his king's enmity to the
Pope, this would demand 'dexterity' indeed. Previous ambassadors at
Charles's court had secretly pledged loyalty to Rome, but each new
move by Henry against the Church made fidelity to the Holy See while
also serving the King less plausible, less possible. At the least, every
ambassador at the Imperial court must attend Mass. On St Luke's Day,
18 October 1537 a solemn procession celebrated the Holy League
against the Turk. As the procession wound through the streets of
Monzón to the church of San Francisco, the Emperor accompanied the

host carried ascendant. At the celebration of Mass, Garcia de Loaysa, Cardinal of Sigüenza and Inquisitor of Toledo, elevated the Corpus Domini in the presence of all the ambassadors. We may imagine Wyatt among them. The nuncio hoped that within the year there would be Mass in Constantinople.[171] But while the Holy League was celebrated circumstances had profoundly, unexpectedly altered. On 15 October the arrival in Monzón of Claude Dodieu, Seigneur de Velly, emissary from the Queen of France, had transformed the prospect of peace or war, disrupted any existing league and shifted every diplomatic balance. He was the herald of peace.[172]

Seeking Wyatt's stance in the long weeks in Monzón or in neighbouring Barbastro, we are caught in a web spun by the Imperial counsellors and peer into the gloom of a diplomacy of desperation. In utter uncertainty, Wyatt sent to England for instructions: first, John Mason rode in post on 16 October, then John Mantell ten days later.[173] It was uncertain whether they would be allowed to pass. In deepest secrecy, negotiations continued between the French envoy and Charles's ministers. No one could discover their nature, and soon no one was allowed to leave Monzón. When the Florentine ambassador rode toward Lleida on the pretext of buying a horse, he was arrested, taken before the Generale of Monzón and forced to swear to his truth on a crucifix. He was ransomed, and survived only by a 'miracle'.[174] The day after the celebration of the Holy League, de Velly departed for France, promising to return within three weeks. On 22 October the Emperor revealed to Wyatt and the Venetian ambassador how matters stood: Francis was inclined to peace, as was Charles himself.[175] Late at night on the 24th Wyatt returned from Monzón to Barbastro with grim news that 'a pestilential fever' was spreading.[176] From bad to worse.

The isolation Henry had so long feared now threatened, for the prospective peace between the two great rivals left him dangerously exposed. Wyatt, without instructions, without his secretary, was left to devise policy and make what shifts he could. In the last days of October an English courier was stopped at Fuenterrabía, the fortress-town on the Spanish border, and escorted to court. This messenger was Rouge Croix. Even a herald was not given free passage. He brought instructions now made obsolete by the overtures of peace which rendered pointless Henry's posturing as arbiter.[177] A disastrous audience with the Emperor ensued. The proposals for a marriage between Mary and the Infante were rebuffed, and Charles rejected any offer of peacemaking from Henry, for the Pope was universal arbiter between Christian princes. When Wyatt spoke dishonourably of the Pope he was dismissed, and his encounter with Cobos and Granvelle also descended to words '*di poco amore et gratia* [of little love and grace]'. Now Wyatt accused the Emperor of 'ingratitude' – the fateful word. The nuncio, Giovanni Poggio, heard from an English '*cavagliero* [gentleman]' that Wyatt was urging many to study '*libretti* [pamphlets]' of his '*piene d'heresie* [full of heresies]'. This 'seemed evil'.[178] At this nadir, Wyatt's 'good friend' John Dudley arrived. He came with news of the birth of the longed-for Prince Edward, Henry's heir, who would save the dynasty but be the death of Queen Jane, who soon succumbed to puerperal fever.[179] Dudley – 'the ambitious and subtle Alcibiades of England'[180] – was an intimate with whom Wyatt could confer, even conspire. Together, they conceived a diplomacy for the times.

In this world of countenances and appearances, we find Wyatt presenting a double face, as he must if he would please two princes. For the first time, we have his own account of 'playing the orator'. In a memorial written for Dudley as he left for England on about 9 November, Wyatt described their long audience with Charles a day or so earlier and we seem to hear their authentic voices. 'After good and long rejoicings and laughings which I never saw in him', the Emperor reported his putative peace with Francis. ('I knew the peace far enough off,' wrote Wyatt dismissively). The crux of the audience was an unspeakable offer: Charles's mediation between Henry and the Pope – 'he thought he would dream such a way to reconcile all those things if the King would'. Wyatt and Dudley were doubtful: 'though the King would, we thought the error so discovered that the people would never return to the yoke, yea, and much less the King, and that that mediation should be but vain'. With Granvelle the following day, they dismissed the offer out of hand – 'we thought it but vain to speak of that'. Still the Emperor offered to mediate, 'with as great secretness as he would for his life', saying that his overture must not be revealed to Henry, unless 'we thought the King would take it of a very friend'.[181]

Reading Charles's account of this audience alongside Wyatt's, we find diverse meanings intended and construed. Certainly, Wyatt and Dudley told him that their king was 'determined never to return to subjection to the Pope' – even if he wished to be reconciled, his subjects did not. 'Nevertheless', so Charles wrote to his ambassadors in England, 'the proposal did not seem altogether distasteful to them'. And he signalled his particular confidence in Wyatt: negotiations for the mediation would be entrusted to 'the English ambassador resident here'.[182] In greatest excitement, in cipher, the nuncio wrote to Cardinal Farnese that the Emperor was determined to return the English King to the faith and reconcile him to the Holy See. The English ambassadors '*si mostrano bravi* [show themselves to be fine men]', they believed that their king might be brought to concord with the Pope. Charles would write to Henry with a proposal. They all lived in hopes.[183] But soon praise of '*l'oratore Anglo*' turned to invective, and Poggio's obsession with the heretical threat to the Church came to be personified in Wyatt.

Poised to say the unsayable, to insist – as they must – that reconciliation was unthinkable, had Wyatt and the duplicitous Dudley allowed by wry smiles, sideways glances and raised eyebrows the possibility that their wayward prince might turn? Or even more. Charles admitted that Wyatt always 'indignantly rejected' the conditions imposed for the mediation as 'against his master's honour and conscience', yet we will discover the press of events causing Wyatt to waver.[184] For the Emperor, the ending of England's schism was part of his Imperial duty to defend Christendom, but there were other reasons. Through all these years the rumbling ground bass of his diplomacy was his enmity with Francis, and that distrust lived on even in the midst of truce and peace negotiations. But not only did he need Henry as a counter to the French King, he also hoped that with English aid the League's crusading fleet might sail into Constantinople. At around this time, hopes were bright even in Rome. 'God has opened a way' whereby the King of England, sharing the 'pious desire' for a crusade against the Turk, might enter the Holy League and be 'united with the Pope'.[185] These hopes were chimerical. By extreme casuistry, Henry might ally with the Bishop of Rome as *temporal* ruler, but could never ally with the Holy Father, spiritual head of Christendom. The Pope, however worldly, could hardly join a schismatic king in a Holy League. Yet burning to lead the crusade against the Turk, Charles hoped to effect reconciliation.[186] As Henry's regal offer to arbitrate was spurned, as his enemies made peace without him and were likely to become foes of foes against him, his ambassadors may have made promises without sanction, seeking any port in a diplomatic storm. When Charles warned that he would withdraw his ambassador from the English court, Wyatt urgently despatched a messenger to England on 20 November. But couriers were especially vulnerable as Francis and Charles were poised between peace and war.[187]

English messengers riding through France were now detained, lest Henry learn that Francis, his 'best friend and brother', was breaking his sworn promises not to treat with another prince. Accident – so it was assumed – delayed John Mason in Lyon, where he lay bed-ridden. Able neither to 'ride nor go', he 'sat him upon his bed' and wrote a self-exculpatory letter.[188] Suspicion attended this illness, rightly. There was nothing accidental about John Dudley's detention. Leaving Monzón on about 11 November, Dudley had ridden fast, but in Lyon he was held by the Cardinal of Tournon and the Chancellor of France, who had received news from Spain of his coming. To ensure that his vital message reached England, Dudley, 'who had perhaps learnt some subtlety in Spain', had sent his own messenger ahead towards Paris, disguised as a merchant. When Gardiner's servant, too, was stopped in Lyon, the incandescent Bishop spoke '*cose di foco* [fiery words]'. Still detained on 26 November, Dudley complained that his news would be 'cold', and that the scandal of his arrest which so dishonoured his king was in 'every mouth'.[189]

Through waiting weeks the ambassadors were all corralled together, first in Monzón, and then from about 7 December in Barcelona, while representatives of the Emperor and the French King conducted talks about talks, and negotiated where to negotiate. On 19 November Charles had left Monzón for Valladolid, to ponder what he could bear to cede.[190] In the making of peace, the King of England had a passive part. Never trusting Francis, Charles still needed Henry's friendship as counter, and held on to the faint hope of his reconciliation with Rome and aid against the Turk. But ominously for Henry, one reason adduced for peace between the Emperor and the French King was 'in case of the Pope fulminating censures or invoking the help of the secular arm against the King of England'.[191] While the plenipotentiaries parleyed in no-man's-land, Charles revolved courses of action so secretly that he revealed them to no one, and said that if he could, he would hide them from his own mind.[192] At the end of December 'all we ambassadors' were still '*al buio* [in the dark]', uncertain what to do, and hopelessly sending messenger after messenger for news and instructions.[193] Wyatt was in the dark also, about events in Spain and at home, and now left to his own devices – even to his poetic devices.

And at the English court, denied audience with the King, Diego Hurtado de Mendoza despaired of his embassy and exile, and longed for home.[194] His desolation took poetic form. To Don Gonzalo Pérez, the royal secretary, at some time unknown, he addressed a verse epistle: 'what good is it to be born in Spain . . . if we have to die in a foreign land'?

> *servir á reyes, residir en corte,*
> *es todo humo de esperanzas vanas,*
> *y no os darán jamás cosa que importe . . .*

> Serving kings, residing at court –
> Smoke and vain hopes.
> They never give you anything important to do . . .[195]

I Restles Rest in Spayne

Off cartage he that worthie warier
    could overcome, but cowld not use his chaunce
    and I like wise off all my long indever
Tho   the sherpe conquest tho fortune did avaunce
    cowld not yt use, the hold that is gyvin over
    I unpossest, so hangith in balaunce
    off warr my pees, reward of all my payne
    At Mountzon thus I restles rest in spayne
               TV

In Wyatt's own poetry manuscript, in his handwriting, is this poem which *seems* to have all to do with his particular circumstances.[1] But much more than an exercise in autobiography, this is an experiment in poetry. He wrote steadfastly in his familiar English vernacular, turning it into something rare and strange by translating it to African Carthage and to the remote Aragonese outpost where Wyatt sometime languished. And he used a novel verse form: ottava rima. Henry Howard, Earl of Surrey, learning from Wyatt 'what might be said in rhyme', found in the concluding lines of 'Off cartage he' the quintessential Wyatt 'that quick could never rest', and he imitated them:

> . . . amidst the hills in base Boulogne;
> Where I am now, as restless to remain,
> Against my will, full pleased with my pain.[2]

Following Wyatt, he used the decasyllabic line. A 'new company of makers' were creating a new poetry for English.

The opening lines of Wyatt's poem lead back to Petrarch's *Rime* 103, where he galvanised Stefano Colonna to learn from Hannibal.

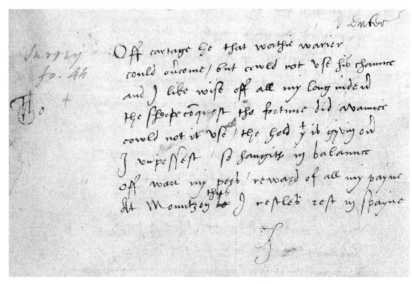

'*Tho*' writes his name alongside 'Off Cartage he' in the Egerton manuscript

Vinse Anibàl, et non seppe usar poi
ben la vittoriosa sua ventura.

Hannibal was victorious, but he did not know
later how to make use of his victorious fortune.[3]

Petrarch adjured Colonna to take up '*l'honorata spada* [the honourable
sword]' in his feud against the Orsini and to follow where fortune led.
But Wyatt, who learnt from Petrarch how enmeshed were the fortunes
of love and war, wrote not a sonnet but a *strambotto* which allowed the
images of war and martial conquest to invoke a lover's despair at his
dispossession and undoing. For Wyatt, as for any Petrarchist, love was
conceived in martial metaphor: love was war, the lover the warrior,
and wounded. As he called to memory the famous general who once
had made Rome tremble, but who was conquered and his city razed
because he failed to follow where fortune led, he contemplated how
'I likewise' could not exploit a victory so keenly fought, so hard won.
Wyatt did not forget that Hannibal and Scipio Africanus were both
undone by the treachery of women.[4] From the first part of the poem,
with its assonance and long lines – where Hannibal's victory and the
speaker's 'sherpe conquest', Hannibal's failure to seize fortune and the

speaker's impotence are juxtaposed – he traverses to the tension of broken lines and to the paralysis of his 'unpossest' persona, whose chance of peace swings like a pendulum in the brilliant antithesis and compression of the closing lines:

> so hangith in balaunce
> off warr my pees, reward of all my payne
> At Mountzon thus I restles rest in spayne.

On '*my peace*' the whole poem – and all the speaker's hopes – turns. That peace, so ardently desired and so elusive, trembles in the balance: if it falls one way there will be a reward for so much 'payne'; if another, that 'payne' will never be palliated. As so often in Wyatt's verse, his 'I' is caught in stasis: here not treading an endless maze nor imprisoned in liberties or standing not fast, but restlessly resting.[5] Wyatt seems to live the paradox. A window seems to open on his life, at this moment when peace and war hung in the balance: opens, only to close again.

The ideas of Carthage, of Hannibal, of the fortunes of war and of love were vivid in the imaginations of poets at Charles's court. When he led the forces of Christendom against the infidel at Tunis in the summer of 1535 Charles had landed near the ruins of ancient Carthage, and in his great victory he was soon compared to Scipio Africanus, the destroyer of Carthage. Poets celebrated this 'worthy warrior'. Garcilaso de la Vega, the great 'maker' of Castilian poetry, fought in the Tunisian campaign. To the friend of his heart, his fellow poet Juan Boscán, Garcilaso addressed his sonnet XXXIII where '*aquí*', here – at the site of Carthage – the images of war and suffering and of incendiary destruction are also images of the poet's suffering, his wounds of love:

> *Aquí donde el romano encendimiento,*
> *dond' el fuego y la llama licensiosa*
> *solo el nombre dexaron a Cartago,*
>   *buelve y rebuelve amor mi pensamiento,*
> *hiere y enciend' el alma temerosa,*
> *y en llanto y en ceniza me deshago.*

Here, where the Roman conflagration, where fire and licentious flame left
  only the name of Carthage,
love turns and turns again my thought, wounds and inflames my fearful
  soul, and in tears and ashes I am undone.

Again in Elegy II, also for Boscán, Garcilaso contemplates Charles's victory and the glories of the Roman past.[6] Garcilaso, Wyatt's exact contemporary though to Wyatt unknown, had died in a skirmish in 1536,
but his memory was bright for those who knew what they, and the life
of poetry, had lost. Another combatant at Tunis was a poet, and he, too,
thought on the example of Hannibal's greatness and his destruction, his
self-destruction. Imitating an epigram of Michele Marullo, Diego Hurtado de Mendoza wrote a famous sonnet, 'De Aníbal'.[7] Bernardo Tasso
also sailed with the Imperial fleet. In sonnet IX of his *Libro terzo de gli
amori* (1537) he, like Garcilaso, thought on the sacred ruins of ancient
Carthage, and his mind turned and turned again to the pains of love:

> *Sacra ruina che 'l gran cerchio giri*
> > *Di Cartagine antica, ignude arene*
> > *D'alte memorie e gloriose piene,*
> > *Dicui convien ch'ancor la fama spiri,*
> *Ascoltate pietose i miei sospiri,*
> > *Che manda il cor a la sua dolce spene,*
> > *Mentre qui Marte sanguinoso tiene*
> > *Lungi da' suoi be' lumi i miei desiri:*

Sacred ruin of ancient Carthage with its great surrounding wall,
bare sand steeped in great and glorious memories,
from which Fame ought still to draw inspiration,
listen with pity to my sighs,
sent by my heart to its tender hope,
while blood-stained Mars keeps my longing
far from her beautiful eyes.[8]

Sailing to Carthage, Tasso had met his Maecenas, Don Luis de Zúñiga
y Ávila, who wrote an eyewitness account of the Emperor's epic victory. To him – 'A Don Luigi Davila' – Tasso dedicated sonnet XVI of
his *Libro terzo*:

I Restles Rest in Spayne

Già veggio Poesia lieta uscir fuori
Al ben seren, col favor vostro solo,
Et obliando ogni passato duolo,
Cantar con dotto stile arme et amori

Now I see poetry emerging happily into good calm times
by your favour alone; forgetting all past pain she sings
of arms and love in learned style.[9]

During long weeks in Monzón, as the French and Imperial counsellors talked endlessly about talks, the ambassadors of other powers were sequestered, cast in each other's company, powerless and bored. How did they pass their time? Were they learning to sing of arms and love in learned style? In November they were awaiting the arrival in Monzón of a man already known at the Spanish court, whose reputation went before him, a poet who had rebelled against the old plaints of courtly love and the excesses of Petrarchism. This was Bernardo Tasso. Rhyming his own name – '*vuestro Lasso*' – with that of '*culto Taso*', Garcilaso had looked to Tasso's poetic inspiration to lead him to the summit of Helicon.[10] Tasso was travelling to Aragon from Venice where he had just published *Libro terzo de gli amori*, with its manifesto for a new poetry. He reached Monzón on 17 November.[11] His mission was desperate: not to teach the poets, but to save Filippo Strozzi from '*il macello* [the slaughterhouse]'. After the defeat of the republican exiles of Florence at the battle of Montemurlo in July 1537, Strozzi had been captured and thrown into Florence's strongest fortress, the opponent of tyranny and its victim.[12] Tasso was secretary to Ferrante Sanseverino, Prince of Salerno, a great prince of the Empire and patron of poetry, but he came to the Emperor's court as envoy of the Strozzi as well as of the Prince.[13]

Perhaps Tasso came trailing clouds of romance. Cast as the lover of the famous courtesan Tullia d'Aragona in Sperone Speroni's *Dialogo dell'Amore*, his character debated with her the nature of love. Though not printed until 1542, this dialogue was set at the fateful moment when Tasso parted from Tullia to serve Sanseverino – a parting which promised to be the inspiration of poetry which would make the lovers and their love immortal – and was first read publicly in Venice in June

1537.[14] In life, Bernardo Tasso may not have been Tullia d'Aragona's lover, but Filippo Strozzi had been, and Tasso came to Spain to save him.[15] Not Bernardo Tasso's poetry, but his son Torquato's, became immortal, yet Bernardo's influence on poetry was considerable, especially in Spain. He proposed a 'poetic revolution', not in metrics, but in freedom from the constraints of medieval courtly love lament, and in free imitation of the subject matter of the best Greek and Roman poets. Classical subjects would be adapted to traditional vernacular verse forms, and in a move to myth and fable, the third-person narrator would replace the pathetic 'I' of the poet–lover.[16] Tasso annotated copies of Horace's *Ars poetica* and would imitate the Horatian ode.[17] Here was a man who personified the lover–warrior, and was also primed to teach a new poetry. Monzón might have become a school for a new 'company of makers'.

Did Wyatt engage in discussion of a new poetry while in Spain? Sometimes we catch glimpses of transfiguring conversations between ambassadors and court poets. 'One day when in Granada with Navaggiero' in 1526, Juan Boscán began talking with him about poetry. Andrea Navagero, the Venetian ambassador and a renowned neo-Latin poet, 'asked me why I did not try to write in the Castilian tongue some sonnets and other art forms used by the good authors of Italy'. Boscán decided 'to be the first that has joined the Castilian tongue with the Italian way of writing'. He and Garcilaso – most devoted of friends, most innovative of poets – began to transform Castilian poetry so radically that Cristóbal de Castillejo called for the Holy Office to censure the Spanish poets who wrote in Italian metres.[18] Torquato Tasso, in his 'Apologia' to *Gerusalemme Liberata* (*Jerusalem Delivered*), claimed that Don Luis de Zúñiga y Ávila and another gentleman of the Spanish court proposed to his father that he turn the Spanish adventures of Amadís de Gaula into an epic poem in Italian. Whether this was first mooted at the time of Tasso's desperate mission to Monzón, or during happier times which followed in Barcelona, or whether later in the Low Countries, is hard to tell.[19] Wyatt, *italianizzato* and so brilliantly versed in Romance languages and Latin, might easily have discussed vernacular poetry and prosody with the most avant-garde poets of Charles's court, might even have discussed with Tasso a new poetry inspired by classical models. Whether he did or not, is quite unknown. Yet homage to conversations in Aragon may perhaps be found in Wyatt's poetry, especially in 'Off cartage he', where a classical subject is translated into a new vernacular and a new form.

If these poets at Charles's court ever deigned to think of English poetry, their ignorance of the language, their conviction of England's irremediable barbarism, prevented any reciprocal debate. For them, English was a language not fitted – literally not fitted – for the new poetry or for the hendecasyllabic line which was its metrical foundation. Later, Thomas Chaloner would compose verse in Latin so that he might converse with poets at the Spanish court, but whether Wyatt did so remains mysterious.[20] When we find Wyatt talking of poetry in Spain, it is within his embassy. His *familia* became a tiny 'company of makers' in exile, and some had a part to play in the poetic enterprise. The Egerton manuscript – Wyatt's personal anthology – went with him and his company to Spain, as perhaps it had travelled with him for years before. During their journeys, in all the lingering weeks of following the court, his servants entered into the manuscript fair copies of Wyatt's verse from his rough drafts. Jason Powell's closest study of the manuscript suggests which poems were copied while in Spain. One of the scribes, writing in a neat secretary hand, was John Brereton, and the handwriting of two other – unknown – copyists appears.[21] In the embassy, Wyatt and Mason nurtured a little school for secretaries and fledgling ambassadors. Thomas Wriothesley sent his young servant Edmund Baker, hoping that Wyatt would be his 'good master' and encourage him in 'the attaining of the Latin tongue': 'I trust you like him well.' Well enough that Baker became tutor to Wyatt's Cobham nephews.[22] Not well enough to make him scribe of his poetry.

The role of Brereton and the other scribes was perhaps simply as amanuensis. But some of Wyatt's *familia* became his poetic companions, and to them he 'taught what might be said in rhyme'. Sometimes, the manuscript reveals Wyatt alone, engaged in the loneliest private process of composition. At other times writing poetry was a shared enterprise to amuse and distract himself and his friends. Perhaps in

Spain, perhaps when he returned to England, the 'rakehell' John Mantell was gathering an anthology of poetry in a manuscript which passed in time to his companion in embassy, George Blage. This manuscript – often called the Blage manuscript – contains verse which may have been Mantell's, and some which was Blage's. And it celebrated the poetry of Wyatt, for these young men – brilliant, but flawed – were the recorders of Wyatt's poetry, and sometimes its editors, determined to keep alight his poetic flame.[23] Mantell entered sixteen poems into the manuscript, six of which are also found in the Egerton manuscript, one of them – 'from thes hye hilles' – in Wyatt's handwriting. There are signs that Mantell carried poems in his head and copied them from memory. One of the six – 'Loo what hytt ys to love' – is a double 'answer' poem: a 'statement' of five stanzas, followed by an 'answer' of five stanzas, and a 'reply' of five stanzas: the quintessential game of the 'courtly makers'.[24] Later, when the manuscript belonged to him, Blage made corrections to the text of twelve Wyatt poems in the manuscript.[25] Another of the poetic adepts was Thomas Chaloner. Though better known as a Latin poet, Chaloner translated into English Ovid, Boethius and Ariosto.[26] In Spain, did these young men divert themselves and their embattled master by challenges in verse?

In the Egerton manuscript is a verse claimed by '*Tho*' which translates a madrigal by Dragonetto Bonifacio (first printed in around 1535). In it Wyatt keeps the steady beat of a musical rhythm. Beneath Wyatt's verse – an entreaty to a pitiless woman – George Blage inscribed his mirroring reply:[27]

> Madame withouten many wordes
> ons I ame sure ye will or no
> and if ye will then leve yor bordes   *games; jests; bantering*
> and use yor wit and shew it so
> And with a beck ye shall me call   *gesture of command*
> and if of oon that burneth alwaye
> *Tho.*   ye have any pitie at all
> aunswer him faire with [ay] or nay
> Yf it be [ay] I shalbe fayne
> if it be nay frendes as before

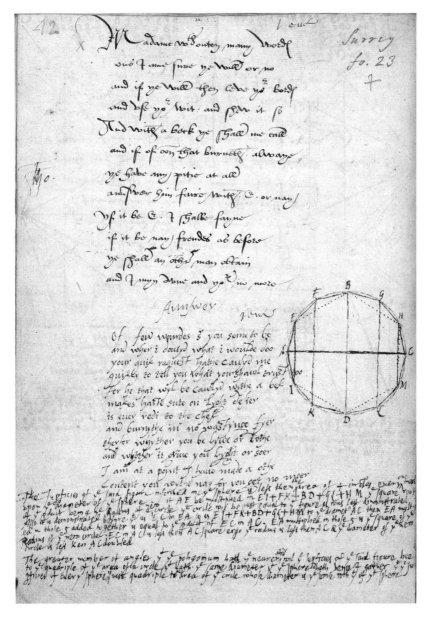

Thomas Wyatt's poetic challenge and George Blage's response. The geometry homework may belong to someone of the Harington family

> ye shall an othr man obtain
> and I myn owne and yors no more

Aunswer

> *Of few wourdes sir you seme to be*
> *and wher i doutyd what i woulde doo*
> *your quik request hathe causyd me*
> *quikly to tell you what you shawl trust too*
> *For he that wyl be cawlyd wythe a bek*
> *makes haste sute on lyght desier*   *easy*
> *is ever redi to the chek*   *rebuff*
> *and burnythe in no wastynge fyer*
> *therfor whyther you be lywe or lothe*   *lief: agreeable*
> *and whyther it griue you lyght or soer*
> *I am at a poynt I haue made a othe*
> *Content you wythe nay for you get no moer*

Whether Blage, as apprentice poet, answered *ex tempore*, with a smiling Wyatt at his side, or whether much later after long pondering his reply, is a matter of conjecture.[28] Blage answers the 'quik request' to 'use yor wit and shew it so' and, taking up Wyatt's challenge, responds within 'few wourdes', within twelve lines, within the page. Playing the scornful lady, he rejects the suitor, point by point, and doubting the sincerity of this lover who 'burnythe in no wastynge fyer', [s]he has no hesitation in saying 'nay'.[29] In the interplay between the two verses we find Wyatt and Blage playing on words, playing on the lack of female company, certainly 'frendes as before'.

Amidst all the deprivations and disappointments of life in Spain, the company of the embassy household was consolation and refuge. Life-long friendships grew among young men cast together in this little band, them against the world. Looking back on his time in Wyatt's service Thomas Chamberlain would record his duty 'to advance all such as were belonging to my old master to whom I was much bound'. In 1545 he was still in close touch with some of his fellows, including John Mason.[30] Mason remembered with piety all his life the duties owed to his friends in Wyatt's household, and he would protect Wyatt's beloved Bess Darrell. At the end of Mason's life 'Quyryne [Quirinus] Blage' – perhaps

George Blage's son – was 'of my Chamber', one of his closest attendants.[31] Friendships were cherished, but nor did enmities fade. Friends
of friends and foes of foes, Wyatt's servants would become enemies of
their master's enemies. Embassy was a kind of exile, bringing separation from family and home comforts, and from the congenial company
of women. In Naples Mason had marvelled at 'the dames in the streets
and churches', 'more like heavenly things than women'. Sadly for him,
'they be shut up. In this only I find fault'. In Spain, women were more
cloistered still. 'Friars and monks be in great reverence, to whom only
it is lawful to speak with a man's wife alone.'[32] Francesco Guicciardini
had chillingly recorded the likely consequences in Spain of adultery: 'a
husband may kill his wife and the lover without jeopardy upon finding
them in the act or proving that it has been committed'.[33]

The young Englishmen, accustomed to the easier exchange between
men and women at home, were now fated to gaze at women from afar
and to pine for beauties forever unavailable to them. Maybe they had
left mistresses at home, but they had not left wives. Mason was bound
for the priesthood, though delaying his entry interminably. George
Blage was still unmarried. Mantell had married Anne Browne, but in
Spain he may have been a widower. By November 1538, he was free to
marry again, and Anne Fiennes, daughter of Lord Dacre of the south,
became his second wife. Peter Rede thought wistfully of 'his old play
fellow, the good wife at the Three Bells'.[34] Life in embassy meant male
camaraderie and the bonding which alternate boredom and shared
danger brought. Celibacy was to be endured, though perhaps there
were furtive visits to ladies of the night. Sometimes, maybe, it was a
relief – despite all the talk, despite all the rhyming – to be free for the
while from the perturbations and perplexities of women. But in Barcelona they could gaze on masked noblewomen like boys in a sweetshop.

The prospect of Christmas in Barcelona held an allure, especially
after the dreariness of Monzón and its attendant tensions. Barcelona
was 'a very beautiful city . . . full of lovely gardens, planted with myrtle,
oranges and cedars' – very beautiful even to Andrea Navagero, who
was accustomed to the glories of Venice. Most 'memorable' among
the beautiful churches and religious houses for Navagero was the royal

monastery of Santa Maria de Jonqueres. The nuns were noblewomen of the Order of Santiago and bore the badge of the red sword, as did its knights. Enticingly for ambassadors, they were not enclosed and were even allowed to marry. Memorable for Wyatt also, who later – and maybe now – enjoyed their company.[35] Cartloads of tapestries and the grandest of grandees had been sent ahead to Barcelona, for the Emperor dreamt of a festival of reconciliation with Francis. Although the peace between them was, as it happened, not a peace – only a truce, and conditional – in the following weeks Barcelona was the scene of great celebrations. At masked balls 'each gallant conversed with the lady he preferred', and noblewomen and courtiers, dressed in brocades and silk, danced to the music of sackbuts and clarions. Even Cardinal Jacobazzi, the papal legate sent to effect the peace, attended the masquerades. There were feasts and tournaments, and courtiers showed their prowess by tilting and running at the ring.[36]

One of the love feasts in Barcelona in that New Year was between Wyatt and the Emperor. Charles was showing extraordinary, 'inexpressible' favour to Wyatt. Sequestered in his chamber following the death of his sister-in-law, the Duchess of Savoy, on 7 January 1538, Charles sent a gentleman every day to treat with Wyatt and to relay secret news of the peace negotiations.[37] Charles's perennial dread of ceding Milan now – and always – stood in the way of peace and led him again to consider investing it as an Imperial fief on Dom Luis married to Mary of England, and to contemplate an English alliance 'to the prejudice and damage of France'.[38] By 12 January 1538 Mason returned from England with letters empowering Wyatt to negotiate. 'Though sundry clouds for the time did obscure and darken our ancient amities', Henry hoped that he and Charles might be 'entire friends', and that he would be included in any peace. The Emperor must be assured that Henry would never do anything not 'quadrant with the word of God'. And Wyatt might promise Henry's aid in the crusade against 'that common enemy the Turk'.[39] In audience with the Emperor on 12 or 13 January Wyatt gave these happy assurances.

The prospect of a General Council of the Church was 'the thing this King dreads most'. The General Council was a representative assembly of Christendom, with power to judge and to condemn, and Henry, who had divorced Katherine of Aragon and broken the unity of the Church, had reason to fear its sanctions. In 1535 Pope Paul III had proclaimed a forthcoming General Council, and by 1537 the convening of the Council, probably at Mantua, had seemed imminent.[40] As Henry admitted in April 1538:

Supposing . . . that all Christian princes . . . attended the Council, which I myself do not intend to do, it would seem as if I wished to make a God of my own . . . separate from the rest of Christendom, which, besides being a great shame, might bring great harm upon me.[41]

The King had been urgently sponsoring the writing of tracts and pamphlets in order to ventilate through the courts of Christendom his arguments that the Pope had no power to summon a General Council. The heretical *libretti* which Wyatt was circulating at the Emperor's court in early November 1537 – to the nuncio's fury – were probably copies of *A protestation made for the most mighty and moste redoubted kynge of Englande*. Here the royal supremacy and the usurpations of the Bishop of Rome were trumpeted: 'He nor his hath no authority nor jurisdiction in England . . . that which he hath usurped against God's law and extorted, by violence, we, by good right, take from him again.'[42] The tract was reissued, with an introductory letter from Henry to Charles, and translated into Latin. Disseminated at royal command, these *libretti* were meant to form the basis of Wyatt's audiences with the Emperor, to enable him to explain precisely the complex political and theological arguments for the royal supremacy, and – crucially – to keep him from diverging from official policy in his oratory.[43] Of course, to explain them at all was to set Wyatt on a collision course with the Emperor.

More than a decade later Charles would still remember with anger an audience with Wyatt. On 17 January Wyatt came armed with arguments from his king which would demand all his 'dexterity', all his oratorical power: papal authority had been 'mere usurpation' since the time of Constantine; the Donation of Constantine was false. His king would never attend a General Council convoked by the Bishop of Rome. So Wyatt argued in the 'most absolute', 'most forcible' manner.

When Charles dismissed Wyatt and his arguments – 'though in moderate terms, and without asperity of any kind' – Wyatt attempted to read out 'certain allegations in writing'. 'Not being a good French scholar' – so he implausibly claimed – he 'had written a paper . . . containing his own ideas', extolling an Imperial authority so absolute that Emperors could 'make and unmake Popes' and convene Councils. Charles 'declined to hear' Wyatt's lecture, refused to receive his essay, 'saying that no doubt they were scholastic compositions'. No doubt they were. Mason had brought from England a – highly partial – history of General Councils, with a refutation of the claims of 'one man which would usurp the power by Christ to Princes only given . . . and take upon him the monarchy of all the world'.[44] That 'one man' was, of course, the Pope. Wyatt's lecture was peculiarly ill-timed, for he delivered it on the day the papal legate came to court.

Cardinal Jacobazzi's mission was to mediate between the French King and the Emperor. At that moment the nuncio anticipated not peace but renewed war, more terrible than ever, and the 'ruin of the whole world'.[45] Jacobazzi also came to persuade Charles to the 'holy and necessary work' of the Council, and when he discovered that the English King attempted to thwart it, he was incensed. Henry's arguments from history – that the first great General Councils had been convened by emperors, not popes – he dismissed as '*pazzie* [lunacies]' and errors, and their proponent – Wyatt – as '*pazzarello*' and '*molto leggiero*', a lunatic and lightweight.[46] Since the Holy Father was universal arbiter, Jacobazzi was enraged by Henry's offers to mediate peace, and he interrogated the chastened Emperor: when had Wyatt proposed this arbitration? At Monzón, and again in Barcelona, answered Charles. The King was trying 'to send a puppy between the Emperor's legs to make him stumble', reported Jacobazzi. Wyatt, a puppy. If peace were made, Henry 'would come running' back to Rome.[47] Cobos and Granvelle assured the legate that they would never listen to the 'dishonest proposals' of the English ambassador.[48]

When the nuncio condemned any alliance with 'that rebel', Charles protested that he could not be 'without friends amidst so many enemies'.[49] He needed to hope – against hope – that Henry might once again be 'the Pope's friend', and offered to mediate. Wyatt became convinced – convinced by necessity, by 'the evil likely to result in future from want of acquiescence' – that Henry must seek papal forgiveness.[50] The story circulating in Barcelona was that Wyatt was persuaded, and that his king did seek reconciliation.[51] On 29 January Alfonso Rossetto visited Wyatt, seeking news. Why ask Wyatt for news? Because he had received a courier a week earlier, and because he was believed to have Charles's confidence. In fact, Wyatt, who 'daily and earnestly solicited' decisions from the Emperor – would there be peace with Francis, would a General Council be called, would Mary marry Dom Luis? – had heard nothing.[52] But at dead of night on 3 February the nuncio reported that Wyatt had at last received news from England: his king was sending a 'favourite' to treat for Christina of Denmark, the dowager Duchess of Milan, to become Henry's fourth queen. On the 7th Charles wrote to his sister that he was minded to support the marriage.[53]

Wyatt urgently sent messengers home. On 3 February an 'English gentleman' – probably George Blage – rode fast from Barcelona. Arriving at the French court at Moulins four days later, he told Gardiner of all that Wyatt had treated in Spain; told him, too, that the Emperor 'was making daily to that ambassador the greatest shows of love that could be desired', and had entrusted him with the making of an alliance. 'Now was the time for the English King to give law to the world', so Cobos and Granvelle had told Wyatt.[54] In England on the 16th, Cranmer and others were granted powers to treat with the Imperial ambassadors for a general peace and a closer alliance between Henry and Charles.[55] In Spain, the arrival of the Infante of Portugal on 17 February seemed to prove the imminence of the marriage alliance.[56] This was the high point of Wyatt's diplomacy.

Charles was now like Hannibal, 'that worthie warier', who 'could overcome, but cowld not use his chaunce'. Victor at Tunis, a new Caesar Africanus, he had planned a crusade against the Turk, and as the Holy League was formed had dreamt of being Emperor of Constantinople by the summer of 1538.[57] Through the winter of 1537 – 'now when it seemeth my successes come something handsomely to pass'

– his hopes were high.[58] In January 1538, following Khair-ad-Din Barbarossa's raids in the Venetian archipelago, Charles and the Venetians were making great preparations in reprisal. Aid from England became vital, and Wyatt was empowered to promise it.[59] All hung in the balance of peace or war with Francis. Early in February Charles sent his favourite, Luis de Zúñiga y Ávila, in post to Rome and then on to Genoa to Admiral Doria.[60] While conceiving overarching Holy, Roman designs for the salvation of Christendom – the defeat of the infidel, the 'reduction' of heretics, the extension of his Christian empire – the Emperor must react to the play of events, to uncertainty. Though he protested that he was 'not a friend of Fortune',[61] he lived in a world of contingency, and the compromise of ideals might be necessary in a greater cause. So it was that the Holy Roman Emperor treated with the English King, through the mediation of the 'English orator'. Appalled by Henry's schism, Charles needed his friendship; incensed by Wyatt's reading him lectures on Church history and political theory, he needed him as agent. So, when Wyatt argued that Charles must 'invalidate the Donation of Constantine and appropriate the temporal possessions of the Pope', he was diverted only 'with moderation', and excused because 'he had no charge . . . the matter was beyond his province'.[62] Years before, Charles had learnt that sometimes it was politic to turn a deaf ear. When Castiglione, as nuncio, had complained in 1525 that 'many unjust complaints were made against the Pope', the Emperor replied – as he did later to Wyatt – 'God had made him king of men and not king of tongues'.[63]

And Wyatt: which evasions, which unkeepable promises did he make? Amidst the smoke and mirrors, his words and actions are clouded. Since arriving in Spain, he had sent messenger after messenger with letters, but of all his official reports sent between April 1537 and June 1538 only the November memorial to Dudley has been found. Two letters to Lord Lisle remain (for grim reasons: Lisle's correspondence would be seized).[64] Otherwise, we hear Wyatt's words relayed by others, extracts from his letters quoted back to him, his moods and actions reported second-hand, not always favourably. In England – so his friends assured him – his initiatives were commended. Yet, writing on 1 March,

Cromwell cast Wyatt's 'fair words' back at him, with a warning of just how much hung upon them: 'Mr Wiat, now handle this matter in such earnest sort with the Emperor as the King, who by your fair words hath conceived a certain to find assured friendship there, be not deceived.'[65] Later, called to answer for his actions, Wyatt protested that the King had often thanked him for 'suche practyses' as he had used to gain intelligence, and asked what else he should have done. 'And yf a mane shulde be dreven to be so scrupulouse to do nothynge withowt warrant, manye occasions of good service shulde schape hym.'[66] This was the ambassador's – especially the resident ambassador's – dilemma: how was he to act when his instructions were remote from the circumstances in which he found himself?

Machiavelli had expressed the problem with typical acuity. Writing to Raffaelo Girolami in 1522, he began: 'How to carry out a commission faithfully [*fedelmente*] is known to everyone who is good, but to carry it out adequately [*sufficientemente*] is the difficulty.' That '*sufficientemente*' suggested a certain deviousness is implied by his advice that 'sometimes it is necessary to conceal a matter with words, but to do so in such a way that it does not appear, or if it is revealed, have a defence prepared'.[67] Dissimulation would be needed – so Dolet acknowledged – where the ambassador had to deal with those who were 'past masters of pretence' (he was thinking of the Pope and Italian powers): 'he should likewise pretend and dissimulate, and should let his speech be greatly at variance with his thoughts'. The ambassador's difficulty was acute where, 'in the making of a treaty of alliance', 'a matter lying beyond the limits of your orders comes into discussion'. In that case, 'see that you merely discuss it, and that you promise to furnish nothing until your king has been advised' and his consent received. 'But', Dolet allowed, 'it often happens that an occasion is so urgent that you cannot wait for a reply.' What then? The ambassador must act, act quickly 'so that no opportunity may pass and be lost through delay'. Dolet turned from realism to happy contemplation of a king who would countenance the mistakes of his well-intentioned ambassador, who used his chance but was overcome by fortune.

Now whether the wisdom of your act will be proved by the outcome is indeed a matter of chance, to be dreaded in some degree, and yet you should not have the slightest anxiety about the result, provided you feel that you have taken no action except when prompted by prudence and induced by an apparent advantage (to the king). For fortune and chance prevail in everything.

If anything should go wrong, that king 'will readily accept the plea that it was a matter of chance, and we shall be upheld by a clear conscience'. A king so indifferent to fortune, so trusting of an ambassador's discretion, was far different from Wyatt's. It would be prudent to keep certain things quiet, advised Dolet: 'for in consultation many matters are discussed for the purpose of observing the various interests of men'.[68] Wyatt had acted like Dolet's prudent ambassador – 'yf in these matters I have presumede to be trustie more then I was trusted, surely the zele of the kinges service drowe [drove, drew] me to yt'[69] – yet when his seizing of *occasioni* came to be distrusted, no excuse would serve.

The ambassador must act according to his discretion, but that discretion was often clouded by his ignorance and by the deception of others. In his *ricordi* Francesco Guicciardini reflected pragmatically on the ambassador's life, drawing on his own youthful experience as ambassador to Ferdinand of Aragon. 'Some princes', he wrote, 'confide to their ambassadors all their secret intentions . . . Others deem it better to tell their ambassador only as much as they want the other prince to believe.' The prince who would use an ambassador in order 'to have others believe a lie, must first deceive the ambassador. For if he thinks he is representing the thoughts of his prince, an ambassador will act and speak more effectively than he would if he knew he were lying.'

Such deception had its own dangers. Since no instructions could be detailed enough to cover every eventuality, 'discretion must teach them to accommodate themselves to the end generally being pursued. But if the ambassador does not fully know that end, he cannot pursue it, and therefore he may err in a thousand ways.'[70] A common way for ambassadors to err was to 'take the side of the prince at whose court they are', and so to be 'suspected either of corruption or of seeking rewards, or at least of having been bedazzled by the endearments and kindnesses' shown to them. But the real reason for such partiality was that 'the ambassador has the affairs of that prince constantly before his eyes', a proximity which obscures his judgement. The ambassador's own prince, however, who observes from a distance, 'quickly detects the mistakes of his minister and will often attribute to evil design what is more probably caused by bad judgement. If you are to become an ambassador, heed this well, for it is a matter of great importance.'[71]

With which necessary compromises, with what dissimulation did Wyatt live, as he persuaded his king by 'fair words', even while he conciliated the Emperor, and was 'bedazzled' by endearments? At the court of his Most Catholic Majesty, he found a way of living which made possible his diplomacy and the gathering of intelligence. This demanded a certain self-presentation. First, the ambassador must 'show himself' to be a devout Christian. If there were a distinction between being a good Christian and appearing to be one, the appearance was essential.[72] As Wyatt bowed before the elevated host in San Francisco in Monzón, he formally observed the ancient worship which had been the visible sign of the unity of Christendom. Every time he communed with Charles after Mass or at some Church festival he led him to believe that they shared the same vision of the path to salvation and the same hope of Christian reconciliation.[73] Attending church and the celebration of Mass was a public duty, and it was in politic terms that Wyatt described this conformity to the King: 'Mason and I by cawse of the name that Inglyshe men then had to be all Lutherans' 'some tymes shewe our selves in the Churche togyther that men conceavyd not an evell opynion of us'.[74] For Pate and Mason, who genuinely longed for the end of schism, there was no hypocrisy. Wyatt, who so hated feigning at the courts of princes, whose persona protests to John Poyntz –

> I cannot crouche nor knele nor do suche wrong
> to wurchippe them like God on erthe alone
> that are like wolfes thes sely Lambes among

– came to hate dissembling in churches more. We will see, at length, how unbearable he found any distinction between 'truth of inward heart' and outward show in religion. Where his religious sympathies lay while he lived in Spain remains his secret, but they may have been changing. On 8 February Rouge Croix rode in haste, carrying Wyatt's letter to Lord Lisle in Calais. At the head of this letter, which was in Mason's hand, not Wyatt's, was a cross.[75] This might protect English letters in Spanish kingdoms, but it also marked a traditional piety – certainly Mason's and Lisle's, and perhaps Wyatt's still.

Even the idea of Henry's reconciliation to Rome would soon be unsustainable, however 'fair' Wyatt's words, however Catholic his behaviour. In December 1537 Henry had promised to send 'doctors' to Spain: 'certain personages, learned and of . . . honest gravity' to present his arguments about popes and Councils. Charles agreed to receive them.[76] Their impending arrival alarmed the legate and intrigued the court. Poggio warned of the scandal and danger of listening to their heresies. 'They came to do evil', judged Jacobazzi, and would be able to reason more powerfully than 'this ambassador whom I consider very frivolous'.[77] No one dreaded their arrival more than Wyatt and Mason. No doubt the mission of the two doctors – Dr Edmund Bonner and Dr Simon Heynes – was very important, very solemn, for they were charged to argue for the royal supremacy and to protest against papal power and the papally summoned General Council. There was no danger that they would take it – or themselves – insufficiently seriously.[78] Pompous and sanctimonious, they would inevitably be set on a collision course with Wyatt and Mason, who had their own learning and were so scornful of clerical pretensions. Wyatt knew, as Guicciardini knew, that princes distrusted their ambassadors and kept watch over them from a distance. This was Cromwell's 'practise': 'by lyke [he] desyered Bonarde to be a spye over me . . . to fynd whether yt were trewe that I dyd so good service as was reported'.[79] With Bonner and Heynes observing their every move and reporting it dutifully home, it would be harder for Wyatt and Mason to act as 'good Christians' and freely attend Mass with His Catholic Majesty, and the doctors' punctilious performance of their duty to the Supreme Head would threaten the security of the English embassy. Yet though their mission was promised at the end of 1537, they were a long time arriving.

Meanwhile in Barcelona the court was, as usual, waiting. Charles departed on 12 February to view his border fortresses, leaving the wider court attending on his return and some decisions. 'What we shall do then God wottith, and I think so doth no man else,' wrote Wyatt. Whether the Emperor would go to Italy, or to Castile, who knew?[80] Charles and Francis were circling with deepest misgivings the proposal that they meet in person, to be reconciled by the Pope, and deliberating where. The place chosen revealed how far they were from concord: Nice, on French soil for Francis's security, but on the coast so that the Emperor could sail there in a great armada, safe in his galley. To England came orders for the Imperial ambassadors to 'temporise', to delay the making of the alliance, and the French ambassador reported delightedly that Henry was likely to 'fall between two saddles and land on his arse'.[81] But Henry continued to present himself as the perfect, impartial arbiter. Wyatt was instructed to offer Henry's 'wise and reasonable order for Duchy of Milan, refusing the Bishop of Rome's means': the Pope could never arbitrate impartially in the disposition of Milan while he advanced his own interests there, as well as in Parma and Piacenza, and 'there is great likelihood that in the doing of it he will follow the steps of his predecessors who in such cases hath ever used to work their own benefit . . .'[82] This claim was – naturally – denied utterly by the papal agents, and the Emperor dismissed it with a smile, but claims of papal aggrandisement and usurpation were all too credible to other Italian powers and to their representatives at the Imperial court.[83] And there were other fears of tyranny in Italy which were the subject of anxious debate in Spain.

Italy had lost the great empire that had once spread from Rome, but had never ceased to feel the loss. As a Holy and Roman empire rose in its place, stretching beyond the old world to the new, Charles V imagined himself as the divinely appointed head of a universal theocratic monarchy, a new Charlemagne. *Plus ultra*: yet beyond. Italy must be at the heart of the renewed empire, so Chancellor Gattinara had convinced him in his youth.[84] Yet the Sack of Rome had epitomized both Italy's abjection and the danger of this monarchy becoming a tyranny. Italians were haunted by the memory of Rome's disaster at the hands of Imperial forces in 1527, and remembered with despair how in 1494 foreign armies had invaded as a consequence of adventitious alliance, and how easily Italy had been overrun. Then, as Italy had imploded, every prince in what was laughingly called Christendom had sought to exploit the divisions. Observers of Italy's disasters and their causes recalled how the powers of Italy, divided against themselves, had been helpless to resist, and feared that, disunited as ever, they would be helpless still. Machiavelli and Guicciardini, most acute of analysts, had been secular prophets of catastrophe.[85] In 1538, seeing Italy's continuing vulnerability and that nothing had changed, Guicciardini began to write the final version of his great *Storia d'Italia*, the history of Italy 'since through the imprudence of princes and her own ill fortune the foreigners from beyond the mountains entered the country . . .'[86] The Duchy of Milan was always the richest prize: it had been a *casus belli* before, and was likely to become so again. Annexed by Charles in 1535, it was the territory which he would never cede, nor Francis cease to claim. Now Henry, too, had ambitions for Milan: envisaging himself arbitrating its control, his daughter married to the Infante of Portugal, with Milan as dowry, and Milan's dowager duchess, Christina of Denmark, as his next queen. Wyatt had vivid memories of Italy as prey to Imperial troops as Bourbon's troops had marched on Rome. Now he and his friends at Charles's court saw the danger, and the *occasione*, of 'kindling a fire' in Italy once more.

As the Republic of Genoa and the Duchy of Milan came under Charles's aegis, and the Republic of Florence fell to Imperial troops, it seemed as though northern Italy as well as the kingdom of Naples and Sicily would be part of the Spanish *imperium*. In Rome, the Pope and Curia were fearful of Spanish control in Italy and wary of this Christian Emperor who should have been the natural ally of the Holy See against infidel and heretic.[87] In Spain, at the Emperor's court, Italian envoys argued about *libertas Italiae* and contested the comparative virtues of republican liberty or princely power. At the New Year of 1538 the Venetian ambassador insisted to Averardo Serristori, ambassador of the new prince Cosimo de' Medici, Duke of Florence, that a condition of the Habsburg–Valois peace must be the Emperor's ceding of all the fortresses he held in Florentine territory, for every power in

Italy distrusted his control. Then, 'we citizens would remain in liberty'. 'How in liberty?' demanded Serristori: Charles had confirmed Cosimo in power. But Cosimo would not be able to withstand the Florentines' desire to recover their republican liberty, said the ambassador of the Most Serene Republic.[88]

Yet the Emperor was not the only aggrandising power in Italy. The Pope himself was not only St Peter's successor with God-given power to bind and loose from sin, monarch of the Universal Church, but also the temporal ruler of the lands of St Peter, a powerful prince of lands in the centre of Italy.[89] The *spirituali* of Italy were not alone in fearing a conflict between the Pope's temporal and spiritual concerns. The dynastic ambitions of Paul III were spectacular. Church patronage was used to establish the ascendancy of his family, and through dynastic marriage and territorial acquisition on the grandest scale the Pope was building a Farnese principality to rival the great princely houses of Italy. Not only did he defend and extend the papal lands and create a Farnese fiefdom, but he began to act as an Italian sovereign supreme over all the other states in the peninsula. Wealth beyond the dreams of avarice came to his pernicious, degenerate son Pier Luigi Farnese, Duke of Castro, and to the Pope's grandsons, Alessandro and Ottavio. In the spring of 1538 negotiations were underway for the marriage of Ottavio Farnese to Margaret of Austria, the Emperor's daughter.[90] Wyatt, who had seen the animosity of Alfonso d'Este towards papal power, now heard Alfonso Rossetto of Ferrara speak disparagingly of the '*papalini* [papalists]' and of the Pope.[91] Wyatt's friendships with the Italian ambassadors mirrored the putative friendships between their principals, and as the Italian powers looked despairingly on the usurpation and tyranny of the Pope, he began to present an alliance between them and the English King as a natural one. The danger to the 'quiet of Italy' and to England came from a common aggressor: the Farnese papacy.

Immured in the Fortezza da Basso of Florence, Filippo Strozzi lived on as a symbol of the cause and cost of resisting tyranny. His name recurs constantly in letters sent from the Imperial court in 1537–8, his plight made vivid by the eloquent efforts of '*il Tasso*' to save him.[92]

Strozzi was accused of complicity in the assassination of Duke Alessandro de' Medici in January 1537, and there were few hopes for his life. '*Uomo morto non fa guerra* [a dead man does not make war]', said Granvelle.[93] Kept alive so that torture would force him to reveal who was behind the assassination, by October 1537 Strozzi had 'sung', telling 'many secrets' about the French King's involvement.[94] Duke Cosimo wanted Strozzi dead; the Pope sought to save him; the Emperor promised his life, so long as he was not proven to have sponsored the assassins. Bernardo Tasso had despaired of his mission, believing that '*sparse al vento dimolte parole* [he scattered so many words to the wind]', but by 1 January he was 'very happy', hopeful at least of saving Strozzi's life. Partly because of Tasso's entreaties Strozzi was 'favoured by everyone' in Barcelona. Waiting with the court, Tasso learnt on 13 February that Strozzi had the Emperor's grace.[95] Strozzi lived on, only to suffer unbearable torture.

In Barcelona in early March Wyatt had an audience with the Emperor – the last for a while. Now descriptions of his diplomacy were always calibrated in metaphors of temperature – from hot to warm, from cold to colder to coldest – with the temperature falling. Faced with setbacks, the prudent ambassador should 'yield gracefully' for the while, 'maintain a good front' and become neither too hopeful nor too discouraged, for circumstances change rapidly, so the advice went.[96] But Wyatt, so averse to dissembling, allowed his feelings to show, and his fellow ambassadors observed his moods. Enter the figure of Wyatt the malcontent. Meeting Alfonso Rossetto 'the English ambassador expressed his dissatisfaction, showed his discontent', because earlier the marriage alliances had been discussed 'more warmly than now'. We hear Wyatt speaking in Italian:

In somma, lo Imperator non fa conto delle genti se non quando è in necessità hora sta bene con questi francesi alli quale da molte buone speranze è ben vero che questi ministri cesarei mi hanno detto che lo Imperator mi vuol parlar' un altra volta innanzi che spazzi questo gentilhuomo che mi è venuto. Ma penso che sara repetermi il medesimo in vano.

The fact is, the Emperor pays no attention to anyone unless he has to. At present he is happy with those Frenchmen, to whom he gives many grounds for hope. It is quite clear that the Emperor's ministers have told me that the Emperor wants to speak to me once more before he sends away this gentleman who has come to see me. But I think for me it will be a repetition of the same things to no purpose.

Rossetto repeated Wyatt's expressions of '*discontentezza*', and would soon report that discontent turning to desperation.[97] At times, Wyatt's manifest displeasure was by order, a representation of that of his king, but here we see his unguarded mood. This is almost all that is heard of Wyatt from the court's observers for months.

A cold wind blew from England too, as English diplomacy and Wyatt's embassy faltered and failed. The conferences of the Imperial ambassadors with Henry's commissioners for the marriage alliances proved a temporizing farce. 'I never heard so many gay words, and saw so little effect . . . there is scant any good faith in this world', wrote Cromwell on 3 April. Icy reproof for Wyatt's 'folly' and 'fault' in sending letters unciphered warned of his failure to fulfil 'his Highness' pleasure'.[98] His 'assured', his 'loving', his 'loving assured friend' Cromwell was the messenger of a fall from grace. 'Much his Majesty doth marvell that you Master Wiat be not more speedy in your advertisements . . . It shall be good that you redub [repair] that negligence.'[99] Wyatt knew too well how quickly his prince's favour turned to disfavour and that when the pretence of friendship between Henry and Charles faded, Henry would cast blame on anyone but himself. By 10 May, as the Emperor's 'coldness' became public, Wyatt was ordered 'either [to] bring things [to] a better stay or decipher the untruth that the malice thereof may be better prevented'.[100] Out in the cold at the Spanish court, Wyatt felt the icy winds from home.

When Wyatt left England he had known that his enemies could, they would, scheme against him in his absence and disparage him to the King, and that his interests at home must be served by those who only intermittently protected them. He never forgot the 'maynie great dyspytes and dyspleasures that I have had done unto me'. Often during his embassy he had felt unqualified 'when I had great matters in hande, medlinge with wysemen, had no councell but my owne folysshe hede'.

'This solicitude, this care trobled me,' so he confessed later.[101] All the while that he basked in the Emperor's favour, and Henry's, some waited for their chance to undermine him. Jealous of Wyatt's seeming success, his own embassy floundering, Gardiner had forwarded Wyatt's letters 'open' in January, knowingly revealing Wyatt's carelessness in not using cipher.[102] More jealous by far was Bonner, who came to Spain with designs on Wyatt's embassy – he was welcome to it, thought Wyatt – 'yf he myght wype me owt of that rowme that hym selffe myghte come to yt, as in dede the man is desyerus of honor'.[103]

Impotent to do anything about it, Wyatt knew that his affairs in England were in chaos. Soon after his departure, Cromwell wrote to tell him that his servants ran wild in his absence, stealing the King's hawks, a capital offence. Their wildness dishonoured their master.[104] At the end of November 1537 Cromwell assured Wyatt of his continuing favour: 'and indeed you had need of friendship, for I have not seen a wise man leave his things so rawly, as yours be left'.[105] Returning home, John Mantell had discovered 'how slenderly Master Wyatt's matters have been handled here and how few assured friends he hath'. 'I will tell you more plainly at our next meeting,' he promised Mason.[106] Partly the failure was mere incompetence, for the letter of attorney to Sir William Haute was insufficient for him to act as Wyatt's agent, but Haute's health was failing. Making his will at the New Year of 1538, Haute was dead by June 1539.[107] But there might also be betrayal. Thomas Wriothesley's letter of 15 February breathes Wyatt's distrust of him:

Where you write unto me to help your friends here in the setting forth of your purposes, you may easily entreat me thereunto who doth, I think, study as much how by some mean to relieve you as any one friend you have here and think assuredly that I cannot forget what I promised at your departure. If such effects follow not as you would, I dare boldly say that it is not for want of good will in me and I would shout so long for you till at the last I will surely hit somewhat, a fat or a lean.

Private transactions for the purchasing of land are never conducive to friendship, and when Wriothesley bargained with Wyatt we observe a faltering in theirs. But on 8 April as Wriothesley justified himself – 'If I

were not better in solicitation of your affairs than most of your agents
be, ye might, I fear, eat your bread there with dishonour to our master,
and dishonesty to yourself' – Wyatt was in danger of being cashiered.
While, in Wyatt's absence, Henry's courtiers contended over the estates of dissolved monasteries, Wyatt fretted that he might miss prizes
that would save him from financial shipwreck.[108] By April Cromwell
warned him: 'I never saw man that had so many friends here, leave so
few perfect friends behind him.'[109]

In Spain Wyatt whiled away the tedium of embassy by writing to his
friends. Few of the letters survive, but their echoes faintly resound. An
ambassador was advised to keep trusted friends around his prince.[110]
Wyatt hoped especially for Cromwell and Wriothesley's friendship,
for a friendship which went beyond utility. Yet his friendship with
Wriothesley was clouded by mutual jealousy. Cromwell, friend and spy-
master, promised him: 'Mistrust not but you shall have as much favour
as I may extend unto you, and indeed you had need of friendship'.[111]
He would prove a truer friend to Wyatt than Wyatt was to him. While
Wyatt was in embassy Cromwell and Wriothesley sent him half-private
letters along with official instructions, and forwarded letters from his
friends at home. 'I send you herewith divers letters from your friends,'
wrote Wriothesley in June 1537.[112] Such letters were eagerly awaited.
In October 1538 George Cobham wrote cheerily from the Blackfriars:
'as for news I have none to write unto you at this time, but I trust that
there shall be never one friar left in England before your coming home
again'.[113] Here was an anticlerical jest best hidden from Wyatt's Spanish hosts. However consoling, private correspondence might become
compromising.

Receiving a letter or two from John Legh in Italy, Wyatt had
responded as a friend would: 'I aunswerde hym . . . exhortinge hym
to come and see Spayne and retorne into Inglande with me.'[114] Legh
was an Englishman *italianato*, living in Italy and 'delighting in pleasant
things like an amorous cortegiano [courtier]'. 'In all things (saving studies) . . . as good company as I could wish,' wrote an anonymous friend.
In November 1538 Legh was in Venice, lodging in a 'fair and honest'
house with a view of the lagoon.[115] Legh was Wyatt's friend from their

childhood and youth. A gentleman of Lambeth in Surrey with family antecedents in Alington, he was born to great wealth and great expectations, as heir to the fortune of his uncle Sir John Legh of Stockwell. By 1526 he was yeoman usher at court, and in the autumn of 1527 joined Wolsey's great retinue to France.[116] Leaving England and travelling to 'divers countries to see the world', Legh was conveniently abandoning a broken marriage, and he was choosing religious exile as well as an exotic education. Pilgrimage to Jerusalem to 'the sepulchre of our master Christ' marked Legh's deep traditional faith, as did his visit to Rome where, with Cardinal Pole and Michael Throckmorton, he lamented the religious desecration in England. At the English hospital of St Thomas of Canterbury, Legh dined with Pole who warned him against reading 'the story of Nicolo Matchavello [Machiavelli], which had already poisoned England and would poison all Christendom'.[117] Legh's Lambeth connections, and his later duel with the Earl of Surrey, make it likely that he was that servant of Surrey's who 'had been in Italy with Cardinal Pole, and was received again at his return'.[118] His suspect allegiances made contact with him suspect also.

The presence of English exiles at the Imperial court threatened to compromise Wyatt both with the Emperor and with his king. Early in November 1537 it was a '*cavagliero di questo regno* [a gentleman of this kingdom]' who had warned the nuncio of Wyatt's proselytizing; that he was passing around *libretti* full of heresy.[119] Since almost no Spaniard understood English, the danger of Wyatt and his household being denounced would come from exiled Englishmen who had a deeper loyalty to the Most Catholic King than to the King of England. Robert Branceter, who had long been in the Emperor's service, was just such a man.[120] In happier times, his friendships in the English embassy in Spain – with Richard Pate and Peter Rede – had been blameless enough, but by the autumn of 1537 he was in the sights of Henry and Cromwell, who made Wyatt the conduit for a collusive correspondence. 'I send you herewith a letter written from Mr Pate to an Englishman in the Emperor's court', wrote Cromwell in October: 'when you have read it, copy it, and so seal and deliver it and solicit the answer with all diligence.' The King 'much desireth to try out that matter of Dignely'. 'Fail not.' 'His grace hath it specially to heart.'[121] The unnamed 'Englishman' was Branceter, and the 'answer' concerned his association with Sir Thomas Dingley.

Dingley was a knight of St John of Jerusalem, sworn to defend Christendom, even by the sword.[122] In November 1536, as the Pilgrims of Grace rose and he understood how desperately the faith needed defending at home, while dining with Richard Pate in Genoa, Dingley spoke treasonably of the succession: 'if anything should fortune to the king otherwise than good in this insurrection . . .' He denounced Henry's murderous extremity.[123] At Christmas 1536 he was with Michael Throckmorton in Calais. Back in England, Dingley found sanctuary in the summer of 1537 with Sir John Walsh and his wife. Lady Walsh was the sister of John Poyntz, who was living nearby in country retreat.[124] Dingley's treason might have gone undetected had not a bitter row within his order laid him open to a malicious – if justified – denunciation. Sent to the Tower on 18 September, he was interrogated until he confessed those conversations and connections which the King had 'specially to heart'.[125] In 1532, at the height of the Submission crisis and the catastrophe for Christendom, Dingley had conferred at length with Sir George Throckmorton in St John's Priory, Clerkenwell, where Throckmorton revealed his agonies of conscience and the conservative opposition mobilizing in the Commons. At midsummer 1537 they met again at St John's, where Dingley told of encounters with Throckmorton's brother Michael.[126] Five years earlier, in another life, Wyatt had been part of the same conservative alignment, and Elizabeth Darrell was connected still – by marriage and by sympathy – to this group. In Paris, Dingley's brother Roger had been John Mason's tutor, and in Oxford they were fellow Fellows of All Souls.*[127] It was politic now to forget any such association, and learn circumspection, even when dealing with countrymen.

In May 1538 Wyatt passed letters from Richard Pate to Branceter, urging him to come home. 'You may tell him', wrote Cromwell, 'I doubt not but he shall find the King's Highness his good and gracious

---

* See above, pp. 173–81 and below, pp. 405–7.

lord.' Wyatt might tell him, but he would surely not believe it. 'Robertto' Branceter replied to Pate on 30 May, recalling Dingley's outburst in Genoa at the time of the Pilgrimage. He promised that he told the truth according to his 'conscience': 'I defy that worldly lucre or favour so dearly bought with the eternal damnation of my poor soul at the dreadful and terrible day of judgement.' Beseeching the King's 'gracious goodness' to pardon him for not returning to England to his service, 'considering the long time I have spent in the diligent and faithful service of my master the Emperor's Majesty', he hoped that Henry would 'graciously accept my faithful heart and humble prayer' and allow him 'with free liberty' to follow the Emperor. Henry, whose reaction may be imagined, knew that only kidnap would bring Branceter home. Since 'Robertto' had turned Spanish in Spain, his letter was written by an English scribe, by John Brereton – whether with Wyatt's knowledge is an open question.[128] What Wyatt had to fear was the presence of other renegade Englishmen in Spain, perhaps even in his service, in his own household. At a vital moment an unnamed Englishman would act as messenger between the nuncio in Spain and Rome.* Any ambassador must be on guard. Dolet warned the ambassador to beware of servants trying 'by indirection or overcurious inquiry to learn his counsels . . . for what involves more risk than the disclosure of your aims through disloyal servants, bribed by the enemy of your prince?' Tellingly, the first action of Diego Hurtado de Mendoza as ambassador in Venice in 1540 was to 'buy a pair a secretaries'.[129] Servants might always be suborned, but now it was usually for reasons of faith that English exiles chose to serve another prince than their own.

Branceter and his scribe wrote from an Imperial galley anchored off the coast of France. On 25 April the Emperor's fleet – twenty of Andrea Doria's Genoese galleys, and eight Spanish galleys – sailed from Barcelona, taking Charles and his court on their voyage to meet the Pope and, so they hoped, the French King.[130] Aboard one of these galleys were Wyatt and his *familia*. The Pope had left Rome on 23 March, with Cardinal Pole, and travelling by land, they made a slow journey

* See below, p. 427.

through Italy.[131] For the Imperial fleet the Mediterranean voyage, always hazardous, turned terrifying on 5 May as ten unknown galleys sailed toward it, giving no signal. Surely, they were Turkish? But when some of the Emperor's galleys gave chase and captured them, they were found to be French, and the peace between the French King and the Emperor was nearly broken before it was made. The fleet sailed on, against a contrary wind, and on the 9th anchored off Villefranche, near Nice, where salvoes of artillery saluted the fleet, and answering salvoes from the Emperor's galleys boomed back. That day half the Emperor's fleet sailed for Savona, carrying his favourite, Jean de Hainin, Sieur de Bossu, sent to kiss the Pope's feet in Charles's name.[132] And to Wyatt, on his galley, came the long-dreaded news that the 'doctors', Bonner and Heynes, were awaiting him in Nice. 'By my truthe, I never leked [liked] them in deade for Embassadours,' so he admitted later.[133]

Wyatt immediately took a boat to find them and to hear their fantastically ill-timed instructions. The first was to show the Emperor 'how Bishops of Rome have of long time usurped upon Princes, how they have wrested scriptures to the maintenance of their lusts, affections and glory'. If their own learned disquisitions should fail to move him, they had a satchel full of pamphlets about the Pope's 'pretended power'. Sent in embassy at the same time as the 'doctors' was the wonderfully incompatible Francis Bryan, with whom they and Wyatt must share 'all occurrants'.[134] But the news was so confused that there was danger in reporting it, or not reporting it. 'I could write many news unto you', Bryan informed Cromwell on 25 April, 'but I [might] write more lies than truth'.[135] The Pope, hearing of these embassies from England, awaited their arrival with greatest suspicion.[136] Bitterly, Wyatt observed the smug inertia of Bonner and Heynes – who believed 'lyttell to be ther charge butt only to converte Themperor by ther leringe' – while he frantically sought news, intelligence, anything. Prickly and tactless, Bonner was hopeless at gaining intelligence. Years afterwards Thomas Chaloner would sarcastically recall for Mason how Bonner was 'fain to go to Granvelle to ask what news from England'.[137] Wyatt remembered with despair the days in Nice when 'an Emperor, a Frenche kinge, a bysshope of Rome beinge so assemblede pretendinge an union of all the worlde to be treated by the handes of my maisters mortall ennimie', Cardinal Pole. And although in the midst of things, with so many sedulously prepared contacts – 'I with all myne acquayntance' – he was completely ignorant of what was happening: an ambassador's nightmare.[138]

Nice was then no glamorous watering hole but a 'doghole' – 'the most doghole I think that be in the world', so Mason wrote to Pate. The weather was scorching, the wine too 'hot and strong', the lodgings dreadful, and worse, it was 'full of the court of Rome'. 'But patience . . .'[139] Restless Wyatt was at his most restless. Later, forced to recall his every move in those desperate days, he gave an account of his actions. 'So restede I not day nor nyght to hunte owte for knowledge . . . I trotted continually up and downe that hell throughe heate and stinke from Councelloure to Embassator, from on frende to an other'.[140] Trotting 'continually' on horseback in the heat was indignity enough; trotting on foot meant dishonour. ('I would not', advised Giovanni della Casa, 'have a gentleman to run in the street, nor go too fast: for that is for lackeys . . . Besides that, it makes a man weary, sweat and puff.')[141] Accompanied by nobles and knights of his court, guarded by five hundred soldiers armed with harquebuses, the Emperor disembarked at Nice on 18 and again on 20 May and went to kiss the Pope's feet. They discussed the troubles of Christendom. This augured badly for the English King, especially because at the Pope's side was Cardinal Pole, whom Charles treated 'as if he were his brother'.[142] Deepest secrecy and confusion surrounded the inner counsels of princes. After nearly a fortnight of fruitless search, thinking 'I shulde leave no stone unmoved to gett sum intelligens', Wyatt conceived a dangerous plan. 'Apone this it chaunced': one night as he dined alone with Bonner, Heynes and Mason, with no servants in attendance, he made a fateful proposition: 'What yf Masone shulde Insinuat hym selffe, dissimblynge with Pole to sucke sume thynge worthy of knowledge in these great matters?' What if? Pole was the King's traitor and any collusion with him was treason. But Wyatt denied any treasonable intent: 'yt was to undermynde hym. Yt was to be a spye over hym. Yt was to lerne an enimmies councell.' Mason, who had been sent to Pole at Saint-Denis the previous spring and 'spake with hym a great space', 'was content to assaye yt when he shulde se tyme and occasione'. The doctors did not demur: this reckless initiative was with their consent.[143]

The frustration of being left in the dark (again), the great anxiety of the moment, the lack of political 'friends', led Wyatt to unguarded conversations in Villefranche with his intimates. Unguarded, because his expostulations to Blage and Mason were – allegedly – in the presence of Bonner and Heynes, who nurtured the memory of his outbursts and blasphemies, and reported them: 'By God's blood, ye shall see the King our master cast out at the cart's tail, and if he so be served, by God's body, he is well served . . . By God's body, I would he might be so served, and then were he well served.' As they remembered, Wyatt's prognosis was made not at Nice, but at Barcelona, and made 'maliciously, falsely and traitorously'. As Wyatt remembered, he said 'arse', not tail. Why would saying that the 'kynge shulde be caste owte of a Cartes arse' be treason?[144] No one understood better than Wyatt how 'in alteringe of one syllable ether with penne or worde that may mayke in the conceavinge of the truthe myche matter or error'. So subtle a poet, who 'tried' and played on the infinite variety which lay in words, knew too well that 'in thys thynge "I fere" or "I truste" semethe but one smale sylbable chaynged and yet it makethe a great dyfferaunce'. After the Treason Act which punished for words alone, whether a man's head stayed on his shoulders might depend on the distinction between 'fall owte', 'caste owte' or 'lefte owte'. Saying that the King was *left* out or might *fall* out of a cart was as unexceptionable as adverting to royal failure could be. Saying that the King was *cast* out was treason, for by analogy the King was like the thief at his hanging, thrown out of the back of a cart: 'that vile deathe that is ordayned for wretchede theves'. 'God forbede' that anyone should wish that, wrote Wyatt. Imagine – put the case – that he ever wished it, that indeed 'I were the naughtieste rancke traytor that ever the grounde bare', would he have expressed that wish in front of 'the doctors', 'with whome I had no great acquayntaunce and myche les truste'? 'Dothe any man thynke that I were so folysshe, so voyde of wytt, that I wolde have tolde Bonar and Haynes?' They already disapproved of him, 'had alreddie lowarde [lowered] at my fasshones'. 'Yet am I not so veri a fole'.[145]

Yet 'yt is a commen proverbe, "I am lefte owte of the cartes ars"'. In Nice, talking with Blage or Mason, Wyatt might well have used it, so he admitted: 'Upon this blessed peace . . . where semed to be an union of moste parte of Christendome. I sawe that wee hunge yet in suspens betwene the two prynces that ware at warre . . . theie wolde conclude amonge them selves and leave us owte.' Neither Francis nor the Emperor would ally with Henry and so challenge the 'Bysshope of Rome', and without that – impossible – promise Henry could ally with neither of them. Seeing the impossibility of his king's position, Wyatt saw that Henry would be excluded. With his friends, revolving these dangers, Wyatt 'paraventure [perhaps]' said: 'I fere for all these menes fayer promyses the kynge shalbe lefte owte of the cartes ars.' And 'paraventure', he admitted, he did lament to Blage and Mason, who had seen the chances offered and not taken, 'that maynie good occasions had bene lett slype of concludinge with one of ther princes'. But by misreporting the tenses which Wyatt used, Bonner and Heynes manifestly lied about the conversation. If – if, 'paraventure' – the conversation did take place and Wyatt's prognosis was in the future tense, it could only have happened in Nice. Yet in Bonner's account the outburst was made in Barcelona, in July, when a novel peace between Francis and the Emperor was *already* made, against all expectations. Henry's hopes of being a third party were in the past: he *had* indeed *been* left out. All speculation in future, conditional tenses was pointless now that Henry did face 'an union of moste parte of Christendome' against him. Was it likely that he – he, Wyatt – would use the future tense for an occasion past? 'Thiei lye and mysreporte the tale or els that I cane [not] speake Inglyshe.'[146]

Here was Wyatt the ambassador, like the 'I' of 'Off cartage he', restless and unpossessed, with peace, the reward of so much pain, hanging in the balance with war. So many chances to seize the initiative had been missed, to his king's detriment and his own. Did he, like the Petrarchan lover, ravel the fortunes of love and war and allow his thoughts to turn, and turn again to love?

13

Friends of Friends and Foes of Foes

In June 1538 Wyatt was back in England. He had been offered – had made for himself – another chance. Riding furiously home on a mission of desperate urgency, he knew that as soon as he arrived he must turn back to France. In fugitive moments he found Bess Darrell. For the first time we see them together, but in their remembered conversations we hear not words of love, but words of death. In Spain, Wyatt told her, 'there was certain kind of poison which being put upon an arrow head and the same pricking any person [he would] die'. This poison's antidote was 'the juice of a quince or else of a peach'. When Wyatt informed the King of the poison, asking 'him whether he should bring any thereof hither', the King replied, 'Nay.' Who was the poison's intended victim? The question was unasked and unanswered, but a name loomed. Bess heard of a strange stand-off in Nice: 'Mr Wyatt saw the Cardinal Pole, but he spake not with him, nor one of them would not look on another.'[1]

Back home, there was hardly time for Wyatt's 'more pleasaunt kynde of lyf', for summer's lease at Alington. Instead, it was time to settle the future of his son who, bereft of his father's supervision and avoiding that of his uncle, George Cobham, seemed likely to turn wayward.[2] Now Wyatt made anxious attempts to shore up his finances, and to claim some of the spoils of the dissolution of the monasteries, which was entering its second phase. A story – perhaps apocryphal, perhaps not entirely so – was told later of Wyatt, the cynical, expedient courtier, the self-seeker, advising his prince. Seeing the Pope 'incensed', 'Christian princes . . . enraged, and King Henry afraid of a revolution', Wyatt offered a solution: *'Butter the Rooks' nests*, (that is, sell and bestow the papal clergy's habitation and land among the nobility and gentry) . . . *and they will never trouble you.*'[3] Who would own Malling Abbey – where his stewardship had been so hard-fought and won – was in dispute, but Wyatt believed that it must be his: '*my* matter of Malling, in which I found at the King's hands so good inclination'.[4] At court, he was a returning hero. 'He was made a God here with the King and his council', the King was eating out of his hand – so Wyatt wrote delightedly to John Mason. But Wyatt put himself in danger by writing too freely, for Mason did not keep these private letters hidden. 'By chance I saw' them, admitted the snooping Bonner.[5]

Wyatt had left Nice on 24 or 25 May, sent by the Emperor with a 'couverture' for Henry. A 'couverture': a covert overture. (Here Wyatt thought in Franglais, as he often thought in Engtaliano). Charles offered Henry – and incidentally Wyatt, as his agent – a great chance. Between wives, Henry saw himself as the greatest prize in the dynastic marriage market, 'wooed on all sides', and now the Emperor promised Milan to the Lady Mary, and Christina of Denmark to Henry as his queen. 'God hath taken away' the 'little cloud' which had darkened the friendship between Henry and Charles. Wyatt sped home, with the proposals of marriages and their attached conditions: 'This my thought was so gladsome unto me to wyne to the kynge, he being unbounde and at libertie.' He had the Emperor's promise that nothing would be concluded until he heard the King's response, *if* Wyatt returned within fifteen or sixteen days. The journeys could not be made faster. Charles and Francis were 'now at the prick' in peace negotiations, and the 'couverture' might prevent them from leaping 'over the brink'. Sparing neither horses nor men, nor himself, in his 'postinge . . . and payne in so hyghe matters', Wyatt rode with five post horses and some of his *familia*, stopping only to confer with Francis Bryan at Aix. He arrived at the English court on 3 June.[6]

To the question why the Emperor suddenly revived the marriage proposals which had gone so cold a predictable answer returns: he feared that Henry would ally with Francis instead. On 17 May in Nice Wyatt had received disquieting news which he reported straight away to the Emperor: the French King was proposing a compact of friendship, whereby Mary would marry not the Infante, but Francis's son, the Duke of Orléans. Milan would be their dowry, a gift from Charles to 'secure the peace of Christendom'. Some might think, wrote Henry, that this was a mere ploy for Francis to gain the prize which otherwise he 'could only gain by the sword'. Quite so. Henry's conditions were that the Pope must not be a 'meddler or a mediator', and that Francis make no peace with the Emperor without Henry being third party.[7] It was to spike this 'friendship' that Charles sent Wyatt so urgently to England with the 'couverture'. Wyatt's agency in this diplomatic coup was widely acknowledged; by the Emperor, and by the Grand Master of France, who blamed Wyatt for nearly wrecking the peace – he had 'well-nigh overturned the whole of King Francis' plans'.[8] But for a resident ambassador to be *sent* home by another prince, rather than *called* home by his own had its dangers. Later, when Henry requested the French ambassador to return to King Francis, he declined: Francis 'would cut off my head if I went without his leave'.[9] Back at the English court 'Master Huyet', 'very desirous of penetrating' the Emperor's intentions, explained Charles's good will and 'seemed as usual to speak frankly'. For the while, Henry seemed content for Wyatt to tell truth to power, content to treat him more as Charles's ambassador than his own.[10] Soon that unlikely sufferance turned to suspicion. Wyatt left England, his departure delayed, carrying equivocal instructions and a more than guarded response. For Henry feared that possession of Milan – always 'the grounds of their contention' – might turn him from a 'maintainer of Christian quiet' to an 'author of war'. This self-avowedly uxorious King – believing that 'marriage is a bargain . . . as may endure for the whole life of man' – would not remarry without first seeing his new wife. On his way to the Emperor, Wyatt must confer with Francis Bryan, because on the state of the King's 'affairs in France' Henry's reply to the Emperor would be calibrated.[11] The King had not accepted Milan when it was offered, and would live to regret it and to cast blame elsewhere. All that followed would be an exercise in damage limitation.

On 21 June Wyatt waited on the coast of Kent for a fair wind for France. Writing to Cromwell, he dated his letter 'the Friday after Corpus Christi': though he did not yet know it, the truce between the French King and Emperor had already been signed on Corpus Christi

Day, the great feast of reconciliation in Christ.[12] As the Pope – 'the Idol of Rome' – left France, the Emperor accompanied him as far as Genoa, with John Mason in his entourage. And in Genoa, sometime between 22 June and 3 July, Mason had his promised and dangerously compromising conversation with Cardinal Pole. But he learnt nothing, so he told Wyatt: 'ther had Masone gotten occasion to entre with Pole and he tolde me that he coulde sucke nothynge owte of hym for that he semed to suspecte hym'.[13] While Mason conferred with Pole, Wyatt rode desperately through France – more posting and pain – not knowing what he would find when he reached the court, not even knowing where to find Bryan or the Emperor. 'For to seek Mr Bryan' he sent Nicholas le Pelle racing ahead from Valence to Avignon in the first days of July, and then from Avignon to Montpellier and along the coast 'to enquire for the Emperor'.[14]

The French court had left Lyon on 7 May travelling by barge down the Rhône to Avignon, and then across country to Aix and Nice. On his headlong journey back to England, Wyatt had met Bryan at Aix, leaving him to save the King from dishonour in the peace, but in Wyatt's absence it was Bryan's dishonour which threatened the royal honour. Once Bryan had tried to suborn the datary's servants in Rome by 'entertaining' them, and now other ambassadors recognised his own susceptibility to 'entertainment', his weakness for wine: 'Good cheer should be made to Brian,' 'Entertain Bryan.'[15] A king's magnificence must be reflected in that of his ambassador: that was universally acknowledged. Now as Bryan accompanied the glorious French court, he was more meanly attended than was usual for him. Even so, when the gilded Bryan with his servants in their 'gorgeous gear', arrived in Villefranche they made a stark contrast to the black-gowned clerics, Bonner and Heynes, whose miserable lodgings they were forced to share.[16] Later, quarrelling with Bonner, Gardiner accused him: 'ye care not for the King's honour, but wretchedly do live with x. shillings a day, as ye did in yonder parts, you and your companion'. Bonner protested: 'For of my fidelity, that week that Master Brian and his servants were with us at Villa Franca, it cost my companion and me £25 in the charges of the house.'[17]

On 19 June Bryan was at Antibes, writing jauntily to Lord Lisle.

'These Courts been so full as all the world were gathered upon a plump [in a company] . . . And in the French court I never saw so many women. I would I had so many sheep to find my house whilst I live!'[18] While the Emperor and the French King circled each other, allowing their grandees and princesses to meet and disport, vying in giving lavish presents, but still avoiding meeting each other, there was a truce but no conclusive peace, and the courts – as usual – waited. In days of feasting Bryan, seeking intelligence as well as entertainment, was cast in the company of his glittering friends at the French court, and was entertained not wisely, but too well. When Étienne Dolet wrote of the ambassadors of his times – 'some long-haired dandy entirely devoted to pleasure . . . devoid of prudence, stupidly greedy for honours (such as a cardinal's hat)' – maybe he had particular ones in mind.[19] Bryan's deep imbibing was the foundation of old friendship with Cardinal Jean du Bellay, who may have been the '*amico grande*' – great friend in a double sense – of Bryan's at the French court.[20] On the journey to Nice du Bellay was gambling with Ippolito d'Este, and on 8 June was the winner. D'Este, soon to be a cardinal, was a spectacular gambler. In his gaming ledger recording his wins and losses, we find d'Este losing to the Cardinal of Lorraine on 1 July at Marseilles, and at Vauvert on the 8th and 10th. A frequent gambling companion was the poet Luigi Alamanni, d'Este's secretary, from whom he won a mule he called 'Alemana'. On 6 June he lost 235 scudi in Nice, his greatest loss in a single day.[21] Although Bryan's name was nowhere in the ledger, it would be '*come fratello*', '*come bon fratello* [as his good brother]' that d'Este wrote to him.[22] Perhaps Bryan played with these princelings – certainly sometime in June or early July he gambled heroically, and lost. When Wyatt arrived to confer with Bryan on great matters of war and peace, he discovered him undone, unable to pay his vast gambling debt of £200. A dismayed Wyatt was forced to borrow from the wealthy merchant Antonio Bonvisi in order to rescue Bryan, and to turn to Cromwell for the debt to be repaid: 'if the King's honour more than his [Bryan's] credit had not been afore mine eyes he should have piped in an ivy leaf for ought of me'.[23] This was not the ivy leaf of the poet's glory, but the proverbial ivy leaf for pointless whistling.

In danger from Moorish corsairs and Mediterranean storms, taking a little bark from Aigues Mortes, Wyatt sailed eastwards toward Hyères in search of the Emperor. The Imperial fleet was sailing west from Nice, and by 13 July was in sight of Marseilles. That morning Wyatt went to find Bonner and Heynes on their galley *La Estrella* (The Star), with no expectation that they knew what was going on. After dining with them he went, alone, to Granvelle and the Emperor, bearing Henry's limp promises. But he came too late. The chance had been taken, fortune seized, and for a moment peace or war in Christendom had seemed to hang upon Wyatt's journey, but the 'couverture' had failed. On the night of the 13th the Emperor sailed to meet Francis.[24] Four days earlier, just as it seemed that the enemies would never meet, never reconcile, Francis had sent a message: 'if the Emperor wishes for peace in Christendom, let him meet me in Aigues Mortes, where I will wait for him'. Francis was now prepared to promise what he had refused in Nice: to join the enterprise against the Turk and renounce any friendship with the Lutherans.[25] On the eve of the meeting the Emperor might have 'contemplated the shortcomings of humanity, and what little hold man has over the sea and elements', for in densest fog, sailing blind, his galley was stranded and struck, and narrowly saved from sinking.[26] In the days that followed the old enemies exchanged priceless rings and pledged sworn brotherhood, not only friends to each other, but friends of friends and foes of foes.[27] This portended badly not only for the Ottoman Sultan, but also for the English King. Some crowed that the Pope would be sick that the princes had reconciled not in his presence, but in his absence.[28] Yet the peace made possible reconciliation in Christendom and the end of the English schism – by war, if pacific means failed.

Bonner and Heynes arrived to denounce the Bishop of Rome just as the Emperor prepared to kiss the Pope's feet. Wyatt had dreaded their mission as ill-timed, ill-judged and disastrous to the careful dynastic diplomacy he had pursued. At first the 'doctors' were denied audience altogether, and in Nice only the anti-papal ambassador of Venice came to find them.[29] The Emperor did see them, but only to repugn them. Wyatt was not surprised; he had told them so. Before and after the audience in which Bonner and Heynes discoursed of papal power and General Councils, Wyatt 'discouraged us greatly, saying, "Ye shall do no good with the Emperor, I know it, and have told the King myself in my letters that he lanceth the sore before it be ripe"'. Since Wyatt's embassy was dependent on the Emperor's good will, he distanced himself from the doctors, doing nothing to help them, 'setting forth old things begun by himself and passing over ours'. As for the Council: 'Sire', so Wyatt told the Emperor, the King 'will repose . . . in your Majesty's former promise'. In Bonner's report we hear Wyatt's proverbial speech as well as his disdain: 'He told us by the way, "Ye have spun a fair thread. I knew well enough how you should speed [succeed];" and he spake the words as though he rejoiced that we had not sped, lest our speeding should have been a dispraise to him.' 'And surely both Mr Wyot and Mason were desirous to have had us gone.' Denying the doctors' status as ambassadors, Wyatt and Mason claimed that their mission was only to denounce papal power and, once they had the Emperor's dusty answer, to depart. So Mason told Bonner.[30]

Between Mason and Bonner lay deepest antipathy and suspicion. According to Bonner, 'in all his facts and doings' Wyatt 'useth Mason as a God almighty', and Mason was responsible for Wyatt's waywardness: 'I . . . am sorry that by evil company, and counsel of that unthrifty body Mason, he is thus corrupted'. Bonner's jealousy that Wyatt confided in Mason, not in him, resentment that Mason was trusted with secret letters, suspicion that Mason might even have forged them, blighted his relations with both men.[31] Since neither of the 'doctors' knew sufficient French they were left – aggrievedly – dependent on Mason. Sending news to the Emperor, Cromwell instructed them to take Mason with them, 'for that having the tongue he may do so more fully then you could percace easily utter the same'.[32] Bonner's disapproval of Mason was comprehensive. 'Mason and other of his [Wyatt's] house spend upon harlots . . . so that all will come to nought.' Beyond all these grievances lay a deeper division over religion and authority in the Church. Bonner was not yet the 'bloody Bonner' of Protestant legend, the persecutor of heretics, but was a committed evangelical and most resolute defender of the royal supremacy. Mason had lamented the supremacy, and he lamented it still. He was, said Bonner, 'as great a papist where he dare utter it'.[33] He had dared utter it at the Emperor's court, to Bishop Gardiner in France, and to his friends at home. As he left Nice for Genoa and his encounter with Pole, Mason wrote affectionately, nostalgically to his old master Richard Pate, remembering 'our travels in time past'. He had sent Pate's commendations to Granvelle, who 'I ensure you was right glad you did well'.[34]

Returning to his *familia* Wyatt found bitter discord. Mason, left in the inimical company of Bonner and Heynes, mortified by their trumpeting of the royal supremacy, was trying to sustain the old rhythms of Wyatt's diplomacy. The gallants of Wyatt's train, excluded from the courts' 'love and entertaining', had been left to watch from the sidelines. Though not respected as ambassadors, the 'doctors' had tried to entertain like ambassadors. At Villefranche they gave hospitality, grudgingly enough, to 'all Master Wyatt's servants to the number of sixteen, all his acquaintance, which dinner and supper continually came to us, sometimes twelve, sometimes ten, and when they were least, six or eight'. 'All his acquaintance' – the 'friends' Wyatt cultivated, in search of intelligence. Worse, Bryan and his train of gallants had joined them. Supposedly abstemious clerics were forced to feast the cuckoo courtiers and to observe some of them sloping off to visit ladies of the night.[35] Wyatt – so conscious of his honour, so open-handed – was outraged when Bonner claimed that he 'had not one penny of Master Wyatt' in repayment, and charged Wyatt with lack of generosity. 'Had ye not in the Gallye the most and beste commodious places?' asked Wyatt. 'Wheare ye were charged with a grote [four pence] was I not charged with v [five pence]?' As for honour: 'I knowe no mane that dyd you dyshonour but your unmanerly behavyour that made ye a laughehynge stocke . . . and me sume tyme to swete for shame to see you.'[36]

A protest addressed to unnamed 'Lordships' tells of a diplomatic disaster and a shift in the diplomacy of Christendom. Although anonymous and undated, it ventilates unmistakably the wounded pride and outrage of Bonner and Heynes, and we witness the impossibility of their embassy. They lamented new limits to the safe-conduct granted to ambassadors from the 'renowned prince the King's grace of England' to the Emperor. 'We marvel not a little' – strong words in diplomacy – given 'the cause considered of our embassade most reasonable (though thereof ye be ignorant as yet undeclared)', that their immunity was restricted, the sanctity of the law of nations broken, in ways unknown among enemies, let alone friends. To their free safe-conduct unprecedented conditions had been added, 'forfending us . . . to promote any strange opinions and specially that we derogate nothing in word nor deed against the authority of the Sacred Holy Church (as ye name it) of Rome'. Strange opinions – only if 'ye account strangeness the reformation of vice and correction of evil manners which may not seem strange but only to them that hate the Christian verity and love no godly virtue'. If denying that they derogated any part of the authority of the Roman Church granted by Scripture seems diplomatic, yet there was doubleness, for it was an evangelical credo that papal claims had no foundation in Scripture. It was because of what they might say, rather than what they might do, that their free safe-conduct was denied. Insisting that 'we . . . may lawfully speak' against the Bishop of Rome's 'wrong usurpation', they feared that some in the Emperor's court waited for them to trap themselves by careless talk: 'we be of purposely provoked by divers of your inquisitive people'.[37] Charles's extreme displeasure 'with two ambassadors' – 'and with one, to such an extent . . . that, but for respect to the King, he would have had him thrown out of the window' – was still remembered thirty years later. Charles requested their recall, though making 'no public demonstration against them'.[38]

In the shipwreck of English diplomacy, and their exclusion from the courts' delights, Wyatt's retinue diverted themselves by teasing 'peevish' Bonner. Imagine the derisive laughter as they procured a prostitute for the portly priest and chortled as he fell from the high moral ground which he claimed. In the English galley no women were allowed before the mast, 'but for your pleasure' – so Wyatt accused Bonner – and 'by cawse the gentell men toke pleasure to see you intertayne her', they invited a woman to dine as a joke. 'Theie leked well your lokes, your carvinge to Madona your drynkynge to here and your playinge under the table.' Anyone would confirm this story. 'Aske Masone, aske Blage –

Rowes is dede. Aske Wolf.' They derided Bonner when he hoarded the drink he should have shared, and played the gallant: 'yt was a playe to them, the kepinge of your bottels that no mane myghte drynke of but your selffe, and that "the lyttell fatt prest were a jollye morsell for the zora [señora]"'.[39] All this play diverted Wyatt and his gentlemen while their galley swayed at anchor outside Aigues Mortes, and Francis and Charles promised undying friendship. On 18 July the Imperial fleet set sail. Running into mistrals, they had a terrible passage, and two days later the Emperor's entourage disembarked at Barcelona, 'all half dead'.[40]

At the making of 'this blessed peace', as Wyatt ironically termed it, the English King was 'left out of the cart's arse'. From Aigues Mortes, in the desolation of his mission, Wyatt sent Henry copies of the 'conclusions and chapiters of the peace whear in he was not mentioned contrarie to themprors promas'.[41] But even there 'in his galleys upon the sea ready to sail', the Emperor dangled the hope that he was free to fulfil his 'overtures'.[42] In Barcelona, Wyatt energetically revived the dynastic diplomacy, and conducted a charm offensive on Charles. Bonner watched with disapproval as Wyatt played the complaisant courtier: 'And surely that is a great mark that he shooteth at, to please the Emperor and Granvelle, and to be noted to be in the Emperor's favour, whom he magnifieth above all measure.' Amphibious Wyatt, trying to please in both the Imperial court and the English, used flattery to talk to power, and conducted a diplomacy parallel to the one commanded. So Bonner accused him. In Barcelona Wyatt received orders to 'expostulate' about the King's exclusion from the peace. On the 23rd he went – alone – to Granvelle. Wyatt's version of the encounter was thus:

Granvelle: 'What! Yet more expostulation?'
Wyatt: 'Yea, faith, for the unkind handling of the King in the treaty of truce.'

'Whether he said so, yea or nay, I cannot tell,' reported Bonner.[43] Doubtless there were ways and ways of expostulating. According to Granvelle, Wyatt did protest – about the truce, about the calling of a General Council – and though assured that Charles and Francis wished to include Henry in the peace, he did not hide his mortification: 'such was the ambassador's general manner and countenance . . . that I am fully convinced that the truce is a morsel not easily digested by the English stomach'. Perhaps, said Wyatt acutely, the reason for excluding Henry from the peace was to 'show that he is not a Christian king, since he has denied obedience to the Church of Rome'.[44]

Seemingly in buoyant mood, Wyatt met Giovanni Bandino, the Florentine agent. He told Bandino that the Emperor was sending powers to his ambassadors in England to arrange the marriage between Mary and the Infante and the crucial donation of Milan. 'Thinking to do me pleasure', reported Bandino, Wyatt had asked Granvelle whether the marriage between Margaret of Austria, the Dowager Duchess of Florence, and the Pope's grandson, Ottavio Farnese, had taken place, and was told not. Bandino did not know whether to believe him or not, knowing that Wyatt was '*non troppo amico al papa* [no great friend of the Pope]', yet he did not disbelieve him.[45] Wyatt's spirits were high, because Bonner and Heynes were leaving. Better still, he had arranged for them to have their parting audience with the Emperor without him attending. Predictably, it was a disaster, for they took 'occasion to expostulate' – again. Showing deepest disfavour to them, and dishonouring their King, the Emperor gave them no conventional parting gift.[46]

The following day – 25 July – was the great feast of St James. Mass was celebrated at the royal monastery of Santa Maria de Jonqueres. Wyatt attended the Emperor to the 'solempnity', talking with him 'all the way, and after such merry sort and fashion that expostulation was turned to oblivion'. So Bonner heard, and so Wyatt boasted that night at dinner.[47] Excluded from the feasting, Bonner's imagination played freely, and he accused Wyatt of living 'viciously amongest the Nunnes of Barsalona'. Many of the nuns were noblewomen who, far from being sequestered, rode gallantly on fine horses and entertained grand visitors to the city. Wyatt described the beguiling recreation. Men 'here and there tawlke with those ladies and when theie will go in and syt companie togyther with them tawlkinge in their Chambres'. Gentlemen of the Emperor's chamber, earls, lords, dukes did so, 'and I amonge them'. 'I used not the pastyme in cumpaynie of Ruffions,' Wyatt protested – scorn for Bonner manifest in his irony – but in 'suche viciouse companye' as the ambassadors of Ferrara, Mantua and of

Venice, 'a man of lx [sixty] yeres olde'.[48] For the first time, we hear
of the Venetian ambassador, Pietro Mocenigo, who will offer Wyatt
'practises' and collude with him in the darkest hours of their embassies. That evening Wyatt spent in the company of Bandino, debating
the meaning of his conversation with the Emperor on the way to Mass.
Perhaps, said Bandino, the Emperor would give the Duchess of Milan
in marriage to Henry, but not allow the marriage of the princess to the
Infante of Portugal? Not so, replied Wyatt: he would not go ahead with
one without the other.

*Et a dirti il vero lo Imperatore mostra haver' grandissimo desiderio di convenir' col mio
Re . . . Dimi piacerebbe . . . perche ti dubiti il mariaggio fra la mia principessa et l'Infante
haverla per il tuo patrone?*

And to tell you the truth, the Emperor shows himself to have the greatest desire
to ally with my king . . . But tell me, would it please you . . . since you doubt
the marriage of my princess with the Infante, to have her for your master?[49]

If Bandino – never the most reliable of envoys – told the truth, Wyatt
now veered from any known instructions. Had Henry really ordered
Wyatt to sound the Florentine ambassador about a marriage between
Duke Cosimo and the Lady Mary, or was Wyatt pursuing a maverick
diplomacy? If he was, it would not be for the last time.

On 29 July the 'doctors' left Barcelona, left ignominiously. Wyatt
declined to escort them from the city, refused to lend them horses. They
rode out on wretched nags – 'such spitell jades as I have not seen',
complained Bonner – while Wyatt's household sniggered. What did
he expect, this fat priest, a caparisoned steed? 'Marye, yt was thought
in dede amongest us' that Bonner wanted 'a genet with gylt harnes'.[50]
Wyatt and Mason were now free to return to their old ways of diplomacy and to conform to Spanish custom. Bonner and Heynes had
compromised the English embassy. Since they were all under suspicion
of being Lutherans, the refusal of the 'doctors' to conform to traditional worship threatened them. Neither Bonner nor Heynes had 'said
masse or offerde to here masse [as] thoughe yt was but a superstition'.
'Theie were more mette to be parysshe prestes then Embassadours', so
Wyatt allegedly said. True, he had scorned them as ambassadors – as

did everyone else – but if ever he said they were better suited to be parish priests, 'on my faythe I never remembre yt': 'And yt is not lyke I shulde so saye for as fare as I coulde see nether of them bothe had greatlye any fancie to masse and that ye knowe were requisyte for a parryshe prest.' Wyatt and Mason 'were fayne to intreate them that we myght som tymes shewe our selves in the churche togyther that men conceavyd not an evell opynion of us'. 'Naughty fellows' 'blazed abroad' that Bonner and Heynes were 'Lutheran', but Wyatt was not called a heretic – not yet.[51]

Bonner now rode fast for France, and his grand new embassy. 'Master Diligence', 'squirting in post': thus Bishop Gardiner described the relentless Bonner, his scorned successor as ambassador to the French King. Wriothesley gleefully reported the 'tragedy between' Gardiner (his old tutor) and Bonner, whom Gardiner called 'fool' as he handed over his embassy.[52] Bonner's seething resentment at his disdainful treatment in Spain was deepened by Gardiner's open contempt. He began to burnish his gathering evidence against both Gardiner and Wyatt, whose loyalty he suspected not least because they shared a dubious dependence on Mason, 'as naughty a fellow, and as very a Papist as any that I know, where he dare express it'.[53] Remembering and misremembering the unguarded talk of Wyatt and his companions, Bonner became a dangerous enemy. In Barcelona, when – so Bonner recalled, though Wyatt did not – Wyatt had talked of his king being 'cast out of the cart's tail', Bonner's 'stomach boiled' and he had a furious row with Wyatt; 'Mason sitting quiet as one at a sermon', and Heynes also keeping silent. 'By my troth,' said Heynes presciently, Wyatt 'is a mad man using us as he doth, and so foolishly speak afore us'.[54] Ominously, the 'doctors' had been present when Wyatt had made his fateful proposal that Mason seek out Pole. With the courier and spy Thomas Barnaby, Bonner compared notes and prepared a story. On 2 September Bonner sent an incendiary report home about Wyatt, and another to condemn Gardiner and Bryan. Heynes had ridden ahead to England with a version of events damning to Wyatt.[55]

The King was already furious, blaming his ambassadors for the peace they had not prevented and the failure of kingly friendships which they should have sustained. He was not only excluded, but also humiliated. In early August the French ambassador challenged Henry about his wish to see the marriageable French princesses paraded before him in Calais, like mares trotted up at a sale – 'Did the Knights of the Round Table treat ladies thus in times past?' Henry had the grace to blush, the only known occasion. According to the French ambassador, he blamed all his ambassadors for his dishonour, but one in particular: 'By God, I will not write until there is another ambassador there, called Dr Boner. The others have deceived me and let themselves be seduced by Hoyet [Wyatt], with whom I am not pleased.'[56]

'Hoyet' was fortunate to be absent. Bryan and Gardiner had been recalled at the end of July, and Bryan left precipitately, with no parting gift from the French King, bringing news which contained 'honey and gall'.[57] The royal fury and his deep disgrace sent Bryan into a decline from which his recovery was doubted. Bryan 'was a drunkard, whom he will never trust', said Henry.[58] At the French court, Bryan had abandoned himself to 'good cheer' and 'entertainment', and his fathomless drinking explains in part his less than diplomatic exchanges, his notorious frankness, his reckless gambling. Early in September the King was waiting pensively, menacingly, for Gardiner's return.[59] While Bryan lay 'sore sick and like to have died' an inquisition began into the embassy in France, and Gardiner and Bryan's purported intrigues.

Amidst the pleasures of summer hunting in Kent, Henry became convinced of his ambassadors' treasons. At the end of August he 'hath spoken much of Mr Bryan', so Thomas Heneage, Bryan's 'bedfellow' in the Privy Chamber, informed Cromwell. 'Surely' Cromwell had sent Thomas Wriothesley – Wriothesley, always privy to the *arcana imperii* – to Bryan 'to know his mind as concerning the Great Matter' that Cromwell knew about.[60] This 'Great Matter' was a shadowy scheme of Gardiner's to effect reconciliation between his king and the Pope, to 'have all things up right with the . . . Bishop of Rome, and his Highness' honour saved'.[61] Wyatt remembered later how Bonner conspired with Barnaby to discredit, even destroy Gardiner: 'what a tragedie and a suspecte theie sturde [stirred] agaynste hym'.[62] In the Curia they believed that Gardiner yearned to see his king return to the true path, and that only lack of courage for martyrdom had led him to write in favour of the royal supremacy. They were not wrong, but Gardiner was too wary 'to be compassed to enter in to dangerous things by any man . . . but would go with and follow', so Wriothesley judged.[63] Back in England, Gardiner was soon restored to royal favour and to a new influence. Bryan, too, was forgiven and restored, and at the end of September he was dreaming that the King had made him Comptroller of Calais to keep company with his old friend Lisle.[64] 'Well, all this is reconciled', wrote Wyatt, but evidence lurked to compromise him.[65] Shared secrets put friends in each other's danger, and the part played by Wyatt's intimates in the investigation which now began left him vulnerable. Wriothesley, the repository of so many secrets, might reveal them. Gardiner should beware: Wriothesley was a 'great expounder of his letters', so Bryan warned him.[66] Wriothesley was a risk Wyatt should never have taken.

John Mason, Wyatt's 'God almighty', had left Valladolid on 19 September. Though neither he nor Wyatt knew it, as Mason travelled home an inquisition awaited him in England.[67] Letters he was carrying from Wyatt's *familia* were confiscated and now rest – forever undelivered – in the national archives.[68] 'In serching Masons papers' a note of infinite threat to Mason and to Wyatt was discovered: a minute of Mason's meeting with Cardinal Pole in Genoa in June. At the time, Mason had sent a report of all that was said between him and Pole, but that letter did not reach Cromwell for almost a year.[69] On 14 October Bonner's 'very loving and great good friend the gentle and good' Wriothesley brought him the not unwelcome news of Mason's arrest and confession, and reminded Bonner that anything he might say to incriminate Wyatt and Mason must stem from his duty to the King rather than 'malice or grudge'. Mason had only confessed to save himself – 'to bring him out of the briars' – judged Bonner. He 'marvell[ed] greatly' that Mason, confessing, extenuated his actions 'as done by commandment and letters of Mr Wyatt', unless this was 'a practise' between them. Bonner recalled three conversations between Mason and the traitor Cardinal or his servant: the first with Pole himself at Saint-Denis in April 1537, the second with Pole at Villefranche, the third with Pole's servant at Nice. 'This is the truth,' so Bonner assured Cromwell. At Saint-Denis, Wyatt had refused to meet Pole, but Mason 'went and spake with him a great space'; as for the other two occasions, Wyatt had been in England. Mason's fault lay in keeping the meetings secret: he never told Bonner or 'my companion Mr Heynes'. Surely, Bonner mused, Wyatt was 'too wise' to send Mason to promise collusion with the traitor Cardinal, or 'to swear and wish that Mason's soul were joined with Pole's soul'?[70]

In Spain, Wyatt awaited Mason's return, but he did not come. By 'chance . . . he is evil diseased of a fever', so Cromwell wrote on 16 October.[71] Perhaps Mason did have a fever, yet interrogation, following the strains of embassy and the posting home, might have sent him, like Bryan, into a decline. But Granvelle told Wyatt something more alarming: Mason was 'in holde', 'detayned by examynation wherin I was suspecte'. Hearing this, Wyatt 'sued to come home for my declaracion'. In England the following year, with all the charges in abeyance, Cromwell assured Wyatt 'how honestlye Masone had declared hym selffe, and how well the kinge toke yt and how good lorde he was to hym'. Yet he warned him: 'thei mente at Masone but theie shote at the Wiatt'. 'Thei': as so often in Wyatt's life and art, the inimical, treacherous 'they' are never named, but that one of Mason's inquisitors was the Duke of Suffolk may set us wondering. Wyatt remembered well how he had answered Cromwell: he could not forgive or forget. 'Theie strake at me but theie hurte me not, therefore I pray god forgive them but I beshrewe [curse] there hartes for ther meaninge.'[72]

In the Arundel Harington manuscript and Tottel's *Songes and Sonettes*, in the sections reserved for Wyatt's verse, is an intriguing double sonnet, with a form and a rhyme scheme unique in his poetry.[73] Tottel entitled it 'The lover describeth his restless state', but here love is not only love, the lost liberty is more than love's ensnarement, and the tertian fever assailing the wasted speaker seems achingly real. If there is indeed sweetness in gall, it is hard to find it:

> The flamyng Sighes that boile within my brest
> Somtyme brake forthe and they can well declare

the hartes unrest and how that it doth fare
the payne thearof the greef and all the rest
the watrid eyes from whence the teares do fall
Do feele some force or ells they wolde be drye
the wasted flesshe of cowlour dead can trye
and Some thing tell what Sweetnes is in gall.
and he that list to see and to discerne   *desires*
How care can force within a weried mynd
Come hee to me, I am that place assynd   *assigned*
But for all this no force it dothe no harme
the wound alas happ in some other place
From whence no toole away, the skarr can race   *erase*
But you that of suche like have had your part
can best be judge, whearfore my frend so deare
I thought it good my state shuld now appeare
to you, and that there is no great desert
and whear as you in weightie matters great
of Fortune saw the shadow that you know
For tasting thinges I now am stryken soo
that thoughe I feele my hart doth wound and beat
I sitt alone save on the second day
my Feaver comes with whome I spend the tyme
in burning heat whyle that she list assigne   *wishes*
and whoe hath health and libertie alwaye
Lett hym thanck god and lett hym not provoke
To have the lyke of this my paynefull stroke
Finis

Wyatt seems to be imagining a speaker shadowed by fortune, as once he himself had been, addressing a 'frend so deare', whose experience seems close to that of Wyatt himself. The speaker's pains and durance are the 'desert' of 'tasting thinges' (or 'trifling thinges' in Tottel's version), whereas the 'frend' has suffered for 'weightie matters great'. The 'weried mynd' recurs in Wyatt's writing. So, too, the unfading scar, which Henry Howard also evoked, an image of especial resonance and force which called to mind the scriptural warning that wounds may be healed and evil words reconciled, but whoever betrays the secrets of a friend is lost.* The 'hartes unrest', the pain, the grief, the 'weried mynd' of the speaker communing solitary with his fever, were agonies Wyatt had known, and so, too, had John Mason.

In Spain Wyatt was left to conduct his mission without Mason's counsel. All to the good, believed Bonner: 'if some things were reformed in him he could do better, as surely he will do, Mason being absent from him'.[74] The endlessly iterated marriage proposals – between Henry and the Duchess of Milan, and Mary and the Infante of Portugal – were still under discussion, and the news in Valladolid early in September (news spread by Wyatt?) was that Charles might visit England to conclude them. In fact, in order to keep the 'affair in suspense and the King of England in balance' – that is, neither quite to renege upon the overture made to Wyatt early in the summer, nor to implement it – the commission to treat was passed to Mary of Hungary, Regent of the Netherlands. It was kicked into the long grass.[75] The nuncio believed the putative alliance, on which '*l'imbassadore d'Inghilterra*' so insisted, to be the Emperor's ploy to effect Henry's reconciliation with Rome.[76] Instead, it revealed the fragility of the peace, and Charles's desire for a crusade against the infidel, and for allies wherever he might find them. His counsellors and grandees, always opposed to grand designs and to paying for them, resisted the Emperor's leaving Castile. 'Everywhere there was murmuring' against his '*fantasia fissa* [fixed fantasy]' to lead the crusade against the Turk in person.[77] Amidst all the uncertainty, left to his own devices, Wyatt began to conceive a lone-wolf diplomacy which had never been fully debated in England. The offer which Wyatt had made in Villefranche, in the King's name, would be of the greatest significance in all his thinking and scheming thereafter – Henry would join with 'the other potentates of Italy' to defend Milan.[78] No despatch from Wyatt survives between June and November, but reports from Italian ambassadors suggest that in the little world of the resident embassies Wyatt increasingly depended on them, and with them found common cause.

Eavesdropping on secret conversations between friends in Valladolid we discover the tenor of Wyatt's diplomacy and his vision of England's

* See above, p. 285 and below, p. 460.

safety. As the grandees of the court jousted magnificently in the first days of September, Wyatt was found confiding in Giovanni Bandino '*come amico et fratello mio* [as my friend and brother]'. Claiming certainty that Princess Mary would be invested with Milan, Wyatt again proposed that Duke Cosimo marry in England, and suggested two alternative beauties: either Lady Margaret Douglas, whom his king loved as a daughter, or 'Maria Duchessa dersmundia [Mary Duchess of Richmond]', one no less beautiful and virtuous than the other. The Duke would surely be pleased to have a '*cognato et fratello et amico* [kinsman, brother and friend]' in Italy to defend him from '*cattivi che ogni giorno ne fanno i papi* [the evils daily perpetrated by popes]'. Evasively, Bandino urged caution, due reflection, etc., etc.[79]

On the 18th Wyatt called on his friendship with Alfonso Rossetto of Ferrara. 'In his judgement', Wyatt confided, since the Emperor could hardly be friends with both the French King and Henry, nor ally with one without leaving the other '*malcontento*', and since he dared not leave a powerful enemy at his back while he crusaded against the infidel, it would be better for him to temporize with both. '*Mi voleva un giorno parlare di cose di molto momento*'. 'One day', he promised Rossetto, he wished to talk to him of matters of great moment. Four days later, reminding him of the ancient '*benivolenza* [benevolence]' between the d'Este and his King, Wyatt ventured a novel '*collegatione* [association]' among the '*potentati d'Italia*'. The princes of Ferrara, Mantua and Urbino, 'resting on the shoulders of his king' and acting in the interests of Henry's daughter and son-in-law, could at little cost defend the principality of Milan, keep it 'in quiet' '*e leverebbe le suspicioni che molte volte accadono e sortiscono* [and would remove the suspicions that many times arise and have an effect]'. Promising to tell all that he heard, Wyatt swore Rossetto to secrecy.[80] Secrecy and friendship were the watchwords of Wyatt's diplomacy. This would be its touchstone: Henry's great power and vast wealth would secure the 'peace of Italy' and defend it from incursion and tyranny.

These conversations raise the question which resounds around the courts of princes: how far did a prince know what was said in his name? Here, we may suppose, Wyatt was implementing a policy ventilated with the King while in England in June. Devising his tortuous diplomacy, Henry cast about for allies. On 16 October he sent to Castile Philip Hoby, Groom of his Privy Chamber and old Spanish hand. Hoby's instructions turned on the vexed question of Milan. Henry had quailed at the prospect of defending Milan: 'who would be glad to put his foot in the briar and take the whole burden in his neck?' But if the marriages were concluded, he would bestow his daughter Elizabeth, Lady Margaret Douglas and the Duchess of Richmond 'upon such of the princes of Italy . . . meet to be retained in alliance for the conservation of Milan and for the defence of Naples and Sicily'. Thus, Henry said, the Emperor's estate in Italy would be assured, and – though he did not say – Henry's influence.[81] In England, this Italian policy was hampered by a haziness of exact intelligence (not least about which princes of Italy were married already), but friendship with the powers of northern Italy offered the best chance for English aggrandisement and – as it happened – defence. No one forgot that the wars which had convulsed Italy and sucked every European power into their vortex might easily come again. Cromwell had fought in the Italian wars, and on the walls of his house in London hung a painted cloth of the 'eversion of Italy' and a 'great table of the misery of Italy, painted'. Henry owned a picture of the siege of Pavia.[82] For Wyatt, the memory of the furies of Bourbon's army was vivid, and he had watched from the papal camp with Machiavelli and Guicciardini as Rome awaited that army's onslaught. 'The revolutions in Italy declareth great war to be in those parts shortly,' so Cardinal Pole had written to his brother Henry, Lord Montague, in 1535.[83]

On the last day of August 1538, as the Imperial ambassador, Diego Hurtado de Mendoza, departed for Spain, he sent news of dark events in England: of a rapprochement with the Lutheran princes of Germany, of the dissolution of the monasteries, and of the King's moves against the family of Cardinal Pole. On 29 August Sir Geoffrey Pole had been sent to the Tower, charged with treasonable correspondence with his traitor brother, amidst rumours that he would flee into exile, 'begone with the next wind', taking an army with him.[84] If Sir Geoffrey fled the realm the dangers would not be his alone. Friends called on higher powers to dissuade him. 'Our Lady had appeared' in a 'marvellous dream' to a Pole family chaplain, telling him to warn Sir Geoffrey that his flight would destroy all his kin.[85] The terrors of the Tower broke Pole, and 'in a frenzy' he attempted suicide. Death would have saved him from interrogation, and from revealing secrets which would destroy his family. That summer Geoffrey had been adjured by his brother Lord Montague 'never to open anything if he should be examined, for if he opened one all must needs come out'.[86] Honour as well as safety demanded that the secrets of a friend be kept sacred. Sir Edward Neville vowed never to reveal anything 'to the hurt of his friend' and, 'liever [rather] to die than to disclose his friend', the Marquess of Exeter had promised never to betray a friend's secrets, 'if it touched not the King'.[87]

Among themselves these 'assured' friends, with their servants and chaplains, had spoken treason. Lamenting that 'the world in England waxeth all crooked, God's law is turned upso-down', they regretted the King's 'incestuous marriage' to Anne, the travesty of the royal supremacy, the deaths of More, Fisher and the Carthusians, and believed that Henry and Cromwell would 'hang in Hell' for dissolving the monasteries. They dreamt of the King's death, and in fevered outbursts, threatened it. 'Yet we should do more, and here whe[n] the time should come', said Montague, 'what with power and friendship.' The 'plucking down' of the 'knaves' around the King would not suffice: 'we must pluck down the head'.[88] Should the King die, his successor must be Princess Mary. She would marry Reginald Pole, who was of the royal blood and, though a cardinal, not in priest's orders.[89] They had not only spoken but written treason. In June – around Corpus Christi – they had burnt correspondence, fearing that 'the keeping of letters m[ight turn a man]'s friend to hurt'.[90] Wyatt, who was in England then waiting for a passage to France, had special reason to fear the keeping of letters.

Elizabeth Darrell, so long a friend of the Pole and Courtenay families, was caught in the web of their treason. When Lord Montague visited her in Hackney on 3 November 1538 she told him 'that his brother Sir Geoffrey had almost slain himself, and lamented that act'.[91] Lamented it, because suicide was a grave sin, and because the breaking of Sir Geoffrey was lethal for his kin and friends, as brother deposed against brother. Both brothers had confided in Bess Darrell, telling her of the horror felt by the most fervent defenders of the old faith, and their opposition, sure of her sympathy: 'Sir Geoffrey saith that he heard the [said] Mistress [Roper and Mistr]ess Clement say within these twelve months that [they liked not] this pulling down of abbeys, images and pilgrima[ges and prayed God] send a change.' These were the daughters of Thomas More, whose death, with those of Fisher and the Carthusians, Geoffrey Pole narrated; 'how, and how patiently, they died'.[92] Now in the Tower, Montague confessed his communication with 'Mistress Darrell'. At Easter 1537 when his chaplain, Thomas Starkey, warned him that the Cardinal was to be brought home from Flanders 'quick or dead', Montague revealed the plot to Bess. She, in turn, told Geoffrey Pole.[93] It was letters from Bess – or from Gertrude, Marchioness of Exeter – which assured them that their 'brother beyond the sea' was not 'slain' but had escaped, and Bess intimated that one of the French King's Privy Chamber 'very familiar with Sir Francis Bryan . . . gave the Cardinal Pole warning'.[94] This she might well have learnt from Wyatt, and in turn she sent news to him. Was it from Bess that Wyatt 'heard such a word' that Robert Branceter 'was secretly once in England with the Marquess of Exeter, and returned'?[95]

In the summer of 1538 a servant of Lord Montague's carried three letters from his master to Bess Darrell, and another, Jerome Ragland, brought her 'assurance of certain lands'. To Ragland she gave news of Wyatt, who 'was then come out of Spain', and of his discovery of a poison, and revealed also that in France Wyatt had seen Cardinal Pole, but not spoken to him.[96] Why had Montague visited her in Hackney, the interrogators asked? To tell her that Sir Anthony Hungerford had left London, for they were trying to obtain £100 due to the impecunious Bess, but 'no good could be done therein'.[97] Hungerford was married to Bess's sister Jane, and had conservative associations which verged on treason. At the height of the Pilgrimage of Grace he and Sir George Throckmorton arranged to meet at the house of Sir William Essex, there to discuss the rebellion and to study the rebel demands. Essex was one of the MPs who once had met at the Queen's Head tavern to resist the King's proceedings, and he also was intimately connected to the Darrells.[98] Bess, in whom the Pole brothers confided, who had taken sanctuary in the Marquess of Exeter's household, was interrogated on 6 November and forced to reveal their secrets. Confessing that she had told Geoffrey Pole that the King had sent Peter Mewtas into France to kill the Cardinal, she insisted that she could not 'call to her remembrance of whom she heard it'. Was she shielding Wyatt, hiding their letters? She did not shield Geoffrey Pole, confessing that he had vowed, hearing of Mewtas's mission: 'By God's blood', if he succeeded, 'I would thrust my dagger in him', even 'at the King's heels'.[99] 'It would be a strange world as words were made treason', mused Lord Montague.[100]

His family and friends had known how vulnerable their connection with the Cardinal made them. Montague had foretold that 'the King to be revenged of Reynold [Reginald], I fear, will kill us all'. Cromwell 'for one Pole's sake would destroy all Poles', so Thomas Starkey told Wriothesley, 'if the King were not of a good nature . . .'[101] The Marchioness of Exeter, who was also examined on 6 November, languished in the Tower – perhaps interminably, no one knew.[102] Bess Darrell, although soon free, was again left without protection, contemplating the consequences of her confessions. For the while, Wyatt was in the dark, knowing nothing yet of the arrests, of Bess's ordeal, or how narrowly his letters escaped the inquisitors. 'At night late' on 13 November Wriothesley – who had his own connections with the 'confederates' – wrote to Wyatt of the disaster. Calling on their shared knowledge of Seneca's *De clementia* (*On Mercy*), he told him that at first, the King had 'passed over' the accusations of 'their own domestics', thinking 'with his clemency to conquer their cankeredness, as Caesar at the last won and overcame Cinna'.[103] But the Pole circle stood too close to the throne for royal clemency to last. Tried for treason at the end of November, Lord Montague, the Marquess of Exeter, Sir Edward Neville and Sir Geoffrey Pole were found guilty, to no one's surprise.[104]

At Mass in Paris on St Andrew's Day, 30 November, it was Bonner's 'fortune' to overhear Cardinal du Bellay's whispered conversation about news from England: 'the Marquess within six days should lose his head . . . Oh! . . . what with hanging, burning, and heading they make there good riddance'.[105] In Toledo the news of the arrests of Pole's brothers proved what was suspected – the depth of Henry's depravity, the extremity of his tyranny.[106] Wyatt knew that he was not beyond his king's reach. Not only did the evidence of Mason – 'my Instrument of my treasones' – remain as a smouldering threat, but soon he understood that he was himself tangled in the mesh of revelations which destroyed the Exeter circle. At the Imperial court 'some here off reputation' told him that 'parventure I was had in suspect'. Pretending to be dismissive of the charges and their terrors, he wrote with irony to Cromwell at the New Year, blaming the malevolence of his enemies perennially stalking and unnamed: 'like as I take it light, so I ascribe it to such invention as some of my good friends would be glad to have it'. Let him, he implored, come home to explain, to justify himself.[107]

In Cardinal Pole's family they had foretold that 'the King would go so far that all the world would mislike him'.[108] So it proved. Now not only the alliance between Francis and the Emperor but his own actions isolated Henry. From the Curia at the end of October came appalled accounts of events in England which would 'sicken a statue'. '*Quel perduto Re*' – that lost King, lost to the Church, damned – had destroyed the shrine of St Thomas of Canterbury, sanctified by 'infinite miracles' over four hundred years. (This was true: Wriothesley had recently 'played a part in that play', and overseen its destruction.) Its jewels were seized, and the bones of the saint burnt and scattered to the winds. Monastic houses were turned into royal palaces and their lands given over to hunting parks. The Pope called on the nuncios at the courts of Charles and Francis to demand swift retribution for such scandals to God, and at a consistory in Rome on 25 October commissioned a group of cardinals to consider the remedy.[109] At Westminster on 16 November, Henry, Supreme Head of the English Church, came clad all in white to dispute concerning the blessed sacrament of the altar with the reformer John Lambert. Cromwell wrote to Wyatt on the 28th of Henry's triumph over the 'miserable heretic sacramentary', and of Lambert's burning at the stake. This was a show of Catholic orthodoxy to display Henry as 'the mirror and light of all other kings and princes of Christendom'.[110] It failed to convince them.

An alliance between Henry and the Emperor still hovered in prospect while Charles held to his 'fixed fantasy' of the crusade against the infidel. At the end of September the Venetian ambassador smilingly asked the Emperor whether he had found a way of including the English King in the Turkish enterprise. Charles replied that he had just been discussing it with Wyatt. Yet Henry's impossible condition for joining a league against the Turk was always that the Emperor declare against the Pope.[111] Philip Hoby arrived in Toledo late in October, with instructions which revealed the weakness of the King's diplomatic hand, how little he had to weigh in the balance. As was 'the office of a perfect friend', Henry offered advice. But little else. Just how untenable was any alliance was clear in Wyatt's account of his audience on 1 November. When he reminded the Emperor of his promise of Milan – 'I stick stiff for the State of Milan, alledging promises and all that I can' – Wyatt was made to understand that 'the occasion is past, and they seem to lament it'. To give Milan to Mary and the Infante would 'despair the Frenchmen and provoke them', and prevent the Turkish crusade. Henry should have accepted Milan 'when time was', when it was offered. Wyatt now accused the Emperor of temporizing – of 'delays farther off and colder than of late it seemed'. True, Charles admitted, he had learnt delaying tactics from the practice of other monarchs, yet he was himself 'no such negotiator'. Rightly, Wyatt suspected that 'Don Diego's coming hath done no good . . . because we find more coldness than afore'.[112]

Don Diego Hurtado de Mendoza returned to the Imperial court on 18 November. Closeted with the Emperor for six hours, he made his 'relation'. Hearing of the English King's tyranny and violence, Charles was '*tutto stomacato contra quello inimico della fe* [totally disgusted by that enemy of the faith]'.[113] He wrote to his sister, Mary of Hungary, that he could not 'with good conscience and honour' treat of marriages with a King 'so notoriously alienated from our faith and religion'. No marriage could be made without papal dispensation, and although Henry took no account of that, Charles must. Her orders were to temporize.

Yet even now, Charles revealed, the English ambassador '*m'a parlé par manière de bonne affection envers moi et en grand secret en jurant que c'est de lui mesmes* [spoke to me affectionately, and in great secret, swearing that he spoke as of himself]'.[114] While relations turned from cold to icy between Henry and Charles, whose 'friendship' with the French King was now blazed abroad, reports came from Toledo of Wyatt's increasing desperation. '*Molto smarito* [very bewildered]', '*più che mai discontento* [more discontented than ever]', he now abandoned the indirections of diplomatic parlance.[115] '*Un di l'Imperator sarà in volontà di concludere che non trovarà il suo Re dello animo che è* [one day the Emperor will wish to conclude the alliance and will find that his king is no longer of the same mind]', so he told Vivaldini of Mantua.[116] Far from home, left to rely on his own doubtful discretion, with events moving too fast for him to receive any instruction, he was forced to act 'as of himself', in full knowledge of the danger that his actions might be disavowed by his king, once he came to hear of them, and would infuriate the Emperor. Suspecting that Wyatt was pursuing a maverick diplomacy, at the end of November Charles sent a message to Genoa for a package for Wyatt to be intercepted as it arrived from Milan.[117] This package, it seems, was sent from the new Duke of Urbino, as Wyatt fanned the flames of a fire 'kindled in Italy'.

In the same letter which told the nuncios of the sacrilege of 'that damned King' of England news came of the death on 21 October of Francesco Maria della Rovere, Duke of Urbino. Though the Curia did not say so, he had been assassinated – like King Hamlet – as poison was dripped in his ear as he slept. This death was as portentous as suspicious, for it laid Italy open to papal ambitions. The Pope's grandson Ottavio Farnese, newly – disastrously – married to Margaret of Austria, the Emperor's daughter, on 12 October was conveniently appointed to succeed to the Duke of Urbino's office of Prefect of Rome on All Saints' Day.[118] There was instant alarm. 'No man in Italy matched better the Roman Bishop, than this Duke,' wrote Cromwell's agent in Venice. By the Duke's death 'it may be that many things will innovate in Italy'.[119] One of the first moves of Paul III as pope had been to intervene in the disputed succession of Camerino, a small but wealthy principality in the marches of Italy. The precariousness of its ruling dynasty of Varano had offered an opportunity for aggrandizement for neighbouring princes, and the della Rovere had seized it. Secretly, without papal consent, in October 1534 Francesco Maria's son, Guidobaldo della Rovere, had married Giulia, heiress of the last Varano duke, and taken possession of Camerino. In 1535 the Pope excommunicated him, and placed Camerino under interdict. As in any dispute in Italian politics, the Emperor and the French King had taken sides in the dispute over Camerino, the Emperor giving his protection to della Rovere.[120] In Genoa in June 1538 the Pope had promised Charles that he would take no action against the Duke of Urbino, a promise which he now broke.[121]

Guidobaldo called upon his allies. On 5 November his envoy, Felice Tiranni, arrived post haste in Toledo with news of the old Duke's death. Granvelle ran round his chamber, crying '*o, o, è morto, è morto*', and promising to do no less for the son than for his father. Letters from Guidobaldo to the Emperor and to ambassadors at his court expressed Urbino's 'bitter plight' and sought justice and protection.[122] In the 'note of remembrance' given to Hoby when he left Spain, Wyatt told of receiving a letter from the new Duke, Guidobaldo, acknowledging the 'ancient amity' between the English King and 'his house, as well for the fellowship of the Garter as other ways', and offering his service 'in anything'. Ordered to confer with Wyatt, to discover 'if I shall practise anything with him, and what', Tiranni had sent back to Urbino for permission 'to commune secreter matters with me if the King will incline to the hearing of them'.[123] This cloak-and-dagger exchange had prompted the mysterious package from Milan. Wyatt's mind now turned to 'practices' and to Italy. Even before the crisis of Camerino, he had proposed a league between the 'potentates of Italy' and his king to defend the 'peace of Italy'.* Hoby's private notes told of conversations with Wyatt in Toledo, and presented a vision of the opportunity offered by the 'division of the potentates of Italy with the Bishop of Rome':

* See above, p. 403.

Concerning the Bishop of Rome, never better time to inflame malice against him than now. And in especial with the potentates of Italy, for all they are already moved against him . . . Wherefore it were very expedient for the King to send some of his Gent[lemen] abroad among them and to fall in familiarity with them, whereby they may the better fall to the knowledge of Christ's Gospel and his abominable abuse.[124]

In Toledo that autumn there were fears – justified fears – that a papal army would invade and seize Camerino, dispossessing the Duke in favour of one of the Farnese family.[125] On 15 November the Pope ordered the Duke and Duchess of Urbino to cede Camerino on pain of confiscation of all their territory and fiefs – not only Camerino but Urbino also. When they refused the Pope's terrible son Pier Luigi Farnese was given the military command to enforce obedience upon the rebellious vassals.[126] Now no Italian prince could feel secure. In Venice the Imperial ambassador told the Duke of Mantua's ambassador that his prince must come to the aid of Guidobaldo, not only through claims of blood but through his own interest. If Guidobaldo were driven from his principality, then no other prince was safe from Farnese tyranny.[127] In Toledo there was universal murmuring, and only the increasingly frantic nuncio defended the Pope's actions.[128] 'The Pope had begun to set his hand to the persecution of the Duke out of time and season' which made it clear that he 'would satisfy his desires', so Rossetto of Ferrara protested.[129] The Pope, leader of the Holy League, was now sending against fellow Christians the forces raised to fight the infidel – so far had he fallen from his apostolic duty.[130] Other powers of Italy – especially the Pope's rebels, those under a papal ban – looked to the Emperor for protection against Farnese aggression. The great Roman prince Ascanio Colonna, whom Paul III had excommunicated, rode fast for Genoa, proposing – to the Emperor's horror – to take ship for Spain and call on Charles's aid against the tyrant Pope.[131] The Duke of Urbino's death had offered an *occasione* for the Pope, but 'the division of the potentates of Italy with the Bishop of Rome' gave a great *occasione* for England also, and Wyatt took it. Here was the prospect of revolution in Italy which Cardinal Pole had foretold.

On 7 December Pietro Mocenigo, the Venetian ambassador, had a remarkable conversation with '*un mio amico* [a friend of mine]', anatomizing the state of Christendom. This friend was a man '*di auttorità et maneggio appresso la Caesarea Maiestà* [of authority and influence with the Emperor]', '*di ottimo animo*' [very well disposed]' to La Serenissima, but for good reasons he insisted that he did not wish to be named. The friend was Wyatt. Revealing all he knew about the preparedness of the Imperial fleet and the likelihood – or not – of the Emperor's leading it against the Turk, Wyatt's first concern was with Italy. He had, he said, no confidence in the peace between Charles and Francis: for all the shows of love, they hated each other, as was natural between the Spaniards and the French. Now that the Pope was about to wage war on Urbino, Wyatt judged that the Duke would call upon the Emperor for help. If Charles *did* give help, the Pope would invite the French King into Italy, and would 'become French', would abandon his neutrality. If the Emperor *did not* help, the Duke must invite the French King to come to his aid. In either case, the French King would come willingly, and would invade Italy. The Italian wars would begin all over again. Wyatt, speaking '*con grande affettione et amore* [with great affection and love]', feared for Italy and for Venice: '*Io vorei vedere quello excellentissimo stato in pace et quiete, perchè da ogni banda vedo angustie et travagli* [I would wish to see that most excellent state in peace and quiet, for from every side I see anguish and travail].' Mocenigo sent this report '*più secretamente che si possa* [as secretly as possible]' to the Doge.[132]

Presenting the contest over Camerino as a great confrontation between the forces of liberty and tyranny, Wyatt lamented the threat which Farnese ambitions posed to 'the quiet of Italy' and condemned the Pope's withdrawal of his forces just as the Holy League was poised to crusade against the Turk. The disaster at Prevesa in September 1538 had already left the League in disarray, for when the League fleet had fled before Barbarossa the Venetians blamed the Imperial admiral Andrea Doria for abandoning them, and Doria blamed the Admiral of the Republic.[133] In mid-December the court was awaiting the arrival of Giannettino Doria, Andrea Doria's nephew, who was sent in post to explain the calamity at Prevesa, to justify Doria's actions, and to reveal the Imperial fleet's unpreparedness for any great action: the worst of news for the Emperor, for the Venetians, and for England. Mocenigo was deeply suspicious of his coming, not least because 'uno Englese [an Englishman]' – Wyatt – warned him of Giannettino's 'sinistri officii [sinister dealings]' in Toledo, and told him 'la verità di molte cose [the truth about many things]'.[134] If Paul III forsook the League in order to pursue Farnese advantage, Venice would be left alone to face the Gran Signor. Thus Venice, most anti-papal of states, and most vulnerable to Turkish attack, bitterly condemned the Pope's aggression against Camerino. In Toledo, Mocenigo spoke 'blazingly', warning that the Pope would incite 'the powers of Italy' to hatred against him. Mocenigo's ardent advocacy of the Duke of Urbino's cause would bring him into furious confrontation with the nuncio, and into the arms of Wyatt.[135] Wyatt and Mocenigo were each other's last chance.

Wyatt was also talking frankly with Rossetto of Ferrara. All the court rumours of the Emperor travelling to Flanders were illusory, said Wyatt. Since the talks of alliance with Henry had frozen, the Emperor would never risk being blown onto the English coast, for he might remember fearfully the fate of his father. Sheltering from Channel storms in 1506, Archduke Philip had become hostage to Henry VII, and been forced to hand over Yorkist exiles – who had found sanctuary in Flanders – to be beheaded.*[136] Isolated, beleaguered, Wyatt understood that his only diplomatic advantage lay in emphasizing the great power and wealth of his king, and insisting on Henry's willingness to deploy them. In Wyatt's vision of England's safety, the fates of Camerino and England became linked, for both needed to defend themselves against papal sanctions and the threat of war. The news from Italy in mid-December was that 'the ambassador of England resident in Spain hath offered many things in favour of the duke [of Urbino]'.[137] Wyatt had promised that his king would underwrite a campaign against papal forces with his vast wealth, and use all his power to damage the Pope. On 26 December Vivaldini of Mantua reported that the Emperor was urgently sending an envoy to Rome to dissuade the Pope from war against Urbino and Camerino. Weighing heavily on Charles was fear

* See above, pp. 69–70.

of worse to come: he had heard of the extravagant promises of the English ambassador '*di aiutare il detto Duca non solo a diffendere il suo, ma a cacciare il Papa di Roma* [to aid the Duke, not only to defend himself, but to hunt, to chase the Pope from Rome]'.[138]

This was the diplomacy of desperation. Here were promises made without royal sanction. In April Henry had blustered that 'even if a league were formed against us, between the Pope, the Emperor, and the King of France, we should not care a fig for it'.[139] Now he learnt otherwise, for that threat became real and imminent as the Pope called for a crusade against the English King. The Pope felt threatened, too. In Nice on 6 June he had asked when Christendom had ever been in greater need of defending. Was not the Turk moving all his forces to threaten it? Were not the Lutherans rising to destroy the 'poor Church'? Was not the English King, indurate in his errors, set against the papacy?[140] In his anxiety, Paul III began to rally the forces of Christendom to defend the embattled Church, and to return the King of England to obedience. The time would come soon when Charles would be forced to choose between an enterprise against the infidel and an enterprise against the schismatic King of England. In the reciprocity of diplomacy, just as the errors of an ambassador dishonoured his prince, so the crimes of a king dishonoured his ambassador. When Henry was shunned and threatened, so would Wyatt be. Bewilderment turned to nightmare. Soon Wyatt was described as '*disperato*', '*disperatissimo* [desperate, very desperate]'.[141]

14

Disperatissimo

At the New Year of 1539 Wyatt wrote to Cromwell imploring his recall:

But out of game I beseech your lordship humbly to help me. I need no long persuasions. Ye know what case I am in . . . I am at the wall. I am not able to endure to March, and the rest shall all be the King's dishonour and my shame beside the going to nought of all my particular things.[1]

The anguish of exile, fears of malevolent enemies working against him in his absence, and the need to vindicate himself called Wyatt home; the nightmarish turn of events in Toledo compelled him to leave. When the violence and sacrilege of the 'perfidious King' of England became known in Toledo, preachers called for punishment, human and divine. On 24 November 1538 the Archbishop of Granada had preached a sermon anathematizing the heretic King. If the animus against Henry turned against his subjects, then his ambassador in Spain and all his embassy were vulnerable. Wyatt's hasty notes sent back to England early in December included these: '. . . my complaining of the bishop's preaching, praying the people to pray for the King's reducing to the faith . . . Item: the burning of the saint's bones, etc.'[2] 'Reducing': the Curia wrote insistently of the need to 'reduce', to draw back, the '*desviati*', those who had left the true path. The 'saint's bones' which Wyatt irreverently dismissed with his laconic 'etc.' were those of the martyred Becket. 'I would I could persuade these preachers' to preach of the Supreme Head's 'grave proceeding' against heretics in his Church as urgently as they denounced his 'burning of the bishop's bones'. By 2 January news of the condemnation of the Marquess of Exeter and Pole's brother had reached Toledo.[3] Trying to justify Henry's actions became ever more dangerous. The Emperor had already warned Wyatt against denouncing papal authority, had counselled silence. If ever he spoke of it again, was even 'tempted to mention it if it came into his mind', Charles would 'make him rue it'.[4] Beware the Grand Inquisitor. In the Spanish kingdoms the Holy Office, a disciplinary institution of extraordinary power, was on guard against any heterodoxy.[5] Still Wyatt dared to protest.[6] Soon the Emperor must decide whether to fulfil his threats, and for how much longer he would tolerate the ambassador of 'that enemy of the faith'. In Spain there was a popular proverb which Wyatt, the lover of proverbs, would have been wise to heed: *Con el rey y la Inquisicion, chiton!* ['With the King and the Inquisition, keep silent!'].[7] Yet Wyatt could not keep silent, for he was bound to obey his king's commands.

At the end of 1538 all the great prelates and grandees of Spain were gathered in Toledo for the holding of the Cortes.[8] Among them was Don Diego Hurtado de Mendoza, whom we find in conversation with Wyatt. The subject was a safe one, of universal and abiding interest for the nobility: finely bred horses. To his letter of 2 January Wyatt added an urgent postscript. With magnificent condescension, Don Diego was sending two genets for Cromwell, riding horses so precious and spirited that Wyatt must accompany and manage them. 'I trust to bring them myself to see them the better ordered': a lure to summon him home.[9] Mendoza, Wyatt's exact contemporary, was scholar, soldier, diplomat – and poet. A famous book collector, he came to own the works of all the classical authors and Italian poets which we know Wyatt read, and much of the divine literature. Mendoza was one of the first to write Horatian verse epistles in Castilian, composing in *tercetos*, like the Italians, like Wyatt, and using colloquial diction. He chose Stoic themes: the search for self-knowledge and invulnerability to fortune, the retreat from the press of courts, the futility of future fears and hopes, the quiet of mind. One was addressed to his friend Don Luis de Zúñiga y Ávila, whom we have met and will meet again. Believed to be the author of the first ever picaresque novel, *Lazarillo de Tormes*, Mendoza told tales of swindling clergy and corrupt sellers of papal indulgences. He was a friend of Pietro Aretino. 'This man appeareth courteous, learned and also witty', so Cromwell heard from his agent in Venice.[10] Mendoza and Wyatt might even have been friends, in other circumstances.

Viatvs desviatvs: wayward Wyatt. Once, the nuncio had believed Wyatt to be '*bravo*', and secretly working towards Henry's reconciliation, but he had learnt differently. Now he demonized him: Wyatt was a '*maligno spirito*', '*diabolicho instrumento*', '*indemoniato* [bewitched]'. In truth, it was not only Wyatt's supposed heresy that horrified Poggio but also his 'evil actions', his promises to 'vex the state of Rome'. On the last day of 1538 Poggio wrote in desperation to Cardinal Farnese:

And in order that you see better the wickedness of this evil spirit, you have to know how closely he practises with the ambassadors of Ferrara and Mantua, and I know that he has said that those two princes could not fail Guidobaldo and he would not lack men: and that his king will send money and make every effort to harm his Holiness, and I am certain that this devilish instrument studies to persuade these ambassadors as much as he can.[11]

'Every day he grew worse,' complained Poggio, urging the Pope to order the Holy Office to enforce Wyatt's obedience. In Toledo, as the nuncio lamented the 'evil actions' of the English ambassador, the Emperor's counsellors assured him that Wyatt had been told to desist. The right moment was awaited to unleash the Inquisitors. 'Perhaps that moment will never come,' the nuncio wrote gloomily on 26 December.[12] Soon it did.

In the last days of 1538 Wyatt did something incendiary. While councillors of the Royal Council of Castile entered the council chamber, 'an unknown man' – a 'demon' – was waiting outside to hand them 'a writing or memorial'. One of the councillors, Diego Escudero, 'a learned and virtuous man', promptly gave the text to his 'very good friend' the nuncio, who judged it to be 'full of Lutheran and English [*sic*] arguments persuading the councillors to diabolical beliefs against the Apostolic See'. Poggio knew that 'some would be displeased' that he pursued the '*indemoniato*' Wyatt, but conscience would not allow him to remain silent. Wyatt never stopped proselytizing to anyone who would listen; he must be stopped from perverting good Christians with his heresies. The Inquisitors now pursued the 'unknown man'.[13] Who was he, this demon, and what was the text? The unknown man was one of Wyatt's household, acting on his orders. The text may have

been Richard Morison's *Apomaxis*, written to defend the royal supremacy and to refute papal authority.[14] At the New Year the Inquisitors
called on the nuncio, commanding him to reveal all he knew about the
'evil doctrine' which the English ambassador was spreading. 'So great
a pestilence could never be allowed in these kingdoms.' There would
be evidence enough to condemn Wyatt, so the nuncio assured them.[15]
Learning of the evangelizing and wild threats of *'l'oratore Anglo'*, the
Pope fulminated. In the margin of a letter from Rome to the nuncio in
Toledo was this scribbled note: *'De la Inquisicione contra al oratore di quel Re
Sua Santità non resta satisfatta, et voi la dovete sollecitare, &c.* [His Holiness is
not satisfied with the Inquisition against the ambassador of that King,
and you must pursue it, etc.]'.[16]

If ever there was a good time to come to the attention of the Spanish Inquisition that time was not the New Year of 1539. Wyatt's proselytizing against the Pope and protests against the preachers came at
a particularly dangerous moment for English *luteranos* in the Spanish
kingdoms. Not only the international politics of Christendom, but the
domestic politics of the Holy Office made it unpropitious to provoke
the Inquisitors. Inquisitor General Alonso de Manrique, the protector
of moderate Erasmian reform in Spain, had retired in disgrace to his
diocese.[17] In 1538 he died, and was replaced by an Inquisitor General determined to seek out heresy, Juan Tavera, Cardinal Archbishop
of Toledo. During Manrique's reclusion, the Suprema – the Supreme
Council of the Inquisition – had gained power, and in these years had
encroached on the functions of the Inquisitor General and was also
extending its authority over the provincial tribunals. In 1539 Fernando
Valdés, a notable hardliner, became president of the Suprema.[18] Just
as the Pope thundered against *l'oratore Anglo* and the Holy Office began
to proceed against him a sea change was occurring in the priorities of
the Spanish Inquisition. From concentrating on the purity of the race
and persecution of *conversos* [converted Jews], it was turning its force to
combat a great threat to the purity of religion: the incursion of foreign
heresy.[19]

Every year on a Sunday in Lent the Edict of Faith was proclaimed in
cathedrals and churches throughout the Spanish kingdoms, and every

Christian was taught the duty to seek out and denounce the heretic, and the terrible penalties, in this world and the next, for those who concealed it. Every Spaniard became an agent of the Inquisition. From the early 1530s anathemas of 'Lutheranism' were added to the traditional denunciations of Jewish and Islamic 'heresies', and from the pulpits the heresies of the English King and his subjects were horribly described to Christians who knew their duty.[20] As pervervid accounts of Henry's alleged apostasy, tyranny and adultery spread, every Englishman became tainted with the reputation of being *luterano*, and it was feared that their heresies would infect anyone with whom they came in contact.[21] It was 'by cawse of the name that Inglysshe men then had to be all Lutherans' that Wyatt and Mason had vainly entreated Bonner and Heynes to be seen at Mass with them.[22] In the autumn of 1537 attacks on English merchants by 'Biscayans' had gone unpunished.[23] Landing at Cadiz in September 1538, Richard Abbis found that since the peace between the French King and the Emperor the English in Spain were despised as heretics and Lutherans and 'hated as Turks'. The Spanish people declared that 'they trust shortly to have war with England and to set in the Bishop of Rome with all his disciples again in England'.[24] The English merchants who had long traded in the Mediterranean ports of the south and the Atlantic ports of the north were now threatened. According to the principle that the heretic had no rights, the merchants' goods were despoiled, their cargoes seized.

Terrifyingly, the beliefs of Englishmen were now attracting the urgent attention of the Inquisition. In 1534 John Mason had saved two English merchants in Valladolid who were discovered with a 'foolish book against the Pope'. 'If we had not made for them great friends and entreatance', they would have been burnt.[25] It was 'infection' from the spread of books from abroad which the Holy Office especially feared, and rightly. In 1528 Humphrey Monmouth, William Tyndale's patron, confessed that he had been given a copy of Luther's *De libertate Christiane* (*The Liberty of a Christian*) by Arnold, a young man serving in the English embassy in Spain.[26] Two English merchants – Hugh Typton and 'Tomas Xipman' (Thomas Shipman) – did public penance in San Sebastián in the summer of 1537 for denouncing the Pope and prayers to saints, and for saying that 'our King did make no laws in England but . . . [they] did stand with God's laws'.[27] By 1538 it was doubtful whether the English embassy would find 'great friends' to save their compatriots – or themselves – from the Holy Office. The long sufferings of Thomas Pery at the hands of the 'fathers of the Inquisition' began in 1539. Incarcerated in the fortress of Tryana by the orders of the Seville tribunal, Pery was tortured by water and hoisted on the dreaded pulleys, the *garrucha*. On 8 February 1540 he and four other Englishmen would do public penance at an auto-da-fé as priests sang the fifty-first Psalm, '*Miserere*'.[28] Physical torture was far from the invariable practice of the Inquisition, but heresy was an error so desperate that desperate remedies were needed.[29] If Wyatt and his household ever forgot the worst terrors of the Inquisition, the trials of their countrymen reminded them. In February 1539, just as Wyatt was under investigation, a Navarrese Inquisitor held an auto-da-fé at Bilbao. There a Lutheran – a Fleming who had become a naturalized Englishman – was burned as a relapsed heretic. This was John Tack who, so it was reported, jumped into the flames as though into a bed of roses.[30] He was the first foreigner to suffer under the Spanish Inquisition, but not the last.

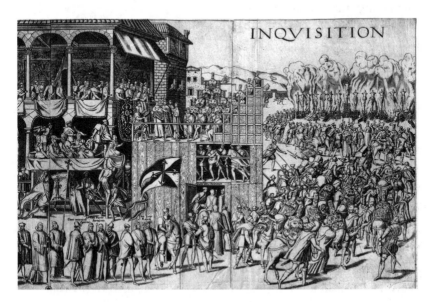

The forces of the Inquisition displayed at an auto-da-fé in Valladolid in 1559

The processes of the Inquisition were mysterious, shrouded in impenetrable secrecy. So dark, so seemingly arbitrary were its investigations that Juan Luis Vives' private name for the Holy Office was 'FORTVNA'. Secrecy heightened its aura of power. The Inquisitors proceeded with a seriousness and deliberation suited to the gravity of their purposes, believing in the exquisite justice of their decisions. Concealment was necessary in the persecution of heresy. A sin as well as a crime, it must be confessed and repented, and the confession and penitence judged to be genuine. The manner of the accusations and the names of witnesses were never revealed, for anonymity protected witnesses, and ignorance of the nature of the denunciation prevented the defendant from framing his admission to confirm or deny it. Secrecy also freed the Inquisitors from outside intervention and allowed them to make unbiased investigations beyond any imputation of corruption. This secrecy was the most feared part of the investigations, torture of an unbearable kind.[31] Later, Wyatt complained to the Emperor: 'though a man live never so uprightly, by their examinations they shall trap him, where there is no publication of witnesses'.[32] The nature of any process against Wyatt or his servants was, and remains, hidden. But some things may be inferred.

Enter the Inquisitors of Toledo: Dr Juan Yanés, the head of the tribunal, Inquisitor Vaquer, and perhaps Dr Blas Ortiz, vicar general of the Archbishop of Toledo. A *consulta da fe* preceded the arrest and trial of heresy suspects. This was not a full-blown interrogation or trial, but the moment when the Inquisitors decided whether there was a case to answer. A *sumaria* or preliminary array of evidence against the accused was collected, and the theological points involved were submitted to three or four *calificadores* (censors) who pronounced whether the acts or words amounted to heresy or suspicion of heresy. A sole *consulta* consists *in extenso* in the records of the Toledo tribunal. Belonging to 1537, it gives an intimate sense of the process and the personnel. This *consulta* took place in the monastery of San Pedro Mártir el Real in Toledo, and the *calificadores* were friars of this Dominican house, learned theologians. Dr Ortiz and some civilian jurists were also involved.[33] Whether the same men began the same process against Wyatt we cannot know, but in January the Inquisitors of Toledo began to investigate him.

The deep secrecy of the Inquisitors' proceedings hardly stopped speculation. The diplomatic community in Toledo was alight with stories that 'certain persons had been secretly examined about the life and morals' of the English ambassador. By 25 January Wyatt had complained '*gagliardamente* [vigorously]' to the Emperor that the Inquisitors were inquiring into private conversations within his household to discover whether he had denounced the Pope. This was, Wyatt protested, to violate the sanctuary of his embassy, to breach the law of nations. He claimed immunity from local jurisdiction. Wyatt's story – according to Alfonso Rossetto and Giovanni Bandino – was that Charles 'marvelled', 'pretended' to know nothing about the Inquisitors' proceedings, claiming that the Holy Office acted without his consent, and promising that he would allow no dishonour either to the ambassador or his King. But they doubted that the pursuit of Wyatt was simply a '*burla* [ruse]' of the nuncio's.[34] The witnesses against Wyatt remain forever unnamed. Since every faithful Christian was bound by the Edict of Faith to denounce impiety, zealous Castilians watched the English embassy. 'We be of purposely provoked by diverse of your inquisitive people,' so Bonner had complained.[35] Because the private discussions in Wyatt's embassy were all in English, the 'certain persons' testifying to the Inquisitors were probably English exiles loyal to Rome. It had been an English '*cavagliero*' who told the nuncio of Wyatt's proselytizing in November 1537.[36]

More vulnerable than the ambassador were his servants, for their immunity was far less certain. The house of an ambassador was 'a sanctuary and a place of retreat to his servants and followers, against all injuries and violences', but there was this crucial proviso: 'that they do nothing against the laws of the country where they are, and against public honesty'.[37] If the ambassador was suspected of speaking illicitly against the Holy Father, then suspicion fell on others within his embassy. Sometime in the spring of 1539 an unnamed servant of Wyatt's was imprisoned by the Inquisitors of Toledo. '*Molto mal contento*', Wyatt pleaded for the man's freedom.[38] While their fellow languished in the secret prison, lonely, disorientated, waiting in terror for the Holy Office to interrogate him, even under torture, the rest of Wyatt's household were fearful for him, and for themselves. Facing the terrible prospect of endless imprisonment, of never returning home, the threat of torture, a prisoner might say anything, incriminate anyone. His friends were especially vulnerable, for in the long months of exile they had joked together, confided in each other, been less than reverent about the Bishop of Rome. They knew the risks of friendship.[39] On 25 January 1539 the exultant nuncio wrote of Wyatt's plaints of persecution by the Holy Inquisition. 'I hope that they will chase him from here. I will not fail'.[40]

Later, Charles told Wyatt that, powerful as he was, he could – or would – not intervene in the decisions of the Holy Office: 'I cannot let [prevent] the Inquisition. This is a thing that toucheth our faith . . . I assure you I will not alter my Inquisition. No, nor if I thought they would be negligent in their offices I would put them out, and put other in the room [office].'[41] 'My Inquisition'. Certainly, the Spanish kings theoretically held power of appointment within the Holy Office and supremacy over it, but whether Charles could halt its processes once begun, especially if the initiative had come from the nuncio, and ultimately from Rome, raises complex questions about the autonomy of the Inquisition in Spain. In practice, it had become an *'imperium in imperio'*, governed by its Suprema, with jurisdiction over all matters connected with the faith.[42] In the investigation of heresy, particularly, the Holy Office came to claim exclusive jurisdiction, even abridging the traditional jurisdiction of the bishops.[43] The Spanish monarchs, since founding the Inquisition in 1487, had fought for its autonomy and to suppress papal interference. By the the time of Charles V, his dominance in Italy and role as 'protagonist of the Church in its struggle with Lutheranism, had enabled him to obtain for the Inquisition virtual, though not acknowledged, independence of Rome'.[44] Yet if the Holy Father himself ordered the Inquisition to proceed against someone under the Emperor's protection, it would be hard for the Emperor to resist. Friends of Alfonso de Valdés had feared in 1531 that if he returned from exile, he would be killed; that even Charles could not save him from the Holy Office. Charles had not been able to protect his favourite preacher, Fray Alonso de Virués, whose long trial and imprisonment by the Inquisition began in 1535. He wrote nine times on Virués's behalf between 1536 and 1538, and finally appealed to the Pope for a brief to annul the Inquisition's sentence.[45]

If the Inquisition imprisoned Wyatt, Charles could hardly appeal to Rome on his behalf, and the Pope would never save him, even for the Emperor. In February Charles admitted that he had allowed Wyatt's heresy to come to the knowledge of the Inquisitors, and that when Wyatt pleaded with him, he had given him a very severe warning to be careful what he said, otherwise he would allow the Holy Office to proceed against him.[46] Later, in the shadow of seemingly arbitrary justice at home, Wyatt recalled: 'what hazarde I was in in Spayne with the Inquisition onlye by spekinge agaynste the Bysshope of Rome . . . The emprore had myche a doe to save me'.[47] Somehow, Charles did intervene to protect Wyatt. But, saved for the while from the Inquisition, Wyatt was now in the eye of a perfect diplomatic storm.

The call for a crusade against England had come. By the winter of 1538 the Pope could no longer tolerate Henry's disobedience and his dishonour to the Holy See: he must be reconciled, 'brought back' – by war.[48] Henry's breaking 'of the mystical body of Christ which is His Church'[49] had invited war in Christendom. The papal diplomats poured forth invective against a 'tyrant so cruel', that 'rebel', 'that enemy of the faith'. 'So wicked an enemy of God and of justice' could not escape punishment.[50] Eternal damnation in the next world was already foretold, for he was 'that lost King' – a lost soul, and damned – but there were penalties in this world also.[51] If Henry was the enemy of God, it was virtuous and a Christian duty to fight him, and holy war against him was justified.[52] Though the Curia sometimes chose to see the English schism as the rebellion of a remote island under a tyrant king, they knew that if Henry was not returned to obedience, then schism could not be prevented elsewhere. The spectre which haunted the papacy – of England allied with German Lutherans – became real in 1537–8 with Henry's rapprochement with the League of Schmalkalden, a defensive alliance of Protestant princes and cities.[53] The bull of excommunication against Henry was finally published on 17

December 1538.[54] It lay with the Emperor as much as himself, insisted the Pope, to remedy 'such great evils, murders, and martyrdoms as the said King daily executes upon the forsaken Christians of that unhappy realm'.[55] This was a call for war.

Late in December the Pope sent the Cardinal of England, Reginald Pole, Henry's traitor, as legate to the Emperor. His mission: to persuade Charles of his Christian, his Imperial duty to undertake 'the reduction of that realm to the true religion and no longer suffer that King with impunity to rage against God and the saints'. That the 'reduction' must be by force was clear from the Pope's order for the Holy League to make a truce with the Turk, lest the chance be lost of 'managing the matter of England'.[56] Henry's schism and disobedience were justification enough for the Pope to call for a crusade, yet there was another compelling reason. Paul III lived in terror of heretic forces massed against him. In the Curia, they had watched with alarm the seizure of the monasteries, because of the sacrilege, but also because of the vast access of wealth which came to the heretic King. Their waking nightmare was that he would use this wealth for martial, evangelical purposes, to send an army against the Holy See. At the New Year of 1539 rumours reached Rome that Henry was raising fifteen to twenty thousand landsknechts.[57] With so vast an army the English King might lead 'some great action' to 'kindle a fire in Italy' which would threaten *pax Italiae* (the peace of Italy) and the Holy See itself. Wyatt's wild promises to defend Camerino and 'to hunt the Pope from Rome', his boasts that his king had more money than 'all of Christendom joined together', began to be believed in the Curia.[58] The Holy Father feared that Henry would assault not only his theoretical authority but his temporal power and possessions:

Il Re Anglo se non sarà molestato lui molestara Noi non pure con seminare la heresia sua, ma colle arme, et non restara di fomentare i lutherani et farli fare qualche gran moto, come già si sente . . .

If the English King is not attacked, *he will attack Us*, not only by spreading his heresy but with arms, and he will not cease fomenting the Lutherans and persuading them to some great action, as is already known . . .[59]

In Toledo in the middle of January 1539 Pietro Mocenigo, the Venetian ambassador, found himself in the inimical company of the nuncio. 'I should know', so Poggio warned him, that he knew of the English ambassador's boasts to aid the Duke of Urbino, but 'before the money could come from England to Italy, the English King would have so much to do at home that he had better save the money for himself . . .'[60]

At the Imperial court the nuncio was urging vengeance on Henry. Now was the time to act, he insisted, because the English people were desperate to remove their tyrant king. The 'islanders', incensed by his sacrilege and tyranny and by the deprivations caused by the stop of commerce, would rise against Henry, depose him, even assassinate him.[61] Before leaving Rome, Pole was already convinced that the Emperor was poised to undertake the crusade against England'.[62] On 16 December an unnamed English 'gentleman' – a fugitive traitor – arrived from Rome bringing letters from Cardinal Farnese, and the nuncio discussed with the Emperor's councillors the publication of the papal censures and the absolution of the English people from their allegiance to their king. Seeking to 'ignite' the Emperor to undertake the '*impresa d'Inghilterra* [enterprise of England]', Poggio always insisted that the enterprise would be quick and 'easy', but Charles's councillors knew too well the dangers of beginning a war from which it might be impossible to retreat. While acknowledging his duty toward Christendom, and his family duty to avenge his aunt, Charles insisted that he could not countenance any action against England while his mind was wholly set on the crusade against the Turk.[63] Yet it seems that in the winter of 1538 Granvelle, Charles's principal counsellor, *had* promised action against Henry.[64]

At the end of December Pole left Rome on his terrible winter journey to Castile, left secretly, travelling incognito in fear of assassination by Henry's agents. Beseeching God to accompany Pole as he rode in post through 'cold, snow and mud', Cardinal Farnese sent him two crucial letters in the Pope's hand, one to the Emperor, the other to the King of France.[65] Pole's desolate journey through the icy passes of the Apennines became more desolate still as he learnt that his brother, Lord Montague, was condemned to death.[66] In Toledo,

Wyatt had terrifying intelligence of Pole's coming: 'afore Pole came owte of Rome', he knew of it, somehow. At this moment of acute danger, as the traitor Cardinal came to levy war on England, Wyatt sent desperately to England with the news, seeking 'to knowe what I shulde do. I hard no thynge'. As Pole travelled on, Wyatt sent another message: 'he is on the see or els as fare as Genes [Genoa] by lande hetherwarde. I harde no worde agayne'.[67] Since his letters of 15 January and despatches sent with George Blage on the 24th are lost, we rely on accounts from Italian envoys who observed with fascination the defiance of this *imp*rudent ambassador. On 9 January a 'desperate' Wyatt told Alfonso Rossetto that Henry no longer knew whom to trust, and was manning ships and arming himself with artillery. 'Very desperate' by the 20th – not least because the Inquisitors were pursuing him in full cry – Wyatt boasted that the Emperor should ally with his king, who was the richest in Christendom. If Charles allowed the censures to be published in his kingdoms, fine: they would have '*un osso molto duro da rossegar* [a very hard bone to gnaw]'.[68] Here Wyatt, 'piping in an ivy leaf', spoke colloquially in Italian, as he did in English.

In Toledo that winter Wyatt and the Venetian ambassador found friendship and common cause in denouncing the tyranny of the Pope. In mid-January Mocenigo learnt of the arrival of a papal brief which gave the English King one hundred days to return to 'Holy Mother Church': should Henry fail, he would be excommunicated, and his subjects freed from their oath of fealty. If the brief were published in the cathedral of Toledo, it would be tantamount to a declaration of war. The prospect of the *impresa d'Inghilterra* appalled the Venetian ambassador: not because of any great desire to protect England, but because it would divert the imminent Turkish campaign, which was so urgently needed to save Venice. Mocenigo went to the Emperor to demand whether it was true; whether he would publish the brief. Temporizing, Charles demurred: he had not seen the brief, he had no desire for war with England, although the King of France did. Mocenigo was left 'scandalized' and 'very confused'.[69] 'At the wall' as Wyatt was 'at the wall', Mocenigo now counted on Wyatt's promises. 'This English ambassador', he assured the Doge, was '*uno gentilissimo signore* [a very fine gentleman]' and Mocenigo's great friend. Speaking to Mocenigo, he had often expressed his king's 'very singular' amity toward Venice, and given him to believe that any time help were needed against the Turk Henry would finance a force of ten thousand landsknechts. Seeing the present turn of events, he would do so even more willingly.[70] 'From a friend of his' – almost certainly Mocenigo – Wyatt learnt of the brief.

Despite the danger, Wyatt dared to protest to the Emperor. At the end of January, in the same audience, in the same breath, as he asserted the sanctity of his embassy and demanded immunity from the Inquisition, he denied the inviolability of Pole's legation. Since Pole was rebel and traitor to his king, the Emperor was bound, by treaty and by honour, to hand him over. Charles must forbid the traitor Cardinal entry to his kingdoms and refuse to receive him. To this outburst, Charles replied 'with the best words in the world': he had not known in advance of Pole's coming, and could neither legitimately countermand his mission nor deliver him to Wyatt. The story of this remarkable audience was reported by Bandino and Rossetto, who probably heard it from Wyatt.[71] In this acute diplomatic crisis, acting on his own initiative, Wyatt remembered and rehearsed the arguments advanced against Pole's first legation to the French King in 1537. *Ius gentium*, which ordered ambassadors 'to have special privilege to be admitted', did not prevail against the treaty promises of Charles and Henry not to harbour each other's traitors. Fortunately – unusually – when instructions arrived from England weeks later they sanctioned what he had already done.[72] For the while Wyatt's safety rested in his ambassadorial immunity, only for the while.

Cardinal Pole was anxiously awaited in Toledo, with hope or dread. Upon his arrival, the Emperor would be charged to publish the papal censures, to allow Henry's public excommunication with full anathemas in Toledo Cathedral. In the first days of February Wyatt had several audiences where he 'labored . . . importunatlie' against Pole's coming, always returning '*molto mal contento*'.[73] On the 5th the anxious nuncio wrote that there was no news of Pole; he had no idea what to do or say until he came.[74] Might the Emperor refuse to publish the bull? In that possibility lay Poggio's fear, and Wyatt's quivering hope. He had little enough hope of his king's favour. When a courier arrived from England on 3 February, news came of the beheading of Pole's brother.[75] And now perhaps Wyatt finally learnt Henry's reaction to his earlier precipitate, reckless diplomacy. On 19 January Henry had written 'as touching Camerino upon occasion whereof ye much harp', assuring Wyatt that he would not neglect 'our right occasion'. But by then the cause of the Duke of Urbino was already lost, and Camerino was surrendered. With the letter came a warning: Wyatt had ventured too far in the King's name. 'It was commonly spoken at Rome, that the ambassador of England, being in Spain, hath made large promises unto the Duke of Urbino's secretary. We cannot think but that like as they meant by you.' Surely, surely, 'ye have not been so large as to offer anything unto them without our advice and pleasure. *We trust your fidelity and discretion better than so . . .*'[76] Terrors of the consequences of acting beyond his powers made Wyatt 'quail', and he also knew that he was meshed in the web of revelations that destroyed the Exeter circle and maybe was still 'had in suspect'. Now he awaited Pole's coming, in the knowledge that if the papal bull were published ambassadorial immunity and *ius gentium* might not save him.

Riding in post from Barcelona, Pole arrived in Toledo on 11 February and went to stay at the nuncio's house. His first legatine audience with the Emperor waited on Charles's definitive answer to the English King. On the 12th Wyatt was summoned and the death blow delivered to any alliance. Pole had a long audience with the Charles on the following day. 'Scandalized', Wyatt protested again, even now, against the Emperor receiving his king's enemy. He sought permission to take his leave but was refused, for if he withdrew so must all the other English ambassadors at the Habsburg courts in Spain and the Netherlands, and the Imperial ambassador at the English court. The other envoys in Toledo watched Wyatt suffering 'great jealousy and doubt'.[77] 'In Spain all things be waxen from colder to coldest,' so Cromwell learnt from Wyatt. Charles countered his protests with 'great vehement grudge and indignation', alleging that Henry happily received envoys from Charles's 'rebels, vassals and enemies'. Even if Pole 'were his own traitor', the Emperor insisted, since he was 'coming from that Holy (*scilicet*) Father of Rome, he cannot refuse him audience'.[78] Yet it was not only Wyatt's mission which failed.

In Rome, the Curia had conceived a grand design to return England to obedience and to end the schism. In France, the French King with Latino Giovenale Manetti, the papal legate, imagined Imperial, French and Scottish armies invading and partitioning England, and Henry's subjects rising to depose their heretic, tyrant king and elect a new one.[79] In Toledo, Wyatt learnt that Cardinal Pole 'devised' with the Emperor to bring 'seven or eight thousande Almaynes [Germans] into the Lowe Cuntreyes, and abowte four thousande Italiens' to encourage Henry's papist subjects – 'the wounded minds' – to join them.[80] Yet the Emperor was firmly opposed to any war except war against the Turk. His insistent refusal to make war on England while the League was poised to begin the enterprise against the infidel had gone unheard by the nuncio. Now Charles also refused the Pope's legate. Leaving the Emperor's palace in despair, Pole asked why he would not 'avenge the cause of God'; 'why is the Emperor less ready than other princes in such a cause?'[81]

The Pope and the Emperor, the spiritual and temporal leaders of Christendom, were at odds. The teaching of the Church, and the argument of the Pope and of Pole, was that 'these hidden dangers' and 'the enemy within', the heretic, posed a greater danger to Christendom than the infidel. For Pole, Henry was a more terrible enemy of God than the Turk, and more insidious, for he invaded the temple from within.[82] Charles presented the counter-arguments. War was far easier to begin than to end, and he doubted the promises of his allies (that is, he doubted his 'sworn brother', Francis). He 'marvelled' that the Pope undermined the Holy League he should have led. For the Pope, Henry was a distant enemy, but for Charles, with lands in Flanders, he was a neighbour. So when Pole argued that heretic England was an '*in*trinsic evil' and the Turk an '*ex*trinsic' one, the Emperor asked this question: if the Turk came to Italy, as far as Ancona, as he certainly would, would the Pope consider him an intrinsic or extrinsic threat? Charles feared that Henry, with his great and growing wealth, could marshal a 'great flood' of Germans, not only to defend his island but to threaten all Christendom.[83] Pole's tragic family history led him to be so '*apassionato*' for the war against England, so Charles suspected; suspected also that Pole was a 'subverter of princes'.[84] Granvelle made a shameful admission to Pole: it was true that they had agreed to obey the censures and withdraw commerce, even hinted that they would go further, but this was now impossible. The Emperor claimed to be waiting on the French King's decision about the enterprise of England, and '*al tempo opportuno* [the opportune time]'.[85] He temporized. There was another reason, a compelling reason, for the abandonment of any offensive enterprise in the spring of 1539, one which Charles never mentioned because it touched his honour. The Spanish nobility resisted his Imperial designs, and the Cortes had just utterly refused to grant him money.[86] All that winter in Toledo Charles was suffering the agonies of gout. In consolation, he spent days closeted with the cosmographer royal, Alonso de Santa Cruz, studying maps and astrology and the movements of the planets.[87]

Pole had friends in Toledo, and he had enemies. The nuncio praised 'so rare a person'. With Juan Ginés de Sepúlveda, the jurist, Pole discussed at length Alberto Pio da Carpi's dispute with Erasmus about Ciceronianism.[88] Ambassadors of the Italian princes paid him courtesy visits. Alfonso Rossetto and Pole had been friends when they studied together at Padua, and now Pole recalled happy times in Ferrara. Vivaldini of Mantua came to pay his duke's respects.[89] But others avoided him. Pietro Mocenigo hoped to subvert Pole's mission. And, of course, Wyatt could not encounter the traitor Cardinal. Instead, he sent two English merchants 'to seke meanes to enter into Poles lodginge and to spye who resorted thyther and what theye coulde learne'. Through this surveillance Wyatt understood at last the treason of Robert Branceter, who was 'not onlie resortinge to Pole but playnely exhortinge' these merchants 'to forsake the kinge and follow Pole', and 'to revolte from thire duty'. Hearing 'of Grandvelas beinge there secretly with hym [Pole]', Wyatt prevailed on Granvelle to tell him further of 'Poles sutes and demaundys' and of his 'practyses'.[90] 'On my own heade' Wyatt did all this, before any instruction came from England. His was the initiative, his was the success. 'I dyd so myche that . . . the bysshope of

Romis legate' failed; he 'dyd nothynge that he came for, nor rewarded'. 'Thus was he by my industrie dyspached owt of Spayne smally to his reputation or contentinge.'[91] So Wyatt claimed later, and at the time. In the spring of 1539 the King believed him and credited his 'great diligence, dexterity and activity' for Pole's departing 'miscontented'.[92] On 23 February Wyatt sent a scribbled message to France, warning Bonner of Pole's coming.[93] The Emperor had promised Wyatt on the 21st that within three days he would give him an answer to delight him.[94]

The unhappy Cardinal left Toledo on 24 February. The first part of his mission failing, he began his journey to the French King, on whose decision about war against England Charles claimed to be waiting. Pole may have taken with him 'owt of Spayne' something more bitter than failure. On 13 February the King had written ordering Wyatt to circulate 'a pretty book printed in our realm'. At the turn of that year Richard Morison had written *An invective ayenste the great and detestable vice, treason*, a book to traumatize Pole. It denounced him as 'the very pool, from whence is poured all this poison', an English Judas and 'archtraitor', and it proved the treason of his family.[95] 'From the heart' Pole wrote to his traitor-friend Morison, who had stayed in his household 'like a brother'.[96] He lived with the knowledge that the King 'for one Pole's sake would destroy all Poles', and that he intended Pole's assassination. The Cardinal rode slowly north, taking Branceter with him, travelling first to Barcelona where he had left his *familia* and horses, and reaching Girona by mid-March. That Pole was not riding in post gave Wyatt and his agents more time, so Wyatt wrote darkly: time to kidnap Branceter, and for 'any other purpose to be devised in France . . . to be the surelier wrought'.[97] Pole lived in terror of ambushes and in fear of an unnamed English exile who was promised pardon if he killed the Cardinal.[98] With furies behind him, Pole suspected that one of them was Wyatt.

In Toledo Granvelle had given Pole warning of the 'impiety and profound malice' the English ambassador expressed against him. Pole knew this already: 'he had known the man before'. But in Spain he learnt how imminent, how precise, how personal, were Wyatt's public threats. If the King would have Pole declared a traitor through the cities of

England and offer a bounty of ten thousand ducats, Wyatt vowed to procure Pole's death within six months. Rome would be the best place for Pole's assassination. That Wyatt required leave from his embassy, pledging his own wealth to increase the King's ransom, suggests that he did not intend to be remote from the deed. At first, Pole dismissed these threats as the 'reckless and impious ravings of a raging young man', but by the autumn he believed them.[99] The depth of Pole's conviction that his king meant to kill him is not in doubt. The closer he came to England, the more he feared it.[100] In the Bodleian Library a manuscript – 'A life of Becket' – bears the inscription 'Reginaldi Poole Liber 1539'. The life and martyrdom of this 'troublesome priest', whose king wished his death but to have no part in it, takes us close to Henry's desecration of Becket's shrine and to his animus against Pole and his family.[101] Wyatt had been in the company of Pole's would-be assassins in 1537, and knew only too well his king's will. If, as pledge of his loyalty, he sought Pole's death, he was as *disperatissimo* as his fellow diplomats imagined – the antithesis of the prudent ambassador.

Hearing rumours of threats to murder the Cardinal, the nuncio in France believed Francis Bryan to be the assassin, as before, but could not believe that even Henry would sanction such sacrilege. The assassination alone would be the cause of war.[102] In 1541, when the French King's ambassadors to the Turk were captured and murdered – allegedly by Diego Hurtado de Mendoza's means and at the Emperor's behest – Francis retaliated by imprisoning Charles's uncle. This violation of immunity did lead to war, and the precedent would reverberate through the theory and practice of Renaissance diplomacy.[103] If a secular ambassador was theoretically safe, more sacred was the papal legate who was protected by canon law. Excommunication and interdict would follow for anyone mistreating him.[104] Suppose a secular ambassador assassinated the Pope's ambassador – what would happen then? Pole had understood in 1537 that, in seeking his capture, Henry acted 'in ways never heard of'. If Granvelle told the Emperor of Wyatt's threats against Pole, it would become impossible for Charles to countenance this ambassador who menaced the papal legate whom he had the highest duty to protect.

In theory, ambassadors were protected in the sanctuary of the laws of nations, even if their principals were at war, 'even amid the weapons of the enemy'.[105] But Wyatt's embassy was challenging all the theories. What would happen at the Reformation, when the ambassador of the 'Most Catholic' King of Spain or 'Most Christian' King of France came to reside at the court of a Protestant prince or – more pertinently – when an ambassador of the Supreme Head of the schismatic Church of England came to the court of a Catholic prince? Was he still protected? Would safe-conducts ensure safety?[106] Charles had famously honoured the safe-conduct granted to Luther at Worms. But the safe-conduct for Bonner and Heynes was limited, and Charles repeatedly warned Wyatt that if he ventured beyond what might licitly be said he would be defenestrated. By the end of the century Jean Hotman admitted that it was 'very certain, that one that is a Protestant should not be so fit to be about the Pope nor the King of Spain'. Yet, he argued, if diplomacy between princes were to continue, 'this false principle, that faith ought not to be kept with heretics' – 'hatched' at the Council of Constance – must be refuted.[107] No one forgot that at Constance Jan Hus, presenting himself before the council under Imperial safe-conduct, had been arrested on papal orders and burned as a heretic. But in 1539, as the Pope called for war against the heretic King of England, theories of diplomatic immunity were tested and very soon ambassadors discovered whether or not the law of nations was a sanctuary. Looking back, the Elizabethan author of *The State of Christendom* recorded that 'Henry the Eighth . . . commanded a French ambassador to depart presently out of his realm, for no other occasion but for that he was the professed enemy of the See of Rome'.[108]

At this climacteric of diplomacy, no ambassador could feel safe. One consequence of the 'enterprise of England' was the breakdown of diplomatic relations. On 2 January 1539 the Pope had called on the Emperor to withdraw his ambassador from the court of 'that impious and heretical tyrant', and a week later Cardinal Farnese reported that Charles and the French King were ready to withdraw 'their secret intelligences' and their ambassadors. The recall must be carefully choreographed and simultaneous.[109] In dark diplomatic times, ambassadors served as hostages for each other's safety, for the *lex talionis* (law of retaliation) might apply as well as the 'laws of nations'.[110] One king would – supposedly – not harm the ambassador of another for fear of reprisal against his own. But the time might come when a king no longer valued his own ambassador's safety sufficiently to restrain his anger. By the end of 1538 Eustace Chapuys, the Imperial ambassador, lived in terror at Henry's court, and late in January 1539 Castillon, the French King's ambassador, was certain that Henry, 'the most dangerous and cruel man in the world', 'in a fury' and with 'neither reason nor understanding left', would harm him. 'Even though his own ambassador may serve as hostage for Castillon', he would not be deterred.[111] In the Netherlands, Mary of Hungary's councillors reminded the English ambassador, Thomas Wriothesley, of the lamentable case of 'Monsieur de Pratt' – Louis de Praet, the Imperial ambassador – who had been 'evil used in England' in 1525. To this Wriothesley lamely replied: 'I was then so young a courtier . . . I meddled in no such matters.' But the reciprocal danger was clear.[112]

In Brussels 'there was a world of rumours'. Wriothesley waited there in torment. From the end of February he was detained, 'a friendly secret prisoner', pledge for the safe return of the Imperial ambassador from England.[113] Dishonoured by the revocation of Chapuys, alleging that his own envoys might be mistreated, Henry now resisted Chapuys's departure, and 'commanded him to tarry, upon pain of his life'. Wriothesley appealed to Cromwell on 7 or 8 March – 'I write in haste, and live in misery' – in terror of spiritual as well as temporal powers.[114] Lured into indiscretion, Wriothesley had joked about the 'abhominations of Rome'. When the Captain of Gravelines said 'our Holy Father marred all', Wriothesley responded, laughing: 'Marry . . . a jolly Father and meet to be called the Devil's vicar.' He scoffed – the way one did – about 'Pope Anne labouring with child, Pope Julius the jolly warrior, &c'.[115] Soon Wriothesley regretted this 'homely jesting', for the Captain was burning heretics. 'We that be here may peradventure broil a faggot'; that is, suffer a heretic's death.[116] By recalling Chapuys, they could 'search our beliefs more familiarly, when he shall be out of England, than they dare now'. 'I am now here taken for a young devil.'[117] So, too, Wyatt was denounced in Toledo as '*diabolicho*', '*indemoniato*'. On 30 March Cardinal Farnese was pleased to report that the Inquisition was proceeding against Wyatt 'very fiercely'. Hearing of the actions of the Holy Office in Castile, the nuncio in France asked for permission likewise to investigate Bonner, who had maligned the Pope. Francis acceded, and later he would remember Wyatt's troubles with the Inquisition.[118]

In desperate negotiations to leave, Wriothesley selflessly pointed out that he might depart and still leave 'one for one to exchange': Wyatt. 'Have you not a pawn of his ambassador in Spain, to countervail Monsieur Chapuis? You may be well assured, that my master will not lose him for more than Monsieur Chapuis.'[119] By the end of March '*Secretary* Voiselay' or 'Vorythesly' was exchanged for Chapuys, and a non-entity sent to serve as Imperial ambassador in England. Wriothesley was disdained in Brussels as 'a man of no estimation, a secretary'. In response, 'I tell them that . . . it may be that I am as noble as the proudest of them.' Doubtless this invited further scorn. Leaving the Low Countries, Wriothesley was not spared the ignominy he feared – 'to be led prisoner through the country'.[120] Now he suspected Wyatt, believing that he thwarted his embassy. 'Forget not the lewd report of Wyatt to your disworship,' so a servant adjured him. Seething with distrust and jealousy, Wriothesley would not forget.[121] Receiving a letter sent from Wyatt to Cromwell containing only 'two words to me', he opened it. 'I found it in cipher so I am never the wiser', but knew that 'we write in cipher when things be either very good or very bad, and of the goodness I have no great [hope]'.[122] So that Wyatt could never keep him in the dark again, Wriothesley – once Clerk of the Signet himself – now suborned a clerk of the ciphers to decipher and copy Wyatt's letters. Soon he received a mystifying missive.

In early March Wyatt was no longer malcontent. Grand court festivities – including the game of canes organized by the Emperor in honour of his pregnant empress, vividly depicted by Jan Cornelisz Vermeyen[123] – might have amused him, but it was the 'trames [*trama*: plot, in Italian]' he was hatching that gave him new hope. For the first time in months he seemed '*assai allegro*', '*più allegro*', '*di meglior animo* [quite happy, happier, in better spirits]' even though 'he had nothing firm in hand'. So his Italian friends reported. Pole had departed in confusion with no promise from the Emperor. Charles now gave encouragement to Wyatt, not that Wyatt trusted it: *'non puo sta col cor contento perche è scotato* [he cannot stay with a happy heart because he is scalded]'.[124] He longed for his recall – not only because he missed home, but because he had been offered a 'practise' so important, so secret that he could not write it. 'Upon the which string he harpeth three or four times', so Wriothesley's creature, the cipher clerk informed him, sending Wriothesley the decipher of Wyatt's gnomic message: 'Send for me . . . it is necessary I speak with you. I say send for me.'[125]

'Me thinketh my head is with child.' Immured in Toledo, with the migraine which felled him when pressures became too great, Wyatt's head also spun with the *occasione*, the great chance offered to him as the politics of Christendom shifted. In mid-March he wrote mysteriously, and in cipher, of what could not be written:[126]

I have promised not to open by writing to the King a practise that is offered me for Italy, to kindle there a fire, but by mouth only, now at my coming home. And then shall be time enough, for about the same time the party doth return thither. It is of importance.

This 'practise' was, Wyatt estimated, 'excellent and will go near . . . to set these great friends both in jealousy, and may fortune further'. It would be 'without note of the King': without Henry's ostensible involvement. Doubtless, the 'great friends' were the French King and the Emperor, never far from 'jealousy'. But who was 'the party', how was the fire to be kindled, and who had 'more particularly declared' the 'practise' to Wyatt?

The question of greatest urgency in Toledo that spring concerned Italy and all Christendom. Would the Holy League undertake the crusade against the Turk? Every court observer was asking whether the League forces could unite in an offensive campaign, and if not offensive, defensive? Would the Emperor go to Italy? Could the League hold together? Could the accord between Francis and Charles be formalized and, if so, would Francis join the League? If the Turkish campaign were abandoned, would the new allies turn to the enterprise against England which the Pope summoned? To these questions, the Emperor and his councillors had given no certain answer, but as the campaign season advanced, soon they must. The representatives of the League were holding fraught negotiations, none more fraught than those between the Venetian ambassador, who held out for a '*gagliarda impresa* [forceful campaign]' against the Turk, and the papal nuncio, who championed the crusade against the heretics.

When its promises were broken with 'calends of excuses' and its purposes failed, the Holy League was finally shown to be neither Holy nor a League.[127] On 10 March the Emperor's councillors summoned Mocenigo and Poggio to tell them that the campaign that year would not be offensive, only defensive. The Emperor was sending his equerry, Jean d'Andalot, to Prince Doria – Doria, whom the Venetians blamed for the disaster at Prevesa. Mocenigo took this as sure sign that he was abandoning the *impresa*, and was fearful. To allow the Turk, this terrifying enemy, to advance unopposed by land and sea, would be 'the ruin of Christendom'. The nuncio came twice to Mocenigo's house, trying to convince him of the virtues of a defensive league, but only incensed him further. On 11 March the Emperor held audience with the 'smiling nuncio' and scowling Mocenigo, and admitted that he could not do 'what God wanted': 'Even though I am Emperor, I can only do what is humanly possible, because I am only a man.' Yet he held out promises for the future.[128] On 16 March Wyatt wrote of these audiences: of the Venetian ambassador 'evil satisfied', of Imperial delays and excuses, of Andalot being sent to Venice 'to declare with fair weather the Emperor's purpose' in order to hold them in alliance and prevent them from making a truce with the Turk alone. From Venice Andalot might ride to Germany: why, 'I cannot tell', but perhaps it was to raise money or troops, or perhaps to 'pass forth the time', a feint to make the Venetians believe that the Emperor did plan a Turkish enterprise after all.[129]

The Holy League also failed because the Pope determined to turn his forces from fighting the Turk to fight the heretics in England and Germany. On 14 March Mocenigo went to protest. 'With many fair words', the Emperor assured him that he wanted 'no war with England' and was confident of peace with Francis which would allow action against the Turk.¹³⁰ Unpersuaded, unplacated, Mocenigo warned: if the Pope deserted them and Venice were left to face the Turk alone, she must invite 'the Most Christian and *other princes* to join the League'. By 'other princes', Charles surmised, 'the Venetian ambassador means, no doubt, the King of England, for just now great intimacy exists between the two ambassadors'. He knew that Mocenigo frequented Wyatt's lodgings in Toledo and suspected their collusion. The Venetian was 'but slightly inclined to papal authority', so Charles believed, and was 'very suspicious and quick to apprehend though not so experienced in State affairs as he ought to be'. ¹³¹ Summoning Mocenigo, Charles's councillors gave him a secret warning. 'If perhaps the King of England should offer some alliance to the Venetians, he was not to be trusted, because he was a bad man'. Twenty years' experience proved that he did not keep his promises: he would never give them 'a ducat' in aid of the 'enterprise against the infidel', never expend '*un quattrino* [a penny]' in their service. Henry had exploited the recent crisis of Camerino to unsettle the fragile peace and disturb the Pope's neutrality, so they alleged. Insinuating that it was not the Pope who was the aggressor, but Charles, who desired to be 'monarch of Italy', Henry invited Francis to ally with him instead. After all, Charles would never cede Milan. Was all this true? Mocenigo did not know.¹³² In fact, it was. At this nadir of their diplomacy, Wyatt and Mocenigo were left to act according to their own doubtful discretion. The two friends were each other's last chance. Now Mocenigo looked to '*il magnifico orator d'Inghilterra*' and listened to his promises: in turn, did he offer Wyatt a 'practise' for Italy?¹³³

Wyatt was promising invasion and immolation in Italy. On 18 March the nuncio, who had never ceased his surveillance of Wyatt, told of his latest vaunting outbursts. In the past few days Wyatt had been bragging publicly that his king would ride at the head of an army, with a great following of German troops. He would invade Italy, where he had allies. These were '*parolazze* [vile words]', and this just 'a dream', insisted Poggio. As he denounced the '*ribalderia de questo deslenguato* [the villainy of this insolent man]', we observe the paradox that Wyatt, the orator, the most skilled manipulator of language, is called *dislenguato*, literally, untongued. But Wyatt promised what Rome most feared, and

it was true that Henry had an understanding with the German Lutherans, and that wealth seized from the English Church could even be used
to 'kindle a fire' in Italy.[134] Sharing his hopes and fears with Mocenigo,
Wyatt told him the same story: his king was in collusion with German Lutherans, and would use his money to send forces into Italy. And
Wyatt told him why: the army was to march against the papacy.[135] Here
was a 'practise' to 'kindle a fire' in Italy. Through the following summer
shadowy rumours persisted of massed armies of German Lutherans,
subsidised by the English King, poised to pour into Italy. The threat
was vivid in the Curia. Henry could, 'with his money and the Lutherans' men, light such a fire in Italy as would be difficult to repair', so
Granvelle told Cardinal Farnese in June.[136] Mocenigo was Wyatt's closest friend in Toledo, seemingly the most likely to offer the 'practise'.
Yet at this moment, despairing of its allies, the Most Serene Republic
prepared to abandon the League and to act alone. On 10 March the
malcontent Mocenigo confided a fateful secret to the Florentine envoy:
'swearing on the Body of Christ, he said that the Signory of Venice will
make a truce with the Turk'.[137]

Wyatt's chimerical scheme to light a fire in Italy promised 'to set
these great friends both in jealousy, and may fortune further'. Bringing German troops into Italy to disrupt the politics of the north would
indeed inflame the old rivalries and 'fortune further'. It might start the
Italian wars all over again. In the spring of 1539 the French King and
the Emperor – 'these great friends' – were as close to amity as they
would ever come, a friendship which threatened to make England –
as Wriothesley put it – 'but a morsel amongst these choppers'.[138] Yet
Milan lay like an unexploded bomb between them. A fire in Italy, if
it licked close to Milan, would incense the great antagonists against
each other. Though a fire which burnt the papacy in the papal lands
might 'fortune further' for England, it was also likely to precipitate the
'enterprise of England' which Francis and Charles had so far avoided.
Wyatt insisted that he could only reveal the 'practise' to the King in
person, 'now at my coming home'. If he reached home fast, 'then shall
be time enough, for about the same time the party doth return thither'.
Who was the unnamed 'party'? Maybe the 'party' was Pole, and Italy

the 'thither' to which he returned. In that case, Wyatt's 'practise' was part of the murky plot to assassinate the Cardinal.[139] Yet the murder of a papal legate would be the cause of war – much more likely to unite Francis and Charles than to set them 'in jealousy'. In fact, it was more likely that the 'party' was Jean d'Andalot, the messenger sent by the Emperor on a mission of terrible importance. Leaving Toledo on 18 March, d'Andalot was to ride to the Pope, to Prince Doria, to Venice, and perhaps also to Germany, and to return 'thither' – to Spain – within forty-five days.[140] D'Andalot was Master of the Horse – he would need to be, for so heroic a journey might break down a man as well as numberless post horses.

In his febrile despatch Wyatt also described the vision from Toledo of 'practises' and 'trames [plots]' in Germany: 'Of Almayne, this I learn.' At that moment Dr Matthias Held, Vice-chancellor of the Empire, was at the Imperial court and so also was a messenger from Philip, Landgrave of Hesse, leader of 'the League which they call the Protestants', the League of Schmalkalden. This German alliance feared that in the new friendship between Francis and the Emperor lay the threat of a Catholic coalition against them, and as a counter looked for Henry's support. As the Emperor tried to borrow money in Germany, and d'Andalot set off on his secret mission, the English and the princes of the League of Schmalkalden had reason to make common cause. Though Cromwell's 'intelligences' from Germany were 'far better then I can give from hence', Wyatt offered all he could learn.[141] So far, so mysterious. Wyatt's 'practise', a thin branch over a diplomatic abyss, remained secret: secret for the while to the King and Cromwell, secret to Wriothesley, who read the deciphered despatch but was none the wiser. It is secret and impenetrable still.

In this nightmare world of morbid dread and possibility, Wyatt waited with quivering anticipation for 'knowledge', abandoned to the territory of imagination. Confined in Toledo, head aching, sickened by its miasmal air, in shuttered desperation, he thought on what might be said, what believed – 'I dare not so surely affirm it. But I believe it.' His closest friends and servants had left, one by one, for England – Mason, Blage, Mantell, Rudston, all gone. 'My secretary is sick, and is scant able to write.' 'Francis the courier is sick, and I have no man that can do anything.' Now his imagination seized upon everything, he hung on 'my friend's secret advertisement', and promised what was not his to promise.[142] Discovering after Pole's departure the true nature of the papal crusade against England, he understood that reality might be as dreadful as his imaginings. In Toledo he heard how seriously his king was taking the threat; that Henry, in his alarm and fury, was seizing and holding to ransom any hapless ship that landed on English shores.[143] In early March, as Wyatt sought leave to return home, Wriothesley and Chapuys were still detained in mutual danger, and he was held in Spain as a pawn – or knight – in the diplomatic game. On 12 April Wyatt's recall, so long desired, was sent from England. 'The King hath much heart to know what is the matter that ye cannot write.' Richard Tate – Richard who? A nonentity – was sailing from Plymouth to replace Wyatt as resident ambassador.[144]

More waiting. Wyatt waited on Tate's arrival and his own leave from the Emperor. The court awaited Andalot's return from his frenetic mission. 'Ambassador, everything rests on Andalò,' Charles told Mocenigo on 23 April.[145] In such uncertainty, there was talk of enterprises against England, or Germany, or Algiers. 'I see so many, varied fantasies here,' wrote Mocenigo.[146] The nuncio heard that Wyatt would depart on 3 May and – to Poggio's dismay – that 'much was forgiven him', and the Emperor's parting gift would be three thousand ducats.[147] Yet Wyatt could not leave then. When Andalot finally arrived in Toledo on 8 May, he found the Emperor distracted from any thought of war. On 1 May his empress had died in childbirth. The Kings of Castile dreamt of burial in Granada. Before leaving on this doleful journey the Empress was laid in state in the church of San Juan de los Reyes. On 2 May her body was taken there from the palace, accompanied by Prince Philip, the Cardinals of Burgos and Toledo, great nobles and 'infinite lords' of the court, all the priests and friars of the city, and the ambassadors. Obsequies began on 10 May and lasted many days. On the 16th all the ambassadors attended a Mass at San Juan de los Reyes.[148] The city was 'in confusion', and the Emperor inconsolable – suffering 'wonderful sorrow', observed Wyatt. 'It would be days, even months' before he gave audience; he was even refusing to see the nuncio. Charles withdrew to the Hieronymite monastery of Sisla to be alone with his grief and his God.[149] Where did this leave Wyatt? He could have no audience with the Emperor. Desperate to depart for England, he was stranded in anguished boredom and uncertainty.

Staying on was not without risk, for the Holy Office did not sleep. Sometime that spring the Inquisition had arrested one of Wyatt's servants for speaking against papal authority, and that unnamed, wretched servant languished in the Inquisition's terrifying secret prison. Furious, Wyatt had pleaded for his freedom.[150] The sins of the master might be visited on his servant. So it was for the servant of Luigi Gonzaga. The poisoning of the old Duke of Urbino – much lamented in Toledo – had been widely blamed on Gonzaga, and in Gonzaga's stead his servant was seized. On the feast of Corpus Christi, 5 June, it was reported ironically that this servant was in the Inquisition's prison, accused of three '*peccatuzzi* [peccadilloes]': blasphemy, heresy and sodomy. 'It will be a great miracle if he is not burnt, for the most rigorous justice is demanded.'[151] But by the last day of May the Inquisition had freed Wyatt's servant, and Wyatt learnt of a remarkable parting grace from the Emperor.

Charles had called off the Inquisition. 'He did not wish the Holy Office to proceed against any Englishman in his kingdoms', so his ministers told Wyatt, 'unless they speak of papal authority.' 'This will not please the Pope when he knows of it,' wrote Rossetto, unerringly.[152] In 'conference' with Cobos, Granvelle and an Inquisitor, Wyatt argued that since his king 'agreed with all notable ceremonies used in the Church with punishments of heresies, as sacramentaries, Anabaptists and other, and the difference alone was but about the Bishop of Rome . . . no such rigour should be used'.[153] In the archives of the Inquisition rests a reply from the Suprema to the English ambassador, dated June 1539, in which the Council of the Inquisition set out the rules which must apply to the English entering the kingdoms of Spain. The Holy Office might proceed, according to law, against any of the English who brought in books of Luther, or his followers, or any books which contained heresies or errors against the holy Catholic faith or derogated from the obedience due to the Holy See. Likewise, it could proceed against anyone who spoke or wrote heresy 'which outraged faithful Christians' or impugned papal authority. If the English were provoked – 'vexed or excited' – to speak in defence of their king, yet not guilty of proselytizing his opinions, the Inquisitors would send evidence to the Council of the Inquisition not only against the English but also against those who incited them. The English must give sureties not to leave without permission, until judgement was given against them *and* their accusers.[154] Here was the Holy Office's answer to the charges that they listened to malicious accusations against the English. Here was a – rare – success for Wyatt's embassy.

The '*gentillissimo cavallier . . . Maestro Thomaso Vugiat*' took leave of the Emperor on 31 May, so Mocenigo reported. Leaving his train to follow 'by sea and by land' Wyatt rode fast from Toledo on 3 June, taking six post horses.[155] Ten days later he was in Paris. At the French court the nuncio reported a revealing conversation. The King of Hungary's ambassador asked Wyatt for a safe-conduct. But admitting that a safe-conduct might be necessary was dishonour. His king would never give one, replied Wyatt in Latin, '*ne videretur consentire violationi iuris gentium* [lest he be seen to consent to a violation of the law of nations]'.[156] Did Wyatt know of the fears that Henry, in his fury, would deny the immunities demanded by the law of nations? Had distance lent enchantment to his king in whose name so many had been censored, proscribed, sequestered, persecuted and condemned? In mid-April the wretched Marchioness of Exeter, who had been in the Tower since the previous autumn, was examined again. 'She pretendeth ignorance' but 'confesseth in substance', so Cromwell assured the vengeful King. 'I shall assay to the uttermost of my power, and never cease till the bottom of her stomach [her inmost knowledge] may be clearly . . . disclosed.'[157] To interrogate the Marchioness was to come close to Bess Darrell. Wyatt's return to court, which he had so long desired, was attended by trepidation. He must at last give his reckoning, '*reddere rationem*'.

In the Egerton manuscript two adjacent poems are written in Wyatt's hand. Above them, later, his son wrote 'In: Spayne', 'In Spayn', as though to fix them in time and place. One – 'So feble is the threde'

– translates, in derided poulter's measure, a canzone of Petrarch; the other – 'Tagus fare well' – is an epigram in pentameter, in genre a protempticon, a poem written on the eve of departure. In the first, the poet writes to his lady who waits for him; in the second, he cries out to his king. Seemingly so different, they are closely linked by adjacency in the manuscript, perhaps by the time and place of composition, and by much more than this. Both are poems of longing and share dreams of leaving, and between them the same images echo and reply.[158] 'So feble is the threde' is an envoy sent by the poet to his beloved to rest in her bosom until he returns, in case he never returns, in this life.[159] In places, Wyatt is composing, amending, rhyming as he writes:

> flete
> the tyme doth [passe] and I perceive thowrs how thei [flye] bend
> so fast [alas] that I have skant the space to marke my comyng end

> The time doth fleet and I perceive th'hours how they bend
> So fast that I have scant the space to mark my coming end[160]

The long lines replicate the pining of the poet, the knowledge of his incompleteness which his beloved's absence has created, his sense of time lost:

> the lyff so short so fraile that mortall men lyve here
> so gret a whaite so hevy charge the body that we bere
> that when I thinke apon the distance and the space
> that doth so ferr devid me from my dere desird face
> I know not how tattayne the wynges that I require
> To lyfft my whaite that it myght fle to follow my desyre[161]

Here, the weighted, earthbound speaker yearns for the wings to fly to his beloved: in 'Tagus fare well', he demands them: 'Of myghty love the winges for this me gyve'. Both poems imagine the diurnal path of the sun and, in imagining it, dream of the speaker's journey homeward: 'from est to west from west to thest so dothe his Jorney ly'.

The last lines are chaotic with emendations. The poet's speaker, who has been haunted by the frailty of the thread on which his 'pore lyff' hangs, how 'the runyng spyndell of my fate anon shall end his cours', who feels that 'full litill doth remayne', understands that if he cannot return to his beloved his 'song' may; if his body fails to fly to her, yet his soul will:

> The resting place of love where virtue lives and grows,
> Where I desire my weary life also may take repose.
> My song, thou shalt attain to find that pleasant place
> Where she doth live by whom I live. May chance thee have this grace:
> When she hath read and seen the dread wherin I sterve,
> Between her breasts she shall thee put; there shall she thee reserve.
> Then tell her that I come; she shall me shortly see;
> If that for weight the body fail, this soul shall to her flee

We see Wyatt's second and third thoughts as he composed those lines:

> wherby I fere
>   and yet I trust to se that I requyre
> The restyng place of love, where vertu lyves and grose
>   also all
>   where I desire my wery lyff may sometyme take repose
> My song you shalt ataine, to fynd that plesant place
>   may
>   where she doth lyve, by whome I lyve, perchaunce
>   the have
>   she shew
>   this grace
> when she hath red and seene the dred wherein I sterve
>   by twene her brestes she shall the put there shall she thee reserve
>   tell her that   she shall me shortly se
> Then [say] I come [for here I may not tary]
>   this
>   yff that for whayte the body fayle [my] sowle shall to her fle
>   *TV*[162]

Reading this poem may be to imagine the poet hastening home to a real beloved, in terrors of the journey and of what he may find when – if – he arrives. Many have read it thus, picturing a real beloved: the long-abandoned Bess Darrell.[163]

Should we imagine Wyatt flying safely home over 'sharp and crag-gyd hilles' on the wings of 'myghty love', and picture a real 'dere desird face'? Should we imagine Bess Darrell waiting for him, at Alington by the River Medway, as he sailed past, down the Thames to the King? Soon she would be under Wyatt's protection. She was desperate now, so desperate that in Wyatt's absence, around the turn of the year, she had begged for help from the man who had helped to destroy her queen, had pursued and was still pursuing her friends, and was dismantling the Church which had her devotion. She wrote to Thomas Cromwell:

Please it your lordship to have me in your remembrances. On my faith it grieveth me to trouble your lordship with my importunate suit, but that extreme necessity driveth me unto it. For I have neither friend nor kin of whom I have any hope or relief, and if I had not found you my singular good lord I had been entirely in despair of anything. But yet of all your goodness I find no fruit but my hope alone . . .

I beseech your lordship to consider my poor case, and to continue your help toward me as ye have begun, and then I thought rather to write unto you than to trouble your lordship with my cumbrous suit.

Thus as I am most bounden
   I shall pray for you during my life.

Yours most bounden
Elysabeth Darrell[164]

Elizabeth's prayers. Once – perhaps still – so pious and resolute in her faith that she confessed her sins to Friars Observant (one by now a martyr), she had been left to seek sanctuary wherever she might find it.[165] Her friends gone, her kin gone, money unforthcoming, all her defences were down. Bess now abandoned herself to the protection of a man who had left the service of her mistress, Queen Katherine, to serve Queen Anne, who was anathematized by the Holy Office in Spain, and was seemingly the most loyal servant of a tyrannical King. Why seek sanctuary with him? There was love. And there was another Wyatt, who sought divine as well as royal favour.

'Tagus fare well' seems to be confessional, but perhaps only seems. In its images of westward leaving and desired winging it responds to its neighbour in the Egerton manuscript, but it is charged with a restless optimism. Here the wayfaring speaker – *viator* – journeys home 'with spur and sayle' to seek the city – London: New Troy: Troynovant – which Brutus sought only in dreams:[166]

in Spayn

Tagus fare well that westward with thy strems
torns up the grayns off gold alredy tryd
with spurr and sayle for I go seke the tems   *Thames*
gaynward the sonne that shewth her welthi pryd   *towards the east*
and to the town wych brutus sowght by drems   *London*
like bendyd mone doth lend her lusty syd   *crescent*
My kyng my Contry alone for whome I lyve
of myghty love the winges for this me gyve

IV

Read simply, read biographically, this epigram seems to be a paean to prince and nation. True, Wyatt, who had chosen Caesar's head as the seal for his ring, and had desperately sought recall from foreign courts grown depressing and disquieting, had reason to vaunt his loyalty, yet 'my king my contry *alone for whom I live*' seems an assertion more than puzzling if we take it literally to be Wyatt's own. But his first purpose was poetic. As before, he was experimenting; he was composing in ottava rima. And in the desolations of embassy, as his imagination played with a transforming power, he may have been learning from the new poetry of Spain and Italy.

Poets have been associated with rivers ever since the head of Orpheus was carried down swift Hebrus to the Lesbian shore. Rivers recurred in Renaissance poetry as poets, especially poets in exile, cleaved to specific places, often identified with the rivers running through them.[167] Echoing behind Wyatt's epigram is Petrarch's sonnet addressed to the Po, king of rivers. While his body is carried powerfully eastward on the Po's stream, the speaker's spirit, beating his wings of love, flies westward towards '*l'aurea fronde*', the golden leaves of Laura, and 'his sweet dwelling'.[168] And echoing behind Petrarch? Perhaps even Bernardo Tasso, who had also addressed sonnets to the Po, where love was transfigured in landscape.[169] The River Tagus with its golden sands, to which Wyatt bade farewell, appeared everywhere in classical and Renaissance verse.[170] There were correspondences between the mysterious processes of the 'maker' and nature's wonder-working in trying and refining gold in the river's bed. Naturally enough, Garcilaso de la Vega's thoughts dwelled on '*felice Tajo*', the river which ran through his home town of Toledo.[171] In his Egloga III the nymphs made cloth of the gold the 'happy Tagus' gave. In homage to the Italian poets who inspired his 'daring steps' to Helicon – including Bernardo Tasso, '*culto Taso*' – Garcilaso promised to channel his 'native, celebrated and rich Tagus', so that the richness of its sparkling sand would pay tribute to their name. The *camino* (path) of the poet 'Lasso' and the *camino* of the gold-bearing Tagus became one.[172] Whether Wyatt contemplated the flame of the late, lamented Garcilaso, or thought on the river poems of Italian contemporaries as he turned to write of Tagus and Thames, we cannot tell. At the end, Wyatt's native English rivers would be associated with him. The Granta joined Wyatt with Leland in friendship, and the nymphs of the Medway mourned his loss.[173]

In 'Tagus fare well', as the Thames flowed eastward, the sun showed 'her welthi pryd'. Such a description of the river and, by association, the City of London was freighted with ambivalence. Only a few folios earlier in Wyatt's poetry manuscript was entered the first page of his paraphrase of Psalm 37: 'Altho thow se thowtragius clime aloft'.[174] Here the Psalmist condemns 'the blinde prosperitye', 'the welth of wretches', 'the cursid welth', which was but seeming, failing wealth – 'such like lucke god sendes/to wicked folke' – and teaches:

> And if with god thow time thy hartie songe
>   he shal the give what soo thy hart can lust[175]   *desire*

Now Wyatt will sing divine poetry to his God. Willing 'no more to sing/Of love nor of suche thing', he will use all the brilliant wordplay that writing balets has taught him in order to forge and file praise for the Lord, praise which is divinely enabled. Practising indirection in his public life, in his private world he seeks the 'truth of thinward heart'.

15

Heart's Jerusalem

> make Syon lord acordyng to thy will
> inward syon, the syon of the ghost
> off hertes Hierusalem strength the walles still[1]

Picture Wyatt. He is alone in his chamber, writing in his poetry manuscript, writing and rewriting. Perhaps he is revising the text, for some
pages are blotted with emendations, perhaps he is copying from a rough
draft. But sometimes he is composing straight into the manuscript, ex-
cising a word, carrying it in his head, and entering it a few lines later.
The second, the third thoughts, the excisions are not all compelled by
metre and rhyme – though some are – for Wyatt is thinking on the
deepest questions of human will and divine grace, of God's mercy and
His justice, and each word has traction and force as a prayer to God
and a revelation of belief. He is paraphrasing the Psalms, the seven
Penitential Psalms. Each psalm and each prologue he signs *TV*.[2] Em-
barking on a journey in the dark, slowly he reveals his faith to himself.[3]
Sinning, doubting Christians have always looked to David's painful,
often backsliding, spiritual journey to find consolation and a way to
meditate and pray. The divine poetry of the Psalmist shows feelings
of deepest despair and solace, of remorse and reassurance, and offers
the stricken believer a path to imitate, the hope of redemption through
faith and trust in God and in His redeeming Word. Contemplating the
divine hand on David and David's attempts to reach his God, Wyatt is
pondering the doctrines at the heart of Reformation debates, and as
he examines David's sin and seeming helplessness before divine grace,
as he tests and tries each contested word, he is discovering his own
belief as he writes. Portraying David, who 'in his hert . . . tornith and
paysith [weighs]', Wyatt is *Viatus viator*: the traveller and pilgrim, a pious seeker.[4]

'Rew on me lord for thy goodnes and grace'. Wyatt is composing his paraphrase of Psalm 51, *Miserere mei domine*. Writing and rewriting, he struggles to understand how God in His justice and His mercy justifies the sinner

David's long confessions to his God and pleas for pardon invite every reader – every sinner – to say 'I' along with the penitent David. This 'I' – so essential to the Psalms – entices to a simple identification between the 'I' of the sinning David and the 'I' of the poet who paraphrases.[5] In expressing David's terrible soliloquies of grief, did Wyatt find expression for grief of his own? Some have imagined that 'clearly' they were 'written in the midst of events they allude to', that David's dark cave where he fled 'the lyght as in pryson or grave' was metaphor for Wyatt's real captivity and some specific abyss.[6] But where he was when he composed his paraphrase, or when he wrote it, is unknown. We cannot know whether he intended his imitation of the Psalms as his personal prayer at a particular moment, or tell the pressures, inner or outer, which bore upon him.[7] Anguished moods and circumstances and anguished works need not be synchronic. Just as sonnets may not be penned in the heat of love's raptures but in recollection, so Scripture may not be paraphrased at the moment of despair. And Wyatt will not allow any easy association between the Psalmist's spiritual plight and his own. Beginning to paraphrase the first Penitential Psalm, he first described divine mercy as 'only confort of *us* synners all', but deliberately turned it to '*wrechid* synners all' as though to distance himself from such complicity.[8] If we seek to find the time when Wyatt wrote his scriptural poetry clues may be more reliably found in his maturity as poet than in any known facts of his life. Writing of David's 'hert in presse', Wyatt achieves, by the end of his paraphrase, perhaps towards the end of his life, that compression which is poetry's quintessence: poetry in press.[9] David, now Prophet, prophesies the coming of Christ:

> In mortall mayd, in mortall habitt made
> Eternall lyff in mortall vaile to shade[10]

Later, another hand entered into Wyatt's manuscript Henry Howard's sonnet 'The great Macedon' as preface to the paraphrase of the Penitential Psalms.[11] Above the sonnet were 'IHS', the sacred initials for *Iesus Hominum Salvator*. If Alexander had placed Homer's epics – 'feigned gestes [deeds] of heathen princes' – in so rich an 'ark', 'what holy grave, what worthy sepulture' could Christians ever find for such treasure as 'Wyatt's Psalms'?

> Where he doth paint the lively faith and pure
> The steadfast hope, the sweet return to grace
> Of just David by perfect penitence.

These words 'grace' and 'just' had become inescapably controversial at the Reformation, freighted with confessional meaning. Profound pondering of the Psalms might be the means of discovering answers to the hardest questions about the nature of salvation, about what a sinner could *do* – if anything – to be saved. So it had been for Luther; so it was for Reginald Pole. And for Wyatt. His paraphrases show him venturing far in the language of Scripture to understand the 'deep secrets' of which David sang and to come to a personal understanding of God's purposes. In the prologue to Psalm 102 Wyatt's narrator observed David astounded by the awful gravity of the questions he was asking:

> Off diepe secretes that david here did sing
> off mercy off fayth off frailte off grace
> off goddes goodnes and off Justyfying
> the grettnes dyd so astonne hym selffe a space   *astound*
> as who myght say: who hathe exprest this thing?
> I sinner I, what have I sayd alas?[12]

If 'Wyatt's Psalms' were lost it would be hard to present Thomas Wyatt as that grave example of Christian piety who inspired contemporaries. Without this 'witness of faith that never shall be dead', left for 'such as covet Christ to know', there would be little enough to reveal Wyatt as inspired teacher, unheeded prophet in his own land.[13] His faith was inward, unknown to those who did not know him well, concealed from outside gaze. He was accused of swearing the most blasphemous of oaths – 'God's blood', 'By God's precious blood', 'By God's body' – oaths to appal any devout believer and to invite divine punishment. And he admitted that 'I am wonte some tyme to rappe owte an othe in an erneste tawlke'.[14] Among friends, he loved jokes against sanctimonious clergy. With his household he had teased Bonner and relished the vision of 'the lyttell fatt prest . . . a jollye morsell for the [señora]'. George Cobham sent a letter to cheer Wyatt in Spain, promising that there would be few friars in England by the time he returned.[15] To Francis Bryan – a far better friend to monks than he was – Wyatt addressed a verse epistle graphically denouncing the idle greed of the monastic life and comparing porcine monks in the cloister, before whom pearls were strewn, to courtiers with their snouts in the royal trough. If Wyatt's conscience was troubled by sharing in the sacrilege at the Dissolution, no trace of remorse remains. His laconic dismissal of the 'saint's bones' scattered as the shrine of Thomas Becket was despoiled, and his blithe acquisition of Boxley Abbey, whose revered Rood of Grace was mocked as it was cut down, leave any regret well hidden. In the race for the spoils of religious houses, Wyatt was one of the front runners.

Superstition, hypocrisy: these were vices he detested. The 'I' of Wyatt's verse epistle to John Poyntz had loathed courtly hypocrisy, and refused to play the game: 'I cannot speake with loke right as a saynt'. Living 'in Spayne wher one must him enclyne/rather then to be owtwardly to seeme' would be torment, he judged. As he translated Petrarch's *Rime* 102 Wyatt thought on the hypocrisy of the powerful. Receiving the head of his enemy, Pompey, whose death he had so long desired, Caesar had wept:

> Caesar when that the traytor of Egipt
> with thonourable hed did him present
> covering his gladnes did represent
> playnt with his teeres owtewarde [. . .][16]

'Teeres owtewarde', feigned worship, outward works without inner piety, 'owtward dede, as men dreme and devyse':[17] all these were hypocrisy which Wyatt particularly condemned. 'If you wil seme honist, be honist, or els seame as you are', so he wrote to his son.[18] Describing to Cromwell how empty were princes' promises Wyatt related a story which revealed their shared contempt for empty vows and superstitious practices:

These things maketh me remember the tale of the Welsh man, when he was in danger on the sea, that vowed a taper as big as the mast, and when he came on land paid a little candle to Our Lady. With that, he offered her to hang him [if] ever she took him on the sea again.[19]

It was not the veneration of the Virgin which was malign but the feigning.

Superstition lay in beliefs and practices which sprang from human invention rather than divine law. Principal among these for Wyatt were the claims for papal primacy. 'If he [Charles V] be superstitious': that is, if he insists on papal approval, wrote Wyatt.[20] Believing that papal authority was not divinely instituted but rested on history and human law, his hatred of papal power and its abuse was heartfelt. In November 1538 he wrote with deepest sarcasm of a man who was 'as good a papist as I'.[21] So many fevered promises to 'chase the Pope from Rome' and 'vex the state of Rome' suggest how he detested the court of Rome under its tyrant bishop. It was politic, of course, to denounce the Holy Father to the Supreme Head he served, and to Cromwell, who called him 'tyrannissimo', but Wyatt's repugnance went deep. Paraphrasing Alamanni's *satira* X in 'Myne owne Jhon poyntz', he sharpened its condemnation of the venality and venom of Rome:

> Nor am I wher Christ is geven in praye
> For mony poyson and treason at Rome
> a common practice used night and daye.[22]

The irony is not lost that Cardinal Pole accused Wyatt of plotting his quietus in Rome, the capital of assassination.

In the most holy sacrament of the Church, the Mass, Wyatt found no superstition. He attended all the great masses and festivals of the Church, together with the Emperor and his court. If he had not bowed with reverence before the elevated Host, and received the Eucharist on festival days, the ever vigilant nuncio and his intelligencers would soon have reported him. Neither Bonner nor Heynes 'had greatlye any fancie to masse' – 'not one of them . . . said masse or offerde to here masse, [as] thoughe yt was but a supersticion' – but Wyatt and Mason attended its celebration.[23] Dating a letter to Cromwell 'Friday after Corpus Christi' was conventional, but Wyatt was acknowledging the great festival which celebrated the Eucharist and reconciliation in Christ.* He ended his letters with religious salutations, as was traditional. Lord Lisle he commended 'to the tuition of the Trinity', and he prayed 'our lord' to have Bonner 'in his keeping', to send Cromwell 'good life and long' and to 'have you in his blessed keeping'. On Shrove Tuesday 1540 he would avow himself Cromwell's 'bond beadsman', bound to pray forever for his spiritual welfare.[24] That such salutations were conventional did not mean that they were insincere.

Bidding his son 'farewell' in the spring and summer of 1537, Wyatt sent 'gods blessing and myne'. In two surviving letters which young Thomas inscribed in filial piety in the Egerton manuscript the errant father belatedly offered moral guidance. The letters attest to an ethical system. As guides for living Wyatt offered 'moral philosophers, among whom I wold Senek were your studye and Epictetus, bicaus it is litel, to be evir in your bosome'. Their teachings would lead young Thomas to 'know goodly things, which when a man knoweth and takith plesure in them, he is a beast that foloweth not them'. He was to think on the nature and dignity of man, to 'consider a mans awne self, what he is and wherfor he is. And herin let him think verilye that so goodly a work as man is, for whom al othir things wer wroght, was not wroght but for goodly things.'[25] Following the light of reason led ineluctably to virtue, so Epictetus taught: 'Socrates became what he was, by paying attention to nothing but his reason'. Epictetus drew the essential distinction between those things under our control – 'everything that is our own doing': choice, desire, aversion – and 'everything that is not our own doing', beyond our control. To understand this and to act accordingly was to be free: 'no one will harm you, for neither is there any harm that can touch you'. The adept, the Stoic philosopher 'looks for all his help or harm from himself'. 'He keeps guard against himself as though he were his own enemy lying in wait'. What lay beyond himself was neither to be feared nor desired: the philosopher must look *within*.[26] These were ethical teachings particularly appropriate for those who

* See above, pp. 387–8.

inhabited the world of power. 'What place, then, shall I have in the State?' The answer came: 'whatever place you *can* have and at the same time maintain the man of fidelity and self-respect that is in you'.[27] The motto ascribed to Epictetus – *sustine et abstine*, bear and forbear – was found often at courts where service was not freedom, unless the servant discovered inner freedom under conditions of external restraint. At the New Year of 1540 a suitor to Cromwell sent him a Latin poem enjoining long-suffering and forbearance, with the refrain *sustine et abstine*.[28]

As for Seneca, his many works, in many editions, attest to his popularity in Wyatt's time. Thomas Lupset adjured his youthful charges to 'specially read with diligence the works of *Seneca*, of whom ye shall learn as much of virtue, as man's wit can teach you'.[29] In the seventh book of *De beneficiis* (*On Benefits*) Seneca describes how the wise man may live safe within the redoubt of his soul:

The soul that can scorn all accidents of fortune, that can rise superior to fears, that does not greedily covet boundless wealth, but has learned to seek its riches from itself; the soul that can cast out all dread of men and gods, and knows that it has not much to fear from man and nothing from God; that, despising all those things which, while they enrich, harass life, can rise to the height of seeing that death is not the source of any evil, but the end of many; the soul that can dedicate itself to Virtue, and think that every path to which she calls is smooth; that, social creature that it is and born for the common good, views the world as the universal home of mankind, that can bare its conscience to the gods, and, respecting itself more than all others, always live as if in the sight of men – such a soul, remote from storms, stands on the solid ground beneath a blue sky, and has attained to perfect knowledge of what is useful and essential. All other matters are but the diversions of a leisure hour . . .[30]

This tranquillity amidst the turbulence of the times, the strength of mind to remain 'philosophical' whatever happened, Wyatt had learnt, perhaps from the Poyntzes, and had taught a decade earlier in *The Quyete of mynde*, a work to influence the coming generation. It was this constant Wyatt that the Earl of Surrey would celebrate:

> A visage stern and mild; where both did grow
> Vice to condemn, in virtue to rejoice;

> Amid great storms whom grace assured so
> To live upright and smile at fortune's choice.[31]

But here the Stoic Wyatt, invulnerable to fortune and inwardly free, is 'assured' not by his self-knowledge or by his will, but by 'grace'. His salvation comes not from philosophy but from God. Wyatt understood that the will is not sovereign, that it was impossible to 'know himself' by the light of reason alone, and that we cannot even pray without divine aid. His David is taught to know himself by a God whose heavy hand extends to correct him, who lifts him up only to throw him down 'to teche me how to know my sellff agayne'.[32]

Writing his first letter to his son in April 1537, Wyatt's final counsel was 'to be sure and have god in your sleve, to cal you to his grase at last . . . We ar not all acceptid of him.' 'Remember', he insisted, 'it is certayn and no imagination that ye are alwaye in the presens and sight of god', although 'he seeth and is not seen'.[33] Again, he wrote adjuring him to remember 'that if god and his grase be not the fundation, nother can ye avoyd evil nor juge wel, nor doo any goodly thing. Let him be fundation of al.' By 'goodly things' Wyatt meant *godly* things. Constant self-examination, 'repining' against evil was vital: 'My son, for our lords love, kepe wel that repining . . . That same repining, if it did punisch as he doth juge, ther wer no such justicer.' That young Thomas should know the teaching of Scripture was apodictic: 'of them of god ther is no question'. When Wyatt warned – 'Here how we think it is no smal grefe of a consciens that condemnith it self. But be wel assurid, aftir this life it is a continual gnawing' – he was calling on his son to think on the torments of Hell, 'where their worm dieth not', assuming his knowledge of the New Testament and of the worm of conscience scorchingly described in the Gospel of St Mark (9:44, 46, 48).[34] When he told of the anguish of the sinner abandoned by God, Wyatt foreshadowed his deep engagement with that sinner who sang of his forsakenness more nakedly than any other. His description of the withdrawing of the divine hand predicted his attempt to sing in verse of David's predicament: 'first the withdrawing of his favour and grase, and in leving his hand to rule the sterne . . . And suffreth so the man

459

that he forsaketh to runne hedlong . . . to evirlasting shame and deth'.*
Paraphrasing Psalm 102, Wyatt returns to this despair:

> do not from me torne thy mercyfull fase
> Unto my sellff leving my government.[35]

By the time he left for Spain, Wyatt believed that sacred truth was
found in Scripture, not in human tradition, but his personal devotion
was still deeply traditional. In his letter to his son he presented a vision
of salvation which measured the value of prayer and the merit of the
supplicant against divine omnipotence. That God 'hath of his goodnes
chastizid me and not cast me cleane out of his favour', he imputed to
his father's prayers 'that I dare wel say purchasid with continual request
of god his grase towards me', and 'a litel part to the smal fear that I
had of god in the most of my rage'.[36] But as he paraphrased the Psalms
Wyatt moved far from any belief that a sinner could bargain with God
for His grace, or that any act of human will could so blithely call down
His 'mesureles marcys to mesureles fawte' or think of 'mesuryng thy
Justice by our Mutation'.[37]

When Queen Katherine's 'most humble subject and slave, Tho.
Wyat', abandoned her service for Anne Boleyn's he became associated
with the evangelical circle of Anne and her brother. If Wyatt was committed to 'true religion' then, there was no evidence at the time, save
by association, and any suspicion that he was one of those gospelling
courtiers who carried both the New Testament and *Troilus and Criseyde*
in his doublet is only suspicion.† Yet in the intimacy of old friendship
Wyatt and Francis Bryan would sometimes converse of Scripture.
'Syghes ar my foode, drynke ar my teares' called on Bryan's knowledge
of Ecclesiasticus, and its warning that whoever betrayed the secrets of
a friend was beyond hope:§

> Sure I am Brian this wounde shall heale agayne
> but yet alas the scarre shall styll remayne.

---

* See above, p. 301.
† See above, p. 200.
§ See above, p. 285.

Bryan, the 'vicar of Hell', might seem an unlikely Bible reader, but he knew Scripture well and was intrigued by the new translations. In Paris he was patron to the scholar Florens Volusenus – Florence Wilson – who dedicated his commentary to Psalm 15 (1531) to Bryan, acknowledging his help.[38] Seeing 'a goodly book' in Bryan's bedchamber in Lent 1538, the Abbot of Woburn asked 'whether it were the bible of the new translation?' 'Yea,' replied Bryan. The Abbot judged that this translation – almost certainly the 'Matthew's Bible' of 1537 – was 'not well interpreted in many places'. Bryan's response revealed his engagement with the New Testament at its most numinous and charged point, at the verse on which the doctrine of the Eucharist was founded: 'interpreters must sometimes follow the letter and some[times] the sense, and with that he opened again the book and turned to the words in Luke of the consecration of the most blessed body and blood of Christ and read the same.'[39] Bryan himself – a linguist but no classicist – could not judge the subtleties of scriptural translation, but he was patron of scholars who could, and within the academy of his household profound study of Scripture led to bitter confessional divisions among the young scholars there.[40]

As Wyatt left for Spain, as he counselled his son, there was little to tell that he would become the grave poet of the Penitential Psalms. Except: known for his elegant Latinity, for being the best 'maker' in England, turning to write scriptural poetry would place him among the supreme 'makers' in a Christian Helicon. In 1542 an evangelical client would claim: 'ye have *ever hitherto* earnestly embraced not only the studies of humane letters but also the grave exercises of divine literature'.[41] Born into the old world of faith, Wyatt and his friends were confronted by a new one, and their religious allegiances were tested. This was 'a strange and dangerous time' for a whole generation who were touched by reform.[42] Of Wyatt's lonely spiritual questioning his Psalm paraphrase is profound witness. At the heart of the religious debates – after the revelation of Luther, and before – was always the great question of how the Christian might be saved; whether the believer was free to strive to be united with Christ through 'that little measure of love we are capable of', or helpless before divine grace.[43] People were coming to new answers to these deep questions, to different understandings of the operation of grace, but religious identities were not yet resolved or resolving. For a few, as the 'veil of Moses' lifted, all the ceremonies and sacraments of the Church became 'very vain', but others hoped to stay within the Church, to reform it but never to leave it.[44] Different choices were being made everywhere, and unthinkable choices forced on the subjects of the Supreme Head of England who advanced his private conscience as a principle to bind their souls as well as their bodies, and set his conscience against all Christendom.

To the works Wyatt was reading which informed his profound questioning we will turn, but there were also intimate conversations with his friends, as they conceived and debated different paths to salvation, paths which might divide them. In the dark imaginings of the papal nuncio, they discoursed of doctrine in the English embassy in Spain, proselytizing to anyone who would listen, handing out little books of 'Lutheran and English' heresies. It was true that in Wyatt's household, as in Bryan's, there were young men of questing intellect primed to study divine literature. Travelling to embassies abroad, men did not leave behind the great matters of faith which preoccupied them at home. So the Lutheran hymn book and the crucifix in Hans Holbein's portrait of the French ambassadors vividly testify. Henry's emissaries debated theology – often dangerously – at foreign courts. In France, Germain Gardiner spoke freely, too freely, about the divisions of Christendom, and in the Low Countries his unguarded talk about the 'abominations' of Rome left Thomas Wriothesley fearful of persecution.* In Nuremberg in 1541 Stephen Gardiner debated the doctrine of justification for three hours with Andreas Osiander.[45] In Valenciennes in October 1538 a servant of Wriothesley met, 'riding by the way, one which is chief about Monsieur Dundego [Don Diego Hurtado de Mendoza]'. They 'contended' over a doctrine of perennial and topical controversy, the Spaniard insisting on the freedom of the will: 'it lieth in every man as well to save himself as to condemn himself'. Mendoza's own engagement with the Psalms appears from his possession of very many commentaries and paraphrases. But with Wyatt he spoke of horses.[46]

* See above, pp. 330, 436.

In what they hoped was the sanctuary of the embassy, did Wyatt and his intimates discuss Scripture and God's promises? With John Mason and George Blage Wyatt might have discussed 'diepe secretes' of 'mercy off fayth off frailte off grace/off goddes goodnes and off Justyfying'.[47] If religious allegiance were proved by choice of friends, then as they rode to Spain together Wyatt's conservatism might have been assumed from theirs. Yet those who thought most deeply about faith were most exercised by the great controversies, those who were best educated and the most elegant linguists were most drawn to biblical translation and exegesis. The minds of such men and women might change, and they were susceptible to persuasion, to evangelism, to conversion. So it was for George Blage whose 'subtle mind' delighted Wyatt. Early in 1536 a letter came to 'Master George Blage, my dearest friend', which revealed a network of friendship and clientage which bound Blage, Wyatt and Bryan. Bishop Gardiner's chaplain, Thomas Runcorn, wrote the letter, sending greetings from Blage's friends in the English embassy in France.[48] Blage had been among the young men nurtured in Gardiner's *familia*, their allegiances conservative, even, in the case of Germain Gardiner, treasonably so.[49] But sometime, somewhere, Blage experienced a religious conversion. By the last years of Henry's reign he was a convinced evangelical, so passionate a reformer that he drew his sword on a friend who reneged on the cause. That friend, Henry Howard, dedicated his paraphrase of Psalm 73 to 'my Blage':

> But now, my Blage, mine error well I see:
> Such goodly light King David giveth me.

One theme of that Psalm is of faltering faith, and Surrey's dedication seems to confess a crisis, engendered by despair; perhaps that his evangelical belief had wavered:

> The sudden storms that heave me to and fro
> Had well near pierced faith, my guiding sail.[50]

Blage's reformed convictions stayed firm. Accused of heretical beliefs concerning the sacrament of the altar, he would certainly have suffered for them, had not the King spared him and saved Blage, his 'pig', from roasting. In ardent religious poetry, Blage expressed the hope that he might serve both God and King, while averring that if forced to choose between them, he must choose 'the living word the bread of life'.[51] When did his dangerous questioning begin? Perhaps in Spain, in Wyatt's embassy.

When Thomas Chaloner 'Englished' from Latin *Moriae Encomium*, *The Praise of Folie* of Erasmus in 1549 maybe he evinced the spiritual questioning and will to challenge conventional pieties which he had learnt in Wyatt's household. Translating this famous satire in which Erasmus had 'thought good between game and earnest' to rebuke 'the vices of our days' through the mouth of the 'Goddess Folly', and hid 'besides the mirth some deeper sense and purpose', Chaloner reviewed how distant true religion and Christ's rule of charity were from the merry-go-round of ceremonies and supersitious practices in the contemporary Church. Were there 'any enemies more pernicious to Christ's Church, than wicked bishops themselves? who suffer Christ's name for lack of their daily remembering, to grow out of the people's knowledge . . . and through the abhominable precedent of their life do eftsoons crucify him.'[52] Letters from Chaloner to Mason written much later revealed their friendship forged in diplomatic exile and a shared understanding, learnt through decades of experience, of how to bow wearily to the superstitious excesses of Spain – 'this preposterous religion' – while 'reserving my opinion to myself'.[53]

'*Maxima amicitia* [greatest friendship]' bound Wyatt and John Mason 'while they lived'.[54] Wyatt was corrupted by him, so Bonner believed, for Mason was a 'great . . . papist where he doth utter it'. If Mason acted as Wyatt's conscience in matters spiritual, his counsels were conservative, for he detested the Break with Rome. A scholar, once intended for the priesthood, Mason engaged deeply with Scripture, as his annotations of Erasmus's *Paraphrases of the New Testament* prove.* Even by the time of Bonner's embassy Mason had learnt to keep silent, but after the terror of the inquisition into his alleged collusion with Pole in the autumn of 1538, his silence became legendary. Now, to all outward appearances,

* See above, pp. 233–4.

he preferred to serve his king before his God. Delayed at Dover from Good Friday until after Easter Sunday 1540 by sailors who 'had more respect to the good day than to serve the King', he wrote darkly, 'it were right well done they were taught wherefore days were made'.[55] It was not until the very end of his life that Mason inscribed his faith. Making his will, beseeching God's mercy on his soul, Mason prayed, like every sinning Christian, that when He came to judge, mercy would temper the exercise of His righteous judgement.

Not to enter into Judgement with me his lewdest servant, knowing that in the sight of him no man can be justified, but be merciful unto mine offences and to crown me in his mercy who hath saved us not according unto the works of Justice that we have done, [but] according unto his mercy.[56]

That same hope inspired Wyatt's paraphrase of the Penitential Psalms.

Through the Christian centuries the Psalter, the Book of Psalms, had been the focus of intense devotion, and especially through contemplation of the seven Penitential Psalms – numbered 6, 32, 38, 51, 102, 130 and 143 in the Psalters used in the English Church – the individual believer found a way of praying and of encountering God. Its influence was pervasive.[57] In their darkest hours Christians turned to the Penitential Psalms for consolation. Sir Thomas More and Margaret Roper had recited them together in the Tower.[58] In Christian exegesis, the events and figures of the Old Testament were seen as types whose true spiritual meaning was realized in Christ. The Psalms might be read by the regenerate believer as prophetic of Christ and the coming of His Church. The Psalter, the most prophetic of prophetic books, was the most cited Old Testament book in the New, a bond between the two Testaments. In the Gospels of Matthew and Mark, Christ on the cross, crying out to the Father, recited the first verse of the twenty-second Psalm: 'My God, My God, why hast thou forsaken me?' The Fathers of the Church – Jerome, Origen, Chrysostom, Augustine – translated and interpreted the Psalms, and through the middle ages there were expositions, meditations, lucubrations, commentaries numberless.[59] In the Renaissance, humanist critical study of the ancient biblical languages encouraged new translations of Scripture. The Psalms, this holy poetry, were the place where the humanist enterprise to set forth Scripture in purer form began, and as early as 1477 a Hebrew edition of the Psalms was printed. For Christian humanists – especially for Erasmus, who wrote expositions of eleven of the Psalms over a period of twenty years – the reading of Scripture would be the way to renewal in Christian life.[60] With new translation came new interpretation.

Intense study of the language of the Psalms brought theological revolution.[61] When Martin Luther, steeped in medieval traditions of thought and exegesis, came to lecture on the Psalms at Wittenberg he had before him the latest textual critical studies: Lefèvre d'Étaples' *Quincuplex psalterium* (1509) and Reuchlin's *In septem psalmos* (1512). Studying these new texts, alongside the Vulgate version of Psalm 32:1–2, Luther discovered the passivity of the sinner in his own justification.[62] The sinner could *do* nothing to save himself: captive to sin, he could never redeem himself, only *be* redeemed. Human works were irrelevant in the face of divine mercy and even his disposition to receive grace was not a work of his own nature, but of grace. Faith was a divine work within man, a work of grace, rather than of his own nature. It was in deepest, most introspective meditation on the Psalms, as he prepared his first series of lectures in 1513–15 – *Dictata super psalterium* – and returned to lecture on them again in 1519–21 – *Operationes super psalmos* – that Luther came to his crucial new understanding of the righteousness of God and of the theology of the cross.[63]

The study of the Psalms was a crucible for the development of the new theology in which suffering and temptation are seen, more than ever, as the way in which the sinner is brought to God. 'The cross alone is our theology.' Through the experience of God's wrath, God's righteousness is revealed: 'whoever totally humiliates himself in the eyes of the world [*coram mundo*] is totally exalted in the sight of God [*coram Deo*]'.[64] Justification is always proleptic, for by virtue of man's own fallen nature and his life he can only be a sinner, always in need of

Titian, *Pope Paul III with Alessandro and Ottavio Farnese,* 1546

Titian, *Nicolás Perrenot de Granvelle*, 1548
Titian, *Don Diego Hurtado de Mendoza*

Sebastiano del Piombo, *Reginald, Cardinal Pole*

El Greco, *Cardinal Juan Pardo de Tavera, Archbishop of Toledo and Inquisitor General.*
This cadaverous portrait is posthumous, and was based on a funerary mask
and a portrait by Alonso Berruguete

Bernardo Tasso, artist unknown

Agnolo Bronzino, *Guidobaldo II della Rovere, Duke of Urbino*

Jan Cornelisz Vermeyen, *The Game of Canes in Toledo in honour of Isabella of Portugal*, March 1539

Uriah the Hittite sent to his death. Tapestry of David and Bathsheba, *c.*1510–15, Flemish School

Taddeo Zuccaro, *The Solemn Entrance of Emperor Charles V, Francis I and Cardinal Alessandro Farnese into Paris in 1540*

Sir Thomas Wyatt the Younger, artist unknown
Sir Thomas Wyatt, *c.*1540, after Hans Holbein the younger

divine forgiveness, of a righteousness which God of His grace may impute to him. The sinner is *semper iustificandi*, always being made just, but always a sinner. Grace transcends nature: the sinner can be at the same time a sinner and righteous: *semel peccator et justus*.[65] From now on, the Psalms – commented on and paraphrased by scholars in what was becoming a doctrinal battleground and by those who sought reconciliation between warring churches, now available in print, in many languages and countless editions – had become innately controversial. Francis Dinham, the young 'Martin Luther scholar' who was interrogated for heresy in the summer of 1528 had been reading 'Savonarola *super Psalmum* "Miserere"', Savonarola's meditation on Psalm 51, and the priest with whom he discussed poetry and Luther had a copy of the Psalter of Pomeranus.[66] Myriad private versions of the Psalms existed, variously translated, never published, forever unknown except to a few friends.[67] 'Wyatt's Psalms' might have been written for no one but himself, or to be shown only to those with whom his most secret thoughts were shared.

'Who indeed has not written on the Psalms?' so Erasmus asked wearily.[68] As Wyatt paraphrased, he was writing alongside other paraphrases, commentaries and sermons – certainly in Latin, in English, in Italian – some of them with him all the time as he composed. One text was read with the aid of another.[69] Beyond the texts before him on his desk were the texts in his memory, for memory training was part of his intellectual discipline. The scholarly endeavour of discovering his sources may not be – may never be – completed, for Wyatt's reading was deep and wide. Of some only echoes of echoes may remain, but some of his 'borrows', his helpers, are evident.[70] Writing alongside his sources – amplifying, omitting, transforming, compressing – he revealed more than the brilliance of creative imitation. To locate his sources is to come closer to locating Wyatt himself, in time if not in place, for publication dates determine the earliest date of composition. Where he stays close to his sources, or ventures from them, we may discover a process of self-discovery in Wyatt, a revelation of the truth of 'inward hert'.[71] As always, the points at which he diverges from his known sources are the most revealing.

First among his sources was, of course, the Bible. The Vulgate, the Scripture of his childhood, was in his head, but which other Bibles or biblical commentaries Wyatt knew is far less certain.[72] The publication of Erasmus's *Novum Instrumentum* (New Testament) in 1516 had been transformative. Travelling to Rome in 1517–18, Thomas Cromwell had taken it with him on his journey and learnt it by heart. In Spain, the Bible became polyglot with the availability of the Complutensian Bible of Alcalá from 1522, and that 'Complutens Editio otherwise called the Spanish Bibles' had reached Kent before 1543, when Dr Richard Champion bequeathed it to a friend in memory of 'old amity and friendships'.[73] Beyond the texts available to Wyatt in Latin, there was a panglossia of Bibles: in French and in Italian.[74] French vernacular Scripture had been close to the heart of Queen Anne and her brother. The Bible was being translated into English: a work of undaunted faith and heroism, as well as of scholarship. There were William Tyndale's translations and those of Miles Coverdale. The first English Bible published under royal licence was the 'Matthew's Bible' of 1537, which was probably the translation that Bryan owned and studied.[75] That Wyatt does not seem to have used the Great Bible of 1539 as he paraphrased may testify to his distance from Kent, his immersion in Christendom.[76]

Enchiridion psalmorum, a Latin paraphrase of the Psalms by the Hebrew scholar Jan van Kampen (Joannes Campensis), was prominent among Wyatt's biblical sources. This European bestseller inspired paraphrases in other languages, and was translated into English in 1535.[77] Almost certainly, Wyatt used the 1533 edition in which Campensis's *Enchiridion* was bound together with Zwingli's Latin prose Psalter.[78] Martin Bucer, too, had translated the Psalms: *Sacrorum psalmorum, libri quinque* (Strasbourg, 1529): freely translated, for both Bucer and Zwingli argued for the freedom of the faithful translator against the too literal translations which made the sense of Scripture impenetrable to the reader. In 1530 an English translation of Bucer's Psalms appeared – *The Psalter of David in Englyshe* – and in 1534 a translation of Zwingli's Psalter: *David's Psalter*. Both were the work of George Joye, and both would resonate in Wyatt's paraphrase.[79] If Joye – and behind him, Zwingli and Bucer – led Wyatt toward the inspired freedom of the translator and toward evangelical reform, some of Wyatt's other sources drew him in quite different directions. As he paraphrased, he turned increasingly to *Psalmi Davidici*, the Psalm commentaries of Tomasso de Vio, Cardinal Cajetan. The papal legate who had faced Luther in 1518, Cajetan was 'orthodox among the orthodox', but believing that translation of Scripture was the way to meet the reformers on their own ground, he was censured by traditionalists for whom his insistence on the literal and grammatical sense of Scripture and rejection of any form of allegory endangered received traditions.[80]

The meditations on the Psalms by a bishop of Kent and Christendom were in Wyatt's heart and head all the time as he wrote: John Fisher's *Treatise concernynge the fruytfull saynges of Davyd the kynge & prophete in the seven penytencyall psalmes* (1509).[81] Fisher had preached ten sermons on the Penitential Psalms as an expository cycle to Lady Margaret Beaufort and her household as early as 1504. A meditation on God's measureless mercy and the efficacy of penance, they offered a message of comfort and hope, reminding the despairing sinner of the truth of the divine promise.[82] Penance must be deep, prayer unceasing, yet without God's mercy and His grace all human repentance was no more than the gnawing of conscience: 'man hath no power of himself, it lieth not in his will to continue or do any goodness, but only by the mercy of God'. God's justice might, in equity, demand 'recompense' for sin, but that recompense had been eternally made by Christ's sacrifice. Fisher's emphasis was on the process of penance rather than the *sacrament* of penance: his wish, to provoke a change of heart. Contrition, the first part of sacramental penance, was dependent on grace, and in sermon IX Fisher defined it thus: 'Contrition is a great inward sorrow coming from the very deepness of the heart with meekness, by a profound consideration and remembrance of our sins . . . an inward sorrow of the mind set in the privy place of the heart.'[83]

Fisher's treatise not only explored divine forgiveness but also examined the nature, the reality of David's sin. Placing the Psalms within the historical setting of David's 'heaping sin upon sin' – his adultery with Bathsheba and his manslaughter in order to achieve his desire – Fisher chiefly lamented David's traduction of his 'true', 'valiant knight' Uriah, whom he contrived to send into the 'foremost ward of the battle, and so for to be slain'.[84] The moment of David's glimpse of Bathsheba in her naked high-breasted loveliness in her bath, the moment of his sin, as he lusts after her and commits adultery in his heart, was portrayed in a woodcut in Fisher's *Treatise* at the head of Psalm 6: *Domine ne in furore*. In the early sixteenth century the depiction of heartbreaking Bathsheba and David the voyeur became so widely known, so resonant an image of the sin to which the flesh is prone, that this one sin came to represent all sin, and David's first glimpse of Uriah's wife – that is, his sin rather than his repentance of it – became the emblem and epitome for the Penitential Psalms as a whole.[85] The image of Bathsheba called to mind both the worldly pleasures of the flesh and their otherworldly dangers. At the courts of Francis I and Henry VIII the sinning David and his paramour were splendidly portrayed. In 1528 Henry had spent a king's ransom on a series of ten tapestries depicting the story of David.[86]

The spiritual counsel of John Fisher and the biblical commentaries of theologians guided Wyatt's contemplation of the Penitential Psalms. So too did the prose paraphrase of Pietro Aretino, the poet.[87] The author of scurrilous satires on court life, pasquinades and obscene sonnets, Aretino was notorious as a libertine, but he shared the 'religious restlessness' of his time and place, of Venice in the 1530s, and from 1534 he began to devote himself to sacred works.[88] Aretino's *I sette salmi* of 1534 inspired the structure of Wyatt's paraphrase. That December Giovanni Guidiccioni delightedly received a copy at the Emperor's court, but though he might have circulated Aretino's Psalm paraphrase only a devious route might bring it from the papal nuncio to Wyatt.[89] Seeking patronage at Charles's court, Aretino dedicated his *Ragionamento delle corti* (*Discourse of Courts*) (1538) to Don Luis de Zúñiga y Ávila, and his poetic lament on the death of the Duke of Urbino and copies of his plays and poems were in Diego Hurtado de Mendoza's library.[90] At the English court Aretino's criticisms of the Church appealed to certain *inglesi italianizzati*. In July 1534 Cromwell wrote to '*miracoloso* Signor Pietro Aretino', and in March 1540 Aretino sent a letter to 'Signor Cromuvello'.[91]

Pietro Aretino introduced his paraphrases to the seven Penitential

Psalms by a sequence of seven prologues which provided a narrative and dramatic setting for David's contrition, his soliloquies, his conversations with his God.[92] From Aretino, Wyatt borrowed the persona of the narrator to tell the story of David captive to the 'tyranny off sin',[93] his progress from despair to true repentance, from exile from God to reconciliation with Him. The narrator interposes judgement on the image of David he presents, and tells what David has learnt and what he has not. Speaking in the third person, Aretino's narrator provides a distance from David's own perturbations and equivocations. But Wyatt's narrator sometimes introduces his own voice – 'it semyth unto me' – or ventriloquizes David's, thus blurring the line between his story and the sacred text.[94] Aretino's historical prologues tell of David, the model penitent, but also of *King* David with '*doppio diadema* [double diadem]' and dominion, with the power to commit sins and crimes particular to a commander of armies, the leader of a people. In his pride David has forgotten God and his duty, but just as a king's sins are greater, so he knows how to make the most perfect penitence.[95] Wyatt follows Aretino in locating the Psalms in the world of royal power and its abuse, where David 'forgott the wisdome and fore cast/(wyche wo to Remes [realms] when that this kynges dothe lakke)'. Like Aretino, he paints David's cave as the place of his penitence: a resonant image for his abyss of despair, his prison of sin and sepulchre of hope.[96] Yet Wyatt's paraphrase is essentially different from Aretino's. Though a poet, Aretino chose prose for his Psalm paraphrase, a prose which by insistent repetition reprised the prayers of penitence: '*mea culpa, mea culpa*'. His style, full of metaphor, was extravagant, even mannerist, intending to evoke '*affettuosa tristizia*' – what Wyatt's narrator called 'hote affect / of god' – in the heart of the penitent.[97] Here was little concision, few plays on words. These prose raptures were a world away from Wyatt's insistent wordplay, even Word play, and his taut images. And Wyatt's paraphrase, unlike Aretino's, was in verse.

> Wyatt the Psalmist
> He translated into our language the songs of David,
> and rendered his verses with great and equal art.[98]

'David's Psalms are a divine poem', 'heavenly poesy', so Philip Sidney would explain, 'fully written in metre . . . although the rules be not yet fully found'.[99] Derived from songs and chants sung in the Temple, the Psalms were vatic, sacred poetry and divine music. 'In the olden time', wrote Erasmus, children in arms would sing Psalms to their nurses 'so great was the love for this divine music'. For Erasmus, the Psalms were sacred rhetoric, with the power to inspire, to *move* sinning Christians to penitence and renewal in faith.[100] Verse paraphrases were appearing in Latin and in vernacular languages: Clément Marot was composing scriptural poetry in French; in Italy, Marcantonio Flaminio began writing Latin Psalm paraphrases in 1533, and continued throughout his life; in Toledo in 1538 *Septem elegiae in septem poenitentiae psalmos* by Alvar Gómez was published.[101] For divine poetry and the rhythms of repentance a perfect metre must be found. Wyatt, teaching 'what might be said in rhyme', chose rhyme schemes hardly used in English before: for the voice of the narrator, stanzaic ottava rima, the heroic rhyme of Italian Renaissance poetry; for the Psalms, terza rima. From the pen of Wyatt 'that quick could never rest', the tercets stream on, with a restlessness that matches David's, and his own.[102]

> In slepe, in wache, In fretyng styll within
> that never soffer rest unto the mynd
> filld with offence, that new and new begyn
> with thowsand feris the hert to strayne and bynd

'The hert to strayne and bynd': Wyatt's first thought here was '*mynd*' not '*hert*': 'mynd' he excised. It was not in his mind that David 'pondered thes thinges' – 'all the glory off his forgyven fault', all undeserved – but 'in his hert'.[103] Paraphrasing the Penitential Psalms, the poet who had so far worn 'Venus' livery' and written of failing human love turned to write of chastening, saving, perdurable divine love. No one had more exquisitely served the court's need to hear of the heart in love, the heart broken and betrayed, the heart of the anguished lover. 'Most wretchid harte why arte thow nott ded?'[104] Now it is the heart as the organ of compunction – what Fisher called 'the privy place of the heart' – which is the intense focus of Wyatt's meditation.[105]

As David prepares to sing the most penitential of Psalms, Psalm 51, *Miserere mei domine*:

> his voyce he strains and from his hert owt brynges
> this song that I not wyther he crys or singes[106]

The heart is the site of redemption, and as God infuses grace into David's heart, as David plays upon the chords of his harp, so Wyatt plays on words at the heart of his paraphrase: *cor* (heart), chord, accord, record:

> tunyng accord by Jugement of his ere
> his hertes botum for a sigh he sowght[107]

In the first stanzas of the first prologue, following Aretino, Wyatt tells the story of David's fall, a story which is still apparently of love and love's dominion. 'Love . . . stode in the Iyes of barsabe the bryght'. But where love in Wyatt's verse before had been unkind, cruel, had imprisoned or stolen hearts, now Love is soul destroyer. Love – like Satan, tempter and tyrant – 'dasd' David's sight, touched his senses 'with venemd brethe', and 'moyst poyson in his hert he launcyd'. As David yielded to this 'cruelly plesant' sight and Bathsheba became his idol, David forgot the worship due to God alone, forgot 'wisdome and fore cast'. Love had made David the kind of shadow king Tyndale denounced, and turned him tyrant. From lust, David degenerated to idolatry, from idolatry to murder in pursuit of his adultery. 'By murder for to clok adulterye', David sent Bathsheba's husband Uriah – 'Urye I say, that was his Idolles mak [mate]' – into the forlorn hope, the front line of the battle, 'for enmys swordes a redy pray to dye'. David's awakening to the horror of his sin – his 'secrete wound' – came not through self-knowledge, but from Nathan the prophet who, in the way of things at courts, 'hath spyd owt this trecherye'. Throwing off his golden crown and purple pall, David is left alone: his harp, his guide: his refuge, the cave.[108] 'With tendre hert Lo thus to god he synges': *Domine ne in furore*.[109]

The biblical Psalms and 'Wyatt's Psalms' are sacred drama in many voices. The David of Wyatt's paraphrase is an orator, using different rhetorical styles according to his labile moods. As Psalm 6 begins David submissively allows God to place His 'myghty name', 'my lord', into his mouth, but then turns to address Him in precatory imperatives, dares to question Him, bargains for his eternal life. Assailed by foes, 'Marmaydes [sirens]' who tempt him with 'baytes off error', by making him remember 'tryumph and conquest' 'dowble Diademe', the 'favor/ of peple frayle, palais, pompe and ryches', David defies them: 'avoyd wreches and fle'.[110] Sometimes David talks to himself: 'I shall, quoth I agaynst my sellff confesse/unto the lord all my synfull plyght'. At times, he conducts an inward dialogue between the self-rebuking and self-restoring parts of his soul. Sometimes it is hard to tell whether David 'crys or singes'; sometimes his prayer is 'not exprest by word/but in his hert'. Even the silence of the cave seems to David 'to argew and replye'.[111] The Psalms dramatize God as present to David. Speaking to him directly, God promises: 'I shall the teche and gyve understondy-ing/and poynt to the what way ye shalt resort'.[112] All these voices echo-ing through the silence provide Wyatt with great poetic and dramatic possibility.

David begins painfully to learn true penitence.[113] In utter abjection, defenceless, he seeks divine pity, asking God to punish him according to His mercy, rather than His justice:

> chastyse me not for my deserving
> Acordyng to thy Just conceyvid Ire.
> O lord I dred, and that I did not dred
> I me repent, and evermore desyre
> The the to dred[114]

Understanding his need to be healed, David admits responsibility for what he is and has become, and welcomes dependence on a therapy beyond his control: 'revyve my sowle be thow the leche [physician]'. As Wyatt's David learns the nature of repentance and of sacrifice, and how divine mercy and justice are applied to the sinner, the shadow of the divine promises fulfilled in Christ resonates in references to Gospel parables.[115] Behind David's argument that those who are whole need no physician echoes the answer Jesus gave to the Pharisees at the feast of Levi: 'I will have mercy and not sacrifice: for I am not come to call the righteous but sinners to repentance'. Distant from his sources, Wyatt adduces the parable of Christ the Good Shepherd: 'the shepe that strayth the sheperd sekes to se/I lord ame strayd, I syke withowt recure [healing]'.[116] Anyone who thought on scriptural exegesis knew that the Psalms may be understood by the regenerate believer as prophetic of Christ and the establishment of His Church. Wyatt does not overtly read Scripture according to its spiritual or mystical senses, but in his paraphrase the promise of Christ's redemptive coming is present from the first.

In the following lines, dwelling on the rebellious flesh, on the prick of death, on the opposition between flesh and spirit, Wyatt may have been thinking on the teachings of St Paul. David has a heart, the repository of feeling, but he also has 'bones', the core of the soul: 'Se how my sowle doth freat it to the bones/Inwarde remorce so sharp'the it like a knife'.[117] The Vulgate version of the first Penitential Psalm ends with the Psalmist revived and assured. Aretino's David is exultant. Not Wyatt's, so the narrator relates. No longer is 'his hert as in dispaire', but deep in sin, he is far from cured: 'esed not yet held [healed] he felith his disese'.[118] In this addition to his sources the soothing sounds belong to words both benign and malign. 'With vapord iyes', the tears of true confession, 'with strayning voyce' David begins to sing Psalm 32.

Psalm 32, the heartland of Luther's discovery of justification by faith alone and of the imputation of God's righteousness, was 'virtually the battle-hymn of the Lutheran republic of the spirit'.[119] Wyatt's paraphrase of these doctrinally freighted words, of whose charge and danger he was well aware, loses poetic grace in defining divine grace:

> Oh happy ar they that have forgiffnes gott
>   off theire offence, (not by theire penitence
>   as by meryt wych recompensyth not
> altho that yet pardone hath non offence
>   withowte the same), but by the goodnes

> off hym that hathe perfect intelligens
> Off hert contrite, and coverth the grettnes
> [under the mantell of mercy]
> Off syn within a marcifull dyscharge[120]

Why had Wyatt first written 'under the mantell of mercy', and re-placed it by 'within a marcifull dyscharge': why did he have second thoughts? Metre was not the reason. The cloaking of human sin, as with a mantle of divine mercy, had become a classic metaphor for Luther's doctrine of the imputation of righteousness. Maybe Wyatt knew it, considered it, and drew back. His tangled, convoluted account of the process whereby righteousness is inferred or imparted or im-puted – the difference in verbs takes us to the centre of Reformation controversy about salvation – suggests his troubled contemplation of this contested doctrine. Here God's merciful grace is freely granted to those 'off hert contrite', regardless of their own merit, which must be accounted negligible, though no sin is pardoned without contrition. As Wyatt loses his readers in a thicket of qualifications and doubling nega-tives – 'not by ... as by ... not/altho that yet ... non ... but by' – is his obfuscation deliberate, or is he lost in wandering theological mazes?[121] Thinking wistfully of the redeemed, cleansed from sin 'As adder freshe new stryppid from his skin', he adds to his sources:

> And happi is he to whom god doth impute
> *No more* his faute *by knoleging his syn*[122]

Choosing the freighted verb 'impute', Wyatt follows Aretino. David feels the weight of divine impingement upon him, a sign of God's chas-tising care:

> thy hevy hand on me was so encrest
> both day and nyght, and held my hert in presse

And he understands that he must keep no sin, no 'secrete wound', hidden, nor 'hide from my gret unryght', but must truly confess. Fol-lowing Campensis, Wyatt shows David praying that others learn by his example, to 'pray and seke in tyme for tyme of grace'. The Psalm ends with David blessing the redeemed: 'Joy and rejoyse I say ye that be Just'.[123] This was the great question of the Reformation: who were the 'just', and how did they become so?[124]

David hears in the silence of the cave his new understanding of the operation of grace echo and echo around him. Here Wyatt imitates, but surpasses Aretino:

> his sylence semid, to argew and replye
> apon this pees. this pees that did rejoyce
> the sowle with mercy, that mercy so did crye
> and fownd mercy at mercy full hand

Peace: this peace: balanced at the caesura is a heavenly peace for which the sinner yearns.[125] Now the darkness of the cave is with divine light illumined, a sign of grace returned to lighten the spiritual darkness of the penitent. The brilliant light 'distendes' onto David's harp, glances on its chords 'as lyght off lampe apon the gold clene tryde', and from the harp into the eyes of David who is 'surprisd with Joye, by penance of the hert'.[126] Kneeling on his right knee, his weight on his left – his heart's side, 'sure hope of helthe' – David 'with sobre voyce did say': Psalm 38.

As the third Penitential Psalm opens, Wyatt's David is haunted by dread of his own mutability, which he contrasts with God's adamantine justice: 'mesuryng thy Justice by our mutation/Chastice me not o lord in thi furour'. While Aretino's stress is on an immutable God, Wyatt's is on human frailty.[127] Using a metaphor borrowed from Aretino, Wyatt examines David's moral passivity by imagining a horse spurred, in its fear and alarm, to free itself from the mud in which it is enmired:

> I lo from myn errour
> Ame plongid up, as horse owt of the myre
> with stroke off spurr, such is thi hand on me[128]

The opposition between steadfastness and mutability, everywhere in Wyatt's love poetry, is found again in David's plaint. In his 'fleshe' there is no 'stabilite', in his 'bones' no 'stedfastnes', 'suche is my drede of mutabilite'. The gnawing of conscience – the 'gruging off the worme

within/that never dyth' of which Wyatt wrote to his son – allows David
no rest. 'My hart pantythe, my force I fele it quaile'.[129] Now he turns to
address traitors within – the worst kind of traitors, traitor friends.

> And when myn enmys did me most assayle
> my frendes most sure wherein I sett most trust
> . . . sonest then did ffaile

Following no known source, Wyatt makes David name his forsaking
friends as 'my own vertus': 'reson and witt unjust', 'kyn unkynd'.[130] If
the philosophical Wyatt had accorded sovereignty to reason and assumed that to know the good was to follow it, here he doubted that
reason could control the will or contain the passion that led to depravity. The Stoic teachings of reliance on reason, which once he thought
virtuous, came to seem a lesson in pride. 'Reson and witt', so far from
perfect friends, abandoned David in his adversity. So, too, in Wyatt's
'My galy charged with forgetfulnes' 'drowned is reason that should me
confort', and in 'Who lyst his welthe and eas Retayne', 'wyt helpythe
not deffence'. Now following Cajetan, Wyatt presents a doubting David
encompassed by enemies and 'provokars' hindering 'my good pursuyte
off grace'.[131] As the Psalm ends, David throws himself on God's mercy
in language of imperative urgency:

> Forsak me not, be not farr from me gone
> hast to my help hast lord and hast a pace
> O lord the lord off all my helth alone[132]

In the prologue to Psalm 51, *Miserere mei Domine*, the narrator describes
David artlessly playing the 'sonour Cordes' of his harp, in dissolving
tears which trickle from him as insensibly as 'he that bledes in baigne
[bath]'.[133] In David's pilgrimage from doubt to hope, from hope to
despair, the darkest lament leads to the next stage of spiritual growth.
As the Psalm begins, David, in deepest humility, cries or sings – the narrator cannot tell which – a paean to the reconciling workings of grace
in nature:

> Rew on me lord for thy goodnes and grace
> that off thy nature art so bountefull

> For that goodnes that in the world doth brace
>> repugnant natures In quiete wonderfull[134]

He pleads for a pity which must be infinite in order to remit sins numberless. Here Wyatt writes independently of his known sources:

> For unto the no nombre can be layd
>> for to prescrybe remissions off offence
>> In hertes retornd[135]

With David's repentance and God's impending judgement poised at the caesura – 'This know I and repent, pardon thow than' – Wyatt reaches a crux in the Psalm, in all Christian theology. This verse which St Paul quoted in his Epistle to the Romans 3:4, and which lay at the heart of Luther's struggle to understand how the Christian was justified, became Wyatt's tortured, baffling statement on justification.[136] All his crossings-out and overwriting testify to his awe and anxiety as he ventures to express the deepest of 'diepe secretes':

> This know I and repent, pardon thow than
>> wherby thow shalt kepe still thi word stable
>> thy Justice pure and clene, by cawse that whan
> I pardond ame, then forthwith Justly able
> Just I ame Jugd, by Justice off thy grace

Here Wyatt delves the Reformation paradox that God's justice is accomplished by His merciful forgiveness, His grace freely given which accords righteousness to the sinner.[137] Here the latent possibility that Wyatt had read Luther's *Enarratio psalmorum LI* (1538) surfaces. Luther's account of justification, too, teems with cognates of justice: '*Sum iustus et iustificatus per iustum et iustificantem Christum* [I am just and justified by a just and justifying Christ]'.[138] The dizzying, twisting wordplay of Wyatt's David deflects from any categorical confessional definition, yet in Wyatt's version and vision God's 'justice' has been transmuted into an understanding of forgiving, merciful justification.[139]

Counterpoising once again divine immutability with human transience, David admits himself to be, in a phrase of Wyatt's invention, 'lo thing most unstable'. He suffers from an ancient dislocation: the Fall:

'Formd in offence, conceyvid in like case/ame nowght but synn'. If David looks back to man's first sin, he also looks forward to his redemption. Wyatt's David begins to speak with the voice of prophecy, and foretells of 'gladsome tydynges', of Christ's coming (in words of Wyatt's invention) 'when from above remission shall be sene/descend on yerthe'. Here Wyatt seems to have adopted Cajetan's messianic interpretation of Psalm 51.[140] The era before Christ's Incarnation is the era of divine justice, of the Old Testament; with His coming will succeed the time of grace, of God's mercy. In another series of imperatives – 'Looke not', 'do a way', 'cast me not', 'nor take', 'rendre to me' – David calls on God to 'conferme with spryte of stedfastnesse', and offers the only thing that he can offer, his praise: 'my tong shall prayse thy Justification'. By God's purging him 'from blood', from the guilt of Uriah's death, David hopes (again in a phrase of Wyatt's invention) 'among the Just that I may have relation'.[141]

Wyatt's David has learnt how to pray: he understands now that God's desire is not for 'the outtward dedes that owtward men disclose', 'off owtward dede, as men dreme and devyse', for He 'loves the trowgh [truth] off inward hert'. The 'sacryfice' – the 'host' – God likes best is of 'mendyng will', 'spryte upryght', 'a clene hert', 'hertes retornd', 'low hert in humble wyse'.[142] Wyatt writes independently of his sources as his David implores the Holy Ghost to suffuse his soul, for divine grace to fortify his heart as a holy shrine:

> make Syon lord acordyng to thy will
> inward syon, the syon of the ghost
> off hertes Hierusalem strengh the walles still[143]

Zion is turned inward and the Jerusalem for which he yearns is within the heart.

Singing numinous secrets, David – as the narrator describes – astounds himself: 'I sinner I, what have I said alas?' In silent prayer, he revolves and weighs in his heart the truth he has learnt: that God's judgement is the efficacious means of His mercy:

> he poyntes, he pawsith, he wonders he praysythe
> the marcy that hydes off Justice the sword

> the Justice that so his promesse complysythe
> for his wordes sake, to worthilesse desert
> that gratis his graces to men doth depert[144]

He finds consolation in calculating an economy of grace in which an infinite supply of mercy is offered unsecured to the bankrupt sinner:

> mesureles marcys to mesureles fawte
> to prodigall sinners Infinite tresure
> tresure termeles that never shall defawte[145]

Irradiating the next lines in the prologue is Christ's promise to St Peter, recorded by St Matthew (16:18–19) – 'thou art Peter, and upon this rock I will build my church; and the gates of hell shall not prevail against it. And I will give unto thee the keys of the kingdom of heaven' –

> Mercy shall reygne, gaine whome shall no assaute
> off hell prevaile by whome lo at this day
> off hevin gattes Remission is the kay

With heaven and hell counterpoised, sin fails and mercy prevails. At the culmination of the crisis which occasioned the fourth Penitential Psalm David 'seith hym sellff not utterly deprivid/from lyght of grace'.[146] God relieves grief with a 'confort' which restores purpose.

By the end of the fifth Penitential Psalm, David's prayer that God will not abandon him is answered: 'the sprite off god retournd that was exild'. David understands that his self-exile from God came from forgetting 'my brede/my brede off lyff'. Distinct from his sources, Wyatt defines this bread as 'the word off trowthe I saye', 'thi Just word'.[147] Again, as David weeps tears which are the sign of continuing penitence, God intervenes to subdue his pride and save him. When Wyatt presents the roughness of the divine hand – 'thou didst lifft me up to throw me downe' – he follows Cajetan and Campensis, but the account of God's purpose is his own invention: 'to teche me how to know my sellff agayne'.[148] Here self-knowledge owes not to Seneca and Epictetus, but perhaps more to Tyndale's prologue to St Paul's Epistle to the Romans. The preacher of 'Christ's glad tidings', 'the daily bread of the soul', must 'prove all men sinners and children of wrath by inheritance . . . and therewith to abate the pride of man, and to bring him into the knowledge of himself . . . that he might desire help'.[149]

Sign of David's regeneration is that he prays no longer 'Rew on me', but 'Rue on Syon'; not 'inward Syon, the syon of the ghost', but for Zion 'the peple that lyve under thy law'. Wyatt is following Fisher's understanding of the second part of the Psalm as a charitable prayer for the 'whole Church of Christian people'.[150] In divinely inspired vatic utterance, David foresees Christ's imminent coming: 'day off redeming syon From sins Aw'. David has become prophet–king as well as individual penitent, and now prophesies of Jerusalem, the holy city, the seat of Christ's Church: 'In this syon hys holy name to stond/and in Hierusalem hys laudes lasting ay'. The Psalm ends with David's hope that the sons of men – 'the sonnes off deth', freed from their 'dedly bond' – will live everlastingly in God's presence.

> the gretest confort that I can pretend   *allege; claim*
>   is that the childerne off thy servantes dere
>   that in thy word ar gott, shall withowt end
> byfore thy face be stabisht all in fere[151]

'All in fere': enjoying the sublime 'fere [friendship]' of Heaven, but in due fear of the Lord. Playing on words, Wyatt plays even on the most sacred Word when he writes of those who are 'gott' – begotten – in the Word, the second person of the Trinity incarnate in Christ.[152]

What stage in his spiritual journey has 'our david' reached? The narrator describes a moment of crucial insight. Having been granted the spirit of prophecy, David begins to interpret this power as a sign of 'remission off offence', of the merit of his own 'payne and penitence'.[153] In his pride, he may be tempted to exalt himself; in his hypocrisy, to invent a worship in which he claims to merit righteousness before God. Teetering toward the spiritual chasm of security, he stops in time. Now as David allows 'all the glory off his forgyven fault' to God, finding 'his owne merytt . . . in deffault' and any 'owtward dede' the sign of the workings of divine grace in him, he is – for all who could hear it – speaking the language of Tyndale:

> wherby he takes all owtward dede in vayne
> to bere the name off ryghtfull penitence
> wich is alone the hert retornd agayne
> and sore contryt that doth his fawt bymone
> and owtward dede the sygne or fruyt alone[154]

Pondering 'thes thinges in his hert', David begins to sing, heartfelt, Psalm 130:

> From depthe off sin and from a diepe dispaire
> from depth of dethe, from depthe off hertes sorow
> from this diepe Cave off darknes diepe repayre
> To the have I cald o lord to be my borow   *ransom; deliverer*

In Wyatt's paraphrase of this Psalm mercy and justice are found conjoined, and again his rewriting reveals the process of revelation, as he discourses beyond his sources. This sixth Penitential Psalm ends with David assured: 'rannzome shall com with hym I say/And shall redeme all our iniquitie'.[155] 'This word redeme' resounding within him sends David into a trance in which he sees in 'the heyght of hevin' 'the word that shold confownd/the sword off deth' transfigured, the Word made flesh, the Annunciation and Incarnation:

> In mortall mayd, in mortall habitt made
> Eternall lyff in mortall vaile to shade[156]

Reading alongside Wyatt writing alongside the Psalms, what has been discovered of his purpose in paraphrase? Becoming *vates*, the poet–prophet, he has learnt to write divine poetry and found a voice for David to sing of 'diepe secretes'. Wyatt, sharing the spiritual anxiety of his time, suffering or remembering grief or some great dislocation, or so we may imagine, searches deeply into Scripture. Yet to align the paraphraser of the Psalms with his protagonist, or assign David's 'secret wounde' as Wyatt's, would be an act of faith alone. If we seek a name for the faith which inspired 'Wyatt's Psalms' and then seek to align it to Wyatt's life we may be confounded. 'The life of a Christian man is inward between himself and God,' wrote Tyndale.[157] Wyatt's paraphrases admit the imputation of no unambiguous doctrine of salvation, adherence to no particular church order. Yet they are eloquent in what they reveal of one formidable mind, one alert conscience, and one 'hert in presse' in this first age of reform, eloquent, too, in what they do not reveal. Unlike Marcantonio Flaminio, Wyatt left no *explanatio* for his Psalms.[158]

Wyatt's paraphrase has been called a 'Hymn to justification'.[159] Between Luther's doctrine of justification *sola fide*, by faith alone, and what Tyndale called the 'cankered heresy of justifying of works'[160] was so deep a chasm that no one could pass insensibly from one belief to another. Breathing the spirit of the evangelical Christian of the early Reformation, Wyatt's paraphrase speaks compellingly 'off mercy off fayth off frailte off grace/off goddes goodnes and off Justyfying':[161] whether it speaks of justification by faith *alone* is far less certain. For Wyatt's David there seems to be no sudden imputation of the alien righteousness of the Lutheran revelation. The very nature of sacred drama and of David's evolving confession and conversation with his God suggests a different theological stance. Wyatt's David, although shadowed and oppressed by sin, is not utterly passive in his salvation, and falling from level to level, falteringly finds 'my will to ryse'. 'The sprite of confort in hym revivid is', but not revived by his personal effort or merit, for God is ever present to him, and within His 'loke thus rede I my confort'.[162] Wyatt depicts the inner impulses inscribed in the heart of the believer by which he is free to obey the spirit of God in him. At times God's 'hevy hand' holds David's 'hert in presse', sometimes roughly lifts him up to throw him down. God speaks through him 'as shalme [shawm] or pype letes owt the sownd inprest/by musikes art forgid', or speaks directly to him.[163] A light of divine benediction illumines the darkness of the cave, and David is 'surprisd with Joye'. He has seen through God's justice the light of His mercy, and is finally granted a vision of the redeeming Word.[164] Divine intervention never annihilates his freedom to strive for holiness. If David were simply helpless before grace, with no power even to do what he had been enabled to do, to strain towards penitence and keep God's commandment, then there would be a different drama of redemption. A transformation of David's will occurs through a process of healing excitation which makes him – his bones, his heart – turn toward God.

All this may seem closer to an Augustinian concept of the *impartation* of righteousness – the interior transformation of the sinner through the presence of God, of human nature renewed through the gradual falling away of sin – than to Luther's radical account of *imputation* of righteousness to fallen human beings still captive to sin and passive in their salvation. For Luther, divine grace and human nature were always opposed, but for those imbued with the spirit of Augustinianism grace and nature might co-operate.[165] For a Catholic Augustinian like Fisher, prevenient grace reveals to the sinner the extent of his sin, and makes possible the process of reconciling him with God and justifying him.[166] For Huldrych Zwingli and Heinrich Bullinger, whose theology was being diffused in England in the 1530s and would influence English Reformed identity, Christ's righteousness was imparted as well as imputed to believers. They formulated a reciprocal concept of covenant: a relationship of mutual agreement and conditional obligation between God and humanity. In Swiss Reformed theology divine grace and human works were held together.[167]

In England, as the Supreme Head and his bishops framed doctrine for the new Church, political exigencies and the King's personal beliefs led to a 'theological mediocrity'. In 1537 *The Institution of a Christian Man* (or *Bishops' Book*) stated explicitly justification *sola fide*, while affirming all seven sacraments. Since it held imputation and impartation in tension, it might have been satisfactory to Zwinglians, but not to Lutherans. Belief in justification by faith alone was not a test of conscience in England, but it was a doctrine which the King profoundly distrusted. As Wyatt paraphrased the Psalms he followed closely the official line.[168] Pondering the nature of David's 'Justyfying' he, like David, 'in his hert . . . tornith and paysith', because he knew how charged were the doctrines upon which he meditated. As he would later write to his judges: 'in some lyttell thynge may apere the truthe which I dare saye you seke for yor consciens sake. And besydys that yt is a smale thinge in alteringe of one syllable ether with penne or worde that may mayke in the con-ceavinge of the truthe myche matter or error.' [169]

At a moment of terrible truth – in the Tower in 1541, with little hope of leaving it alive – Wyatt declared his faith in language self-reflexive and elliptical even for him. Accused of being papist – Wyatt, papist – and of treasonable intelligence with the traitor Cardinal who believed that Wyatt sought his death, he protested: 'Besydes this, ye bring in now that I shulde have this intelligens with Pole bycawse of our opinions that are lyke and that I am papyshe.'[170] If Wyatt was a papist, it was his best kept secret. Everything he said outwardly, as his master's servant, condemned the tyrant Bishop of Rome. Only Bonner doubted him, suspecting Wyatt's intimacy with the 'very papist' Mason. Pole was the most stalwart defender of the Church Universal, determinedly obedi-ent to Rome and to the institutions of the visible Church, despite his fervent desire for reform. But as Wyatt and Pole circled each other in Toledo, they had spiritual affinities greater than they can have known, and shared the unhap of being mistrusted in their faith and misunder-stood, not least because the ambiguities and dangers of the times led them to equivocation. By the end of Pole's life the Roman Inquisition suspected that he was 'averse from the right faith' and began to pre-pare charges against him.[171] It was remarked that 'in the eyes of the world' he died unhappily, 'being regarded in Rome as a Lutheran and in Germany as a Papist'.[172] Pole ardently believed in the centrality of Scripture, diminished the human element in salvation, exalted Christ's merits and His atonement as a way of alleviating 'unholy fear', and conceived justification to be by faith alone. This spirit was evident by 1538, and by 1546 he had accepted a doctrine of justification very hard to distinguish from Luther's.[173] Belief in justification by faith *alone* separated Pole from a Catholic reformer like Erasmus; belief that he could remain still within the Roman communion in the hope of hold-ing Christendom together separated him from Luther. The sustaining hope of Pole and all those who thought like him was that a General Council would bring reconciliation between diverging faiths and return the *desviati* to the Church. That dream was disappointed at Regensburg and shattered at Trent.[174]

In their vision of the Church Pole and Wyatt were violently opposed, but in their understanding of salvation and their contemplation of Scripture they had more than a little in common. In circumstances of grief and strain, they both sought consolation in the Psalms. The Psalms were at the heart of the sacred studies and devotions of Pole and his friends.[175] In 1537 Pole's company had awaited the return of Jan van Kampen, and Flaminio hoped to show Pole his Latin paraphrase of thirty Psalms, the paraphrase which was his lifelong endeavour.[176] At Carpentras in May 1539 as Pole pondered the failure of his mission to the Emperor, the impossibility of doing 'what the Pope wishes', he was reading the Psalms of David for spiritual comfort, where he found 'that prudent simplicity' which a servant of God needs.[177] Perhaps then he began his exposition of the fifth and seventh Penitential Psalms and of Psalms 89–93 and 102 (90–4 and 143 in the numbering of the English Psalter). At a moment of unspeakable tribulation, as the vengeful King made Pole's mother a martyr, Pole again turned to the Psalms. Through them he meditated on 'justification, faith, works [and] law', and contemplated God's justice.[178] In Pole's *famiglia* in Viterbo in 1541 Flaminio owned a copy of the *Commentary on the Psalms* of Juan de Valdés, the exiled Spanish humanist and mystic.[179] For Pole and his friends the study of sacred literature and the life of poetry were not wholly divorced, to the concern of those of more austere judgement. At the New Year of 1533 Gian Pietro Carafa – the future Pope Paul IV – had doubted that Pole distinguished clearly enough between sacred and secular literature, and two decades later the life of Pole's household in Viterbo, and of Italian reform more generally, would still be characterized by what has been judged 'this unstable mix of poetry and piety'.[180]

Wyatt, like Pole, turned to the Psalms for consolation and in search of understanding of God's justice and His mercy. He may have contemplated them at some dire moment of undoing, though more likely in recollection, and very late in his life. We might imagine him returned to England, in his chamber, composing in the Egerton manuscript. In England, private contemplation of Scripture and of David's 'sweet return to grace' was safe enough, or so it seemed. Yet 'Wyatt's Psalms'

– especially the prologues – charting King David's world of power, his sins of idolatry and adultery, and his crimes of imagining and plotting Uriah's death, his tyranny in order to possess his 'idol', would soon be held up as a moral to all kings, and perhaps to one in particular: Henry VIII, who identified himself so closely with David, King of the Jews, the father of a chosen people. So the Earl of Surrey would praise Wyatt's paraphrase,

> Where rulers may see in a mirror clear
> The bitter fruit of false concupiscence,
> How Jewry bought Uriah's death full dear.

But in Wyatt's examination of the guilt of the sinning David there could be nothing so certain as a direct allusion to the affairs of his own king. He wrote openly of no tyranny other than the 'tyranny off sin'.[181]

Theological uncertainty alone may not account for all the convolutions of these Psalm paraphrases. Wyatt knew well that in England, by the 'law of words', words alone might condemn anyone and only silence offered safety. In Spain, learned jurists wrote treatises about ways of keeping and detecting secrets. For Domingo de Soto an absolute secret was an act which only the author, God and the confessor knew. Next came the secret offence which only one person apart from its author knew, and to prove it would be difficult.[182] The Holy Office was, of course, exquisitely able to extract secrets. If Wyatt had been paraphrasing the Psalms while in Spain, would the Inquisitors have found there the evidence of his heresy that they sought? Later, even possession of Psalms in English or in French, or singing them in the Inquisition's secret prisons, was taken as proof of heresy.[183] Early in the reign of Elizabeth a ship sailed into San Lucar. On board was 'a little boy not passing 10 or 11 years of age', who was arrested by the Inquisition for 'having in his hand David's Psalms in English'. When his gaoler 'beheld him lifting up his eyes to heaven, saying some Psalm . . . in English, now surely (said he) this boy is become a pretty heretic already'.[184] Was the little boy reading 'Wyatt's Psalms'? By then, they were published. In 1549 John Harington, one of the guardians of Wyatt's verse, had produced an edition of his paraphrase so that 'the noble fame of so worthy a knight, as was the author hereof, Sir Thomas Wyatt, should not perish but remain'.[185]

Wyatt's faith intrigued his contemporaries. The King of France asked 'whether he was of the Lutherian sect or not'?[186] Knowing that this question was asked about him, Wyatt turned it back upon the questioners, disdained to answer it: 'I thynke I shulde have more adoe with a great sorte in Inglande to purge my selffe of suspecte of a Lutherane then of a papyst'.[187] Though Wyatt chose to keep any confessional allegiance private, and even he might have found it hard to label his faith precisely, it was true that evangelicals claimed him as one of their own. Finding Wyatt's paraphrase breathing the spirit of the Gospel, Henry Howard, Earl of Surrey, would eulogise 'Wyatt's Psalms' in the pure language of the evangelical. This was the work for which Wyatt should be venerated, the monument of his faith and religious example,

> Which left with such as covet Christ to know
> Witness of faith that never shall be dead;
> Sent for our health, but not received so.[188]   *health: safety, welfare*

As he lamented Wyatt's death, Surrey was sure that the dead could claim no more than tears from the living. This was to deny the efficacy of prayers for souls departed and the doctrine of Purgatory:[189]

> In days of truth if Wyatt's friends then wail
> (The only debt that dead of quick may claim)
> That rare wit spent employed to our avail
> Where Christ is taught, deserve they man's blame?

We have seen that Wyatt's deepest meditation upon the Psalms allows no imputation of Lutheranism. If he was won to a different strain of reformed belief, there are glimmers of signs of who might have influenced him.

The reformer Thomas Becon owned a copy of Wyatt's Psalm paraphrase: 'Thomas Wyat . . . *psalmos penitentiales rhithmice edidit*'.[190] Under the shadow of persecution, in the early summer of 1541 Becon retreated into Kent, where he 'lurked', changing his vocation from preaching to writing, and his name to 'Theodore Basille'. There families of evangelical sympathies sheltered him. To these protectors Becon dedicated his first works.[191] Trusting that Sir Thomas Wyatt would accept 'my little gift with that benevolence, which all men commend and praise in you', Becon dedicated *The new pollecye of war* to this man who had 'ever hitherto earnestly embraced not only the studies of humane letters, but also the grave exercises of divine literature'. The work began as a paean to patriotism, but soon turned to warn of 'the tokens and signs of the day of judgement' of these latter days: 'wonderful battles', pestilences, the 'tyrannical persecution . . . of the true preachers of God's Word', 'the Christian public weal rent and torn, and miserably deflowered'.[192] Only repentance and Christian living could avert God's due wrath. 'Lurking' in Kent', writing this jeremiad and drawing on examples from history and Scripture, Becon knew that Wyatt, grave paraphraser of 'the Psalmograph', contemplated deeply the consequences of sin, and he believed that Wyatt would welcome this 'little gift'. Perhaps, home from embassy and in retreat at Alington, Wyatt welcomed Becon himself. John Hooper, who became the most renowned exponent of Zurich theology in England and a martyr, would mourn Wyatt's loss. From religious exile in Strasbourg in January 1546 Hooper wrote to Heinrich Bullinger that 'the chief supporters of the gospel in England are dying every hour'. He particularly named 'Sir Thomas Wyat, known throughout the whole world for his noble qualities, and a most zealous defender of yours and Christ's religion'.[193] 'In days of truth', in Kent and Christendom, Wyatt would be acknowledged as a patron of reform by his fellow evangelicals. But in the midst of courts, Wyatt kept his faith concealed, even though he knew that equivocation brought moral hazard. At court, this was one among many other moral hazards.

16

The Slipper Toppe of Courtes Estates

Paraphrasing the Psalms Wyatt kept inviolate that part of him that did not play the orator and did not try to serve both God and King, 'inward Syon'. But once his paraphrases left the privacy of his chamber for the edification of his friends, they were susceptible to new interpretation. The Earl of Surrey, who found in 'Wyatt's Psalms' an animating evangelical intent, also placed them deliberately amidst the royal excesses of the second Book of Samuel, with its lessons for all kings:[1]

> The great Macedon that out of Persia chased   *Alexander*
> Darius, of whose huge power all Asia rang,
> In the rich ark if Homer's rhymes he placed,
> Who feigned gests of heathen princes sang;   *deeds; exploits*
> What holy grave, what worthy sepulture
> To Wyatt's Psalms should Christians then purchase?
> Where he doth paint the lively faith and pure,   *living*
> The steadfast hope, the sweet return to grace
> Of just David by perfect penitence,
> Where rulers may see in a mirror clear
> The bitter fruit of false concupiscence,
> How Jewry bought Uriah's death full dear.
>> In princes' hearts God's scourge yprinted deep
>> Might them awake out of their sinful sleep.

Wyatt's paraphrase may have been his refuge from the world of courts, but reflecting on the Old Testament history of King David led him inescapably to think on royal power and its abuse. David's majesty, as portrayed in Wyatt's first prologue, is lapped in the 'tyranny of sin', his unrestrained authority turned to malign purposes, tyranny becomes treachery. David repents, deeply repents, and renounces 'tryumphe and conquest' and 'dowble Diademe', but in the prologue to the seventh Penitential Psalm Wyatt's David is contemplating once again the threat of worldly enemies and the resumption of dominion. David has been vouchsafed a vision of redemption: to see in 'the heyght of hevin', the Word Incarnate, the sword of death confounded, and by light of divine grace – 'the glint of lyght that in the ayre doth lome [loom]' – the promise of forgiveness. He is sure that he, the sinner, is forgiven: 'David assurance off his iniquite'. Now Wyatt departs from Aretino, his source,[2] to imagine a newly confident David making demands of his God: he instantly turns to 'frame' – a word freighted with doubleness – 'this reson in his hert', to present a 'suit of his pretence'. His heart seems to be less the 'new heart' of contrition than the seat of 'reson', that failing friend he had earlier renounced as 'unjust'. Since God has vouchsafed His 'larger grace' – the death of His Son to convert 'my dethe to lyff, my synn to salvation' – surely, He can grant 'a smaller grace'?[3] King David aspires again to earthly command and to victory over his rebel son Absalom, and seems to have acquired a parodic security in his salvation:

> Alas my sonne porsuys me to the grave
> sufferd by god my sinne for to correct
> but of my sinne sins I my pardonne have
> my sonnes porsuyt shall shortly be reject
> then woll I crave with suryd confidence
> and thus begynnes the suyt off his pretence[4]

Psalm 143 begins with a series of precatory imperatives: 'Here my prayer', 'complyshe my bone', 'answere to my desire'. Now David thinks not only of keeping 'thy word stable', or of himself 'lo thing most unstable', but of God's promise for 'myn Empyre/to stond stable', for his rule to prevail against the rebellion of Absalom.[5] In his pride, his royal pride, David is tempted to believe that divine favour will bring worldly success. His spiritual pilgrimage finds no end in the Penitential Psalms.

❦

When we find Wyatt contemplating Scripture again it is with direct application to the secular realm and with dark intimation. Warning the Chancellor of France in January 1540 that to intervene between a king and his subject was 'to put a sickle in another man's corn', he was adducing Deuteronomy 23:25. This text – 'thou mayst not move a sickle unto thy neighbour's corn' – had always been used for the protection of frontiers and jurisdictions, but in Reformation political theory was employed to teach Christian princes their duty in piety and justice to save stricken people from religious persecution and tyranny.[6] In Spain Wyatt had talked 'oftimes' of royal power with the English exile Robert Branceter. When their paths crossed again in Paris, Wyatt spoke menacingly of the hand of the King and the hand of God stretching out together over the errant. After 'a little dump' – gloomy musing – Branceter told Wyatt that he had 'heard me *oftimes* say that kings have long hands'. But God, said Branceter, 'hath longer'. Wyatt responded: 'I asked him then what length thought he that would make when God's and kings' hands were joined together?'[7]

Thinking on Scripture, Henry's subjects often contemplated Proverbs 21:1: 'The king's heart is in the hand of the Lord, as the rivers of water: he turneth it whithersoever he will.' In 1539, lauding the royal promotion of the Gospel, George Constantine exulted: 'Wonderful are the ways of the Lord, kings' hearts are in the hand of God. He turneth them as he lusteth.'[8] Others, lamenting the royal acts of these latter days, bowed to the unsearchable will of God who held the hearts of princes in His hand. In the Tower, Thomas More had reflected often on this text: '(*Nam in manu Dei*) saith the scripture (*cor regis est*)'.[9] With John Mason, Wyatt spoke of Henry's unsearchable purposes and of the heavy hand of God impinging on the will of princes, believing that if their conversations were private they might stay beyond the King's reach, even if they discussed laws that it was treason to impugn. But as the royal hand stretched over Mason, he would be forced to reveal their secret, dangerous conversations. Wyatt adroitly turned his account of the Act of Supremacy into a paean to a prince who deserved such power: 'yt was a godlye acte, the acte of supreme hede speciouslye the kynges maieste beinge so vertiouse so wyse so lerned and so good a prynce'. Yet he allowed that it might be used malignly, by divine permission: 'yf yt shulde fall into an evell prince that yt were a sore roode'. 'Sore rood': a sorrowful cross.

I suppose I have not myssayde in that, for all powers namelye absolute ar so[re] roodes when theie fall into evell mens handes and yet I saye theie ar to be obeied by expres lawe of good [God] for that ther is no evell prence but for deserte of the people and no hande over an evell prynce but the hande of god.[10]

Wyatt's choice of 'rood' to describe a grievous penalty is full of significance, for the rood was the cross used as an instrument of execution.

Amphibious Wyatt tried to serve God and King. Soon he would be ambassador again. Meanwhile, released from his embassy in Spain, where was he? At the end of September 1539 Cardinal Pole was wondering. Sequestered in the monastery of Montélimar at Carpentras and still living in fear of Wyatt as his assassin, Pole knew of Wyatt's recall from Spain, but no more: 'he has not yet landed in England, and nobody knows where on earth he is. Consequently I suspect that he has the time for this business.'[11] 'This business': the murder of Pole. Wyatt had returned to England and the court by 17 June *reddere rationem* – to present his reckoning, financial and otherwise. For months, ever since the dangerous inquisition into Mason's intelligences with Pole, he had been waiting to vindicate himself. Cromwell advised him 'to lett yt pas. I was clered well inoughe, and he tolde me myche.' Henry 'had so good opinion of me' that he chose to believe Wyatt rather than his accusers, the shadowy 'they' who waited their chance: 'at my commynge home *theye* were punysshed that had sowne that noyse on me'.[12] For the while, only for the while, Wyatt was in the King's grace, favoured and rewarded. 'They' who maligned and sought to harm him were in disfavour. Though the passage of the conservative Act of Six Articles in the summer of 1539, reaffirming the Real Presence in the 'blessed Sacrament of the altar' and confirming traditional practices, had signalled reaction, these reversals for the evangelicals had not overthrown Cromwell. By the autumn he was again high in the counsels of the King.

'Nor does anyone know where he is'. Maybe Wyatt was at court on 18 June to watch the mock naval battle on the Thames, where the King's galley sank the ship of fools of a pretend pope and cardinals.[13] Certainly, he was found enjoying the cock-fighting among the court's gamblers. At the cockpit at Whitehall sometime in the summer or autumn of 1539 Don Andrés de Laguna, a Spanish doctor and naturalist, encountered 'Thomas Huuyat', a 'man of rare wit'. An amphitheatre, a colosseum worthy the heroism of the doomed fighting cocks, had been built at this royal palace for the cruel pleasure of the King and his courtiers. As the cocks came out to fight to the death, courtiers placed jewels as bets. So valued were the cocks that the wounded victors were sent – in vain – to be cured. Laguna could 'not stop marvelling' at the sport – so valorous the little birds, so childish, so vulgar the spectators – until Wyatt grace-fully explained, probably in Latin, that this was more, much more, than diversion. To see how 'fervently these little animals seek for victory at the expense of their own lives' must inspire even the most cowardly to recover a 'strength of spirit to vanquish his foe or to die bravely' fight-ing for 'children's sake, for religion, for one's sacred places, or for the honour and salvation of one's country'. Here Wyatt was rehearsing the argument used by Themistocles to rally his troops.[14]

As the King went on his long summer progress there was no sign of Wyatt following the chase.[15] Flush with the profits of favour, he was buying himself a City mansion. On 23 October his friends signed and sealed a livery of seisin for Wyatt's new house and garden – 'Pekes Garden' – in the parish of St Olave in Tower Ward. His friends George Blage, Sir Thomas and Adrian Poynings, Sir Anthony Lee, Robert Rudston and John Basset were all there to witness it. In his own hand Wyatt endorsed it: 'the dede off my hows at the towre hill'.[16] The pros-pect from Tower Hill would darken the months to come.

Perhaps Wyatt was enjoying summer freedom at Alington, his 'more pleasaunt kynde of lyf'.[17] At last he was with Elizabeth Darrell, but as their past had been shadowed so would be their future. Bess would bear a child, their son Francis, born into all the uncertainties of illegitimacy, though to the great wealth and privilege of life at Alington, while his father lived.[18] Wyatt's son Thomas and his wife Jane were probably also resident at Alington with their growing family. Their first son, Wyatt's grandson Henry – named after his great-grandfather – was followed by Charles, Arthur, George, Anne, Jane and Mary.[19] Thomas Cromwell, who was constantly sued by his friends to favour their children, may have kept a watchful eye on young Thomas and given him patronage. In 1538 this youth was named among 'gentlemen of my Lord Privy Seal' who might be preferred to the royal service, and in May 1539 Cromwell sent a christening present 'by Wiat'.[20] By 1545 the politic William Paget would judge young Thomas Wyatt as 'already a sage man albeit he be young in years', who 'will prove the best man of war with time and experience'. He 'hath been many days a good husband, a strait keeper of discipline military, a great forseer in fortification'. Paget promised that if young Thomas could avoid the fault which marred his father – '(I mean too strong opinion)' – 'he will undoubtedly be excellent'.[21] If. But young Thomas could not and did not avoid 'strong opinion'. In the reign of Queen Mary he turned traitor and led the men of Kent in rebellion.

Magnanimous, gregarious, great men supported great households: the greater the man, the greater the household. Wyatt, always generous to the point of folly, gathered to Alington friends and family, and servants to serve them. In his will Henry Wyatt had charged Thomas to provide for his nephews, Henry and Robert Lee, the sons of his sister Margaret, 'to find them to school'. In his childhood spent at Alington Henry Lee was trained to become so perfect a knight that he would be chosen as Queen Elizabeth's champion. And in Wyatt's household he learnt how to keep himself 'right and steady in many dangerous shocks and three utter turns of State'. Young Henry Savile was also left to Thomas Wyatt's care: from the household in Alington he went on to study at Oxford.[22] At Alington, too, was the family of Wyatt's old friend, Sir Thomas Poynings: if not yet, certainly later. Writing to his son in 1537, Wyatt had sent greetings to 'my daughter Jane and my daughter Besse'. Jane was his new daughter-in-law, and 'Besse' probably her sister Elizabeth Haute.[23]

The life of Wyatt's daughter Frances is obscure. Her childhood and youth are lost to us, but from the dubious custody of her mother she may have passed to the care of Lucy Harper. Lucy, the heiress of great lands in Kent, was married – catastrophically married – to George Harper. Abandoning her husband, she became the mistress of Richard Morison and the mother of his children. In time Frances would inherit part of Lucy Harper's estate.[24] By 1537–8 Frances was married to Thomas Leigh, doctor of law, of distant Calder in Cumberland. With Leigh Frances had a son, Henry, another grandson for Wyatt. Whether Wyatt ever saw his daughter is unknown, but if he forgot her she did not forget him. When she died in July 1578, having remarried after Leigh's death in 1556, her memorial brass in Ponsonby Church bore this inscription:

Here lyeth the body of Frances Patrickson, daughter of Sir Thomas Wyatt, knight, one of the most honourable Privy Council to King Henry VIII – sometime wife of Thomas Leigh of Calder, and at the day of her death, wife of William Patrickson, gentleman.

> God gave this wife a mind to pray in groans and pangs of death;
> And to heaven elevating hands and eyes, smilingly to yield breath
> And thus at age of 56 to grave she took her way . . .[25]

In the wings was the shadowy presence of Wyatt's wife Elizabeth, grandmother to all these grandchildren, observing the new domestic arrangements at Alington while excluded from them, wherever she was. Maybe she was not the least of the clogs which hung at Wyatt's heel in the country. The allurements of life at Alington might have have palled; Wyatt might have become bored, had they lasted. But in November the call came for him to return to embassy, with all its endless waiting, the ache of boredom and exile, and the chance it offered for service and for honour.

The Emperor had left his Burgundian territories for his Spanish kingdoms so many years before. When he returned there it was for grim reasons. Ghent had been in revolt since 1537 and must be shown the consequences of its disobedience.[26] But even Charles was not lord of the whole world, and to reach the Low Countries he must make himself vulnerable to other princes. 'The way thither by sea', wrote Wyatt, 'besides the danger of the winter, must be to him suspected by landing peradventure where he would not'. The storm which had blown Charles's father on to the Channel coast and made him hostage of Henry VII was never forgotten.[27] Nor had Charles and Francis visited each other's realms since Francis had been Charles's prisoner in Spain after the battle of Pavia in 1525. Memories of these unhappy precedents lived on. But travelling north through Italy would present Charles with the unwelcome prospect of a meeting with the Pope, and yet more exhortations to his Imperial duty. Finally, he accepted the French King's invitation to pass through France, what Francis called 'your kingdom and mine'.[28] At the end of November Charles departed Spain, accompanied by a small band of grandees all dressed in mourning black. The Duke of Orléans met them at the border and, joined by the Dauphin and the Constable of France, they journeyed north, celebrated by magnificent entries in the cities they passed.[29] To assist the peace between this 'duumvirate' who would share the world between them and make the enemies of Christendom tremble, the Pope sent his young grandson Cardinal Alessandro Farnese as legate, with Marcello Cervini, the future Pope Marcellus: 'a young god' from Rome with his minder, the 'legate's governor', so Wyatt disparagingly called them.[30] Farnese had instructions to discover any secret dealings between Francis or Charles and the English King, and to order them to deny a safe-conduct to Anne of Cleves, Henry's prospective fourth queen, 'if it be true that she is a Lutheran'. The English dreaded the legate bringing the bull of excommunication.[31]

Who should Henry send to this festival of universal harmony? Who but Wyatt? 'I was sent agayne Embassadoure to themperour at his commynge into Fraunce . . . yt was saide unto me that I was used for the necessite.'[32] Time was that Wyatt was 'cherished' by the Emperor. 'A man of wit and reputation' was sent 'in diligence' to France – so the French ambassador reported on 14 November – his name, 'Hoyet'.[33] Dishonoured by his exclusion from the festivities, the King charged Wyatt to 'ensearch and investigate by all ways and means . . . how things do stand' with the friendly rival princes, and to pretend to rejoice at their 'amity'. With Wyatt went John Mason – 'ye[a] . . . the Instrument of my treasons' – and they were to act in concert with Bonner, now ambassador to the French King.[34] They hardly forgot how comprehensively they had been calumnied by Bonner, so this co-operation would be an exercise in hypocrisy and patience, the more trying because the French King, no less than they, was irritated by him. On 28 November they reached Paris and sought news from English scholars there. Riding south, they overtook Bonner, 'Master Diligence', at Orléans, and sped on to intercept the royal entourage as Francis travelled towards the Emperor. By 2 December four exhausted post horses had carried them to Blois.[35] After supper and a 'little hearing his music', Wyatt and Mason, with Bonner in tow, accompanied the Cardinal of Lorraine to an audience with the King. By the light of a great candle held by the Cardinal, Francis read their letters of credence. Wyatt declared his King's delight at the 'reconciliation, friendship and confidence' between the princes on whom the peace of Christendom depended. Doffing his bonnet, Francis acknowledged the honour that 'his good brother' Charles did him in visiting his realm. The Emperor knew him to be 'a prince of honour and Christian', replied Wyatt. 'Oh . . . we have among us all nothing but our honour,' said the King, and 'laying his hand on his breast', protested – protested too much – his trust in the Emperor, and that Henry was as 'dear as the ball of his eye'.

'I will spur afore the French King', promised Wyatt, 'and get access and insert myself into the Emperor's band afore they meet.' Yet he feared being 'cast far behind', for the hiring of horses was forbidden on pain of death, to prevent anyone following the royal entourages.[36] Wyatt being Wyatt, 'what by force, what by means', he found a horse and did 'spur afore'. Late at night on 10 December the Emperor arrived at Châtellerault, and the next morning received Wyatt 'very gently, with his hat in his hand'. All the while, Constable Montmorency hung around to prevent any double-dealing between Charles and Henry. At the entry of the Dauphin and the Duke of Orléans, 'bidding them good morrow', Charles 'smilingly' dismissed Wyatt. 'But I began again', wrote Wyatt, insisting that the treaty promises be kept 'stable'. Charles offered a warning: just as Henry wished his sovereignty to be respected, so he must not aid the Duke of Cleves in his usurping claim to the Duchy of Gelderland. 'I assure you, Monsieur l'embassadeur, I shall show him [Cleves] that he hath played but the young man.' The Duke did not understand with whom he dealt; the Emperor's threat was his promise. 'Laying his hand on his breast', Charles averred that although in him the Duke had 'a sovereign, a neighbour and a cousin', if he persisted in this claim, he 'shall lose all three'. 'Surely', Wyatt judged, the Emperor 'mindeth more Gelder[land] in his heart then he doth Milan or all Italy.' 'And in my conscience, his coming out of Spain in this haste' was because he had heard of Henry's alliance with Cleves, 'to prevent things that might succeed'. This explained Charles's terrible winter journey through France, with all its dangers and its speed. His speaking openly, 'discovering his courage', when usually he kept everything so close, made Wyatt suspect 'some further assurance with France' than either he or Francis was admitting. 'Again he bade me welcome and that we should see oftener. And thus he went to mass, and forthwith to horse.' Our elegant courtier meanwhile made his way to Losches late that night 'with much ado upon plough horse in the deep and foul way'.[37]

It was now Wyatt's fortune to be a knight without a horse and an ambassador without intelligence. 'I wot not, by Our Lord, what I may write . . . of any certainty, for I see little appearance which way I may come to knowledge; all that I may do is conjecture.' Since the Emperor's entourage was so small, 'here is come few or none of my familiars'.[38] In the French court, Mason encountered a man – never named – they knew before, who was once almoner to the Duke of Bourbon who had sacked Rome. He had served the Emperor in Spain until driven by Charles's 'falsehood and trumpery' to 'return to his natural country'. Charles, the man insisted, 'cometh to deceive us'. Here was a man whom Wyatt could trust – 'of wit and judgement, and a round [plain-speaking] man' – and there were few enough of these.[39] Friendships which had sustained Wyatt in his first mission in Spain proved fleeting. Often now his information came by roundabout means and from dubious sources: 'we had it in a right good place that the Queen of Navarre advertised a friend of hers . . .' Or from unnamed 'friends': 'a secretary of Granvela told a friend of mine'. He even discovered what Cardinal Farnese's 'governor' Marcello Cervini told 'a near friend of his'. Silence led Wyatt to surmise: 'the [vain] glory of the Constable and the very nature of the Frenchmen would not hide the conclusion if there were any'; they would declare 'a bare likelihood for a certainty if there were any likelihood at all'. A visiting ambassador 'could not be hidden from them that would not hide it from me'.[40] As the rival princes prepared to meet – not this time on a swaying galley in the Mediterranean, but with magniloquent ceremony – all the emissaries of other powers were excluded. At Losches Wyatt lodged 'in evil favoured lodging and worse bedding' until 'dislodged', because 'no ambassador should tarry'. Charles and Francis met privately on the 12th: they 'do that they do by themselves'.[41]

On 12 December '*Magistro VViet orator Anglo*' arrived in Amboise.[42] This notice from the papal nuncio at the French court is one of few sightings of Wyatt in the reports of foreign ambassadors, for he became sidelined. Wyatt now dwelt in the suburbs of the Emperor's affections and of his court. Even Poggio, the papal nuncio, encountering Wyatt on the road to Amboise, sent no fevered report of his malignant purposes. 'They say he offers great alliances and seeks to sow jealousy', but so far as Poggio could discover the Emperor would not listen.[43] Wyatt eloquently told the – often picaresque – story of his embassy, scripted in many voices, in twenty extant letters written to the King or Cromwell. But behind the story told in letters lay another one, and behind that another, often too dangerous to tell. A man who professed plain speech and openness, whom dread never intimidated, so the Earl of Surrey would claim, was now driven to invent a diplomatic literature and performance of duplicity. 'To sett spies over traytors, yt ys I thynke no newe practys with Imbassadours.'[44] Spying on the confederacy of English exiles was the duty of Henry's ambassadors, but they all ran the risk of being suspected of collusion with these shadowy intelligencers of the Pope. Wyatt discovered in Blois, 'here in the tail' of the Emperor's train, a man he had known before: Robert Branceter. He planned 'secretly to trap him' – 'he shall never escape my hands'.[45]

As the Emperor and the French King travelled in state, under canopies of cloth of gold, from town to town and palace to palace – from Chenonceaux to Amboise, from Chambord to Châlon, from Orléans to Fontainebleau – feasting, sometimes hunting (unsportingly shooting harts with hand guns), Wyatt and every other ambassador were 'all driven still afore, afore', forced in 'corners [to] lie hidden'. 'In a cave being in [an or]chard, which for lack of wine was filled [with] horses' Bonner's servant penned his report.[46] Their discomfiture and humiliation speaks through all the letters home.[47] In Paris on Christmas Day, while the princes disported themselves at Fontainebleau, Wyatt forecast with weary cynicism that the Emperor would practise his usual delays 'to win time till they have wound themselves honestly out of France': 'But we see not for all these entries, for all this joining of arms, knitting of crowns, and such ceremonies, that they should determine to part the world between them.'[48] At one of the most resplendent court festivals of the Renaissance, while the Emperor was received in triumph, Wyatt, 'far off lodged', observed from a distance. During all these ceremonies and all the feasting in glittering palaces, he was desperately chasing an English renegade through the back streets of Paris.

Last seen, Robert Branceter was leaving Toledo with Cardinal Pole in February 1539. During Pole's retreat at Carpentras and at his return to Italy, Branceter had been at his side.[49] Now in France, he 'practised' with Poggio 'for Pole'. Although never tried for treason, Branceter was attainted in his absence, and if ever he were captured and taken to England, there would be no way for him but one. Stealthily, Wyatt stalked him, waiting his chance. If his first attempt should 'quail', his quarry would be forewarned and seek the Emperor's protection. Since Branceter was in the realm of the French King, his capture, if known, was likely to raise large questions of immunity. 'I have sure watch over him, both where he lodgeth, whither he goeth, and what he intendeth,' so Wyatt assured Cromwell. His agents, appointed to 'entertain' Branceter in Paris, constantly to report his whereabouts ready for his 'sudden apprehension', were two English scholars: William Swerder, Cranmer's servant, and William Welden, whose patron was Richard Pate. They would guard Branceter, the better to kidnap him. Mason had declined to 'entertain' Branceter, because 'he had once swerved from him' before.

As the waiting game palled, stalking somehow turned to hotter pursuit, and Wyatt injured himself in the chase, 'hurt my leg with a fall, that in deed I fear me will not be whole this month'. 'Long standing' in formal audience now pained him; he could not sleep. But thanking the King for having 'my jeopardy more dear than his traitor's destruction', he promised still to 'hazard', to venture to seize Branceter.[50]

On 3 January, in the aftermath of the triumphant entries of the Emperor and legate into Paris, Wyatt and Bonner asked for audience with the French King to demand that Branceter be handed over. After evasions of speech and action by the Constable – who 'escaped us by a back door' – he gave assurances. So did the King, but Wyatt deceived Francis by describing Branceter as 'a man of small quality . . . a merchant's factor' who had robbed his master, an outlaw 'desperate of his country', turned conspirator and traitor. As Branceter said, 'it was greater matters than creditors'. At dead of night, with no lantern to light their way, Wyatt and the Provost of Paris went secretly to Branceter's lodgings where they found him quietly writing letters while Welden kept watch over him. 'Since he would not come to visit me, I was come to seek him . . .' Hearing Wyatt's voice, Branceter blanched; 'his colour changed'. As Wyatt grabbed for his letters, Branceter 'flung them backward into the fire', and Wyatt reached into the flames to save them. Claiming to be the Emperor's servant, Branceter took from his doublet 'a bag of cere [wax] cloth with writings therein' as proof. Wyatt confronted Branceter, who recalled how he would 'oftimes say that kings have long hands'. When the Provost took Branceter 'to his lodging and not to mine', Wyatt was powerless to act.

This blundered arrest precipitated a diplomatic maelstrom, for it raised lofty principles of immunity and touched princely honour. To give refuge to another king's 'vassal, subject and rebel' was a breach of treaties, a violation of sovereignty: it was, said Wyatt, 'to put his sickle in another man's corn'. Yet to capture the servant of another prince, under his protection, was to violate the law of nations and to dishonour the prince. The French King's consent to hand over Branceter – not debtor and thief, but the Emperor's servant – was gravely embarrassing. Earlier, Granvelle had denied that Branceter was travelling in the

Imperial suite, but hearing of Branceter's arrest, Granvelle claimed him and sought his freedom.[51] If Charles and Francis were angry, Henry would be more furious still. His ambassadors again required the delivery of the 'rebel Branceter'.

On Twelfth Night Wyatt and his successor, Richard Tate, had an audience with the Emperor which Wyatt reported in vivid, excruciating detail, each succeeding exchange a humiliation for the English King and his ambassadors. There was a man 'that seemed to hang about his court', a fugitive from Henry, so Wyatt told the Emperor: '"Ah", quod he, "Robert". "That same, Sir", quod I. "I shall tell you", quod he, "Monsieur l'embassadour; it is he that hath been in Persia." "As he saith, Sir", quod I.' Charles fondly recounted the many services Robert had performed for him from Turkey to Persia, and beyond. 'And I have had him following me this ten or twelve years in all my voyages in Africa, in Provence, in Italy, and now here'.[52] He expressed 'no little marvel' that Wyatt had had him arrested, without warning: '"And I promise you it was evil done of you" . . . "What!" quod he, "would ye that I should consent to the destruction of a man that followeth me . . . ? I will set him at liberty," quod he, "Monsieur l'embassadeur".' With telling reference to the English King's disregard for conscience, Charles promised: 'though your master had me in the Tower of London, I would not consent so to change mine honour and my conscience'.

Wyatt dared to raise more delicate jurisdictions and more cosmic authority. '"Sir", quod I, "I have also to complain . . . of the evil entreating by the Inquisition of the English merchants that traffic in your countries of Spain".' To Charles's response that 'the authority of the Inquisition depended not upon him', that those who lived in his realms must live under their laws, Wyatt recalled his 'conference' in Toledo with Granvelle and an Inquisitor. Charles forgot, or chose to forget, the agreement of the Holy Office to moderate its rigours, the agreement which still rests in the Inquisition archives: 'Though, as you say, there were communication upon this it was not agreed to.'*[53] This dispute about the powers of the Inquisition led to deeper contention

* See above, pp. 444–5.

over papal primacy and the Petrine succession, human law and divine, the authority of the Church and the authority of Scripture. Charles insisted: "'I cannot let [prevent] the Inquisition. This is a thing that toucheth our faith". "What, Sir," quod I, "the primacy of the Bishop of Rome?"' Wyatt answered, against the Emperor, that papal power was not divinely instituted – 'almost they themselves durst never claim that *de jure divino* [by divine law]' – but rested on history and human law. "'What!" quod he, "Monsieur l'embassadeur, shall we now come to dispute that of *tibo dabo claves* [I will give you the keys]? I assure you I will not alter my Inquisition. No, nor if I thought they would be negligent in their offices I would put them out".'

That the Inquisition which 'depended not upon him' now became '*my* Inquisition' shows the extent of Wyatt's provocation and Charles's outrage. Seeking to calm the Emperor, distancing himself from such incendiary arguments, Wyatt said submissively: "'I come not to dispute. I am not learned. But there is yet more, Sir," quod I, "preachers be set forth that defame the King and the nation and provoke your subjects against the King's".' Charles replied: 'I will tell you, Monsieur l'embassadour . . . kings be not kings of tongues.' But Wyatt's experience, at his own King's court and the Emperor's, had taught otherwise. Wyatt, who had once basked in Imperial favour, now experienced an unaccustomed 'vehemence'. 'I noted his louder voice, his earnester look, and specially his imperious fashion in his words.' As he presumed too far on diplomatic privilege, he had reason to fear defenestration. Now Wyatt wrote suggesting to the King that 'some man of authority, wisdom and learning' – a man, though he did not say so, conservative in religion – afforce his embassy. This would lighten him 'of a great burden I feel by fear of my error and folly'.[54] Wyatt's folly: the French King, 'pointing his hand to his head' in the universal gesture indicating derangement, recalled Wyatt speaking 'very audaciously' to the Emperor while in France, and judged him 'somewhat fantastic'.[55]

As his king's messenger Wyatt felt the force of the Imperial fury intended for his master as well as that directed towards him 'as of himself'. The animus against Henry intensified with the arrival of Cardinal Farnese, who had made his solemn entry into Paris on New Year's Eve, attended by five cardinals. Never countenancing the English schism, still fearing Henry's militant enmity, the Pope continually urged the Catholic powers to move against him, and had sent his grandson to consider ways and means.[56] The apprentice legate, under the tutelage of Cervini and Poggio, sent an extraordinary report on New Year's Day which seemed to reveal Wyatt as no ordinary messenger. The English ambassador – the one 'chased from Spain as a heretic' – had secretly proposed the marriage of Mary, 'daughter of England', to the Emperor. Charles's response had been 'between sweet and sour': unless Henry returned to papal obedience he could hope for neither alliance nor protection.[57] This was a proposal too secret to appear in any extant royal instruction, and almost too delicate to be made, lest the King and his daughter be dishonoured by its refusal. But since rumours of the proposal would surface in the coming months, this was more than a figment of Farnese's excited imagination.

While the Emperor 'wound [himself] honestly out of France' Wyatt followed disconsolately.[58] Henry's fury once he discovered the sanctuary offered to Branceter resulted in incendiary instructions to his ambassadors to protest. Protest turned to insult. Bonner's zeal in protesting was soon the talk of the diplomatic community: he dared tell Francis that it was impossible to have justice in his kingdom. If Henry himself had said so, declared Francis, he would have punched him in the eye; he must presume that Bonner spoke 'as of himself', not by order of his king. An envoy rode in post to England to discover the truth, and Bonner's recall soon followed.[59] Wyatt's instructions made him quail: 'surely I durst never have done it unless your majesty had commanded me, the matter being perilous for such a fool as I to deem upon'. Obeying this command left him in nervous prostration, suffering from migraine, as before in times of greatest anxiety: 'I was not able scant to write three lines together for my head that so pain[ed] me.'[60] The command: to charge the Emperor with *ingratitude*.

The diplomatic disaster which was Wyatt's audience with the Emperor in Brussels on 1 February was variously reported and long remembered.[61] Wyatt, in his king's name, accused the Emperor of a grave dishonour: 'ye had broken promas'.[62] This encounter was so heated that Wyatt could hardly report it: 'often, he clipped my tale with imperious and brave words enough'; 'we had quarrels enough'; 'I often pricked him with words'. Words were said from which there was no going back, words which Wyatt did not dare report to his king. The fateful word 'ingrate' provoked from Charles a furious denial: 'I cannot be toward him [Henry] ingrate. The inferior may be ingrate to the greater, and the term is scant sufferable between like. But peradventure because the language is not your natural tongue, ye may mistake the term.' This rebuke was an exquisite insult to so perfect a linguist as Wyatt, even if it seemed to offer an exit from a diplomatic impasse. To Charles, Holy *Roman* Emperor, who might command the empire more easily than its language, Wyatt condescended to give a lecture on etymology, on the derivation of 'ingrate' from Latin:

'Nor I see not', quod I, 'Sir . . . that that term should infer prejudice to your greatness. And though yourself, Sir, excuseth me by the tongue, yet I cannot render that term in my tongue into the French tongue by any other term which I know also to descend out of the Latin, and in the original it hath no such relation to lesserness or greaterness of persons.'

As Wyatt accused Charles of giving Henry 'fair words' – lies, in diplomatic parlance – Charles 'kekid': he cackled. A darker exchange, a seemingly irrecoverable breach, was reported by Charles, but not by Wyatt. It was unreasonable, said Charles, to deliver Branceter to the hangman without knowing why. Did he mean to call Henry hangman, Wyatt asked? Even the words of Charles's retraction – he would rather call Henry 'cruel prince' – Wyatt could not send to a king who had instituted the 'law of words'. The charge of ingratitude and Charles's response precipitated a 'tragedy', for these words 'sound so evil' that Henry did not think 'they should be left unanswered'. If the Emperor believed 'himself pricked on so high a pin as though he had no peer in Christendom', he might learn that 'the world is but slipper, and will sometime have his turns'. Henry sought the French King's advice how to answer.[63] Delightedly, Poggio reported Wyatt's dishonour.[64] Having sent Mason racing home to England to explain matters too sensitive even for cipher, Wyatt was left alone in the shipwreck of his embassy, in an underworld of spies and fantasists.

The Emperor departed for Ghent on 9 February, escorted by three thousand landsknechts and six hundred horsemen, a display of Imperial power to awe his rebel subjects.[65] Stuck in Brussels, Wyatt occupied himself worrying about his debts and longing for recall, but also divining the diplomatic state of play, especially in Germany – 'Almain matters'. He rediscovered a man 'who penetrateth far into matters of state': Dr Udalricus of Strasbourg, alias 'Hulrik thalmayne', whom he had trusted in grim days in Toledo as 'a right honest man and that understandeth right well the things of his country'. With the largesse he could never afford, Wyatt had given him a horse. Now he proposed to recruit him to send back 'continual letters' on the state of affairs in Germany, and soon they began to arrive. One letter, addressed to the '*Magnifico et generoso domino, D. Thome Wiat, equiti aurato* [the magnificent gentleman, Sir Thomas Wiat, knight]', survives.[66] Other contacts were more clandestine. In the shadows, Wyatt was observing and orchestrating a band of spies. Two men offered to serve the King 'for the truth's sake . . . and for the advancement of the word of God'. One was a Gascon – 'Robert Valle, but his name must be secret' – both were 'men of war'.[67] These would-be spies were evangelical in religion, but most others were not. Cardinal Pole's intelligencers were closely watched.

In Brussels, 'Mr Wriothesley's jewel hath made alliance with mine and the third insinuates himself very well.'[68] Wriothesley's jewel was Harry Phillips, an English exile, who had betrayed Tyndale and offered his allegiance to Rome and his service to Pole. Earlier, Wriothesley had been charged with arranging the arrest and extradition of Phillips, but in February 1539 he had escaped, in circumstances so implausible that Wriothesley's complicity seemed likely.[69] Wyatt's 'jewel' was Branceter. The third was John Torre, Sir John Wallop's servant, secretly recruited by Wyatt as double agent to go undercover. 'Tor is here still about Branceter, and with him keepeth company Phillips,' so Wyatt reported on 14 February: 'they take him to be in as evil case as themselves, whereby he creepeth well into their company. And they warn him greatly to beware of me.' They had reason. Finding 'no way to convey' Branceter, Wyatt was devising 'the other way'; he was arranging for Branceter's assassination. Even while Branceter's quietus was prepared, Wyatt provided subventions to him.[70] Rescuing Branceter, the Emperor sent him to Rome, to Pole's safe keeping, so Branceter told Cardinal Farnese.[71] He was not the only English traitor visiting Farnese in these days or travelling from France to Rome.

These were Lenten days in Ghent. Wyatt arrived on 1 March, just as the Emperor punished the town with exemplary justice to show the consequences of rebellion and his terrible power. On 12 March the town surrendered its privileges. Many fled as the rebel leaders were rounded up 'to the number of three or four score' and the ghastly public executions began. Nine rebels were beheaded in the marketplace on the 18th and fourteen more were expected to die that week. Hundreds of the citizenry paraded barefoot, and knelt before the Emperor, crying, 'Mercy!'[72] For whatever reason, Charles was 'in great melancholy, in so much that he confessed he could not sleep on nights'. This Wyatt learnt from a friend, who heard it from Granvelle's secretary.[73] Banished from the Emperor's grace and from his presence, Wyatt rested his diplomacy upon intelligence gleaned at a distance. Ambassadors sent reports of his exile. In France the – exaggerated – story was that Wyatt was ordered to stay ten leagues distant from the Imperial court.[74] Yet, in his king's isolation and his own, he was still bound to report, even to advise. Hearing rumours in Ghent of 'matter of great suspect toward some secret thing' planned against the King, Wyatt dismissed them as 'common drunkards' talks'. And yet, if all the truces and accords then current – with the Turks, between the French King and the Emperor, between the Emperor and the German Protestants – held, there was reason to credit the rumours. While Henry was not firmly 'comprehended with the Germans', he was without allies, 'destitute of any foreign assurance', and vulnerable to the Pope's continued attempts to rally the Catholic powers against him.[75] Now Wyatt ventured to advise his king on policy, and he urged him to fuller alliance with the German Protestant alliance, the League of Schmalkalden.

Rapprochement between England and the Schmalkaldic League had seemed likely as Wyatt left for France.[76] The King had long been intrigued by theological discussions with the League which would help him to further the moderate reformation of his Church. Those discussions had foundered a year previously, in the spring of 1539, when the truce between the League and the Emperor – the Frankfurt Interim – blocked Henry's entry to the League, and when the Act of Six Articles had so threatened the evangelical cause, but in November League ambassadors were preparing to return to England. They were to seek Cromwell's advice: 'how he thinks that matters between the Christian league of the German nation with respect to religion might be brought to a good agreement'.[77] 'Pious men' in England ardently hoped that Henry's marriage to Anne of Cleves would be the way to return England to the true path, to the advancement of the 'true doctrine of religion', and that it would also prepare the way for an alliance with the League. But, meeting his fourth queen on New Year's Day 1540, Henry felt an instant, insurmountable revulsion.[78] The marriage proved disastrous, though not fatal, or not to her. Cromwell understood just how dangerous its failure was to himself and to his cause. On 10 January 1540 he told the Lutheran envoys that 'he sees our opinions in matters of the faith, but the world standing now as it does, whatever his lord the king does, so too will he hold'. Cromwell would follow royal policy: how could a counsellor to the King do otherwise? But he was acknowledging, too, his adherence to the same faith as these ambassadors, and his will to advance that faith when the world turned again.[79] Also waiting for the world to turn, for their chance to subvert the evangelicals, was the 'papistical faction'[80] of their conservative enemies led by Bishop Gardiner. Thus, when Wyatt advised further alliance with the Germans, he was urging royal policy, but a policy to which 'pious men' in Henry's counsels – Cromwell and Cranmer – were far more committed than was the King himself, who was preparing to abandon it. Wyatt's advice came at an impolitic moment.

These were times of great volatility and danger in England. Religious divisions at court and in the capital grew bitter, and political fortunes were shifting. The evangelicals had brought the Gospel to the people, but their own downfall was prefigured in their triumph. Lenten sermons by leading evangelicals who preached sedition along with Scripture spurred Gardiner to reply, and that pulpit contest endangered as well as furthered the evangelical cause.[81] The inwardness of events was hard to read, the signs conflicting. Even Gardiner and Cromwell seemed reconciled, 'perfect entire friends'. At a long, private dinner in London on 30 March 'they opened their hearts', 'all displeasures be forgotten'.[82] It was pretty to think so. This love feast which Wriothesley reported to Wallop was not what it seemed, for Gardiner, Wallop and Wriothesley countenanced the removal of Cromwell in order to save the Church from further reform. Their chance would come in London, and also in Calais.

Calais had become an enclave of gospellers as well as a conservative redoubt. So fearful was Lord Lisle that religious division would turn to violence that, reportedly, he slept in armour.[83] As deputy he had been unable to contain the dissension, partly because Cromwell, ignoring his pleas for help, his warnings that heresy was spreading, had protected the reformers. Indeed, Cromwell wrote 'taxing him for persecuting those who favour and set forth God's word and favouring those who impugn it'.[84] Two visits in February 1540 prompted action: a commission to enquire into the affairs of Calais. When the Earl of Hertford came to view its military preparedness and the Duke of Norfolk passed through on his way to the French court both were shocked by what they found.[85] That Calais was so riven was the more dangerous because the fortress was already so vulnerable that 'forty Frenchmen in a morning might win the Castle without any jeopardy'.[86] For Cromwell, the best solution would be to replace Lisle as deputy by a man who was at once martial *and* sympathetic to the Gospel. Therein lay the fear of Lisle and the conservatives – and Wyatt's hope, Wyatt's 'practise'. On 14 March the conservative Wallop wrote gnomically to his old friend Lisle, Wyatt's old friend Lisle, of the possibility of Wyatt's return to Calais: 'if he should supply you in your place, that I would much mislike, and soundeth much contrary to those good purposes that you, I, and other hath travailed in'.[87] For them, Wyatt was clearly aligned with Cromwell and the evangelical cause. High Marshal once, with military experience in Calais, Wyatt's elevation to be deputy would be a fitting glory for him. Lisle's allegiances would soon provide the occasion for his fall, the chance to remove him. In March 1539, Wriothesley had feared subversion in Calais, for '*Judas non dormit* [Judas does not sleep]'.[88]

Enter Gregory 'Sweetlips' Botolf.[89] Thwarted, so far, in their plans for holy war against England, the Pope and Pole were receptive to more adventitious schemes. A conspiracy devised in Calais and countenanced in Rome touched Wyatt and his *familia* in the spring of 1540. Gregory Botolf, once a canon at St Gregory's Priory in Canterbury, with allegiances all to the old faith and to Rome, had become a domestic chaplain in the household of the Lisles in 1538. A man of plausible charm – hence the nickname – he found followers in Calais, especially his 'bedfellow' Clement Philpot. Late in January Botolf, Philpot and a friend departed, seemingly for England, with Lisle's leave. Botolf spent the night at the Rose Tavern, ostentatiously gambling, winning and waiting for a Channel crossing.[90] But he did not intend to go to England: instead, he sought Cardinal Farnese in Amiens. According to Farnese, 'Gregorio', an English priest, steward to 'Arthur, natural son of King Edward [IV]', came to declare a conspiracy: he knew 'an easy way to capture Calais'. In the herring time – between Michaelmas and St Andrew tide – many ships came from France and Flanders to fish. When the bridge was raised, this priest, 'moved by zeal and love of God', planned to go secretly by night with a band of twenty companions through a little door to the guardhouse. Surprising the guard, they would open the Lantern Gate to allow waiting forces to enter and seize Calais. Suspicious of Gregorio and his scheme, Farnese and Cervini sent him to Rome for the Pope and Pole to decide whether he was '*savio ò matto, ò buono ò cattivo* [wise or stupid, good or wicked]'.[91] In Rome, so Sweetlips boasted to Philpot, 'I declared everything of my mind unto them, no more but we three together, in the Pope's chamber.' As he left, the Pope gave him two hundred crowns, sang Mass and prayed for him.[92] The words of a fantasist? Not entirely.

On 27 February news was sent from Rome to Farnese that the English priest was returning, '*molto satisfatto*'. Having interrogated Gregorio and his story, Pole believed that he and his conspiracy would serve well if Francis and Charles could be persuaded, at last, to levy war against England. Pole was convinced that Gregorio was genuine because 'Arthur, his master, and his wife' supported him. The Lisles were Pole's friends, 'good Christians' who abhorred the actions of 'that bad King'.

The plot must remain deadly secret until the autumn herring season. On 1 March Gregorio left Rome, riding fast toward Calais.[93] At Boulogne Sweetlips persuaded Wallop to lend him a horse, and he reached Calais on 17 March.[94] There, in the Lisles' chapel, he showed Edward Corbett the coins he would make into rings: the pledge of their brotherhood and confederacy.[95] On the walls at Bourbourg on 25 March – propitiously, the day of the Annunciation and Maundy Thursday in that year – Botolf imparted to Philpot, 'my most joy of the world', the secret purpose of his journey to Rome. Promising Philpot that they would deserve 'the merits of Heaven', 'we be the elect of God', Botolf also assured him: 'gold ye shall have plenty . . . This world shall be ours'. Philpot vowed 'whatsoever you will do, I shall take part to live and die as you do', the vow of perfect friendship.[96]

In the last days of March Botolf was riding 'like a gallant abroad' for Ghent. Outside Bruges he and a servant, John Browne, were overtaken by John Mason and Francis, the King's messenger, riding post haste to find Wyatt.[97] Following 'apace' Botolf spoke to them, making some secret arrangement, but fell behind as they rode furiously on. He gave Browne the slip and went to find the Pope's ambassadors. Searching all through Ghent the hapless Browne 'had lost Sir Gregory two days of three', until finally 'as I was going to Mr Wyatt's lodging for to seek for him', he found him. Botolf 'prayed me for to go to Mr Wyatt's with him' to recover letters he had – unwisely – entrusted to Wyatt's servant, Robert Rudston.[98] Rudston – 'no honest man', thought Botolf – deceived them, telling them they must call back later, for his 'bedfellow' had the keys of the chamber where they were kept. Returning, they were told that the 'bedfellow' had given the letters to Mr Gresham, who was 'riding into Englandward'. In vain, Clement Philpot waited for Botolf's letter 'sent by Mr Wyatt's servant'.[99] But the letters were now in the hands of Wyatt who, discovering the conspiracy, 'browght them to the Kinge'.[100] Wyatt's household, keeping watch, saw that 'amongst the Cardinal's servants Sir Gregory was well known'.[101]

In Ghent Botolf haunted Wyatt's lodgings, and the legate's. On 7 April he told Farnese that 'Clemente Wilpot [Philpot]' was sworn to the conspiracy and that they needed £50 urgently. But Farnese suspected

Botolf to be '*ò spia ò mariolo* [either spy or fool]', because he knew that he 'frequented the lodgings of the English ambassador familiarly'.[102] Somehow, very likely from Botolf, Wyatt learnt of Lord Lisle's secret communication with the Emperor. 'Post scriptum: My Lord Deputy wrote of late to the Emperor by the conveyance of the Captain of Gravelines.' 'I suppose not without knowledge of the King', so Wyatt wrote to Cromwell on 2 April, supposing nothing of the sort. By the 12th he had discovered something of the letter's contents and would 'enquire further for the truth. It is but well if it be none other than I can learn yet.' 'Well' for whom: for Cromwell, for Wyatt? Surely, not for Lisle.[103] While Pole's frantic intelligencer tried to penetrate the English embassy, Wyatt in turn sought intelligence from sources close to the papal ambassadors. On 9 March he had reported Farnese's communication with the King of the Romans and his audience with the French King, reports to be trusted: 'I have it out of a good place', for Cervini told it 'to a near friend of his', 'true it is in so good a place that I have it'.[104] Wyatt's success was now measured not by intimate exchanges with the Emperor but by secret intelligence and the discovery of traitors and treason. Botolf's conspiracy was aborted by Rome's disowning of him and perhaps by Philpot's terrified confession, but also by Wyatt's revelations.[105] Botolf's accomplices were rounded up, and Philpot would pay for his friendship and his treason with his life.[106] Fleeing to Louvain, Botolf, '*quel povero homo Inglese* [that poor Englishman]', was imprisoned. At the end of August Cervini sent an emissary to procure the release of 'Gregorio Anglo', with a message that the English ambassador still pursued him.[107]

Diplomacy was following its accustomed rhythms. As the French King's accord with the Emperor 'waxeth colder and colder every day' – prevented as usual by the 'non donation of Milan', '*neque in hoc seculo neque in futuro* [neither in this world nor the next]' – the legate's mission failed, and the Emperor delayed. Envoys plied back and forth.[108] So far: so predictable. But relations between Francis and Charles had not reached the nadir that would compel Charles to renewed amity with Henry or cordiality to his ambassador, not yet. On 21 March – Palm Sunday – Wyatt had again pleaded for recall: 'I begin to wax unnac-

ceptable here.'[109] But on 4 April came a sign of the Emperor's returning grace. The Prince of Salerno sent an emissary to Wyatt, telling him
that the Emperor gave the Prince leave to visit the King of England, as
he had long desired. 'I suppose he would tarry there to see hunting and
such pastime for one month,' wrote Wyatt. Ferrante Sanseverino, Prince
of Salerno, was 'greatly esteemed in all Italy', of legendary wealth and
culture, and the only reason for him to visit Henry's benighted island
would be for some clandestine purpose of the Emperor's.[110] Summoned
from the kingdom of Naples to add lustre to the Imperial entourage,
the Prince had been amusing himself in the company of Cardinal Farnese and the Duke of Orléans. On 13 February they had spent the day
hunting in Amiens, and the evening being entertained by King Francis
and telling tales from history and romance.[111] In the Prince's retinue
was a man who was exquisitely able to recite chivalric romance: his
secretary, Bernardo Tasso. Perhaps it was during this journey through
the Low Countries that Don Luis de Zúñiga y Ávila and Francisco de
Toledo persuaded Tasso to write the adventures of Amadís de Gaula.
According to his son Torquato, Tasso's other Spanish patron was Francisco de Toledo. But in the Emperor's entourage that spring were Don
Fernando Álvarez de Toledo, third Duke of Alva, and 'Don Henrico de
Toledo'. *L'Amadigi di Gaula* began at the behest of these courtiers, began
slowly, shaped into form as a mother bear licks her cub, so Bernardo
Tasso wrote, composed not as epic in blank verse as he wished, but in
ottava rima to please his prince.[112]

Wyatt longed to accompany the Prince of Salerno to England: 'would
God I were then ready . . . I would make him such company as should
not be unhonourable to the King'.[113] But grubbier duties awaited in
Ghent. There was the matter of John Legh. Wyatt had urged Legh to
join him in Spain to see the country, for Legh was good company, 'an
amorous cortegiano'. It was just a pity that he lacked judgement. By
March 1540 Legh was summoned home under a cloud, for his long
exile seemed 'contemptuous' and he was suspected of collusion with
Pole. 'I know no malice in the man but rather weakness of reason and
imprudency,' wrote Edmund Harvel, beseeching 'pardon and clemency'
for him.[114] In the 'way of old friendship and acquaintance' from their

time together in Wolsey's service, Cromwell might show some lingering favour, so Legh hoped. From Wyatt he had reason to hope for stronger support, for they were friends from youth and, distantly, cousins. In Ghent, Wyatt treated Legh 'like the King's true servant and my friend' and, so far as he could tell, Legh 'hath such confidence in his innocence' that he was prepared to come home, even though he knew he was under suspicion.[115] There was an urgent reason for Legh to return to England. In the spring of 1540 the conservatives had presented the King with a prospective fifth queen. Henry's young inamorata, Katherine Howard, was Legh's cousin.[116] Legh's clandestine connections with Cardinal Pole could not be allowed to compromise her (though she had clandestine connections enough of her own, as it turned out). Cousinhood became cozenage as Wyatt, who coveted Legh's lands, obeyed orders for his return to be '*compassed* in such wise as he shall not stick at it'.[117]

'All this year shall pass with practises and no declaring openly'. Wyatt, weary of diplomatic duplicities, was increasingly impatient and showing lack of judgement. As the balances shifted and Charles's pretended amity with Francis faltered, he turned toward Henry again – in the person of his ambassador, Wyatt. The papal ambassadors looked on suspiciously. They had never known the Imperial counsels so impenetrable, and they feared new practices with England. Early in April Granvelle and Wyatt were conferring frequently and familiarly for hours at a time.[118] In Ghent on 11 April Wyatt had audience with the Emperor – the first for months – and it 'passed sweetly with smilings and good countenances'. The Emperor 'laughed' – Charles *laughed*. In what passed for 'brotherly' royal affection, he nudgingly referred to the vigour of the King newly married to Anne of Cleves, seemingly unaware of the connubial catastrophe which had rocked the English court. Passing to the incendiary question of sovereignty in Gelderland, Charles insisted that the Duke of Cleves 'relinquish the possession which is yet no possession', and Wyatt drew back, claiming ignorance: a claim that the Emperor knew to be disingenuous, if tactful.

'Sir', quod I, 'I know not the law'. 'Yes, mary, do ye', quod he, and laughed. 'Nay, in good faith, Sir', quod I, 'I am no legist'. 'Well', quod he, 'I have learned so far . . .' 'Sir', quod I, '. . . I have no commission, nor will not detain your Majesty in pleading of that I cannot skill of'. Thus with good and gentle fashions we parted friends.

To amuse his harassed friend, Wyatt related to Cromwell the 'tale of the Welshman' who, in peril on the sea, vowed a great candle to Our Lady if ever he reached land, but disembarking, gave her only a tiny candle and a promise that she might hang him if 'ever she took him on the sea again'. So it was for the Emperor and the French King, for princely promises and courtly bargains in general.[119] But even as Wyatt wrote Cromwell, the master of courtly 'practises', who had feigned in order to set forth the Gospel, was 'tottering'. His favoured evangelical preachers were being imprisoned. Conservatives, returning from exclusion, now cherished '*une bonne pensee* [a happy thought]' of their revenge.[120] As Wyatt prepared to return, the patron in whom all his hopes were founded might no longer be able to advance him. On 9 April a passport was granted to Richard Pate to replace Wyatt as resident ambassador, while the King and Cromwell debated whether the Prince of Salerno should come to England privately, or with Wyatt as escort.[121] The Prince stayed with the Emperor, for the while, and so did Wyatt, with new companions: Pate and Nicholas Wotton, his neighbour from Kent. On 16 April he wrote his last letter from embassy, explaining the untoward, quite unexpected arrival in Ghent of the Duke of Cleves.[122] By the 20th he had taken leave of the Emperor for the last time. At this parting audience Charles declined to honour Henry by wearing the Order of the Garter on the coming St George's Day, but on Wyatt he bestowed '*carezze*', and showed 'the greatest cheer', 'extraordinary favours'. And it seems that he gave him a remarkable, secret commission.[123]

'The world is but slipper, and will sometime have his turns.' Cromwell's fortune now proved forcibly the truth of his warning. In early April he and Cranmer did not 'know where they are', but by the 18th Cromwell was at the zenith of his power. When he was created Earl of Essex and given the office of Great Chamberlain and thereby formal mastery of the royal household, the conservative nobility saw Nature turning in her course.[124] In early May, as Wyatt returned to

court, Cromwell, seemingly ascendant, was moving against the conservatives, not without Wyatt's help. Summoned from Calais, Lord
Lisle was sent to the Tower for his alleged complicity with Pole; the
hapless John Legh, his return carefully 'compassed' by Wyatt, joined
him on 6 May; and soon after Richard Sampson, Bishop of Chichester,
and Dr Nicholas Wilson followed. Cromwell moved urgently, lethally,
to strike before he was struck down. By 1 June the French ambassador
foresaw that 'things are brought to such a pass that either Cromwell's
party or that of the Bishop of Winchester must succumb'.[125] A poem
purportedly by Stephen Gardiner – though written by a reformer –
describes the Bishop's plot to discover Cromwell's secret counsels. He
'sought for Judas and found him', suborning a man whom Cromwell
trusted. 'As God would have it', Gardiner found 'my secret friend and
of old acquaintance', a man whom Cromwell loved.

> And Crumwell him thought my mortal enemy
> the more him loved, above all other
> and on my part, I showed not contrary
> yet were we friends as brother to brother.

Who was this false friend? The suspicion falls first on Thomas Wriothesley.[126] But there may have been other traitor friends.

For weeks, perplexing accounts of arrests and likely coups in England were circulating at foreign courts. To Brussels on 10 June came
a rumour that the King of England had been assassinated and the
Duke of Norfolk discovered at the head of a conspiracy.[127] It was far
otherwise, but a coup did occur on that day in which Norfolk was
instrumental. In the Council Chamber at Westminster Cromwell was
arrested, and from there led to the Tower, the victim of a noble and
conservative conspiracy. The charges against him were many, accusing
him of overweening power and abuse of office, of treason, and above
all of heresy. Allegedly, at St Peter le Poor in London in March 1539
he had defended the most fervent evangelical preachers, saying that if
the King should turn from the Gospel 'yet I would not turn; and if the
King did turn and all his people I would fight in the field in my own
person with my sword in my hand against him and all other'. Vowing

to 'die in that quarrel', he had promised that 'if I live one year or two it shall not lie in the King's power' to prevent the advance of reform.[128] In the Tower, denied access to the King, he wrote with 'quaking hand and most sorrowful heart' protesting that he never acted treasonably, 'never *thought* treason'. Yet as for protecting reformers, this he did confess: 'if I have heard of any combinations, conventicles or such as were offenders of your laws I have *though not as I should have done, for the most part*, revealed them'.[129] For the making of the Cleves marriage and finding no way out of it, he 'was very sorry . . . and so God knoweth I was', but his agency was not forgiven. 'I cry for mercy mercy mercy.'[130] Once the King was persuaded that Cromwell had impugned the Mass, there would be no way but one for him. For so long Cromwell had been Wyatt's patron, his protector and his friend, but friendship made them hostage to each other. They shared secrets which imperilled both of them. As the conservatives' trap closed around Cromwell and the evangelicals, and evidence was desperately sought of collusion, heresy and treason, what would be Wyatt's hap or unhap?

Foreign ambassadors at Henry's court and his ambassadors in the courts of other princes were informed post haste of Cromwell's many treasons.[131] The Most Christian King of France and the papal envoys exulted at his fall: it was 'the judgement of God', a divine miracle, because he had been the 'wicked and unhappy instrument' of England's schism.[132] That the minister's removal offered the way for the King to return to the true path, to reconciliation with Rome, some of his own ambassadors allowed, even hoped. In London the rumour spread that Wallop was fled to Rome, and his allegiance remained suspect.[133] If there were no suspicions yet of Richard Pate, there should have been. At the Imperial court, he was assuring Marcello Cervini that his king was Catholic in everything apart from his false belief that the papal primacy was not *de iure divino* (by divine law). If he was shown to be in error, he would be reconciled. Cervini enumerated the signs of Henry's will to return to the Roman obedience – the arrest of Cromwell, the Act of Six Articles – and saw only the *'peccadiglio'* of his supremacy in the English Church standing in the way. Now was the time to work toward his reconciliation.[134]

'The whole world of Christendom hangeth yet in balance,' so Cromwell had written on 11 May.[135] As the world turned, Cromwell's fall was part of a reversal in alliances, a necessary sacrifice. It seemed 'marvellously strange' that the Emperor would unite with the King of England, against the faith, yet if he did not make this 'unholy alliance' the French King would. An Imperial alliance with Henry would block any alliance between Henry and the League princes.[136] Sir Thomas More had understood long before that if his head could win the King a castle in France, he would lose it. Now Cromwell waited in the Tower as the price of Henry's alliance with the Emperor, the pledge that he was a true Christian prince. Charles 'these years and days past' praised the gifts of body and mind which made Henry the image of his Creator, so Pate gushed.[137] It was rumoured that the new royal friends would soon meet, 'whether by land or sea'. Insisting, as ever, that there could be no friendship with the English King until his return to the faith, Charles now held out hope, but everything must be kept secret.[138] On 3 July the Prince of Salerno sailed for England on a secret mission. Accompanied by Luis de Zúñiga y Ávila, the Emperor's most trusted confidant, and by forty men liveried in grandest black, Salerno came 'from the Emperor, as some said; other some said he came for his own pleasure for to see the King of England'.[139] The given story – the Prince was visiting for pleasure and pastime, to hunt and 'see the island' – was hardly believed in Charles's court or in Henry's. They went for a deeper purpose than '*solazzo* [pastime]', so everyone surmised, but could not tell what, save that matters were 'heating up'.[140] Don Francesco d'Este, brother of the Duke of Ferrara, with leave from the Emperor and papal nuncio to 'see that island', sailed from Calais on 18 July.[141]

And the true purpose of the mission? The Prince and Zúñiga went to inspect 'the daughter of that King' as a prospective empress for her cousin the Emperor. Thus the Florentine, Giovanni Bandino, reported. Lest Duke Cosimo dismiss this as '*capriccio mio* [my little joke]', Bandino recalled Charles two months earlier making 'the greatest cheer' and cherishing the English ambassador, Wyatt. Lest we dismiss it, we might remember Cardinal Farnese's story at the New Year, of Wyatt as broker of this glittering dynastic marriage. Rumours of this starry proposal were also spreading at the English court.[142] There was murmuring at the Imperial court that Henry and Charles would meet, either by land or sea, with no ambassadors in attendance.[143] Feasting at Greenwich, Windsor and Hampton Court, 'the most beautiful places this King has', entertained grandly by the nobility of the kingdom, the 'strangers' had 'great cheer' and generous entertainment, yet they were 'taken as half spies' and never allowed to see the Lady Mary.[144] And they were appalled by what they found. The Prince of Salerno returned to the Imperial court on 23 July, urgently seeking absolution for the sin of communing with heretics. His relation of his time in England was also his confession. When the King called the Pope the 'Bishop of Rome', they had called him 'Papa' with deliberate intent, but Henry grew angry, as did his nobles, who were invested in the royal supremacy by their sacrilege and seizure of the spoils of the monasteries, and so opposed to the Holy See that unless God intervened it would be impossible to return the realm to obedience. The Howards were ascendant and the Earl of Surrey seemed, even to such grand grandees, 'very proud'. Henry himself was 'like a pig, and showed little emotion'. Although the Mass was still celebrated, priests were now ordained by the King and marrying. Salerno spoke darkly of the Cleves divorce and of the King's impending marriage to Katherine Howard. 'Everything is descending into chaos and it seems like Hell.' As for Cromwell, although he was not yet dead, sentence was passed: 'they would tear out his heart and stuff it in his mouth'.[145]

Whether Wyatt was among the *grandi* who entertained the Prince of Salerno in England is unknown, but in Ghent he had prepared the way for this visit and in Spain he knew Ávila. Few at the English court were *italianizzati* and none, save the Earl of Surrey, as graceful as Wyatt or as able to provide 'pastime with good company'. Certainly Wyatt was among the sacrilegious favourites to whom the King doled out monastic prizes. Leaving for France, he had received 'a good pece of landes above my deservinge'. At his return he was royally, munificently rewarded. An exchange of lands with the King was confirmed by a private Act. By another he was assured of lands he had purchased in Hoo in Kent and Greys Thurrock in Essex, whose possession had been long and fiercely contested.[146] Writing to an unnamed 'lord-ship', Wyatt complained of burdens of wealth and business that many envied, 'I have so much a do to prepare my bills into the Parliament'.[147] Rewards for his services as ambassador may also have acknowledged some darker service. By an exchange of lands with the King dated 14 June 1540 – four days after Cromwell's arrest – Wyatt gained monastic lands to dream of from the abbeys of Boxley, Malling and Reading, from the priories of St Mary Graces in London and St Mary Overy in Southwark, and from St Saviour in Bermondsey. The site of the priory of the Crossed Friars was the ultimate prize for a courtier. Overlooking Tower Hill and its dreadful scaffold, the grand London mansion which Wyatt would begin to build offered an unforgettable prospect of the consequences of power, the reversals of fortune.[148]

The Parliament which enriched Wyatt condemned Cromwell. That Cromwell must suffer under the same laws that he had made was an irony not lost on Wyatt and his friends. Later, John Mason would tes-tify that he and Wyatt discussed 'the lawe of wordes', and that Wyatt thought the law 'verie harde, and that the fyrst devysers were well served in fawlinge into yt'. 'He thynkethe I ment by the lorde Rocheforde or the lorde of Estsex': 'And yet', wrote Wyatt, 'I never remembre I said so unto hym.'[149] Henry now determined to 'abolish all memory' of Cromwell.[150] Only the method of execution was unsure; people specu-lated grimly whether he would burn alive as a heretic or suffer the terrible death of a traitor.[151] His fall left his friends bereft, vulnerable. Wagers were laid in London that Cranmer, his partner in the evangeli-cal cause since the beginning, would be 'laid up with Cromwell . . . in the Tower'. Cranmer wrote with great bravery to the King: 'I loved him as my friend . . . I am very glad that his treason is discovered in time; but again I am very sorrowful', for whom could the King trust now? Cranmer's 'friends' whom he had 'most trusted to', 'his familiars' Bishops Skip and Heath 'left him in the plain field' to defend the Gos-pel alone.[152] Cromwell's friends, distancing themselves, failed the test of true friendship: constancy in adversity. On 18 April 1540, at the 'slipper toppe' of his fortune, Cromwell had secured the appointment of Ralph Sadler and Thomas Wriothesley as joint principal secretaries

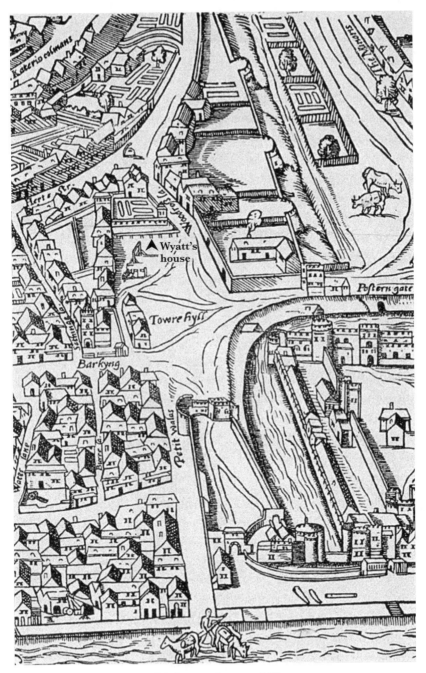

'My hows at the towre hill'

to the King, and on that day they were knighted. Two months later, 'ever trusty and faithful' to his old master, Ralph Sadler dared to take a letter to the King. Otherwise Cromwell, who had so valued the claims and consolations of friendship, faced his death friendless. He had 'not one friend in the whole island'.[153] Powerless to help Cromwell, Wyatt had the power to harm him, may already have harmed him. He knew perfectly how necessary was the sacrifice of 'Cramuello' to ease the alliance with the Emperor for which he himself had worked. Now he awaited the death of his patron, knowing that the secrets between them also endangered him, and that 'they', his old enemies, did not sleep. How could friendship be sustained in times of such danger? The last duty of friendship might be to console a friend at the scaffold. Wyatt, who had vowed to Cromwell 'I always your bond beadsman', was bound to pray for him, at least at the hour of his death.

The scaffold was more than usually close to home to Thomas Wyatt in the summer of 1540, as he looked towards the Tower from his new property in the Crossed Friars. On 28 July Cromwell was led to the scaffold on Tower Hill.[154] Addressing the crowd – 'Masters, I am come hither to die . . . justly condemned by the law to die' – he admitted his offence to 'my Prince', and confessed his sin, 'I have lived a sinner'. He besought the people to pray with him for his forgiveness: 'O Father forgive me, O Christ forgive me, O Holy Ghost forgive me, O three persons in one Godhead forgive me.' Confuting all who slandered him by saying that he maintained those who held 'evil opinions' and held them himself, he asked the crowd to bear witness: 'I die in the Catholic faith not doubting of any article of my faith, no nor doubting of any sacraments of the Church.' But facing the Last Judgement, he confessed that he had been led astray: 'yet all were not slanders, for as God hath instruct so hath the Devil seduced'. 'Whilst that the flesh departeth', he urged them to pray 'that I waver not'. Kneeling, he said his last prayer – 'when this mouth shall lose his use that my heart may see thee. *O Pater in manus tuas commendo spiritum* [Father, into your hands I commend my spirit].' This prayer finished, he asked for prayers for King and Council, for the clergy and commonalty. 'And he turned him about and said: "Farewell Wyatt, and gentle Wyatt pray for me."' Pray for him at his departing, but perhaps not beyond, where no human prayer availed.

Another contemporary witness tells of Wyatt at Cromwell's execution. The Spanish chronicler – usually unwaveringly unreliable – may veer toward truth as he relates Cromwell's farewell to his grief-stricken friend. 'Oh, gentle Wyatt, good-bye, and pray to God for me.' 'Wyatt could not answer him for tears', and as he wept, according to the chronicler, Cromwell feared that Wyatt would be compromised by such open grief. Once before, he had been arrested to disclose treason, and he might be again. 'Oh, Wyatt, do not weep, for if I were no more guilty than thou wert when they took thee, I should not be in this pass'.[155] If these words were accurate, there may have been a doubleness in them. If Cromwell bade farewell to Wyatt, knowing that Wyatt's testimony from foreign courts had helped to condemn him, they may be among the most bitter words ever spoken at the scaffold, and Wyatt's the tears most bitterly shed.

Wyatt's tears: tears of grief, tears of remorse. There had been executions enough that year. In Ghent, he had witnessed the terror which brought rebels to obedience. In London, friends of Queen Katherine of Aragon suffered at last for treason, and evangelical preachers were burnt for heresies concerning the blessed sacrament. He watched the ghastly death of his friend and patron, Cromwell. Perhaps in the life left to him after these horrors, Wyatt would turn to paraphrase the Penitential Psalms, and seek the truth of the inward heart. But he knew searingly that the Christian, the evangelical imperative to truthfulness proved lethal when it met the demands of his king. Courtierly indirection and duplicity were the way to advance, and safety and self-knowledge were not to be sought at court, amidst its 'wanton toys'.[156] Translating the second chorus of Seneca's *Thyestes*, Wyatt suppresses the calm leisure and soft quiet of the Roman countryside for a rural reclusion less idle, and finds alliterative, cropped Anglo-Saxon folk words to describe a manner of death not found in Seneca. 'Use me quyet', asks his speaker who, seeking to 'dye aged after the common trace', imagines a life yoked in harness to rural toil, lived hidden. Only with retreat comes the ability to know oneself. With a dying fall, in words of his addition – 'dazed with dreadfull face' – Wyatt presents death's terrible, sudden assault on the great man at court who, living and dying in the public gaze, lacks – 'alas' – the virtue of self-knowledge.[157]

> Stond who so list upon the Slipper toppe   *desires*
> of courtes estates, and lett me heare rejoyce
> and use me quyet without lett or stoppe   *impediment*
> unknowen in courte, that hath suche brackishe joyes
> in hidden place, so lett my dayes forthe passe
> that when my yeares be done withouten noyse
> I may dye aged after the common trace
> For hym death greep'the right hard by the croppe
> that is moche knowen of other, and of him self alas
> Doth dye unknowen, dazed with dreadfull face
> ffinis

Standing, if he chose, 'upon the Slipper toppe/of courtes estates', basking in the royal favour for the while, Wyatt understood the moral hazard. 'The slipper wheel of high estate's' swift turning in the summer of 1540 left him rewarded, but at a high moral price and with all his certainties shaken. The bewilderment of great men at their fall was due partly to astonishment that they could have been so misled in those they trusted. The friends who traduced them were also numbed. Wyatt might now abandon the 'brackishe joyes' of the court, but the clog would hang at his heel in the country.[158]

17

Myne Unquyet Mynde

Contemplating destiny and loss and 'dreadfull death' Wyatt looked to a sonnet of Petrarch's, '*Rotta è l'alta colonna e 'l verde lauro*'.[1] Here Petrarch mourned the destruction of the high column and the green laurel, the death of his '*doppio tesoro* [double treasure]', his patron Colonna and his beloved Laura. As Wyatt imitated, the irreversible loss shrank to a single loss, and the speaker's lament turned from sorrowful fatalism inward to bitter remorse and endless self-blame.

> The piller pearisht is whearto I Lent
> the strongest staye of myne unquyet mynde
> The lyke of it no man agayne can fynde
> From East to west still seking thoughe he went
> To myne unhappe for happe away hath rent *misfortune fortune*
> Of all my joye the vearye bark and rynde
> And I (alas) by chaunce am thus assynde
> Dearlye to moorne till death do it relent
> but syns that thus it is by destenye
> What can I more but have a wofull hart
> My penne in playnt, my voyce in wofull crye
> My mynde in woe, my bodye full of smart
> And I my self, my self alwayes to hate
> Till dreadfull death, do cause my dolefull state *cease*

Though the sonnet assigns no time or place or person – except 'I my self' – it has been read as 'the elegy for Cromwell'.[2] True, as the waters closed over his fallen patron there may have been reason enough for Wyatt to feel mortification and remorse. But here we discover a more essential alienation and a self to whom unhap has happed.[3] In this un-hap – '*myne* unhappe' – his persona has '(alas) by chaunce' been 'thus assynde', but is not wholly passive; otherwise, why 'I my self, my self always to hate'? He is capable of, guilty of actions of unintended consequence. Here 'dreadfull death' – the death which inspires awe – is not another's, but his own, and he longs for it.

Henry Howard, the poet Earl of Surrey, chose to be portrayed leaning upon a broken pillar, the emblem of his disappointed hope.[4] But to hope at all was to be disappointed. This Wyatt had profoundly known, and he had taught and sought the rational freedom which indifference gave. This was why he counselled his son to have Epictetus 'evir in your bosome', and why he translated Plutarch's *Quyete of mynde*, which taught that what lay beyond an individual's control was neither to be feared nor desired, that it was worse than pointless to live in hope and dread of the future and allow 'thoughtes [to] gape gredily after thynges to come'. In a verse epistle which was tribute to John Poyntz and all that he had learnt from him, he insisted that it was 'madde' and self-destructive to 'let present passe and gape on tyme to com'.[5] Yet in Wyatt restlessness – the defining quality of 'Wyatt . . . that quick could never rest'[6] – was always in contention with quietness of mind. 'I restless rest': this image, using the figure of *traductio*, recurred in Wyatt's writing and in Surrey's, representing their particular fear of being cast into inactivity. If we imagine Wyatt easily embowered in shady bliss at Alington through the long summer of 1540 we misunderstand him and his times. Restlessness, somnolence, idleness were children of *acedia*, one of the seven deadly sins, which spans states from listlessness and boredom to dejection and melancholy, and ultimately to despair. Idleness was no innocent pleasure, but a diversion from the active path to virtue, leading down the rosy path to sin. The problem of *otium* (leisure, idleness or repose) received exhaustive – exhausting – consideration in Petrarch's *De remediis utriusque fortunae* (*Of the Remedy of Both Kinds of Fortune*), the work too tedious for Wyatt to translate, even at Queen Katherine's behest. It began with Reason's call to 'wake up you sleepyheads, it is time'. In *The Quyete of mynde* Wyatt had addressed the crucial question: 'What if that same, nothyng to do, hath troubled many from the ryght order of the mynde?'[7] Writing to his son, Wyatt had warned against complacency: it was not enough to avoid evil: 'can not a gentle corage be content to be Idle and to rest without doing enything'.[8] Virtue must be active. Life in the country offered rustic freedoms and 'untroubled peace'

to farmers living in harmony with the 'just earth', 'happy beyond measure, could they but know their blessings!' Yet a Virgilian idyll of honest
toil was denied to the English gentleman who could not, in honour, work
with his hands, 'after the common trace'. He might never come closer
to agriculture than knocking his tenants' heads together or counting his
country chattels down to the last spade and rabbit.

Reeling from some unspeakable 'unhappe', Wyatt's poet persona had
no recourse – 'What can I more?' – except to lament, and become a
man who weeps and writes: 'My penne in playnt, my voyce in wofull
crye'. Idleness and self-absorption were also, of course, cause and consequence of falling in love, and love was the mortal condition celebrated
by poet–lovers.[9] Love-in-idleness would divert any lover – save Aeneas
– from following duty and destiny. In Wyatt's poetry smitten lovers, often
versions of Petrarchan lovers, faintingly follow the object of desire away
from the path of who knows what duty. If not 'in hold' to Love 'that
spurreth with fyer and bridilleth with Ise', they might have been martial
and active, but now they are driven back by 'armed sighes', in a paralysed state of 'forced sighes and trusty ferefulnes', left 'wailing or sighing continuelly'.[10] The Muses might lure Wyatt to the delusive delights
of reading and rhyming, but he knew that sterner critics would judge
how he did 'dispende [spend, squander]' his time. Perhaps it was during
some real retreat late in his life that Wyatt – in his imagination at least –
invited John Poyntz to join him in Kent which was not in Christendom.

In the shires, gentlemen born to serve the public good performed
the melancholy duties imposed on them by royal command. In 'Myne
owne Jhon poyntz' Wyatt venerated the self-immolating example of
the younger Cato who 'did his hart the comon welthe applye', but his
speaker admitted a more self-serving desire for honour, 'I graunt somtyme that of glorye the fyer/dothe touche my harte'. Living unphilo-
sophically in hope, Wyatt awaited some grand opportunity to serve,
some great office which might come his way. Even while at Alington
he was only a short ride and boat trip from Westminster, within easy
distance by river from the royal palaces and the world of power to
which he was drawn like a moth to a flame. But royal favour swung like
a weathervane and glory might never come, even to 'such an unscru-

pulous agent of the King'.[11] Wyatt's hopes of the deputyship of Calais, for which he had schemed, were disappointed. Appointment to Kent's commission of sewers counted as duty rather than glory.[12] Meanwhile there were newly acquired lands to administer, and a new mansion to build: 'I have so muche a do', so he wrote at the beginning of that long summer.[13] Yet early in 1541 he would write, with deepest irony, to the King's Council: 'myghte I well spare some of my *leasure* to move your lordshippes hartes to be favorable unto me'.[14] By then he had more leisure than he can ever have wanted, such hap he was happed in.

In November 1540 the call came for a special ambassador to go to the Emperor. But it came not to Wyatt, but to Stephen Gardiner. Travelling in magnificent legation, he was accompanied by Henry Knyvet and a hundred horsemen, all dressed in grey velvet, wearing gold chains. This conservative bishop had all the necessary credentials to explain the nature of religion in England; to insist that 'things are as before in religion', that Henry had innovated nothing 'upon the doctrines of the primitive church'. 'Some said' Gardiner went to attend the religious debates at the Diet of Worms, 'some said' he went to treat for the marriage between the Lady Mary and the Emperor. Like any of Henry's ambassadors, his mission was to keep the 'two chiefs of Christendom in discord'. As Gardiner's great suite embarked for Calais, the Duke of Suffolk was also on his way there.[15] Wyatt may have been in Calais too – so we hear from an inimical source. Poggio, the papal nuncio, reported from Valenciennes that Gardiner had landed at Calais 'at the same time as that heretic, formerly ambassador in Spain'.[16] Why and whether Wyatt was there, whether leaving or arriving, remains mysterious. Ominously for Richard Pate, resident ambassador with the Emperor, on 9 November Wyatt's servant had delivered him a packet for forwarding to the Lord Privy Seal. In 'dark writing', Pate's letter of the 12th fulsomely, anxiously expressed his devotion to the King. The discovery of correspondence between Pate and his chaplain and the 'wicked traitor', John Heliar, might have condemned them, Pate knew, were it not for the King's 'gracious interpretation' of it. Perhaps, Pate hoped, Henry trusted in his 'faith and perseverance in the truth', or in his 'sincere judgement in learning not lightly corrupted by the persuasion of such false prophets that cometh unseen'. Perhaps his truth would deliver him. Perhaps, but Pate knew his king too well to believe it.[17]

While Henry's suspicions of Pate grew, Wyatt may have been at work in the shadows. A letter 'to Mr Wyatt which is thought to be of some weight' came to Gardiner.[18] From Calais on 28 November Pate's 'loving friends' Gardiner and Knyvett wrote to him with a secret warning. They carried – so misleadingly termed – royal 'letters of comfort', demanding his return to England immediately on their arrival.[19] Forewarned, forearmed, Pate did not yield to the summons. Although, like Pole, he came to accept a doctrine of salvation very close to Luther's, like Pole, Pate was committed to the papal primacy as the way to keep Christendom united. The royal supremacy was unbearable to him.[20] On 27 December the Emperor wrote that Pate had taken his leave. But Pate departed not for England, but for Rome. Leaving secretly and by night, he rode from Namur via Cologne and Spires, and would soon, Poggio hoped, arrive safely to kiss the feet of his Holiness.[21] In horror and mortification, Henry's councillors tried to keep this defection secret.[22]

Pate was now 'out of his King's power': not so his servants or other ambassadors. A search began for the complicity of fellow travellers. Even Pate's uncle, the Bishop of Lincoln, was arrested, and the writings of Pate's relations and friends were searched for 'practices of Cardinal Pole in England'.[23] In the tsunami which swelled from this dangerous defection Wyatt was swept away. 'They' – his 'good frendes' who were his 'back friends' – had been waiting their chance. That it was the Duke of Suffolk's players who entertained the King and his court at Twelfth Night brought no joy to Wyatt.[24] When the Privy Council met at Hampton Court on 16 and 17 January its business went unrecorded, the sign of secret emergency deliberation and continuing crisis.[25] Among the councillors present on those days were men whom Wyatt had counted as patrons or friends – Russell, Cheyne, Wriothesley – but they were powerless to save him, even if they wished. 'Voyzelay' had very recently been in great danger of descending as fast as he had risen, but after interrogation, he was rewarded and returned to the Council board, his presence ominous for Wyatt.[26] On the Council were Wyatt's known enemies: the Duke of Suffolk and his allies – Sir Anthony Browne and Sir William Fitzwilliam (now Earl of Southampton), who were half-brothers; Sir John Gage, Comptroller of the Household, and Sir Anthony Wingfield, Vice-chamberlain.[27] Here were the malevolent 'they', sequestered together with the power to do Wyatt hurt. On the night before the cataclysm which he was expecting, Wyatt challenged Suffolk. Blaming him for his arrest in 1536, blaming him still five years later, he told him: 'for his favor to remytte his olde undeservyd evyll will and to remembre lyke as he was a mortall mane so to bere no immortal hate in his brest'.[28]

'Mr Huet' was arrested in his house and taken to the Tower on 17 January 1541. 'And what is worse', his house was searched and the King's seal placed on his chest and cupboards.[29] 'A new and strange' event had occurred at court, 'unexpected and of great consequence'. The story of the French ambassador Marillac was that on the night of the 17th Wyatt and a gentleman of the north (Sir Ralph Sadler) were arrested at Hampton Court, and the following morning they were escorted as prisoners, with hands bound, by twenty-four archers. Walk-ing – not riding – they were led through the City to the Tower. A greater humiliation could hardly have been inflicted. Marillac was puzzled. Neither earl nor lord, Wyatt was nevertheless among the richest gentle-men in England, with a patrimony of six or seven thousand ducats a year. No lord in the whole kingdom enjoyed the King's grace more than he did; there was no one to whom the King showed greater favour and love. Not a month before, Wyatt had received a royal gift. Marillac had been unable to discover the cause of their arrests, nor would it be easy to find the truth, for they were likely to be condemned without being heard, by attainder. Once a man was imprisoned in the Tower, no one would dare intervene or speak in his favour, for fear of falling under suspicion of the same crime as the accused. These arrests might be the 'relics of Cromwell', Marillac judged. Wriothesley had already been interrogated.[30] Others were in danger. John Mason was travelling on a mission to Spain, with open instructions and 'Remembrances secret', but this honour was short-lived. Messengers were urgently despatched to ride after him – haste, post haste – and bring him back to testify. Riding home, did Mason know what melancholy duty awaited him?[31]

Wyatt's plight was desperate. His being led to the Tower bound and fettered was universally taken as a dire sign, for political prisoners were usually trusted not to escape. This was 'the third time' that Wyatt was in the Tower and 'it will certainly be his last'. In fact, it was the second, but Marillac's expectation of a fatal outcome to this 'great matter' was widely shared. Many wished Wyatt ill, including all those who had been in league against Cromwell whose 'mignon' he was. Marillac was, in general, correct though in detail misinformed. He believed that Wyatt's principal enemy was his father-in-law, the Earl of 'Rotellan' of the house of Clarence, who was determined to avenge the wrong Wyatt had done long before when he discovered his wife in adultery and defamed her. The name was wrong, but it was true that the Cobham family wanted redress. Although Wyatt was better loved among great men, and his arrest more lamented and regretted by both the English and foreigners than that of any other of the last few years, no one dared say a word for him, so Marillac reported. 'By these fine laws he must be judged without knowing why.' Marillac had never seen people look more troubled.[32] By 6 February the Imperial ambassador, Chapuys, heard that no substantial charge had been made against Wyatt. 'With the exception of words, which elsewhere than here would not have been noticed, nothing has been proved against him.'[33] Words. Under the 'law of words', words alone would condemn the speaker, even guarded words, words between friends. It was 'familiar secret talk, nothing affirming' which had destroyed Sir Thomas More, under the law.[34]

As Wyatt restlessly rested in the Tower, he was left to imagine in anguish the fate of his family at Alington. Perhaps he learnt how soon the family was dispersed and his household dismantled. On 19 January the Privy Council gave orders for John Mason's wife and servants to be sent up to London, and for Mason's coffers to be brought from Alington to be searched.[35] Richard Southwell, scholar and hatchet man, was the agent assigned to ransack Wyatt's household, as once before he was sent to Thomas More in the Tower 'to fetch away his books from him'.[36] Wyatt's letters from embassy had been his private property, but now they were scrutinized.[37] On the 20th Southwell was sent to Alington. Any plate or 'household stuff' which 'by his discretion' he thought most attractive, he was to send for the King's use. As always, Henry was first to benefit from a favourite's fall. Guns from the armoury, fine riding horses and military chargers from Wyatt's stables were to be reserved for the royal pleasure. Although the only goods of Wyatt's recorded in the royal inventory were a silver 'signet of Sir Thomas Wyatt's arms with a steel of bone' and 'xiiij little varvells of silver upon a roll which were Mr Wiattes' these take us pathetically close to him, for with the signet he stamped his letters, and the varvels were the metal rings attached to the jess of a falcon.[38] Did he remember then the fidelity of his falcons: 'Lux, my faire fawlcon, and thy felowes all'?[39]

Summoning all Wyatt's servants, some of whom had been at Alington since Henry Wyatt's time, Southwell was to dismiss them with half a year's wages, and 'a good lecture to use themselves honestly' and be duly grateful for the King's 'most gracious reward'. The ladies of the household Southwell must send elsewhere – wherever that might be. 'Young Wyatt's wife' and Lady Poynings, whose husband was serving in Calais, were 'discharged'. As for Bess Darrell, she was expecting a child. All Southwell's subtlety would be needed to interpret the instructions of a Council acting for a king who, seemingly, feared having the death of Wyatt's unborn child on his conscience, and who was uncertain how to treat the pregnant mistress of a man whose life might soon be forfeit:

also to enquire of Mistress Darrell whether she intended to go to any such place, whereas she should be ordered, as that, wherewhithall she appeared to be, might be preserved, and in case she would not declare unto him the same, whereby he might conjecture that might perish therein which she had conceived, then to stay her there until the King's Highness' further pleasure were known.

Bess Darrell, who had suffered so much at the hands of the King and waited so long for a child, would not so easily be cast out of Alington – not least because she had nowhere else to go, unless perhaps by the King's doubtful 'further pleasure'.[40] By 12 February Marillac had learnt that all Wyatt's goods were given to others, 'a sign that his life is in great danger'.[41]

It was the depth of winter, cold, damp, endlessly dark, and Wyatt was in the Tower. How far the consolations of philosophy or of Scripture sustained him, we can only imagine, but he was restless. 'God knowethe what restles tormente yt hathe byne to me sens my hether commynge to examen my selffe, perusinge all my dedes to my remembraunce.'[42] As evidence was collected to condemn him, he racked his brains for ways to confute it. Ominously, on 21 January his old adversaries Bonner and Heynes were ordered to bring in immediately 'the depositions concerning Mason, &c' – the charges dropped in 1538 and now revived. By the 22nd Mason was arrested on his journey to Spain and brought home under armed guard. In the Tower, kept apart from Wyatt, he was sent 'bedding and things for [his] necessary relief' by the Council, solicitous because on Mason's testimony rested the best hope of convicting Wyatt. Constantly occupied in examining Wyatt's 'accomplices', the councillors acquitted them one by one, until only Mason was detained.[43] In Nuremberg Granvelle and Poggio had a sinister conversation about events in England. Gardiner, they said, longed for reconciliation with Rome, but he knew that it was death to urge it to his king. Still, it would be opportune to persuade him to write, believed Granvelle, even if the King did cut off Gardiner's head if his counsel failed. This was a king who had his best-loved servants murdered on the least pretext. Take the case of '*quel ribaldo ambassatore*' – that rogue, that scoundrel – who had been in Spain: Gardiner said that they would cut off his head. Best keep this secret, said Granvelle. By the end of February the news at the Imperial court was that Wyatt was beheaded.[44]

The King's mood was grim. A tertian fever had lowered him, and the suppurating lesion on his leg was causing grave (literally) concern. A *mal d'esprit* overwhelmed him. His 'unhappy people' resisted his will, he said, but he would make them so poor that they would be too undermined to oppose him. This was the story of Marillac's mole at court. Henry believed that most of his councillors were false: pretending to be loyal and faithful servants, they temporized and dissembled, acting only in self-interest. Shrovetide turned to Lent without the accustomed pastime at court or the music which usually delighted the King. Now Henry brooded on Cromwell's death. On light pretexts and by false accusations '*they made* him' – so he claimed – 'put to death the most faithful servant he ever had'.[45] Henry revolved in his mind the treachery of his ambassadors whom he had trusted to 'set forth his princely nature' at the courts of foreign princes. Richard Pate had betrayed him. Sir John Wallop was now recalled from France with a 'letter of comfort', secretly 'sent for' to answer to his fidelity.[46] By 10 March 'poor Master Wallop' was in the Tower, and with him Thomas Palmer, Wyatt's old friend from Calais.[47] Immured in the Tower at the same time as Wyatt were a company of his old friends – Lord Leonard Grey, with whom he had jousted at the Castle of Loyalty in happier times, John Legh, John Mason. If not a traitor to his king, Wyatt had been to some of them a traitor friend.

Five long years before, Anne Boleyn had punned as Wyatt arrived in the Tower: they 'might make balets well now'.[48] In the desperate mid-winter of 1541 Wyatt was not writing balets, but writing for his life. First, he wrote what a sixteenth-century editor called 'A Declaration . . . of his innocence'.[49] The King's 'pleasure' and the Council's 'commaundment' – so the Lieutenant of the Tower instructed him – was that he declare in writing 'suche thynges as have passed me' at the Emperor's court 'whearby I knowe my selffe to have offended or whear by I myght rune in suspecte of offence'. Sure that 'a malicious enimye myghte tayke advantage by evell interpretation' of anything he wrote, he sought to compose an account to exonerate himself, knowing that it might more easily condemn him. Writing his 'Declaration' before the endless examinations began, perhaps after only a single examination, still ignorant of the precise charges against him, he understood the travesty of their general tenor, and protested his innocence and his outrage that his truth, his *troth* was doubted: 'As I complayned before your lordshipes yt had greved me the suspectes I have byn in beinge in Spayne that yt was noysed that I was ronne a way to the bysshope of Rome.'[50] He wrote the story of fevered days in Nice and Villefranche in the summer of 1538 that we have already heard in his words, taken in pieces and patches from this later testimony. It was always the fate of his writing to be appropriated by others, and left unedited by him.

'This withowte correctinge, sendinge, or overseinge' he sent for the Council to frame and file as they would, beseeching them:

Fyrste, lyke as I tayke God to recorde, in whome I truste to be saved and whose redemtion I forsake yf wyttinglie I lye: so do I humbly in his name besyche you all that in those thinges that beinge [not] fresshe in my memorie no captious advantage to be taken of me . . . I declare affirminglie at all proffes whearby a Christian man may be tried that in my lyf in Cryme towarde the maieste of the kinge my master . . . in dede worde wrytinge or wysshe I never offended . . .[51]

He presented an unembellished list of contacts with a motley crew who, unknown to him at the time, turned out to be traitors: Michael Throck-morton and Robert Branceter; 'a lyght fellowe, a gunner' who came of Ireland with an Irish traitor called James; 'a fole, an Iryshe mane that was lame' who took the name of Rosarossa because he wore a red rose. He had received letters from Cromwell, from Pate, from John Legh, and intercepted letters from Gregory Botolf. If anyone believed that he had communed with rebels or traitors, 'lett yt be provede and impute yt to me for Treasone': a challenge he offered not because 'I have done yt so secreatlie that yt cane not be provede, but as god judge me I am clere of thought'. He pleaded for latitude for a resident ambassador sent to discover secrets by whatever means: 'the credet that an Imbas-sadoure hathe or owte to have myghte well dyscharge as great stretches as these'.[52] And he ended by pleading 'lett not my lyf were awaye here', and beseeching 'Our Lorde put in your hartes to do with me as I have deservyd towarde the kinges Maiestie'. He signed himself the King's 'humble Orator, T. Wiatt', but he had not revealed in this 'Declaration' the gifts of oratory that made him famous. Soon he would.

Wyatt believed that he was facing trial for high treason. Since Parlia-ment was not in session the way to condemn him would not be by Act of Attainder but by the common law, trial by jury. In the 'Declaration' he promised that when 'yt shall please your Lordshippes to examen me' they would learn his innocence. Soon examination after examination fol-lowed. Thirty-eight interrogatories – written questions, now lost – were put to him. He knew that his friends were interrogated; 'familier frendes examined in holde and aperte'. 'What worde gave I unto the, Mason? What message? I defye all familiarite and fryndshipe betwexte us – say thie worste.'[53] In the Tower, John Mason was subjected to intense interrogation. George Blage was summoned, and others also. 'Masone, Blage, Mr Hobbye, Mr Dudeleye and other that were with me can testyfie,' so Wyatt offered, and perhaps they did, though not necessarily in his favour.[54] Forced to reveal the secrets they had shared, they might turn traitor friends in adversity. No one knew the risk better than Wyatt, who had witnessed against Anne Boleyn and his friends. When they protectively encircled the name of '*Viat*' with his virtues – Innocence, Truth, Faith – Blage and Mantell knew of what they wrote, and may even have written ironically.[55] Wyatt now surrounded himself with words in defence against his encircling enemies, and to move the jury in his favour.

De profundis he composed an oration 'to the judges after the indictement and the evidence': his *Defence*. Indictment required a bill of accusation put before the jury on the crown's behalf, and its technicalities were formidable. Here Wyatt was assuming that a jury had been empanelled and had found a *vera billa* ('true bill') against him. At the trial the crown's case had to be proved. If the jury found a verdict of guilty, the man convicted would be given a chance to speak – or so it seems, for much remains obscure.[56] Imprisoned in the Tower with Wyatt, another prisoner was preparing a speech to defend himself against a charge of treason by words. At his trial at the Kent Assizes Dr Richard Benger spoke eloquently, denying that his words could be construed as incitement to rebellion, and charging Archbishop Cranmer with malicious accusation. Successfully convincing the jury that it would be 'against conscience' to condemn him, Benger was set free.[57] If Wyatt was writing alongside Benger in the Tower, perhaps he was also writing alongside Lord Leonard Grey. In June 1541 Grey, arraigned in King's Bench, convicted and judged, would defend himself, using as his 'buckler' the fact that he had acted with the Council's consent. He was at the bar from nine in the morning until four in the afternoon.[58] But no speech would save Grey. And no pleading could save the Earl of Surrey. In January 1547 he would plead not guilty, and 'had such pleading for himself' that

Wyatt's *Defence*, copied by a scribe. Here Wyatt answers 'this malyce of my accusars', and considers the new Treason Act: 'What say I then to the lawe of wordes?'

it took all day 'or he had judgement'. Challenging his accusers, Surrey 'defended himself many ways', sometimes denying their truth, 'sometimes interpreting the words he said, in a far other sense than in that in which they were represented'.[59] Wyatt's *Defence* did the same.

As he began his *Defence* Wyatt impugned the justice of the Council who charged him with treason. In his youth, he had studied the common law at the Middle Temple, and might have studied more assiduously had he known how desperately he would now need this knowledge, especially since he was denied the advice of counsel. He knew that the trial of the facts lay with the jury who, once elected, tried and sworn, were to be regarded as judges, and that the ultimate responsibility for a conviction depended on their consciences. Yet he also knew that the judges could exert influence on a jury, and now called on their Christian duty to 'interprete lawe syncerely':

I beseke you onlye att the reverence of god whose place in Judgemente you occupie under the kinges maiestie . . . that you be not bothe my Judges and my accusars, that is to say that you aggravate not my cawse unto the queste . . . For altho yt be these men that muste pronounce uppone me yet I knowe right well what a smale worde may of anye of your mouthes that syttes in your places to these mene that sekethe lyght at your handes.[60]

Wyatt could call no one to speak for him, nor have his witnesses sworn to their testimony. 'Call forthe Masone, swere hym,' he challenged, pretending to forget that 'he is defendant: his othe cane not be taken. What sayethe he at the leste?'[61]

As he prepared to defend himself at the bar, Wyatt knew that he must give the rhetorical performance of his life to save his life. Beyond any hope save the justice of his jury, he must sway their feelings and *move* their consciences to believe him and his truth, rather than his accusers and their falsehood, and bring them to his side. He would use all his power of oratory, all his control of language to this persuasive end.[62] His speech to defend his *troth* and honour, as dear as life itself, must be delivered from memory, in absolute control of voice and gesture, in language and argument perfectly suited to his case. A lifetime of training in the arts of eloquence had made him oratory's master; the classical rules of rhetoric, the hundreds of figures and tropes learnt by rote and by heart since childhood had become so deeply impressed as to be second nature.[63] Armed with the weapons of oratory, he would deliver his *Defence* as his last public utterance, a fighter going down fighting in a war to the death. Teachers of rhetoric used such military metaphors to explain the force and nature of their art. *Elocutio* – expression of language fitting to the argument – was hardest of all, wrote Quintilian, yet 'without this power all the preliminary accomplishments of oratory are as useless as a sword that is kept permanently concealed within its sheath'. 'Ornament' signified not adornment, but a soldier's weapons ready for any challenge – 'the speaker who possesses it fights not merely with effective, but with flashing weapons'.[64] Wyatt will use rapier rather than broadsword.

He had learnt, above all, that consummate art of the orator, the art of concealing art. He would play the plain man, a man with faults certainly, which the jury would understand, but never infidelity to his king, never treason. As he prepared his brilliant *Defence*, Wyatt claimed that it was not he who was eloquent or a challenger in rhetoric, but his accusers: 'these be the two markes wheare unto myn accusers directe all ther shott of eloquence. A dede and a sayinge.' His accusers, not he, were the spinners and weavers of tales:

Th'accusation comprehendythe the Indightmente and all these worshipfull mens tales annexed therunto, the lengthe wheare of, the cunning wheare of, made by lerned mene, weavyd in and owte to perswade you and troble me . . . may bothe deceave you and amase me, yf god put not in your heades honeste wysdome to waye these thynges.[65]

Wyatt's tactic must be to set the 'honeste wysdome' of the men of the jury and his own 'truth' against the 'cunning', the 'suttell craft' of his accusers and the 'lernede mene' of the Council, who were 'craftelye and wyttinglie' devising a case which no 'symple man' could try. The perfect orator, so Quintilian taught, will be 'natural and unaffected', 'give the impression of simplicity and reality', and appeal to 'the common feeling of mankind' while preserving 'the natural current of our speech'.[66] Accordingly, to the jury, 'simple' men like himself – 'I saye unto you my good maisters and Christian brotherne' – Wyatt would not speak like a gilded ambassador, but in plain language, his native English. 'But ye knowe, maisters, yt is a commen proverbe'.[67] And he will tell them a story:

thinke, I besyke you, that yf yt be sufficiente for the condemnation of anye mane to be accused only, that then there is no man giltles, but yf for condemnation is requisyte prof and declaration, then tayke me as yet not condemned tell throughely . . . ye have harde and marked my tale.[68]

Swinging like a bell through the *Defence* was *antithesis*: Wyatt's truth against 'their' lies. 'But, maisters, this is more of lawe then of equite, of livinge [lying] then of uprightnes, with suche intricate aparances to blynde mens consciens'; 'for his [Bonner's] craftie malice I suppose in my consciens abusethe the others symplenes'.[69] He will now play on words for his life depended on it. 'I doute not, I doute not but the reste of there proffes wilbe but reproffes in everie honeste mans judgmente'; 'yt gatt me so myche credet that I am in dett, yet in dett for yt'.[70] Here he was using *agnominatio*, bringing together two words of different meanings but similar sound. Those who copied and read the *Defence* long after Wyatt wrote it would have recognised his easy deployment of all the figures and schemes and techniques of argument. Again and again, he used *anthypophora* (or *rogatio*), asking a question and answering it himself:

Who then accused me . . . ? No mane. Whye so? For ther is no suche thynges. Why arte thou brought hether then? Yt ys but a bare condemnatyon to say, yf I had not offended I hade not byne brought hethere. That was ther saying agaynste Chryste that had nothing to saye agaynst hym els.[71]

Most natural to him were the figures which seem to say one thing and mean another. The perfect courtier was master of the art of indirection, of the mocking answer, the disdainful reply. Now, driven by hardly suppressed fury at the injustice and travesty of the charges and by contempt for his accusers, Wyatt used his wit, his *sprezzatura*, to scorn them. His principal accusers – and principal targets – were 'the doctors', 'the right *reverende* father in god, the bysshope of London and Mr *Dr* Haynes, the kynges chaplayne', whose very titles might condemn them since their lies belied the spirituality they professed. Ranging against Bonner all the figures of derision, Wyatt mischievously, disdainfully, hilariously belittled the hypocrite bishop, his pomposity, his tight-fistedness, his absurdity. 'The lyttell fatt prest were a jollye morsell for the zora [señora]'.[72] Using the figure *paralepsis* or *occultatio* – pretending to pass over a matter and so drawing attention to it – he called into doubt the integrity of this Bishop who began to persecute the common people for reading the Bible he had once wanted them to have: 'Yt was not lyke then that the Bysshope of Londone shulde sue to have the scripture in Inglyshe taken owt of the churche. But I have not to do withall'. In the end, it would be the word of Bonner and Heynes against that of Wyatt and Mason, and Wyatt the gambler now offered odds: 'theye are ij [two], we ar also ij . . . lett us trie our fames for our honesties – and we will give them oddes'.[73]

The *Defence* opposed Wyatt's honesty to the malice of his accusers and adduced the intrinsic unlikelihood of their charges, for the jury to weigh and ponder, just as the jury which had acquitted Lord Dacre of Gilsland had 'wayede I suppose the malice of his accusars, the unlyklyhood of the thynges hanginge togyther'. The remarkable acquittal of Lord Dacre in his treason trial in 1534 offered Wyatt hope, and gave the crown cause for alarm.[74] The deed alleged against Wyatt made no sense: 'Wiatt in so greate truste with the kinges maiestie that he made hym his Imbassadoure . . . hathe hade intelligens with the kinges rebell and traytor, Pole'? Nor did his alleged saying: 'he feryd that the kinge shulde be caste owte of a Cartes arse and that by goddis bloude yf he were so, he were well served, and he wolde he were so'.[75] Since neither 'goddes lawe nor mans lawe nor no equite condemnethe a man for suspectes', where was their proof? 'Before yt had come as fare as accusation yt shulde have byne proved betwene Pole and me kynne, acquayntaunce, familiaritie or els accorde of opinions.' 'But what, there is none. Whie so? Thou shalte as sone fynde owte oyle owte of a flynte stone as fynde any suche thynge in me.'[76] All Wyatt's 'pollicy', all his 'dexteritie' had been directed to 'com to knowledge and intelligence' of Pole. Yet now Wyatt, who had thwarted Pole's legation, whom Pole most feared as his assassin, was charged with collusion with him. In circumstances less desperate, cynical, mordant Wyatt might have found irony in the accusation, but now it was bitter to him: 'as god judge me this vii yere I suppose came no gladder newes unto hym [Pole] then this of my troble, and one my trothe yt is no smale troble unto me that he shulde rejoyce in hyt'.[77] Venturing into the maze of suspicion encircling the truth of his faith, he diverted the parodic charge of papistry by adverting to a Lutheranism which he might also need to deny, in language more self-reflexive than ever:

Besydes this, ye bringe in now that I shulde have this intelligens with Pole by cawse of our opinions that are lyke and that I am papyshe. I thynke I shulde have more a doe with a great sorte in Inglande to purge my selffe of suspecte of a lutherane then of a papyst.

The 'hazarde I was in in Spayne with the Inquisicion' for dutifully denying the Bishop of Rome might surely have countered any charge of papistry.[78]

'Reherse here the lawe of wordes.' The jury must decide whether Wyatt's spoken words would bear treason, whether they were words treasonable by the statute. Always dark and doubtful, the interpretation and application of this novel and complex law would be more difficult than ever in the case of Wyatt.[79] His tangled language the sign of his anger, Wyatt protested: 'Were yt so I had saide the wordes, yet that remaynethe unproved but tayke yt not that I graunt them for I meant not so, but onlye that I had so saide.' On a word misstated, misremembered, or 'yet worst of all altered by an examyner', the verdict upon his guilt or innocence would hang.

Yt is a smale thynge in alteringe of one syllable ether with penne or worde that may mayke in the conceavinge of the truthe myche matter or error. For in thys thynge 'I fere', or 'I truste', semeth but one smale sylbable chaynged, and yet it makethe a great dyfferaunce. ... Agayne 'fall owte' 'caste owte', or 'lefte owte' makethe dyfferaunce . . .

But, he asked, was it likely that he would speak treasonably before Bonner and Heynes, with whom his relations were already so inimical? 'Yet am I not so veri a fole'.[80] Finding a metaphor for their 'fasshone', he described their simple method of defaming him. The bedizened courtier chose an image of the 'guard', an ornamental trimming of a garment:

But by cawse I am wonte some tyme to rappe owte an othe in an erneste tawlke, looke howe craftylie theie have put in an othe to the matter to mayke the matter seme myne and bycawse theie have garded an nowghttie garmente of thers with on of my nawghttie gardes theie wyll swere and face me downe that that was my garment. But bringe me my garment as yt was.

No one would believe, surely, 'that I understonde Inglyshe so evell to speake so owte of purpose'. 'To you, my good maisters . . . I dowte not but you see alreddie that in this sayinge, yf I had so saide, I mente not that nowghtie interpretacion that no Devell wolde have imagined upone me'. His jurors would see through the double negatives, beyond that 'so dysguysed sayinge' to the true Wyatt.[81]

What would have been his motive for treason? His accusers alleged that 'Wyat grudged at his fyrst puttinge in the tower. Ergo (say theie) he bare malyce in his harte', and sought revenge. 'Yf by grudginge theie meene moninge, theie nead not prove yt, I graunt yt': so would anyone moan about being in the Tower.[82] But, Wyatt claimed, 'yt ys fare from my nature to studie to revenge', for all the 'maynie great dyspytes and dyspleasures that I have had done unto me'. 'Here agayne theye have garded my tale with an othe' to make it seem true. A sartorial metaphor recurred: 'as yf a mane shulde tayke one of my dublet sleves and one of my cote and sowe them togyther after a dyguysed fasshion and then saye "Loke, I pray you whatt apparrell Wyat werethe!"'[83] His accusers charged him 'that I shulde wysshe the kynge had sent me to Newgatte when he sent me Embassadoure'. True, he had never sought the office, had feared that he would fail, but why would anyone seeking revenge wish himself in Newgate? It made no sense. Charged with repining against the 'lawe of wordes', he claimed not to remember what he had, allegedly, once discussed with Mason, save that 'yf yt shulde fall into an evell prince that it were a sore roode [sorrowful cross]. I suppose that I have not myssayde in that'. He now stated the most orthodox of political theory: 'all powers' are to be obeyed by the 'expres lawe of good [God]: for that ther is no evell prence but for deserte of the people and no hande over an evell prynce but the hande of god'.[84]

Wyatt's conclusion of his *Defence* was devastating. Should the jury be fearful of freeing him, this was tantamount to denying that their king was a prince of mercy and justice:

And yt is a nawghtie fere yf any man have any suche, to thynke a queste dare not acquyte a man of treason when theie thynke hym clere for yt were a fowle sclaunder to the kynges maieste. God be thanked he is no tyrant. He woll no suche thynges agaynst mens consciens. He will but his lawes and his lawes with mercie.[85]

The King had shown no disfavour to Lord Dacre's jurors, 'nor woll not unto you yf you do as your consciens leades you'. The appeal to conscience rang through the *Defence* as Wyatt's only hope of freedom. 'Will any man that hathe Chrystiane charite and any conscience upone suche a malicious getheringe frame an accusation upone a mans lyf?'[86] With a plea which was also a warning, he charged them to think beyond this worldly inquest to the Great Inquest, to remember that if they betrayed his 'innocent truthe' they would stand accused at the Last Judgement which awaited them all: 'afore god and all these men I charge you with my innocente truthe that incase, as God defende, ye be gyltie of myne innocent bloude, that ye before his tribunall shalbe inexcusable.'[87] Praying God to 'put in your hartes to pronounce upone me accordinge as I have willed to the kinge . . . in harte, wyll and wyshe', he signed himself: 'T.W.'

T.W. never did plead at the bar, never delivered his defence in court. Danger lay in allowing so dazzling an orator, a man so closely observed by his contemporaries, to speak freely, and there were signs that some were turning against the King's injustice. If a jury ever did indict Wyatt, he escaped trial. He pleaded his innocence by other means. Confessing under examination 'in lamentable and pitiful sort', 'delivering his submission in writing, declaring the whole history of his offences', he protested that these 'proceeded from him in his rage and foolish vainglorious fantasy, without spot of malice'. So the Council reported. Wyatt yielded to the King's mercy.[88] And he had a powerful intercessor. In the springtime of her marriage, Queen Katherine pleaded for Wyatt's freedom. On 19 March when she passed through London for the first time as queen, travelling along the Thames on the royal barge the *Lyon*, as the guns of the Tower saluted and her people welcomed her, she took the occasion of her triumph to seek the royal grace. By 'humble suits and intercessions', by 'great and continual suit', she prevailed on the King for mercy toward Wyatt.[89]

Queens might ask for pity, especially queens consort who, unlike queens regnant, were not sworn by their coronation oath to be the fount of justice. Katherine of Aragon had sought pardon for the Evil May Day rioters in 1517, when the King still listened to her. A leader of the Pilgrimage of Grace besought Queen Jane to intercede for his life.[90] Chivalric romance celebrated pitiful queens. In *The Castle of Love*, translated by Lord Berners for Elizabeth Carew (whom no pity saved), Leriano entreated the Queen to plead for the life of Laureola. 'I found her in an hall accompanied with many noble ladies and other, who were sufficient to have attained their desires.' She went before her royal husband and 'showed him the moderation that a king ought to have', unavailingly.[91] Reading in romance of pardons for sorrowful lovers, despairing lovers at Henry's court besought pity in their real plights. When Mary Boleyn, once the King's mistress, married secretly and beneath her, she disparaged herself and her sister Anne. 'Love overcame reason', 'I loved him as well as he did me; and was in bondage', so she entreated: 'And being that I have read in old books that some for as just causes have by kings and queens been pardoned by the suit of good folks, I trust it shall be our chance . . . to come to the same.'[92] Maybe 'friends and lovers' of Wyatt pleaded to Katherine Howard, who might well have been reading romance in her giddy youth. Maybe one of them was her cousin, the Earl of Surrey. 'At the contemplation' of Wyatt's submission, and 'at the great and continual suit' of his queen, the King 'being of his own most godly nature inclined to pity and mercy', granted him pardon.[93]

Wyatt was summoned to Dover, to the royal presence, 'with a very favourable and amicable letter'. He was pardoned '*pour estre personage de bonne esprit* [for his wit]', according to Marillac, and for services past and to come.[94] Yet his freedom came at a bitter price. The King granted him pardon of life and goods, so Chapuys heard, but granted it on 'very painful and heavy conditions'. The first was not unusual – that he should confess his guilt. The second was unprecedented. Wyatt must take back the wife from whom he was so long separated and live with her as a good husband. If ever he were found in the company of another woman, '*mesmes de deux quil a ayme* [even of the two he had loved]', he would lose both life and goods.[95] Wyatt had cast out Elizabeth Brooke so long before, had never forgiven her nor ever wanted to see her. There was inwardness to the forced restoration of his faithless wife to bed and board. Maybe the sanctimonious King thought to reform the morals of his courtier accused of 'vicious living', but it is more likely that the Brooke family were seeking Elizabeth's rehabilitation, demanding that Wyatt acknowledge her. Suspicions of the Cobham family's animus against Wyatt may have had foundation. A new beauty – Elizabeth's niece, another Elizabeth Brooke – was poised to captivate the court. Witty, talented, worthy the grandest marriage, she must not be compromised by the scandals swirling around her aunt. In February 1542, as the King took a fancy to the young Elizabeth Brooke and showed her special favour, Chapuys described her as 'a beautiful young girl' with 'the spirit to enterprise to do as badly as the others'.[96]

Farewell Bess Darrell? If Wyatt now abandoned Elizabeth Darrell, it was not as once Aeneas abandoned Dido to fulfil his imperial destiny and found Rome. This was a separation forced and cynical. If Chapuys's story was true, Bess Darrell faced another grim dislocation, another search for protection, though now with a child in arms, her young son Francis. Was this the final cruel parting for Wyatt and Bess? Thinking on last things, on 12 June 1541 Wyatt made his will. How he bequeathed his soul is unknown, for his will is lost. But his bequests of transitory things, the disposition of his property, tell of where his responsibilities and where his heart lay. To Bess Darrell he bequeathed for the term of her life the dissolved monastic site of Montacute Priory in Somerset, with all its manors and lands.[97] His hope was to protect her against the reversals of fortune. Some hope.

The excesses of a sanguinary summer in England might have caused those in high places to bear low. On 28 May 1541 ancient Margaret Plantagenet, Countess of Salisbury, was beheaded for the treason of communicating with her son, Cardinal Pole. Now the son of a martyr, Pole compared Henry to Herod, Caligula and Nero.[98] At the end of May also the young Lord Dacre of the south, his brother-in-law John Mantell, Wyatt's former servant, and other young bloods were indicted for murder committed during an illegal hunting party which had gone disastrously wrong. In Star Chamber, the lords were in disarray and 'made great conscience' over Dacre's indictment, weeping as they found him guilty, for they 'could not agree to wilful murder'. George Brooke, Lord Cobham, especially, was 'vehement and stiff' against it. Though Dacre confessed and submitted, he was not pardoned.[99] On 28 June Lord Leonard Grey was beheaded at the Tower and John Mantell and two of the renegade huntsmen were hanged at Tyburn. Dacre was hanged the following day. Seeing Mantell, the 'handsomest and best bred man in England', and the young nobleman dragged through the streets and shamed by public hanging aroused great pity.[100] The outrage was heightened by awareness that the King, who gained by accrual of their property and wardships, was reinforcing his legal victory in the great case of Lord Dacre of the south which had been so ominous for English landowners.[101] Dacre's bereft widow and sister sought explanation and precedent by reading Lydgate's *Fall of Princes*.[102] Mantell, the companion of Wyatt's travels, the bearer of his most secret messages, who carried Wyatt's poetry in memory and recorded it, did not live to fulfil so much youthful promise.

After the King's fury came his grace, for some. John Legh, Queen Katherine's cousin, was pardoned in May, and Thomas Palmer reprieved.[103] For unnamed services rewards came to John Mason and Philip Hoby, who had been caught up in Wyatt's catastrophe.[104] Royal menace, as well as Wyatt's perennial financial exigency, may have lain behind the exchanges of land from Wyatt to the King in April, and from the King to Wyatt in November 1541. At the end of June Wyatt sold the hundred and manor of Hoo in Kent for £300, signing the receipt '*Tho. Wiat*' (the same '*Tho.*' who signed his poems), and in July he leased away the site and precinct of the dissolved Carmelite priory of Aylesford in Kent which he had so determinedly sought.[105] Yet one transaction in that melancholy year signified a friendship which had survived the anguish of the Tower. Granting to John Mason and his wife Elizabeth a house with gardens and a courtyard within the Crossed

Friars for an annual rent of five artichokes at midsummer, Wyatt made them his City next-door neighbours.[106]

Wyatt was free. But whether this was freedom with honour – the only freedom – was uncertain. His 'troth' was tainted by his imprisonment, and time alone would vindicate him. Once, 'of glorye the fyer' had touched his heart, a glory which might – or might not – come again. Rumours of war with France led to massive mobilization of troops in the marches of Calais in the spring of 1541, and offered the chance of military service. With John Wallop's pardon came martial command: in April 1541 he was appointed Captain of Guînes, to lead thousands of men. Sir Thomas Palmer was his deputy. Wyatt was given the command of three hundred light horse to be stationed at Calais to hold the garrison until its new-built fortifications were defensible.[107] Leadership of cavalry in war was fitting for a knight, the service for which Wyatt had prepared since childhood, but never yet performed. Writing *The new pollecye of warre* in 1542, a paean to the love of virtuous men for their country, Thomas Becon dedicated it 'To the right worshipful Sir Thomas Wyatt knight', praising him as 'apt for the godly administration of the public weal no less in the perfect knowledge of the diversity of Languages than in the activity of martial affairs'.[108] Martial command returned Wyatt to the Calais garrison – not sunk in peaceful torpor, as during his previous command, but preparing for war. Also in Calais early in May were his old friend Lord Russell, with whom he had travelled to Italy in 1527, and a 'back friend', William Fitzwilliam, the Earl of Southampton. With them arrived two young men of princely aspiration. With twenty-four 'gentlemen and yeomen' in attendance, they made a brief visit 'only for their pastime and disport'. One was the King's brother-in-law, Sir Thomas Seymour, the other Henry Howard, Earl of Surrey.[109]

In Calais, did Wyatt and Surrey sing of arms and the man? In retrospect, they would be hailed as the 'chieftains' and makers of a new poetry for England, adepts and disciples of Petrarch. The principal evidence of their mutual inspiration lies in the poetry itself, and in the salutations of fellow 'makers', but sometimes they found themselves in the same place at the same time. Perhaps in Calais, as war threatened, it was Surrey's 'pastime and disport' to read and rhyme with Wyatt. In

Tottel's *Songes and Sonettes* (and only there) is a poem of love and war which contains Surrey's internal dedication to WIATT:[110]

The lover comforteth himself
with the worthiness of
his love.

When raging love with extreme pain
   Most cruelly distrains my heart:
When that my tears, as floods of rain,
Bear witness of my woeful smart:
When sighs have wasted so my breath,
That I lie at the point of death:

  I call to mind the navy great,
That the Greeks brought to Troy town:
And how the boisterous winds did beat
Their ships, and rent their sails adown,
Till Agamemnon's daughter's blood
Appeased the gods, that them withstood.

   And how that in those ten years war,
Full many a bloody deed was done,
And many a lord, that came full far,
There caught his bane (alas) too soon:
And many a good knight overrun,
Before the Greeks had Helen won.

   Then think I thus: since such repair,
So long time war of valiant men,
Was all to win a lady fair:
Shall I not learn to suffer then,
And think my life well spent to be,
Serving a worthier wight than she?

   Therefore I never will repent,
But pains contented still endure.
For like as when, rough winter spent,
The pleasant spring straight draweth in ure:
So after raging storms of care
Joyful at length may be my fare.

This is the work of the apprentice-poet, far from Surrey's mature achievement (not that he lived to full maturity). Yet the poem's ravelling of the fortunes of love and war, its engagement with the grandest of classical themes, not only foretell Surrey's great translation of the *Aeneid* but also advert to Wyatt's thoughts of love and war in Carthage and to his composing of 'Iopas song':

> When Dido feasted first the wand'ring Trojan knight
> Whom Juno's wrath with storms did force in Libyc sands to light.[111]

There is also a *strambotto* – 'Dydo am I, the fownder first of Cartage' – which 'could be by Wyatt'.[112] Surrey soon departed Calais, and perhaps Wyatt followed him not long after.

There were other contexts for Wyatt and Surrey's encounters. At court, they may often have met, though Wyatt's long absences and Surrey's princely eminence divided them.[113] Perhaps Wyatt had taken part with Surrey in the festivities to entertain the Prince of Salerno in July 1540.* Less grandly, they both played poetically on their strange relationship with Anne Stanhope, the wife of Edward Seymour, Earl of Hertford – Surrey by writing a parodic satire, 'Each beast can choose his fere [companion], according to his mind', and Wyatt by composing 'Accusyd tho I be without desert', where her name appears in an acrostic.[114] When we find Wyatt and Surrey translating the same sonnet of Petrarch – '*Amor, che nel penser mio vive e regna* [Love who lives and reigns in my thought]' – the possibility that they had discussed it together is enticing.[115]

We may imagine the two 'chieftains' of the new poetry entertaining and being entertained by Charles Blount, fifth Baron Mountjoy, at his London house in Silver Street. This household was praised as 'home of the Muses' by the scholar Roger Ascham, who compared Mountjoy's patronage of learning to that of the Medici.[116] Splendidly educated himself, Mountjoy cherished the poetic enterprise of Wyatt and Surrey and hoped to preserve Wyatt's fame. So a manuscript associated with Mountjoy attests. Within it are inscribed not only Wyatt's *Defence* and *Declaration*, and various of his poems – headed 'T. Wyat of love',

* See above, pp. 520–1.

'T.W', 'A balad of Wiatt', 'A Ridell' – but also verse and a letter by Surrey, and the epitaphs for Wyatt which Surrey and Anthony St Leger wrote to honour his memory.[117] Mountjoy's epitaph for himself was included in his will, 'The testament of my Lord Mountjoy's'. Blount placed his trust in his cousin, Richard Blount, leaving him his London house – where Mary, Duchess of Richmond, had been living – until his heir came of age.[118] Richard Blount, who had been the King's messenger to Wyatt in the Low Countries in 1540, deserved Wyatt's trust also. When Elizabeth Darrell was left in desperate financial straits after Wyatt's death, despite his best endeavour to protect her, Blount came to her rescue. In May 1546 a servant sent news to Bess at Montacute of help in her calamity: Mr Blount – by then in the service of John Legh – had lent her four marks, 'or else ye had been outlawed and that had been a great shame'.[119] Mountjoy's manuscript illumines a company bound by honour, faith, friendship, and poetry.

Wyatt's life was now lived away from the world of camps and courts, in London or in Kent. No longer in Christendom. In December 1541 he was elected knight of the shire for Kent, though nothing is known of his role in the House of Commons. Local lands and offices – not entirely to be despised – came his way: he became bailiff of the manor of South Frith and in March 1542, described as the King's servant, was appointed chief steward of the manor of Maidstone. As Fortune's wheel turned, perquisites which once belonged to Thomas Culpeper, a gentleman of Kent and of the Privy Chamber, reverted to Wyatt, for in February 1542 Culpeper and Queen Katherine were executed for their adultery.[120] Free from the great demands of high office, Wyatt might leave the busy companies of men to devote himself to private affairs and retreat to his study. Yet it was easier to know than to live by the classical ideal of the virtuous man, never less idle than with nothing to do, never less lonely than when he was alone.[121] Exiled in the countryside, forgotten, forgetting, the poet would take up his pen. In the loneliness of his study, in retirement, the virtuous man would turn to writing philosophy or to Christian contemplation. Wyatt, who sought to follow Christian Stoic teachings, thought on Boethius's *De consolatione philosophiae* (*The Consolation of Philosophy*) and translated passages which taught – as Tottel expressed it – 'He ruleth not, though he reign over realms, that is subject to his own lusts':[122]

> If thou wilt mighty be, flee from the rage
> Of cruell wyll, and see thou kepe thee free
> From the foule yoke of sensuall bondage,
> For though thy empyre stretche to Indian sea,
> And for thy feare trembleth the fardest Thylee,   *Thule*
> If thy desire have over thee the power,
> Subject then art thou and no governour.
> [. . .]

Self-knowledge is the way to self-control which assures constancy. More than ever, Wyatt aspired to the Roman virtue of *constantia*, the strength to withstand the blows of adversity and the seductions of success, to live beyond the power of Fortune. The insistence that the mind is its own place, refuge and redoubt, and that the virtuous man must look within to find self-knowledge recurs in Wyatt's writings. 'He that wyll obey the poesy of Appollo must first knowe hym self', so he had written in his youth, translating Plutarch.[123] By the end of his life, the ideal of the antique Roman, armed within, immoveable, invulnerable, had become Wyatt's self-image.

Portraiture's master, Hans Holbein the younger, portrayed the mature Wyatt as the noble Roman. In a tondo or roundel, as on a coin, Wyatt is in almost-profile, gazing into the distance, untroubled by life's vicissitudes. The surrounding inscription – SYR . THOMAS . WYAT – and toga-like drapery add to the classical effect. Here, as in so much else, Wyatt was innovator and experimenter, for this was the first such portrait known in England.[124] The usual clutter of crests and signs of honour which decked the portraits of his contemporaries, and the resplendent garments, are absent, though Wyatt still wears a distinctly un-Roman beard (as Henry's courtiers were bound to do). This alone adverted to the Englishness of his virtues: of being steadfast, stable, unfeigned, unswayed. Yet even here, there might be reversal. When a woodcut of this image was used to head *An excellent Epitaffe of Syr Thomas Wyat* and Leland's *Naeniae*, Wyatt was shown facing the other way:

On Wyatt's Portrait

> Holbein, the chiefest of that curious Art,
> Drew Wyatt's lively Image in each part
> With matchless skill; but no Apelles can
> Portray the wit and spirit of that man.[125]

Surrey would describe the virtuous Wyatt, constant in a stormy world:

> Vice to contemn, in virtues to rejoice
> Amid great storms, whom grace assured so
> To live upright and smile at fortune's choice.[126]

Not only the classical virtues of self-knowledge and constancy saved Wyatt, but 'grace'; divine grace freely imparted to the sinner. Meditating on deep questions of human will and divine grace, of God's mercy and His justice, in prayer to God and in self-revelation of his belief, Wyatt paraphrased the seven Penitential Psalms. This divine poetry, composed perhaps as profound product of his retreat and in consequence of some great distress, may well belong to this period when introspection was forced upon him. Perhaps by the time Wyatt wrote a heavier hand than that of any mortal king taught him 'how to know my sellff agayne'.[127] The compression, the wordplay, the poetic achievement of 'Wyatt's Psalms' suggests that they came late in his life. Here was a work worthy of a noble mind, to keep his name alive, the divinely inspired work of the prophet–poet: 'witness of faith that never shall be dead'.

When we find Wyatt for the last time, he is riding desperately in the King's service, as so often before. Learning in early October 1542 of the sudden arrival in Cornwall of the Imperial ambassador, Philippe de Montmorency, Sieur de Courrières, the King chose a man of trust to welcome him with honour, and to journey without sparing himself. Riding westward, Wyatt caught a fever. A few days later he died at the house of Sir John Horsey in Clifton Maybank in Dorset, so the epitaph of his devoted friend John Mason attests.[128] On 11 October Wyatt was buried in Sherborne Abbey, though precisely where is unknown.[129] Wyatt is elusive in death, as in life. In Surrey's epitaph he is forever stilled in death: 'Wyatt resteth here, that quick could never rest.' But in life Wyatt had carried his restlessness with him, like lightning in a cloud. He might have chosen another figure for himself: the galloping horseman, image of death and of desire.[130]

'*E Cosi Desio me Mena* [And so Desire carries me along]'. The unbridled horse, the image of desire, bears a rider in classical dress who would not halt him, even if he could.

Manuscript Sources

AUSTRIA

Vienna

Haus-, Hof- und Staatsarchiv

England, Korrespondenz,   Correspondence of the Imperial ambassadors in England
4–8   with Emperor Charles V and Mary of Hungary, Regent
of the Netherlands, 1530–41

BELGIUM

Brussels

Archives Générales du Royaume

Audience, 50, 64, 67, 69   Correspondence between Charles V and Mary of
Hungary (nineteenth-century copies from the Haus-, Hof-
und Staatsarchiv, Vienna)
123–4   Correspondence between Nicolas Perrenot, Seigneur de
Granvelle, and Mary of Hungary
358   Instructions to Ambassadors in England
Papiers Gachard, 643,   Correspondence between the papal nuncio at the
644, 645   Imperial court and the Cardinal Secretary of State,
1535–44 (transcribed by M. L-P. Gachard from the
Farnese archive in Naples. This archive was later
destroyed by enemy action).

ENGLAND

Cambridge

Christ's College

Account Book, 1530–45

Corpus Christi College

Parker MS 168   Documents relating to Richard Cox, Bishop of Ely

Trinity College

MS R 3. 33   Poem on Stephen Gardiner: 'The disclosinge of the practyse of Stephen Gardyner, byschope of Wynchester'

University Library

EDR, D5/8   Household book of Thomas Goodrich, Bishop of Ely

Doncaster

Doncaster Archives

DD Yar/C/1/84–113   Manor of Conisbrough Court Rolls, 1509–42

Kent

Centre for Kentish Studies

DRa/Vb 4   Visitation book of the Archdeacons of Rochester, 1504–65
DRb/AR1   Bishopric of Rochester, Bishops' Registers
DRb/AR1/13   Register of Richard Fitzjames and John Fisher, 1497–1535
DRb/AR1/14   Register of John Hilsey, 1535–9
DRb/Pwr/   Wills proved in the Rochester Consistory Court
DRb/Pwr/5   Register of Wills, 1482–1502
DRb/Pwr/7   Register of Wills, 1514–25
DRb/Pwr/8   Register of Wills, 1525–31
DRb/Pwr/9   Register of Wills, 1531–42
DRb/Pwr/10   Register of Wills, 1543–7
DRb/Pwr/11   Register of Wills, 1547–56
DRb/Pwr/12   Register of Wills, 1556–61
U 301/E1   Terrier of Sir Henry Wyatt's estates

London

British Library

Additional MSS   17012, 17492, 18741, 21564, 24965, 25114, 28576, 28590, 28591, 33514, 36529, 38692, 45131, 62135
Cottonian MSS   Caligula D ix, D x, D xi, E ii
    Cleopatra E iv, E vi
    Galba B x
    Nero B vii
    Otho C x

Titus B i

Vespasian C iv, C vii, C xiii, F xiii

Vitellius B ix, B x, B xiv, B xxi

Cotton Appendix   lxv

Egerton MSS   2603, 2711

Harley MSS   41, 69, 78, 282, 283, 304, 419

Royal MSS   17 A xxii, 19 A xx, 20 B xxi, 7 C xvi, 17 D ii, 17 D xi, 14 E iii, 16 E xiv, 16 E xxxi, 7 F xiv

Sloane MS   1523

Stowe MSS   396, 956

The College of Arms

MS M.6

MS I. 2

London Metropolitan Archives

COL/CA/01/01/09   Repertory of the Court of Aldermen, 14 May 1533–
28 October 1537

The National Archives

C 1   Court of Chancery: Six Clerks Office: Early Proceedings, Richard II to
Philip and Mary

C 2   Court of Chancery: Six Clerks Office: Pleadings, Series II

C 4   Court of Chancery: Six Clerks Office: Answers

C 43   Chancery: Common Law Proceedings, Rolls Chapel series

C 82   Chancery: Warrants for the Great Seal, Series II

C 142   Chancery: Inquisitions Post Mortem, Series II

DL 41   Duchy of Lancaster: Miscellanea

E 30   Exchequer: Treasury of the Receipt: Diplomatic Documents

E 36   Exchequer: Treasury of the Receipt: Miscellaneous Books

E 40   Exchequer: Treasury of the Receipt: Ancient Deeds, Series A

E 101   Exchequer: King's Remembrancer: Accounts Various

E 154   Exchequer: King's Remembrancer and Treasury of the Receipt:
Inventories of Goods and Chattels

E 192/2   Exchequer: Private Papers and Exhibits, Supplementary: Heneage Papers

E 210   Exchequer: King's Remembrancer: Ancient Deeds, Series D

E 305   Exchequer: Courts of Augmentations: Deeds of Purchase and Exchange

E 314   Exchequer: Court of Augmentations and Court of General Surveyors:
Miscellanea

E 315   Exchequer: Court of Augmentations and Predecessors and Successors:
Miscellaneous Books

E 326   Exchequer: Augmentation Office: Ancient Deeds, Series B

KB 9   Court of King's Bench: Crown Side: Indictments Files, Oyer and
Terminer Files and Informations Files

KB 27   Court of King's Bench: Plea and Crown Sides: Coram Rege Rolls
LR 14   Officers of the Auditors of Land Revenue: Ancient Deeds, Series E
PRO 31   Public Records Office: Rome Archives Series I
PROB 2   Prerogative Court of Canterbury: Inventories compiled before 1661
PROB 11 Prerogative Court of Canterbury: Will Registers
PROB 51 Prerogative Court of Canterbury: Administration Bonds before 1601
SC 2   Special Collections: Court Rolls
SC 6   Special Collections: Ministers' and Receivers' Accounts
SC 12   Special Collections: Rentals and Surveys
SP 1   State Papers: Henry VIII: General Series
SP 7   Wriothesley Papers
SP 9   State Paper Office: Williamson Collection, Pamphlets, Miscellaneous
SP 46   State Papers Domestic: Supplementary
STAC 2   Court of Star Chamber: Proceedings, Henry VIII
WARD 2   Court of Wards and Liveries: Deeds and Evidences

Sotheby's

Western Manuscripts and Miniatures, London, Tuesday 4 December 2007.
36. Letterbook of Marcellus Cervini (subsequently Pope Marcellus II)

Oxford

All Souls College

SR 79 f. 9   John Mason's copy of Erasmus's paraphrase of the New
                 Testament, printed in Basle in 1535

Bodleian Library

Fol. Δ 624   The chronicle of Anthony Anthony
MS Ashmole 858
Jesus College MS 74

York

Borthwick Institute, University of York

Jurisdiction of the Archbishops of York
          Archbishops' Registers
                    Reg. 27   Thomas Wolsey, 1514–30
          Consistory Wills
                    Probate Registers 8, 10, 11

REPUBLIC OF IRELAND

Dublin

Trinity College

MS 160   The 'Blage' Manuscript

ITALY

Florence

Archivio di Stato

Archivio Mediceo del Principato, 335, 4296, 4297, 4300
Ducato di Urbino, Classe Prima, filza 183

Mantua

Archivio di Stato

Archivio Gonzaga
  Francia, 638, 639
  Spagna, 589
  Ferrara, 1206
  Venezia, 1426, 1472, 1473

Modena

Archivio di Stato

Cancelleria Ducale, Estero
  Ambasciatori Francia, 14, 15, 16
  Ambasciatori Germania, 4, 5A
  Ambasciatori Spagna, 3, 4
Camera Ducale, Amministrazione Principi, 999: Ippolito d'Este's gaming book

Parma

Archivio di Stato

Carteggio Farnesiana Estero
  Francia, 7, 8, 10
  Spagna, 124
  Roma, 421, 422
  Toscana, 565
  Venezia, 608

SPAIN

Madrid

Archivo Histórico Nacional
Inquisición, libro 322, libro 785

Simancas

Archivo General
Segretaría de Estado
  Castile   legajos 39, 41, 42, 44
  Alemania   638
  Francia   K 1642, 1691, 1693
  Genova   1371, 1372
  Inglaterra   806
  Milano   1185
  Roma   866, 867, 868
  Venecia   1310, 1311, 1313, 1314, 1315, 1316
  Estados pequeños de Italia 1458, 1459
Guerra Antigua   legajos 9, 15

UNITED STATES OF AMERICA

The Huntington Library, San Marino
MSS, EL 1113, 1115

VATICAN CITY

Archivio Segreto Vaticano

Archivium Arcis, Armarium I-XVIII, 6530, 6533, 6535, 6537, 6538
Carte Farnesiane, 1(ii), 2, 8, 11, 12
Fondo Pio, 55, 56, 92, 95, 247
Miscellanea Armaria, II, 10, 46, 49
Segretaria di Stato
  Francia 1A
  Germania 52, 58
  Principi 4, 9, 10, 12, 13, 14A
  Spagna 1A

Biblioteca Apostolica Vaticana

MSS Vaticani Latini, 5826, 5967, 5970

Abbreviations

Place of publication is London, unless otherwise specified.

AC	*Archaeologia Cantiana*
AGR	Archives Générales du Royaume, Brussels
AGS	Archivo General, Simancas
AGS, E	Archivo General, Simancas, Segretaría de Estado
AGS, GA	Archivo General, Simancas, Guerra Antigua
AHN	Archivo Histórico Nacional, Madrid
AHN, Inquisición	Archivo Histórico Nacional, section Inquisición
ANG	*Acta Nunciaturae Gallicae*
ANG, 1	*Correspondance des nonces en France: Carpi et Ferrerio, 1535–1540*, ed. J. Lestoquoy, *ANG*, 1 (Rome and Paris, 1961)
APC	*Acts of the Privy Council of England*, ed. J. R. Dasent (1890–1907)
Arundel Harington	*The Arundel Harington Manuscript of Tudor Poetry*, ed. R. Hughey, 2 vols. (Columbus, Ohio, 1960)
ASF	Archivio di Stato, Florence
ASF, MP	Archivio di Stato, Florence, Mediceo del Principato
ASMn	Archivio di Stato, Mantua
ASMn, AG	Archivio di Stato, Mantua, Archivio Gonzaga
ASMo	Archivio di Stato, Modena
ASMo, CDAP	Archivio di Stato, Modena, Camera Ducale, Amministrazione Principi
ASMo, CD	Archivio di Stato, Modena, Cancelleria Ducale
ASPr	Archivio di Stato, Parma
ASPr, CFE	Archivio di Stato, Parma, Carteggio Farnesiana Estero
ASV	Archivio Segreto Vaticano
ASV, SS	Archivio Segreto Vaticano, Segretaria di Stato
BAV	Biblioteca Apostolica Vaticana
BIHR	*Bulletin of the Institute of Historical Research*
BL	British Library, London
Blage	Trinity College, Dublin, MS 160
Bodleian	Bodleian Library, Oxford
Book of the Courtier	*The Book of the Courtier by Count Baldassare Castiglione, done into English by Sir Thomas Hoby, Anno 1561*, intro. W. H. D. Rouse (Everyman's Library, 807)
Borthwick	Borthwick Institute, University of York

BRAH   *Boletín de la Real Academia de la Historia*

BRUO   A. B. Emden, *A Biographical Register of the University of Oxford, AD 1501 to 1540* (Oxford, 1974)

CAD   *A Descriptive Catalogue of Ancient Deeds in the Public Record Office*, 6 vols. (1890–1915)

Cardauns, *Legationen Farneses und Cervinis* *Legationen Farneses und Cervinis. Gesandtschaft Campegios. Nuntiaturen Morones und Poggios, 1539–1541, ND*, 1. Abteilung, 1533–1559, ed. L. Cardauns (Berlin, 1909)

Carteggi di Guicciardini *Carteggi di Francesco Guicciardini*, a cura di P. G. Ricci (Roma, 1968–9), vol. 13 (6 Marzo–22 Aprile 1527), vol. 14 (24 Aprile–8 Marzo 1534)

Cavendish, *Wolsey* George Cavendish, *The Life and Death of Cardinal Wolsey*, ed. R. S. Sylvester (EETS, 243, 1959)

CCR   *Calendar of the Close Rolls Preserved in the Public Record Office: Henry VII*, 2 vols. (1955–63)

CIPM   *Calendar of Inquisitions Post Mortem . . . Preserved in the Public Record Office: Henry VII*, 3 vols. (1898–1955)

Chronicle of Calais *The Chronicle of Calais in the Reigns of Henry VII and Henry VIII to the year 1540*, ed. J. G. Nichols (Camden Society, 1846)

Chronicle of King Henry VIII *Chronicle of King Henry VIII of England. Being a Contemporary Record of some of the Principal Events of the Reigns of Henry VIII and Edward VI, Written in Spanish by an Unknown Hand*, trans. M. A. S. Hume (1889)

CKS   Centre for Kentish Studies

Collected Poems of Wyatt *Collected Poems of Sir Thomas Wyatt*, ed. K. Muir and P. Thomson (Liverpool, 1969)

Constantine, 'Memorial' 'A memorial from George Constantine', ed. T. Amyot, *Archaeologia*, 23 (1831)

Contarini, Regesten und Briefe *Regesten und Briefe des Cardinals Gasparo Contarini*, ed. F. Dittrich (Braunsberg, 1881)

Correspondance du Bellay *Correspondance du Cardinal Jean du Bellay*, ed. R. Scheurer, ii, *1535–1536* (Paris, 1973)

Correspondance de Castillon et Marillac *Correspondance politique de MM. de Castillon et de Marillac, ambassadeurs de France en Angleterre (1537–1542)*, ed. J. Kaulek (Paris, 1885)

Correspondenz Karl V *Correspondenz des Kaisers Karl V*, ed. K. F. W. Lanz, 3 vols. (Leipzig, 1844–6)

CPR   *Calendar of the Patent Rolls Preserved in the Public Record Office: Edward IV, Edward V, Richard III* (1901), *Henry VII*, 2 vols. (1914–16), *Philip and Mary*, 4 vols. (1936–9)

CSPFor   *Calendar of State Papers, Foreign Series, of the Reign of Elizabeth, Preserved in the State Paper Department of her Majesty's Public Record Office*, ed. J. Stevenson *et al.* (1863–1950)

CSPFor, *1547–1553* *Calendar of State Papers, Foreign Series, of the Reign of Edward VI, 1547–1553*, ed. W. B. Turnbull (1861)

CSPMilan	*Calendar of State Papers and Manuscripts Existing in the Archives and Collections of Milan*, ed. A. B. Hinds (1912). Reference is to document numbers
CSPSp	*Calendar of Letters, Despatches and State Papers Relating to the Negotiations between England and Spain, Preserved in the Archives at Simancas and Elsewhere*, ed. G. A. Bergenroth *et al.*, 13 vols. in 20 (1862–1954)
CSPVen	*Calendar of State Papers and Manuscripts Relating to English Affairs, Existing in the Collections of Venice and in Other Libraries of Northern Italy*, ed. R. Brown *et al.*, 38 vols. in 40 (1864–1947). Reference is to document numbers
CWE	*Collected Works of Erasmus* (Toronto, 1974–)
CWM	*The Yale Edition of the Complete Works of St Thomas More*, 15 vols. in 21 (New Haven, 1963–c.1997)
CWTW	*The Complete Works of Sir Thomas Wyatt the Elder*, ed. Jason Powell, vol. i, *Prose Works* (Oxford, forthcoming)
DA	Doncaster Archives
DBI	*Dizionario biografico degli Italiani*, ed. A. M. Ghisalberti (Rome, 1960–)
Declaration	'A Declaration made by Sir Thomas Wiatt knight of his Innocence' (*Harley 78*, fos. 5r–6v)
Defence	TW: 'To the Judges after the Indictmente and the evidence' (*Harley 78*, fos. 7r–15r)
Devonshire	BL, Additional MS 17492
Dictionary of Proverbs	M. P. Tilley, *A Dictionary of the Proverbs in England in the Sixteenth and Seventeenth Centuries: a Collection of the Proverbs Found in English Literature and the Dictionaries of the Period* (Ann Arbor, 1950)
EC	*Essays in Criticism*
EEBO	Early English Books Online
EETS	Early English Text Society
Egerton	BL, Egerton MS 2711
EHR	*English Historical Review*
ELH	*English Literary History*
ES	*Essays and Studies*
Estancias y viajes	*Estancias y viajes del Emperador Carlos V*, ed. Don Manuel de Foronda y Aguilera (Madrid, 1914)
Faculty Office Registers	*Faculty Office Registers, 1534–1549: A Calendar of the First Two Registers of the Archbishop of Canterbury's Faculty Office*, ed. D. S. Chambers (Oxford, 1966)
Florio, *A Worlde of Wordes*	*A Worlde of Wordes, or most copious, and exact dictionaries in Italian and English, collected by Iohn Florio* (1598)
Foxe, *AM*	*The Acts and Monuments of John Foxe*, ed. G. Townsend and S. R. Cattley, 8 vols. (1837–41)
Foxe's Book of Martyrs	*John Foxe's Book of Martyrs, Variorum Edition Online* (Version 1.1, summer 2006)
Gardiner, *Letters*	*The Letters of Stephen Gardiner*, ed. J. A. Muller (Cambridge, 1933)

Gentleman's Magazine	'Recovery of the Lost Accusation of Sir Thomas Wyatt, the Poet, by Bishop Bonner', ed. John Bruce, *Gentleman's Magazine*, 33 (June 1850), pp. 563–70
Guidiccioni: Lettere	*Giovanni Guidiccioni: le lettere*, a cura di M. T. Graziosi, 2 vols. (Roma, 1979)
Hall	Edward Hall, *The Vnion of the two noble and illustre famelies of Lancastre & Yorke* (1548)
Harley 78	A miscellany, associated with Charles Blount, fifth Lord Mountjoy, containing epitaphs for Wyatt and some of his poetry
Harley 282	Original papers and letters relating to the negotiations of Sir Thomas Wyatt, ambassador of King Henry VIII to Emperor Charles V
Harrier, *Wyatt's Poetry*	Richard Harrier, *The Canon of Sir Thomas Wyatt's Poetry* (Cambridge, Mass., 1975)
HHL	Henry Huntington Library, San Marino, California
HHStA	Haus-, Hof- und Staatsarchiv, Vienna
HJ	*Historical Journal*
HLQ	*Huntington Library Quarterly*
HMC	*Historical Manuscripts Commission*
House of Commons	*The House of Commons, 1509–1558*, ed. S. T. Bindoff, 3 vols. (1982)
HR	*Hispanic Review*
Inventory	*The Inventory of King Henry VIII: the Transcript*, ed. D. Starkey (1998)
JEH	*Journal of Ecclesiastical History*
JWCI	*Journal of the Warburg and Courtauld Institutes*
KFF	*Kent Feet of Fines, Henry VIII*, ed. M. L. Zell (Kent Archaeological Society, 1998)
Legazioni di Serristori	*Legazioni di A. Serristori, con note di G. Canestrini* (Firenze, 1853)
Leland, *Encomia*	*Principum, ac illustrium aliquot & eruditorum in Anglia virorum, encomia, trophaea, genethliaca, & epithalamia. A Ioanne Lelando antiquario conscripta* (1589)
Leland, *Itinerary*	*The Itinerary of John Leland in or about the Years 1535–1543*, ed. J. Toulmin Smith, 5 vols. (Carbondale, Ill., 1964)
Leland, *Naeniae*	John Leland, *Naeniae in mortem Thomae Viati equites incomparabilis* (1542)
Letters of Cromwell	*Life and Letters of Thomas Cromwell*, ed. R. B. Merriman, 2 vols. (Cambridge, 1902)
Lirici Europei	*Lirici europei del cinquecento: ripensando la poesia del Petrarca*, a cura di G. M. Anselmi, K. Elam, G. Forni, D. Monda (Milano, 2004)
Literae ad Craneveldivm	*Literae virorvm ervditorvm ad Franciscvm Craneveldivm, 1522–1528: a Collection of Original Letters*, ed. H. de Vocht (Louvain, 1928)
LL	*Lisle Letters*, ed. Muriel St Clare Byrne, 6 vols. (Chicago and London, 1981)
L&L	K. Muir, *The Life and Letters of Sir Thomas Wyatt* (Liverpool, 1963)

LMA	London Metropolitan Archives
LP	*Letters and Papers, Foreign and Domestic, of the Reign of Henry VIII, 1509–1547*, ed. J. S. Brewer, J. Gairdner and R. H. Brodie, 21 vols. in 33 (1862–1932). Reference is to document numbers throughout, unless otherwise stated.
MLN	*Modern Language Notes*
MLR	*Modern Language Review*
More, *Correspondence*	*The Correspondence of Sir Thomas More*, ed. E. F. Rogers (Princeton, 1947)
ND	*Nuntiaturberichte aus Deutschland*: 1. Abteilung, 1533–59
Nott, *Surrey*	G. F. Nott, *The Works of Henry Howard, Earl of Surrey, and of Sir Thomas Wyatt the Elder*, 2 vols. (1815–16), i
Nott, *Wyatt*	G. F. Nott, *The Works of Henry Howard, Earl of Surrey, and of Sir Thomas Wyatt the Elder*, 2 vols. (1815–16), ii
NQ	*Notes and Queries*
Nunz. Ven.	*Nunziature di Venezia*, vol. ii, *1536–1542*, a cura di F. Gaeta (Roma, 1960)
ODNB	*Oxford Dictionary of National Biography* (online version)
OED	*Oxford English Dictionary* (online version)
Papers of George Wyatt	*The Papers of George Wyatt Esquire of Boxley Abbey in the County of Kent*, ed. D. M. Loades, Camden Society, 4th series, 5 (1968)
Parker	Parker Library, Corpus Christi College, Cambridge, MS 168
Pastor, *History of the Popes*	L. Pastor, *The History of the Popes from the close of the Middle Ages*, ed. and trans. F. I. Antrobus *et al.*, 40 vols. (1901–33)
PBA	*Proceedings of the British Academy*
Penguin Book of Renaissance Verse	*The Penguin Book of Renaissance Verse, 1509–1659*, selected and introduced by D. Norbrook, ed. H. R. Woudhuysen (1992)
Petrarch's Lyric Poems	*Petrarch's Lyric Poems: The* Rime Sparse *and Other Lyrics*, trans. and ed. R. M. Durling (Harvard, 1976)
Pole's Correspondence	*The Correspondence of Reginald Pole, volume 1. A Calendar, 1518–1546: Beginnings to Legate of Viterbo*, ed. T. F. Mayer (Aldershot and Burlington, Vermont, 2002)
PMLA	*Publications of the Modern Language Association of America*
PP	*Past and Present*
PPE	*Privy Purse Expenses of King Henry VIII*, ed. N. H. Nicolas (1827)
PPE Mary	*Privy Purse Expenses of the Princess Mary*, ed. F. Madden (1831)
Pr.	Prologue
Ps.	Psalm
Puttenham	George Puttenham, *The Arte of English Poesie* (1589) in *English Reprints* (1869)
Quyete of Mynde	*Tho. Wyatis translatyon of Plutarckes boke / of the Quyete of mynde* (1528)
RES	*Review of English Studies*
Ribier	*Lettres et mémoires d'estat, des roys, princes, ambassadeurs, et autres ministres, sous les règnes de François premier, Henry II & François II*, ed. G. Ribier, 2 vols. (Paris, 1666)

Römische dokumente	*Römische dokumente zur Geschichte der Ehescheidung Dokumente Heinrichs VIII von England, 1527–1534*, ed. S. Ehses (Paderborn, 1893)
RQ	*Renaissance Quarterly*
RRR	*Reformation and Renaissance Review*
RS	*Renaissance Studies*
RSTC	*A Short-Title Catalogue of Books Printed in England, Scotland and Ireland, and of English Books Printed Abroad, 1475–1640*, 2nd edn., ed. W. A. Jackson, F. J. Ferguson and K. F. Pantzer, 2 vols. (1976 and 1986)
Rymer	T. Rymer, *Foedera, conventiones, litterae*, ed. J. Caley (1816–30)
Salinas	'El Emperor Carlos V y su Corte', *Boletín de la Real Academia de la Historia*, XLIII (1903), XLIV–XLV (1904)
Santa Cruz, *Crónica*	Alonso de Santa Cruz, *Crónica del Emperador Carlos V*, vol. iv, ed. A. Blázquez y Augelera and R. Beltrán y Rozpide (Madrid, 1928)
Sanuto	*I diarii di Marino Sanuto*, ed. R. Fulin *et al.*, 58 vols. (Venice, 1879–1903). Reference is to column numbers throughout
SCJ	*Sixteenth Century Journal*
SEL	*Studies in English Literature*
SHC	Surrey History Centre
Singer	*The Life of Cardinal Wolsey by George Cavendish*, ed. S. W. Singer (1827)
SP	*State Papers, King Henry VIII*, 11 vols. (1830–52)
Spelman's Reports	*The Reports of Sir John Spelman*, ed. J. H. Baker, vols. xciii–xciv (Selden Society, 1977)
Surrey: Poems	*Henry Howard, Earl of Surrey: Poems*, ed. E. Jones (Oxford, 1964)
TCD	Trinity College, Dublin
Testamenta Vetusta	*Testamenta Vetusta: Being Illustrations from Wills*, ed. N. H. Nicolas, 2 vols. in 1 (1826)
TM	*Tottel's Miscellany* (1557–87), ed. H. E. Rollins, 2 vols. (Cambridge, Mass., 1966)
TNA	The National Archives, London
TRHS	*Transactions of the Royal Historical Society*
TSLL	*Texas Studies in Literature and Language*
Unpublished Poems	*Sir Thomas Wyatt and his Circle: Unpublished Poems, edited from the Blage manuscript*, K. Muir (Liverpool, 1961)
Ven. Dep.	*Venetianische Depeschen vom Kaiserhofe (Dispacci di Germania)*, ed. G. Turba, 3 vols. (Vienna, 1889–1901)
Wyatt: Poems	*Sir Thomas Wyatt: The Complete Poems*, ed. R. A. Rebholz (1978)
YAS	*Yorkshire Archaeological Journal*

All references to the New Testament are taken from *Tyndale's New Testament* (1534), introduced by David Daniell (New Haven and London, 1989).

Notes

In references to manuscripts in foreign archives the writer, the intended recipient, the date and place of composition are given. Not so for manuscripts in English archives, which are more readily accessible. References to *LP*, *CSPMilan* and *CSPVen* are to document numbers, unless otherwise stated. *I diarii di Marino Sanuto* is cited by column numbers. Folio references are always to recto, unless otherwise stated.

In anticipation of Jason Powell's authoritative *Collected Works of Sir Thomas Wyatt the Elder*, vol. i, which was not available to me as I wrote, I have given references to Wyatt's letters in this edition. For Wyatt's 'Declaration' and 'Defence' I have referred to an older edition: K. Muir, *The Life and Letters of Sir Thomas Wyatt* (Liverpool, 1963).

WYATT'S WORDS: A NOTE ON TRANSCRIPTION

1 *Sir Thomas Wyatt: Poems selected by Alice Oswald* (2008), pp. xi, xviii.

2 *Devonshire*, fo. 81.

FORGET NOT YET

1 *Declaration*; *Harley 78*, fo. 5v (*L&L*, p. 180).

2 Ps. 32.69–70. Harrier, *Wyatt's Poetry*, p. 226.

3 *Defence*; *Harley 78*, fo. 9 (*L&L*, p. 193); 'Syghes ar my foode'; *Harley 78*, fo. 27.

4 'Who lyst his welthe and eas Retayne': *Blage*, fo. 183.

5 'Some tyme I fled': *Egerton*, fo. 40; *Devonshire*, fo. 38v.

6 *Egerton*, fo. 23. See 'rememberer', n. 2, *OED*. This is one of few citations of Wyatt in *OED*. For a valuable discussion of the poem, see E. Heale, *Wyatt, Surrey and Early Tudor Poetry* (Harlow, 1998), pp. 98–100.

7 'O restfull place', entered by Nicholas Grimald into *Egerton*, fo. 7v.

8 *Blage*, fo. 150; Harrier, *Wyatt's Poetry*, p. 74.

9 *Egerton*, fo. 21v. *Petrarch's Lyric Poems*, 189. 'Forgetfulness', n. 3, *OED*. For a persuasive reading of this sonnet, see A. Ferry, *The 'Inward' Language: Sonnets of Wyatt, Sidney, Shakespeare, Donne* (Chicago, 1983), pp. 82–3, 107–10.

10 'Who lyst his welthe and eas Retayne', 'Quondam was I': *Blage*, fos. 183, 150; 'Love and fortune and my mynde', 'My galy': *Egerton*, fos. 23, 21v.

11 *An excellent Epitaffe of Syr Thomas Wyat: with two other compendious dytties, wherein are touchyd, and set furth the state of mannes lyfe* (printed by John Herford, *c.*1542), sig.

A1r–v. Another version of the epitaph survives in a manuscript associated with Wyatt and Surrey's circle: *Harley 78*, fo. 15v; see above, pp. 553. For the circumstances and poetic achievement of this epitaph, see W. A. Sessions, *Henry Howard, the Poet Earl of Surrey: A Life* (Oxford, 1999), pp. 245–59; F. B. Tromly, 'Surrey's Fidelity to Wyatt in "Wyatt Resteth Here"', *SP*, 77 (1980), pp. 376–87.

12 R. A. Quinones, *The Renaissance Discovery of Time* (Cambridge, Mass., 1972).

13 *Tho. Wyatis translatyon of Plutarckes boke / of the Quyete of mynde* (1528), sig. D2v.

14 *Quyete of mynde*, sig. D1v. Sessions, *Henry Howard*, p. 253. Virgil, *Georgics*, trans. H. R. Fairclough, rev. G. P. Goold (Cambridge, Mass., 1999), 2. 458–9, 467.

15 *Surrey: Poems*, 29, 30, 31 (the quotation is at 29. 9–12).

16 *Ibid.*, 30. 9, 11–12; 29. 1.

17 Puttenham, pp. 74, 76, 139, 185.

18 For the 'new poetry' which was collaborative, see Richard Helgerson's beautiful, valedictory *A Sonnet from Carthage: Garcilaso de la Vega and the New Poetry of Sixteenth-Century Europe* (Philadelphia, 2007), especially ch. 6.

19 *De rep. Anglorvm instauranda libri decem, authore Thoma Chalonero* (1579), pp. 358–9; printed in Nott, *Wyatt*, pp. cxii–cxiii. This English translation was made for George Wyatt, Thomas Wyatt's grandson: BL, Additional MS 62135, fo. 80. I am indebted to Chris Stamatakis for his transcription.

20 *Harley 78*, fo. 15.

21 *Naeniae in mortem T. Viati, equitis incomparabilis* (1542). For an English translation, see *L&L*, pp. 261–9 (the quotations are at pp. 268–9).

22 *Egerton*, fo. 71v (*CWTW*, i, letter 1); Wyatt to his son, 14 April 1537, Paris. I have benefited greatly from reading Jason Powell's transcriptions of Wyatt's letters: 'The Letters and Original Prose of the Poet Sir Thomas Wyatt: A Study and Critical Edition' (unpublished University of Oxford D.Phil. thesis, 2003).

23 These judgements are those of the scholar who knew the sources best: James Gairdner, the great editor of the *Letters and Papers, Foreign and Domestic, of the Reign of Henry VIII*: xiii(1), p. xli; xvi, p. xxv. According to Miss St Clare Byrne, editor of the *Lisle Letters*, Gairdner 'rightly called' Wyatt 'an unscrupulous agent': *LL*, vi, p. 223.

24 'So feble is the threde': *Egerton*, fo. 68v (l. 88).

25 ASMo, CD, Ambasciatori Spagna, busta 4; Alfonso Rossetto to the Duke of Ferrara, 12 March 1539, Toledo.

26 'The flaming sighes': *TM*, 101.

27 L. Forster, *The Icy Fire: Five Studies in European Petrarchism* (Cambridge, 1969), p. 62.

28 So Wyatt described King David's melancholy stance in his prologue to his paraphrase of Psalm 130: Pr. VI.31.

29 'Balet' was the word which Wyatt's contemporaries used for verse: see *LP*, iii (2), p. 1533, and above, p. 35. John Stevens, Elizabeth Heale and Chris Stamatakis use 'balet' when referring to Wyatt's courtly verse, avoiding 'lyric' which is anachronistic: J. Stevens, *Music and Poetry in the Early Tudor Court* (1961), pp. 14, 120–1; E. Heale, *Wyatt, Surrey, and Early Tudor Poetry* (1998); C. Stamatakis, '"Turning the Word": Sir Thomas Wyatt and Early Tudor Literary Practice' (unpublished University of Oxford D.Phil. thesis, 2008).

30 The following version is from *Egerton*, fo. 37v. Other versions are found in *Devonshire*, fos. 22v, 24r–v.

31 For Wyatt and music, see Stevens, *Music and Poetry*, pp. 27–8, 32, 110–11, 132–8 (the quotation is at p. 133); I. L. Mumford, 'Sir Thomas Wyatt's Verse and Italian Musical Sources', *English Miscellany*, 14 (1963), pp. 9–26; Heale, *Wyatt, Surrey, and Early Tudor Poetry*, pp. 76–83.

32 For a brilliant account of the protean making of the 'makers', see C. Stamatakis, '"Turning the Word"', soon to be published in a revised version: *Sir Thomas Wyatt and the Rhetoric of Rewriting: Turning the Word* (Oxford, forthcoming). E. Heale, *Autobiography and Authorship in Renaissance Verse: Chronicles of the Self* (Basingstoke, 2003); M. A. Skura, *Tudor Autobiography: Listening for Inwardness* (Chicago and London, 2008).

33 'Thou hast no faith of him that hath none': *Egerton*, fo. 16.

34 The quotation is from Quinones, *The Renaissance Discovery of Time*, p. 498. H. A. Mason, *Humanism and Poetry in the Early Tudor Period* (1959).

35 Suzanne Woods provides a lucid introduction to Wyatt's versification: *Natural Emphasis: English Versification from Chaucer to Dryden* (San Marino, California, 1984), ch. 3 (the quotation is at p. 72). Although Chaucer wrote verse epistles, they are not explicitly Horatian. I am grateful to Paul Keegan and Chris Stamatakis for elucidation of this point.

36 Richard Harrier scrupulously described and transcribed the manuscripts and sought to establish a canon of Wyatt's poetry: *The Canon of Sir Thomas Wyatt's Poetry* (Cambridge, Mass., 1975). Every Wyatt scholar is indebted to Jason Powell for fastidious, imaginative work on Wyatt's manuscripts which allows us to trust which poems might be Wyatt's: 'Marginalia, Authorship, and Editing in the Manuscripts of Thomas Wyatt's Verse', *English Manuscript Studies*, 15 (2009), pp. 1–40. Dr Powell prepares a scholarly edition of the poetry which Wyatt's readers eagerly await: *The Complete Works of Sir Thomas Wyatt the Elder*, vol. ii (Oxford, forthcoming).

37 For the practice of rescription in courtly manuscripts more generally, see A. F. Marotti, *Manuscript, Print and the English Renaissance Lyric* (Ithaca and London, 1995). John Stevens and Chris Stamatakis wonderfully evoke the world of the courtly makers: Stevens, *Music and Poetry*; C. Stamatakis, '"Turning the Word"'.

38 H. Baron, 'Mary (Howard) Fitzroy's Hand in the Devonshire Manuscript', *RES*, 45 (1994), pp. 318–35; E. Heale, 'Women and the Courtly Love Lyric: The Devonshire MS (BL Additional 17492)', *MLR*, 90 (1995), pp. 296–313.

39 H. Baron, 'The "Blage" Manuscript: the Original Compiler Identified', *English Manuscript Studies*, 1 (1989), pp. 85–119.

40 For revelatory forensic study of this manuscript, see J. Powell, 'Thomas Wyatt's poetry in Embassy: Egerton 2711 and the Production of Literary Manuscripts Abroad', *HLQ*, 67 (2004), pp. 261–82. For the significance of the '*Tho.*' inscriptions, see Powell, 'Marginalia, Authorship, and Editing', especially pp. 15–25.

41 *Surrey: Poems*, 31. 5–6.

42 Whether the nobility scorned or embraced the medium of print is a matter of scholarly controversy: J. W. Saunders, 'The Stigma of Print: A Note on the

Social Bases of Tudor Poetry', *EC*, 1 (1951), pp. 139–64; S. W. May, 'Tudor Aristocrats and the Mythical "Stigma of Print"', *Renaissance Papers*, 11, ed. A. L. Deneef and M. T. Hester (1980), pp. 11–18.

43 Uncertainty reigns. Harrier cast doubt on the assertion that some of Wyatt's verse was printed in *The Courte of Venus. Newly and diligently corrected with many proper Ballades newly amended* (c.1537–9). Only a fragment of this text survives. See *The Court of Venus*, ed. R. A. Fraser (Durham, North Carolina, 1955), especially pp. 31–46, 140–2; *Thomas Wyatt's Poetry*, pp. 80–5.

44 For the intractable problems of editing Wyatt, see H. A. Mason, *Editing Wyatt: an examination of* Collected Poems of Sir Thomas Wyatt *together with suggestions for an improved edition*, The Cambridge Quarterly (Publications, Cambridge, 1972); C. Burrow, 'An Augustan Wyatt', *English*, 36 (1987), pp. 148–58; J. Powell, 'Editing Wyatts: Reassessing the Textual State of Sir Thomas Wyatt's Poetry', *Poetica*, 71 (2009), pp. 93–104.

45 *Songes and Sonettes, written by the right honorable Lorde Henry Haward late Earle of Surrey, and other* (1557).

46 *TM*, i, p. 2. This is Tottel's title for Wyatt's 'My lute awake performe the last': *TM*, 87. For Tottell's transformations, see particularly Skura, *Tudor Autobiography*, pp. 40–8; Woods, *Natural Emphasis*, pp. 82–5.

47 Puttenham, p. 142 (my italics). The version in Tottel differs slightly: *TM*, 97. The version in *Egerton* is different again: fo. 24.

48 For Wyatt among the theorists, see above, pp. 354–7. The discussions of Wyatt's versification and style which I have found particularly helpful are Woods, *Natural Emphasis*, ch. 3, appendix A; M. Nolan, 'Style' in *Cultural Reformations: Medieval and Renaissance in Literary History*, ed. B. Cummings and J. Simpson (Oxford, 2010), pp. 396–419.

49 Hallett Smith, 'The Art of Sir Thomas Wyatt', *HLQ*, 4 (1946), pp. 323–55. Stevens, *Music and Poetry*, p. 16.

50 *Defence*, Harley 78, fo. 10v (*L&L*, p. 197).

51 *L&L*, p. 266.

52 G. F. Nott, *The Works of Henry Howard, Earl of Surrey, and of Sir Thomas Wyatt the Elder*, 2 vols. (1815–16).

53 *Collected Poems of Sir Thomas Wyatt*, ed. K. Muir and P. Thomson (Liverpool, 1969).

54 Mason, *Editing Wyatt*. The quotation is from the preface.

55 *Devonshire*, fo. 54v. *Collected Poems of Wyatt*, CCIII, p. 420.

56 J. Kerrigan, 'Wyatt's Selfish Style', *ES*, 34 (1981), pp. 1–18 (the quotation is at p. 8).

57 The art of imitation and Wyatt's Petrarchism are discussed further in ch. 5 below. The quotation is from *Sir Thomas Wyatt: Poems Selected by Alice Oswald* (2008), p. xii.

58 This is the contention of Ferry, *The 'Inward' Language*, especially ch. 2.

59 *Egerton*, fo. 5r–v. For the history of criticism of this poem, and a new interpretation, see H. Smith, 'The Art of Sir Thomas Wyatt', pp. 333–7. I am particularly indebted to the readings of P. Thomson, *Sir Thomas Wyatt and His Background* (Stanford, California, 1964), pp. 169–79; Ferry, *The 'Inward' Language*, pp. 114–

16; Heale, *Wyatt, Surrey and Early Tudor Poetry*, pp. 94–7; M. Holahan, 'Wyatt, the Heart's Forest, and the Ancient Savings', *English Literary Renaissance*, 23 (1993), pp. 46–80 (though I am very far from accepting Professor Holahan's political reading or his suggestion that this sonnet is Wyatt's 'assurance of continuing service to the King, of a good life that will end in faithfulness' (p. 47)).

60 For an analysis of the metre and scansion of this sonnet, see Woods, *Natural Emphasis*, pp. 74–7.

61 *Petrarch's Lyric Poems*, 140. For the linguistic virtuosity of Petrarch's sonnet and the interpretations of it by Renaissance commentators, see W. J. Kennedy, *Authorizing Petrarch* (Ithaca, New York, 1995), pp. 5–11.

62 Ferry, *The 'Inward' Language*, pp. 114–16.

63 *Devonshire*, fo. 19.

64 'Still', *adj.* and *n.* 2; *v.* 1, *OED*.

1: THEY FLE FROM ME

1 *Egerton*, fo. 26v.

2 For the mutability of words and the force of history upon them, see T. M. Greene, *The Light in Troy: Imitation and Discovery in Renaissance Poetry* (New Haven and London, 1982), ch. 2; J. Biester, *Lyric Wonder: Rhetoric and Wit in Renaissance English Poetry* (Ithaca and London, 1997), especially pp. 1–6.

3 Seemingly, every critic has essayed an interpretation of this elusive poem. The readings to which mine is especially indebted are: J. H. Prynne, *They That Haue Powre to Hurt; a Specimen of a Commentary on Shake-speares Sonnets, 94* (Cambridge, 2001); S. Greenblatt, *Renaissance Self-Fashioning: From More to Shakespeare* (Chicago and London, 1980), pp. 150–4, 156; C. Stamatakis, '"Turning the Word": Sir Thomas Wyatt and Early Tudor Literary Practice' (unpublished University of Oxford D.Phil. thesis, 2008); A. Fowler, 'Obscurity of Sentiment in the Poetry of Wyatt' in *Conceitful Thought: the Interpretation of English Renaissance Poems* (Edinburgh, 1975); Greene, *The Light in Troy*, pp. 256–8.

4 'Wild', *adj.*, *OED*.

5 In 1540 John Palsgrave noted 'how much the name of novelty or newfangledness is behated': *The Comedy of Acolastus*, ed. P. L. Carver (EETS, 202, 1937), pp. 15–16.

6 C. E. Nelson, 'A Note on Wyatt and Ovid', *MLR*, 58 (1963), pp. 60–3. M. A. Skura, *Tudor Autobiography: Listening for Inwardness* (Chicago and London, 2008), pp. 45–8.

7 P. J. Frankis, 'The Erotic Dream in Medieval English Lyrics', *Neuphilologische Mitteilungen*, 27 (1956), pp. 228–37. For an erotic dream vision contemporary with 'They fle from me', see *The Welles Anthology: MS. Rawlinson C. 813*, ed. S. L. Jansen and K. H. Jordan (Binghamton, New York, 1991), 36, pp. 27–8.

8 'Newfangledness' recurs in Wyatt's verse with connotations of falsehood: *Wyatt: Poems*, CC. 8; CCXXIII. 27. The evangelical reformers were accused of 'newfangledness' in faith: J. Frith, *A disputacion of purgatorye* (1531), i, sig. Dr; *LP*, xi. 354.

9 'It may be good like it who list': *Egerton*, fo. 17.

10 *Devonshire*, fo. 70 (my italics). The suggestion of the ordering of the versions is Jason Powell's: 'Editing Wyatts: Reassessing the Textual State of Sir Thomas Wyatt's Poetry', *Poetica*, 71 (2009), pp. 98–100.

11 For plays on serving and deserving, see for example, 'Suche happe as I ame happed in'; 'If fansy would favor'; 'Tho I cannot yor crueltie constrain' (*Egerton*, fos. 25v–6, 30r–v, 38); 'Ye know my heart my lady dear' (*Devonshire*, fo. 73v). Serving and 'sterving [starving]' is another common play.

12 The 'game of love' is beautifully expounded by J. Stevens, *Music and Poetry in the Early Tudor Court* (1961), ch. 9.

13 *The castell of love, translated out of Spanishe into Englyshe, by Johan Bowrchier knyght, lorde Bernis* (1552?), sigs. A2v–A3r, C6v. Lord Berners translated the romance at the request of his niece, the widowed Lady Elizabeth Carew.

14 E. Heale, 'Women and the Courtly Love Lyric: The Devonshire MS (BL Additional 17492)', *MLR*, 90 (1995), pp. 296–313, especially pp. 296–8, 306.

15 *Surrey: Poems*, 27. 10.

16 Geoffrey Chaucer, *Troilus and Criseyde*, ed. B. Windeatt (2003), 1. 15. Stevens, *Music and Poetry*, pp. 157–9, 188, 206, 213. S. Lerer, *Chaucer and His Readers* (Princeton, 1993).

17 More, *Correspondence*, p. 529; Chaucer, *Troilus and Criseyde*, 3. 390.

18 *Devonshire*, fo. 30. Chaucer, *Troilus and Criseyde*, 4. 323–9. Ethel Seaton first identified the borrowings from Chaucer: '"The Devonshire Manuscript" and its Medieval Fragments', *RES*, 7 (1956), pp. 55–6.

19 D. C. Kay, 'Wyatt and Chaucer: They Fle From Me Revisited', *HLQ*, 47 (1984), pp. 211–25. P. Fussell, *Poetic Meter and Poetic Form* (rev. edn., New York, 1979), pp. 145–6.

20 Puttenham, p. 74. R. Southall, *The Courtly Maker: an Essay on the Poetry of Wyatt and His Contemporaries* (Oxford, 1964); Stevens, *Music and Poetry*, p. 147.

21 Puttenham, pp. 74, 76.

22 H. Baron, 'Mary (Howard) Fitzroy's Hand in the Devonshire Manuscript', *RES*, 45 (1994), pp. 318–35. Ludovico Ariosto, *Orlando Furioso* (Vinegia [Venice], 1539). This book is my prized possession, thanks to the generosity of Jeremy Wormell.

23 *Surrey: Poems*, 28. 14.

24 *Devonshire*, fos. 6v–7; Stamatakis, '"Turning the Word"', pp. 234–5.

25 *Devonshire*, fos. 70v–71. *TM*, 91.

26 'Myne olde dere enmy'; *Wyatt: Poems*, LXXIII. 68, p. 386. 'The languishment' is Wyatt's addition to Petrarch.

27 *Egerton*, fo. 13; *Devonshire*, fo. 74v.

28 For this, see especially Stamatakis, '"Turning the Word"', pp. 215 ff.

29 For example, *The castell of love*, sigs. E1v, E2v–3r; *A certayn treatye moste wyttely deuysed orygynally wrytten in the Spanysshe, lately traducted in to frenche entytled, lamant mal traicte de samye. And nowe out of frenche in to Englysshe, dedicat to the ryght honorable lorde henry Erle of Surrey* (1543?), sigs. B2r–B3v, H1r–H3r.

30 B. Windeatt, '"Love that oughte ben secree" in Chaucer's Troilus', *The Chaucer Review*, 14 (1979), pp. 116–31.

31 Stevens, *Music and Poetry*, pp. 189–91, 216 (the quotation is at p. 216).

32 D. Javitch, *Poetry and Courtliness in Renaissance England* (Princeton, 1978), especially pp. 35–6, 55–8; R. A. Lanham, *Motives of Eloquence: Literary Rhetoric in the Renaissance* (New Haven and London, 1976).

33 Puttenham, pp. 196, 201.

34 *Wyatt: Poems*, XLIX. 7.

35 Biester, *Lyric Wonder*, pp. 75–7, 109; F. Whigham, 'Interpretation at Court: Courtesy and the Performer–Audience Dialectic', *New Literary History*, 14 (1983), pp. 623–39.

36 *The Book of the Courtier*, p. 46. P. Burke, *The Fortunes of the Courtier: The European Reception of Castiglione's* Cortegiano (Cambridge, 1995), especially pp. 30–1, 38.

37 Burke, *The Fortunes of the Courtier*, pp. 68–72.

38 Florio, *A Worlde of Wordes*, p. 392.

39 See Greene, *The Light in Troy*, p. 259.

40 Javitch, *Poetry and Courtliness*, p. 58.

41 *Devonshire*, fo. 18 (my italics). Puttenham, pp. 186–7. The stanza embodies further figures: *parison* (the use of parallel phrases) and *traductio* (the repetition of a word under different forms): Stevens, *Music and Poetry*, p. 67.

42 'Myne owne Jhon poyntz': *Parker*, fo. 200v.

43 'Thou hast no faith of him that hath none': *Egerton*, fo. 16. Greene, *The Light in Troy*, p. 256.

44 *Wyatt: Poems*, LXVIII. 4.

45 Stamatakis, '"Turning the Word"', especially pp. 206–7, 214.

46 *Devonshire*, fo. 45v.

47 'Suche vayn thought as wonted to myslede me': *Egerton*, fo. 38.

48 Ps. 102.91. Harrier, *Wyatt's Poetry*, p. 242.

49 *Letters of Cromwell*, ii, p. 135.

50 *An excellent Epitaffe of syr Thomas Wyat, with two other compendious ditties, wherin are touchyd, and set furth the state of mannes lyfe* (*c.*1542), sig. A2r.

51 *The Book of the Courtier*, p. 21.

52 T. Stemmler, *Die Liebesbriefe Heinrichs VIII. an Anna Boleyn* (Zürich, 1988), brief 6 (also brief 10). S. Lerer, *Courtly Letters in the Age of Henry VIII* (Cambridge, 1997), pp. 94–5.

53 BL, Additional MS 31922, fo. 22v; printed in Stevens, *Music and Poetry*, p. 390.

54 Stemmler, *Die Liebesbriefe Heinrichs VIII*, briefe 12, 6.

55 'Peult estre que cestoit certaines balades que le dict Roy a compose desquelles la putain et son frere comme de chose innepte et bouffe se gaudissoient que leur fut objecte pour grand et grief cryme': HHStA, England, Korrespondenz, 7, fo. 108 (*LP*, x. 908, p. 378); Chapuys to Charles V, 19 May 1536. Cited in P. Friedmann, *Anne Boleyn: a Chapter of English History, 1527–1536*, 2 vols. (1884), ii, pp. 267–8.

56 *Egerton*, fo. 33v. *Devonshire*, fo. 67v.

57 So his contemporaries noticed: BL, Sloane 1523, fo. 26.

58 BL, Cotton MS Otho D x, fo. 222v (Singer, p. 455).

59 Quintilian, *Institutio oratoria*, trans. H. E. Butler, 4 vols. (Cambridge, Mass., 1920–2), iii, 9.2.68; cited in Biester, *Lyric Wonder*, p. 116.

60 For the Treason Act of 1534 and its implementation, see above, pp. 203, 538–40. See also G. Walker, *Writing under Tyranny: English Literature and the Henrician Reformation* (Oxford, 2005).

61 *LP*, xiii(2). 829(2), p. 339.

62 Thomas Wilson, *Art of Rhetorique* (1553), p. 182. For the importance of rhetoric in Renaissance England, see Q. R. D. Skinner, *Reason and Rhetoric in the Philosophy of Hobbes* (Cambridge, 1996), especially part i.

63 'Avysing the bright bemes of these fayer Iyes': *Egerton*, fo. 22.

64 TNA, PRO 31/9/65, fo. 253 (*LP*, xiv(1). 561). For *dislenguare*: to untongue, see Florio, *A Worlde of Wordes*, p. 107. See above, p. 440.

65 *Defence*; *Harley 78*, fos. 10v–11 (*L&L*, pp. 197–8).

66 *Egerton*, fo. 52 r-v, *Wyatt's Poetry*, pp. 176–7. See below, ch. 9.

67 Stamatakis, '"Turning the Word"', pp. 151–68.

68 For Wyatt's portraiture, see R. Strong, 'Holbein's Thomas Wyatt the Younger', *Apollo* (March 2006), pp. 48–56. Professor Lerer identifies 'a sidelong quality' in Wyatt's poetry: Lerer, *Courtly Letters*, p. 165. *Surrey: Poems*, 28. 12.

69 *Egerton*, fos. 71–3 (*CWTW*, i, letters 1 and 2); Wyatt to his son, 14 April 1537, Paris; summer 1537, from Spain.

70 *Surrey: Poems*, 28. 35.

71 For eloquent and due warning of the difficulties in seeking Wyatt and of finding the life in the work, see C. Shrank, '"But I, that know what harbred in that hed": Sir Thomas Wyatt and his posthumous interpreters', *PBA*, 154 (2007), pp. 375–401.

72 Chaucer, *Troilus and Criseyde*, 5.1433; *Harley 282*, fo. 227 (*CWTW*, i, letter 11); Wyatt to Cromwell, 2 January 1539, Toledo.

73 Fowler, 'Obscurity of Sentiment', pp. 7–10.

74 *Parker*, fos. 200v–201v; see below, ch. 9.

2: THE CASTLE OF LOYALTY

1 The Castle of Loyalty is discussed by S. Anglo, *The Great Tournament Roll of Westminster*, 2 vols. (Oxford, 1968), i, pp. 43, 44, 69–72; D. Starkey, *Six Wives: the Queens of Henry VIII* (2003), pp. 271–3, 277; *A European Court in England* ed. D. Starkey (1991), pp. 41, 48. For Greenwich Palace, see *ibid.*, pp. 20–5; S. Thurley, *The Royal Palaces of Tudor England* (New Haven and London, 1993), pp. 35–6, 48–50.

2 The description of the Castle is found in the Revels accounts: *LP*, iv(1). 965, and the quotation in Hall, fo. 133v.

3 For the challenge and the rules of engagement, see College of Arms, MS M. 6, fos. 57v–58; Hall, fo. 133r.

4 Hall, fos. 133v–134r. For Henry's long friendship with the Duke of Suffolk, see S. J. Gunn, *Charles Brandon, Duke of Suffolk, 1484–1545* (Oxford, 1988).

5 Anglo, *Great Tournament Roll*, i, pp. 18, 71–2.

6 Hall, fo. 133r.

7 *Ibid,,* fo. 134v.

8 The King's side are named by Hall, fo. 134r.

9 J. P. D. Cooper, 'Courtenay, Henry, marquess of Exeter (1498/9–1538)', *ODNB.* For the friendship of the Order of the Garter, see *CSPVen, 1202–1509,* 790; cited in D. Starkey, 'King Henry and King Arthur', *Arthurian Literature,* xvi, ed. J. P. Carley and F. Riddy (1998), p. 180.

10 T. F. Mayer, 'Pole, Henry, Baron Montagu (1492–1539)'; M. M. Norris, 'Manners, Thomas, first earl of Rutland (*c.*1497–1543)', *ODNB.*

11 S. Lehmberg, 'Carew, Sir Nicholas (*b.* in or before 1496, *d.* 1539)'; S. Brigden, 'Bryan, Sir Francis (*d.* 1550)'; E.W. Ives, 'Norris, Henry (*b.* before 1500, *d.* 1536)', *ODNB.*

12 'Letters of the Cliffords, Lords Clifford and Earls of Cumberland, *c.*1500–*c.*1565', ed. R. W. Hoyle, *Camden Miscellany,* xxxi (Camden Society, 4th series, 44, 1993), pp. 95–6; R. W. Hoyle, 'Percy, Henry Algernon, sixth earl of Northumberland (*c.*1502–1537)', *ODNB.*

13 Their names are recorded by Hall, fo. 133r. M. A. Lyons, 'Lord Leonard Grey, Viscount Graney (*c.*1490–1541)'; C. S. Knighton, 'Brooke, George, ninth Baron Cobham (*c.*1497–1558)'; M. Riordan, 'Carey, William (*c.*1500–1528)'; D. Loades, 'Dudley, John, duke of Northumberland (1504–1553)'; A. Hawkyard, 'Sir Francis Poyntz (*c.*1487–1528)'; W. B. Robison, 'Browne, Sir Anthony (*c.*1500–1548)'; B. L. Beer, 'Seymour, Edward, duke of Somerset (*c.*1500–1552); V. R. Bainbridge, 'Newdigate, Sebastian (1500–1535)', *ODNB.*

14 For loyalty, see M. Keen, 'Chivalry and Courtly Love' in his *Nobles, Knights and Men-at-Arms in the Middle Ages* (1996), p. 33; R. W. Kaeuper, *Chivalry and Violence in Medieval Europe* (Oxford, 1999), p. 185.

15 S. J. Gunn, 'Chivalry and the Politics of the Early Tudor Court' in *Chivalry in the Renaissance,* ed. S. Anglo (Woodbridge, 1980), pp. 120–1. These were the mottoes of the Duke of Suffolk, Sir Edward Guildford and Sir Edward Poynings.

16 For the role of the Esquires and Knights of the Body, see J. Guy, 'Wolsey and the Tudor Polity' in *Cardinal Wolsey: Church, State and Art,* ed. S. J. Gunn and P. G. Lindley (Cambridge, 1991), pp. 66–8; Starkey, *Six Wives,* pp. 691–2.

17 Hall, fo. 100v.

18 N. Orme, *From Childhood to Chivalry: the Education of the English Kings and Aristocracy, 1066–1530* (1984), ch. 6.

19 For the relationship between war and chivalry, and the dangers of the tournament, see M. G. A. Vale, *War and Chivalry* (1981), pp. 63–87, 101–28.

20 D. Starkey, *The Reign of Henry VIII: Personalities and Politics* (1985), pp. 68–9.

21 'The Ordre of Knyghtod': TNA, SP 9/31, fo. 7v.

22 Cited in Kaeuper, *Chivalry and Violence,* pp. 171–2.

23 Hall, fo. 98r.

24 *Ibid,,* fo. 146v; Anglo, *Great Tournament Roll,* i, pp. 69, 72.

25 'The Ordre of Knyghtod': TNA, SP 9/31, fo. 12.

26 TNA, SP 9/31, fo. 15.

27 *Surrey: Poems,* 27. 3, 17–18, 51.

28 Orme, *From Childhood to Chivalry,* pp. 25, 189–90 (the quotation is at p. 190);

S. Brigden and N. Wilson, 'New Learning and Broken Friendship', *EHR*, 112 (1997), pp. 396–411.

29 J. P. Carley, *The Books of King Henry VIII and His Wives* (2004), p. 133. This gift postdates George Boleyn's elevation to the title of Viscount Rochford in 1529.

30 'The Ordre of Knyghtod': TNA, SP 9/31. The translator was Thomas Wall, Windsor Herald. *The Boke of the Ordre of Chyvalry*, translated and printed by William Caxton, ed. A. T. P. Byles (EETS, 168, 1926). J. Hillgarth, *Ramon Lull and Lullism* (Oxford, 1971).

31 J. P. Carley, 'Bourchier, John, second Baron Berners (*c*.1467–1533)', *ODNB*. *Sir John Froissart's Chronicles . . . translated by John Bourchier, Lord Berners*, 2 vols. (1812), preface, cited in S. J. Gunn, 'The French Wars of Henry VIII' in *The Origins of War in Early Modern Europe*, ed. J. Black (Edinburgh, 1987), p. 34.

32 BL, Harley MS 419, fo. 382v. For Lady Carew, see B. J. Harris, *English Aristocratic Women, 1450–1550* (Oxford, 2002), pp. 142–3, 222, 227, 234, 236.

33 Leland, *Itinerary*, iv, p. 116. The work was bequeathed to Poyntz by his friend Thomas Matston: TNA, PCC, Prob 11/28, fos. 205v–206.

34 Starkey, 'King Henry and King Arthur', pp. 171–96; Keen, 'Chivalry and Courtly Love', p. 26.

35 Francis Poyntz's tomb is in Hunsdon church in Hertfordshire. It was while the court was staying at Hunsdon Palace that Poyntz died in 1528. For the poly-hedral sundial which Sir Robert or Anthony Poyntz commissioned from the astronomer Nicolaus Kratzer in *c*.1520, see K. Rodwell and R. Bell, *Acton Court: the Evolution of an Early Tudor Courtier's House* (2004), pp. 260–1.

36 *LP*, iii. 206, 704, 1554. Francis Poyntz's name is not mentioned among the retinue. The plate was returned to him in Sir Robert Poyntz's will: TNA, PCC, Prob. 11/19, fo. 223v.

37 *The table of Cebes* (1531?, printed *cum privilegio* by Thomas Berthelet). For modern editions, see *Epictetus' Handbook and The Tablet of Cebes: Guides to Stoic Living*, ed. K. Seddon (2005); *Cebes's Tablet: Facsimiles of the Greek Text, and of Selected Latin, French, English, Spanish, Italian, German, Dutch and Polish Translations*, ed. S. Sider (New York, 1979); H. B. Lathrop, *Translations from the Classics into English from Caxton to Chapman* (New York, 1967), pp. 46–8. Poyntz translated from Constantine Lascaris's Latin translation.

38 *SP*, i, p. 225; J. Maclean, *Historical and Genealogical Memoir of the Family of Poyntz* (Exeter, 1886), pp. 69–71, 95; Rodwell and Bell, *Acton Court*, p. 24.

39 A. Hawkyard, 'Poyntz, Sir Robert (*b*. late 1440s, *d*. 1520); Poyntz, John (*c*.1485–1544); Poyntz, Sir Francis (*c*.1487–1528)', *ODNB*.

40 Thurley, *Tudor Royal Palaces*, p. 182; Thomas Malory, *Le Morte D'Arthur*, ed. J. Cowen, 2 vols. (1969), i, p. 88, ii, p. 246.

41 Keen, 'Chivalry and Courtly Love', pp. 63–82; Kaeuper, *Chivalry and Violence*, ch. 10. The quotation comes from a song sung at Henry's court: J. Stevens, *Music and Poetry at the Early Tudor Court* (1961), p. 218.

42 *CSPVen, 1509–1519*, 316, 328–9, 340; Starkey, *Six Wives*, p. 145.

43 Anglo, *Great Tournament Roll*, i, pp. 51, 74–5, 91–2, 109–15; Starkey, *Six Wives*, pp. 133–4.

44 J. P. D. Cooper, 'Courtenay (née Blount), Gertrude, marchioness of Exeter (*d.* 1558)', *ODNB*.

45 Harris, *English Aristocratic Women*, pp. 210, 219–21, 234–6; *CSPVen, 1527–1533*, 105 (pp. 59–60); Gasparo Spinelli, Venetian Secretary in London, to his brother Lodovico in Venice, 7 May 1527.

46 *Surrey: Poems*, 27.

47 Harris, *English Aristocratic Women*, pp. 234–5, 307; J. G. Russell, *The Field of the Cloth of Gold: Men and Manners in 1520* (New York, 1969), pp. 164, 170; Maclean, *Memoir of the Family of Poyntz*, pp. 115, 131.

48 J. S. Block, 'Boleyn, George, Viscount Rochford (*c.*1504–1536)'; C. Davies, 'Boleyn (née Parker), Jane, Viscountess Rochford (*d.* 1542)', *ODNB*.

49 She was the Queen's maid of honour in 1530, and perhaps had been so earlier: *LP*, v, p. 319.

50 That Anne was present, and the tournament partly a 'battle for a woman' is David Starkey's suggestion: *Six Wives*, pp. 271–3.

51 B. A. Murphy, 'Blount (married names Tailboys, Fiennes de Clinton), Elizabeth (*c.*1500–1539x41)'; J. Hughes, 'Stafford (née Boleyn; other married name Carey), Mary (*c.*1499–1543)'; *ODNB*.

52 Cavendish, *Wolsey*, p. 29. For a thrilling account of Anne's life and influence, see E. Ives, *The Life and Death of Anne Boleyn, 'the Most Happy'* (Oxford, 2004). For her return to court and its éclat, see pp. 37–45.

53 For the promise of marriage between Lord Henry Percy and Anne Boleyn, see Cavendish, *Wolsey*, pp. 29–34; Ives, *Life and Death of Anne Boleyn*, pp. 63–7.

54 For the chronology of this love which became more than courtly love, see Starkey, *Six Wives*, ch. 41, Ives, *Life and Death of Anne Boleyn*, ch. 6.

55 Lady Courtenay's father was Katherine of Aragon's chamberlain by May 1512 until his death in 1534: J. P. Carley, 'Blount, William, fourth Baron Mountjoy (*c.*1478–1534)', *ODNB*.

56 Rodwell and Bell, *Acton Court*, p. 22; *LP, Addenda*, 165, 177.

57 *LP*, i. 674, 885(8), 1862. Starkey, *Six Wives*, p. 121.

58 *LP*, iv(1). 1032; Queen Katherine to Wolsey, 25 January 1525.

59 *West Kent and the Weald*, ed. J. Newman in *The Buildings of England*, ed. N. Pevsner (Harmondsworth, 1976), p. 483. *LP*, xvi. 947(42).

60 *Devonshire*, fos. 29v–30r. The borrowing was first noticed by Ethel Seaton, 'The Devonshire Manuscript and its Medieval Fragments', *RES*, n.s., 7 (1956). See also Harrier, *Wyatt's Poetry*, pp. 23–55, especially pp. 25–6; P. G. Remley, 'Mary Shelton and her Tudor Literary Milieu' in *Rethinking the Henrician Era: Essays on Early Tudor Texts and Contexts*, ed. P. C. Herman (Urbana and Chicago, 1994), pp. 54–7.

61 J. Kerrigan, 'Wyatt's Selfish Style', *ES*, 34 (1981), pp. 1–18 (the quotation is at p. 1).

62 *Egerton*, fos. 42v–43r.

63 *Ibid*, fos. 25v–26r. A. Ferry, *The 'Inward' Language: Sonnets of Wyatt, Sidney, Shakespeare, Donne* (Chicago and London, 1983), p. 94. I have benefited from the wonderful play of Chris Stamatakis's mind upon this poem.

64 *LP*, iv(2). 4404, 4408–9, 4429, 4440; Leland, *Encomia*, p. 21.

65 J. G. Bellamy, *The Tudor Law of Treason: an Introduction* (Toronto, 1979).

66 C. M. Meale and J. Boffey, 'Gentlewomen's Reading' in *Cambridge History of the Book in Britain*, vol. iii, *1400–1557*, ed. L. Hellinga and J. B. Trapp (Cambridge, 1999), p. 538. For the quotation, *CSPSp*, iv(1), *1529–1530*, p. 366. See above, pp. 289, 549, 687 n.102.

67 'Carey, William', *ODNB*. A. Conway, 'The Maidstone Sector of Buckingham's Rebellion', *AC*, 37 (1925), p. 114.

68 'Norris, Henry', *ODNB*; Rodwell and Bell, *Acton Court*, p. 21.

69 S. J. Gunn, 'The Accession of Henry VIII', *Historical Research*, 64 (1991), pp. 284–7.

70 *LP*, iii(1). 1284.

71 *Ibid,*, iii(1), 1268, 1293, p. 499.

72 Sir Robert Poyntz was surveyor general to the Duke, and steward of his estates in Gloucestershire, Hampshire and Wiltshire: C. Rawcliffe, *The Staffords, Earls of Stafford and Dukes of Buckingham, 1394–1521* (Cambridge, 1978), pp. 200, 210. *A Relation . . . of the Island of England, c.1500*, trans. and ed. C. A. Sneyd (Camden Society, 1847), pp. 93, 95; *LP*, iii (1). 1284 (iv, vi).

73 TNA, SP 60/10, fos. 106–8 (*LP*, xvi. 1487).

74 Eustace Chapuys to Granvelle, 21 November 1535: cited in P. Friedmann, *Anne Boleyn: a Chapter of English History, 1527–1536*, 2 vols. (1884), ii, p. 148.

75 Lord Montague's brother owned 'a chronicle of More's making of Richard III': *LP*, xiii(2). 828. Thomas More, *The History of King Richard III*, ed. G. M. Logan (Bloomington and Indianapolis, 2005), p. 47. Later, Nicholas Throckmorton quoted More's words verbatim: S. Alford, *Kingship and Politics in the Reign of Edward VI* (Cambridge, 2002), p. 91.

76 D. E. Hoak, *The King's Council in the Reign of Edward VI* (Cambridge, 1976), ch. 7.

77 *Surrey: Poems*, 27. 39.

78 TNA, SP 1/138, fo. 145 (*LP*, xiii(2). 772, p. 300); examination of Lord Montague, 7 November 1538.

79 College of Arms, MS I 2, fo. 76.

80 G. Walker, 'The Expulsion of the Minions of 1519 Reconsidered', *HJ*, 32 (1988), pp. 1–16.

81 *Arundel Harington*, 311.

82 Harte was sent in embassy to France in 1519, and was Sewer of the Chamber by 1520: *LP*, iii(1). 246, 273, p. 408. TNA, E101/420/11, fo. 8v. Harte's memorial in Lullingstone, Kent is dated 1581: *West Kent and the Weald*, p. 387.

83 'The Ordre of Knyghtod': TNA, SP 9/31, fos. 18v, 24.

84 Malory, *Le Morte D'Arthur*, ii, pp. 37, 289.

85 Gunn, 'Chivalry and the Politics of the Early Tudor Court', p. 122

86 A tract upon the four virtues of chivalry, *c.*1550: HHL, MS EL 1115.

87 'The Ordre of Knyghtod': TNA, SP 9/31, fo. 22r–v.

88 Statutes of the Order of the Garter, transcribed *c.*1550: HHL, MS EL 1113.

89 For Newdigate's life and martyrdom, see Dom Bed Camm, *Courtier, Monk and Martyr: a Sketch of the Life and Sufferings of Blessed Sebastian Newdigate of the London Charterhouse* (1891).

90 *The Lyfe of Sir Thomas Moore, knighte . . . by William Roper*, ed. E. V. Hitchcock (EETS, 197, 1935, repr. 1958), pp. 6, 80–1; Nicholas Harpsfield, *The Life and Death of Sir Thomas Moore, Knight*, ed. E. V. Hitchcock (EETS, 186, 1932), pp. 179–80) the quotation is at p. 179).

91 For the Oath of Supremacy, see G. R. Elton, *Policy and Police: the Enforcement of the Reformation in the Age of Thomas Cromwell* (Cambridge, 1972), pp. 229–30, and above, pp. 203–4.

92 TNA, SP 1/237, fo. 78 (*LP, Addenda*, 752); Sebastian Newdigate to Antony Denny, date unknown.

93 *LP*, iv(1). 965. S. Brigden, *London and the Reformation* (Oxford, 1989), pp. 279, 319, 349, 384, 418, 420.

94 *Foxe's Book of Martyrs* (1563 edn.), 3, pp. 517–18. *A booke called in latyn Enchiridion militis christiani, and in englysshe the manuell of the christen knyght . . . made by the famous clerke Erasmus of Roterdame* (1533).

95 *Tyndale's Old Testament*, ed. D. Daniell (New Haven and London, 1992), pp. 4–5.

96 K. Dockray, 'Guildford, Sir Henry (1489–1532)', *ODNB*; see above, pp. 174ff.

97 This phrase Henry Howard borrowed from Virgil's *Georgics* and used in his epitaph for Wyatt: *Surrey: Poems*, 28. 30.

3: YOUNG WIAT

1 For general accounts of the affairs of Christendom, see J. Hook, *The Sack of Rome, 1527* (1972); *Charles V, 1500–1558, and His Time*, ed. H. Soly (1999); M. J. Rodríguez-Salgado, 'Obeying the Ten Commandments: the First War between Charles V and Francis I, 1520–1529' in *The World of Emperor Charles V*, ed. W. Blockmans and N. Mout (Amsterdam, 2004), pp. 15–68; M. Gattoni, *Clemente VII e la geo-politica dello Stato Pontifico* (Città del Vaticano, 2002); R. J. Knecht, *Francis I* (Cambridge, 1982), chs. 11–14; J. J. Scarisbrick, *Henry VIII* (1968), ch. 6.

2 TNA, SP 1/37, fo. 214 (*LP*, iv(1). 2037); Wolsey to Francis I, *c.*20 March, 1526.

3 *LP*, iv(1). 2075, 2079.

4 Sanuto, 41: 274–5, 318–20 (*CSPVen, 1520-1526*, 1243, 1245: an incomplete transcript); Andrea Rosso to the Doge and Signory, 10 April 1526; papal nuncio to the Marquis of Mantua, 12 April 1526, Bordeaux.

5 Cheyne's instructions: BL, Cotton MS Caligula, D ix, fos. 164–70.

6 BL, Cotton MS Caligula D ix, fos. 187–9 (*LP*, iv(1). 2087, 2091); Cheyne to Henry VIII, 12 April 1526; Taylor and Cheyne to Wolsey, 13 April 1526, Bordeaux.

7 BL, Cotton MS Caligula D ix, fo. 179 (*LP*, iv(1). 2087). For the manners of the French court, and the nature of English diplomacy with Francis I, see L. McMahon, 'Courtesy and Conflict: the Experience of English Diplomatic Personnel at the Court of Francis I' and R. J. Knecht, 'Sir Nicholas Carew's Journey through France in 1529' in *The English Experience in France, c.1450–1558: War, Diplomacy and Cultural Exchange*, ed. D. Grummitt (2002), pp. 182–99, 160–80.

8　BL, Cotton MS Caligula D ix, fo. 190 (*LP*, iv(1). 2092).

9　D. Starkey, 'Representation through Intimacy: a Study in the Symbolism of Monarchy and Court Office in Early Modern England' in *The Tudor Monarchy*, ed. J. Guy (1997), pp. 42–77; D. Biow, 'Castiglione and the Art of Being Inconspicuously Conspicuous', *Journal of Medieval and Early Modern Studies*, 38 (2008), pp. 35–55.

10　See, for example, *LP*, ii(1). 2406; *CSPVen, 1520–1526*, 1105.

11　One of the code names for Francis was '*celluy que n'a dens* [he who has no teeth]': *LP*, viii. 431.

12　Sanuto, 41: 349 (*CSPVen, 1520–1526*, 1265); Rosso to the Doge and Signory, 1 May 1526, Cognac.

13　TNA, SP 1/38, fo. 62 (*LP*, iv(1). 2136); Cheyne to Henry VIII, 1 May 1526.

14　Sanuto, 41: 440; Lorenzo Orio to the Doge and Signory, London, 7 May 1526.

15　TNA, SP 1/38, fo. 124 (*SP*, i, p. 159: miscalendared to 1525). Wolsey to Henry VIII, York Place, 9 May 1526. The arrival of a messenger from the English King with letters dated the 11th was reported on 19 May: Sanuto, 41: 441.

16　BL, Cotton MS Caligula D ix, fo. 224 (*LP*, iv(1). 2194); Cheyne to [Henry VIII], 21 May 1526.

17　*HMC, Salisbury MSS*, i, 27 (copy of Francis I's oath); Sanuto, 41: 442–6; Hook, *Sack of Rome*, pp. 60–2.

18　TNA, SP 1/38, fo. 162 (*LP*, iv(1). 2205); Taylor to Wolsey, 27 May 1526.

19　BL, Cotton MS Caligula D ix, fos. 195–6 (*LP*, iv(1). 2135).

20　*Surrey: Poems*, 30. 11. Ingenious scholars – not altogether convincingly – have found Wyatt 'signing' his verse, using his initials to open each new stanza: E. P. Hammond, 'Poems "Signed" by Sir Thomas Wyatt', *MLN*, 37 (1922), pp. 505–6.

21　BL, Sloane MS 1523, fo. 26v. This passage was used in D. Lloyd, *State-worthies, or, the states-men and favourites of England since the Reformation* (1679), p. 80.

22　Theodore Basille [Thomas Becon], *The new pollecye of warre* (1542), sig. B6v.

23　BL, Additional MS 62135, fo. 50v.

24　*Quyete of mynde*, sig. D2v.

25　*Surrey: Poems*, 28. 11–12.

26　George Vertue, *Vertue Note Books*, v (Walpole Society, 26, 1937–8), pp. 38–9; M. Conway, 'Allington Castle', *AC*, xxviii (1909), p. 355.

27　D. C. Kay, *Melodious Tears: the English Funeral Elegy from Spenser to Milton* (Oxford, 1990), p. 10.

28　'The Ancestors of Sir Henry Wiat', *Miscellanea Genealogica et Heraldica*, viii (1932–4), pp. 133–5.

29　*Annals of the House of Gainsford*, ed. W. D. Gainsford (Horncastle, 1909).

30　*Papers of George Wyatt*, appendix ii. In 1532 Margaret Wyatt married Anthony Lee of Quarrendon, Buckinghamshire: E. K. Chambers, *Sir Henry Lee: an Elizabethan Portrait* (Oxford, 1936), pp. 19, 23.

31　CKS, U908/T454; TNA, C 1/232/65; PCC, Prob. 11/13, fo. 142r–v. Since there is no indication of an earlier marriage, the presumption is that all the children were born of this marriage.

32　For Roger and John Wilde, see *BRUO*, p. 644. CKS, DRb/AR1–14, fo. 16v;

TNA, C 1/1144/37; SP 1/117, fo. 164 (*LP*, xii(1). 766). *Egerton*, fo. 71 (*CWTW*, i, letter 1); Wyatt to his son, 14 April 1537, Paris.

33 *The Visitations of the County of Surrey ... 1530 ... 1572 ... 1623*, ed. W. Bruce Bannerman (1899), p. 15.

34 Mill Stephenson, *A List of Monumental Brasses in Surrey* (rev. edn., Bath, 1970), pp. 17–18; I. Nairn and N. Pevsner, *The Buildings of England: Surrey* (rev. edn., 1971), p. 104; O. Manning and W. Bray, *The History and Antiquities of the County of Surrey*, 3 vols. (1804–14; repr. 1974), iii, p. 326.

35 BL, Additional MS 62135 (especially fos. 359–66). For a descriptive catalogue of the contents of the Wyatt commonplace book, see *Papers of George Wyatt*, appendix i, and the description in the BL manuscripts catalogue.

36 BL, Additional MS 62135, fos. 364, 361. R. Strong, 'Holbein's Thomas Wyatt the Younger', *Apollo* (March 2006), p. 56.

37 BL, Additional MS 62135, fos. 362v–363; College of Arms, MS I. 2, fo. 95. For the barnacle, see *Boutell's Heraldry*, rev. C.W. Scott-Giles (London and New York, 1958), p. 268.

38 *Materials for a History of the Reign of Henry VII*, ed. W. Campbell, 2 vols. (Rolls Series, 60, 1873), ii, pp. 112, 116, 446.

39 *CPR, 1485–94*, p. 136; *Materials for a History of the Reign of Henry VII*, ii, pp. 296, 297, 304. G. R. Elton, *The Tudor Revolution in Government: Administrative Change in the Reign of Henry VIII* (Cambridge, 1953), pp. 99, 104–5.

40 Henry Wyatt is the seemingly unlikely dedicatee and hero of Agnes Conway's *Henry VII's Relations with Scotland and Ireland, 1485–1498* (Cambridge, 1932). Her admiration owes to his saving of Alington Castle, her family home, as well as his redoubtable service. P. H. Hansen, 'Conway, (William) Martin, Baron Conway of Allington (1856–1937)', *ODNB*.

41 Conway, *Henry VII's Relations with Scotland and Ireland*, pp. 16–22, 28–30.

42 *Ibid.*, pp. 36, 100. H. Summerson, 'Carlisle and the English West March in the Later Middle Ages' in *The North of England in the Age of Richard III* (Stroud and New York, 1996), pp. 89–114.

43 Conway, *Henry VII's Relations with Scotland and Ireland*, pp. 54–9, 65–7, 74–5, 86; appendices xi–xii; BL, Royal MS, 14 B xlv.

44 Conway, *Henry VII's Relations with Scotland and Ireland*, pp. 100–3, appendix xlv; I. Arthurson, *The Perkin Warbeck Conspiracy, 1491–1499* (Stroud, 1994), pp. 134–5, 140.

45 *Egerton*, fo. 71v (*CWTW*, i, letter 1); Wyatt to his son, 14 April 1537, Paris; *LP*, xii(2). 205.

46 *LP*, ii(1). 842.

47 See for example, *LP*, ii(1). 120. With remarkable scholarship, Steven Gunn reveals the grim detail of Henry Wyatt's dealings. The description is his. *Henry VII's New Men and the Making of Tudor England* (forthcoming). I am extremely grateful to Dr Gunn for his generosity in allowing me to read this important book before its publication.

48 *CPR, 1485–94*, p. 219; *CPR, 1495–1509*, p. 16.

49 *Chronicle of Calais*, pp. 5–6; BL, Additional MS 38692, fo. 52v.

50 D. Starkey, *Henry: Virtuous Prince* (2008), pp. 206–10, 216–17.

51 *CSPSp*, iv(2), *1531–1533*, p. 930; Jean de la Sauch and Eustace Chapuys to the Emperor, December 1532. *LP*, iii(1). 734.

52 ASMo, CD, Ambasciatori Spagna, busta 3; Alfonso Rossetto to the Duke of Ferrara, 7 December 1538.

53 BL, Additional MS 62135, fos. 366v–367.

54 For the mind-bendingly complex genealogies of Skinner and Gaynesford, see *Visitations of Surrey*, pp. 59–60, 91–5; *Annals of the House of Gainsford*, pp. 36–44, 86–99; W. B. Robison III, 'The Justices of the Peace in Surrey in National and Gentry Politics, 1483–1570' (unpublished Louisiana State University Ph.D. thesis, 1984), pp. 450ff, 495–9. For the brasses at Reigate church, *Visitations of Surrey*, p. 111; Stephenson, *Monumental Brasses*, pp. 427, 431.

55 So John Stevens suggested: *Music and Poetry at the Early Tudor Court* (1961), p. 133. For the custom of fosterage, see N. Orme, *From Childhood to Chivalry: the Education of English Kings and Aristocracy, 1066–1530* (1984), ch. 2.

56 *Testamenta Vetusta*, pp. 548–9, 551–3. *A Dispraise of the life of a Courtier, and commendacion of the life of the labouryng man* (1548), sig. A3r, cited in D. Starkey, *Six Wives: the Queens of Henry VIII* (2003), p. 694. S. Brigden and N. Wilson, 'New Learning and Broken Friendship', *EHR*, 112 (1997), pp. 396–411.

57 *LP*, xvi. 272.

58 Chambers, *Sir Henry Lee*, pp. 27, 305.

59 TNA, PCC Prob. 11/22, fos. 171–2v (will of John Barret, October 1526).

60 The *locus classicus* for this teaching is Cicero's speech *Pro Sestio*, 138–9, but is also found in *De republica* and *De officiis*. For the *vita activa* and the consequences of idleness, see B. Vickers, 'Leisure and Idleness in the Renaissance: the Ambivalence of Otium', *Renaissance Studies*, 4 (1990), pp. 1–37, 107–54.

61 ASF, MP, 4297, fo. 16; secretary of the Florentine ambassador to the Duke of Florence, 2 January 1540, Paris.

62 TNA, E 36/120, fo. 137 (*LP*, xiii(2). 1011); William Wise, Sheriff of Waterford to [Chancellor of Ireland], 8 December 1538.

63 For the training in chivalry, see A. J. Pollard, *North-Eastern England during the Wars of the Roses: Lay Society, War, and Politics, 1450–1500* (Oxford, 1990), ch. 8; Orme, *From Childhood to Chivalry*, ch. 6.

64 *Book of the Courtier*, p. 41.

65 *CSPVen, 1534–1554*, p. 25.

66 For example, *LP*, iv(1). 1647; TNA, SP 1/233, fo. 18.

67 *LP*, iv(1). 2136.

68 *CSPSp*, iv(2), *1531–1533*, p. 212.

69 For Sir Anthony Browne's authoritative account of hunting, see *SP*, vi, pp. 598–9.

70 *LP*, xv. 449; TNA, PCC, Prob. 11/33, fo. 181.

71 *Egerton*, fo. 54; *Wyatt: Poems*, XXVII, pp. 354–6. See also 'Like as the bird in the cage enclosed': *Wyatt: Poems*, XC.

72 *TM*, 92.

73 BL, Additional MS 62135, fos. 361–2.

74 R. Graziani, 'Sir Thomas Wyatt at a Cockfight, 1539', *RES*, 27 (1976), pp. 299–303.

75 *LP*, i. 4307, 4314, 4800.

76 See, for example, *Testamenta Vetusta*, pp. 563, 621–2, 658, 676, 703.

77 TNA, PCC Prob. 11/39, fo. 88; 11/23, fos. 141–2v; E 154/2/36, fo. 11.
Sir Edward Ringley, Wyatt's successor as marshal of Calais, bequeathed arms
to his nephew: *Kentish Wills: Genealogical Extracts from Sixteenth-Century Wills in the
Consistory Court at Canterbury*, ed. A. W. Hughes Clarke (1929), p. 39.

78 Becon, *The new pollecye of warre*, sigs. A4v–A5r.

79 *Harley 78*, fos. 18v–19.

80 *CPR, 1495–1509*, pp. 660–1. The nature of Surrey society and its politics are
explained by Robison, 'The Justices of the Peace in Surrey', especially chs. 1–3.

81 For the dispute and alignments, see *ibid.*, pp. 67, 81–6, 108–9, 120–4.

82 See, for example, *CPR, 1495–1509*, pp. 517, 557; Robison, 'The Justices of the
Peace in Surrey', pp. 94, 134, 160, 516.

83 The evidence for the affray appears in a series of Star Chamber depositions,
elucidated by Robison, 'The Justices of the Peace in Surrey', pp. 134–42; J. A.
Guy, *The Cardinal's Court: the Impact of Thomas Wolsey in Star Chamber* (Hassocks,
1977), pp. 72–4.

84 For Wyatt's landholding in Barnes, see TNA, E 314/79, fos. 27, 225, 584.

85 J. P. Carley, 'Bourchier, John, second Baron Berners (*c*.1467–1533)', *ODNB*;
J. Boro, 'Lord Berners and His Books: A New Survey', *HLQ*, 67 (2004), pp.
236–49.

86 *Chronicle of Calais*, p. 22.

87 Bodleian, MS Ashmole 858, fo. 28.

88 Conway, 'Allington Castle', pp. 337–62; A. Conway, 'The Owners of Allington
Castle, Maidstone (1086–1279)', *AC*, 29 (1911), pp. 1–39; G. O. Bellewes, 'The
Cobhams and Moresbys of Rundale and Allington', *AC*, 29 (1911), pp. 154–63.

89 A. Conway, 'The Maidstone Sector of Buckingham's Rebellion', *AC*, 37 (1925),
pp. 116–18; *British Library, Harleian Manuscript 433*, ed. R. Horrox and P. W.
Hammond, 4 vols. (Gloucester, 1979–83), ii. pp. 79, 126; *CPR, Edward IV and
V, Richard III*, p. 478; C. Ross, *Richard III* (1981), pp. 106–7, 113, 181; *Annals of
the House of Gainsford*, pp. 86–93.

90 *CIPM, Henry VII*, i, p. 336; Bellewes, 'The Cobhams and Moresbys', pp. 161–3.
TNA, PCC Prob. 11/9, fo. 12 (will of Robert Brent, proved December 1491).
In 1498 John Alygh (a Legh) was described as 'of Alyngton': TNA, PCC Prob
11/11, fo. 27 (will of Nicholas Gaynesford, 1498); Robison, 'The Justices of
the Peace in Surrey', p. 450. Martin Conway, and others following him, state
that Wyatt purchased Alington from Robert Gaynesford's trustees in 1492:
'Allington Castle', p. 354. I have found no evidence of this.

91 TNA, PCC Prob 11/9, fo. 12 (will of Robert Brent, October 1491); CKS,
DRb, Pwr 5, fo. 245 (will of Joan Brent, 1492).

92 *Select Cases in the Council of Henry VII*, ed. G. C. Bayne and W. H. Dunham
(Selden Society, 75, 1956), pp. 141ff; A. Dunn, 'Inheritance and Lordship in
Pre-Reformation England: George Neville, Lord Bergavenny (*c*.1470–1535)',
Nottingham Medieval Studies, 48 (2004), pp. 116–40; especially pp. 121–6.
Bergavenny's second marriage was to Margaret Brent: A. Hawkyard, 'Neville,

George, third Baron Bergavenny (c.1469–1535)', *ODNB*. See the will of Amy Brent, May 1516: *Testamenta Vetusta*, pp. 536–7.

93 *LP*, i. 1664. In 1511 Robert Gaynesford acquired Wood Place, Coulsdon, Surrey from Henry Wyatt – hardly fair exchange for Alington: CKS, U908/T454.

94 Conway, 'Allington Castle', pp. 355–6.

95 CKS, DRb, AR1/13, fo. 54.

96 *LP*, ii(2). 4391.

97 CKS, DR, U 301/E1.

98 TNA, SC 6/Hen VIII/1684; *LP*, iii(2). 2020; Robison, 'The Justices of the Peace in Surrey', p. 160.

99 14 & 15 Henry VIII, c. 32. William Lambarde, *A Perambulation of Kent, 1570* (Chatham, 1970), pp. 475–513, 531 (the quotation is at p. 485).

100 Dunn, 'Inheritance and Lordship', pp. 131–4.

101 See, for example, *LP*, iii(1). 1286, pp. 507–8; iii(2). 3214(3). *Hadlow: Life, Land and People in a Wealden Parish, 1460–1600*, ed. J. Thirsk (Kent Archaeological Society, 2007), pp. 44, 101–2.

102 BL, Royal MS 7 cxvi, fos. 104–5 (*LP*, xiii(2). Appendix 7). Thomas Boleyn said that he had lived in Kent since 1505: *LP*, xiii(1), 937. For the culture of poaching in Kent, see I. M. W. Harvey, *Jack Cade's Rebellion of 1450* (Oxford, 1991), pp. 3–4, 65, 138.

103 Leland, *Itinerary*, iv, pp. 46–7. According to Leland, Sir John Cutt, under-treasurer, had bought from 'one Savelle, a man of fair lands in Yorkshire, then being in trouble', the lordship of Goudhurst in Kent: *Itinerary*, ii, p. 30.

104 *Materials for a History of the Reign of Henry VII*, ii, p. 112; *LP*, i. 54(61), 2022; ii(1). 699; iii(2), 2074(16), 2214, p. 943. For Conisbrough and Tickhill, see R. B. Smith, *Land and Politics in the England of Henry VIII: The West Riding of Yorkshire* (Oxford, 1970), pp. 51–2, 194, 197. H. Wayment, 'Sir John Savile, Steward of Wakefield 1482, d. 1505', *YAJ*, 68 (1996), pp. 181–9. A case was brought against Sir John Savile, and John Savile, 'bastard', in 1497–8 for a cattle raid in Southowram, the home of the Wyatts: TNA, REQ 2/2/80.

105 Borthwick Institute, Abp. Reg. 27, fo, 159; *Visitation of Yorkshire*, p. 275; 'Savile, Henry (1517/18–69)', *House of Commons*, iii, pp. 279-80.

106 TNA, SP 1/233, fo. 55 (*LP, Addenda*, 317); PCC, Prob. 11/26, fo. 50. Henry Savile was being educated at Oxford at this time: *BRUO*, p. 505.

107 TNA, PCC, Prob. 11/30, fos. 196–7. John Savell (Savile) made a bequest to his cousin Henry Savile of Lupset. His tomb, with a brass in new Renaissance fashion, was at Aylesford church: W. D. Belcher, *Kentish Brasses*, 2 vols. (1905), ii, p. 7.

108 R. W. Hoyle, 'The Fortunes of the Tempest Family of Bracewell and Bowling in the Sixteenth Century', *YAJ*, 74 (2002), pp. 169–89.

109 T. W. Beastall, *Tickhill: Portrait of an English Country Town* (Doncaster, 1995), p. 57; W. B. Robison, 'Browne, Sir Anthony (c.1500–1548)', *ODNB*.

110 Wyatt has been found at court in 1516, serving as sewer – wrongly, for this list belongs to c.1533: BL, Royal MS 7 F xiv, fo. 100v (*LP*, ii(1). 2735).

111 *Visitation of Yorkshire*, p. 104; TNA, C 1/690/36. V. H. H. Green, *The Commonwealth of Lincoln College, 1427–1977* (Oxford, 1979), pp. 46–7, 595, 601.

112 TNA, STAC 2/13/81–2 (*Yorkshire Star Chamber Proceedings*, ed. W. Brown, *YAS Record Series*, xli (1909), pp. 110–15). *A Handlist of Star Chamber Pleadings before 1558*, ed. R. W. Hoyle and H. R. T. Summerson (List and Index Society, 299, 2003), p. 220.

113 DA, DD Yar/C/1/92, 95.

114 DA, DD Yar/C/1/59, 86, 87, 89, 91. For the tourn in neighbouring Wakefield, see *The Court Rolls of the Manor of Wakefield from 1537 to 1539*, ed. A. Weikel (*The Wakefield Court Rolls Series*, YAS), ix, pp. xxi–xxii.

115 He was present and sworn on 8 October 1522, 17 March and 15 April 1523, 6 April and 5 October 1524, 26 April 1525, 2 October 1527, 21 April 1528, 7 April 1529: DA, DD Yar/C/1/95, 96, 97, 100, 101.

116 *LP*, iv(1), p. 85. On his second journey, Wyatt reached York by 29 November: BL, Additional MS 24965, fos. 195v–6, 68 (*LP*, iii(2). 3574, 3597). Lord Dacre's receipt was dated 6 December: TNA, E 101/58/6. For the usual route from London to Newcastle, see *LP*, iv(1). 694.

117 *LP*, v. 278(10). Starkey, *Six Wives*, p. 269.

118 Lloyd, *State-worthies, or, the states-men and favourites of England*, p. 76.

119 Chambers, *Sir Henry Lee*, p. 19; 'Lee, Sir Anthony (1510/11–1549)', *House of Commons*, ii, pp. 505–6.

120 Conway, *Henry VII's Relations with Scotland and Ireland*, p. 100, appendix xlv.

121 *Quyete of mynde*, sig. A3v. See, for example, A. N. Brilliant, 'The Style of Wyatt's "The Quyete of Mynde"', *ES*, 24 (1971), pp. 1–21; J. Biester, *Lyric Wonder: Rhetoric and Wit in English Renaissance Poetry* (Ithaca, 1997), pp. 38ff.

122 *CAD*, iii, D. 1308; *KFF*, pp. 43, 44, 54, 55; *CPR, 1485–1494*, p. 45; TNA, PCC, Prob. 11/21 (will of John Wyat, priest, parson of St Margaret, Cley by the Sea, 16 June 1525).

123 *CPR, 1495–1509*, pp. 46, 218, 266, 272; J. Peile, *Biographical Register of Christ's College, 1505–1905, and of the Earlier Foundation, God's House, 1448–1505*, 2 vols. (Cambridge, 1910) i, p. 6; Venn, p. 480.

124 *CCR, Henry VII*, pp. 269, 270, 278, 354, 369; *KFF*, pp. 6, 10, 12, 26, 28, 42, 43, 44, 45; *CAD*, vi, C. 7345. S. Gunn, 'The Structures of Politics in Early Tudor England', *TRHS*, sixth series, v (1995), p. 78.

125 Borthwick, Abp. Reg. 27, fo. 159.

126 *BRUO*, p. 644; *Grace Book B, Part II, Containing the Accounts of the Proctors of the University of Cambridge, 1511–1544*, ed. M. Bateson (Cambridge, 1905), p. 177. L. L. Duncan, 'The Renunciation of the Papal Authority by the Clergy of West Kent, 1534', *AC*, 22 (1897), p. 302. In 1539 Thomas Wyatt presented Roger Wilde to the parish of Wouldham; CKS, DRB/AR1–14, fo. 16v.

127 *Middle Temple Register of Admissions, July 1501 to December 1544*, p. 9; *Minutes of Parliament of the Middle Temple*, trans. and ed. C. T. Martin, i, *1501–1603* (1904), p. 52. That William Wyat, who had a legal career as an attorney, was not admitted to the Middle Temple until 1523–4 makes it more likely that the 'Wyot' admitted in 1517 was Thomas: *Year Books of Henry VIII, 12–14 Henry VIII*, ed. J. H. Baker (Selden Society, 119, 2002), p. 178; *Minutes of Parliament of the Middle Temple*, i, p. 76.

128 *Lincoln's Inn Admission Register, 1420–1893*, pp. 17, 33.

129 *Gray's Inn Admission Register, 1521–1887*, p. 8.

130 For the learning at the Inns of Court, see especially E. W. Ives, *The Common Lawyers of Pre-Reformation England* (Cambridge, 1983); M. McGlynn, *The Royal Prerogative and the Learning of the Inns of Court* (Cambridge, 2003); J. H. Baker, 'The Books of the Common Law' in *The Cambridge History of the Book in Britain*, vol. 3, *1400–1557* (Cambridge, 1999), ch. 20; *Spelman's Reports*, ii, pp. *131–5*.

131 *Spelman's Reports*, i, pp. 223–4, ii, pp. 130–1. S. Brigden, *London and the Reformation* (Oxford, 1989), pp. 116–17; Biester, *Lyric Wonder*, pp. 80–9, especially p. 81; P. J. Finkelpearl, *John Marston of the Middle Temple: an Elizabethan Dramatist in his Social Setting* (Cambridge, Mass., 1969).

132 *Minutes of Parliament of the Middle Temple*, i, pp. 56, 61.

133 A. Wijffels, 'The Civil Law' in *Cambridge History of the Book*, iii, pp. 399–410.

134 *Harley 282*, fo. 249v (*CWTW*, i, letter 33); Wyatt to Cromwell, 12 April 1540, Ghent.

135 A. W. Clapham, 'On the Topography of the Dominican Priory of London', *Archaeologia*, 53 (1912), pp. 57–83. For burials in the Blackfriars, see A. R. Wagner, *Heralds and Heraldry in the Middle Ages* (Oxford, 2nd edn. 1956), p. 142; *Testamenta Vetusta*, pp. 490, 548, 588, 600, 650; *LP*, iii(1), pp. 50, 51, and above, pp. 174, 179. For a joust there, see *LP*, ii(2), p. 1494; for the anchoress, TNA, C1/538/13.

136 TNA, SP 1/25, fo. 222; *LP, Addenda*, 493. A survey showed some of these families living in Blackfriars still *c*.1540: Folger Shakespeare Library, Lb. 362, 370.

137 For the importance of the Blackfriars connection, and the household of Lady Parr, see Starkey, *Six Wives*, pp. 690–5. For Lady Guildford, W. G. Davis, *The Ancestry of Mary Isaac, c.1549–1613* (Portland, Maine, 1955), pp. 86–90. G. Anstruther, *Vaux of Harrowden: a Recusant Family* (Newport, Mon., 1953), chs. 2–3, appendices A, B.

138 *LP*, iii(2). 3649; Starkey, *Six Wives*, pp. 694–5.

139 BL, Additional MS 38692, fo. 52v.

140 *LP*, i. 5483, 5489, 5517, 5553. TNA, PCC, Prob. 11/27, fo. 161.

141 TNA, PCC, Prob. 11/16, fos. 223v–224v; Prob. 11/27, fo. 161. This I learnt from Steven Gunn, *Henry VII's New Men*.

142 Lady Guildford and Anthony Poyntz had married by 1519: *LP*, iii(1). 206(12). K. Rodwell and R. Bell, *Acton Court: the Evolution of an Early Tudor Courtier's House* (2004), pp. 22–4, and above, pp. 249–50.

143 TNA, SP 1/232, fo. 54 (*LP, Addenda*, 196); Wolsey to Henry VIII (undated). Bryan was Master of the Henchmen from 1526 to 1549: 'Bryan, Sir Francis (by 1492–1550)', *House of Commons*, i, p. 527.

144 *CWE*, vi, p. 365.

145 *Naeniae*; *L&L*, p. 263.

146 J. P. Carley, 'Leland, John (*c.*1503–1552)', *ODNB*; J. P. Carley, 'John Leland in Paris: the Evidence of His Poetry', *SP*, 83 (1986), p. 7; Peile, *Biographical Register of Christ's College*, i, p. 13; *LP, Addenda*, i, p. 107.

147 I am most grateful to Dr Malcolm Underwood for revealing to me Wyatt's ab-

sence from the records of St John's. Peile, *Biographical Register of Christ's College*, i, pp. 6, 10. John Wyatt's name appears throughout Christ's College, Cambridge, Account Book, 1530–1545. He was admitted BA, 1517–18; MA, 1519–20: *Grace Book B, Part II*, pp. 152, 179, 241, 286–7, 302, 311, 321.

148 D. R. Leader, *A History of the University of Cambridge*, i, *The University to 1546* (Cambridge, 1988), pp. 281–91; M. Dowling, *Humanism in the Age of Henry VIII* (Beckenham, 1986), pp. 10–11; *Fisher of Men: A Life of John Fisher, 1469–1535* (Basingstoke, 1999), pp. 12–14, 19.

149 Leader, *History of the University of Cambridge*, i, pp. 297–319; L. Bradner, 'The First Cambridge Production of *Miles Gloriosus*', *MLN*, 70 (1955), pp. 400–3.

150 *CWE*, vi, pp. 316–17; Leader, *History of the University of Cambridge*, i, p. 317; Dowling, *Humanism in the Age of Henry VIII*, p. 91; R. Rex, 'The Early Impact of Reformation Theology at Cambridge University, 1521–1547', *RRR*, 2 (1999), pp. 38–71 (especially p. 44); see above, pp. 179–80, 204, 518. Richard Reynolds and John Feron of Christ's may have been associated with the monastery of Syon: Peile, *Biographical Register of Christ's College*, i, pp. 8, 12.

151 Peile, *Biographical Register of Christ's College*, i, pp. 8, 13; J. Hogg, 'Exmew, William (c.1507–1535)'; K. Carleton, 'Wilson, Nicholas (d. 1548)'; T. S. Freeman, 'Dusgate (Benet), Thomas (d. 1532)', *ODNB*.

152 Dowling, *Fisher of Men*, pp. 60–2; R. Rex, *The Theology of John Fisher* (Cambridge, 1991), p. 56.

153 L. E. Whatmore, 'A Sermon of Henry Gold, Vicar of Ospringe, 1525–27, Preached before Archbishop Warham', *AC*, 57 (1944), pp. 34–43; R. Rex, 'Gold, Henry (d. 1534)'; *ODNB*.

154 TNA, SP 1/47, fo. 152 (*LP*, iv(2). 4117: where the date is wrong); Henry Guildford to Cromwell, 30 March 1525. P. J. Ward, 'The Origins of Thomas Cromwell's Public Career: Service under Cardinal Wolsey and Henry VIII, 1524–1530' (unpublished London School of Economics Ph.D thesis, 1999), pp. 64–72.

155 TNA, SP 1/25, fo. 51 (*LP*, iii(2). 2390).

156 Ps. 51.77–9, Harrier, *Wyatt's Poetry*, p. 236.

157 The panoply of worship is recorded in *Testamenta Cantiana: a series of extracts from fifteenth and sixteenth century wills relating to church building and topography*: L. L. Duncan, *West Kent* (1906); A. Hussey, *East Kent* (1907).

158 *Holbein in England*, ed. S. Foister (2006), 142.

159 A royal licence was granted by letter patent on 1 April 1524: TNA, C 82/543 (*LP*, iv(1). 297(1)).

160 CKS, DRb, Pwr 11, fo. 256 (will of William Broadbent); DRb, Pwr 9, fo. 353 (will of Richard Tuttisham). Duncan, 'Renunciation of the Papal Authority by the Clergy of West Kent', pp. 302–3. TNA, C1/1144/37.

161 That Thomas Wyatt the younger was of age by the time of the inquisition post mortem for his father in 1542 gives an approximate date for the marriage and his birth: 'Wyatt, Sir Thomas II (by 1521–54)', *House of Commons*, iii, pp. 670–2; I. W. Archer, 'Wyatt, Sir Thomas (b. in or before 1521, d. 1554)', *ODNB*.

162 N. Saul, *Death, Art and Memory in Medieval England: the Cobham Family and their Monuments* (Oxford, 2001), pp. 116–22.

163 *Ibid.*, pp. 32, 119. For the descent of the Cobham and Neville families, see P. Fleming, 'Cobham family (*per. c.*1250–1530)', *ODNB*; Dunn, 'Inheritance and Lordship', p. 117.

164 Saul, *Death, Art and Memory*, p. 116, fig. 22. BL, Harley MS 6157, fo. 10.

165 For Frances, who married Thomas Leigh (or Legh), esquire, of Calder, see R. P. Littledale, 'Some Notes on the Patricksons of Ennerdale', *Transactions of the Cumberland and Westmorland Antiquarian and Archaeological Society*, n.s., 26 (1925), pp. 135–7. In 1551 an indenture records a bargain between Thomas Wyatt the younger and Thomas Legh: 'between mi brother legh and me': TNA, E 40/6566.

166 HHStA, England, Korrespondenz, 8, fo. 7v; AGR, Audience, 380, fo. 5v (a copy) (*CSPSp*, vi(1), *1538–1542*, p. 314); Chapuys to Mary of Hungary, 27 March 1541. *Correspondance de Castillon et Marillac*, p. 263 (*LP*, xvi. 467); Marillac to Montmorency, 18 January 1541.

167 W. Harrington, *In this booke are conteyned the commendations of matrimony* (1528), sig. D1r. *Marriage and Society: studies in the social history of marriage*, ed. R. B. Outhwaite (1981). In 1548, when John Foxe brought out a tract arguing that adultery should not be a capital crime, this was a controversial stand: T. Freeman, 'Foxe, John (1516/17–1587)', *ODNB*.

168 *LP*, iv(1). 1547, 2319. In 1526 Erasmus published *Christiani matrimonii institutio* and dedicated it to Katherine.

169 BL, Cotton MS Cleopatra E iv, fo. 99 (*LP*, vi. 923); Brigden, *London and the Reformation*, p. 214. Widowed, Elizabeth Amadas would take as her second husband Sir Thomas Neville, brother-in-law of Mary, Lady Bergavenny.

170 *Surrey: Poems*, 18. 13–20.

171 TNA, SP 9/31, fo. 34.

172 *CWTW*, i, letter 1; Wyatt to his son, 14 April 1537, Paris. Transcribing his father's letter in *Egerton* (fo. 72), Thomas Wyatt the younger omitted his father's aspersions of his mother.

173 For the sting in the tail, see C. Shrank: '"But I, that know what harbred in that hed": Sir Thomas Wyatt and his posthumous interpreters', *PBA*, 154 (2007), p. 384.

174 TNA, PCC Prob. 11/23, fos. 191–2 (will of Thomas Brooke, Lord Cobham, 7 July 1529).

175 BL, Additional MS 62135, fos. 55r–v (Singer, pp. 432–4).

176 G. L. Harriss, 'Eleanor (*née* Eleanor Cobham), duchess of Gloucester (*c.*1400–1452)', *ODNB*; see above, pp. 548.

177 TNA, PCC, Prob. 11/25, fos. 259v–60; Hawkyard, 'George Neville (*c.*1469–1535)', *ODNB*. Elizabeth's aunt, Mary Brooke, married at least three times: first, Robert Blagge (d. 1522); second, John Barret (d. 1526); third, Sir Richard Walden (d. 1539): TNA, PCC, Prob. 11/20, fos. 112–13; 11/22, fos. 171–2v; 11/27, fos. 225v–226v (dates of death are estimated from dates of probate). She married Walden sometime between 1529 and 1532: TNA, C1/621/1.

178 *Defence; Harley 78*, fo. 14 (*L&L*, p. 206).

179 HHStA, England, Korrespondenz, 8, fo. 7v; AGR, Audience, 380, fo. 5v (a

copy) (*CSPSp*, vi(1), *1538–1542*, p. 314); Chapuys to Mary of Hungary, 27 March 1541.

180 *Devonshire*, fo. 14.

181 For brilliant light on this poem, see T. M. Greene, *The Light in Troy: Imitation and Discovery in Renaissance Poetry* (New Haven and London, 1982), pp. 258–9.

182 *Egerton*, fo. 66v.

183 Shrank, '"But I, that know what harbred in that hed"', p. 390.

184 Puttenham, p. 187.

185 BL, Royal MS 20 B xxi. George Boleyn's inscription is on fo. 2v; Wyatt's are on fos. 99v–100. J. P. Carley, *The Books of King Henry VIII and His Wives* (2004), fig. 119, p. 133. *Les Lamentations de Matheolus et le livre de Leesce de Jehan le Fèvre, de Ressons: poèmes français du XIVe siècle*, ed. A.-G. van Hamel (Paris, 1905); R. Blumenfeld-Kosinski, 'Jean le Fèvre's "Livre de Leesce": Praise or Blame of Women?', *Speculum*, 69 (1994), pp. 705–25.

186 *Arundel Harington*, i, p. 53; ii, p. 51. This is the English translation of an Italian proverb: G. Giusti, *Raccolta di proverbi Toscani*, ed. G. Capponi (Firenze, 1871), p. 286.

187 For the reasons to doubt that the JP who signed this manuscript was the John Poyntz to whom Wyatt addressed his verse epistles, see above, ch. 9.

4: VIATUS VIATOR: WYATT THE TRAVELLER

1 *Papers of George Wyatt*, p. 27.

2 D. Willen, *John Russell, First Earl of Bedford: One of the King's Men* (1981), ch. 1.

3 BL, Cotton MS Vitellius B ix, fo. 94v (*LP*, iv(2). 3011). For English travellers, see G. B. Parks, *The English Traveler to Italy*, 2 vols. (Roma, 1954).

4 For the League, see J. Hook, *The Sack of Rome* (1972), pp. 59–62; M. Gattoni, *Clemente VII e la geo-politica dello Stato Pontifico* (Vatican City, 2002), pp. 339–46.

5 Luigi Guicciardini, *The Sack of Rome*, ed. and trans. J. H. McGregor (New York, 1993), p. 9.

6 For the first stages of the war of the League of Cognac, see F. Guicciardini, *Storia d'Italia*, a cura di S. Seidel Menchi, 3 vols. (Torino, 1971), 3, pp. 1722–63; L. Guicciardini, *The Sack of Rome*, pp. 14–33; M. Arfaioli, *The Black Bands of Giovanni: Infantry and Diplomacy during the Italian Wars* (Pisa, 2005), part i.

7 Francesco Guicciardini, *Maxims and Reflections*, trans. M. Domandi (Philadelphia, 1965), pp. 78–9.

8 *Machiavelli and his Friends: their Personal Correspondence*, trans. and ed. J. B. Atkinson and D. Sices (De Kalb, Ill., 1996), pp. 403–6.

9 *CSPVen*, *1520–1526*, 1412–13; Hook, *Sack of Rome*, pp. 63–76; Pastor, *History of the Popes*, ix, ch. 9.

10 For the campaign, see Guicciardini, *Storia d'Italia*, 3, pp. 1799–1800; L. Guicciardini, *The Sack of Rome*, pp. 32–40; Hook, *Sack of Rome*, pp. 103–15; Arfaioli, *The Black Bands of Giovanni*, p. 30.

11 *Lirici europei*, p. 343.

12 *CSPVen, 1520–1526*, 1447; *LP*, iv(2). 2657. By the end of November Duke Alfonso was supplying artillery to the landsknechts: *LP*, iv(2). 2699.

13 *LP*, iv(2). 2662–3, 2684–5, 2700, 2715–16, 2731; L. Guicciardini, *The Sack of Rome*, pp. 37–8.

14 *CSPMilan*, 757–9; Sanuto, 43: 701; Guicciardini, *Storia d'Italia*, 3, p. 1818.

15 *LP*, iv(2). 2790, 2805–6; *CSPVen, 1527–1533*, 7, 9; *CSPMilan*, 771; TNA, SP 1/41, fo. 38v (*LP*, iv(2). 2891).

16 ASV, SS, Principi, 9, fo. 220; Francis I to Clement VII, 11 January 1527, St Germain en Laye.

17 *SP*, vi, p. 565; *LP*, iv(2). 2774, 2822. Parks, *The English Traveler to Italy*, i, ch. 11.

18 TNA, SP 1/40, fo. 225 (*SP*, vi, pp. 561–2).

19 TNA, SP 1/41, fo. 1 (*LP*, iv(2) 2875); Sanuto, 44: 182. It was perhaps significant that the datary, not Campeggio, the Cardinal Protector, welcomed Russell to Rome: W. E. Wilkie, *The Cardinal Protectors of England: Rome and the Tudors before the Reformation* (Cambridge, 1974), pp. 134, 176–8. For the protocol, D. E. Queller, *The Office of Ambassador in the Middle Ages* (Princeton, 1967), pp. 193–4.

20 For Casali, see C. L. Fletcher, 'Renaissance Diplomacy in Practice: the Case of Gregorio Casali, England's Ambassador to the Papal Court, 1525–33' (unpublished University of London Ph.D thesis, 2008). Russell and Casali had been together on missions before: at Milan, at the siege of Marseilles and at Rome: *LP*, iv(1). 604, 1085–6, 1410; iv(2). 2720.

21 TNA, SP 1/40, fos. 397–9; SP 1/41, fos. 1–3 (*SP*, vi, pp. 563–5; *LP*, iv(2). 2875).

22 *Paolo Giovio: Lettere*, a cura di G. G. Ferrero, 2 vols. (Roma, 1956), i, p. 116; Sanuto, 44: 103.

23 H. D. Fernández, 'The Patrimony of St Peter: the Papal Court at Rome, *c.*1450–1700' in *The Princely Courts of Europe: Ritual, Politics and Culture under the Ancien Régime, 1500–1700*, ed. J. Adamson (1999), ch. 5.

24 *LP*, iv(2). 2819; *CSPVen, 1527–1533*, 18; *CSPSp*, iii(2), *1527–1529*, pp. 54–5.

25 TNA, SP 1/41, fo. 2 (*LP*, iv(2). 2875).

26 ASMo, CD, Ambasciatori, Roma, 31, letter of 11 February.

27 BL, Cotton MS Vitellius B ix, fo. 57 (*LP*, iv(2). 2879); *SP*, vi, pp. 163–7, 174–5, 331, 353–4, 406–7; *LP*, iv(1). 604, 606, 608, 1017, 1086, 1175, 1326, 1339, 1357, 1410, 1425, 1479, 1534.

28 BL, Cotton MS Vitellius B ix, fos. 61–3 (*LP*, iv(2). 2912); Sanuto, 44: 98, 148; *CSPSp*, iii(2), *1527–1529*, p. 77.

29 BL, Cotton MS Vitellius B ix, fos. 61–3, 73 (*LP*, iv(2). 2912, 2921); *Correspondenz Karl V*, i, p. 230; *CSPMilan*, 775–6. For Venice's caution, see R. Finlay, 'Fabius Maximus in Venice: Doge Andrea Gritti, the War of Cambrai, and the Rise of Habsburg Hegemony', *RQ*, 53 (2000), pp. 988–1031.

30 *Foxe's Book of Martyrs* (1570 edn.), 8, p. 1348; *LP*, iv(1). 570, 909, 1086; TNA, SP 1/41, fo. 2; BL, Cotton MS Vitellius B ix, fo. 57v (*LP*, iv(2). 2875, 2879); Sanuto, 44: 164.

31 Sanuto, 44: 186; *CSPSp*, iii(2), *1527–1529*, p. 87.

32 *CSPMilan*, 778; BL, Cotton MS Vitellius B ix, fo. 80 (*LP*, iv(2). 2931); *LP*, iv(2).

2918. Fletcher, 'Renaissance Diplomacy in Practice', p. 87. *'Molto inepto e non pratico di stato'*: *CSPVen, 1520–1526*, 1215.

33 *CSPMilan*, 782; Guicciardini, *Storia d'Italia*, 3, p. 1824; Sanuto, 41: 84.

34 Sanuto, 44: 187.

35 For a contemporary description of the College, see *Venice: A Documentary History, 1450–1630*, ed. D. S. Chambers and B. Pullan (Oxford, 1992), pp. 43–4.

36 So the papal nuncio, Verallo, described his duty as orator in Venice in January 1536: ASV, AA, Arm. I–XVIII, 6535, fo. 18.

37 BL, Cotton MS Vitellius B ix, fo. 80v (*LP*, iv(2). 2931(2)); Sanuto, 44: 187; *CSPMilan*, 782.

38 Sanuto, 44: 198, 203.

39 *Carteggi di Guicciardini*, 13, pp. 39–40. To Altobello Averoldi, 12 March 1527, Bologna.

40 Sanuto, 44: 209; Rymer, *Foedera*, vi(2), p. 78.

41 The lost capital is reconstructed by T. Tuohy, *Herculean Ferrara: Ercole I d'Este (1471–1505) and the Invention of a Ducal Capital* (Cambridge, 1996). See above, pp. 123–5. For Alfonso's conclusive way with traitors, see *CSPSp*, iii(2), *1527–1529*, p. 851; de Soria to Charles V, 21 November 1528.

42 Sanuto, 44: 325.

43 G. M. Zerbinati, *Chroniche di Ferrara, quali commenzano del anno 1500 sino al 1527*, a cura di G. Muzzarelli (Ferrara, 1989), p. 163.

44 Sanuto, 44: 208.

45 *CSPSp*, iii(2), *1527–1529*, pp. 95–6, 130–1; Sanuto, 44: 245; Zerbinati, *Chroniche*, pp. 162–3.

46 *CSPSp*, iii(2), *1527–1529*, pp. 88–9, 95, 130–1; *LP*, iv(2). 2699.

47 Sanuto, 44: 249. On 4 April Alfonso wrote to Henry VIII of his response to Casali: Rymer, *Foedera*, vi (2), p. 78.

48 *CSPSp*, iii(2), *1527–1529*, pp. 69–71, 87–8, 96. For Bourbon's march south, see Hook, *Sack of Rome*, ch. 8.

49 *CSPSp*, iii(2), *1527–1529*, pp. 131–2; BL, Cotton MS Vitellius B ix, fos. 85–6 (*LP*, iv(2). 2971); Guicciardini, *Storia d'Italia*, 3, pp. 1835–6; Sanuto, 44: 257–8, 271–2, 273–4, 293, 302–3, 325, 326–9, 353. A *paga* ('pay') was a month's wages for one man: J. D. Tracy, *Emperor Charles V, Impresario of War: Campaign Strategy, International Finance and Domestic Politics* (Cambridge, 2002), pp. 33–4.

50 *Correspondenz Karl V*, i, p. 231. Tracy, *Emperor Charles V*, pp. 46–7.

51 BL, Cotton MS Vitellius B ix, fo. 94v (*LP*, iv(2). 3011).

52 For the importance of safe-conducts, see R. A. de Maulde-la-Clavière, *La Diplomatie au temps du Machiavel*, 3 vols. (Genève, 1970), ii, pp. 46–67.

53 BL, Cotton MS Vitellius B ix, fo. 94v (*LP*, iv(2). 3011); BL, Additional MS 28576, fo. 141v (*CSPSp*, iii(2), *1527–1529*, p. 133); *Carteggi di Guicciardini*, 13, p. 51; Sanuto, 44: 272; Brigden and Woolfson, 'Thomas Wyatt in Italy', *RQ*, 58 (2005), appendix 1.

54 BL, Additional MS 28576, fo. 141v (*CSPSp*, iii(2), *1527–1529*, p. 133).

55 TNA, SP 1/41, fo. 2 (*LP*, iv(2). 2875); Sanuto, 44: 325.

56 Brigden and Woolfson, 'Thomas Wyatt in Italy', appendix 1.

57 *CSPSp*, iii(2), *1527–1529*, pp. 188–9.

58 BL, Cotton MS Vitellius B ix, fo. 94v (*LP*, iv(2). 3011). In Russell and Casali's letters of 20 and 29 March there is no mention of Wyatt's capture.

59 *Carteggi di Guicciardini*, 13, p. 103.

60 *Correspondenz Karl V*, i, p. 232; *CSPSp*, iii(2), *1527–1529*, pp. 134–5.

61 For their biographies, see *DBI*, 57, pp. 711–22, 734–44. P. V. Murphy, *Ruling Peacefully: Cardinal Ercole Gonzaga and Patrician Reform in Sixteenth-Century Italy* (Washington, D.C., 2007); A. Ulloa, *Vita del Valorissimo e Gran Capitano don Ferrante Gonzaga, Principe di Molfetta* (Venice, 1563).

62 Brigden and Woolfson, 'Thomas Wyatt in Italy', appendix 2.

63 *Ibid.*, appendix 3.

64 *Ibid.*, pp. 489–93.

65 *SP*, vi, p. 577.

66 BL, Cotton MS Vitellius B ix, fos. 45, 149 (*LP*, iv(2). 3241).

67 ASMn, AG, 1461: Giovan Battista Malatesta to Federigo Gonzaga, 1 March; Brigden and Woolfson, 'Thomas Wyatt in Italy', p. 491 n. 183.

68 Fletcher, 'Renaissance Diplomacy in Practice', p. 75.

69 ASMn, AG, 1903, 26; 1461. Brigden and Woolfson, 'Thomas Wyatt in Italy', p. 491 n. 183.

70 Brigden and Woolfson, 'Thomas Wyatt in Italy', appendix 1.

71 Sanuto, 44: 325.

72 *SP*, vi, pp. 569–70.

73 *CSPSp*, iii(2), *1527–1529*, p. 134; *Correspondenz Karl V*, i, p. 232.

74 Machiavelli had been with Guicciardini since early February 1527: N. Machiavelli, *Legazioni e commissarie*, a cura di S. Bertelli, 3 vols. (Milano, 1964), iii, pp. 1638–43; R. Ridolfi, *The Life of Francesco Guicciardini*, trans. C. Grayson (1967), pp. 168–71.

75 Machiavelli, *Legazioni*, iii, p. 1641.

76 *Carteggi di Guicciardini*, 13, p. 140; Guicciardini to Giberti, 27 March 1527, Bologna.

77 Sanuto, 44: 329, 347, 379; *Carteggi di Guicciardini*, 13, pp. 158–9.

78 Machiavelli, *The Prince*, ed. Q. Skinner and R. Price (Cambridge, 1988), pp. 87, 103–6.

79 *Carteggi di Guicciardini*, 13, pp. 146–8 (the quotations are at p. 148).

80 Sanuto, 44: 350, 361.

81 *Carteggi di Guicciardini*, 13, pp. 141, 149–51, 154–5.

82 Machiavelli, *Legazioni*, iii, p. 1643; *Carteggi di Guicciardini*, 13, p. 145.

83 BL, Cotton MS Vitellius B ix, fo. 94v (*LP*, iv(2). 3011).

84 Finlay, 'Fabius Maximus in Venice', pp. 1016–23; M. Mallett and J. R. Hale, *The Military Organization of a Renaissance State: Venice, c.1400 to 1617* (Cambridge, 1984), pp. 225–6.

85 *Carteggi di Guicciardini*, 13, pp. 157–255; 14, pp. 3–25; *SP*, vi, p. 570; *LP*, iv(2). 3045.

86 *CSPSp*, iii(2), *1527–1529*, p. 138; Hook, *The Sack of Rome*, pp. 141ff.

87 BL, Cotton MS Vitellius B ix, fos. 57, 106 (*LP*, iv(2). 2879, 3065); *CSPVen, 1527–1533*, 74.

88 BL, Cotton MS Vitellius B ix, fo. 85 (*LP*, iv(2). 2971); *Correspondenz Karl V*, i, p. 230.

89 BL, Cotton MS Vitellius B ix, fos. 85, 86v (*LP*, iv(2). 2971).

90 *CSPVen, 1527–1533*, 71; T. C. P. Zimmermann, *Paolo Giovio: the Historian and the Crisis of Sixteenth-Century Italy* (Princeton, 1995), p. 81.

91 *Carteggi di Guicciardini*, 13, p. 165; to Cardinal Passerini, 2 April 1527, Imola.

92 Sanuto, 44: 577; BL, Cotton MS Vitellius B ix, fo. 106 (*LP*, iv(2). 3065).

93 The account of the Easter ceremonial, which was virtually unchanged from the fifteenth to the eighteenth century, is drawn from the diary for 1497 of Johann Burchard, Papal Master of Ceremonies: *At the Court of the Borgia*, ed. and trans. G. Parker (1963), pp. 136–41.

94 Brigden and Woolfson, 'Thomas Wyatt in Italy', p. 495 n. 212.

95 *Carteggi di Guicciardini*, 13, p. 250; to Giberti, 21 April 1527.

96 BL, Cotton MS Vitellius B ix, fo. 106r–v (*LP*, iv(2). 3065).

97 *SP*, vi. p. 577; *LP*, iv(2). 3112; *CSPVen, 1527–1533*, 100.

98 Domenico Orano, *Il Sacco di Roma*, i, *I ricordi di Marcello Alberino* (Roma, 1901), pp. 230–6; *LP*, iv(2). 3089–90.

99 *SP*, vi, pp. 576–7.

100 This was the judgement of the papal nuncio in England: *LP*, iv(2). 3200. For Rome as worse than Hell, see Sanuto, 45: 219, and for the terrible details of its sack, Sanuto, 45: 86–189, 206–22.

101 *Papers of George Wyatt*, p. 27.

102 G. Masson, *Courtesans of the Italian Renaissance* (1975).

103 'A Poem on Bishop Stephen Gardiner': Trinity College, Cambridge, MS R 3.33, fos. 22v–23.

104 *SP*, vii, p. 272. She had left Rome for France before the end of 1526 – her journey financed by 'Signor Bonvisi of Lucca' – and returned to Rome by 1528: Masson, *Courtesans of the Italian Renaissance*, pp. 70–1, 84–6. Bryan's embassy to Rome was in 1528–9: see above, pp. 169–70.

105 *Papers of George Wyatt*, p. 28.

106 *Ibid.*, pp. 28–9. M. Conway, 'Portraits of the Wyat Family', *The Burlington Magazine*, 16 (1909), pp. 154–9. For the iconography of the papal minotaur and the maze, see Jonathan Woolfson's explication in Brigden and Woolfson, 'Thomas Wyatt in Italy', pp. 497–9. I am most grateful to the Earl and Countess of Romney for so generously showing me this picture and allowing me to reproduce it here.

107 *Defence*; *Harley 78*, fo. 12v (*L&L*, p. 202); *Egerton*, fo.71v (*CWTW*, i, letter 1); Wyatt to his son, 14 April 1537, Paris.

108 For the best guides, see J. Woolfson, *Padua and the Tudors: English Students in Italy, 1485–1603* (Cambridge, 1998); A. Overell, *Italian Reform and English Reformations, c.1535–c.1585* (Aldershot, 2008).

109 *Foxe's Book of Martyrs* (1570 edn.), 8, pp. 1346–7; *Letters of Cromwell*, i, pp. 9–11, 19–23. H. Leithead, 'Cromwell, Thomas, earl of Essex (*b.* in or before 1485, *d.* 1540)', *ODNB*.

110 TNA, SP 1/57, fo. 80 (*LP*, iv(3). 6346).

111 D. Javitch, '*Il Cortegiano* and the Constraints of Despotism' and J. Hale,

'Castiglione's Military Career' in *Castiglione: the Ideal and the Real in Renaissance Culture*, ed. R. W. Hanning and D. Rosand (New Haven and London, 1983), pp. 17–28, 143–64.

112 *LP*, v. 574.

113 BL, Cotton MS Vitellius B ix, fo. 103 (*LP*, iv(2). 3090). *Carteggi di Guicciardini*, 14, pp. 3–7; to Giberti, 24 and 26 April 1527, Florence. For the 'Friday tumult', see J. N. Stephens, *The Fall of the Florentine Republic, 1512–1530* (Oxford, 1983), pp. 198–201; Hook, *Sack of Rome*, pp. 152–4.

114 F. Gilbert, *Machiavelli and Guicciardini: Politics and History in Sixteenth-Century Florence* (Princeton, 1984), ch. 7; Finlay, 'Fabius Maximus in Venice', pp. 1021–2.

115 *The Satires of Ludovico Ariosto: A Renaissance Autobiography*, trans. and ed. P. DeSa Wiggins (Athens, Ohio, 1976), pp. 27–9, 42–3, 48. For the literary and social context, see A. R. Ascoli, 'Ariosto and the "Fier Pastor": Form and History in *Orlando Furioso*', *RQ*, 44 (2001), pp. 487–522.

116 Alamanni, *Opere toscane* (Lyons, 1532); printed in Nott, *Wyatt*, p. 460.

117 *Parker*, fo. 201v. C. Burrow, 'Horace at Home and Abroad: Wyatt and Sixteenth-Century Horatianism' in *Horace Made New: Horatian Influences on British Writing from the Renaissance to the Twentieth Century*, ed. C. Martindale and D. Hopkins (Cambridge, 1993), pp. 27–49.

118 M. Catalano, *Vita di Ludovico Ariosto*, 2 vols. (Genève, 1930), i, pp. 554, 573.

119 Tuohy, *Herculean Ferrara*; M. Folin, 'L'architettura e la città nel Quattrocento' in *Un Rinascimento singolare: la corte degli Este a Ferrara* (Milano and Köln, 2003), pp. 73–94; W. L. Gundersheimer, *Ferrara: The Style of a Renaissance Despotism* (Princeton, 1973); C. M. Rosenburg, *The Este Monuments and Urban Development in Renaissance Ferrara* (Cambridge, 1997).

120 C. Hope, 'The "Camerini d'Alabastro" of Alfonso d'Este', *Burlington Magazine*, 113 (1971), pp. 641–50, 712–18, and 'The Camerino d'Alabastro: a reconsideration of the evidence' in *Bacchanals by Titian and Rubens*, ed. G. Cavalli-Björkman (Stockholm, 1987), pp. 25–42.

121 M. Gattoni, 'L'antagonismo ponitifico-Ferrarese come *exemplum* di conflitto tra potere ecclesiastico e laico nell'Italia del Rinascimento', *Ricerche storiche*, 26 (1996), pp. 619–74.

122 Pastor, *History of the Popes*, vi, pp. 327–9, 331, 419–20; Catalano, *Vita di Ludovico Ariosto*, i, p. 329.

123 *LP*, iv(2). 3956; Prothonotary Gambara to Wolsey, February 1528.

124 Titian's portrait is now lost, but is preserved in a copy by Il Bastianino, *c*.1563; *Lucrezia Borgia*, a cura di L. Laureati (Ferrara, 2002), pp. 112–13; Catalano, *Vita di Ludovico Ariosto*, i, p. 468; J. Bridgeman and K. Watts, 'Armour, Weapons and Dress in Four Paintings by Dosso Dossi', *Apollo*, 151 (2000), pp. 20–7.

125 G. J. M. Weber, 'La collezione di pittura ferrarese a Dresda' in *Il Trionfo di Bacco: Capolavori della Scuola Ferrarese a Dresda, 1480–1620* (Torino and London, 2002), pp. 38–9.

126 Giorgio Vasari, *Lives of the Painters, Sculptors and Architects*, trans. G. du C. de Vere, intro. D. Ekserdjian, 2 vols. (1996 edn.), ii, p. 785. C. E. Gilbert, 'Some Findings on Early Works of Titian', *The Art Bulletin*, 62 (1980), pp. 36–75,

especially pp. 62–5; P. P. Fehl, 'The *Bacchanals* for Alfonso I d'Este' in *Decorum and Wit: The Poetry of Venetian Painting: Essays in the History of the Classical Tradition* (Vienna, 1992), pp. 46–87, 355–61, especially pp. 48–9; C. Hope, 'The Camerino d'Alabastro' in *Bacchanals*, pp. 38–9.

127 *Titian* (National Gallery, 2003), catalogue, ed. D. Jaffé *et al.*, pp. 98, 156.

128 *LP*, iv(2). 3112.

129 *LP*, iv(2). 2805–6, 4645.

130 D. Baker-Smith, 'Florens Wilson and His Circle: Émigrés in Lyons, 1539–1543' in *Neo-Latin and the Vernacular in Renaissance France*, ed. G. Castor and T. Cave (Oxford, 1984), pp. 83–97.

131 W. G. Zeeveld, *Foundations of Tudor Policy* (1969), pp. 58–65; J. A. Gee, *The Life and Works of Thomas Lupset* (New Haven and London, 1928), pp. 121–30.

132 J. P. Carley, 'John Leland in Paris: the Evidence of His Poetry', *Studies in Philology*, 83 (1986), pp. 1–50; L. Bradner, 'Some Unpublished Poems by John Leland', *PMLA*, 71 (1956), pp. 827–36.

133 Carley, 'John Leland in Paris', p. 11; *Pole's Correspondence*, p. 61 n. 110; *LP*, iv(1). 481.

134 *CSPSp*, iii(2), *1527–1529*, p. 208; *CSPVen*, *1527–1533*, 98–9, 101, 105, 115.

135 Leland, *Encomia*, pp. 9, 11, 21, 25, 50, 77; Carley, 'John Leland in Paris', pp. 29–33.

136 Carley, 'John Leland in Paris', p. 22.

137 Bodleian, Tanner MS 464d, fo. 31v; Leland, *Encomia*, p. 77. This translation is Professor Tony Woodman's and I am very grateful to him.

138. TNA, SP 1/49, fo. 99v; SP 1/48, fo. 197 (*LP*. iv(2). 4493, 4407).

139. *Middle Temple Register of Admissions*, p. 12; *Minutes of Parliament of the Middle Temple*, p. 76. *LP*, iv(1). 1143.

140 *An exhortacion to young men* in Gee, *Life and Works of Thomas Lupset*, pp. 180–1, 244, 257, 262.

141 TNA, SP 1/48, fos. 185r–v (*LP*, iv(2). 4396). The elegance of Dinham's humanist script in this confession does credit to his tutor, Henry Gold.

142 TNA, SP 1/48, fos. 196–7v (*LP*, iv(2). 4407).

143 TNA, SP 1/48, fo. 91 (*LP*, iv(2). 4326). John Corbett was admitted to Lincoln's Inn on 8 February 1524, four days after Dinham's admission to the Middle Temple: *Lincoln's Inn Admissions Register*, p. 42.

144 TNA, SP 1/48, fos. 92–3, 123 (*LP*, iv(2). 4327–8, 4338).

145 *Foxe's Book of Martyrs* (1563 edn.), 3, p. 502; D. Daniell, 'Frith, John (1503–1533)', *ODNB*.

146 TNA, SP 1/38, fo. 162 (*LP*, iv(1). 2205).

147 *CSPSp*, iii(2), *1527–1529*, pp. 189–90; Iñigo de Mendoza to the Emperor, 18 May 1527.

148 DA, DD Yar C1/100.

149 'The manuscripts of William More Molyneux, Esquire of Loseley Park, Guildford, County Surrey', *HMC*, *7th report, part 1, Appendix* (1879), pp. 600–1. The account book was kept by Robert Hall, who was probably chamberlain to the ambassador. Other records pertaining to Sir Anthony Browne and his

train in embassy to France were also part of this collection. In the dispersal of the Loseley manuscripts in the early twentieth century, some of the early volumes, which included the expenses kept by Robert Hall and those of Browne's 1532 embassy, were sold into private ownership. Since the nineteenth-century transcription is prevailingly accurate, the account of Wyatt's presence in Browne's embassy taken from this lost volume may be trusted. I am grateful to Isabel Sullivan of the Surrey History Centre and Heather Wolfe of the Folger Shakespeare Library for their efforts to trace these manuscripts.

150 *LP*, iv(2). 3124; *SP*, vi, p. 584. *A Handlist of British Diplomatic Representatives, 1509–1688*, ed. G. Bell (1990), p. 71.

151 W. B. Robison, 'Browne, Sir Anthony (*c.*1500–1548)', *ODNB. LP*, iv(2). 3244, 3328, 3484, 3502, 3548; *SP*, vi, pp. 596–9; vii, pp. 6–10, 12–13. None of these letters mentions Wyatt.

152 Cited in 'Browne, Sir Anthony (*c.*1500–48)', *House of Commons*, i, pp. 518–21.

153 George Vertue, *Vertue Note Books*, v (Walpole Society, 26, 1937–8), pp. 38–9. The third Earl of Stafford died in 1751.

154 Leland, *Encomia*, p. 47. The verse is printed in Nott, *Wyatt*, p. xv, and Nott ascribes it to this period. The manuscript version of the poem, collected by John Stow, does not bear the inscription to 'Thomas Wyatt, knight' that it bears in the published version, which led Kenneth Muir to date it to post 1535: Bodleian, Tanner MS 464d, fo. 28v. I am greatly indebted to Professor James Carley for help in dating this verse. Some of the Latin is rebarbative, and I owe deepest thanks to Professor Tony Woodman and to Richard King for translating it for me.

155 Carley, 'John Leland in Paris', pp. 2–5.

156 *LP*, iii(2). 2390.

157 *LP*, iv(2). 3216. The journey began on 3 July, and the Cardinal returned in October: *SP*, i, pp. 196, 235–60, 262–81.

5: DEPE WITTED WYAT

1 *The Book of the Courtier*, p. 50. For 'The New Idiom of Sir Thomas Wyatt', see V. L. Rubel, *Poetic Diction in the English Renaissance* (New York, 1941), ch. 4.

2 For the poet and marvels, see J. Biester, *Lyric Wonder: Rhetoric and Wit in Renaissance English Poetry* (Ithaca and London, 1997).

3 *Quyete of mynde*, sig. A3r.

4 *Ibid.*, sig. A3r.

5 *Ibid.*, sig. C7r.

6 *Ibid.*, sig. C5r.

7 C. Fantazzi, 'Vives, Juan Luis (1492/3–1540)', *ODNB*. For Vives's importance to the Queen, see D. Starkey, *Six Wives: the Queens of Henry VIII* (2003), pp. 174–9, 212–13.

8 *Literae ad Craneveldivm*, 90, ll. 26–39; from Vives, 25 January 1524. The translation is that of C. G. Noreña, *Juan Luis Vives* (The Hague, 1970), p. 87. J. K. McConica, *English Humanists and Reformation Politics under Henry VIII and Edward VI*

(Oxford, 1965), p. 54. *Vives: On Education, a Translation of the* De tradendis disciplinis *of Juan Luis Vives*, trans. and intro. F. Watson (Cambridge, 1913), p. lxxx.

9   *LP*, iv(1). 1547, 2319.

10 J. L. Vives, *De officio mariti*, ed. C. Fantazzi (Leiden and Boston, 2006), p. 43. Noreña, *Juan Luis Vives*, pp. 93, 106.

11 *SP*, i., pp. 196–204. Starkey, *Six Wives*, p. 296.

12 *Literae ad Craneveldivm*, 243, pp. 620–36; from John de Fevyn, 21 July 1527, Bruges. *LP*, iv(2). 3263.

13 BL, Cotton MS Vitellius B ix, fo. 158 (*SP*, i, p. 230); *SP*, i, p. 198.

14 For the early stages of the 'Great Matter', 'our matter', see Starkey, *Six Wives*, ch. 43.

15 For reports on Wolsey's mission, see *Literae ad Craneveldivm*, 241, 243, 248; N. Sander, *The Rise and Growth of the Anglican Schism*, trans. and ed. D. Lewis (rev. edn., Rockford, Ill., 1988), pp. 20–2.

16 Cavendish, *Wolsey*, pp. 44–64, 210–21.

17 For Wolsey's stately progress through France in August and September, see *SP*, i, pp. 235–60, 262–81. David Starkey writes with his usual penetration about Wolsey's mission, and the static royal progress and the plot in England: *Six Wives*, ch. 44.

18 Cavendish, *Wolsey*, pp. 58–9; Starkey, *Six Wives*, pp. 301–3.

19 Cavendish, *Wolsey*, pp. 64, 221.

20 *CSPSp*, iii(2), *1527–1529*, p. 432; Don Iñigo de Mendoza to the Emperor, 26 October 1527. Starkey, *Six Wives*, pp. 303–4, 786 n. 19.

21 By the end of April 1528 news circulated that Brian Tuke would succeed Wyatt as treasurer: *LP*, iv(2). 4194. See, for example, TNA, KB 9/523, fo. 79 (February 1533); KB 9/526, fo. 41 (February 1534).

22 *LP*, iv(2). 3216.

23 *Literae ad Craneveldivm*, 248, pp. 636–9.

24 Thomas More, *Utopia*, ed. E. Surtz and J. H. Hexter, *CWM*, iv, p. 183.

25 *I due primi registri di prestito della Biblioteca Apostolica Vaticana*, a cura di M. Bertolà (Città del Vaticano, 1942), pp. 72, 81.

26 *Opuscula Plutarchi . . . Richardo Paceo anglico interprete* (Roma, n.d.). C. M. Curtis, 'Richard Pace on Pedagogy, Counsel and Satire' (unpublished University of Cambridge Ph.D. thesis, 1996), pp. 41–2.

27 R. Pace, *De fructu qui ex doctrina percipitur*, ed. and trans. F. Manley and R. S. Sylvester (New York, 1967), pp. 134–7.

28 Noreña, *Juan Luis Vives*, pp. 92, 98, 203–5, 305–6.

29 *Vives: On Education*, pp. 158, 230, 253; Noreña, *Juan Luis Vives*, p. 196; D. O. McNeil, *Guillaume Budé and Humanism in the reign of Francis I* (Genève, 1975), p. 14 n. 50.

30 Noreña, *Juan Luis Vives*, pp. 32, 46–7; McNeil, *Guillaume Budé*, pp. 56, 58–9. Budé dedicated his *De contemptu* to his brother Dreux, perhaps the Drogo for whom Leland wrote an encomium: J. P. Carley. 'John Leland in Paris: the Evidence of His Poetry', *Studies in Philology*, 83 (1986), pp. 46–7.

31 *Plutarchi . . . ex interpretatione G. Budei . . . De tranquillitate & securitate animi* (Paris, 1505). *The Prefatory Epistles of Jacques Lefèvre d'Étaples*, ed. E. F. Rice Jr (New York and London, 1972), pp. 137–9.

32 H. de Vocht, 'Vives and His Visits to England', *Monumenta Historia Lovaniensia* (Louvain, 1934), pp. 22–3, 28–34.

33 *Ibid.*, pp. 8, 11, 16. *LP*, iv(1). 481. Leland, *Encomia*, p. 61.

34 *Literae ad Craneveldium*, 251–2; pp. 645–50.

35 De Vocht, 'Vives and His Visits to England', p. 28.

36 *LP*, iv(2). 3140, 3143–4. *CSPSp*, iii(2), *1527–1529*, pp. 179, 185; Mendoza to the Emperor, 9 May 1527.

37 *CSPSp*, iii(2), *1527–1529*, pp. 185–6. Queen Katherine to the Emperor, 10 May 1527.

38 *Ibid.*, pp. 206, 208; Mendoza to the Emperor, 25 May 1527.

39 H. B. Lathrop, *Translations of the Classics into English from Caxton to Chapman, 1477–1620* (New York, 1967), ch. 2, especially pp. 29, 39–40.

40 Curtis, 'Richard Pace', pp. 245–7; R. Rex, *The Theology of John Fisher* (Cambridge, 1991), pp. 149–50, 256.

41 Rex, *Theology of John Fisher*, pp. 148–51, 153–5, 157, 160–1, 165–6.

42 *CSPSp*, iii(2), *1527–1529*, pp. 440–2; Mendoza to the Emperor, 26 October 1527. For the spies, see de Vocht, 'Vives and His Visits to England', p. 28. For this episode, see Starkey, *Six Wives*, ch. 34.

43 *LP*, iv(2). 4990 (miscalendared to November 1528), printed in de Vocht, 'Vives and His Visits to England', pp. 29–32; *CSPSp*, iii(2), *1527–1529*, p. 443; Mendoza to the Emperor, 26 October 1527.

44 *Literae ad Craneveldium*, 251–2, 254; BL, Cotton MS Vespasian F xiii, fo. 150 (*LP*, iv(2). 3943); Russell to [Wolsey], 20 February 1528.

45 De Vocht, 'Vives and His Visits to England', pp. 29–32.

46 *CSPSp*, iii(2), *1527–1529*, pp. 443–4; Mendoza to the Emperor, 26 October 1527.

47 Hall, fo. 171v (where the arrest is dated the 12th); *CSPSp*, iii(2), *1527–1529*, pp. 587–8.

48 *LP*, iv(2). 3844, 3857, 3873, 3876, 3897, 3916; *CSPSp*, iii(2), *1527–1529*, pp. 549–52, 562–3.

49 Noreña, *Juan Luis Vives*, pp. 86, 307; de Vocht, 'Vives and His Visits to England', pp. 29–33; BL, Cotton MS Vespasian F xiii, fo. 150 (*LP*, iv(2). 3943).

50 N. Mann, 'La fortuna del Petrarca in Inghilterra' in *Il Petrarca ad Arquà*, a cura di G. Billanovich and G. Frasso (Padua, 1975), pp. 279–89; *idem*, *Petrarch Manuscripts in the British Isles* (Padua, 1975).

51 *Quyete of mynde*, sig. A2r–v.

52 *Ibid.*, sig. A2v.

53 *Ibid.*, sig. A2r.

54 For the insight, and the phrase, see D. Javitch, *Poetry and Courtliness in Renaissance England*, especially pp. 57, 60.

55 For Wyatt's style, see Lathrop, *Translations of the Classics*, pp. 39–40; P. Thomson, 'A Note on Wyatt's Prose Style in *Quyete of Mynde*', *HLQ*, 25 (1962), pp. 147–56; A. N. Brilliant, 'The Style of Wyatt's "The Quyete of Mynde"', *ES*, 24 (1971), pp. 1–21.

56 *Quyete of mynde*, sig. A1v.

57 *Ibid.*, sig. A3v. B. Vickers, *In Defence of Rhetoric* (Oxford, 1998), pp. 1–3.

58 For Greek rhetorical theory, see Biester, *Lyric Wonder*, pp. 18–19, 37–58, 110–11.

59 *Quyete of mynde*, sig. A3r.

60 *Ibid.*, sig. A3v.

61 *Ibid.*, sig, A3v.

62 *Ibid.*, sig, A3v.

63 A. Ferry, *The 'Inward' Language: Sonnets of Wyatt, Sidney, Shakespeare, Donne* (Chicago, 1983), p. 12.

64 *Quyete of mynde*, sig. A4v.

65 *Ibid.*, sig. A5r.

66 *Ibid.*, sig. A6v.

67 *Ibid.*, sig. A7r.

68 *Ibid.*, sig. A8r.

69 *Ibid.*, sig. A8v.

70 *Ibid.*, sig. B5r.

71 *Ibid.*, sig. B6v.

72 *Ibid.*, sig. B6v.

73 *Ibid.*, sig. C1r.

74 *Ibid.*, sig. B7v.

75 *Ibid.*, sig. C2v.

76 The correspondences were noticed by Brilliant: 'The Style of Wyatt's "The Quyete of Mynde"', pp. 15–16.

77 *Quyete of mynde*, sigs. C5r–v.

78 *Ibid.*, sig. C8v.

79 *Ibid.*, sig. D2v.

80 *An excellent Epitaffe of Syr Thomas Wyat* (printed by John Herford, *c.*1542), sig. A1r.

81 For Katherine's patronage, see McConica, *English Humanists and Reformation Politics*, pp. 7, 53ff; M. Dowling, *Humanism in the Reign of Henry VIII* (Beckenham, 1986), pp. 16–18, 20–6, 30, 223–31, 238–9.

82 McConica, *English Humanists and Reformation Politics*, p. 54.

83 Dowling, *Humanism in the Reign of Henry VIII*, pp. 26, 30; de Vocht, 'Vives and His Visits to England', p. 9 n. 8.

84 De Vocht, 'Vives and His Visits to England', pp. 8–9. J. P. Carley, 'Blount, William, fourth Baron Mountjoy (*c.*1478–1534)'; 'Blount, Charles, fifth Baron Mountjoy (1516–1544)', *ODNB*. For *Harley 78* as the treasury of Wyatt's verse and memory, see above, pp. 552–3.

85 BL, Cotton Appendix lxv. Sir Henry Wyatt's name appears in fos. 45v, 57v, 60v, 83. TNA, SC 6/HENVIII/777, 908.

86 TNA, C 1/723/45; 939/19, 20–2.

87 G. G. Gibbs, 'Abell, Thomas (*d.* 1540)', *ODNB*.

88 BL, Cotton Appendix lxv, fo. 45.

89 Nicholas Harpsfield, *A Treatise on the Pretended Divorce between Henry VIII and Catharine of Aragon* (Camden Society, 1878), pp. 253, 332.

90 T. S. Freeman, 'Harpsfield, Nicholas (1519–1575)'; C. T. Martin, rev. B. Morgan, 'Bonvisi, Antonio [Anthony] (1470x75–1558)', *ODNB*.

91 Sander, *Rise and Growth of the Anglican Schism*, pp. 23–4, 27–8. The work was originally published as *De origine ac progressu schismatis anglicani* (1585). T. F. Mayer, 'Sander, Nicholas (*c.*1530–1581)', *ODNB*.

92 Sander, *Rise and Growth of the Anglican Schism*, pp. 28–30.

93 BL, Additional MS 62135, fo. 52v. 'Extracts from the Life of the virtuous Christian and renowned Queen Anne Boleigne by George Wyatt, Esquire' are printed in Singer, and reprinted in *Papers of George Wyatt*, pp. 19–30, 181–7. Both editions omit some parts of the manuscript which pertain to Thomas Wyatt.

94 BL, Additional MS 62135, fo. 48v. *LP*, iv(2). 4477; TNA, SP 1/25, fo. 222r–v.

95 BL, Additional MS 62135, fo. 48v. The valor of the property of the late Lady Elizabeth Warner was dated 1561–2: TNA, E 315/368/2. For the suggestion that Wyatt's sister was the informant, see M. Dowling, 'William Latymer's Chronickille of Anne Bulleyne' in *Camden Miscellany*, xxx (Camden, 4th series, 39, 1990), p. 41.

96 *Chronicle of King Henry VIII*, p. 63. This chronicler's intelligence came from those close to the Wyatts.

97 Sander, *Rise and Growth of the Anglican Schism*, p. 28.

98 Harpsfield, *A Treatise on the Pretended Divorce*, p. 253.

99 BL, Additional MS 62135, fo. 52v.

100 Starkey, *Six Wives*, ch. 44.

101 BL, Additional MS 62135, fo. 53v (Singer, p. 429).

102 *Defence*; *Harley 78*, fo. 12 (*L&L*, p. 201).

103 BL, Additional MS 62135, fo. 54v (Singer, pp. 431–2).

104 BL, Additional MS 62135, fos. 54–5 (Singer, pp. 430–2).

105 BL, Additional MS 62135, fo. 53v (Singer, p. 429).

106 BL, Additional MS 62135, fo. 50.

107 BL, Additional MS 62135, fos. 55r–v (Singer, pp. 432–4).

108 *Harley 282*, fo. 123v (*CWTW*, i, letter 27); Wyatt to Henry VIII, 9 March 1540, Ghent.

109 G. Pollini, *L'Historia ecclesiastica della rivoluzion d'Inghilterra* (1594), p. 28. See Nott, *Wyatt*, p. xix.

110 *Chronicle of King Henry VIII*, p. 63.

111 BL, Additional MS 62135, fo. 50r–v.

112 For Anne's life, splendidly told, see E. Ives, *The Life and Death of Anne Boleyn: 'the Most Happy'* (Oxford, 2004).

113 BL, Additional MS 62135, fos. 50–1.

114 Thomas Malory, *Le Morte D'Arthur*, ed. J. Cowan, 2 vols. (1969), ii, p. 374.

115 BL, Cotton MS Vespasian C xiii, fos. 327–8v (*LP*, vii. 945); John Mason to Thomas Starkey, 3 July 1534, Valladolid.

116 *Vives: On Education*, pp. 126–7.

117 *Egerton*, fo. 59. J. Stevens, *Music and Poetry in the Early Tudor Court* (1961), pp. 209–10. Hans Holbein made a tiny drawing of a courtly lover proffering the gift of a heart to his lady: *Holbein in England*, ed. S. Foister (2006), 60a.

118 J. Kerrigan, 'Wyatt's Selfish Style', *ES*, 34 (1981), p. 15.

119 *Vives: On Education*, p. 127.

120 R. A. Leaver, *'Goostly Psalmes and Spirituall Songes': English and Dutch Metrical Psalms from Coverdale to Utenhove, 1535–1566* (Oxford, 1991), p. 3.

121 J. Schofield, *Philip Melanchthon and the English Reformation* (Aldershot, 2006), p. 22.

122 D. Fenlon, *Heresy and Obedience in Tridentine Italy: Cardinal Pole and the Counter Reformation* (Cambridge, 1972), p. 29.

123 Richard Smith, preface to George Gascoigne, *Posies* (1575); *TM*, ii, p. 83.

6: WHO SO LIST TO HOUNTE

1 It is a woeful thing to try and describe Petrarch's *Rime* in a paragraph. Perhaps it would be better done in a limerick. Those who have not yet read Petrarch's poetry are urged to race to Robert Durling's edition, with the text and facing translation: *Petrarch's Lyric Poems*. Here, I have made one exquisite canzone (129) stand for many. For a beautiful account of the Petrarchan vision, see D. Kalstone, *Sidney's Poetry: Contexts and Interpretations* (Cambridge, Mass., 1965). L. W. Forster, *The Icy Fire: Five Studies in European Petrarchism* (Cambridge, 1969). For Petrarchan love, see G. Braden, *Petrarchan Love and the Continental Renaisssance* (New Haven and London, 1999). My principal guides to Wyatt's Petrarchism have been P. Thomson, *Thomas Wyatt and his Background* (Stanford, California 1964), ch. 6; A. Ferry, *The 'Inward' Language: Sonnets of Wyatt, Sidney, Shakespeare, Donne* (Chicago and London, 1983), ch. 2; D. L. Guss, 'Wyatt's Petrarchism: an Instance of Creative Imitation in the Renaissance', *HLQ*, 29 (1965), pp. 1–15; M. Domenichelli, *Wyatt: il Liuto Infranto: Formalismo, convenzione e poesia alla corte Tudor* (Verona, 1975), ch. 3; R. W. Dasenbrock, 'Wyatt's Transformation of Petrarch', *Comparative Literature*, 40 (1988), pp. 122–33; R. Kirkpatrick, *English and Italian Literature from Dante to Shakespeare: A Study of Source, Analogue and Divergence* (London and New York, 1995), pp. 124–45.

2 *Egerton*, fo. 70.

3 *Petrarch's Lyric Poems*, 190. 'Doe' refers specifically to the female of the fallow deer; 'hind' more generically to the female of the deer, though particularly of the red deer, and to a deer in and after its third year: *OED*.

4 *Egerton*, fo. 7v Of all the criticism of this elusive sonnet, I have faintingly followed T. M. Greene, *The Light in Troy: Imitation and Discovery in Renaissance Poetry* (New Haven and London, 1982), ch. 12, especially pp. 261–2, 334; A. Fowler, *Conceitful Thought: the Interpretation of English Renaissance Poems* (Edinburgh, 1975), pp. 2–6; S. Greenblatt, *Renaissance Self-Fashioning: from More to Shakespeare* (Chicago and London, 1980), pp. 145–50; J. Kerrigan, 'Wyatt's Selfish Style', *ES* (1981), pp. 15–16; Ferry, *The 'Inward' Language*, pp. 111–13; Thomson, *Thomas Wyatt and his Background*, pp. 196–200.

5 For Petrarchan metamorphosis and the myth of Narcissus, see *Petrarch's Lyric Poems*, pp. 26–32.

6 The reader will find me imitating, uncreatively enough, Greene, *The Light in Troy*. See also B. Weinberg, *A History of Literary Criticism in the Italian Renaissance*, 2 vols.

(Chicago, 1961); M. L. McLaughlin, *Literary Imitation in the Italian Renaissance: the Theory and Practice of Literary Imitation in Italy from Dante to Bembo* (Oxford, 1995); T. Cave, *The Cornucopian Text: Problems of Writing in the French Renaisssance* (Oxford, 1979), ch. 2.

7 For the apian metaphor, see Greene, *The Light in Troy*, pp. 68, 73–6, 95–9, 307, n. 33. The wonder-working bee is celebrated by Claire Preston: *Bee* (2006).

8 Seneca, *Ad Lucilium epistulae morales*, trans. R. M. Gummere, 3 vols. (Cambridge, Mass., 1953), ii, 84; cited in Greene, *The Light in Troy*, p. 74.

9 Cited in Greene, *The Light in Troy*, p. 99.

10 J. Blevins, *Catullan Consciousness and the Early Modern Lyric in England: From Wyatt to Donne* (Aldershot, 2004), ch. 2; Leland, *Encomia*, 10.

11 Canto x.7. Anyone who did find this similitude was reading the 1532, not the 1516 or 1521 editions, for this canto was a later addition. Ariosto, *Orlando Furioso* (Vinegia [Venice], 1539), fo. 39v (this is the copy annotated by Mary, Duchess of Richmond).

12 Horace, *Satires*, I. II. 105–8. I owe the identification of Horace as Ariosto's source to the scholarship and kindness of Dr Marco Dorigatti, to whom I am extremely grateful.

13 See P. Thomson's important article: 'Wyatt and the Petrarchan Commentators', *RES*, x (1959), pp. 225–33 (the description is at p. 230). W. T. Rossiter, *Chaucer and Petrarch* (Cambridge, 2010); W. Kennedy, *Authorizing Petrarch* (Ithaca, New York, 1994).

14 Thomson, 'Wyatt and the Petrarchan Commentators', p. 227 n. 3. Pietro Bembo's *Gli Asolani*, trans. R. B. Gottfried (Bloomington, Ind., 1954), pp. xviii, 35–6.

15 Kennedy, *Authorizing Petrarch*, pp. 55–62.

16 *Petrarch's Lyric Poems*, p. 336; Fowler, *Conceitful Thought*, p. 4.

17 *Il Petrarcha: con l'espositione d'Alessandro Vellutello* (Venice, 1544), fo. 149r–v.

18 *Il Petrarcha colla spositione di Misser Giouanni Andrea Gesualdo*, fo. 236r–v; Thomson, 'Wyatt and the Petrarchan Commentators', p. 231.

19 *LP*, ii(1). 2205.

20 TNA, SP 9/3, fo. 4.

21 R. Goffen, *Titian's Women* (New Haven and London, 1997), pp. 171–92; M. Mosco, *La Maddalena fra sacro e profano* (Milano, 1986).

22 Goffen, *Titian's Women*, pp. 172, 185–6; Mosco, *La Maddalena*, pp. 231–2.

23 S. Foister, 'Paintings and Other Works of Art in Sixteenth-century English Inventories', *Burlington Magazine*, 123 (1981), p. 276. There is also a fragment of a *Noli me tangere* in the internal fittings of the Wolsey closet at Hampton Court: *Cardinal Wolsey: Church, State and Art*, ed. S. J. Gunn and P. G. Lindley (Cambridge, 1991), p. 47.

24 *LP*, iv(2). 3197, p. 1457; 3759; TNA, E 154/2/36; BL, Cotton Appendix 89, fos. 154–68 (*LP*, xv. 650).

25 *Holbein in England*, ed. S. Foister (2006), 86; S. Foister, *Holbein and England* (New Haven and London, 2004), p. 85.

26 The royal inventory lists images of Mary Magdalen, and tiny flagons of shell and crystal picturing her: *Inventory*, 219, 268, 3462. Vessels with covers, shaped

like Mary Magdalen's jar of spikenard, were called Magdalens: *Inventory*, 474, 557–8, 613, 647, 650–2, 694–6, 714–15, 727.

27 Whether the 1527 image was painted or sculpted is unknown: *LP*, iv(2). 3085. *Inventory*, 10601. Sir Oliver Millar doubts that the *Noli me tangere* in the inventory is Holbein's: *The Tudor, Stuart and Early Georgian Pictures in the Collection of Her Majesty the Queen* (1961), p. 61.

28 Foister, *Holbein and England*, pp. 42–6. J. Rowlands, *Holbein: the Paintings of Hans Holbein the Younger* (Oxford, 1985), pp. 61–2. Technical discoveries point to the picture having been painted *c*.1526–7, at the same time, and upon panels from the same oak as the portrait of Sir Henry Guildford: J. Fletcher and M. Cholmondeley Tapper, 'Hans Holbein the Younger at Antwerp and England, 1526–28', *Apollo*, 117 (1983), pp. 87–93; V. Pemberton-Pigott, 'Holbein's *Noli me tangere*: "so much reverence expressed in picture"', *Apollo*, 155 (2002), pp. 34–9. In 1527 Henry Wyatt as Treasurer of the Chamber and Henry Guildford as Comptroller of the Household employed Holbein to decorate the banqueting house at Greenwich: TNA, E 36/227 (*LP*, iv(2). 3104) (the catalogue entry mistakenly names Thomas, instead of Henry Wyatt). For the portrait of Sir Henry Guildford, see Foister, *Holbein and England*, pp. 51, 231–2, 233, 241–6.

29 S. Gardiner, *De vera obedientia* (1536), sig. D4r.

30 TNA, SP 1/18, fo. 15 (*LP*, iii(1). 48). The parson of Great Coates brought a case in Star Chamber when his pet fawn was killed: TNA, STAC 2/3.

31 *PPE*, p. 149.

32 BL, Additional MS 62135, fo. 58.

33 For the literary hunt, see, for example, G. Walker, *Writing under Tyranny: English Literature and the Henrician Reformation* (Oxford, 2005), pp. 287–8.

34 The quotation is from 'My herte I gave the not to do yt payne': *Devonshire*, fo. 75v. Kerrigan, 'Wyatt's Selfish Style', p. 16 n. 32.

35 D. Watt, *Secretaries of God: Women Prophets in Late Medieval and Early Modern England* (Woodbridge, 1997), p. 57.

36 '*Et dit lon quil en est banny pour quelque temps a cause quil revela au Roy que la Dame avoit este trouvee au delict avec ung gentilhomme de court que desia en avoit autreffois este chasse par suspicion, et ceste derniere foys lon avoit faict vuyder de court a linstance de la dicte dame qui faignoit estre fort courroussee contre luy; mais enfin le Roy a intercede vers elle que le dicte gentilhomme retournast a la court*': HHStA, England, Korrespondenz, 4, fo. 313r–v (*CSPSp*, iv(1), *1529–1530*, p. 535). For the likely identification of the gentleman as Wyatt, see P. Friedmann, *Anne Boleyn: a Chapter of English History, 1527–1536*, 2 vols. (1884), i, pp. 46, 121; E. Ives, *The Life and Death of Anne Boleyn, 'the Most Happy'* (Oxford, 2004), pp. 77, 140.

37 *Chronicle of King Henry VIII*, p. 68.

38 DA, DD Yar C1/100–1.

39 The first official mention of Wyatt's office came in September 1529: *LP*, iv(3). 5978(26). *LL*, i, p. 679. The warrant for the Great Seal was not dated until 6 October 1530 (TNA, C82/635), but the King often conferred office orally upon his intimate servants.

40 *The Obedience of a Christian Man* (1528) in *Doctrinal Treatises . . . by William Tyndale*, ed. H. Walter (Parker Society, Cambridge, 1848), p. 239.

41 My knowledge of the topography, government and military organization of Calais rests on D. Grummitt, 'Calais, 1485–1547: a Study in Early Tudor Politics and Government' (unpublished London School of Economics Ph.D. thesis, 1997); Viscount Dillon, 'Calais and the Pale', *Archaeologia*, 53 (1892), pp. 289–388; P. T. J. Morgan, 'The government of the Pale, 1485–1558' (unpublished University of Oxford D.Phil. thesis, 1966), and Miss St Clare Byrne's great edition of the Lisle letters: *LL*. I am extremely grateful to Dr Grummitt for sending me a copy of his thesis.

42 *Chronicle of Calais*, p. xxv.

43 *SP*, viii, p. 166; Wriothesley to Cromwell, 3 March 1539, Brussels.

44 For the decline of good government and of the martial strength of the retinue, *c*.1500–36, see Grummitt, 'Calais', pp. 118–25, 152–4.

45 *Ibid.*, pp. 102–5, 153–4.

46 TNA, SP 1/51, fo. 195 (*LP*, iv(2). 5102, p. 2226).

47 Grummitt, 'Calais', pp. 126, 154–5; Dillon, 'Calais and the Pale', p. 305.

48 *LL*, i, pp. 528, 531–43. Miss St Clare Byrne may particularly stress the decline of Calais in order to exonerate Lord Lisle, Deputy between 1533 and 1540, from charges of incompetence.

49 *Chronicle of Calais*, pp. 111–12; Dillon, 'Calais and the Pale', p. 326. John Leland was absentee rector of Pepeling in the marches of Calais from 1530: J. P. Carley, 'Leland, John (*c*.1503–1552)', *ODNB*.

50 H. M. Colvin, 'Calais and the King's Works, 1485–1558' in *The History of the King's Works*, iii, *1485–1660* (Part I), ed. H. M. Colvin, D. R. Ransome, J. Summerson (1975), pp. 343–6.

51 *LP*, iv(2). 3835, 3865.

52 W. G. Davis, *The Ancestry of Mary Isaac, c.1549–1613* (Portland, Maine, 1955), pp. 263–300. Wyatt later patronized Gilbert Whetehill.

53 M. L. Robertson, 'Wingfield, Sir Robert (*b*. in or before 1464, *d*. 1539)', *ODNB*; TNA, PCC Prob. 11/27, fos. 262–3. The book of hours is now in the Pierpoint Morgan Library, New York.

54 The existence of several Thomas Palmers has caused confusion from which Muriel St Clare Byrne extricates this Thomas Palmer: *LL*, ii, pp. 3–6; vi, appendix i, pp. 253–6. The quotation is from *LL*, i, p. 96.

55 *LP*, iv(2). 4601–2. Palmer had been granted the reversion of the office of Knight Porter in June 1526, but did not succeed to it until 1534.

56 TNA, SP 3/8, fo. 61 (*CWTW*, i, letter 5); Wyatt to Lord Lisle, 7 February 1538, Barcelona.

57 *LL*, iv, pp. 429–30, 432–3.

58 *LL*, iv, pp. 429, 432.

59 *LL*, i, p. 424.

60 *LL*, ii, p. 256; John Husee to Lord Lisle, 20 September 1534.

61 Grummitt, 'Calais', pp. 24, 30, 68–84, 209–16.

62 *LP*, iv(2). 4127, 4199; Grummitt, 'Calais', p. 158.

63 The lament is John Taylor's to Wolsey on 20 September: *LP*, iv(2). 4752. See also TNA, SP 1/49, fos. 99–100 (*LP*, iv(2). 4493); *LP*, iv(2). 4492, 4494, 4887, 4936.

64 BL, Cotton MS Caligula E ii, fo. 148 (*LP*, iv(2). 4988).

65 *LP*, iv(2). 4928, 4961, 4985, 5008; *CSPVen, 1527–1533*, 377.

66 De Vocht, 'Vives and His Visits to England', pp. 34–6; *LP*, iv(2). 4938–9, 4943–6; *Römische Dokumente*, p. 58.

67 BL, Cotton MS Caligula E ii, fo. 148 (*LP*, iv(2). 4988). The editors of *LP* refer to 'Mr. Wat', and the editor of *Chronicle of Calais* to 'master water[-bailiff]' (p. 206), but the name 'Wiat' can just be deciphered.

68 TNA, SP 1/51, fo. 110v (*LP*, iv(2). 5051); *LP*, iv(2). 5008.

69 BL, Cotton MS Caligula E ii, fo. 148 (*LP*, iv(2). 4988); *LP*, iv(2). 5009.

70 BL, Cotton MS Caligula E ii, fo. 151 (*LP*, iv(3). 5171); *LP*, iv(2). 5103.

71 When the Queen sent Mendoza warning that he would be interrogated, he prepared to answer in such a way that he would not 'make it appear as if she had stated an untruth': *CSPSp*, iii(2), *1527–1529*, p. 845.

72 For the Spanish brief, see G. de C. Parmiter, *The King's Great Matter: a Study of Anglo-Papal Relations, 1527–1534* (1967), ch. 4; H. A. Kelly, *The Matrimonial Trials of Henry VIII* (Stanford, 1976), ch. 3; D. Starkey, *Six Wives: the Queens of Henry VIII* (2003), ch. 36.

73 N. Pocock, *Records of the Reformation*, 2 vols. (Oxford, 1870), i, pp. 213, 215; *CSPSp*, iii(2), *1527–1529*, pp. 849, 860.

74 *CSPSp*, iii(2), *1527–1529*, p. 854.

75 *Ibid.*, p. 849.

76 *LP*, iv(2). 4977; *SP*, vii, pp. 117–40.

77 *LP*, iv(3). 5213, 5230.

78 *CSPSp*, iii(2), *1527–1529*, pp. 854–5, 860. Felipe had been Katherine's messenger to the Emperor before, in 1527: *LP*, iv(3). 5307.

79 TNA, SP 1/113, fo. 123 (*LP*, xi. 1436); *LP*, iv(2). 5065; iv(3). 5182; *Römische Dokumente*, p. 70; *CSPSp*, iii(2), *1527–1529*, pp. 877, 882; BL, Additional MS 28578, fos. 16–17 (*CSPSp*, iii(2), *1527–1529*, p. 884).

80 Katherine's letter asking Charles's favour for Montoya was dated 9 January: *LP*, iv(3). 5154. Mendoza wrote on the 16th stating that Montoya had already sailed: *CSPSp*, iii(2), *1527–1529*, pp. 877, 885. Here my account diverges from that of David Starkey, who judged Abell, not Curson, to be 'the King's own servant, in whom she placed no trust': *Six Wives*, p. 230.

81 TNA, SP 1/52, fo. 218 (*LP*, iv(3). 5283); *LP*, iv(3). 5154(ii). Curson was made to wait for his safe-conduct until Abell had had his audience: *LP*, iv(3). 5298–9, 5311

82 *LP*, iv(3). 5283, 5301, 5425; *SP*, vii, pp. 158–64.

83 *Chronicle of King Henry VIII*, p. 5.

84 TNA, C 82/638 (*LP*, v. 119(71)).

85 TNA, C 1/521/27; E 210/9437.

86 *CSPSp*, iii(2), *1527–1529*, pp. 845, 848, 850, 861–2, 974.

87 *Ibid.*, pp. 845–6, 861–2, 881; Pocock, *Records of the Reformation*, i, p. 213. S. Brigden, *London and the Reformation* (Oxford, 1989), pp. 169, 208–10.

88 *CSPSp*, iii(2), *1527–1529*, p. 861; Pocock, *Records of the Reformation*, i, pp. 429–33.

89 BL, Cotton MS Caligula D x, fo. 276v (*LP*, iv(3). 5332); Wingfield to Brian Tuke.

90 DA, DD Yar C1/101.

91 *LP*, iv(3). 5978(26), 6490(23), 6751(24). In September Wyatt received a lucrative licence to import a thousand tuns of Gascon wine or Toulouse woad. A year later there was still some argument about money: TNA, SP 1/237, fo. 81 (*LP, Addenda*, 746).

92 *LL*, iv, p. 432.

93 Satires, II. vii, 28–9, in *Horace: Satires Epistles, Ars Poetica*, tr. H. R. Fairclough (Cambridge, Mass., 1926).

94 TNA, PCC Prob. 11/24, fos. 175v–176; Prob 2/484.

95 CKS, U120/T1/24/1.

96 TNA, Prob 2/484.

97 K. Dockray, 'Guildford, Sir Henry (1489–1532)', *ODNB*.

98 S. E. Lehmberg, *The Reformation Parliament, 1529–1536* (Cambridge, 1970), p. 82; Pocock, *Records of the Reformation*, i, pp. 429–33.

99 *CSPSp*, iv(2), *1531–1533*, pp. 176–7. Chapuys to the Emperor, 6 June 1531. Ives, *The Life and Death of Anne Boleyn*, p. 143.

100 *LP*, iii(1). 206(12); iv(3). 5774(5 and 5(iii)); B. J. Harris, *English Aristocratic Women, 1450–1550* (Oxford and New York, 2002), pp. 217–18; J. Maclean, *Historical and Genealogical Memoir of the Family of Poyntz* (Exeter, 1886), pp. 66–71, 95, 113–16; A. Conway, 'The Maidstone Sector of Buckingham's Rebellion', *AC*, 37 (1925), pp. 107–8, 115.

101 K. Rodwell and R. Bell, *Acton Court: the Evolution of an Early Tudor Courtier's House* (2004), pp. 20–2.

102 *CSPSp*, iii(2), *1527–1529*, pp. 185–6; Katherine to the Emperor, 10 May, 1527.

103 *LP*, iii(1). 704 (3ii).

104 Poyntz's name appears throughout Griffith Richards' account book: BL, Cotton Appendix lxv, fos. 27, 30, 32, 39, 42, 44, 49, 52, 53v, 54, 56, 58, 63v, 65, 71, 75, 78, 80.

105 These were, apparently, the Queen's own words: *CSPSp*, iv(1), *1529–1530*, p. 351; Chapuys to the Emperor, 6 December 1529.

106 *CSPSp*, iv(1), *1529–1530*, pp. 599–600. The editor proposes 'the wife of the young Marquis' (of Dorset?), but the Marquess of Exeter and his wife were far closer to the Queen: Ives, *The Life and Death of Anne Boleyn*, pp. 139–40.

107 *CSPSp*, iv(1), *1529–1530*, p. 710.

108 *CSPSp*, iv(2), *1531–1533*, pp. 177, 214, 239.

109 The phrase is John Guy's: *The Public Career of Sir Thomas More* (Brighton, 1980), p. 198.

110 *CSPSp*, iv(1), *1529–1530*, p. 327. TNA, SP 1/142, fo. 201v (*LP*, xiv(1). 190(6)). For this Parliament, see Lehmberg, *Reformation Parliament*, ch. 5. For Fisher's dissidence, see M. Dowling, *Fisher of Men: a Life of John Fisher, 1469–1535* (Basingstoke, 1999), ch. 7.

111 *CSPSp*, iv(1), *1529–1530*, p. 366; Chapuys to the Emperor, 13 December 1529.

112 'Poyntz, John (*c.*1485–1544)'; *House of Commons*, iii, pp. 147–8.

113 *CSPSp*, iv(1), *1529–1530*, p. 853; Chapuys to the Emperor, 21 December 1530.

114 *CSPVen*, *1527–1533*, 760; Carlo Cappello to the Signory, 13 April 1532. *CSPSp*, iv(2), *1531–1533*, pp. 427–8; Chapuys to the Emperor, 16 April 1532.

115 *CSPVen*, *1527–1533*, 761; Cappello to the Signory, 23 April 1532.

116 *CSPSp*, iv(2), *1531–1533*, p. 440; Chapuys to the Emperor, 2 May 1532. 'Temys, Thomas (by 1508–75)', *House of Commons*, iii, pp. 434–6. Lehmberg, *Reformation Parliament*, pp. 147–8.

117 Guy, *Public Career of Thomas More*, ch. 9.

118 *CSPVen*, *1527–1533*, 773; Cappello to the Signory, 31 May 1532.

119 *LP*, v. 1064.

120 P. Marshall, 'Crisis of Allegiance: George Throckmorton and Henry Tudor', in *Catholic Gentry in English Society: the Throckmortons of Coughton from Reformation to Emancipation* (Aldershot, 2009), pp. 31–67.

121 *LP*, iii(2). 3352; TNA, Prob 2/484.

122 TNA, SP 1/125, fos. 247–56. The confession is printed and discussed in Guy, *Public Career*, pp. 198–9; appendix B, pp. 207–12. See also G. R. Elton, 'Sir Thomas More and the Opposition to Henry VIII' in his *Studies in Tudor and Stuart Politics and Government*, 4 vols. (Cambridge, 1974–92), i, pp. 155–72.

123 *House of Commons*, i, appendix vii. Charles Bulkeley, who was John Poyntz's cousin and in the Queen's service with him, was named in this list: BL, Cotton Appendix lxv; 'Bulkeley, Charles (by 1493–1549/50)', *House of Commons*, i, pp. 537–8.

124 For Wilson, see J. Peile, *Biographical Register of Christ's College, 1505–1905, and of the Earlier Foundation, God's House, 1448–1505*, 2 vols. (Cambridge, 1910), i, p. 8; K. Carleton, 'Wilson, Nicholas (*d.* 1548)', *ODNB. LP*, iv(2). 4521, 4546, 4562. M. Dowling, *Humanism in the Age of Henry VIII* (Beckenham, 1986), pp. 91, 98; R. Rex, *The Theology of John Fisher* (Cambridge, 1991), p. 84.

125 *LP*, v. 529–30.

126 *Correspondence of Pole*, pp. 70–1. Edward Wotton to Reginald Pole, end June 1532. A. F. Pollard, rev. P. Wallis, 'Wotton, Edward (1492–1555)', *ODNB*; *BRUO*, p. 639.

127 In the early summer of 1537 Throckmorton left seeds and a letter for Wotton in Paris: *LP*, xii(2). 45; Henry Cole to Dr Wotton, 6 June 1537, Paris.

128 L. Bradner, 'Some Unpublished Poems by John Leland', *PMLA*, 71 (1956), p. 832; J. P. Carley, 'John Leland in Paris: the Evidence of His Poetry', *Studies in Philology*, 83 (1986), p. 8; Leland, *Encomia*, p. 51.

129 *Egerton*, fo. 40.

130 Most scholars follow G. F. Nott, who dated this epigram to 1532, when the King took Anne Boleyn to Calais: Nott, *Wyatt*, p. xxiii. I have not found the evidence that Wyatt was in their train.

7: IMPRISONED IN LIBERTIES

1 *Egerton*, fo. 17. *Wyatt: Poems*, pp. 400–1. *TM*, 58. A. Ferry, *The 'Inward' Language: Sonnets of Wyatt, Sidney, Shakespeare, Donne* (Chicago, 1983), pp. 76–7. 'Quaint', *n*. 1: *OED*.

2 *CSPSp*, iv(2), *1531–1533*, p. 602; Chapuys to Charles V, 15 February 1533.

3 For the date of the marriage, see D. MacCulloch, *Thomas Cranmer* (New Haven and London, 1996), appendix ii, pp. 637–8; D. Starkey, *Six Wives: The Queens of Henry VIII* (2003), chs. 59–60. E. Ives, *The Life and Death of Anne Boleyn, 'the Most Happy'* (Oxford, 2004), p. 162. David Starkey establishes the time and place of the formal marriage: *Six Wives*, p. 475.

4 *The maner of the tryumphe at Caleys and Bulleyn* (1532); BL, C. 21.b.20.

5 D. Watt, *Secretaries of God: Women Prophets in Late Medieval and Early Modern England* (Woodbridge, 1997), p. 69.

6 *PPE*, p. 273; Hall, fo. 209v.

7 *PPE*, pp. 273–5.

8 *CSPSp*, iv(2), *1531–1533*, p. 618; Chapuys to Charles V, 15 March 1533.

9 HHStA, Korrespondenz, 5, fo. 23; Chapuys to Granvelle, 23 February 1533. This story is not calendared, but Dr Friedmann, who found it in the Vienna archives, tells it: *Anne Boleyn: a Chapter of English History, 1527–1536*, 2 vols. (1884), i, pp. 189–90.

10 BL, Royal MS 7F xiv, fo. 100v (*LP*, ii(1). 2735; calendared in 1516, but properly belonging to *c*.1533).

11 CUL, EDR/D5/8, fo. 13; BL, Additional MS 62135, fo. 52. 'Myne owne Jhon poyntz', l. 53.

12 *LP*, vi. 563.

13 Starkey, *Six Wives*, pp. 462–3.

14 BL, Harley MS 41, fos. 9v–15; Additional MS 6113, fo. 37; Hall, fos. 212–17; *LP*, vi. 395–6, 562, 601, 701. Starkey, *Six Wives*, ch. 62; Ives, *Life and Death of Anne Boleyn*, ch. 12.

15 *LP*, vi. 613.

16 S. Brigden, *London and the Reformation* (Oxford, 1989), p. 211.

17 *LP*, vi. 1468(7).

18 BL, Additional MS, 62135, fos. 53v–54 (Singer, p. 429).

19 TNA, SP 1/81, fo. 67 (*LP*, vi. 1599).

20 *CSPSp*, v(1), *1534–1535*, p. 573; Ives, *The Life and Death of Anne Boleyn*, p. 198.

21 *CSPSp*, iv(2), *1531–1533*, p. 700; Chapuys to Charles V, 29 May 1533.

22 *SP*, i, p. 398.

23 N. Pocock, *Records of the Reformation*, 2 vols. (Oxford, 1870), i, pp. 473–4.

24 TNA, E 30/1025.

25 Pocock, *Records of the Reformation*, i, p. 491.

26 *SP*, i, pp. 397–401 (the quotations are at pp. 398–9); Pocock, *Records of the Reformation*, i, pp. 497–501.

27 *SP*, i, pp. 408–9.

28 *Ibid.*, pp. 415–17. For Abell, see J. E. Paul, *Catherine of Aragon and Her Friends* (1966), ch. 11.

29 *LP*, vii. 135; *The Chronicle of King Henry VIII*, pp. 11, 39–41.

30 'Darrell, Sir Edward (1465/6–1530)', *House of Commons*, ii, pp. 18–19. For the Darrell pedigree, see C. E. Long, 'Wild Darrell of Littlecote', *Wiltshire Archaeological Magazine*, iv (1858), pp. 209–32.

31 *LP*, iii(1). 957.

32 Lord Howard de Walden, *Banners, Standards and Badges from a Tudor Manuscript in the College of Arms* (1904), p. 213.

33 TNA, SP 46/45, fos. 266–7.

34 TNA, SP 1/26, fos. 103, 123 (*LP*, iii(2). 2614, 2636).

35 TNA, PCC Prob. 11/23, fos. 141–2 (will of Sir Edward Darrell, dated 25 July 1528).

36 'Essex, Sir William (*c*.1470–1548)'; *House of Commons*, ii, pp. 106–7.

37 TNA, PCC Prob. 11/23, fos. 141–2. N. Pevsner, rev. B. Cherry, *Wiltshire* in *The Buildings of England* (Harmondsworth, 2nd edn., 1975), p. 378. W. G. Davis, *The Ancestry of Mary Isaac c.1549–1613* (Portland, Maine, 1955), pp. 151, 153. P. Fleming, 'William [i] Haute (*c*.1390–1462)', *ODNB*.

38 TNA, E 154/2/36.

39 BL, Additional MS 45131, fo. 75 (a herald's drawing of Darrell's funeral pennon).

40 Ives, *Life and Death of Anne Boleyn*, p. 147.

41 *LP*, vii. 1013, p. 387.

42 BL, Cotton MS Otho C x, fo. 216. In November 1539 the King paid £66 13s 4d to Blanche Twyford 'for her long and painful service done unto the Princess Dowager': *PPE*, pp. xxxvi–xxxvii.

43 *Defence*; *Harley 78*, fo. 14 (*L&L*, p. 206).

44 HHStA, England, Korrespondenz, 8, fo. 7v; AGR, Audience, 380, fo. 5v (*CSPSp*, vi(1), *1538–1542*, p. 314); Chapuys to Mary of Hungary, 27 March 1541.

45 For exquisite distinctions between the Lover-as-Poet and the Poet-as-Lover in the 'game of love', see J. Stevens, *Music and Poetry in the Early Tudor Court* (1961), pp. 206ff.

46 *TM*, 65; *Collected Poems of Wyatt*, LII, p. 307; Nott, *Works*, p. 547. See above, pp. 146–7, 186. The version included here is from *Devonshire*, fo. 16v.

47 *TM*, 74; *Blage*, fo. 70. R. M. Warnicke, 'Seymour [née Stanhope], Anne, duchess of Somerset (*c*.1510–1587)', *ODNB*.

48 *Devonshire*, fos. 6v–7.

49 *Ibid.*, fos. 70v–71.

50 *Egerton*, fos. 42v–43r.

51 I am very grateful to Dr Susan Foister for her generous advice concerning the portrait of 'Lady Heneghem'. For the complex problem of the hands in *Devonshire*, and the nature of the game of love played within it, see H. Baron, 'Mary (Howard) Fitzroy's Hand in the Devonshire Manuscript', *RES*, 45 (1994), pp. 318–35; E. Heale, 'Women and the Courtly Love Lyric: The Devonshire MS (BL Additional 17492)', *MLR*, 90 (1995), pp. 296–313; J. Powell, 'Marginalia, Authorship, and Editing in the Manuscripts of Thomas

Wyatt's Verse', *English Manuscript Studies*, 15 (2009), especially pp. 3–8. Professor Remley provides a vivid portrayal of Mary Shelton, although he mistakes for hers the hand which almost certainly belonged to Lady Margaret Douglas: P. G. Remley, 'Mary Shelton and her Tudor Literary Milieu' in *Rethinking the Henrician Era: Essays on Early Tudor Texts and Contexts*, ed. P. C. Herman (Urbana and Chicago, 1994), pp. 40–77. E. Heale, 'Shelton, Mary (married names Mary Heveningham, Lady Heveningham; Mary Appleyard) (1510x15–1570/1)', *ODNB*.

52 *LP*, vii. 1193, 1279, 1297 (p. 498), 1554; viii. 263 (p. 104). The *demoiselle* was said to be the Queen's cousin, daughter of the governess of the Lady Mary. This leaves two candidates: Mary and Margaret Shelton. Mary is the more likely. Professor Ives explains the circumstances of this courtly romance: *Life and Death of Anne Boleyn*, pp. 192–5.

53 *LL*, v, p. 10; John Husee to Lord Lisle, 3 January 1538.

54 *SP*, viii, p. 7; John Hutton to Cromwell, 9 December 1537, Brussels.

55 TNA, SP 1/223, fo. 36 (*LP*, xxi(1). 1426); *Surrey: Poems*, 35. 5–6.

56 The date of the dinner is given as Tuesday 13 May, but in 1534 Tuesday fell on the 12th. CUL, EDR, D5/8, fo. 13. Nicholas Shaxton had been appointed the Queen's almoner in April 1534: *LP*, vii. 549.

57 For Goodrich, Shaxton and Butts, and Anne's patronage, see Ives, *Life and Death of Anne Boleyn*, especially pp. 261, 266, 275. In the Tower, Anne hoped that her bishops would appeal to the King for her: Singer, p. 457.

58 This discussion closely follows the sensitive accounts of Anne's promotion of reform and her personal religion in Ives, *Life and Death of Anne Boleyn*, chs. 18–19, and M. Dowling, 'Anne Boleyn and Reform', *JEH*, 35 (1984), pp. 30–46; 'William Latymer's Cronickille of Anne Bulleyne', ed. M. Dowling, *Camden Miscellany*, xxx (Camden Society, 4th series, 39, 1990), pp. 29–44.

59 *CSPFor, 1558–9*, 1303, p. 532.

60 'William Latymer's Cronickille', p. 63.

61 These works have been brilliantly identified and described by James Carley and Eric Ives: J. P. Carley, '"Her moost loving and fryndely brother sendeth gre-tyng": Anne Boleyn's manuscripts and their sources' in *Illuminating the Book*, ed. M. P. Brown and S. McKendrick (1998), pp. 261–80; Ives, *Life and Death of Anne Boleyn*, pp. 240–4, 270–3, 279–83.

62 S. Bentley, *Excerpta Historica, or, Illustrations of English History* (1831), p. 263; Constantine, 'Memorial', p. 65.

63 Carley, '"Her moost loving and fryndely brother"', p. 277 n. 43.

64 BL, Cotton MS Vespasian F iii, fo. 15v (*LP*, iv(3), appendix 197).

65 Brigden, *London and the Reformation*, pp. 106–28.

66 *LP*, vii. 664; x. 876(8).

67 Carley, '"Her moost loving and fryndely brother"', p. 272; Ives, *Life and Death of Anne Boleyn*, pp. 278–9.

68 Louis le Brun, 'Ung Petit Traicte en Francoys', cited by Ives, *Life and Death of Anne Boleyn*, p. 269.

69 *The Courte of Venus* (*c.*1537–9), fo. 4r–v. *The Court of Venus*, ed. R. A. Fraser

(Durham, North Carolina, 1955); Harrier, *Wyatt's Poetry*, pp. 80–5. Robert Singleton, *A sermon preached at Poules Crosse . . . 1535*. Brigden, *London and the Reformation*, pp. 348–52; A. Ryrie, 'Singleton, Robert (*d.* 1544)', *ODNB*.

70 *LP*, vi. 585.

71 Ives, *Life and Death of Anne Boleyn*, pp. 6–7, 37–9; 'William Latymer's Cronickille', pp. 62–3.

72 *Egerton*, fos. 43v–44. It was attributed 'By the Earl of ROCHEFORD. In Manuscript, dated 1564': *Arundel Harington*, i, pp. 392–3, 24–5, 391; *TM*, ii, pp. 83, 87. This song is also copied in *Devonshire*, fo. 14v, and *Blage*, fo. 125v.

73 For doubt about the ascription, see J. Powell, 'Editing Wyatts: Reassessing the Textual State of Sir Thomas Wyatt's Poetry', *Poetica*, 71 (2009), pp. 100–1.

74 *The Court of Virtue by John Hall*, ed. R. A. Fraser (New Brunswick, 1961), pp. 164–9; Stevens, *Music and Poetry*, pp. 135–8; *Wyatt: Poems*, pp. 407–8.

75 *CSPSp*, v(2), *1536–1538*, p. 91.

76 *Pasquil the Playne* in Thomas Elyot, *Four Political Treatises*, ed. L. Gottesman (Gainesville, 1967), pp. 41–100. For this tract, see G. Walker, *Writing under Tyranny: English Literature and the Henrician Reformation* (Oxford, 2005), pp. 180–95.

77 *Pasquil the Playne*, pp. 46–51.

78 S. Foister, *Holbein and England* (New Haven and London, 2004), fig. 157, pp. 151–2.

79 TNA, SP 1/123, fos. 125–8 (*LP*, xii(2). 361). The editors of *LP* date his examination to 1537, but the interrogation of Phillips took place a year earlier: Brigden, *London and the Reformation*, pp. 261–3.

80 *Egerton*, fo. 4r–v. Peculiar difficulties attend the transcription of this poem. For a revelatory discussion, see M. Nolan, 'Style' in *Cultural Transformations: Medieval and Renaissance in Literary History*, ed. B. Cummings and J. Simpson (Oxford, 2010), especially pp. 409–19.

81 *Devonshire*, fo. 74v.

82 CCC, Parker MS 168, fo. 209. See below, p. 682 n.154.

83 CUL, EDR, D5/8, fo. 4v. *LL*, ii, p. 130; John Husee to Lord Lisle, 20 April 1534.

84 For the law of treason, see G. R. Elton, *Policy and Police: the Enforcement of the Reformation in the Age of Thomas Cromwell* (Cambridge, 1972), ch. 6.

85 *LL*, ii, p. 130; Elton, *Policy and Police*, pp. 222–3.

86 LMA, COL, CA/01/01/09, fos. 55, 56v. Brigden, *London and the Reformation*, pp. 222–4.

87 *LP*, vii. 665.

88 Elyot, *Pasquil the Playne*, pp. 43, 65. The figure of Harpocrates may have been inspired by the new Archbishop of Canterbury: MacCulloch, *Cranmer*, pp. 80–2.

89 For the enforcement and acceptance of the Reformation, see especially Elton, *Policy and Police*; E. Shagan, *Popular Politics and the English Reformation* (Cambridge, 2003).

90 TNA, SP 1/162, fo. 127 (*LP*, xv. 1029(21)).

91 *Correspondence of More*, pp. 537, 542, 550.

92 *Ibid.*, p. 552.

93 For the oath contrived for More and the case against him, see Elton, *Policy and Police*, pp. 222–5, 227, 400–20.

94 *Correspondence of More*, pp. 536, 542.

95 *Ibid.*, pp. 532–8.

96 Christ's College, Cambridge, Account Book, 1530–1545, fo. 68v (22 April 1533–21 April 1534).

97 Juan Luis Vives to Erasmus, 10 May 1534, Bruges. Cited in M. Bataillon, *Érasme et l'Espagne*, ed. C. Amiel and D. Devoto, 3 vols. (Genève, 1991), i, p. 529.

98 *LL*, ii, p. 158.

99 See, *inter alia*, *LP*, ii(2). 4114; iii(1). 644(1); iv(1). 390(30), 521; v. 1139(11); vii. 951; viii. 149(83); x. 806; TNA, SP 1/112, fos. 222–5v (*LP*, xi. 1334); xiii(1). 696; xiii(2). 578; xv. 1029(39), 1030(67); xvi. 760; *Addenda*, 1074, 1201, 1516. R. W. Hoyle, 'The Fortunes of the Tempest Family of Bracewell and Bowling in the Sixteenth Century', *YAJ*, 74 (2002), p. 180.

100 *LL*, v, p. 95; Thomas Warley to Lady Lisle, 7 April 1538.

101 S. Brigden, 'Henry Howard, Earl of Surrey, and the "Conjured League"', *HJ*, 37 (1994), pp. 520–1, 532. For Legh, see above, pp. 135, 377–8, 515–16; for Knyvet's poetry, see Harrier, *Wyatt's Poetry*, pp. 36, 51.

102 Foister, *Holbein and England*, fig. 234, pp. 140, 234, 236; TNA, SP 1/92, fo. 9 (*LP*, viii. 618).

103 The phrases are Henry Howard's: *Surrey: Poems*, 26.8; 34.1; 36.1.

104 Foxe, *AM*, vii, p. 508.

105 *CSPVen, 1527–1533*, 761; Carlo Capello to the Signory, 23 April 1532; *LP*, v. 1139(11), 1183. In 1564 Southwell left this cross to Surrey's son, the fourth Duke of Norfolk: Foister, *Holbein and England*, p. 240.

106. *APC*, i, pp. 17, 19; Nott, *Surrey*, pp. xlix–l, 167–9.

107 Brigden, 'Henry Howard, Earl of Surrey, and the "Conjured League"', pp. 521–2.

108 Florencius Voluscenus, *De animi tranquillitate dialogus* (Lyon, 1543), pp. 94–5; D. Starkey, 'The Court: Castiglione's Ideal and Tudor Reality: Being a Discussion of Sir Thomas Wyatt's *Satire addressed to Sir Francis Bryan*', *JCWI*, 45 (1982), p. 236.

109 *LP*, v. 431, 1334; S. J. Gunn, *Charles Brandon, Duke of Suffolk* (Oxford, 1988), p. 204.

110 TNA, KB 9/523/105; SP 1/238, fo. 73 (*LP*, *Addenda*, 848).

111 *LP*, vii. 761(11); viii. 149(83).

112 TNA, SP 1/88, fo. 110r–v (*LP*, vii. 1672(2)). M. L. Bush identified the hand of the scribbled notes: 'The Rise to Power of Edward Seymour, Protector Somerset, 1500–1547' (unpublished University of Cambridge Ph.D. thesis, 1965), pp. 55–9.

113 *PPE*, pp. 17, 32, 33, 37, 190, 204, 205, 267, 270, 315–16; *LP*, x. 869; TNA, PCC, Prob 11/29, fos. 120v–121 (will of Sir William Pickering senior); C 1/347/16; 349/38; 351/74; 355/69; 906/26–8; 1022/57.

114 TNA, Prob 2/484; *LP*, v. 1285(v). In a mysterious bill belonging to *c.*1534 Wyatt's name appears at the head of a list with £200 – almost certainly of debt – recorded: TNA, SP 1/88, fo. 115v (*LP*, vii. 1674).

115 *Egerton*, fo. 71v (*CWTW*, i, letter 1); Wyatt to his son, 14 April 1537, Paris.

116 TNA, E 210/9917.

117 For the legal status of uses, the crown's campaign against them and Lord Dacre's case, see E. Ives, 'The Genesis of the Statute of Uses', *EHR*, 82 (1967), pp. 673–97; *Spelman's Reports*, ii, pp. 140, 195–204; M. McGlynn, *The Royal Prerogative and the Learning of the Inns of Court* (Cambridge, 2003), ch. 4; A. Hawkyard, 'Neville, George, third Baron Bergavenny (*c.*1469–1535)', *ODNB*.

118 Geoffrey Chaucer, *Troilus and Criseyde*, ed. B. Windeatt (2003), 2: 50, 57–8.

119 *Egerton*, fo. 64v. P. Thomson, *Sir Thomas Wyatt and His Background* (1964), appendix D.

120 D. Starkey, 'King Henry and King Arthur' in *Arthurian Literature*, xvi, ed. J. P. Carley and F. Riddy (1998), pp. 171–96 (the quotation is at p. 189).

121 Thomas Malory, *Le Morte D'Arthur*, ed. J. Cowan, 2 vols. (1969), i, pp. xx–xxii, 58–9, 155; ii, pp. 103, 425, 456, 509.

122 *LL*, ii, p. 158.

123 *LP*, vii. 922(17). For the seven hundreds, see *Early Modern Kent, 1540–1640*, ed. M. L. Zell (Woodbridge, 2000), p. 10.

124 Ives, *Life and Death of Anne Boleyn*, pp. 106–7.

125 M. Mercer, 'Sir Richard Clement, Ightham Mote, and local disorder in the early Tudor period', *AC*, 115 (1995), pp. 155–74.

126 TNA, SP 1/88, fo. 76v (*LP*, vii. 1647); xiii(2), 702, 804 (p. 317).

127 TNA, SP 1/84, fos. 138, 140; SP 1/88, fo. 145 (*LP*, vii. 788, 789, appendix 27); Mercer, 'Sir Richard Clement', p. 169.

128 *LP*, vii. 922(16), 823.

129 *LP*, vii. 789. The description is Sir William Fitzwilliam's, writing to Cromwell in August 1533: *LP*, vi. 965.

130 TNA, SP 1/84, fo. 156; SP 1/86, fo. 30v (*LP*, vii. 813, 1251). Wyatt acted as intermediary in 1535 when Cromwell sent a command to Dudley.

131 Cavendish, *Wolsey*, p. 105; *Gabriel Harvey's Marginalia*, ed. G. C. Moore-Smith (Stratford on Avon, 1913). For the best appraisal of Cromwell's character, intellect, and aspirations, see G. R. Elton, *Reform and Renewal: Thomas Cromwell and the Common Weal* (Cambridge, 1973), ch. 2; 'Thomas Cromwell Redivivus' in his *Studies in Tudor and Stuart Politics and Government*, 4 vols. (Cambridge, 1974–92), iii, pp. 183–215.

132 For a powerful vision of the King's own strategy and mastery of policy, see G. Bernard, *The King's Reformation: Henry VIII and the Remaking of the English Church* (New Haven and London, 2005).

133 MacCulloch, *Cranmer*, p. 135.

134 *LP*, ix. 862.

135 *Letters of Cromwell*, i, pp. 56–63; *LP*, vi. 299, pp. 136, 137, 139; x. 979; *KFF*, p. 106; M. L. Robertson, 'Profit and power in the development of Thomas Cromwell's landed estates', *JBS*, 29 (1990), pp. 317–46.

136 *LP*, viii. 142, 366. *LL*, iv, p. 174; John Husee to Lady Lisle, 16 October 1537.

137 TNA, SP 1/84, fo. 156 (*LP*, vii. 813).

138 The complex story is told by M. C. Erler, 'The Abbess of Malling's Gift Manuscript (1520)' in *Prestige, Authority and Power in Late Medieval Manuscripts and Texts*, ed. F. Riddy (Woodbridge, 2000), pp. 147–57.

139 TNA, SP 1/90, fos. 142, 151, 170–1; SP 1/91, fo. 61 (*LP*, viii. 230, 249, 275, 349).

140 TNA, SP 1/90, fo. 170 (*LP*, viii. 275). The italics are mine.

141 Elton, *Reform and Renewal*, p. 10. *LP*, xii(2). 445.

142 TNA, E 36/143, fos. 1–22; E 36/139, fos. 42–88 (*LP*, vi. 299; vii. 923). The bulk of this material belongs to 1532–3: Elton, *Reform and Renewal*, pp. 12–14.

143 Gardiner, *Letters*, p. 44.

144 *LP*, ix. 42.

145 S. Brigden, 'Thomas Cromwell and the "Brethren"' in *Law and Government under the Tudors*, ed. C. Cross, D. Loades and J. J. Scarisbrick (Cambridge, 1988), pp. 39–40.

146 TNA, C1/1218/49.

147 *LP*, xiii(2). 800, p. 313.

148 TNA, C1/1218/49. The threat belonged to a period after Cromwell was appointed Lord Privy Seal in July 1536. *KFF*, 1336, p. 101. The transfer was dated 1536–7.

149 TNA, SP 1/91, fo. 103 (*LP*, viii. 415).

150 *LP*, i. 82, p. 41; iii(1), p. 245. Frogenhall was named Esquire for the Body extraordinary: BL, Royal MS 7F xiv, fo. 100v (LP, ii(1). 2735); TNA, SP 1/91, fo. 103 (LP, viii. 415).

151 TNA, SP1/239, fo. 336 (*LP, Addenda*, 1070). *L&L*, p. 202.

152 In June and August 1535 Thomas Wyatt purchased property, which remained in the possession of his widow: TNA, E 315/368/2 (The valor or extent of all manors &c in the possession of Queen Elizabeth after the death of Lady Elizabeth Warner, 1561–2).

153 *LP*, viii. 1158(16); TNA, STAC 2/20/162; 23/211 (*Yorkshire Star Chamber Proceedings*, iii, ed. W. Brown, *YAS, Record Series*, li (1914), pp. 71–4). Hoyle, 'The Fortunes of the Tempest Family', pp. 169–89.

154 *English Manuscript Studies*, 4 (1993), p. 290. I am extremely grateful to Professor Henry Woudhuysen for this reference. BL, Cotton MS Vespasian F xiii, fo. 117 (*LP*, vii. 631).

155 D. Grummitt, 'Thomas Poynings (1512?–1545)'; H. R. Woudhuysen, 'Vaux, Thomas, second Baron Vaux (1509–1556)'; *ODNB*.

156 G. Anstruther, *Vaux of Harrowden: A Recusant Family* (Newport, Mon., 1953), pp. 38–67.

8: FRIENDSHIP

1 The *locus classicus* for the ideal is Montaigne's beautiful essay 'On Friendship': *The Essayes of Michael Lord of Montaigne, translated by John Florio*, 2 vols. (1910), i, ch. 27. For an exquisite modern study, see A. Bray, *The Friend* (Chicago and London, 2003). L. J. Mills was the first systematically to consider this theme in English literature: *One Soul in Bodies Twain: Friendship in Tudor Literature and Stuart Drama* (Bloomington, Indiana, 1937). I have learnt much from U. Langer, *Perfect Friendship: Studies in Literature and Moral Philosophy from Boccaccio to Corneille* (Genève,

1994); D. V. Kent, *Friendship, Love and Trust in Renaissance Florence* (Cambridge, Mass., 2009); D. Wootton, 'Francis Bacon: Your Flexible Friend' in *The World of the Favourite*, ed. J. H. Elliott and L. W. B. Brockliss (New Haven and London, 1999), pp. 184–204; A. Stewart, '"The Proofe of Frends": Reading *Amicitia* in 1548' in *Close Readers: Humanism and Sodomy in Early Modern England* (Princeton, 1997), pp. 122–60.

2 T.-L. Pebworth and C. J. Summers, '"Thus Friends Absent Speake": the Exchange of Verse Letters between John Donne and Henry Wotton', *Modern Philology*, 81 (1984), pp. 361–77.

3 D. Wootton, 'Friendship Portrayed: A New Account of *Utopia*', *History Workshop Journal*, 45 (1998), pp. 29–47.

4 A. McGrath, *Iustitia Dei: A History of the Christian Doctrine of Justification* (2nd edn., Cambridge, 1998), p. 240.

5 For Christ and His family, see especially J. Bossy, *Christianity in the West, 1400–1700* (Oxford, 1985), ch. 1. For St John as the friend of Christ, see Bray, *The Friend*, pp. 116–122. For Christ the ironist, see D. Knox, *Ironia: Medieval and Renaissance Ideas on Irony* (Leiden, 1989), p. 53.

6 *Foxe's Book of Martyrs* (1570), 11, p. 2027; Horace, *Epistles*, I. xi. 27.

7 Thomas Elyot, *The Boke named the Gouernour*, ed. H. H. S. Croft, 2 vols. (1883), ii, pp. 119–66.

8 Thomas Lupset, *An exhortation to yonge men* (1538), fo. 23r–v. The treatise was written nearly a decade before its publication: 'Fare ye well. At More, a place of my lord Cardinal's, in the feast of St Bartholomew, 1529' (fo. 40).

9 John Harington, *The Booke of Freendeship of Marcus Tullie Cicero*, in R. Hughey, *John Harington of Stepney: Tudor Gentleman: His Life and Works* (Columbus, Ohio, 1971), part iii. The work was published in 1550. The quotation is at p. 137.

10 See, for example, Thomas Elyot, 'The Bankette of Sapience' in *Sir Thomas Elyot: Four Political Treatises*, intro. L. Gottesman (Gainesville, Florida, 1967). The commonplace book of Thomas Paynell; Hatfield House, MS 332 (without folio numbers). See above, pp. 235–6.

11 Miguel de Cervantes Saavedra, *The Adventures of Don Quixote*, trans. J. M. Cohen (Harmondsworth, 1985 edn.), p. 28.

12 *The History of Oliver of Castile, reprinted from the unique copy of Wynkyn de Worde's edition of 1518*, ed. R. E. Graves (1898).

13 *Surrey: Poems*, 27. 39, 46.

14 *Book of the Courtier*, p. 119.

15 *Surrey: Poems*, 28. 22.

16 TNA, SP 1/236, fo. 339 (*LP, Addenda*, 703).

17 Harington, *The Booke of Freendeship*, p. 139.

18 BL, Royal MS 19 A xx. John Poyntz's signature is found in fos. 1 and 152v, and the section on friendship in fos. 85–91, 97–9v. This work had been translated into French, probably for Charles V of France, from the Latin tract *De administratione principum*, which itself mainly derived from *De regimine principum* of Giles of Rome. C. F. Briggs, *Giles of Rome's* De regimine principum: *Reading and Writing Politics at Court and University, c.1275–c.1525* (Cambridge, 1999).

19 For the protean Bryan, see D. Starkey, 'The Court: Castiglione's Ideal and Tudor Reality: Being a Discussion of Sir Thomas Wyatt's *Satire addressed to Sir Francis Bryan*', *JCWI*, 45 (1982), pp. 232–9; S. Brigden, 'Bryan, Sir Francis (*d.* 1550)', *ODNB*. For Bryan's infernal title, see *Letters of Cromwell*, ii, p. 12.

20 *CSPVen, 1534–1554*, 1019; Giovanni Antonio Venier to the Doge and Senate, 10 October 1531, Paris.

21 *LL*, i, pp. 593–6.

22 *LL*, ii, pp. 30, 267.

23 *Ibid.*, pp. 153, 256.

24 *A Dispraise of the life of a Courtier, and a comendacion of the life of the labouryng man* (1548), sig. A3v; cited D. Starkey, *The Reign of Henry VIII: Personalities and Politics* (1985), p. 70. *LP*, v. 548.

25 *Sir John Froissart's Chronicles . . . translated . . . by John Bourchier, Lord Berners*, 2 vols. (1812, edn), i, preface, cited in S. Gunn, 'The French Wars of Henry VIII' in *The Origins of War in Early Modern Europe*, ed. J. Black (Edinburgh, 1987), p. 40.

26 *The Golden Boke of Marcvs Avrelivs* (1535), fo. 167v.

27 *Ibid.*, fos. 167, 18–19v, 40–1v.

28 HHL, MS 183. The manuscript is transcribed, edited and elucidated by R. S. Kinsman, '"The Proverbes of Salmon do playnly declare": a sententious poem on wisdom and governance, ascribed to Sir Francis Bryan', *HLQ*, 42 (1979), pp. 279–312. Thomas Elyot, *The Bankette of Sapience* (1534), *Four Political Treatises*, pp. 101–202.

29 Bryan, 'The Proverbes of Salmon do playnly declare', ll. 166–7.

30 *Ibid.*, ll. 105–6

31 *Ibid.*, ll. 78, 119, 125, 132–3, 173.

32 *Ibid.*, ll. 55–6.

33 Lord Howard de Walden, *Banners, Standards and Badges from a Tudor Manuscript in the College of Arms* (1904), pp. 106, 285.

34 TNA, SP 1/111, fo. 142v; BL, Cotton MS Cleopatra E iv, fo. 109 (*LP*, xi. 1086; xiii(1). 981(2)).

35 *Letters of Cromwell*, ii, pp. 92, 124.

36 R. A. Lanham, *The Motives of Eloquence: Literary Rhetoric in the Renaissance* (New Haven and London, 1976), especially pp. 4, 27.

37 See Knox, *Ironia*, especially pp. 7–19, 32–57, 72–7, 87–93, 100–5.

38 *LP*, x. 670, p. 270. Richard Pate to Henry VIII, Good Friday 1536, Rome.

39 BL, Additional MS 62135, fo. 52.

40 *LP*, i. 1404; ii(2). 3864.

41 T. F. Mayer, *Reginald Pole: Prince and Prophet* (Cambridge, 2000), p. 24.

42 TNA, SP 1/25, fo. 55 (*LP*, iii(2). 2394).

43 TNA, SP 1/25, fo. 154 (*LP*, iii(2). 3249).

44 For this problem, see Wootton, 'Francis Bacon: Your Flexible Friend'.

45 TNA, SP 1/241, fos. 54–7v (*LP*, *Addenda*, 1215).

46 Giovanni della Casa, *Trattato de gli vffici commvni tra gli amici svperiori et inferiori* (1561) in *Baldassar Castiglione, Giovanni della Casa, opere*, a cura di G. Prezzolini (Milano, 1937), pp. 739–72.

47 Seneca, *De beneficiis*, VI. xxxiv. 1, in *Seneca: Moral Essays*, iii, trans. J. W. Basore (Cambridge, Mass., 1935), p. 437.

48 *Letters of Cromwell*, ii, p. 145.

49 TNA, SP 1/236, fo. 339 (*LP*, Addenda, 703).

50 For a disavowal of flattery, see *LP*, x. 224. *LP*, vii. 862; St Leger to Cromwell, 20 June 1534, Slendon.

51 TNA, SP 1/133, fo. 246 (*LP*, xiii(1). 1297).

52 See F. W. Conrad, 'The problem of counsel reconsidered: the case of Thomas Elyot' in *Political Thought and the Tudor Commonwealth*, ed. P. A. Fideler and T. F. Mayer (1992), pp. 75–107.

53 E. W. Ives, *Faction in Tudor England* (2nd edn., 1986).

54 TNA, SP 1/241, fos. 54–7v (the quotations are at fos. 54, 55) (*LP*, Addenda, 1215); Thomas Knight to Wriothesley, 8 April 1537.

55 *SP*, viii, p. 147; Wriothesley to Henry VIII, 1 February 1539, Brussels.

56 For Wriothesley's career and importance, see G. R. Elton, *The Tudor Revolution in Government: Administrative Changes in the Reign of Henry VIII* (Cambridge, 1969), pp. 307ff (the quotation is at p. 308); M. A. R. Graves, 'Wriothesley, Thomas, first earl of Southampton (1505–1550)', *ODNB*.

57 For the role of principal secretary, and Cromwell's transformation of the office, see Elton, *Tudor Revolution in Government*, pp. 31ff, 56ff, 298ff.

58 *CSPFor, 1547–1553*, 491 (cited in 'Wriothesley', *ODNB*).

59 L. Bradner, 'The first Cambridge production of *Miles Gloriosus*', *MLN*, 70 (1955), pp. 400–3.

60 TNA, SP 1/137, fo. 110v (*LP*, xiii(2). 542); *SP*, viii, p. 184; *Harley 282*, fos. 271, 281v (Nott, *Wyatt*, pp. 428, 422).

61 *Letters of Gardiner*, p. 211.

62 *Harley 282*, fo. 281v (Nott, *Wyatt*, p. 423); Wriothesley to Wyatt, 10 October 1537.

63 TNA, SP 1/142, fos. 226–7 (*LP*, xiv(1). 208); Wriothesley to Cromwell, 2 February 1539.

64 *LL*, v, p. 241.

65 TNA, SP 1/143, fo. 35v (*LP*, xiv(1). 247).

66 TNA, SP 1/52, fo. 144 (*LP*, iv(3). 5184).

67 *Letters of Gardiner*, p. 102.

68 For their early letters: *Letters of Cromwell*, i, pp. 323, 340–1, 434–4, 380; *Letters of Gardiner*, pp. 44, 50–3. For amity expressed in the midst of dissension, see *Letters of Cromwell*, ii, pp. 19–21, 23–4.

69 *LL*, vi, p. 58; Sir John Wallop to Lord Lisle, 31 March 1540.

70 Bray, *The Friend*, p. 137.

71 Harington, *The Booke of Freendeship*, p. 149.

72 More, *Correspondence*, pp. 559–63.

73 *Commentary on the Seven Penitential Psalms by John Fisher, Bishop of Rochester*, ed. J. S. Phillimore, 2 vols (1914), i, p. 8.

74 S. Brigden, *London and the Reformation* (Oxford, 1989), pp. 106–18; 'Thomas Cromwell and the "Brethren"' in *Law and Government under the Tudors*, ed. C. Cross, D. Loades and J. J. Scarisbrick (Cambridge, 1988), pp. 31–50.

75 TNA, SP 1/141, fos. 125–6v (*LP*, xiii(2). 1223); G. R. Elton, *Reform and Renewal: Thomas Cromwell and the Common Weal* (Cambridge, 1973), pp. 26–9.

76 *LP*, vii. 1559.

77 TNA, SP 1/134, fo. 218v (*LP*, xiii(1). 1428(3)). For the letter, its circumstances, and its consequences, see S. Brigden and N. Wilson, 'New Learning and Broken Friendship', *EHR*, 112 (1997), pp. 396–411.

78 Bray, *The Friend*, pp. 136–7.

79 P. Marshall, 'The Making of the Tudor Judas: Trust and Betrayal in the English Reformation', *Reformation*, 13 (2008), pp. 77–101.

80 More, *Correspondence*, pp. 533–6.

81 *Ibid.*, p. 564.

82 *Ibid.*, pp. 531, 543.

83 *Gentleman's Magazine*, p. 567.

84 All Souls College, Oxford, SR 79 f. 9. E. Craster, *The History of All Souls College Library*, ed. E. F. Jacob (1971), ch. 3.

85 All Souls College, Oxford, SR 79 f. 9, fos. 172–84.

86 *Paraphrase on Mark*, translated and annotated by E. Rummel, *CWE*, xlix (Toronto and London, 1988), p. 168; *Paraphrase on John*, translated and annotated by J. E. Phillips, *CWE*, xlvi (Toronto and London, 1991), p. 201.

87 J. K. McConica, *English Humanists and Reformation Politics under Henry VIII and Edward VI* (Oxford, 1965), p. 110; J. Woolfson, *Padua and the Tudors: English Students in Italy, 1485–1603* (Cambridge, 1998), pp. 256–7; All Souls College, Oxford, SR 79 f. 9, fo. 178.

88 Payments for an exhibition for Mason, the King's scholar in Paris, are recorded from December 1529. The last payment for a year's exhibition was in October 1532: *PPE*, pp. 8, 71, 119, 190, 263.

89 *Thomas Starkey: A Dialogue between Pole and Lupset*, ed. T. F. Mayer (Camden Society, 4th series, 37); T. F. Mayer, 'Starkey, Thomas (*c.*1498–1538)', *ODNB*.

90 Bray, *The Friend*, p. 120.

91 BL, Cotton MS Vespasian C xiii, fos. 327–8v (*LP*, vii. 945).

92 *LP*, xiii(2). 772.

93 Wootton, 'Francis Bacon: Your Flexible Friend', p. 189.

94 *The Book of the Courtier*, p. 119.

95 Elyot, *The Bankette of Sapience* in *Four Political Treatises*, pp. 189–90. The commonplace book of Thomas Paynell; Hatfield House, MS 332 (without folio numbers).

96 S. Brigden, 'Henry Howard, Earl of Surrey, and the "Conjured League"', *HJ*, 37 (1994), pp. 533–4.

97 BL, Sloane MS 1523, fo. 32v. *Surrey: Poems*, 45. 19; 50. 22–5. Marshall, 'The Making of the Tudor Judas', pp. 87–9.

98 Harington, *The Booke of Freendeship*, pp. 156–7.

99 BL, Cotton MS Cleopatra E iv, fo. 260 (*LP*, xiii(2). 854). G. Walker, *Writing under Tyranny: English Literature and the Henrician Reformation* (Oxford, 2005), pp. 129–30.

100 *Adages II vii 1 to III iii 100*, translated and annotated by R. A. B. Mynors, *CWE*, xxxiv (Toronto and London, 1992), III ii 10, pp. 228–9.

101 TNA, SP 1/142, fo. 154 (*LP*, xiv(1). 141).

102 Richard Morison, *An inuectiue ayenste the great and detestable vice, treason* (1539), sigs. B6r, B7r.

103 BAV, MS Vat Lat 5970, fo. 377r–v (*Pole's Correspondence*, pp. 208–9).

104 Aristotle, *The Nichomachean Ethics*, trans. D. Ross, rev. L. Brown (Oxford, 2009), VIII. 11, pp. 156–7.

105 *Devonshire*, fo. 31. C. Stamatakis, '"Turning the Word": Sir Thomas Wyatt and Early Tudor Literary Practice' (unpublished University of Oxford D.Phil. thesis, 2008), especially pp. 206–7, 214.

106 *Devonshire*, fo. 66.

107 *Ibid.*, fo. 22.

108 *Ibid.*, fos. 44v–46.

109 R. K. Marshall, 'Douglas, Lady Margaret, countess of Lennox (1515–1578)', *ODNB*.

110 *Devonshire*, fo. 79r–v.

111 I follow the interpretation of this poem by D. M. Ross, *Self-Revelation and Self-Protection in Wyatt's Lyric Poetry* (New York and London, 1988), pp. 162–7. Rebholz places this among 'Poems attributed to Wyatt after the Sixteenth Century': *Wyatt: Poems*, pp. 507–8.

112 See E. Heale, '"An Owl in a Sack Troubles No Man": Proverbs, Plainness and Wyatt', *Renaissance Studies*, 11 (1997), pp. 421–33.

113 *Egerton*, fo. 25 (Harrier, *Wyatt's Poetry*, p. 130).

114 *Quyete of mynde*, sigs. A4v, C5v.

115 *Devonshire*, fo. 81v. *Wyatt: Poems*, pp. 380–1.

116 *Egerton*, fo. 33.

117 Ps. 38.41–3. Harrier, *Wyatt's Poetry*, p. 230. See *Wyatt: Poems*, p. 469.

118 Ps. 102.88–91. Harrier, *Wyatt's Poetry*, p. 242.

119 J. Powell, 'Thomas Wyatt's Ivy Seal', *NQ*, 54:3 (September 2007), pp. 242–4.

9: 'MYNE OWNE JHON POYNTZ'

1 'Myne owne Jhon poyntz' is 'the most frequently recopied item' in the 'manuscript corpus of the Henrician courtier writing'. See D. R. Carlson, 'The Henrician Courtier Writing Manuscript and Print: Wyatt, Surrey, Bryan and Others' in *A Companion to Tudor Literature*, ed. K. Cartwright (Chichester, 2010), pp. 151–77 (the quotation is at p. 151). Great difficulties attend the choice of version. The first versions of 'Myne owne Jhon poyntz' are found in *Egerton*, fo. 49r–v (where the first fifty-one lines are missing); *Devonshire*, fos. 85v–87 (where ll. 28–30 are omitted), and Corpus Christi College, Cambridge, Parker MS 168, fos. 200v–201v. I have transcribed the last, the only complete version. Parker MS 168 belonged to Bishop Cox of Ely. Thomas Goodrich, with whom Wyatt dined in May 1534, had been Cox's chaplain, and Wyatt's name recurs within the manuscript. See above, p. 203. I have introduced functional indentation, as in the versions of 'Myne owne John poyntz' and 'My mothers maydes'

in *Egerton*. The incomplete version of 'Myne owne John poyntz' from *Egerton* is transcribed in Harrier, *Wyatt's Poetry*, pp. 167–72. An immaculate composite version and edition is found in *The Penguin Book of Renaissance Verse*, 223. 'My mothers maydes' below is transcribed from *Egerton*, fos. 50–2v. Following Hallett Smith, I refer deliberately to verse epistles, rather than to epistolary satires, since *satire* suggests a different form and style: 'The Art of Sir Thomas Wyatt', *HLQ*, 4 (1946), p. 337. For valuable discussion of these epistles, see P. Thomson, *Sir Thomas Wyatt and his Background* (Stanford, 1964), ch. 8; H. A. Mason, *Sir Thomas Wyatt: A Literary Portrait* (Bristol, 1986), pp. 256–326; C. Burrow, 'Horace at Home and Abroad: Wyatt and Sixteenth-century Horatianism' in *Horace Made New: Horatian Influences on British Writing from the Renaissance to the Twentieth Century*, ed. C. Martindale and D. Hopkins (Cambridge, 1993), pp. 27–49; J. Scattergood, 'Thomas Wyatt's Epistolary Satires and the Consolations of Intertextuality' in *Building the Past (Konstruktion der eigenen Vergangenheit)*, ed. R. Suntrup and J. R. Veenstra (Frankfurt am Main, 2006), pp. 67–83. Also C. Z. Hobson, 'Country Mouse and Towny Mouse: Truth in Wyatt', *TSLL*, 39 (1997), pp. 230–58; J. Gleckman, 'Thomas Wyatt's Epistolary Satires: Parody and the Limitations of Rhetorical Humanism', *TSLL*, 43 (2001), pp. 29–45.

2 For the development and nature of the verse epistle in the Renaissance, see C. K. Le Vine, 'The Verse Epistle in Spanish Poetry of the Golden Age' (unpublished Johns Hopkins University Ph.D. thesis, 1974).

3 Geoffrey Chaucer, *The Riverside Chaucer*, ed. L. D. Benson (3rd edn., Oxford, 1987), p. 653.

4 J. A. Kingdon, *Incidents in the Lives of Thomas Poyntz and Richard Grafton* (1895); E. Ives, *The Life and Death of Anne Boleyn, 'the Most Happy'* (Oxford, 2004), p. 263. Even the most distinguished Wyatt scholars have believed that the John Poyntz he addressed was the one from Essex, or conflated the two: Nott, *Wyatt*, pp. lxxxiii–lxxxiv; C. Burrow, 'Horace at Home and Abroad', pp. 38–9.

5 J. Roberts, *Holbein and the Court of Henry VIII: Drawings and Miniatures from the Royal Library, Windsor Castle* (National Galleries of Scotland, 1993), 23. An oil portrait of Poyntz at Sandon Hall, owned by the Earl of Harrowby, bears the inscription *Aet. Suae 42*: K. T. Parker, *The Drawings of Hans Holbein at Windsor Castle* (Oxford and London, 1945), p. 50. Poyntz, born in *c*.1485, was aged forty-two in 1527, the date of Holbein's first visit to England, and of Holbein's painting of Poyntz's friend and patron, Sir Henry Guildford: see above, p. 161.

6 For the marriage settlement of Margaret Wydeville and Robert Poyntz of 1479, see BL, Sloane MS 3424, fo. 7v. For the 'rise of the Poyntzes', see K. Rodwell and R. Bell, *Acton Court: the Evolution of an Early Tudor Courtier's House* (2004), pp. 20–3.

7 M. Hicks, 'Woodville (Wydeville), Anthony, second Earl Rivers (*c*.1440–1483)', *ODNB*; *CPR, Edward IV. Henry VI, 1467–1476*, p. 417; E. W. Ives, 'Andrew Dymmock and the Papers of Anthony, Earl Rivers, 1482–3', *BIHR*, 41 (1968), pp. 216–29.

8 A. Hawkyard, 'Poyntz, Sir Robert (*b*. late 1440s, *d*. 1520)', *ODNB*; A. Conway, 'The Maidstone Sector of Buckingham's Rebellion, Oct. 18, 1483', *AC*, 37 (1925), pp. 97–119.

9 *LP*, iv(3), 5774(5). For the Haute family, and its connections through marriage with the Wydevilles, see W. G. Davis, *The Ancestry of Mary Isaac, c.1549–1613* (Portland, Maine, 1955), pp. 157–8; P. W. Fleming, 'Haute family (*per. c.*1350–1550)', *ODNB*.

10 *LP*, iv(3). 5774(5).

11 *LP*, iii(1). 206(12); B. J. Harris, *English Aristocratic Women, 1450–1550* (Oxford and New York, 2002), pp. 217–18; J. Maclean, *Historical and Genealogical Memoir of the Family of Poyntz* (Exeter, 1886), pp. 115, 131; Conway, 'The Maidstone Sector', pp. 107–8, 114.

12 P. W. Fleming, 'The Hautes and their "Circle": Culture and the English Gentry' in *England in the Fifteenth Century: Proceedings of the 1986 Harlaxton Symposium*, ed. D. Williams (Woodbridge, 1987), pp. 85–102.

13 The ownership of the manuscript and the complexities of the connections between the Hautes and Guildfords are explained by C. M. Meale, 'The Manuscripts and Early Audience of the Middle English Prose *Merlin*' in *The Changing Face of Arthurian Romance: Essays on Arthurian Prose Romances in Memory of Cedric E. Pickford*, ed. A. Adams *et al.* (Cambridge, 1986), pp. 92–111. Eleanor may have been the Eleanor Haute who married Edward Guildford, or Eleanor, daughter of Sir Richard Guildford, who married Edward Haute. In either case, she was related to the Poyntzes.

14 Fleming, 'The Hautes and Their "Circle"', pp. 88–91; BL, Royal MS 14 E iii, fo. 162. D. Gray, 'Roos (Ros), Sir Richard (*c.*1410–1482)', *ODNB*.

15 BL, Royal MS, 19 A xx, fo. 152v. *CPR, Edward IV. Henry VI, 1467–1476*, pp. 460–1; Davis, *Ancestry of Mary Isaac*, pp. 163, 180.

16 G. S. J. White, 'A stone polyhedral sundial dated 1520, attributed to Nicholas Kratzer and found at Iron Acton Court, near Bristol', *Antiquaries Journal*, 67 (1987); Rodwell and Bell, *Acton Court*, pp. 260–1.

17 *LP*, iii(1). 228; *CWE*, vi, p. 365.

18 Fleming, 'The Hautes and Their "Circle"', pp. 91–3; BL, Royal MS 16 E xiv.

19 *The table of Cebes* (1531? Printed *cum privilegio* by Thomas Berthelet). For modern editions, see *Epictetus' Handbook and The Tablet of Cebes: Guides to Stoic Living*, ed. Keith Seddon (2005); *Cebes's Tablet: Facsimiles of the Greek Text, and of Selected Latin, French, English, Spanish, Italian, German, Dutch and Polish Translations*, ed. Sandra Sider (New York, 1979). H. B. Lathrop, *Translations from the Classics into English from Caxton to Chapman* (New York, 1967), pp. 46–8. Poyntz translated from Constantine Lascaris's Latin translation.

20 D. T. Starnes, 'The Figure Genius in the Renaissance', *Studies in the Renaissance*, 11 (1964), pp. 234–44.

21 For the adoption of neo-Stoicism later in the century by those who lived around rulers, see P. N. Miller, *Peiresc's Europe: Learning and Virtue in the Seventeenth Century* (New Haven and London, 2000), especially pp. 12–13, 36–7, 109–17.

22 BL, Additional MS 17012, fos. 179v–180. The manuscript is described in E. Duffy, *Marking the Hours: English People and their Prayers, 1240–1570* (New Haven and London, 2006), pp. 51–2. M. M. Norris, 'Manners, Thomas, first earl of Rutland (*c.*1497–1543)', *ODNB*. Roos was created earl in 1525.

23 BL, Additional MS 17012, fo. 20v.

24 *CSPSp*, iii(2), *1527–1529*, pp. 185–6; Katherine to Charles V, 10 May, 1527. Leland, *Encomia*, p. 21.

25 *LP, Addenda*, 803; Rodwell and Bell, *Acton Court*, pp. 24, 38, appendix B.

26 *CSPSp*, iv(2), *1531–1533*, p. 863; Eustace Chapuys to Charles V, 20 November 1533. John Poyntz's name appears throughout the account book of Katherine's receiver general as one of her receivers and principal officers: BL, Cotton Appendix lxv, fos. 9, 27, 30, 32, 39, 42, 44, 49, 52, 53v, 54, 56, 63v, 65, 71, 75, 78, 80.

27 TNA, PCC, Prob. 11/19, fos. 223–6 (will of Sir Robert Poyntz, 1520). N. Pevsner, *North Somerset and Bristol* in *The Buildings of England* (Harmondsworth, 1958), p. 393.

28 Rodwell and Bell, *Acton Court*, pp. xiv, 26, 188–93. TNA, SP 1/103, fo. 213 (*LP*, xv. 629).

29 Matston bequeathed his copies of Froissart and Enguerrand de Monstrelet to Poyntz: TNA, PCC Prob 11/28, fo. 205v.

30 TNA, PCC Prob. 11/30, fo. 150v; C 142/70/27.

31 G. M. Murphy, 'Poyntz, Robert (*b. c*.1535, *d.* in or after 1568)', *ODNB*; T. B. Trappes-Lomax, 'The Family of Poyntz and its Catholic Associations', *Recusant History*, 6 (1961), pp. 68–79.

32 BL, Additional MS 17012, fo. 180; Royal MS 19 A xx, fos. 1 and 152v.

33 This verse may be by Jacopone da Todi: H. Walther, *Initia carminum ac versuum medii aevi posterioris latinorum* (Gottingen, 1959), 3934.

34 I am extremely grateful to Mr James Morwood for help on this point.

35 M. Gale, *Virgil on the Nature of Things: The* Georgics, *Lucretius and the Didactic Tradition* (Cambridge, 2000). The translation is Professor Gale's, from *Georgics* 2.490–4, 458–9, 467.

36 *The Praise of Folie by Thomas Chaloner*, ed. C. H. Miller (EETS, 257, 1965), p. 5.

37 C. Guillén, *Literature as System: Essays toward the Theory of Literary History* (Princeton, 1971), pp. 248–50; Le Vine, 'The Verse Epistle in Spanish Poetry', pp. 7off.

38 For example, H. A. Mason, *Humanism and Poetry in the Early Tudor Period: an Essay* (1959), p. 221; A. Fox, *Politics and Literature in the Reigns of Henry VII and Henry VIII* (Oxford, 1989), pp. 270–1.

39 Burrow, 'Horace at Home and Abroad', pp. 32–49; D. Marsh, 'Horatian Influence and Imitation in Ariosto's Satires', *Comparative Literature*, 27 (1975), pp. 307–26.

40 H. Hauvrette, *Luigi Alamanni (1495–1556): sa vie et son oeuvre* (Paris, 1903), pp. 207–15. *CSPSp*, iv(1), *1529–1530*, pp. 375–7, 521–3; Luigi Alamanni to the Republic of Florence, 25 December 1529; to the Ten[?] of Florence, April 1530.

41 'Cappello, Bernardo (1498–1565); Cappello, Carlo (1492–1546)'; *DBI*, 18, pp. 765–72.

42 Leland, *Encomia*, p. 61.

43 *LP*, vi. 584, 601, 653; vii. 49, 214, 1057; viii. 199, 234. The quotation is from Cappello's 'Report of England' made to the Venetian Senate, 3 June 1535:

CSPVen, 1534–1554, 54.

44 *DBI*, 18, p. 768. BL, Cotton MS Nero B vi, fo. 54 (*LP*, xiii(2). 813); Thomas Theobald to Cromwell, 12 November 1538, Padua.

45 'Myne owne John Poyntz'; *Devonshire*, fos. 85v–87 (where ll. 28–30 are omitted); 'My mothers maydes'; *Devonshire*, fo. 87v (the opening lines).

46 For brilliant forensic study of this manuscript, see J. Powell, 'Thomas Wyatt's Poetry in Embassy: Egerton 2711 and the Production of Literary Manuscripts Abroad', *HLQ*, 67 (2004), pp. 261–82 (especially pp. 275–6, 269–71, 279–80). The quotation is from J. Daalder, 'Are Wyatt's Poems in Egerton Manuscript 2711 in Chronological Order?', *English Studies*, 3 (1988), pp. 205–23 (at p. 209).

47 *The Satires of Ludovico Ariosto: a Renaissance Autobiography*, trans. P. DeSa Wiggins (Athens, Ohio, 1976).

48 C. A. Mayer, *Clément Marot* (Paris, 1964), pp. 35, 124–7.

49 *Rime di G. Guidiccioni e F. Coppetta Beccuti*, a cura di E. Chiorboli (Bari, 1912), pp. 81–9.

50 R. Helgerson, *A Sonnet from Carthage: Garcilaso de la Vega and the New Poetry of Sixteenth-Century Europe* (Philadelphia, 2007), ch. 6, pp. 74–9.

51 *A ti, Doña Marina : the Poetry of Don Diego Hurtado de Mendoza*, ed. M. C. Batchelor (Havana, 1959), pp. 163–77; A. González Palencia and E. Mele, *Vida y obras de don Diego Hurtado de Mendoza*, 3 vols. (Madrid, 1941–3); A. González Palencia, *Don Luis de Zuñiga y Avila: Gentilhombre de Carlos V* (Madrid, 1932); le Vine, 'The Verse Epistle in Spanish Poetry of the Golden Age', pp. 41ff; D. H. Darst, *Diego Hurtado de Mendoza* (Boston, Mass., 1987), pp. 46–54; A. G. Reichenberger, 'Boscán's *Epístola a Mendoza*', *HR*, 17 (1949), pp. 1–17; E. L. Rivers, 'The Horatian Epistle and Its Introduction into Spanish Literature', *HR*, 22 (1954), pp. 175–94. Mendoza owned copies of Alamanni, *Opere toscane* (Florence, 1532); Ariosto, *Satire* (Venice, 1537); Horace, *Poemata omnia* (Venice, 1527): 'Catalogue of Diego Hurtado de Mendoza's Library of Printed Books', 19, 87, 611 in A. Hobson, *Renaissance Book Collecting: Jean Grolier and Diego Hurtado de Mendoza, their Books and Bindings* (Cambridge, 1999).

52 For the possibility that Wyatt met Marot and Ariosto, see Thomson, *Thomas Wyatt and his Background*, pp. 54, 58, 280. For the encounters with Guidiccioni and Mendoza, see above, pp. 344–5, 409, 417.

53 M. R. Watson, 'Wyatt, Chaucer and *Terza Rima*', *MLN*, 68 (February 1953), pp. 124–5.

54 H. A. Mason, 'Wyatt's Greatest Adventure?' *Cambridge Quarterly*, 7 (1977). The quotations are at pp. 156, 160.

55 Le Vine, 'The Verse Epistle in Spanish Poetry', pp. 36–7.

56 A. Ferry, *The 'Inward' Language: Sonnets of Wyatt, Sidney, Shakespeare, Donne* (Chicago and London, 1983), pp. 89–90.

57 Chris Stamatakis, figuring this revolving word as *subintellectio* for all Wyatt's wordplay, entitled his doctoral thesis '"Turning the Word": Sir Thomas Wyatt and Early Tudor Literary Practice'.

58 Quentin Skinner explains the importance of this figure in Renaissance rhetoric:

'Moral Ambiguity and the Renaissance Art of Eloquence', *EC*, 44 (1994), pp. 267–92; *Reason and Rhetoric in the Philosophy of Hobbes* (Cambridge, 1996), pp. 10–11, 142–53, 156–72; 174–80; 'Paradiastole: Redescribing Virtues as Vices' in *Renaissance Figures of Speech*, ed. S. Adamson, G. Alexander and K. Ettenhuber (Cambridge, 2007), ch. 8.

59 See, especially, Skinner, *Reason and Rhetoric*, pp. 152ff.

60 Skinner, 'Moral Ambiguity and the Renaissance Art of Eloquence', p. 278.

61 *Book of the Courtier*, p. 31. H. A. Mason found the resemblance: *Sir Thomas Wyatt: a Literary Portrait*, pp. 283–4.

62 *Magnificence*, ed. P. Neuss (Manchester, 1980), ll. 1606–8. For dating and inter-pretation of the play, see pp. 1–64.

63 This is the suggestion of M. Dowling, 'Scholarship, Politics and the Court of Henry VIII' (unpublished London School of Economics Ph.D. thesis, 1981), pp. 104–8, and G. Walker, *Plays of Persuasion: Drama and Politics at the Court of Henry VIII* (Cambridge, 1991), ch. 3.

64 *A booke called in latyn Enchiridion militis christiani, and in englysshe the manuell of the christen knyght . . . made by the famous clerke Erasmus of Roterdame* (1533). This resem-blance was discovered by Mason, *Sir Thomas Wyatt*, p. 284.

65 Skinner, *Reason and Rhetoric*, pp. 166–7.

66 BL, Additional MS 62135, fo. 60.

67 More, *Dialogue Concerning Heresies*, *CWM*, i, p. 399; More, *Correspondence*, p. 521.

68 Skinner, 'Moral Ambiguity and the Renaissance Art of Eloquence', p. 280.

69 Cited in Ferry, *The 'Inward' Language*, pp. 6, 90.

70 *The Essayes of Michael Lord of Montaigne*, translated by *John Florio*, 2 vols. (1910), i, ch. 36.

71 G.-B. Niccolini, *Filippo Strozzi, tragedia (corredata d'una vita di Filippo e di documenti in-editi)* (Firenze, 1847), pp. cxix. M. M. Bullard, *Filippo Strozzi and the Medici: Favour and Finance in Sixteenth-Century Florence* (Cambridge, 1980), pp. 175–6. Hauvrette, *Luigi Alamanni*, p. 187.

72 *Quyete of mynde*, sig. B7r.

73 See, for example, Mason, *Sir Thomas Wyatt: A Literary Portrait*, pp. 259, 292.

74 Seneca, 'On the Happy Life' in *Seneca: Moral Essays*, ii, trans. J. W. Basore (Cambridge, Mass., 1932), xvi. 3, pp. 140–3; *Juvenal and Persius*, ed. and trans. S. M. Braund (Cambridge, Mass., 2004), *Persius*, Satire 5.159–60.

75 *KFF*, pp. 84, 152.

76 *Oxford Dictionary of English Proverbs*, 3rd edn., rev. F. P. Wilson (Oxford, 1970), p. 420; *Dictionary of Proverbs*, K 16, p. 353.

77 *LP*, xi. 235. For Aesop's influence on a later life lived in Kent and Christendom, see B. Worden, *The Sound of Virtue: Philip Sidney's* Arcadia *and Elizabethan Politics* (New Haven and London, 1996).

78 See Seamus Heaney's beautiful translation: *Robert Henryson: The Testament of Cresseid and Seven Fables* (2009).

79 Philip Sidney, *A Defence of Poetry*, ed. J. A. Van Dorsten (Oxford, 1966), p. 34.

80 Virgil, *Georgics*, 2. 458–60.

81 The similarities to *The Quyete of mynde* and the reference to Luke 6:44 were

noted by A. N. Brilliant, 'The Style of Wyatt's "The Quyete of Mynde"', *ES*, 24 (1971), pp. 1–21 (at pp. 15–16). For the echo of Boethius, see Scattergood, 'Thomas Wyatt's Epistolary Satires', p. 79.

82 *Quyete of mynde*, sig. B7v.

83 *Ibid.*, sig. C2v.

84 Horace, *Ep.* I. 11. 29–30. Burrow, 'Wyatt and Sixteenth-century Horatianism', pp. 42–4.

85 See D. M. Friedman's important article: 'The "Thing" in Wyatt's Mind', *EC*, 16 (1966), pp. 375–81.

86 In *Paradise Lost* John Milton would borrow the same lines to curse the Devil: Nott, *Wyatt*, p. 562.

87 BL, Additional MS 48126, fo. 16v. *Arundel Harington*, 295.

10: CIRCA REGNA TONAT

1 The poem now exists only in one version, in one manuscript: *Blage* (TCD, MS 160), fo. 183. The 'Blage' manuscript is described by K. Muir, *Sir Thomas Wyatt and His Circle: Unpublished Poems* (Liverpool, 1961); Harrier, *Wyatt's Poetry*, pp. 55–75; S. O'Keeffe, 'TCD MS 160: A Tudor Miscellany' (unpublished Trinity College, Dublin M. Litt. thesis, 1986); H. Baron, 'The "Blage" Manuscript: the original compiler identified' in *English Manuscript Studies*, 1, ed. P. Beal and J. Griffiths (Oxford, 1989), pp. 85–119.

2 *Seneca: Phaedra*, ed. and trans. J. G. Fitch (Cambridge, Mass., 2002), 1123–40. The quotations are at ll. 1140 and 1134.

3 J. W. Binns, 'Seneca and Neo-Latin Tragedy in England' in *Seneca*, ed. C. D. N. Costa (London and Boston, 1974), pp. 205–34.

4 A. Keay, *The Elizabethan Tower of London: the Haiward and Gascoyne Plan of 1597* (London Topographical Society, 158, 2001), pp. 33, 41, 51 n. 120–3. I am greatly indebted to Historic Royal Palaces for allowing me to visit the Bell Tower.

5 *Spelman's Reports*, i, p. 71.

6 I have relied especially upon E. Ives, *The Life and Death of Anne Boleyn, 'the Most Happy'* (Oxford, 2004), part iv. David Starkey is, as always, illuminating: *Six Wives: the Queens of Henry VIII* (2003), chs. 68–9. G. W. Bernard, 'The Fall of Anne Boleyn', *EHR*, 106 (1991), pp. 584–610; *Anne Boleyn: Fatal Attractions* (New Haven and London, 2010); E.W. Ives, 'Anne Boleyn and the Early Reformation in England: the Contemporary Evidence', *HJ*, 37 (1994), pp. 389–400; G. Walker, 'Rethinking the Fall of Anne Boleyn', *HJ*, 45 (2002), pp. 1–29.

7 *LL*, iii, p. 324.

8 D. Starkey, 'King Henry and King Arthur', *Arthurian Literature*, xvi, ed. J. P. Carley and F. Riddy (1998), pp. 175, 189–90.

9 *Chronicle of King Henry VIII*, p. 63.

10 Lancelot de Carles, 'Poème sur la mort d'Anne Boleyn' in G. Ascoli, *La Grande Bretagne devant l'opinion Français* (Paris, 1927), appendice ii, pp. 246–8, pp. 66–7.

11 Hall, fo. 227v.

12 Constantine, 'Memorial', p. 64.

13 *LP*, x. 782, 785.

14 *LP*, x. 785; Constantine, 'Memorial', p. 65.

15 BL, Cotton MS, Otho C x, fo. 225 (Singer, p. 451).

16 Sir William Kingston's letters to Cromwell, though badly damaged in the fire in the Cottonian library in 1731, survive: BL, Cotton MS Otho, C x, fos. 222–5. They were transcribed in the nineteenth century by S. W. Singer, who incorporated missing words, and printed by the ecclesiastical historian John Strype – who saw the letters before the fire – in his *Ecclesiastical Memorials* (1721): Singer, pp. 451–61. See also *LP*, x. 793, 797–8, 910. I have also used my own transcriptions.

17 BL, Additional MS 25114, fo. 160 (*Letters of Cromwell*, ii, p. 12). For Anne and her ladies, see Ives, *Life and Death of Anne Boleyn*, pp. 329–34.

18 *LL*, iii, p. 378; iv, p. 50.

19 BL, Cotton MS Otho C x, fo. 209v (Singer, p. 458).

20 *Spelman's Reports*, i, p. 71; *Chronicle of King Henry VIII*, pp. 66. Ives, *Life and Death of Anne Boleyn*, pp. 329–31. Wyatt knew Lady Wingfield from Calais, where her husband had been deputy.

21 BL, Cotton MS Otho C x, fo. 225 (Singer, pp. 451–2).

22 *Ibid.*, p. 452.

23 Greg Walker's interpretation is persuasive: 'Rethinking the Fall of Anne Boleyn', pp. 21–8.

24 Singer, p. 453.

25 BL, Additional MS 25114, fo. 160 (*Letters of Cromwell*, ii, pp. 11–13).

26 TNA, SP 1/103, fo. 251 (*LP*, x. 819).

27 The time was recorded in the chronicle of Anthony Anthony, an official in the Tower: Bodleian, Fol. Δ 624, facing p. 384. I am grateful to Gary Hill for giving me a copy of his transcription.

28 BL, Cotton MS Otho C x, fo. 222v (Singer, p. 455).

29 BL, Cotton MS Otho C x. fo. 209v.

30 BL, Additional MS 25114, fo. 160 (*Letters of Cromwell*, ii, p. 12).

31 BL, Cotton MS Cleopatra E iv, fo. 110 (*LP*, xiii(1). 981).

32 The Spanish chronicler, who relied upon some informant close to the Wyatt family, revived the old stories of Wyatt's revelations about Anne at this chronological point in his narrative. That he allied his account of Wyatt's plain speaking and banishment with a fevered story from Boccaccio undermines it, but there are shadows of plausibility: *Chronicle of King Henry VIII*, pp. 63–4, 68–70.

33 *Defence*; *Harley 78*, fo. 12 (*L&L*, p. 201).

34 *LL*, iii, p. 360.

35 TNA, SP 1/103, fo. 281 (*LL*, iii, p. 361).

36 *LL*, iv, p. 48; *LP*, x. 909.

37 *LL*, iii, p. 460; *LP*, x. 1135; *PPE Mary*, pp. 30–2.

38 BL, Additional MS 62135, fo. 368.

39 TNA, SP 1/103, fo. 266 (*LP*, x. 840). My italics.

40 *LP*, x, p. 379.

41 *Unpublished Poems*, XXVII, pp. xv, xvi. Rebholz includes this among 'Poems Attributed to Sir Thomas Wyatt after the Sixteenth Century': *Wyatt: Poems*, pp. 255–6, 512–13. *Chronicle of King Henry VIII*, p. 68. Ives, *Life and Death of Anne Boleyn*, pp. 362–4.

42 Singer, p. 457.

43 D. MacCulloch, *Thomas Cranmer* (New Haven and London, 1996), pp. 157–8.

44 BL, Cotton MS Otho C x, fo. 260 (*LP*, x. 942).

45 Singer, pp. 456–7.

46 *Ibid*, p. 452.

47 De Carles, 'Poème sur la mort d'Anne Boleyn', ll. 339ff, in Ascoli, *La Grande Bretagne*, pp. 242–3.

48 Bernard, 'The Fall of Anne Boleyn', pp. 596–9; Walker, 'Rethinking the Fall of Anne Boleyn', pp. 16–20; Ives, *Life and Death of Anne Boleyn*, pp. 326, 332–4, 337, 339, 342.

49 This interpretation is David Starkey's: *The Reign of Henry VIII: Personalities and Politics* (1985), pp. 112–13.

50 *Chronicle of King Henry VIII*, pp. 63–4.

51 For the judgement that Wyatt was witness, rather than suspect, see P. Friedmann, *Anne Boleyn: a chapter of English history, 1527–1536*, 2 vols. (1884), ii, p. 263; W. B. Robison, 'The Justices of the Peace in Surrey in National and County Politics, 1483–1570' (unpublished Louisiana State University Ph.D. thesis, 1984), p. 193; 'Wyatt, Sir Thomas I (by 1504–1542)', *House of Commons*, iii, p. 669.

52 *Defence*; *Harley 78*, fo. 8v (*L&L*, p. 192).

53 *Harley 78*, fo. 27.

54 *Petrarch's Lyric Poems*, 1.

55 The biblical source was identified by Dr Nott: Nott, *Surrey*, p. 359. Wyatt recalled the image of the unfading scar again: *Defence*; *Harley 78*, fo. 9 (*L&L*, p. 193). Meaningfully, the Earl of Surrey remembered Wyatt's use of the image and its warning: *Surrey: Poems*, 34. 6. S. Brigden, 'Henry Howard, Earl of Surrey, and the "Conjured League"', *HJ*, 37 (1994), pp. 533–4.

56 *Reginae Utopiae falso adulterii crimine damnatae* in *Epigrammata* (Lyon, 1538), bk. iii, 162; Ascoli, *La Grande Bretagne*, p. 71; Ives, *Life and Death of Anne Boleyn*, p. 421.

57 *CSPFor, Elizabeth, 1558–1559*, 1303, pp. 524–34; Alexander Alesius to the Queen.

58 *LP*, xi. 988; Foxe, *AM*, v, p. 136.

59 BL, Additional MS 62135, fo. 60.

60 *LP*, x. 615. For Skip's sermon and its significance, see Ives, 'Anne Boleyn and the Early Reformation', pp. 395–400.

61 BL, Additional MS 25114, fo. 350 (*LP*, x. 761). Gardiner's courier from France was Robert Massy.

62 ASV, Carte Farnesiane, 11, fo. 45v; Rodolfo Pio di Carpi, papal nuncio, to Ambrogio Ricalcati, 10 March 1536, Montplaisant.

63 TNA, SP 1/239, fo. 294 (*LP, Addenda*, 1064). The messenger was Thomas Barnaby.

64 *LP*, x. 908, p. 380; 956.

65 HHStA, England, Korrespondenz, 7, fo. 108 (Friedmann, *Anne Boleyn*, ii, pp. 267–8; *LP*, x. 908, p. 378); Chapuys to Charles V, 19 May 1536.

66 *Spelman's Reports*, i, p. 59; *LP*, x. 902, 956; Ives, *Life and Death of Anne Boleyn*, pp. 351, 357–9.

67 *LP*, x. 1134(1).

68 *Spelman's Reports*, i, p. 59.

69 For the marriage and the surrounding plots, see Starkey, *Six Wives*, ch. 70.

70 *LP*, x. 908, p. 379.

71 Wriothesley, *Chronicle*, i, p. 43.

72 *LP*, x. 1079, 1083, 1108–10.

73 *LP*, vii. 1172 (miscalendared); x. 1110, 1134, 1150; xi. 222. Starkey, *Six Wives*, p. 598; Ives, *Life and Death of Anne Boleyn*, pp. 361–2.

74 AGS, Guerra Antigua, legajo 9/95, 105; Conde de Cifuentes to Charles V, 4 August and 8 October 1536, Rome.

75 Starkey, *Six Wives*, p. 550; *LP*, x. 871.

76 BL, Cotton MS Otho C x, fos. 174v–175 (*LP*, x. 1134 (4)).

77 *PPE Mary*, pp. 14, 59. The references in the King's payments may be to a different Elizabeth Darrell; see below, p. 664 n.164.

78 TNA, SP 1/104, fo. 165 (*LP*, x. 1131).

79 *LP*, xi. 108, 385 (5, 6).

80 There were two alternative designs for the prayer book cover: S. Foister, *Holbein and England* (New Haven and London, 2004), p. 144, fig. 150; *Holbein in England*, ed. S. Foister (2006), 90.

81 For the history of the Hautes of Kent, see W. G. Davis, *The Ancestry of Mary Isaac, c.1549–1613* (Portland, Maine, 1955), pp. 99–193.

82 R. Strong, 'In Search of Holbein's Thomas Wyatt the Younger', *Apollo* (March, 2006), pp. 48–56; E. Foucart-Walter, *Les Peintures de Hans Holbein le jeune au Louvre* (Paris, 1985), pp. 48–52; *Holbein in England*, ed. Foister, 142.

83 TNA, SP 1/113, fo. 189 (*LP*, xi. 1492).

84 TNA, PCC Prob. 11/26, fos. 49v–50.

85 K. T. Parker, *The Drawings of Hans Holbein . . . at Windsor Castle* (Oxford, 1945), 63, p. 53.

86 Strong, 'In Search of Holbein's Thomas Wyatt's the Younger', p. 51.

87 The identification was made by the Hon. C. Stuart Wortley: 'Holbein's Sketch of the Wyat Coat of Arms', *Burlington Magazine*, 56 (April, 1930), pp. 211–13.

88 *Defence*, Harley 78, fo. 12v (*L&L*, p. 201); *LP*, xi. 1217(23).

89 See particularly R. W. Hoyle, *The Pilgrimage of Grace and the Politics of the 1530s* (Oxford, 2001); M. L. Bush, *The Pilgrimage of Grace: A Study of the Rebel Armies of October 1536* (1996).

90 *LP*, xi. 580(1, 2), appendices 8–9.

91 *Defence*, Harley 78, fo. 12v (*L&L*, p. 201). In June 1534 Wyatt had been granted for life the 'conduct and command of all men able for war in the liberty of the seven hundreds of the weald' of Kent, and licensed to retain twenty men in his livery. The weavers in the seven hundreds were complaining in 1536, for economic reasons: *LP*, xi. 520.

92 *LP*, xi. 670, 751, 753, 1406, p. 558.

93 *LP*, xi. 803, 821, 824, 874, 918, 926, 1405–6.

94 *SP*, i, p. 468; *LP*, xi. 759.

95 *LP*, xi. 1244.

96 *LP*, xi. 519(4). Ancient Sir John Melton, who had held the office jointly with Henry Wyatt since 1522, lived on: *LP*, xi. 1475.

97 TNA, SP 1/111, fo. 35 (*LP*, xi. 1026).

98 *LP*, xii(1). 306. For Tickhill in the rebellion, see R. B. Smith, *Land and Politics in the England of Henry VIII: the West Riding of Yorkshire* (Oxford, 1970), pp. 194, 198; T. W. Beastall, *Tickhill: Portrait of an English Country Town* (Doncaster, 1995), p. 83.

99 *LP*, xi. 593.

100 *LP*, xi. 911; TNA, SP 1/111, fo. 199 (*LP*, xi. 1136(2)); TNA, SC 12/17/63.

101 *LP*, xi. 846, 997, 1051, 1058, 1113–4, 1122, 1167. For the feud and the role of the Tempests and Saviles in the revolt, see R. W. Hoyle, 'The Fortunes of the Tempest Family of Bracewell and Bowling in the Sixteenth Century', *YAJ*, 74 (2002), especially pp. 176–83; Smith, *Land and Politics*, pp. 190–4.

102 Hoyle, *The Pilgrimage of Grace*, p. 410.

103 *LP*, xi. 754–5, 766, 768, 800, 803; *SP*, i, p. 489. For detailed accounts of Browne's receipts and expenses in his journey north, 17 October to 15 December 1536, see Folger Shakespeare Library, L.b. 336.

104 The quotations are from *LP*, xi. 888, 1016. Hoyle, *The Pilgrimage of Grace*, pp. 170–1, 175.

105 *LP*, xi. 1079.

106 TNA, SP 1/111, fo. 153v (*LP*, xi. 1103).

107 *LP*, xi. 1086 (p. 437), 1196–7, 1224; *SP*, i, pp. 511–12.

108 *LP*, xi. 663.

109 TNA, SP 1/112, fo. 245 (*LP*, xi. 1319). S. Brigden, *London and the Reformation* (Oxford, 1989), pp. 248–52.

110 *LP*, xi. 714.

111 *LP*, xi. 841(iv).

112 *LP*, xii(2). 907–8.

113 *LP*, xii(2). 752, 959.

114 TNA, SP 1/118, fos. 231–2 (*LP*, xii(1). 990); G. R. Elton, *Policy and Police: the Enforcement of the Reformation in the Age of Thomas Cromwell* (Cambridge, 1972), pp. 65–6. For Lewes's marriage: *LP*, xii(2). 450.

115 *LP*, vi. 1164 (p. 486); Chapuys to Charles V, 27 September 1533. M. Dowling, *Fisher of Men: A Life of John Fisher, 1469–1535* (Basingstoke, 1999), ch. 7, especially pp. 150–1.

116 N. Pocock, *Records of the Reformation*, 2 vols. (Oxford, 1870), i, p. 133.

117 *LP*, iv(3). 5177.

118 AGS, Estado, legajo 1311/137; Reginald Pole to Charles V, 17 June 1535, Venice. *Pole's Correspondence*, pp. 81–3. AGS, Estado, legajo 1311/138; Cardinal Contarini to Charles V, 5 June 1535, Venice. *CSPSp*, v(2), *1536–1538*, pp. 490–1.

119 TNA, SP 1/204, fos. 1–280. For the deepest analysis of the work, see T. Mayer, *Reginald Pole, Prince and Prophet* (Cambridge, 2000), ch. 1.

120 *Ibid.*, pp. 19–20, 28.

121 *LP*, ix. 207.

122 *ANG*, 1, pp. 217–18; *LP*, xi. 1250. For Pio and Pole, see T. F. Mayer, *Cardinal Pole in European Context* (Aldershot, 2000), pp. 307–10.

123 *LP*, xi. 1143, 1353(2), 1354. For Throckmorton and his dramatic mission, see A. Overell, 'Cardinal Pole's Special Agent: Michael Throckmorton, *c.*1503–1558', *History*, 94 (2009), pp. 265–78.

124 *LP*, xii(1). 779. G. B. Parks, 'The Parma Letters and the Dangers to Cardinal Pole', *Catholic Historical Review*, 46 (1960), pp. 310–11; Mayer, *Cardinal Pole in European Context*, especially pp. 296, 311–13.

125 *LP*, xiii(2). 996.

126 *Correspondance de Marillac*, p. 22 (*LP*, xiii(1). 205); *SP*, viii, p. 189. BL, Cotton MS Vespasian C vii, fo. 24 (*CWTW*, i, letter 14); Wyatt to Cromwell, 15 March 1539, Toledo.

127 TNA, SP 1/111, fo. 189r–v (*LP*, xi. 1131).

128 *Estancias y viajes*, p. 431. TNA, SP 1/132, fo. 164 (*LP*, xiii(1). 1104). In March 1536 Dingley had been granted royal licence to depart the realm 'to serve the duties of his religion': *LP*, x. 775(8); xi. 849. He was with Michael Throckmorton in Calais at the end of 1536, leaving on 28 December: *LL*, iii, p. 589.

129 *Declaration; Harley 78*, fo. 6v (*L&L*, p. 184).

130 *Defence; Harley 78*, fo. 12v (*L&L*, p. 202); *LP*, xii(1). 274; Nott, *Wyatt*, p. 312. Cromwell's first letter to Wyatt in embassy is addressed to 'Sir Thomas Wyatt, Knight': *Letters of Cromwell*, ii, p. 61.

131 *Egerton*, fos. 71–2 (*CWTW*, i, letter 1); Wyatt to his son, 14 April 1537, Paris. For a persuasive discussion of the letters, see J. Powell, 'Thomas Wyatt and Francis Bryan: Plainness and Dissimulation' in *The Oxford Handbook of Tudor Literature, 1485–1603*, ed. M. Pincombe and C. Shrank (Oxford, 2009), pp. 187–92.

132 For the word's breadth and habit of satire, see William Empson, 'The Honest Man' in *The Structure of Complex Words* (1952).

133 *Egerton*, fos. 72v–73 (*CWTW*, i, letter 2); Wyatt to his son, summer 1537.

134 For an exquisite account of truth in Wyatt's poetry: T. Greene, *The Light in Troy: Imitation and Discovery in Renaissance Poetry* (New Haven and London), pp. 254–9.

135 *CWTW*, i, letter 1; Wyatt to his son, 14 April 1537, Paris.

136 TNA, SP 1/117, fo. 164 (*LP*, xii(1). 766).

137 *PPE Mary*, pp. 14, 59.

138 TNA, SP 1/138, fo. 180 (*LP*, xiii(2). 804(3)).

11: AMBASSADOR

1 *Gentleman's Magazine*, p. 566.

2 J. D. Tracy, *Emperor Charles V, Impresario of War: Campaign Strategy, International Finance, and Domestic Politics* (Cambridge, 2002). Charles is described as 'paladin' at p. 307.

3 See D. Starkey, 'Representation through Intimacy: a Study in the Symbolism of Monarchy and Court Office in Early Modern England', in *Tudor Monarchy*,

ed. J. Guy (1997), pp. 42–78; D. Biow, 'Castiglione and the Art of Being Inconspicuously Conspicuous', *Journal of Medieval and Early Modern Studies*, 38 (2008), pp. 35–56 (the quotation is at p. 49).

4 Torquato Tasso discussed the ethical and political responsibilities of the ambassador in *Il messaggiero*. *Torquato Tasso: opere*, a cura di E. Mazzali, 2 vols. (Napoli, 1969), ii, pp. 417–502. See T. Hampton, *Fictions of Embassy: Literature and Diplomacy in Early Modern Europe* (Ithaca and London, 2009), pp. 50–62. Torquato's father, Bernardo Tasso, was an emissary at the Imperial court: see above, pp. 354–6, 373–4, 515.

5 Stephanus Doletus, *De officio legati* (Lyon, 1541); 'Étienne Dolet on the Functions of the Ambassador, 1541', intro. J. S. Reeves, *American Journal of International Law*, 26 (1933), pp. 80–92 (the quotation is at pp. 84–5).

6 Francis Thynn, *The Application of Certain Histories concerning Ambassadours* (1651), pp. 18–19.

7 *Letters of Cromwell*, ii, p. 92.

8 *CSPSp*, iv(1), *1529–1530*, p. 223.

9 *Defence*, *Harley 78*, fo. 12v (*L&L*, p. 202).

10 *LP*, xiii(1). 1215.

11 My principal guides to Renaissance diplomacy have been the classic works of G. Mattingley, *Renaissance Diplomacy* (Boston, 1954); R. A. de Maulde-la-Clavière, *La Diplomatie au temps du Machiavel*, 3 vols. (Genève, 1970). I have also relied on E. R. Adair, *The Extraterritoriality of Ambassadors in the Sixteenth and Seventeenth Centuries* (1929); D. E. Queller, *The Office of Ambassador in the Middle Ages* (Princeton, 1967); G. Alexander, 'The Life and Career of Edmund Bonner, Bishop of London, until his Deprivation in 1549' (unpublished University of London Ph.D. thesis, 1960). Renaissance diplomacy is the subject of renewed scholarly enquiry: *Politics and Diplomacy in Early Modern Italy: the structure of diplomatic practice, 1400–1800*, ed. D. Frigo, trans. A. Belton (Cambridge, 2000); *Ambasciatori e nunzi: figure della diplomazia in età moderna*, ed. D. Frigo, *Cheiron*, xxx (Brescia, 1999); D. Biow, *Doctors, Ambassadors, Secretaries: Humanists and Professions in Renaissance Italy* (Ann Arbor, 2002); M. J. Levin, *Agents of Empire: Spanish Ambassadors in Sixteenth-century Italy* (Ithaca and London, 2005); J.-M. Ribera, *Diplomatie et espionnage: Les ambassadeurs du roi de France auprès de Philippe II* (Paris, 2007); T. A. Sowerby, *Renaissance and Reform in Tudor England: the Careers of Sir Richard Morison c.1513–1556* (Oxford, 2010), ch. 6.

12 *CSPVen*, *1520–1526*, pp. 33, 46, 55, 73.

13 *Il messagiero*, cited in Hampton, *Fictions of Embassy*, p. 59. D. Frigo, 'Prudence and Experience: Ambassadors and Political Culture in Early Modern Italy', *Journal of Medieval and Early Modern Studies*, 38 (2008), pp. 15–34. 'Étienne Dolet on the Functions of the Ambassador, 1541', p. 90.

14 *SP*, viii, p. 267.

15 'Myne owne Jhon poyntz', ll. 53–4.

16 *CSPFor, Elizabeth, 1561–1562*, pp. 521, 567–8; Thomas Chaloner to Sir John Mason, 9 February, 26 March 1562.

17 Nicholas Harpsfield, *The Life and Death of Sir Thomas Moore, Knight*, ed. E. V. Hitchcock (EETS, 186, 1932), pp. 33–4.

18 *SP*, vi, pp. 449–50; *LP*, iv(1). 1555, 1632. M. L. Robertson, 'Wingfield, Sir Richard (*b.* in or before 1469, *d.* 1525)', *ODNB*.

19 D. G. Newcombe, 'Hawkins, Nicholas (*c.*1495–1534)', *ODNB*.

20 *LP*, iii(2). 2908.

21 See, for example, *LP*, iii(2). 2281, 2661; iv(1). 1132, 1555, 1684, 1839.

22 Hall, fo. 200v; AGR, Papiers Gachard, 643, fo. 157; Giovanni Poggio to Cardinal Farnese, 20 November 1538, Toledo.

23 I am very grateful to Dr Ben Hazard for this information.

24 *Harley 282*, fo. 255v (*CWTW*, i, letter 4); Wyatt's memorandum for Dudley, first week of November 1537.

25 AGS, Guerra Antigua, legajo 9/95, 105; Conde de Cifuentes to Charles V, 4 August and 8 October 1536, Rome.

26 See P. Marshall, 'The Other Black Legend' in *Religious Identities in Henry VIII's England* (Aldershot, 2006), pp. 103–24.

27 *Defence*; *Harley 78*, fos. 12v–13r (*L&L*, p. 202).

28 So he would ironically refer to them: *Harley 282*, fo. 227v (*CWTW*, i, letter 11); Wyatt to Cromwell, 2 January 1539.

29 *LP*, iv(2). 4078.

30 *LP*, xiv(2). 782, p. 318; E. K. Chambers, *Sir Henry Lee: an Elizabethan Portrait* (Oxford, 1936), p. 20.

31 *LP*, xii(1). 539(1). Egerton, fo. 71 (*CWTW*, i, letter 1); Wyatt to his son, 14 April 1537, Paris. In 1559 Wyatt's widow Elizabeth and her second husband were still seeking administration of Sir Henry's goods, and in 1576 George Wyatt sought the same: TNA, PCC, Prob. 11/26, fo. 50. *Index of Wills Proved in the Prerogative Court of Canterbury Wills, 1558–1583*, iii, ed. L. L. Duncan (British Record Society, 1898), p. 350.

32 TNA, C 2/Eliz/B21/29; *CPR, 2 & 3 Philip and Mary*, p. 159.

33 For example, TNA, C 54/422, mm. 6–7d; C 54/423, m. 33d; C 54/432, m. 20d. I owe this information to the scholarship and generosity of Steven Gunn, both great. I am very grateful to him for showing me his forthcoming book: *Henry VII's New Men and the Making of Tudor England*.

34 TNA, SP 1/126, fo. 83 (*LP*, xii(2). 1048). *Letters of Cromwell*, ii, p. 102.

35 CKS, DRb/Pwr/9, fo. 254. Hawte's will, dated January 1538, was proved in June 1539: TNA, PCC, Prob. 11/26, fos. 107v–108v.

36 *Letters of Cromwell*, ii, p. 64.

37 Most famous of all was A. Gentili, *De legationibus libri tres*, intro. E. Nys (New York, 1924). J. J. Jusserand, *The School for Ambassadors* (1924); B. Behrens, 'Treatises on the Ambassador Written in the Fifteenth and Sixteenth Centuries', *EHR*, 51 (1936), pp. 616–27. Bodleian, BB 12 Art. For Pickering's inscriptions, see fos. 12, 12v, 16v, 81v, 89v.

38 C. M. Curtis, 'Richard Pace on Pedagogy, Counsel and Satire' (unpublished University of Cambridge Ph.D. thesis, 1996), pp. 139–40.

39 Nott, *Wyatt*, p. 312; *LP*, xii(1). 637.

40 Jean Hotman, *The Ambassador* (1603), sig. K2v; Adair, *Extraterritoriality*, pp. 102–4. *Surrey: Poems*, 28. 20.

41 Leland, *Naeniae* (*L&L*, p. 264). Leland may have received the patronage of Blage's stepfather, John Barret: J. P. Carley, 'Leland, John (*c.*1503–1552)', *ODNB*.

42 Mary Brooke married first, Sir Robert Blage (d. 1522); second, John Barret (d. 1526); third, Sir Richard Walden (d. 1539): TNA, PCC, Prob. 11/20, fos. 112–13; 11/22, fos. 171–2v; 11/27, fos. 225v–226v (dates of death are estimated from dates of probate). Her personal wealth – and her determination to hold onto it – appears in Barret's will and in her involvement in several Chancery suits: TNA, C1/465/9; C1/478/17; C1/621/1; C1/793/9–10.

43 *LP*, xviii(2). 190; *Blage*, fos. 58, 101, 124, 152, 177. Blage's 'A voice I have' is printed in *L&L*, appendix C. *Foxe's Book of Martyrs* (1570), 8, p. 1427.

44 For Gardiner's household, see TNA, SP 1/129, fos. 71–82 (*LP*, xiii(1). 327); Germain Gardiner to Thomas Wriothesley, 21 February 1538. TNA, SP 1/101, fo. 149r–v (*LP*, x. 177); Thomas Runcorn to 'Georgio Blaag, *amico meo charissimo* [my dearest friend]', 25 January 1536.

45 *LP*, xiii(1). 659.

46 Bryan bothered to write in his own hand this letter requesting favour for his 'old friend', Lettice Lee: TNA, SP 1/143, fo. 176 (*LP*, xiv(1). 387). 'Knollys, Henry I (by 1521–83)'; 'Lee, Sir Anthony (1510/11–49)', *House of Commons*, ii, pp. 481, 505; J. Woolfson, *Padua and the Tudors: English Students in Italy, 1485–1603* (Cambridge, 1998), pp. 176, 249.

47 For Mantell fighting at the barriers, see BL, Harley MS 69, fo. 18v. TNA, SP 1/240, fo. 308 (*LP, Addenda*, 1201).

48 TNA, C 1/495/46; W. G. Davis, *The Ancestry of Mary Isaac, c.1549–1613* (Portland, Maine, 1955), pp. 186, 297. When his father, Sir Walter Mantell, made his will in August 1523 John was not yet of age: TNA, PCC, Prob. 11/23, fo. 73v. Mantell was perhaps about twenty-one in 1537.

49 Hall, fo. 244r; *LL*, v, p. 95. Helen Baron identified Mantell as the custodian of Wyatt's verse: 'The "Blage" Manuscript: the Original Compiler Identified', *English Manuscript Studies, 1100–1700*, 1 (Oxford, 1989), pp. 85–119.

50 For the hand of Brereton in *Egerton*, see J. Powell, 'Thomas Wyatt's Poetry in Embassy: Egerton 2711 and the Production of Literary Manuscripts Abroad', *HLQ*, 67 (2004), pp. 261–8.

51 'Rudston, Robert (1514/15–90)', *House of Commons*, iii, pp. 226–7.

52 'Household and Privy Purse Accounts of the Lestranges of Hunstanton', *Archaeologia*, 25 (1834), pp. 548–50. C. Oestmann, *Lordship and Community: the Lestrange Family and the Village of Hunstanton in Norfolk in the First Half of the Sixteenth Century* (Woodbridge, 1994), pp. 13ff.

53 C. H. Miller, 'Chaloner, Sir Thomas, the elder (1521–1565)', *ODNB*; *The Praise of Folie by Sir Thomas Chaloner*, ed. C. H. Miller (EETS, 257, 1965), pp. xxix–xlv. J. Lock, 'Chamberlain, Sir Thomas (*c.*1504–1580)', *ODNB*. Chamberlain returned to Spain in January 1562 as 'minder' of Anthony Browne; Chaloner as ambassador in the winter of 1561. Their correspondence appears in *CSPFor, Elizabeth, 1561–1562; 1562*.

54 Chaloner wrote regularly to Mason (by then Sir John Mason) from Spain: *CSPFor, Elizabeth, 1561–1562*, pp. 492–4, 521, 567–8, 610–11; *1562*,

pp. 135–6, 274–5, 588 (the quotations are at *1562*, p. 275; *1561–1562*, p. 521). See above, pp. 8, 358, 360–1, 464.

55 *L&L*, p. 204; Hotman, *The Ambassador*, sig. C7r.

56 Ribier, i, p. 386 (*LP*, xiv(1). 371).

57 'Étienne Dolet on the Functions of the Ambassador', p. 86.

58 *Foxe's Book of Martyrs* (1563), 4, pp. 816–18.

59 TNA, SP 1/136, fo. 123 (*LP*, xiii(2). 348); *LL*, v, p. 95.

60 For Wyatt's diplomatic correspondence and use of secretaries, see Powell, 'Thomas Wyatt's poetry in embassy', pp. 264–5. Wyatt's lament was made in mid-March 1539; see above, pp. 442–3. 'Étienne Dolet on the Functions of the Ambassador', p. 86; Hotman, *The Ambassador*, sig. C6v–C7r.

61 *CSPSp*, v(2), *1536-1538*, p. 422; *LP*, xiii(1). 131, 329, 330; xiv(1). 1123.

62 *LP*, ix. 459, 490. Rede's private letters survive, for dark reasons: *LP*, viii. 908; x. 1066; *LP*, *Addenda*, 942.

63 *Gentleman's Magazine*, p. 567.

64 P. Chaplais, *English Diplomatic Practice in the Middle Ages* (London and New York, 2003), pp. 168–9; A. Bray, *The Friend* (Chicago and London, 2003), pp. 116–22.

65 *Pole's Correspondence*, p. 36.

66 M. Jaffé, 'The Picture of the Secretary of Titian', *Burlington Magazine*, 108 (1966), pp. 114–26; *Titian*, ed. D. Jaffé (National Gallery, 2003).

67 D. Biow, *Doctors, Ambassadors, Secretaries*; M. L. Doglio, *Il secretario e il principe: studi sulla letteratura italiana del Rinascimento* (Alessandria, 1993); S. Kolsky, '"The Good Servant": Mario Equicola. Court and Courtier in Early Sixteenth-century Italy', *The Italianist*, 6 (1986), pp. 34–60.

68 For Mason's career, see P. R. N. Carter, 'Mason, Sir John (*c.*1503–1566)', *ODNB*; D. G. E. Hurd, *Sir John Mason, 1503–1566* (1975).

69 Leland, *Naeniae* (*L&L*, p. 264).

70 *Gentleman's Magazine*, p. 567.

71 BL, Cotton MS Vespasian, C xiii, fo. 328 (*LP*, vii. 945); T. F. Mayer, 'Starkey, Thomas (*c.*1498–1538)', *ODNB*.

72 R. Ascham, *The scholemaster* (1570), sig. B1v; cited in 'Mason, Sir John', *ODNB*.

73 *LP*, *Addenda*, 1019; ix. 838.

74 BL, Cotton MSS, Vitellius B xiv, fos. 157–60; Nero B vii, fo. 106 (*LP*, ix. 981, 927). AGS, Estado, legajo 1311/137; Pole to Charles V, 17 June 1535, Venice.

75 *LP*, x. 687 (in Mason's hand); x. 670 (the quotations are at pp. 269, 274).

76 *CSPSp*, v(2), *1536–1538*, pp. 122–3.

77 *Faculty Office Registers*, p. 57; *BRUO*, p. 386; *LP*, xi. 1186.

78 *Letters of Cromwell*, ii, p. 144.

79 'Étienne Dolet on the Functions of the Ambassador', p. 85.

80 *Harley 282*, fos. 36v, 58v; *Letters of Cromwell*, ii, pp. 114, 133, 140, 144, 179.

81 *Harley 282*, fos. 36v, 281v; *Letters of Cromwell*, ii, pp. 63, 92, 102.

82 Hotman, *The Ambassador*, sigs. K2v–K4; Adair, *Extraterritoriality*, pp. 11–12, 102–4, 115–76. The quotation is taken from the title of Maulde-la-Clavière's great work.

83 BL, Cotton MS Vespasian C xiii, fo. 328v (*LP*, vii. 945).

84 TNA, SP 1/117, fo. 164 (*LP*, xii(1). 766) (the letter is dated Maundy Thursday, which fell on 13 April in 1536). *Defence, Harley 78*, fo. 8 (*L&L*, p. 191). On the 15th the papal nuncio in France knew of Wyatt's coming: see above, p. 329.

85 Nott, *Wyatt*, p. 449. F. Wasner, 'Fifteenth Century Texts on the Ceremonial of the Papal "Legatus a Latere"', *Traditio*, 14 (1958), pp. 295–358.

86 ASV, SS, Principi, 12, fos. 27v–9; cited in C. Höllger, 'Reginald Pole and the Legations of 1537 and 1539: Diplomatic and Polemical Responses to the Break with Rome' (unpublished University of Oxford D.Phil. thesis, 1989), p. 40; *Pole's Correspondence*, pp. 150–1; *LP*, xii(1). 988. For Francis's attestation of undying friendship: *LP*, xii(1). 625. For Pole's legation of 1537, see T. F. Mayer, 'If Martyrs Are to Be Exchanged with Martyrs: the Kidnappings of William Tyndale and Reginald Pole' and 'A Diet for Henry VIII: the Failure of Reginald Pole's 1537 Legation' in his *Cardinal Pole in European Context: a* via *media in the Reformation* (Aldershot, 2000), chs. 6–7, and *Reginald Pole: Prince and Prophet* (Cambridge, 2000), pp. 62–70; C. Capasso, *Paolo III, 1534–1549*, 2 vols. (Messina, 1924), i, pp. 387–97; G. M. Monti, 'La legazione del Polo e del Giberti in Francia e in Fiandra nel 1537', *Archivio storico italiano*, ser. 7, 12 (1929), pp. 293–309.

87 *LP*, xii(1). 869, 884. Bryan had been at Dover on 8 April, and in Calais by the next day.

88 BL, Additional MS, 25114, fo. 255 (*LP*, xii(1). 865); *LP*, xii(1). 988; *ANG*, 1, p. 263.

89 M. Rodríguez-Salgado, 'Charles V and the Dynasty', and G. Parker, 'The Political World of Charles V' in *Charles V, 1500–1558, and His Time*, ed. H. Soly (Antwerp, 1999), especially pp. 80–1, 167–8.

90 ASV, SS, Principi, 12, fos. 187v–203; cited in Höllger, 'Reginald Pole and the Legations of 1537 and 1539', p. 42. *LP*, xii(1). 923.

91 He first openly mentioned his fear to the King on 15 July 1536; *Pole's Correspondence*, pp. 101–2. G. B. Parks, 'The Parma Letters and the Dangers to Cardinal Pole', *Catholic Historical Review*, 46 (1960–1), pp. 299–317. Mayer, *Reginald Pole*, pp. 91–2, 96, 98.

92 *Pole's Correspondence*, pp. 152–3. Höllger, 'Reginald Pole and the Legations of 1537 and 1539', p. 47.

93 ASPr, CFE, Francia, busta 7 (*LP*, xii(1). 949); Cardinal Carpi to Ricalcati, 15 April 1537, Amiens.

94 *ANG*, 1, p. 253 (*LP*, xii(1). 996); Carpi to Ricalcati, 21 April 1537, Amiens.

95 BL, Additional MS 25114, fo. 257 (*LP*, xii(1). 939).

96 BL, Cotton MS Caligula E i, fo. 46 (*LP*, xii(1). 953); Mewtas to [Cromwell], 16 April 1537.

97 *ANG*, 1, p. 252; *LP*, xii(1). 987; *Nine Historical Letters*, p. 17 (*LP*, xii(1). 1123).

98 *LP*, xii(1). 987.

99 *LP*, xiii(2). 797, p. 310. Mewtas was a gentleman usher of the Privy Chamber, now given an annuity of £20 blood money: *LP*, xii(1). 795(41).

100 TNA, SP 1/138, fo. 134; SP 1/139, fos. 29, 47v (*LP*, xiii(2). 766, 829(3). 830(vii)); examination of Elizabeth Darrell, 6 November 1538.

101 TNA, SP 1/138, fos. 181v–182 (*LP*, xiii(2). 804(5)); fifth examination of Sir Geoffrey Pole, 7 November 1538.

102 TNA, SP 1/138, fo. 180 (*LP*, xiii(2). 804(3)); third examination of Sir Geoffrey Pole, 3 November 1538.

103 TNA, SP 1/137, fo. 203 (*LP*, xiii(2). 615).

104 A. Overell, 'Cardinal Pole's Special Agent: Michael Throckmorton, *c.*1503–1558', *History*, 94 (2009), pp. 265–78; 'An English Friendship and Italian Reform: Richard Morison and Michael Throckmorton, 1532–1538', *JEH*, 57 (2006), pp. 478–98.

105 *Declaration*; *Defence*; *Harley 78*, fos. 5, 8 (*L&L*, pp. 179, 191).

106 BL, Additional MS 25114, fo. 263 (*LP*, xii(1). 1032).

107 *LL*, iv, p. 300.

108 *LP*, xii(1). 1235, 1242; xii(2). 795.

109 *The State of Christendom* (1667 edn.), p. 209. For immunity, see Gentili, *De legationibus libri tres*, Book II; Adair, *The Extraterritoriality of Ambassadors*; Queller, *The Office of Ambassador*, pp. 175–84. Book 2 of Dolet's treatise concerned the immunities of ambassadors – not in his own vitiated times, but in the ancient world: 'Étienne Dolet on the Functions of the Ambassador', pp. 91–5.

110 *LP*, xii(1). 988, 1123.

111 *SP*, vii, pp. 693–4.

112 *ANG*, 1, p. 449.

113 *Delle lettere di M. Bernardo Tasso*, a cura di A.-F. Seghezzi, 2 vols. (Padova, 1733), i, pp. 260–1.

114 BL, Cotton MS Vespasian C xiii, fo. 258 (*LP*, xii(2). 131); Brereton to Wriothesley, 23 June 1537, Valladolid.

115 *CSPSp*, v(2), *1536–8*, pp. 351–2, 357, 366–7; *LP*, xii(2). 104.

116 AGS, Estado, Francia, legajo K 1691, fo. 2. *LP*, xii(1). 696. E. Spivakowsky, *Son of the Alhambra: Diego Hurtado de Mendoza, 1504–1575* (Austin, Texas and London, 1970), pp. 60–9.

117 BL, Cotton MS Vespasian C xiii, fo. 258r–v (*LP*, xii(2). 131); Nott, *Wyatt*, p. 449. *Chronicle of King Henry VIII*, pp. 15–16.

118 *Egerton*, fo. 66. Mantell's version is found in *Blage*, fo. 73. For the possible sources of this poem – Ariosto, Petrarch and Serafino – see P. Thomson, *Sir Thomas Wyatt and his Background* (Stanford, 1964), pp. 280–3. For Wyatt's poetry written in embassy, and the exciting revelation of the significance of the pale ink, see J. Powell, 'Thomas Wyatt's Poetry in Embassy: Egerton 2711 and the Production of Literary Manuscripts Abroad', *HLQ*, 67 (2004), pp. 261–81. For Mantell's 'carrying' of this poem in his head: H. Baron, 'The "Blage" Manuscript: the Original Compiler Identified', pp. 99–101.

119 Salinas, *BRAH*, 45 (1904), p. 468; Guidiccioni, *Lettere*, i, p. 316.

120 Guidiccioni, *Lettere*, i, pp. 317–18. The messenger who reported Mendoza's treatment left England on 7 June.

121 BL, Cotton MS Vespasian C xiii, fo. 327v (*LP*, vii. 945).

122 'Francesco Guicciardini's Report from Spain', trans. S. ffolliott, *Allegorica* (1982), pp. 60–114 (the quotation is at pp. 74–5).

123 For Valladolid, and its festivities, see B. Bennassar, *Valladolid au siècle d'or: une ville de Castille et sa campagne au XVIe siècle* (Paris, 1967). For an illustration of a game of canes in 'la plaza mayor' in 1506, see M. del Rosario Fernandez Gonzalez, *Edificios Muncipales de la Cuidad de Valladolid de 1500 a 1561* (Valladolid, 1985), pp. 18–19.

124 *CSPSp*, viii, *1545–1546*, pp. 604–5. For Don Pedro de la Cueva, see *CSPSp*, iv(2), *1531–1533*, pp. xiv–xx. That night Wyatt sent news of this meeting to Cromwell, by Bartholomew Butler, Rouge Croix pursuivant: *Letters of Cromwell*, ii, p. 63.

125 BL, Cotton MS Vespasian C xiii, fo. 258v (*LP*, xii(2). 131).

126 M. Rodríguez-Salgado, 'Charles V and the Dynasty', pp. 78–9. F. Sansovino, *Il simolacro di Carlo Quinto Imperadore* (Venice, 1567), p. 21, cited in P. Burke, *The Fortunes of the* Courtier: *the European Reception of Castiglione's* Cortegiano (Cambridge, 1995), p. 58. For Boscán's translation, see *ibid.*, pp. 62–3, 73, 104–5, 148.

127 J. Powell, 'Thomas Wyatt and the Emperor's Bad Latin', *NQ*, 49:2 (June 2002), pp. 207–9.

128 *Legazioni di Serristori*, p. 24. Charles conversed with Richard Morison in Italian: Sowerby, *Renaissance and Reform in Tudor England: the Careers of Sir Richard Morison*, p. 194.

129 *CSPSp*, vi(1), *1538–1542*, p. 215.

130 Pedro Salazar y Mendoza, *Chrónica de el Cardenal don Juan Tavera* (Toledo, 1603).

131 *CSPSp*, viii, *1545–1546*, pp. 604–5.

132 *LP*, xii(2). 245; *CSPSp*, v(2), *1536–1538*, p. 97. Pate returned to London via Calais, and wrote to Lord Lisle upon his return: *LL*, iv, pp. 294–5 (misdated to 10 May). For Pate's career, see T. A. Sowerby, 'Richard Pate, the Royal Supremacy, and Reformation Diplomacy', *HJ*, 54 (2011), pp. 265–85.

133 Guidiccioni, *Lettere*, i, p. 292.

134 TNA, SP 1/129, fo. 76v (*LP*, xiii(1). 327); Germain Gardiner to Wriothesley, 21 February 1538. P. Friedmann, *Anne Boleyn: a Chapter of English History, 1527–1536*, 2 vols. (1884), i, pp. 150–2, 179.

135 *LP*, xii(1). 705; *ANG*, 1, pp. 239, 247.

136 *ANG*, 1, p. 265.

137 ASV, SS, Principi, 12, fos. 210–11v; cited in Höllger, 'Reginald Pole and the Legations of 1537 and 1539', pp. 70–1.

138 *CSPVen, 1520–1526*, 902; Contarini to the Council of Ten, 4 December 1524. Guidiccioni, *Lettere*, i, p. 205.

139 *Harley 282*, fos. 7–14v (*SP*, vii, pp. 683–8). This letter was endorsed by Wyatt: 'The Kynges grace to my predecessor, the last lettre afore my coming'. *CSPSp*, v(2), *1536–1538*, p. 412.

140 Nott, *Wyatt*, pp. 311–15. The italics are mine.

141 *LP*, xii(1). 815; *ANG*, 1, pp. 267–8.

142 *Harley 282*, fo. 279 (Nott, *Wyatt*, p. 421).

143 Guidiccioni, *Lettere*, i, pp. 271, 298.

144 *LP*, xii(2). 245; Guidiccioni, *Lettere*, i, p. 322.

145 M. Rodríguez-Salgado, 'Charles V and the Dynasty', pp. 78–9, 86.

146 For the quotation: *Ven. Dep.*, i, p. 202. K. M. Setton, *The Papacy and the Levant, 1204–1571*, 4 vols. (Philadelphia, 1976–84), iii, pp. 395–7, 406. Tracy, *Emperor Charles V, Impresario of War*, pp. 144–9.

147 R. J. Knecht, *Francis I* (Cambridge, 1982), pp. 224–5, 233–4; Capasso, *Paolo III*, i, ch. 6; R. Finlay, 'I Am the Servant of the Turkish Sultan': Venice, the Ottoman Empire and Christendom' in *Venice Besieged: Politics and Diplomacy in the Italian Wars, 1494–1534* (Aldershot, 2008), ch. 10.

148 K. Brandi, *The Emperor Charles V*, tr. C. V. Wedgwood (1939), p. 383; *LP*, vi. 859.

149 Francis Poyntz had described the discomforts of the journey a decade earlier: BL, Cotton MS Vespasian C iv, fo. 188 (*LP*, iv(2). 3375); Poyntz to Wolsey, 23 August 1527, Valladolid.

150 ASMo, CD, Ambasciatori Spagna, busta 3; Rossetto to the Duke of Ferrara, early August 1537, Zaragoza.

151 Salinas, *BRAH*, 45 (1904), pp. 470–1.

152 Guidiccioni, *Lettere*, i, p. 324.

153 *Correspondance de Castillon et Marillac*, p. 58; Castillon to Montmorency, 4 June 1538.

154 ASMo, CD, Ambasciatori Spagna, busta 3; Rossetto to the Duke of Ferrara, 22 September 1538, Valladolid. *CSPSp*, v(2), *1536–1538*, p. 499; ASF, MP 4296, fos. 227, 250v; Bandino to the Duke of Florence, 23 July 1538, Barcelona; 5 September 1538, Valladolid.

155 ASMo, CD, Ambasciatori Francia, busta 14; Alberto Turco to the Duke of Ferrara, 8 February 1538, Moulins.

156 AGR, Audience, 67, fo. 262.

157 *Harley 282*, fos. 281, 267 (Nott, *Wyatt*, pp. 422, 427); *Letters of Cromwell*, ii, pp. 92–3, 95.

158 ASMo, CD, Ambasciatori Spagna, busta 3; Rossetto to the Duke of Ferrara, end of September 1537, Monzón.

159 *Defence; Harley 78*, fo. 9v (*L&L*, p. 194); *Letters of Cromwell*, ii, pp. 92–3.

160 *Letters of Gardiner*, pp. 81–91 (especially pp. 88–9).

161 'Memoriale a Raffaelo Girolami quando ai 23 d'Ottobre partì per Spagna all'Imperatore' in *Tutte le opere di Niccolò Machiavelli*, a cura di F. Flora and C. Cordié, 2 vols. (Milano, 1949–50), ii, pp. 515–18 (the quotation is at p. 516).

162 TNA, SP 1/129, fo. 77 (*LP*, xiii(1). 327).

163 R. McEntegart, *Henry VIII, the League of Schmalkalden, and the English Reformation* (2002); *LP*, xv. 419.

164 For ambassadors and history, see for example, Gentili, *De legationibus libri tres*, book ii, ch. 8; Hotman, *The Ambassador*, sig. B8r. For an illuminating discussion, Hampton, *Fictions of Embassy*, pp. 25–9.

165 ASMo, CD, Ambasciatori Spagna, busta 3; Rossetto to the Duke of Ferrara, 22 September 1538, Valladolid.

166 *G. Guidiccioni & F. Coppetta Beccutti: Rime*, a cura di E. Chiorboli (Bari, 1912); *Novelle del cinquecento*, a cura di G. Salinari (Torino, 1955), i, pp. 231–45.

167 Guidiccioni, *Lettere*, i, pp. 191, 275, 292, 323–4 (the quotation is at p. 292).

For Poggio as papal tax collector, see J. M. Carretero Zamora, 'La colectoría de España en época de Carlos V: cuentas del nuncio y colector General Giovanni Poggio (1529–1546)', *Cuadernos de Historia de España*, 78 (2003).

168 P. Richard, 'Origines des nonciatures permanentes: la représentation pontificale au xvie siècle (1450–1513)', *Revue d'Histoire Ecclésiastique*, 7 (1906), pp. 52–70, 317–38; L. Riccardi, 'An Outline of Vatican Diplomacy in the Early Modern Age', in *Politics and Diplomacy*, ed. Frigo, pp. 95–108. H. C. Lea, *A History of the Inquisition of Spain*, 4 vols. (1906), iii, pp. 533–4.

169 J. E. Longhurst, *Erasmus and the Spanish Inquisition: the Case of Juan de Valdés* (Albuquerque, 1950), p. 12.

170 AGR, Papiers Gachard, 643, fo. 150; Poggio to Cardinal Farnese, 20 November 1538, Toledo.

171 ASV, AA, Arm. I–XVIII, 6533, fo. 45; ASMn, AG, Spagna 589; Vivaldini to the Duke of Mantua, 25 October 1537. For the making of the Holy League, see Capasso, *Paolo III*, i, pp. 443–61; Setton, *The Papacy and the Levant*, iii, pp. 422–30.

172 ASV, AA, Arm. I–XVIII, 6533, fo. 44v.

173 Nott, *Wyatt*, p. 449.

174 ASF, MP, 4296, fos. 24–5; Serristori to the Duke of Florence, 22 October 1537.

175 ASF, MP, 4296, fo. 30; Lorenzo Pagni to the Duke of Florence, 22 October 1537. ASV, AA, Arm. I–XVIII, 6533, fo. 46.

176 ASMn, AG, Spagna 589; Vivaldini to the Duke of Mantua, 25 October 1537.

177 *Letters of Cromwell*, ii, pp. 92–4. Wyatt's reckoning includes a payment of twenty ducats to 'Bartholomew, the Herald, that he borrowed to come into Aragon': Nott, *Wyatt*, p. 449. ASV, SS, Principi, 12, fo. 36.

178 ASV, AA, Arm. I–XVIII, 6533, fos. 55v–57 (*LP*, xii(2). 1031); Poggio to Cardinal Farnese, 4 November 1537, Monzón.

179 ASPr, CFE, Spagna 124; Poggio to Cardinal Farnese, 10 November 1537. *Letters of Cromwell*, ii, p. 95.

180 [John Ponet], *A short treatise of politike pouuer* (1556), sig. I3r.

181 *Harley 282*, fos. 255–62v (*CWTW*, i, letter 4); Wyatt's memorandum for Dudley, first week of November 1537.

182 *CSPSp, Supplement, 1513–1542*, p. 455. Capasso, *Paolo III*, i, p. 682. *LP*, xiv(1). 321, pp. 125–6.

183 ASPr, CFE, Spagna 124; Poggio to Cardinal Farnese, 20 November 1537.

184 *CSPSp*, v(2), *1536–1538*, pp. 501–2.

185 *Contarini, Regesten und Briefe*, p. 296; Cardinal Contarini to the papal nuncio in Venice, undated.

186 *ANG*, 1, p. 330; Ricalcati to Ferrerio, 7–8 January 1538, Rome.

187 ASV, AA, Arm. I–XVIII, 6533, fo. 57 (*LP*, xii(2). 1031). Adair, *Extraterritoriality of Ambassadors*, pp. 110–12; Maulde-la-Clavière, *La Diplomatie au temps du Machiavel*, ii, pp. 34–5.

188 TNA, SP 1/126, fos. 126, 133, 162, 164 (*LP*, xii(2). 1087, 1098, 1135, 1137).

189 BL, Cotton MS Caligula E ii, fos. 240–1 (*LP*, xii(2). 1133); *LP*, xii(2). 1253. Germain Gardiner was the source of the report from Alberto Turco, the Ferrarese ambassador at the French court: ASMo, CD, Ambasciatori Francia, busta 14 (27 December 1537).

190 For the peace negotiations, see K. Hayward, *Francisco de los Cobos: Secretary of the Emperor Charles V* (Pittsburgh, 1958), pp. 194–202; Capasso, *Paolo III*, i, pp. 462–77.

191 *CSPSp*, v(2), *1536–1538*, pp. 412–13.

192 Hayward, *Francisco de los Cobos*, p. 200.

193 Serristori, *Legazioni*, pp. 47–8; ASMo, CD, Ambasciatori Spagna, busta 3; Rossetto to the Duke of Ferrara, 17, 28 December 1537.

194 *CSPSp*, v(2), *1536–1538*, pp. 438–41; Diego Hurtado de Mendoza to Francisco de los Cobos, 28 February 1538, London.

195 W. Knapp (ed.), *Obras Poéticas de D. Diego Hurtado de Mendoza* (Madrid, 1877), p. 467; cited Spivakovsky, *Son of the Alhambra*, p. 66.

12: I RESTLES REST IN SPAYNE

1 *Egerton*, fo. 54v.

2 *Surrey: Poems*, 28. 13; 10. 13–14, p. 110.

3 *Petrarch's Lyric Poems*, 103.

4 See 'Myne olde dere enmy'. P. Thomson, 'Wyatt and the Petrarchan Commentators', *RES*, 10 (1959), p. 228.

5 For sensitive criticism of the poem, see D. M. Ross, *Self-Revelation and Self-Protection in Wyatt's Lyric Poetry* (New York and London, 1988), pp. 40–4. *Wyatt: Poems*, pp. 368–9.

6 Richard Helgerson's essay is inspiring: *A Sonnet from Carthage: Garcilaso de la Vega and the New Poetry of Sixteenth-Century Europe* (Philadelphia, 2007). The translation is his. See also *Selected Poems of Garcilaso de la Vega*, ed. and trans. J. Dent-Young (Chicago, 2009), pp. 52–3; D. L. Heiple, *Garcilaso de la Vega and the Italian Renaissance* (Pennsylvania, 1994), pp. 222–6, 319–20.

7 D. H. Darst, *Diego Hurtado de Mendoza* (Boston, 1987), pp. 54–6.

8 *Bernardo Tasso: Rime*, a cura di D. Chiodo, 2 vols. (Torino, 1995), i, p. 308. For the life of Tasso, see E. Williamson, *Bernardo Tasso* (Roma, 1951).

9 *Bernardo Tasso: Rime*, i, p. 315. The translations are Nigel Wilson's, and I acknowledge them with great gratitude. Williamson, *Bernardo Tasso*, pp. 35–6; A. González Palencia, *Don Luis de Zuñiga y Avila: Gentilhombre de Carlos V* (Madrid, 1932).

10 Helgerson, *A Sonnet from Carthage*, p. 44.

11 *Delle lettere di M. Bernardo Tasso*, a cura di A.-F. Seghezzi, 2 vols. (Padova, 1733), i, pp. 260–1. ASF, MP, 4296, fos. 67, 81 (*Legazioni di Serristori*, pp. 39, 44).

12 For the Romantic period, Strozzi was a tragic hero: see G.-B. Niccolini, *Filippo Strozzi, tragedia (corredata d'una vita di Filippo e di documenti inediti)* (Firenze, 1847). For his career, see M. M. Bullard, *Filippo Strozzi and the Medici: Favour and Finance in Sixteenth-Century Florence* (Cambridge, 1980).

13 Williamson, *Bernardo Tasso*, pp. 8–10.

14 Sperone Speroni, *Dialogo d'Amore*, trans. C. Gruget (Poitiers, 1998); J. L. Smarr, 'A Dialogue of Dialogues: Tullia d'Aragona and Sperone Speroni', *MLN*, 113 (1998), pp. 204–12.

15 For Williamson, the love between Tullia and Tasso was only fictional: *Bernardo Tasso*, pp. 11–12. For Georgina Masson, they were 'passionately in love': *Courtesans of the Italian Renaissance* (1975), ch. 5.

16 Heiple, *Garcilaso de la Vega*, ch. 5 (the quotation is at p. 106).

17 R. Altrocchi, 'Tasso's Holograph Annotation to Horace's *Ars poetica*', *PMLA*, 43 (1928), pp. 931–52.

18 See Boscán's manifesto on the adoption of Italianate metres addressed 'To the Duchess of Somma', and Castillejo's censure: D. H. Darst, *Juan Boscán* (Boston, 1978), pp. 21–6, 133–9. *Andrea Navagero: Lusus: Text and Translation*, ed. A. E. Wilson (Nieuwkoop, 1973).

19 H. Thomas, *Spanish and Portuguese Romances of Chivalry* (Cambridge, 1920), p. 183. Williamson argues that the proposal was made in 1540: *Bernardo Tasso*, pp. 35–6, 99ff.

20 *The Praise of Folie by Sir Thomas Chaloner*, ed. C. H. Miller (EETS, 257, 1965), p. xli.

21 Helen Baron suggested that the Egerton manuscript went to Spain with Wyatt: 'The "Blage" Manuscript: the Original Compiler Identified', *English Manuscript Studies*, 1 (1989), pp. 85–119 (at p. 102). Jason Powell provides a convincing account of how Wyatt's poetry was copied and compiled: 'Thomas Wyatt's Poetry in Embassy: Egerton 2711 and the Production of Literary Manuscripts Abroad', *HLQ*, 67 (2004), pp. 261–8; 'Marginalia, Authorship, and Editing in the Manuscripts of Thomas Wyatt's Verse', *English Manuscript Studies*, *1100–1700*, 15 (2009), pp. 1–40 (especially pp. 15–25).

22 Nott, *Wyatt*, pp. 422, 425; BL, Harley MS 283, fo. 171; TNA, SP 1/209, fo. 91v (*LP*, xx(2). 518, 637). Baker's handwriting by 1545 does not accord with the unknown hands in *Egerton*.

23 TCD, MS 160: the 'Blage' manuscript. *Unpublished Poems*; S. O'Keeffe, 'TCD MS 160: A Tudor Miscellany' (unpublished Trinity College, Dublin M.Litt. thesis, 1986). That the original compiler was John Mantell was Helen Baron's discovery: 'The "Blage" Manuscript'. For the great complexity of the making of this anthology and its relation to the Egerton manuscript, see Baron, 'The "Blage" Manuscript' and Powell, 'Marginalia, Authorship, and Editing', pp. 17–28.

24 Baron, 'The "Blage" Manuscript, pp. 96–102.

25 Powell, 'Marginalia, Authorship, and Editing', p. 27.

26 *De rep. anglorvm instauranda libri decem, authore Thoma Chalonero* (1579). For Chaloner's English verse, see *The Praise of Folie by Sir Thomas Chaloner*, pp. xlvii–xlix.

27 *Egerton*, fo. 24v. The source was identified by J. Newman, 'An Italian Source for Wyatt's "Madame, withouten many wordes"', *Renaissance News*, 10 (1957), pp. 13–15; *Collected Poems of Wyatt*, pp. 297–8; S. Woods, *Natural Emphasis: English Versification from Chaucer to Dryden* (San Marino, 1984), pp. 78–9. Dr Baron

established that Blage wrote the 'Aunswer', and found another version in *Blage*, fo. 128: 'The "Blage" Manuscript', pp. 103–6.

28 *Egerton* was certainly in Blage's possession for a time, for in it he made corrections, added ascriptions. It is possible that he was working under Wyatt's supervision, but – since he mistakenly 'improved' certain poems – this is unlikely. Probably he made most of his insertions into *Egerton* after Wyatt's death: Powell, 'Marginalia, Authorship and Editing', pp. 17–20.

29 The most subtle reading of the interplay between the two verses is by C. Stamatakis, '"Turning the Word": Sir Thomas Wyatt and Early Tudor Literary Practice' (unpublished University of Oxford D. Phil. thesis, 2008), pp. 235–8. For the male game of ventriloquizing a female voice, see E. Heale, 'Women and the Courtly Love Lyric: the Devonshire MS (BL Additional 17492)', *MLR*, 90 (1995), pp. 302–4.

30 TNA, SP 1/209, fo. 91v (*LP*, xx(2). 637).

31 In 1552 Mason granted the rectory and church of Tintinhull in Somerset to Elizabeth Darrell and her husband Robert Strode: TNA, LR 14/769. TNA, PCC, Prob. 11/49, fo. 10 (will of Sir John Mason, proved 25 January 1566).

32 BL, Cotton MSS Vitellius B xiv, fos. 157–60; Vespasian C xiii, fo. 327 (*LP*, ix. 981; vii. 945).

33 'Francesco Guicciardini's Report from Spain', trans. S. ffolliott, *Allegorica* (1982), pp. 60–114 (the quotation is at p. 77).

34 For Mantell's marriage to Anne Browne: Baron, 'The "Blage" Manuscript', p. 90. Perhaps she was related to the Browne family of Surrey. On 4 November 1538, Mantell and Anne Fiennes were granted dispensation for marrying without banns. In July 1540 Blage was dispensed to marry Dorothy Badbye in a private chapel or oratory: *Faculty Office Registers*, pp. 154, 221. After his dalliance with the 'good wife', Rede married Wyatt's niece Jane, daughter of Anthony and Margaret Lee: TNA, SP 1/136, fo. 144 (*LP*, xiii(2). 382); E. K. Chambers, *Sir Henry Lee: an Elizabethan Portrait* (Oxford, 1936), p. 24.

35 *Il viaggio fatto in Spagna et in Francia dal Magnifico M. Andrea Navagiero* (Venice, 1563), pp. 3–4.

36 ASMo, CD, Ambasciatori Spagna, busta 3; Rossetto to the Duke of Ferrara, December 1537; *Relaciones de Pedro de Gante, Secretario del Duque de Nájera (1520 1544)* (Madrid, 1873), pp. 15–20 (*CSPSp*, v(2), *1536–1538*, pp. 531–4). H. Keniston, *Francisco de los Cobos: Secretary of the Emperor Charles V* (Pittsburgh, 1958), pp. 201–4.

37 ASMo, CD, Ambasciatori Francia, busta 14; Alberto Turco to the Duke of Ferrara, 8 February 1538, Moulins.

38 *CSPSp*, v(2), *1536–1538*, pp. 419, 423.

39 Henry's letter to Wyatt is dated 23 December 1537. Letters came from Cromwell and Wriothesley, dated the 26th. Nott, *Wyatt*, pp. 464–9, 423–4; *Letters of Cromwell*, ii, pp. 110–11.

40 H. Jedin, *A History of the Council of Trent*, trans. E. Graf, 2 vols. (1957–61), i, pp. 290–312; C. Capasso, *Paolo III, 1534–1549*, 2 vols. (Messina, 1924), i, ch. 5.

41 *CSPSp*, v(2), *1536–1538*, p. 526; Chapuys to the Queen of Hungary, 13 April 1538.

42 *A protestation made for the most mighty and most redoubted kynge of Englande and his hole counsel and clergie wherin is declared that neyther his highenes, nor his prelates, neyther any other prynce, or prelate, is bounde to come or sende, to the pretended councell, that Paule bysshoppe of Rome, first by a bul indicted at Mantua, a citie in Italy, [and] nowe a late by an other bull, hath prorogued to a place, no man can tell where* (1537). A Latin version was also printed: *Illustris.ac potentis. Regis, senatus, populi que Angliae, sententiae, et de eo concilio, quod Paulus episcopus Roma Mantuae futurum simulauit, et de ea bulla* (1537). Tracey Sowerby explains the importance of such propaganda in English diplomacy, and its official dissemination: 'All our books do be sent into other countreys and translated': Henrician Polemic in its International Context', *EHR*, 121, 494 (2006), pp. 1271–99.

43 *Henrici Octaui . . . ad Carolum Caesarem Augustum* (1538); Sowerby, 'All our books do be sent', pp. 1277, 1282–7.

44 Charles gave three different accounts of his audiences with Wyatt in January 1538: *CSPSp*, v(2), *1536–1538*, pp. 421–2, 498–506; *CSPFor*, *1547–1553*, pp. 312, 315; Nott, *Wyatt*, p. 467. In audience with Richard Morison in March 1551 the Emperor remembered Wyatt's audacity: see T. A. Sowerby, *Renaissance and Reform in Tudor England: the Careers of Sir Richard Morison c.1513–1556* (Oxford, 2010), pp. 197–200.

45 *ANG*, 1, pp. 327ff; AGS, Estado, legajo 867/192; *CSPSp*, v(2), *1536–1538*, pp. 424–5; AGR, Papiers Gachard, 643, fo. 51v. For Jacobazzi's mission, see Capasso, *Paolo III*, i, pp. 477–9, 658–60. Diego Hurtado de Mendoza owned a copy of Jacobazzi's *De concilio tractatus* (Roma, 1538): 'Catalogue of Diego Hurtado de Mendoza's Library of Printed Books', 549 in A. Hobson, *Renaissance Book Collecting: Jean Grolier and Diego Hurtado de Mendoza, their Books and Bindings* (Cambridge, 1999).

46 ASV, SS, Principi, 12, fos. 32–3; Jacobazzi to Cardinal Farnese, 1 February 1538, Barcelona.

47 ASV, SS, Principi, 12, fos. 36–8; Misc. Arm. II. 10, fos. 4–13; Jacobazzi to Cardinal Farnese, 6 and 7 March 1538.

48 AGR, Papiers Gachard, 643, fo. 65v; Poggio to Cardinal Farnese, 3 February 1538.

49 AGR, Papiers Gachard, 643, fos. 49, 52v; Poggio to Ambrogio Ricalcati, 17–23 January 1538.

50 *CSPSp*, v(2), *1536–1538*, pp. 501–2.

51 AGR, Papiers Gachard, 643, fo. 66; Poggio to Cardinal Farnese, 3 February 1538; ASF, MP 4296, fos. 160–1.

52 ASMo, CD, Ambasciatori Spagna, busta 3; Rossetto to the Duke of Ferrara, 29 January 1538.

53 AGR, Papiers Gachard, 643, fo. 66v; Poggio to Cardinal Farnese, 3 February 1538; AGR, Audience, 69, fos. 172–3; Charles V to Mary of Hungary, 7 February 1538.

54 ASMo, CD, Ambasciatori Francia, busta 14; Alberto Turco to the Duke of Ferrara, 8 February 1538, Moulins. The King referred to a letter of Wyatt's of 2 February: *LP*, xiii(1). 329.

55 TNA, E 30/1029.

56 ASF, MP, 4296, fo. 190; ASMo, CD, Ambasciatori Spagna, busta 3; Rossetto to the Duke of Ferrara, 16 February 1538.

57 Setton, *The Papacy and the Levant*, iii, pp. 422–30.

58 Charles's own words, reported by Wyatt, were quoted back at him: *Letters of Cromwell*, ii, p. 103.

59 *LP*, xiii(1). 31, 139; *Letters of Cromwell*, ii, p. 114. Cromwell's letter of 11 February arrived with Wyatt in Barcelona on the 24th.

60 *CSPSp*, v(2), *1536–1538*, pp. 433–7; ASV, SS, Principi, 12, fo. 34v; AGR, Papiers Gachard, 643, fo. 66v.

61 *Ven. Dep.*, i, p. 237; Mocenigo to the Doge, 22 November 1538.

62 *CSPFor, 1547–1553*, p. 312.

63 *CSPVen, 1520–1526*, 960; Gasparo Contarini to the Signory, 16 March 1525.

64 We know, from reports of their recipients, that Wyatt sent letters on 20 November 1537, 18 January, 3 February, 14 March, 25 April, 17–25 May 1538.

65 *Letters of Cromwell*, ii, p. 125.

66 *Defence; Declaration; Harley 78*, fos. 9v, 6v (*L&L*, pp. 194, 184).

67 'Memoriale a Raffaelo Girolami quando ai 23 d'Ottobre partì per Spagna all'Imperatore' in *Tutte le opere di Niccolò Machiavelli*, a cura di F. Flora and C. Cordié, 2 vols. (Milano, 1949–50), ii, pp. 515–18. See Hampton, *Fictions of Embassy*, p. 21.

68 'Étienne Dolet on the Functions of the Ambassador, 1541', pp. 88–9.

69 *Declaration; Harley 78*, fo. 6v (*L&L*, p. 184).

70 Francesco Guicciardini, *Maxims and Reflections (Ricordi)*, trans. M. Domandi (Philadelphia, 1965), C2, B 24, pp. 40, 103.

71 Guicciardini, *Maxims and Reflections*, C 153, p. 80.

72 D. E. Queller, 'How to Succeed as an Ambassador: a Sixteenth-century Venetian Document', *Studia Gratiana*, 15 (1972), pp. 653–71.

73 For Wyatt attending Mass with the Emperor, see for example: *Gentleman's Magazine*, p. 566; ASF, MP, 4300, fo. 55; Giovanni Bandino to the Duke of Florence, 22 July 1538, Barcelona. See above, pp. 345–6. G. Mattingley, *Renaissance Diplomacy* (Boston, 1955), p. 242.

74 *Defence; Harley 78*, fo. 13v (*L&L*, p. 204).

75 For Rouge Croix's departure, see Wyatt's reckoning: Nott, *Wyatt*, p. 449. For the letter with a cross: TNA, SP 3/8, fo. 61 (*LL*, v, pp. 29–30; *CWTW*, i, letter 5). Other members of Wyatt's household in Spain – John Mason, Anthony Barker, and William Wolfe – sent letters headed with a cross: TNA, SP 1/126, fo. 126; SP 1/135, fo. 234; SP 1/136, fo. 123 (*LP*, xii(2). 1087; xiii(2). 191, 348).

76 Nott, *Wyatt*, pp. 468–9; *CSPSp*, v(2), *1536–1538*, pp. 501, 506.

77 ASV, SS, Principi, 12, fo. 32v; AGR, Papiers Gachard, 643, fo. 66; ASMo, CD, Ambasciatori Spagna, busta 3; Rossetto to the Duke of Ferrara, 29 January 1538.

78 K. Carleton, 'Bonner, Edmund (d. 1569)'; C. S. Knighton, 'Haynes (Heynes), Simon (d. 1552)', *ODNB*. For their mission, see G. Alexander, 'The Life and Career of Edmund Bonner, Bishop of London, until his Deprivation in 1549' (unpublished University of London Ph.D. thesis, 1960), ch. 6.

79 *Defence*; Harley *78*, fo. 14 (*L&L*, p. 207).

80 *LL*, v, pp. 29–30.

81 *CSPSp*, v(2), *1536–1538*, pp. 433–7, 450–4; AGR, Papiers Gachard, 643, fos. 69–70; *Correspondance de Castillon et Marillac*, p. 25 (*LP*, xiii(1). 274).

82 *Letters of Cromwell*, ii, pp. 113–14.

83 ASV, SS, Principi, 12, fo. 36; *ANG*, 1, p. 315.

84 J. M. Headley, 'The Habsburg World Empire and the Revival of Ghibellinism', in *Theories of Empire, 1450–1800*, ed. D. Armitage (Aldershot, 1998), pp. 45–79.

85 *Italy and the European Powers: the Impact of War, 1500–1530*, ed. C. Shaw (Leiden and Boston, 2006); T. C. Price Zimmermann, *Paolo Giovio: the Historian and the Crisis of Sixteenth-Century Italy* (Princeton, 1995), ch. 4.

86 R. Ridolfi, *The Life of Francesco Guicciardini*, trans. C. Grayson (1967), pp. 255ff (the quotation is at p. 255).

87 C. Capasso, *Paolo III, 1534–1549*, 2 vols. (Messina, 1924), i, chs. 1–3; Tracy, *Emperor Charles V, Impresario of War*, ch. 6.

88 ASF, MP 4296, fos. 112–113v (Serristori, *Legazioni*, p. 50).

89 P. Prodi, *The Papal Prince, One Body and Two Souls: The Papal Monarchy in Early Modern Europe* (Cambridge, 1982).

90 C. Robertson, *Il Gran Cardinale: Alessandro Farnese, Patron of the Arts* (New Haven and London, 1992), ch. 1; Capasso, *Paolo III*, i, ch. 1.

91 ASMo, CD, Ambasciatori Spagna, busta 3; Rossetto to the Duke of Ferrara, 15 and 17 April 1538, Barcelona.

92 Niccolini, *Filippo Strozzi*, pp. 270–92.

93 Serristori, *Legazioni*, p. 18.

94 ASMo, CD, Ambasciatori Spagna, busta 3; Rossetto to the Duke of Ferrara, 4 October 1537, Monzón.

95 For Tasso's letters from the Imperial court, see Niccolini, *Filippo Strozzi*, pp. 265–7, 269, 270–7, 280–1, 282–6, 289 (his lament is at p. 280). For reports on Tasso's efforts: Serristori, *Legazioni*, pp. 42, 44, 48–50, 61, 71; ASMo, CD, Ambasciatori Spagna, busta 3 (1 and 31 January 1538; cited in *Lettere inedite di Bernardo Tasso*, a cura di G. Campori (Bologna, 1869), pp. 54–6).

96 Queller, 'How to Succeed as an Ambassador', p. 659.

97 ASMo, CD, Ambasciatori Spagna, busta 3; Rossetto to the Duke of Ferrara, 4 March 1538, Barcelona.

98 *Letters of Cromwell*, ii, pp. 133–4. For the conferences, see *LP*, xiii(1). 640; xiii(2), appendices 14–15.

99 *Letters of Cromwell*, ii, pp. 117, 133, 135, 137–8.

100 *Ibid,*, pp. 140–1.

101 *Defence*; Harley *78*, fos. 12r, 12v (*L&L*, pp. 201, 202).

102 *LP*, xiii(1). 131.

103 *Defence*; Harley *78*, fo. 14 (*L&L*, p. 207).

104 *Letters of Cromwell*, ii, p. 64; *LP*, xii(2). 774, 811, 977, 1151.

105 *Letters of Cromwell*, ii, p. 102.

106 TNA, SP 1/126, fo. 162 (*LP*, xii(2). 1135); John Mantell to John Mason, 27 November 1537, London.

107 TNA, PCC, Prob. 11/26, fos. 13v–14v.

108 *Harley 282*, fos. 267–85 (Nott, *Wyatt*, pp. 424–9). The quotations are at fos. 267 and 273 (pp. 426, 428).

109 *Letters of Cromwell*, ii, p. 135.

110 Queller, 'How to Succeed as an Ambassador', p. 662.

111 *Letters of Cromwell*, ii, p. 102.

112 *Harley 282*, fo. 279 (Nott, *Wyatt*, p. 421); *Letters of Cromwell*, ii, pp. 64, 93–4, 102, 114–15, 124–5, 133–5, 157, 161, 167, 179, 186.

113 TNA, SP 1/137, fo. 118 (*LP*, xiii(2). 553).

114 *Declaration*; *Harley 78*, fo. 5 (*L&L*, p. 180).

115 TNA, SP 1/158, fos. 48, 52; BL, Cotton MS Vitellius B xiv, fo. 264v (*LP*, xv. 358, 369; xiii(2). 847).

116 For the Leghs of Stockwell, and the John a Lygh who lived at Alington in the 1490s, see W. B. Robison III, 'The Justices of the Peace in Surrey in National and Gentry Politics, 1483–1570' (unpublished Louisiana State University Ph.D. thesis, 1984), pp. 50, 60, 450. In his uncle's will of June 1523 Legh was left a bequest which he would receive at the age of twenty-four. The rest of his fortune was left in reversion, to be inherited after the death of his aunt: TNA, PCC, Prob. 11/21, fos. 112–14v (will of Sir John Legh); Prob 11/22, fos. 143–4 (will of Dame Isabel Legh). *LP*, iv(1), p. 867; iv(2). 3216.

117 BL, Cotton MS Cleopatra E vi, fos. 380–1 (*LP*, xv. 721). There are problems of chronology in Legh's testimony – perhaps unsurprisingly, since he gave it in the Tower: *Pole's Correspondence*, pp. 189–90. He asked for the cross of Jerusalem to be engraved on the breast of his image for his tomb: TNA, PCC, Prob. 11/48, fo. 281v. For Legh and his family, see W. G. Davis, *The Ancestry of Mary Isaac, c.1549–1613* (Portland, Maine, 1955), pp. 340–55.

118 Edward, Lord Herbert of Cherbury, *The Life and Raigne of King Henry the eighth* (1649), p. 564.

119 ASV, AA, Arm. I–XVIII, 6533, fo. 57 (*LP*, xii(2). 1031).

120 For Branceter's life, see J. J. Scarisbrick, 'The First Englishman Round the Cape of Good Hope?' *BIHR*, 34 (1961), pp. 165–77.

121 *LP*, ix. 490; *Letters of Cromwell*, ii, pp. 94, 95, 103.

122 G. J. O'Malley, 'Dingley, Sir Thomas (1506x8–1539)', *ODNB*.

123 *LP*, xi. 849; TNA, SP 1/132, fo. 164 (*LP*, xiii(1). 1104); *LP*, xiii(1). 230. *Estancias y viajes*, p. 431.

124 *LP*, xii(2). 427; *Addenda*, 1095, 1157.

125 TNA, SP 1/240, fo. 295 (*LP*, *Addenda*, 1191); *LP*, *Addenda*, 1269; xii(1). 78, 207, 975, 1103(28); xii(2). 663; xiii(1). 230, 627.

126 *LP*, xii(2). 921, 1023. Sir George Throckmorton's confession is printed in J. Guy, *The Public Career of Sir Thomas More* (Brighton, 1980), pp. 207–12. P. Marshall, 'Crisis of Allegiance: George Throckmorton and Henry Tudor', in *Catholic Gentry in English Society: the Throckmortons of Coughton from Reformation to Emancipation* (Aldershot, 2009), pp. 31–67.

127 *PPE*, p. 8.

128 TNA, SP 1/132, fo. 164r–v (*LP*, xiii(1). 1104). Jason Powell, whose recogni-

tion of the handwriting of these scribes is masterly, told me that Brereton was Branceter's scribe. I am very grateful.

129 'Étienne Dolet on the Functions of the Ambassador, 1541', p. 86. M. J. Levin, *Agents of Empire: Spanish Ambassadors in Sixteenth-Century Italy* (Ithaca and London, 2005), p. 170.

130 For narratives of the journeys and the meetings, see *Relaciones de Pedro de Gante*, pp. 22–49, 174–91 (*CSPSp*, v(2), *1536–1538*, pp. 535–66); *CSPSp*, v(2), *1536–1538*, pp. 475–90.

131 *CSPSp*, v(2), *1536–1538*, p. 458. On that day Pole wrote to Cardinal Farnese, leaving his affairs in Farnese's care: *Pole's Correspondence*, p. 194.

132 *CSPSp*, v(2), *1536–1538*, pp. 475–7, 535–7.

133 *Declaration*; *Defence*; *Harley 78*, fos. 5v, 13 (*L&L*, pp. 180, 204).

134 *SP*, viii, pp. 22–7; Henry VIII to Wyatt, 7 April 1538, and to Haynes and Bonner; *CSPSp*, v(2) *1536–1538*, p. 526. Thomas Barnaby followed them 'into Spain with certain protestations newly imprinted': *LP*, xiii(2), p. 580.

135 *LP*, xiii(1). 842.

136 *LP*, xiii(1). 897.

137 *CSPFor, Elizabeth, 1562*, pp. 274–5; Thomas Chaloner to John Mason, August 1562.

138 *Declaration*; *Defence*; *Harley 78*, fos. 5v, 8v (*L&L*, pp. 181, 191).

139 BL, Cotton MS Vitellius B xiv, fo. 27v (*LP*, xiii(1). 1165); *LL*, v, pp. 124–5.

140 *Declaration*; *Harley 78*, fo. 5v (*L&L*, p. 181).

141 *Il Galateo* (1558) of Giovanni della Casa (1503–56) was translated into English in 1576: Robert Peterson, *Galateo of Manners and Behaviours (1576)* (Bari, 1997), p. 151.

142 *CSPSp*, v(2), *1536–1538*, pp. 482–3, 538. *Pole's Correspondence*, p. 193.

143 *Declaration*; *Defence*; *Harley 78*, fos. 5v–6, 8v–9v (*L&L*, pp. 181–2, 191–4).

144 Bonner's charges against Wyatt are found in Inner Temple Library, Petyt MS 47, fos. 9ff (printed in *Gentleman's Magazine*, pp. 565–8; *L&L*, pp. 64–9). For Wyatt's version, see *Defence*; *Harley 78*, fo. 7v (*L&L*, p. 189).

145 *Defence*; *Harley 78*, fo. 10v (*L&L*, pp. 197–8). This may have been a common expression: *The Comedy of Acolastus*, ed. P. L. Carver (EETS, 202, 1937), p. 18.

146 *Defence*; *Harley 78*, fos. 10v–11 (*L&L*, pp. 198–9).

13: FRIENDS OF FRIENDS AND FOES OF FOES

1 TNA, SP 1/138, fo. 29v (*LP*, xiii(2). 702); examination of Jerome Ragland, [28 October] 1538.

2 TNA, SP 1/137, fo. 118 (*LP*, xiii(2). 553).

3 D. Lloyd, *State-worthies, or, the states-men and favourites of England since the Reformation* (1679), p. 79 (cited in *L&L*, p. 271).

4 TNA, SP 1/133, fo. 155 (*LP*, xiii(1). 1228). *LP*, xiii(1). 1024, 1177–9, 1202, 1228; TNA, SP 1/133, fo. 186; SP 1/242, fo. 65 (*LP*, xiii(1). 1251; *Addenda*, 1343).

5 *Gentleman's Magazine*, pp. 565–6.

6 *Declaration*; *Harley 78*, fo. 6 (*L&L*, p. 182). 'Mr Wiattes Articles': TNA, SP 1/132, fos. 201–3v (*SP*, viii, pp. 34–8). Nott, *Wyatt*, p. 449; TNA, SP 1/132, fo. 140; SP 1/133, fo. 4 (*LP*, xiii(1). 1062, 1146); *Correspondance de Castillon et Marillac*, p. 55; *Letters of Cromwell*, ii, p. 143.

7 Nott, *Wyatt*, pp. 490–4; *Letters of Cromwell*, ii, pp. 137–8; *Correspondance de Castillon et Marillac*, p. 45.

8 AGR, Audience, 69, fos. 187–90v. *CSPSp*, vi(1), *1538–1542*, p. 30.

9 *LP*, xiv(1). 72.

10 *CSPSp*, v(2), *1536–1538*, p. 529; *Correspondance de Castillon et Marillac*, p. 55 (*LP*, xiii(1). 1134).

11 Nott, *Wyatt*, pp. 485–9; *Correspondance de Castillon et Marillac*, p. 63.

12 TNA, SP 1/133, fo. 155 (*CWTW*, i, letter 7).

13 *LP*, xiii(1). 1213; *CSPSp*, v(2), *1536–1538*, p. 547; *Estancias y viajes*, p. 453. *Declaration*; *Harley 78*, fo. 6v (*L&L*, p. 183).

14 Nott, *Wyatt*, p. 449.

15 *LP*, xiii(1). 1102, 1135.

16 TNA, SP 1/132, fo. 140 (*LP*, xiii(1). 1062); *LL*, v, pp. 138–9; Geoffrey Loveday to Lord Lisle, 25 May 1538, Aix. For Bryan's servants in 'gorgeous gear', see TNA, SP 1/134, fos. 188–90 (*LP*, xiii(1). 1402–3).

17 *Foxe's Book of Martyrs* (1570), 8, p. 1243.

18 *LL*, v, pp. 145–6.

19 'Étienne Dolet on the Functions of the Ambassador, 1541', ed. J. S. Reeves, *American Journal of International Law*, 27 (1933), pp. 80–95 (the quotation is at p. 91).

20 'L'amitié entre Francis Bryan et le cardinal Jean du Bellay' in C. Michon, '"De Bons Frères, cousins et Parfaits Amys?" Les anglais et la France sous François Ier' in *Les idées passent-elles la Manche? Savoirs, représentations, pratiques*, ed. J.-P. Genet et F.-J. Ruggiu (Paris, 2007), annexe, p. 322. I am very grateful to Dr Tracey Sowerby for this reference. For Bryan's 'great friends': ASV, AA, Arm. I–XVIII, 6538, fo. 77v; Nuncio in France to Farnese, 8 August 1538, Moulins.

21 D'Este's Conto del Giuoco: ASMo, CDAP, 999, fos. 3v, 6v–7v, 11r –v. For d'Este and his gambling, see M. Hollingsworth, *The Cardinal's Hat: Money, Ambition and Housekeeping in a Renaissance Court* (2004), especially pp. 201–3, 207.

22 *LP*, xiv(1). 267.

23 *Harley 282*, fo. 227 (*CWTW*, i, letter 11); Wyatt to Cromwell, 2 January 1539, Toledo. *Letters of Cromwell*, ii, p. 161. Among the King's payments in December 1538 was 'so much money paid and allowed to Sir Francis Bryan, knight, upon a letter of exchange of Anthony Bonvix . . . £165.6s.8d': *LP*, xiii(2), p. 537.

24 *Declaration*; *Harley 78*, fo. 6r–v (*L&L*, p. 183); *Gentleman's Magazine*, p. 566; AGR, Audience, 69, fo. 187v; *Estancias y viajes*, p. 454; Nott, *Wyatt*, p. 449. I am grateful to Dr Jason Powell for telling me the name of the galley.

25 *CSPSp*, v(2), *1536–1538*, pp. 548–9, 557 (the quotation is at p. 548); *Ven. Dep.*, i, pp. 179–80, 185; Pietro Mocenigo to the Doge, 11 and 16 July 1538, Hyères and Aigues Mortes.

26 *CSPSp*, v(2), *1536–1538*, pp. 549–50; *Ven. Dep.*, i, pp. 185–6; ASMo, CD,

Ambasciatori Spagna, busta 3; Rossetto to the Duke of Ferrara, 15 July 1538, Aigues Mortes.

27 *CSPSp*, v(2), *1536–1538*, pp. 550–4, 561–6; *Ven. Dep.*, i, pp. 186–90; Mocenigo to the Doge, 22 July 1538, Barcelona.

28 ASMo, CD, Ambasciatori Spagna, busta 3; Rossetto to the Duke of Ferrara, 15 July 1538, Aigues Mortes.

29 *Ven. Dep.*, i, p. 110; Mocenigo and Giovanni Antonio Venier to the Doge, 6 June 1538, Nice. C. Capasso, *Paolo III (1534–1549)*, 2 vols. (Messina, 1924), i, p. 683.

30 *Gentleman's Magazine*, pp. 565–6. For an account of the mission, see G. Alexander, 'The Life and Career of Edmund Bonner, Bishop of London, until his Deprivation in 1549' (unpublished University of London Ph.D. thesis, 1960), ch. 6.

31 *Gentleman's Magazine*, pp. 565–7.

32 TNA, SP 1/133, fo. 4 (*Letters of Cromwell*, ii, p. 144). (This letter bears the inscription: 'Item, delivered to Thomas Wriothesley, the xth of September: John Mason'.)

33 *Gentleman's Magazine*, p. 567.

34 *Foxe's Book of Martyrs* (1570 edn.), 8, p. 1244; BL, Cotton MS Vitellius B xiv, fos. 27v–28v (*LP*, xiii(1). 1165).

35 *Foxe's Book of Martyrs* (1570 edn.), 8, p. 1243; *Gentleman's Magazine*, p. 567.

36 *Defence*; Harley *78*, fo. 13 (*L&L*, p. 203).

37 BL, Cotton MS Vespasian C xiii, fos. 249–50.

38 *Calendar of Letters and State Papers relating to English Affairs*, ed. M. A. S. Hume, 4 vols. (1868–79), ii, p. 38. Cited in T. A. Sowerby, 'Richard Pate, the Royal Supremacy and Reformation Diplomacy', *HJ*, 54 (2011), p. 272. It may be, as Dr Sowerby judges, that Wyatt was the more likely candidate for defenestration than the 'doctors'.

39 *Defence*; Harley *78*, fo. 14 (*L&L*, p. 206).

40 *Ven. Dep.*, i, pp. 188–91; Mocenigo to the Doge, 22 July 1538, Barcelona; AGR, Papiers Gachard, 643, fos. 94–7; Poggio to Cardinal Farnese, 17 July 1538, Aigues Mortes, 22 July, Barcelona.

41 *Defence*; Harley *78*, fo. 11 (*L&L*, p. 198). Nicholas le Pelle was sent: Nott, *Wyatt*, p. 449.

42 Nott, *Wyatt*, pp. 499–500.

43 *Gentleman's Magazine*, p. 566.

44 *CSPSp*, vi(1), *1538–1542*, pp. 2–4, 68; AGR, Audience, 69, fos. 189–90v.

45 ASF, MP, 4296, fo. 227r–v; Giovanni Bandino to the Duke of Florence, 23 July 1538, Barcelona.

46 *Gentleman's Magazine*, p. 566; AGR, Papiers Gachard, 643, fo. 103; Poggio to Cardinal Farnese, 28 July, Barcelona. *LP*, xiii(2). 59–60; *Foxe's Book of Martyrs* (1570 edn.), 8, p. 1240.

47 *Gentleman's Magazine*, p. 566.

48 *Defence*; Harley *78*, fos. 13v–14 (*L&L*, pp. 205–6). For the monastery of Santa Maria de Jonqueres, see *Il Viaggio fatto in Spagna et in Francia dal Magnifico M. Andrea Navagiero* (Venice, 1563), pp. 3–4.

49 ASF, MP 4300, fo. 55; Bandino to the Duke of Florence, 25 July 1538, Barcelona.

50 *Gentleman's Magazine*, pp. 567–8; *Defence*; Harley *78*, fo. 13 (*L&L*, pp. 203–4).

51 *Defence*; Harley *78*, fo. 13r–v (*L&L*, p. 204); *Foxe's Book of Martyrs* (1570 edn.), 8, p. 1240 (*LP*, xiii(2), 59–60).

52 *Foxe's Book of Martyrs* (1570 edn.), 8, pp. 1244, 1243. For Gardiner's letters of instruction to Bonner, see *Letters of Gardiner*, pp. 81–91. *SP*, viii, p. 52; Wriothesley to Cromwell, end of September 1538.

53 *Foxe's Book of Martyrs* (1570 edn.), 8, p. 1244.

54 *Gentleman's Magazine*, p. 567. For Wyatt's version, see above, pp. 383–4.

55 *Foxe's Book of Martyrs* (1570 edn.), 8, pp. 1241–4; *Gentleman's Magazine*, pp. 565–8. Barnaby was the courier who carried the reports: *LP*, xiii(2). 270; *Foxe's Book of Martyrs* (1570 edn.), 8, p. 1240.

56 *Correspondance de Castillon et Marillac*, pp. 80–1 (*LP*, xiii(2). 77).

57 TNA, SP 1/135, fo. 6 (*LP*, xiii(2). 8); *LP*, xiii(1). 1451; xiii(2). 77, 78, 1120.

58 TNA, SP 1/135, fo. 246; SP 1/136, fo. 32 (*LP*, xiii(2). 210, 258); *LP*, xiii(2). 243, 280, 312 (the quotation is at 280).

59 *LP*, xiii(1). 1451; xiii(2). 23, 280.

60 TNA, SP 1/136, fo. 7 (*LP*, xiii(2). 233).

61 BL, Cotton MS Titus B i, fos. 94v–95.

62 *Defence; Harley 78*, fo. 14v (*L&L*, p. 207). For the meeting between Bonner and Barnaby at the end of August, see *Foxe's Book of Martyrs* (1570 edn.), 8, p. 1241. For Barnaby's later account of Gardiner's hopes for reconciliation, see BL, Lansdowne MS 2, fos. 87–90v.

63 *ANG*, 1, p. 151; Carpi to Ricalcati, Montplaisant, 27 March 1536. *SP*, viii, p. 52; Wriothesley to Cromwell, end of September 1538.

64 *SP*, viii, pp. 51–2; *LL*, v, p. 224.

65 *Defence; Harley 78*, fo. 14v (*L&L*, p. 207).

66 *SP*, viii, p. 52; Wriothesley to Cromwell, end of September 1538.

67 BL, Additional MS 5498, fo. 7 (*CWTW*, i, letter 9); Wyatt to Henry VIII, 9 November 1538, Toledo; Nott, *Wyatt*, p. 450. Mason travelled with Nicholas le Pelle, the courier.

68 TNA, SP 1/136, fos. 123, 144 (*LP*, xiii(2). 348, 382). William Wolfe wrote to his brother Edward, and John Brereton to Alexander Mather (enclosing a letter from Peter Rede). Mason also carried John Ratcliff's letter to Cromwell of 18 September: *LP*, xiii(2). 383.

69 *Declaration; Defence; Harley 78*, fos. 6v, 8v (*L&L*, pp. 183, 192–3).

70 TNA, SP 1/137, fos. 203–4 (*LP*, xiii(2). 615).

71 *Letters of Cromwell*, ii, pp. 157–8. Cromwell forwarded letters from Mason.

72 *Declaration; Defence; Harley 78*, fos. 6v, 8v–9, 14v (*L&L*, pp. 183, 193, 208).

73 The version given here is *Arundel Harington*, i, 310. *TM*, 101.

74 *LP*, xiii(2). 615.

75 *CSPSp*, vi(1), *1538–1542*, pp. 20–2, 391.

76 AGR, Papiers Gachard, 643, fo. 118; Poggio to Cardinal Farnese, 8 September 1538, Valladolid.

77 ASMo, CD, Ambasciatori Spagna, busta 3; Rossetto to the Duke of Ferrara, 4 September 1538, Valladolid.

78 AGR, Audience, 69, fo. 187v; Charles V to Mary of Hungary, 28 July 1538; *CSPSp*, vi(1), *1538–1542*, p. 67.

79 ASF, MP, 4296, fos. 250v–252; Bandino to the Duke of Florence, 5 September

1538, Valladolid.

80 ASMo, CD, Ambasciatori Spagna, busta 3; Rossetto to the Duke of Ferrara, 22 September 1538, Valladolid.

81 Nott, *Wyatt*, pp. 499–504 (*LP*, xiii(2). 622(1)); BL, Cotton MS, Vespasian C vii, fos. 71–83 (*LP*, xiii(2). 622(3)). The quotations are at fos. 76 and 81.

82 *LP*, v. 574, xv. 1029(6); *Inventory*, 10709.

83 *LP*, xiii(2). 702(2), p. 270.

84 *CSPSp*, vi(1), *1538–1542*, p. 31; *LP*, xiii(2). 392, 393. For the 'Exeter conspiracy', see M. H. and R. Dodds, *The Pilgrimage of Grace, 1536–7, and the Exeter Conspiracy*, 2 vols. (1915). J. P. D. Cooper, 'Courtenay, Henry, marquess of Exeter (1498/9–1538)'; A. Hawkyard, 'Neville, Sir Edward (*b.* in or before 1482, *d.* 1538)'; T. F. Mayer, 'Pole, Sir Geoffrey (*d.* 1558)'; 'Pole, Henry, Baron Montagu (1492–1539)', *ODNB*.

85 *LP*, xiii(2). 828, 829, 830(5); examination of George Croftes, [12 November] 1538.

86 *LP*, xiii(2). 796, 804(6).

87 *LP*, xiii(2). 961(2); TNA, SP 1/138, fo. 145 (*LP*, xiii(2). 772); *LP*, xiiii(2). 804(4).

88 Their treasonable speech is recorded in a series of depositions, best summarized in Sir Geoffrey Pole's statement: *LP*, xiii(2). 800. For God's law turned 'upsodown' and the King in Hell, see *LP*, xiii(2). 797, p. 309, 827(1).

89 *LP*, xiii(2). 827(1); examination of John Collins, 14 November 1538.

90 TNA, SP 1/138, fo. 145 (*LP*, xiii(2). 772); examination of Lord Montague, 7 November 1538; *LP*, xiii(2). 829(2).

91 TNA, SP 1/138, fo. 145r–v; SP 1/139, fo. 46 (*LP*, xiii(2). 772, 830).

92 TNA, SP 1/139, fo. 62 (*LP*, xiii(2). 830 v); Elizabeth Darrell's confession. This article is crossed through in the manuscript.

93 TNA, SP 1/138, fos. 145, 179 (*LP*, xiii(2). 772, 804(2)); examinations of Lord Montague, 7 November, and of Sir Geoffrey Pole, 2 November 1538.

94 TNA, SP 1/138, fos. 180, 181v–182 (*LP*, xiii(2). 804(3, 5)); third and fifth examinations of Sir Geoffrey Pole, 3 and 7 November 1538; *LP*, xiii(2). 831.

95 *Harley 282*, fo. 152v (*CWTW*, i, letter 17); Wyatt to Henry VIII, 16 December 1539, Blois.

96 *LP*, xiii(2). 827(3); examination of William Brent, 14 November 1538; TNA, SP 1/138, fo. 29v (*LP*, xiii(2). 702); examination of Jerome Ragland, [28 October], 1538.

97 TNA, SP 1/138, fo. 145 r–v; SP 1/139, fo. 46 (*LP*, xiii(2). 772, 830).

98 *LP*, xi. 1406. Edward Darrell, heir of Sir Edward Darrell, was the ward, then son-in-law, of Sir William Essex: TNA, PCC, Prob. 11/23, fos. 141–2; *LP*, xvi. 550. 'Sir Edward Darrell (1465/6–1530)'; 'Sir William Essex (*c.*1470–1548)'; 'Sir Anthony Hungerford (by 1492–1558)', *House of Commons*, ii, pp. 18–19, 106–7, 409–10.

99 TNA, SP 1/138, fo. 134; SP 1/139, fos. 29, 47v (*LP*, xiii(2). 766, 829(3), 830(vii)); examination of Elizabeth Darrell, 6 November 1538.

100 *LP*, xiii(2). 829(2), p. 339.

101 *LP*, xiii(2). 800, 804(2); confessions of Sir Geoffrey Pole.

102 *LP*, xiii(2). 765.

103 BL, Cotton Appendix L, fo. 71 (*L&L*, pp. 82–3). For Augustus's clemency to-
    wards Gnaeus Cornelius Cinna, see *De clementia*, I. viii.5–ix.12, in *Seneca: Moral
    Essays*, trans. J. W. Basore (Cambridge, Mass., 1928), i, pp. 381–7. Wyatt might
    also have learnt the news via conduits between the Pole circle and the Imperial
    ambassadors in England: *LP*, xiii(2). 797, p. 311; 828(2), p. 338.

104 *LP*, xiii(2). 979, 986.

105 *LP*, xiii(2). 948.

106 *CSPSp*, vi(1), *1538–1542*, p. 77; AGR, Papiers Gachard, 643, fo. 184; Poggio
    to Cardinal Farnese, 31 December 1538, Toledo.

107 *Harley 282*, fo. 228 (*CWTW*, i, letter 11). For this description of Mason, see
    Harley 78, fo. 14v. Via his friend Thomas Starkey, Montague's chaplain, Mason
    was apprised of Montague's affairs: for example, BL, Cotton MS Nero B vii, fo.
    106 (*LP*, ix. 927).

108 *LP*, xiii(2). 804(7).

109 ASV, SS, Principi, 13, fo. 91r–v; *LP*, xiii(2). 542, 684, 1280, fo. 34b.

110 *Letters of Cromwell*, ii, p. 162.

111 *Ven. Dep.*, i, p. 214; Mocenigo to the Doge, 26 September 1538, Valladolid;
    CSPSp, vi(1), *1538–1542*, p. 64.

112 Wyatt's accounts of the audience appear in his letter of 9 November, and his
    'note of remembrance' sent home with Hoby: BL, Additional MS 5498, fos.
    6v–12v (*CWTW*, i, letters 9–10).

113 AGR, Papiers Gachard, 643, fos. 151, 158; Poggio to Cardinal Farnese, 20
    November 1538, Toledo.

114 AGR, Audience, 67, fos. 245–65 (the description of Wyatt is at fo. 262).

115 ASMn, AG, Spagna 589, fos. 118, 127, 143; Vivaldini to the Duke of Mantua,
    20 October, 12, [26] November 1538; ASMo, CD, Ambasciatori Spagna,
    busta 3; Rossetto to the Duke of Ferrara, 12 December 1538, Toledo. *Ven. Dep.*,
    i, p. 217; Mocenigo to the Doge, 20 October 1538. Ribier, pp. 263–4.

116 ASMn, AG, Spagna 589, fo. 143; Vivaldini to the Duke of Mantua, [26]
    November 1538.

117 AGS, Estado, legajo 1371/103; BL, Additional MS 28590, fo. 279 (*LP*, xiii(2).
    939); to Gómez Súarez de Figueroa, 29 November 1538, Toledo.

118 ASV, SS, Principi, 13, fos. 91v–92. AGR, Papiers Gachard, 643, fo. 132;
    Cardinal Farnese to Poggio, 12 October 1538, Rome. Extensive charges and
    depositions concerning the poisoning remain in Simancas: AGS, Estado, legajo
    1459/121–3, 150.

119 *SP*, viii, pp. 80–1; Edmund Harvel to Cromwell, 15 November 1538, Venice.

120 J. Law, 'The Ending of the Duchy of Camerino' in *Italy and the European Powers: the
    Impact of War, 1500–1530*, ed. C. Shaw (Leiden and Boston, 2006), pp. 77–90;
    Pastor, *History of the Popes*, xi, pp. 304–9, 320–3; Capasso, *Paolo III*, i, pp. 625–31.

121 *CSPSp*, v(2), *1536–1538*, p. 556.

122 ASF, Ducato di Urbino, Classe prima, filza 183, fos. 10–11v; Felice Tiranni to
    Guidobaldo II, Duke of Urbino, 9 November 1538, Toledo. ASF, MP, 4296,
    fos. 294, 308; Bandino to the Duke of Florence, 13 and 23 November 1538.
    Guidobaldo wrote insistently to the Emperor and to fellow princes of north-

ern Italy: AGS, Estado, legajo 1459/120, 117; to the Emperor, 22 October, 20 November 1538; ASMn, AG, Urbino 1073; to the Duke of Mantua, 21 October and 4 November 1538.

123 BL, Additional MS 5498, fo. 12 (*CWTW*, i, letter 10); Wyatt's memorandum for Hoby, [early] December 1538.

124 BL, Additional MS 5498, fo. 14v (*LP*, xiii(2). 974(2)).

125 See, for example, *CSPSp*, v(2), *1536–1538*, p. 494; ASMo, CD, Ambasciatori Spagna, busta 3; Rossetto to the Duke of Ferrara, 14 October 1538, Toledo. ASV, SS, Principi, 13, fos. 178v–179; Duke of Castro to Paul III, [27?] October 1538.

126 Pastor, *History of the Popes*, xi, p. 320.

127 ASMn, AG, Venezia 1472, fos. 427, 429.

128 AGR, Papiers Gachard, 643, fos. 148v–150, 151v–152; Poggio to Cardinal Farnese, 20 November 1538, Toledo.

129 ASMo, CD, Ambasciatori Spagna, busta 3; Rossetto to the Duke of Ferrara, 12 December 1538, Toledo.

130 BL, Cotton MS Nero B vii, fo. 135r–v (*LP*, xiii(2). 1047).

131 AGS, Estado, legajo 1371/107, 137, 137–57. *LP*, xiii(2). 686.

132 *Ven. Dep.*, i, pp. 248–9; Mocenigo to the Council of Ten, 7 December 1538, Toledo. That the friend was English appears from Mocenigo's letter of 30 December: *ibid.*, p. 264.

133 *SP*, viii, pp. 79–83; Harvel to Cromwell, 25 October and 15 November 1538, Venice. *Ven. Dep.*, i, pp. 250–3; Mocenigo to the Doge, 12 December 1538. For Prevesa, see Capasso, *Paolo III*, i, ch. 8; J. D. Tracy, *Emperor Charles V, Impresario of War: Campaign Strategy, International Finance and Domestic Politics* (Cambridge, 2002), pp. 164–5.

134 *Ven. Dep.*, i, pp. 259, 262–4; Mocenigo to the Doge, 18 and 30 December 1538, Toledo (the quotations are at p. 264).

135 *Ven. Dep.*, i, pp. 256–7, 260–1; Mocenigo to the Doge, 14 and 18 December 1538, Toledo. ASV, AA, Arm. I–XVIII, 6533, fo. 74r–v; AGR, Papiers Gachard, 643, fo. 170; Poggio to Cardinal Farnese, 8 and 20 December 1538, Toledo.

136 ASMo, CD, Ambasciatori Spagna, busta 3; Rossetto to the Duke of Ferrara, 7 December 1538, Toledo.

137 BL, Cotton MS Vitellius B xiv, fo. 25v (*LP*, xiii(2). 1068).

138 ASMn, AG, Spagna 589, fo. 152v; Vivaldini to the Duke of Mantua, 26 December 1538, Toledo.

139 *CSPSp*, v(2), *1536–1538*, p. 525.

140 *Ven. Dep.*, i, p. 112; Mocenigo and Venier to the Doge, 7 June 1538, Nice.

141 ASMo, CD, Ambasciatori Spagna, busta 4; Rossetto to the Duke of Ferrara, 9 and 20 January 1539, Toledo.

14: DISPERATISSIMO

1 *Harley 282*, fo. 227v (*CWTW*, i, letter 11); Wyatt to Cromwell, 2 January 1539, Toledo.

2 BL, Additional MS 5498, fo. 13v (*LP*, xiii(2). 974(2)); Philip Hoby's private notes of remembrance. MS 5498, fo. 12 (*CWTW*, i, letter 10; Wyatt's memorandum for Hoby (early December 1538).

3 *Harley 282*, fo. 227 (*CWTW*, i, letter 11); Wyatt to Cromwell, 2 January 1539, Toledo.

4 *CSPFor, 1547–1553*, pp. 312, 315; Charles V to Scheyfve, 29 June 1551, Augsburg.

5 For an account of its awesome power, see F. Bethencourt, *The Inquisition: A Global History, 1478–1834* (Cambridge, 2009).

6 AGR, Papiers Gachard, 643, fo. 182v; Poggio to Cardinal Farnese, 31 December 1538, Toledo.

7 H. C. Lea, *A History of the Inquisition of Spain*, 4 vols. (1906), ii, p. 477; iv, p. 515.

8 Santa Cruz, *Crónica*, iv, ch. 1. J. D. Tracy, *Emperor Charles V, Impresario of War: Campaign Strategy, International Finance, and Domestic Politics* (Cambridge, 2002), p. 297.

9 *Harley 282*, fo. 228 (*CWTW*, i, letter 11); Wyatt to Cromwell, 2 January 1539, Toledo.

10 A. González Palencia and E. Mele, *Vida y obras de don Diego Hurtado de Mendoza*, 3 vols. (Madrid, 1941–3); D. H. Darst, *Diego Hurtado de Mendoza* (Boston, Mass., 1987); A. Hobson, *Renaissance Book Collecting: Jean Grolier and Diego Hurtado de Mendoza, their Books and Bindings* (Cambridge, 1999). *SP*, viii, p. 199.

11 For vexing Rome, see BL, Additional MS 5498, fo. 7v (*CWTW*, i, letter 9); Wyatt to Henry VIII, 9 November 1538, Toledo. AGR, Papiers Gachard, 643, fo. 183; Poggio to Cardinal Farnese, 31 December 1538, Toledo.

12 AGR, Papiers Gachard, 643, fos. 180, 181v; Poggio to Cardinal Farnese, 26 December 1538, Toledo.

13 AGR, Papiers Gachard, 643, fos. 182v, 183v; Poggio to Cardinal Farnese, 31 December 1538. *La Corte de Carlos V*, dir. J. Martínez Millán, 5 vols. (Madrid, 2000); vol. 3, *Los Consejos y los consejeros de Carlos V*, p. 8.

14 For the *Apomaxis*, see T. A. Sowerby, *Renaissance and Reform in Tudor England: the Careers of Sir Richard Morison, c.1513–1556* (Oxford, 2010), pp. 53–64.

15 ASV, SS, Principi, 13, fo. 209; AA, Arm. I–XVIII, 6533, fo. 61; Poggio to Cardinal Farnese, 4 January 1539, Toledo.

16 ASPr, CFE, Roma, busta 422; Cardinal Farnese to Poggio, 27 January 1539, Rome.

17 M. Bataillon, *Érasme et l'Espagne*, ed. D. Devoto and C. Amiel, 3 vols. (Genève, 1991), i, pp. 177, 203–7, 253–7, 260–5, 288–90, 293–4, 341, 368, 486, 540; J. E. Longhurst, *Erasmus and the Spanish Inquisition: the Case of Juan de Valdés* (Albuquerque, 1950), pp. 35–6, 40–4, 72–4; Lea, *Inquisition of Spain*, i, pp. 304–5.

18 Lea, *Inquisition of Spain*, ii, pp. 165–7, 179–81, 184–5, 188–9.

19 W. Monter, *Frontiers of Heresy: The Spanish Inquisition from the Basque Lands to Sicily* (Cambridge, 1990), pp. 37–45, 128, 146–9, 236–43.

20 Lea, *Inquisition of Spain*, ii, pp. 91–8; iii, pp. 422, 482.

21 P. Marshall, 'The Other Black Legend' in *Religious Identities in Henry VIII's England* (Aldershot, 2006), pp. 103–24.

22 *Defence*; *Harley 78*, fo. 13v.

23 See above, p. 342. *LP*, xii(1). 873.

24 BL, Cotton MS Vespasian C vii, fo. 87r–v (*LP*, xiii(2). 429).

25 BL, Cotton MS Vespasian C xiii, fo. 328v (*LP*, vii. 945).

26 *LP*, iv(2). 4282.

27 AHN, Inquisición, lib. 785, fos. 25v, 29; lib. 833, fos. 4, 7v, 8, 10. The discoveries in the Inquisition archives were made by Dr Ciaran O'Scea, and I very gratefully acknowledge his brilliant research. TNA, SP 1/124, fo. 251 (*LP*, xii(2). 716(2)).

28 Thomas Pery described the horrors of his experiences in the Inquisition's prison to Richard Field and to Wyatt's servant Ralph Vane: BL, Cotton MS Vespasian C vii, fos. 91v–95, 102–6 (*LP*, xv. 281); Marshall, 'The Other Black Legend', pp. 110–11. For concern in England at his ill-treatment, see *LP*, xv. 859, 977; xvi. 138, 284, 312.

29 Lea, *Inquisition of Spain*, iii, ch. 7.

30 AHN, Inquisición, lib. 785, fos. 1r–v, 3; Monter, *Frontiers of Heresy*, pp. 37, 146.

31 C. Fantazzi, 'Vives, Juan Luis (1492/3–1540)', *ODNB*. Lea, *Inquisition of Spain*, ii, pp. 470–8; Monter, *Frontiers of Heresy*, pp. 72–3; J.-P. Dedieu, *L'Administration de la Foi: L'Inquisition de Tolède (XVIe–XVIIIe siècle)* (Madrid, 1992), pp. 80–4; C. Griffin, *Journeymen-Printers, Heresy and the Inquisition in Sixteenth-Century Spain* (Oxford, 2005), ch. 3.

32 *Harley 282*, fo. 102r (*CWTW*, i, letter 20); Wyatt to Henry VIII, 7 January 1540, Paris.

33 Dedieu, *L'Administration de la Foi*, pp. 171–2.

34 ASMo, CD, Ambasciatori Spagna, busta 4; Rossetto to the Duke of Ferrara, 25 January 1539, Toledo. ASF, MP, 4296, fo. 363; Bandino to the Duke of Florence, c.24 January 1539, Toledo.

35 BL, Cotton MS Vespasian C xiii, fo. 249v.

36 ASV, AA, Arm. I–XVIII, 6533, fo. 57; SS, Principi, 13, fo. 316 (*LP*, xii(2). 1031); Poggio to Cardinal Farnese, 4 November 1537, Monzón. It would be a member of his own household who betrayed Richard Morison in 1551: Sowerby, *Renaissance and Reform in Tudor England: the Careers of Sir Richard Morison*, p. 201.

37 Hotman, *The Ambassador*, sig. K3r–v.

38 ASMo, CD, Ambasciatori Spagna, busta 4; Rossetto to the Duke of Ferrara, 31 May 1539, Toledo.

39 For the terrors of the Inquisition's proceedings, described for an avid Elizabethan audience, see Anon., *A Discovery and playne Declaration of sundry subtill practises of the Holy Inquisition of Spayne* (1569). See also Griffin, *Journeymen-Printers, Heresy and the Inquisition*, especially pp. 45–8, 199–204.

40 ASV, AA, Arm. I–XVIII, 6533, fo. 67v.

41 *Harley 282*, fos. 100v–101r (*CWTW*, i, letter 20); Wyatt to Henry VIII, 7 January 1540, Paris.

42 For the establishment of the Inquisition, and the conflicting jurisdictions, see Lea, *Inquisition of Spain*, i, especially pp. 157ff, 181–2 (the quotation is at p. 182), 289–98, 302–5, 322–6. A copy of the *Instruciones Antiguas* was reissued by Inquisitor General Manrique in 1537.

43 Lea, *Inquisition of Spain*, ii, pp. 1–11.

44 *Ibid.*, p. 127.

45 Bataillon, *Érasme et l'Espagne*, i, pp. 504–5, 519–20; Longhurst, *Erasmus and the Spanish Inquisition*, pp. 47, 76.

46 TNA, PRO 30/26/54, fo. 2v; ASV, SS, Principi, 12, fo. 19v; Pole to Cardinal Farnese, 25 March 1539.

47 *Defence*; Harley *78*, fo. 10 (*L&L*, p. 196).

48 For the enterprise of England and Cardinal Pole's second legation, see T. Mayer, *Reginald Pole: Prince and Prophet* (Cambridge, 2000), pp. 91–102; *Pole's Correspondence*, pp. 201–26; C. Höllger, 'Reginald Pole and the Legations of 1537 and 1539: Diplomatic and Polemical Responses to the Break with Rome' (unpublished University of Oxford D.Phil. thesis, 1989), ch. 5; C. Capasso, *Paolo III (1534–1549)*, 2 vols. (Messina, 1924), i, pp. 681–93.

49 '*Il corpo mystico di christo cioe de la chiesa sua*': AGS, Estado, legajo 1311/137; Cardinal Contarini to Charles V, 5 June 1535, Venice.

50 See, for example, ASV, SS, Principi, 14A, fos. 115, 215v; Cardinal Farnese to Poggio, 12 February 1539, and to the nuncio in France, 30 March 1539. AGR, Papiers Gachard, 643, fos. 47, 158; Poggio to Cardinal Farnese, 17 January, 20 November 1538.

51 For '*quel perduto Re*', '*quel Re perso*': ASV, SS, Principi, 13, fos. 91, 213; Cardinal Farnese to the nuncios with the King of the Romans, 28 October 1538; Poggio to Cardinal Farnese, 13 January 1539.

52 S. Brigden, 'Henry VIII and the Crusade against England' in *Henry VIII and his Court*, ed. T. Betteridge and S. Lipscomb (forthcoming, 2012). For this crusade, within a wider history, see C. Tyerman, *England and the Crusades, 1095–1588* (Chicago and London, 1988), ch. 13.

53 R. McEntegart, *Henry VIII, the League of Schmalkalden, and the English Reformation* (Woodbridge, 2002), ch. 3.

54 *LP*, xiii(2). 1087.

55 AGS, Estado, legajo 867/138 (*LP*, xiii(2). 1148); Marqués de Aguilar to Charles V, 26 December 1538, Rome.

56 *Pole's Correspondence*, pp. 201–4; *LP*, xiii(2). 1110; P. van Dyke, 'The Mission of Cardinal Pole to Enforce the Bull of Deposition against Henry VIII', *EHR*, 37 (1922), pp. 422–3.

57 *ANG*, 1, p. 425; Ferrerio to Cardinal Farnese, 26 December 1538.

58 ASMn, AG, Spagna 589, fo. 152r–v; Vivaldini to the Duke of Mantua, 26 December 1538, Toledo; ASMo, CD, Ambasciatori Spagna, busta 4; Rossetto to the Duke of Ferrara, 20 January 1539, Toledo.

59 ASPr, CFE, Roma 422; Cardinal Farnese to Poggio, 27 January 1539 (cited in Capasso, *Paolo III*, i, p. 687 n. 4). The italics are mine.

60 *Ven. Dep.*, i, p. 277; Mocenigo to the Doge, 16 January 1539, Toledo.

61 AGR, Papiers Gachard, 643, fos. 151v, 157–8v, 160v–161, 165v, 172–5v, 351–2v, 196r–v; Poggio to Cardinal Farnese, 20 and 30 November, 8, 13 and 20 December 1538, Toledo.

62 *Pole's Correspondence*, p. 219.

63 ASV, AA, Arm. I–XVIII, 6533, fos. 72–5v; SS, Principi, 13, fos. 211v–215v; Poggio to Cardinal Farnese, 20 December 1538. ASMo, CD, Ambasciatori Spagna, busta 4 [undated, December 1538].

64 ASV, SS, Principi, 12, fo. 17; Pole to Cardinal Farnese, 22 February 1539, Toledo; Ribier, i, p. 287. Höllger, 'Reginald Pole and the Legations of 1537 and 1539', p. 130.

65 *CSPSp*, vi(1), *1538–1542*, pp. 97–8; ASPr, CFE, Roma, busta 422; Cardinal Farnese to Pole, 2 January 1539. Further copies, in the Pope's hand, were sent on the 28th: *Pole's Correspondence*, p. 206.

66 *Pole's Correspondence*, pp. 205–6; Mayer, *Reginald Pole*, p. 93.

67 *Defence*; Harley *78*, fo. 9v (*L&L*, pp. 194–5).

68 ASMo, CD, Ambasciatori Spagna, busta 4; Rossetto to the Duke of Ferrara, 9 and 20 January 1539, Toledo.

69 *Ven. Dep.*, i, p. 276; Mocenigo to the Doge, 16 January 1539. ASMo, CD, Ambasciatori Spagna, busta 4; Rossetto to the Duke of Ferrara, 25 January 1539, Toledo.

70 *Ven. Dep.*, i, p. 277; Mocenigo to the Doge, 16 January 1539, Toledo.

71 ASMo, CD, Ambasciatori Spagna, busta 4; Rossetto to the Duke of Ferrara, 25 January 1539, Toledo. ASF, MP, 4296, fos. 363–4; Bandino to the Duke of Florence, *c*.24–25 January 1539.

72 Nott, *Wyatt*, p. 509.

73 *Defence*; Harley *78*, fo. 9v (*L&L*, p. 195); *Ven. Dep.*, i, pp. 281–2; Mocenigo to the Council of Ten, 6 February 1539, Toledo.

74 ASV, AA, Arm. I–XVIII, 6533, fo. 69; AGR, Papiers Gachard, 643, fo. 201v; Poggio to Cardinal Farnese, 25 January and 5 February 1539, Toledo.

75 ASF, MP, 4296, fo. 384v; Bandino to the Duke of Florence, 4 February 1539. ASMo, CD, Ambasciatori Spagna, busta 4; Rossetto to the Duke of Ferrara, 4 February 1539, Toledo.

76 Nott, *Wyatt*, pp. 506–7; Henry VIII to Wyatt, 19 January 1539. My italics.

77 ASV, SS, Principi, 12, fo. 15v; Pole to Cardinal Farnese, 22 February 1539, Toledo. AGR, Papiers Gachard, 643, fos. 208, 210v; Poggio to Cardinal Farnese, 28 February 1539. ASMo, CD, Ambasciatori Spagna, busta 4; Rossetto to the Duke of Ferrara, 20 February 1539. *CSPSp*, vi(1), *1538–1542*, pp. 114–15.

78 TNA, SP 1/143, fo. 208 (*SP*, viii, p. 155); *Letters of Cromwell*, ii, p. 188. On 14 February Nicholas le Pelle was despatched with a letter to the King: Nott, *Wyatt*, p. 450. Mocenigo also sent his letter of the 14th 'by the means of the English ambassador': *Ven. Dep.*, i, p. 285.

79 *ANG*, 1, pp. 437–40, Latino Giovenale to Cardinal Farnese, 21 January 1539, Paris. Ribier, i, p. 350. ASV, SS, Principi, 14A, fo. 116; Cardinal Farnese to Poggio, 12 February 1539, Rome. AGS, Estado, legajo 868/1; Marqués de Aguilar, 14 February 1539, Rome.

80 BL, Cotton MS Vespasian C vii, fo. 24r (*CWTW*, i, letter 14); Wyatt to Cromwell, 15 March 1539, Toledo.

81 *LP*, xiv(2). 212.

82 TNA, PRO, 30/26/54, fo. 3; Pole to Cardinal Farnese, 25 March 1539. *Pole's Correspondence*, pp. 210, 213.

83 *Ven. Dep.,,* i, p. 287; Mocenigo to the Doge, 18 February 1539. ASV, SS, Principi, 12, fos. 16v–17v; Pole to Cardinal Farnese, 22 February 1539. AGR, Papiers Gachard, 643, fos. 211–12; Poggio to Cardinal Farnese, 28 February 1539, Toledo. ASF, MP, 4296, fo. 404v; Bandino to the Duke of Florence, 6 March 1539. Höllger, 'Reginald Pole and the Legations of 1537 and 1539', pp. 147–8.

84 AGR, Papiers Gachard, 643, fo. 212; Poggio to Cardinal Farnese, 28 February 1539. *Ven. Dep.,* i, p. 288; Mocenigo to the Doge, 18 February 1539. Pole denied the allegation that his family's sufferings impelled him to act: *Pole's Correspondence*, pp. 221–3. The phrase is Professor Mayer's: *Reginald Pole: Prince and Prophet*, pp. 95–6.

85 ASV, SS, Principi, 12, fos. 17r–v; Pole to Cardinal Farnese, 22 February 1539, Toledo.

86 *LP*, xiii(2). 974(2). *Ven. Dep.,* i, pp. 283–4; Mocenigo to the Ten, 14 February 1539. H. Keniston, *Francisco de los Cobos: Secretary of the Emperor Charles V* (Pittsburgh, 1958), pp. 216–22; Tracy, *Emperor Charles V*, pp. 296–8.

87 Santa Cruz, *Crónica*, iv, p. 24.

88 TNA, PRO 31/9/65, fos. 252–3 (*LP*, xiv(1). 561); *Pole's Correspondence*, p. 234.

89 ASMo, CD, Ambasciatori Spagna, busta 4; Rossetto to the Duke of Ferrara, 20 February 1539, Toledo. ASMn, AG, Spagna 589, fo. 289v; Vivaldini to the Duke of Mantua, 27 February 1539.

90 *Declaration*; *Harley 78*, fo. 6 (*L&L*, p. 182). *Harley 282*, fo. 95v (*CWTW*, i, letter 20); Wyatt to Henry VIII, 7 January 1540, Paris.

91 *Defence*; *Harley 78*, fo. 9v (*L&L*, p. 195). The note added to Cromwell's letter of 13 February – 'by Francis at Toledo the xix of January' – makes no sense, but the letter may have arrived before Pole's departure on the 24th: *Letters of Cromwell*, ii, p. 179.

92 Nott, *Wyatt*, p. 511; Henry VIII to Wyatt, 10 March 1539.

93 TNA, SP 1/143, fo. 154 (*CWTW*, i, letter 12); Wyatt to Bonner, 23 February 1539, Toledo.

94 ASMo, CD, Ambasciatori Spagna, busta 4; Rossetto to the Duke of Ferrara, 21 February 1539, Toledo.

95 *Invective*, sigs. C8r, B8r–v. The tract was printed by Berthelet, the King's printer, in January 1539. Nott, *Wyatt*, p. 510; *LP*, xiv(1). 72, 233. For its genesis and dissemination, see Sowerby, *Renaissance and Reformation in Tudor England: the Careers of Sir Richard Morison*, pp. 90–100.

96 BAV, Vat. Lat. 5970, fos. 376r, 377–9v, 380r–382v, 384 (*Pole's Correspondence*, pp. 207–9).

97 TNA, PRO 30/26/54, fo. 1 (transcript PRO 31/9/65; calendar *LP*, xiv(1). 603); Pole to Cardinal Farnese, 25 March 1539, Carpentras. BL, Cotton MS Vespasian C vii, fo. 24r (*CWTW*, i, letter 14); Wyatt to Cromwell, 15 March 1539, Toledo.

98 AGS, Guerra Antigua, legajo 15 (unfoliated) (*CSPSp*, vi(1), *1538–1542*, p. 145);

Marqués de Aguilar to Charles V, 16 April 1539. G. B. Parks, 'The Parma Letters and the Dangers to Cardinal Pole', *Catholic Historical Review*, 46 (1960–1), pp. 299–317.

99 BAV, MS Vat. Lat. 5826, fo. 7ov (*LP*, xiv(2). 212); Pole to ?Cardinal Contarini, 22 September 1539. Professor Mayer reads this damaged manuscript slightly differently: *Pole's Correspondence*, p. 243. For Wyatt as assassin, see *LP*, xiv(1), pp. viii–x.

100 TNA, PRO 30/26/54, fo. 1 (*LP*, xiv(1). 603); Pole to Cardinal Farnese, 25 March 1539, Carpentras. AGR, Papiers Gachard, 643, fo. 222; Cardinal Farnese to Poggio, 16 April 1539.

101 Bodleian, MS Bodl. 493. Mayer, *Reginald Pole: Prince and Prophet*, pp. 91–2.

102 ASV, AA, Arm. I–XVIII, 6530, fo. 141; Ferrerio to Cardinal Farnese, 18 March 1539.

103 *CSPSp*, vi(1), *1538–1542*, pp. 336–8, 345, 359, 361, 369–70, 380, 386–9, 392, 397, 404–5, 421–4, 426; J. Zeller, *La Diplomatie Française vers le milieu du XVIe siècle* (Paris, 1881), chs. 8, 10; A. Gentili, *De legationibus libri tres*, intro. E. Nys, trans. G. J. Laing, 2 vols. (New York, 1924), ii, p. 63; *The State of Christendom* (1667 edn.), p. 210; Jean Hotman, *The Ambassador*, sig. H3r; F. Thynn, *The Application of Certain Histories concerning Ambassadours* (1651 edn.), sigs. F3r–F4r.

104 D. E. Queller, *The Office of Ambassador in the Middle Ages* (Princeton, 1967), pp. 65–6, 176; E. Adair, *The Extraterrioriality of Ambassadors in the Sixteenth and Seventeenth Centuries* (1929), p. 6.

105 Here Gentili quotes Cicero: *De legationibus libri tres*, ii, p. 58; Queller, *The Office of Ambassador*, pp. 90, 179.

106 See Adair, *Extraterritoriality*, pp. 11–12, ch. 10.

107 Hotman, *The Ambassador*, sigs. B5v; I7v–8r.

108 *The State of Christendom*, p. 210.

109 BL, Additional MS 28591, fo. 4 (*CSPSp*, vi(1), *1538–1542*, p. 97); *LP*, xiv(1). 36; *ANG*, 1, pp. 438–9.

110 Hotman, *The Ambassador*, sigs. H5r–H7r.

111 *LP*, xiii(2). 1055; xiv(1). 72, 144 (the quotation is at 144); *CSPSp*, vi(1), *1538–1542*, p. 95.

112 *SP*, viii, p. 181. For the case see *SP*, vi, pp. 388–409.

113 TNA, SP 1/143, fos. 134–5, 142–5; SP 1/144, fos. 21–7v, 30–1, 40–1v, (*SP*, viii, pp. 148–51, 159–69, 173–5); *SP*, viii, pp. 176–91 (the quotation is at p. 189).

114 *SP*, viii, pp. 152–5, 175 (the quotation is at p. 175).

115 *LP*, xiv(1). 308.

116 TNA, SP 1/143, fos. 131–2 (*LP*, xiv(1). 336).

117 *SP*, viii, pp. 151, 182.

118 ASV, SS, Principi, 14A, fo. 216; Cardinal Farnese to Ferrerio, 30 March 1539; AA, Arm. I–XVIII, 6530, fos. 15–16v; Ferrerio to Cardinal Farnese, 20 February 1539.

119 *SP*, viii, p. 174; *CSPSp*, vi(1), *1538–1542*, p. 126.

120 *CSPSp*, vi(1), *1538–1542*, pp. 134–7; TNA, SP 1/142, fos. 226–7 (*LP*, xiv(1). 208); AGR, Audience, 50, fos. 49v–50; Audience 358, fo. 89. The passport for Chapuys was dated 11 March: *LP*, xiv(1). 651(33).

121 John Parker wrote to his unnamed master on 14 April 1539, reporting events in Brussels, and Wyatt's 'malice' towards him. Wriothesley had a servant called Parker, and the letter's contents indicate that it was addressed to Wriothesley: BL, Cotton MS Galba B x, fos. 124–5v (*LP*, xiv(1). 768). *SP*, viii, p. 159.

122 TNA, SP 1/143, fo. 111 (*LP*, xiv(1). 321).

123 H. J. Horn, *Jan Cornelisz Vermeyen, Painter of Charles V and His Conquest of Tunis: Paintings, Etchings, Drawings, Cartoons and Tapestries*, 2 vols. (Doornspijk, 1989), i, pp. 25–7, 83, n. 247–9.

124 ASF, MP, 4296, fos. 393–4, 404v; Bandino to the Duke of Florence, 10 and 6 March 1539, Toledo. ASMo, CD, Ambasciatori Spagna, busta 4; Rossetto to the Duke of Ferrara, 12 March 1539.

125 TNA, SP 1/150, fo. 118r–v (*LP*, xiv(1). 757); John Godsalve to Wriothesley, 13 April 1539.

126 BL, Cotton MS Vespasian Cvii, fos. 24r–33v (*CWTW*, i, letter 14). The final page lacks. This letter to Cromwell was written episodically, between *c.*14 and 18 March. A merchant's courier was sent with letters to the King on 23 March and Nicholas le Pelle, the courier, on the 30th with Wyatt's missing letter of the 29th: Nott, *Wyatt*, p. 450. The great James Gairdner attempted to unravel the plot: *LP*, xiv(1), pp. ix–xi; *LP*, xiv(2), pp. v–vi.

127 The phrase is Wyatt's: BL, Cotton MS Vespasian C vii, fo. 24v (*CWTW*, i, letter 14).

128 *Ven. Dep.*, i, pp. 293–8; Mocenigo to the Doge, 12 March 1539. Mocenigo's audiences were related by Wyatt, Bandino and Rossetto. ASF, MP, 4296, fos. 394, 408–9; Bandino to the Duke of Florence, 10 and 18 March 1539. The Emperor's words were reported by Rossetto: ASMo, CD, Ambasciatori Spagna, busta 4; Rossetto to the Duke of Ferrara, 14 March 1539. Poggio related the audience to Cardinal Farnese on 18 March: TNA, PRO 31/9/65, fos. 246–52 (*LP*, xiv(1). 561).

129 BL, Cotton MS Vespasian C vii, fo. 31r–v (*CWTW*, i, letter 14).

130 *Ven. Dep.*, i, pp. 297–301; Mocenigo to the Doge, 12 and 14 March 1539, Toledo. ASMo, CD, Ambasciatori Spagna, busta 4; Rossetto to the Duke of Ferrara, 14 March 1539. BL, Cotton MS Vespasian C vii, fo. 31v–32r (*CWTW*, i, letter 14).

131 AGS, Estado, Roma, legajo 868/117 (BL, Additional MS 28591, fos. 75–7v; *CSPSp*, vi(1), *1538–1542*, pp. 132–3); Emperor to Marqués de Aguilar and to the Imperial ambassador in Genoa, 17 March 1539.

132 ASMo, Ambasciatori Spagna 4; Rossetto to the Duke of Ferrara, 16 March 1539, Toledo. *Ven. Dep.*, i, pp. 304–5; Mocenigo to the Doge, 18 March 1539. For Henry's machinations with the French King, see *LP*, xiv(1). 72.

133 This is how Mocenigo described Wyatt to the Doge, after a meeting on 17 March: *Ven. Dep.*, i, p. 305.

134 TNA, PRO 31/9/65, fo. 253 (*LP*, xiv(1). 561). Florio, *A Worlde of Wordes*, p. 107.

135 *Ven. Dep.*., i, pp. 307–8; Mocenigo to the Doge, 28 March 1539, Toledo.

136 *LP*, xiv(1). 1168. See also *LP*, xiv(1). 1261.

137 ASF, MP, 4296, fos. 393v–394; Bandino to the Duke of Florence, 10 March 1539, Toledo.

138 *SP*, viii, p. 166; Wriothesley to Cromwell, 3 March 1539.

139 This was James Gairdner's contention: *LP*, xiv(1), p. x.

140 BL, Cotton MS Vespasian C xiii, fo. 260 (*LP*, xiv(1). 550).

141 BL, Cotton MS Vespasian C vii, fos. 24v–27v (*CWTW*, i, letter 14). *Letters of Cromwell*, ii, pp. 202–7. McEntegart, *Henry VIII, the League of Schmalkalden*, pp. 145–9. For d'Andalot's journey, see *LP*, xiv(1). 767–8, 786, 834, 851.

142 The quotations are from BL, Cotton MS Vespasian C vii, fos. 28v–30r, 28v (*CWTW*, i, letter 14).

143 *Ven. Dep.*, i, p. 307; Mocenigo to the Doge, 28 March 1539. *CSPSp*, vi(1), *1538–1542*, p. 129.

144 *SP*, viii, pp. 183–4; i, p. 614; Nott, *Wyatt*, p. 350; *LP*, xiv(1). 746.

145 *CSPSp*, vi(1), *1538–1542*, pp. 139, 140, 146; AGR, Papiers Gachard, 643, fo. 229; *Ven. Dep.*, i, p. 315.

146 *Ven. Dep.*, i, pp. 309–10; Mocenigo to the Doge, 12 April 1539.

147 AGR, Papiers Gachard, 643, fo. 236; Poggio to Cardinal Farnese, 3 May 1539, Toledo.

148 AGR, Papiers Gachard, 643, fo. 233; Poggio to Cardinal Farnese, 3 May 1539, Toledo. ASMo, CD, Ambasciatori Spagna, busta 4; Rossetto to the Duke of Ferrara, 1, 2 and 6 May 1539. *Ven. Dep*, i, p. 321; Mocenigo to the Doge, 17 May 1539. Santa Cruz, *Crónica*, iv, pp. 24–6.

149 Wyatt's remark is from ASV, SS, Francia 1A, fo. 200; Ferrerio to Pope Paul III, 13 June 1539. ASV, Principi, 13, fos. 17v–18v; Alessandro Guidiccioni to Cardinal Farnese, 3 May 1539; Fondo Pio, 247, fo. 242; Poggio to Pole, 17 May 1539. ASMo, CD, Ambasciatori Spagna, busta 4; Rossetto to the Duke of Ferrara, 16 and 21 May 1539. *Ven. Dep.*, i, p. 323; Mocenigo to the Doge, 18 May 1539. *Estancias y viajes*, p. 466.

150 ASMo, CD, Ambasciatori Spagna, busta 4; Rossetto to the Duke of Ferrara, 31 May 1539, Toledo.

151 ASF, Ducato di Urbino, Classe I, f. 183, fos. 15r–v, 17r–v; Felice Tiranni to Guidobaldo della Rovere, Duke of Urbino, 31 May and 5 June 1539, Toledo. For the alleged poisoning of Francesco Maria, Duke of Urbino, by Gonzaga, who had been in the Emperor's service, see AGS, Estado, legajo 1459/121–3, 150; ASV, AA, Arm. I–XVIII, 6530, fos. 200v–201.

152 ASMo, CD, Ambasciatori Spagna, busta 4; Rossetto to the Duke of Ferrara, 31 May 1539, Toledo.

153 *Harley 282*, fo. 100 (*CWTW*, i, letter 20); Wyatt to Henry VIII, 7 January 1540, Paris.

154 AHN, Inquisición, lib. 322, fo. 241r–v. This letter was the discovery of Dr Ciaran O'Scea, and his is the transcription and translation. A reference to this reply is found in Inquisición, lib. 1232, fo. 122r.

155 *Ven. Dep.*, i, p. 330; Mocenigo to the Doge, 31 May 1539. Nott, *Wyatt*, p. 450.

156 ASV, SS, Francia 1A, fo. 200 (*ANG*, 1, pp. 462–3); Ferrerio to Pope Paul III,
13–14 June 1539, Paris.

157 *Letters of Cromwell*, ii, p. 214. She was not pardoned until December 1539: *LP*,
xiv(2). 780(2).

158 *Egerton*, fos. 67r–69r. See the text of 'So feble' and its analysis in *Wyatt: Poems*,
pp. 109–12, 390–4. The most illuminating criticism of these poems is found
in S. M. Foley, *Sir Thomas Wyatt* (Boston, Mass., 1990), pp. 53–5; C. Shrank,
'"But I, that know what harbred in that hed": Sir Thomas Wyatt and his posthumous interpreters', *PBA*, 154 (2007), pp. 375–401; C. Stamatakis, '"Turning
the Word": Sir Thomas Wyatt and early Tudor literary practice' (unpublished
University of Oxford D. Phil. thesis, 2008), pp. 55–65.

159 Professor Rebholz's version is given alongside transcriptions from *Egerton*, fos.
67–8v: *Wyatt: Poems*, LXXVI.

160 *Egerton*, fo. 67; *Wyatt: Poems*, LXXVI, ll. 15–16.

161 *Egerton*, fo. 67; *Wyatt: Poems*, LXXVI, ll. 21–6. I follow Cathy Shrank's beautiful
rehabilitation of this scorned poem: '"But I, that know"', pp. 389–92.

162 *Wyatt: Poems*, LXXVI, ll. 93–100. *Egerton*, fo. 68v.

163 To Stephen Foley 'the poem clearly evokes Wyatt's personal longing for
Elizabeth Darrell': *Thomas Wyatt*, p. 39. Cathy Shrank finds a 'plausible autobiographical motive': '"But I, that know"', p. 388.

164 TNA, SP 1/143, fo. 3 (*LP*, xiv(1). 212). Two Elizabeth Darrells wrote to
Cromwell, in two different holograph hands. One was Elizabeth Darrell of
Scotney, Kent, a widow, with a son who was a priest: TNA, SP 1/143, fo. 1
(*LP*, xiv(1). 211). The other was kinless, friendless Bess Darrell. Her suit con-
cerned George Hastings, Earl of Huntingdon, who was closely related to Lord
Montague and had only narrowly escaped implication in the alleged Exeter con-
spiracy: LP, xiv(1). 513. C. Cross, 'Hastings, George, first earl of Huntingdon
(1486/7–1544)', *ODNB*.

165 For the names of the Friars Observant coming to confess the 'ladies and gentlewomen' of Katherine's household, see TNA, SP 1/142, fo. 201v (*LP*, xiv(1). 190).

166 *Egerton*, fo. 69.

167 R. Helgerson, *A Sonnet from Carthage: Garcilaso de la Vega and the New Poetry of
Sixteenth-Century Europe* (Philadelphia, 2007), p. 45.

168 *Petrarch's Lyric Poems*, 180. See Stephen Foley's convincing identification of this
source-text: *Thomas Wyatt*, pp. 54–5.

169 See, for example, *Bernardo Tasso: Rime*, vol. i, *I tre libri degli Amori*, a cura di D.
Chiodo (Torino, 1995), *Libro primo*, CVI; *Libro secondo*, XLV; *Libro terzo*, XX.

170 'Contrive to work in some mention of the river Tagus into your story', counselled a friend of Cervantes, showing him how to vaunt a scintilla of learning
'in the humanities and in cosmography': Miguel de Cervantes Saavedra, *The
Adventures of Don Quixote*, trans. J. M. Cohen (Harmondsworth, 1950), pp. 28–9.
Dr Stamatakis examines the stock literary topos, '"Turning the Word"', p. 59.
For pertinent examples, see, for example, Juvenal, Satires 3: 55; 14: 299; *Juvenal
and Persius*, ed. and trans. S. M. Braund (Cambridge, Mass., 2004), pp. 171,
481; *Andrea Navagero: Lusus: Text and Translation*, ed. A. E. Wilson (The Hague,

1973), XXXV, p. 65. Wyatt's principal source may have been Boethius, perhaps in Chaucer's translation: *TM*, ii, p. 212.

171 *Selected Poems of Garcilaso de la Vega*, ed. and trans. J. Dent-Young (Chicago, 2009), pp. 181–205 (the 'happy Tagus' is at l. 106).

172 Helgerson, *Sonnet from Carthage*, pp. 44–5.

173 Leland, *Naeniae* (*L&L*, pp. 263, 266).

174 *Egerton*, fo. 65v. John Brereton, Wyatt's servant and scribe (Hand *D* in *Egerton*), was the copyist, probably in Spain: J. Powell, 'Thomas Wyatt's Poetry in Embassy: Egerton 2711 and the Production of Literary Manuscripts Abroad', *HLQ*, 67 (2004), Figure 3 and pp. 278–9.

175 *Egerton*, fo. 65v; Harrier, *Wyatt's Poetry*, p. 201, ll. 2, 3, 17, 22–3, 10–11.

15: HEART'S JERUSALEM

1 Ps. 51.77–9.

2 I remember with gratitude my tutorial with Dr Jason Powell in the Manuscripts Room of the British Library as we read Egerton MS 2711 together. I particularly acknowledge my great debt to continuing conversations with Dr Chris Stamatakis. Robert Wainwright, who has written an Oxford doctoral dissertation on the influence of the Swiss reformers on the making of the English Reformation, 'Covenant and Reformed Identity in England, 1525–1555', very kindly read this chapter. I am grateful for all that he has taught me. Transcribing from *Egerton*, I have relied on Harrier, *Wyatt's Poetry* to confirm my readings and for the lines of Psalm 6 missing from *Egerton*. I have used modern numbering, and numbered separately the lines of each prologue (I–VII) and each Psalm (6, 32, 38, 51, 102, 130, 143). Dr Helen Baron's dissertation – sadly still unpublished – is a remarkable edition of Wyatt's paraphrase and exploration of his sources: 'Sir Thomas Wyatt's Seven Penitential Psalms: a Study of Textual and Source Materials' (University of Cambridge Ph.D. thesis, 1977).

3 Crucially, Brian Cummings insists that belief is not antecedent to language, and that for Wyatt it is the text on which belief is founded: *The Literary Culture of the Reformation: Grammar and Grace* (Oxford, 2002), p. 228.

4 Pr. V.10. My unfailing guides to Wyatt's paraphrase have been Baron, 'Wyatt's Seven Penitential Psalms'; Cummings, *Literary Culture*; H. A. Mason, *Humanism and Poetry in the Early Tudor Period* (1959) and *Sir Thomas Wyatt: A Literary Portrait* (Bristol, 1986); C. Stamatakis, '"Turning the Word": Sir Thomas Wyatt and early Tudor literary practice' (unpublished University of Oxford D.Phil. thesis, 2008); A. W. Taylor, 'Psalms and Early Tudor Humanism' (unpublished University of Cambridge Ph.D. thesis, 2002); R. G. Twombly, 'Sir Thomas Wyatt's Paraphrase of the Penitential Psalms of David', *TSLL*, 12 (1970), pp. 345–80; R. Zim, *English Metrical Psalms: Poetry as Praise and Prayer, 1535–1601* (Cambridge, 1987); E. Heale, *Wyatt, Surrey and Early Tudor Poetry* (Harlow, 1998), ch. 5.

5 In his exposition of the Psalms, Calvin stated that 'although I follow David at a great distance . . . I have no hesitation in comparing myself with him'. Cited in

E. A. Gosselin, *The King's Progress to Jerusalem: Some Interpretations of David during the Reformation Period* (Malibu, 1976), p. 69. For the temptation to read the 'I' of Psalm paraphrase biographically, see P. Larivaille, *Pietro Aretino: fra Rinascimento e manierismo* (Roma, 1980), pp. 259–62; E. Boillet, *L'Arétin et la Bible* (Genève, 2007), pp. 277–8, 374.

6 Pr. I.62. For the most emphatic statement of the time and place of the paraphrase, see Mason, *Humanism and Poetry*, pp. 204–5 (the quotation is at p. 204). For vivid biographical readings, see S. Greenblatt, *Renaissance Self-Fashioning: from More to Shakespeare* (Chicago and London, 1980), pp. 115–28; G. Walker, *Writing under Tyranny: English Literature and the Henrician Reformation* (Oxford, 2005), ch. 15.

7 Zim, *English Metrical Psalms*, pp. 46–7.

8 Ps. 6.6.

9 Ps. 32.30. J. Kerrigan, 'Wyatt's Selfish Style', *ES*, 34 (1981), pp. 16–18.

10 Pr. VII.7–8.

11 *Egerton*, fo. 85v.

12 Pr. V.1–6.

13 *Surrey: Poems*, 28. 35; 30. 11.

14 *Gentleman's Magazine*, pp. 566–7; *Defence*; Harley *78*, fo. 11 (*L&L*, p. 199).

15 *Defence*; Harley *78*, fo. 14 (*L&L*, p. 206). *LP*, xiii(2). 553.

16 *Egerton*, fos. 4v–5r.

17 Ps. 51.73.

18 *Egerton*, fo. 72v (*CWTW*, i, letter 2); Wyatt to his son, summer 1537. Cromwell wrote, then crossed out, 'we be . . . of such sort in heart as the shape showeth outward': *Letters of Cromwell*, ii, p. 208 n. 5.

19 *Harley 282*, fo. 250v (*CWTW*, i, letter 33); Wyatt to Cromwell, 12 April 1540.

20 BL, Additional MS 5498, fo. 12r (*CWTW*, i, letter 10); Wyatt's memorandum for Hoby, [early December] 1538.

21 BL, Additional MS 5498, fo. 7 (*CWTW*, i, letter 9); Wyatt to Henry VIII, 9 November 1538, Toledo.

22 'Myne owne Jhon poyntz': *Parker*, fo. 201v.

23 *Defence*; Harley *78*, fo. 13r–v (*L&L*, p. 204).

24 *CWTW*, i, letters 5, 8, 11, 14, 24.

25 *Egerton*, fos. 72v–73 (*CWTW*, i, letter 2); Wyatt to his son, summer 1537.

26 Epictetus, *Encheiridion* in *The Discourses*, Books III–IV, trans. W. A. Oldfather (Cambridge, Mass., 1928), pp. 535, 483, 531, 533. How did Wyatt read his Epictetus? Probably in the Latin translation of Angelo Poliziano. See T. Lupset, *An exhortation to yonge men* (1534), pp. 38v–39.

27 Epictetus, *Encheiridion*, p. 503.

28 *LP*, xiv(2). 758.

29 See the 'Catalogue of Diego Hurtado de Mendoza's Library of Printed Books', 992–6, in A. Hobson, *Renaissance Book Collecting: Jean Grolier and Diego Hurtado de Mendoza, Their Books and Bindings* (Cambridge, 1999). Lupset, *An exhortation to yonge men*, pp. 16, 28r–v. T. Sowerby, *Renaissance and Reformation in Tudor England: the Careers of Sir Richard Morison, c.1513–1556* (Oxford, 2010), p. 34.

30 *De beneficiis* in *Seneca: Moral Essays*, iii, trans. J. W. Basore (Cambridge, Mass., 1935), VII.1.7, pp. 457–9.

31 *Surrey: Poems*, 28. 9–12.

32 Ps. 102.36. The words quoted are Wyatt's addition: *Wyatt: Poems*, p. 479.

33 *Egerton*, fos. 71–2 (*CWTW*, i, letter 1); Wyatt to his son, 14 April 1537, Paris.

34 *Egerton*, fo. 73 (*CWTW*, i, letter 2); Wyatt to his son, summer 1537.

35 Ps. 102. 3–4. Helen Baron draws the comparison: 'Wyatt's Seven Penitential Psalms', p. 298. The second line is, again, Wyatt's addition.

36 *Egerton*, fo. 71v (*CWTW*, i, letter 1); Wyatt to his son, 14 April 1537, Paris.

37 Pr. V.18; Ps. 38.4.

38 D. Baker-Smith, 'Florens Wilson and his Circle: Émigrés in Lyons, 1539–1543' in *Neo-Latin and the Vernacular in Sixteenth-Century France*, ed. T. Cave (1983), pp. 86–7.

39 BL, Cotton MS Cleopatra E iv, fo. 109 (*LP*, xiii(1). 981(2)). Luke 22:17–20.

40 S. Brigden and N. Wilson, 'New Learning and Broken Friendship', *EHR*, 112 (1997), pp. 396–411.

41 Theodore Basille [Thomas Becon], *The new pollecye of war* (1542), sig. B6v (the italics are mine).

42 *LP*, xii(1). 430. Cited in A. Overell, 'An English friendship and Italian reform: Richard Morison and Michael Throckmorton', *JEH*, 57 (2006), p. 493.

43 For a moving account of such spiritual striving, see Contarini's letters to his friends: J. B. Ross, 'Gasparo Contarini and his Friends', *Studies in the Renaissance*, 17 (1970), pp. 192–232. The quotation is at p. 207.

44 For the 'infinite variety in experiments we call "reform"', see Anne Overell's subtle, beautiful account: *Italian Reform and English Reformations, c.1535–c.1585* (Aldershot, 2008). For the most perceptive account of the nature and manner of conversion in these years, see P. Marshall, 'Evangelical conversion in the reign of Henry VIII' in *The Beginnings of English Protestantism*, ed. P. Marshall and A. Ryrie (Cambridge, 2002), pp. 14–37. This book, partly dedicated to me, is my treasure.

45 *LP*, xvi. 667.

46 TNA, SP 1/137, fo. 110 (*LP*, xiii(2). 542); Thomas Knight to Cromwell, 5 October 1538. 'Catalogue of Diego Hurtado de Mendoza's Library of Printed Books', 175, 243, 347, 479, 512, 514, 515, 702, 846, 1015, 1065, 1092, 1145 in Hobson, *Renaissance Book Collecting*.

47 Pr. V.1–3.

48 TNA, SP 1/101, fo. 149 (*LP*, x. 177).

49 Gardiner, *Letters*, pp. 55, 80, 218–9, 286–7, 507–8, 511, 513, 514, 516, 558, 564; Foxe, *AM*, vi, pp. 121, 125, 136, 192, 199, 202, 221, 242, 249, 253.

50 *Surrey: Poems*, 49; 37. 11–12, 1–2. S. Brigden, 'Henry Howard, Earl of Surrey, and the "Conjured League"', *HJ*, 37 (1994), pp. 521–2, 533.

51 *Foxe's Book of Martyrs* (1570), 8, p. 1427; *L&L*, appendix C, p. 273.

52 *The Praise of Folie by Thomas Chaloner*, ed. C. H. Miller (EETS, 257, 1965). The quotations are at pp. 4–5, 100.

53 *The Praise of Folie*, pp. xxxix–xl.

54 Mason's epitaph for Wyatt: *L&L*, p. 217.

55 BL, Cotton MS Galba B x, fo. 103 (*LP*, xv. 449).

56 TNA, PCC, Prob 11/49, fo. 107r (will of John Mason, knight, proved 25 January 1566).

57 M. P. Kuczynski, *Prophetic Song: the Psalms as Moral Discourse in Late Medieval England* (Philadelphia, 1995).

58 More, *Correspondence*, p. 515.

59 B. Smalley, *The Study of the Bible in the Middle Ages* (Oxford, 1952).

60 *The Cambridge History of the Bible*, vol. 3, *The West from the Reformation to the Present Day*, ed. S. L. Greenslade (Cambridge, 1963), chs. 1–4. *Expositions of the Psalms*, *CWE*, lxiii–lxv, ed. D. Baker-Smith *et al.* (Toronto 1997–2010).

61 For this process, see Brian Cummings' profound, illuminating study: *Literary Culture*.

62 See, especially, Cummings, *Literary Culture*, pp. 77–8, 83–5, 96–7.

63 My indispensable guides to this development at the heart of Luther and Reformation studies have been A. E. McGrath, *Luther's Theology of the Cross: Martin Luther's Theological Breakthrough* (Oxford, 1985) and *idem, Iustitia Dei: A History of the Christian Doctrine of Justification*, 2nd edn. (Cambridge, 1998). For Luther's crisis of doubt which he worked out theologically in his lectures on the Psalms, see B. Hamm, *The Reformation of Faith in the context of Late Medieval Theology and Piety*, trans. H. Heron, G. Wiedermann and J. Frymire (Leiden and Boston, 2004), pp. 163–77, 212–13. The Psalms had the most profound influence on the development of the doctrine of justification, and the two most influential verses in the Psalter on the Western conception of *iustitia Dei* are Ps. 32.1 and 72.2: *Iustitia Dei*, pp. 17–18.

64 Cited in McGrath, *Theology of the Cross*, pp. 152, 155.

65 Cummings, *Literary Culture*, pp. 98–9.

66 TNA, SP 1/48, fos. 185r–v, 196–7v (*LP*, iv(2). 4396, 4407).

67 See, for example, the Psalm manuscript in John Croke's girdle book: BL, Stowe MS 956.

68 *CWE*, lxiii, *Expositions of the Psalms*, p. xv.

69 For Psalm translations in Italian, see A. Jacobson Schutte, *Printed Italian Vernacular Religious Books, 1465–1550: A Finding List* (Genève, 1983), pp. 86–90. In Spain, vernacular Psalm paraphrases were multiplying to meet a growing popular demand: M. Bataillon, *Érasme et l'Espagne*, ed. C. Amiel and D. Devoto, 3 vols. (Genève, 1991), i, pp. 53, 308–9, 596–7, 648–50. For the process of reading and interpretation, see T. Cave, *The Cornucopian Text: Problems of Writing in the French Renaissance* (Oxford, 1979), ch. 3.

70 For the identification of Wyatt's sources I have relied on Baron, 'Wyatt's Seven Penitential Psalms'; Mason, *Wyatt: Literary Portrait*, pp. 164–220; Taylor, 'Psalms and Early Tudor Humanism', ch. 4. Dr Baron judged, even after her own exhaustive search, that the discovery of Wyatt's textual influences was not 'full or final': p. 256. For Wyatt's divergences from his sources, I have relied on Dr Baron's edition, and Professor Rebholz's: *Wyatt: Poems*, pp. 452ff.

71 Ps. 51.35.

72 Wyatt 'must have known it well': Baron, 'Wyatt's Seven Penitential Psalms', p. 255. For Dr Taylor, 'the source awaiting proper analysis in relation to Wyatt's work is the Bible': 'Psalms and Early Tudor Humanism', p. 173.

73 *Kentish Wills: Genealogical Extracts from Sixteenth-Century Wills in the Consistory Court at Canterbury*, ed. A. W. Hughes Clarke (1929), p. 39.

74 In French, there were Lefèvre d'Étaples' New Testament of 1523, and the vernacular translations of Olivetan. For Italian translations of the Bible, see Schutte, *Printed Italian Vernacular Religious Books, 1465–1550*, pp. 84–90.

75 S. L. Greenslade, 'English Versions of the Bible, 1525–1611' in *The Cambridge History of the Bible*, iii, ch. 4.

76 Mason, *Editing Wyatt*, pp. 178–87.

77 For an illuminating study of Campensis' *Enchiridion*, and of the complex problem of *how* Wyatt used it, see Taylor: 'Psalms and Early Tudor Humanism', especially ch. 1 and pp. 163ff. *A Paraphrasis upon all the Psalmes of David made by Joannes Campensis* ([Antwerp], 1535). Miles Coverdale was probably the translator.

78 Mason, *Wyatt: Literary Portrait*, pp. 158–9.

79 *The Psalter of David* (Aretius Felinus), facsimile, introduced by G. E. Duffield (Appleford, Abingdon, 1971); *David's Psalter, diligently and faithfully translated by George Joye* [Antwerp, 1534]. Mason, *Editing Wyatt*, pp. 180–4.

80 Dr Baron proved Wyatt's reliance on Cajetan's Psalter, published first in Venice (1530), and in Paris (1532, 1540): 'Wyatt's Seven Penitential Psalms', commentaries on Ps. 32, 38, 51, 102, 130, and pp. 243, 245–7, 324. For the description of Cajetan, see Cumming, *Literary Culture*, p. 385. *Cambridge History of the Bible*, iii, pp. 64–5, 92.

81 John Fisher, *This treatise concernynge the fruytfull sayinges of Davyd the kynge & prophete in the seuen penytencyall psalmes* (1509). I have used the *Commentary on the Seven Penitential Psalms*, ed. J. S. Phillimore, 2 vols. (1914). Mason insisted that Wyatt translated with Fisher's Psalms 'before him *all the time*': *Editing Wyatt*, p. 179. Fisher's *Psalmi seu precationes*, meditations inspired by themes of the Psalms, were published in Latin in Cologne in 1525. M. Dowling, *Fisher of Men: A Life of John Fisher, 1469–1535* (Basingstoke, 1999), p. 129. Mendoza owned a copy of an edition of Fisher's Psalms of 1544: 'Catalogue of Diego Hurtado de Mendoza's Library of Printed Books', 512, in Hobson, *Renaissance Book Collecting*.

82 For the message and theology of Fisher's sermons on the Penitential Psalms, see R. Rex, *The Theology of John Fisher* (Cambridge, 1991), pp. 32–40.

83 Cited in Rex, *Theology of John Fisher*, p. 39.

84 *Commentary on the Seven Penitential Psalms*, i, p. 5.

85 C. L. Costley, 'David, Bathsheba and the Penitential Psalms', *RQ*, 57 (2004), pp. 1235–77; Twombly, 'Wyatt's Paraphrase', pp. 350–1.

86 T. P. Campbell, *Henry VIII and the Art of Majesty: Tapestries at the Tudor Court* (New Haven and London, 2007), pp. 146, 177–87; J. Adamson, 'The Making of the Ancien-Régime Court, 1500–1700' in *The Princely Courts of Europe: Ritual, Politics and Culture under the Ancien Régime, 1500–1750*, ed. J. Adamson (1999), pp. 21–4.

87 For an extensive scholarly study of Aretino and the Penitential Psalms, see Boillet, *L'Arétin et la Bible*, part iii. For Wyatt's use of Aretino, see Twombly,

'Wyatt's Paraphrase', pp. 353–5; Zim, *English Metrical Psalms*, 43–57; Heale, *Wyatt, Surrey and Early Tudor Poetry*, pp. 160–70; M. Palermo Concolato, 'Il viaggio del testo. I "Salmi Penitentiali" dall'Aretino al Wyatt', *Filologia e Critica*, 18 (1993), pp. 321–33. That Wyatt used the 1534 edition was proved by Dr Baron: 'Wyatt's Seven Penitential Psalms', p. 324.

88 C. Cairns, *Pietro Aretino and the Republic of Venice: Researches on Aretino and his Circle in Venice, 1527–1556* (Firenze, 1985), ch. 4. For the 'religious restlessness' of this period, see P. Grendler, *Critics of the Italian World, 1530–1560: Anton Francesco Doni, Nicolò Franco and Ortensio Lando* (Madison, Milwaukee and London, 1969), pp. 104–35.

89 *Guidiccioni: Lettere*, i, pp. 185–6.

90 Cairns, *Pietro Aretino*, p. 86; *Pietro Aretino: Lettere*, a cura di P. Procaccioli, 2 vols. (Roma, 1997–8), ii, pp. 36, 93–8, 110–11, 205–7, 209. 'Catalogue of Diego Hurtado de Mendoza's Library of Printed Books', 82–5, in Hobson, *Renaissance Book Collecting*. Aretino's works may have come into Mendoza's possession in Venice, where their friendship began.

91 Palermo Concolato, 'Il viaggio di testo', p. 332; *Pietro Aretino: Lettere*, ii, pp. 197–8.

92 Boillet, *L'Arétin et la Bible*, pp. 242–6.

93 Ps. 38.25.

94 Pr. VII.2. For the role of Wyatt's narrator, see A. Halasz, 'Wyatt's David' in *Rethinking the Henrician Era: Essays on Early Tudor Texts and Contexts*, ed. P. C. Herman (Urbana and Chicago, 1994), pp. 193–218, especially pp. 196–8.

95 Boillet, *L'Arétin et la Bible*, pp. 282–4.

96 Pr. I.17–18. Boillet, *L'Arétin et la Bible*, pp. 248–52.

97 Pr. III.25–6. Boillet, *L'Arétin et la Bible*, pp. 354–73, especially pp. 358–9, 364, 370.

98 Leland, *Naeniae*, sig. A4v.

99 Philip Sidney, *A Defence of Poetry*, ed. J. A. Van Dorsten (Oxford, 1966), p. 22.

100 *Expositions of the Psalms*, CWE, lxiii, pp. lix, xxxiii.

101 M. Jeanneret, 'Marot traducteur des Psaumes entre le néo-platonisme et la Réforme', *Bibliothèque d'Humanisme et de Renaissance*, 27 (1965), pp. 629–43. For Flaminio, see above, pp. 484, 487; B. J. Gallardo, *Ensayo de una biblioteca Espanola de libros raros y curiosas* (Madrid, 1862), cols. 61–6; Bataillon, *Érasme et l'Espagne*, pp. 170, 389, 596, 648–50.

102 *Surrey: Poems*, 28. 13. For the use Wyatt makes of terza rima, see Twombly, 'Wyatt's Paraphrase', pp. 345–6, 349.

103 Ps. 32.67–70; Pr. VI.27, 30.

104 'Moste wretchid hart most myserable': *Egerton*, fo. 63v.

105 For the heart in the process of salvation in Augustinian theology, see W. J. Bouwsma, 'The Two Faces of Humanism: Stoicism and Augustinianism in Renaissance Thought' in *Itinerum Italicum: the Profile of the Italian Renaissance in the Mirror of its European Transformations*, ed. H. A. Oberman and T. A. Brady (Leiden, 1975), pp. 1–60, especially pp. 10–11, 36–42.

106 Pr. IV.31–2.

107 Pr. II.29–30. For the playing on words at the heart of Wyatt's verse, see especially Stamatakis, '"Turning the Word"', ch. 2.

108 Pr. I; Ps. 32.25.

109 Pr. I. 72; Ps. 6.

110 Ps. 6.90–7.

111 Ps. 32.38–9; Pr. IV.31–2; Pr. V.9–10; Pr. III.4.

112 Ps. 32.56–7.

113 For an extensive commentary on Psalm 6, see Mason, *Wyatt: Literary Portrait*, pp. 166–86.

114 Ps. 6.9–13.

115 Ps. 6.46. For the crucial significance of the New Testament allusions, see Taylor, 'Psalms and Early Tudor Humanism', pp. 170–3.

116 Matthew 9:12–13, 18:11–13; Ps. 6.24–5.

117 Mason, *Wyatt: Literary Portrait*, pp. 171, 175. Ps. 6.50–1.

118 Pr. II.12,16

119 Cummings, *Literary Culture*, pp. 88–101 (the wonderful phrase is at p. 225).

120 Ps. 32. 1–8.

121 For Wyatt's grammar and grace here, and the 'self-censoring burden of Henrician prohibition', see Cummings, *Literary Culture*, pp. 225–6.

122 Ps. 32. 19, 16–17. The italics are mine.

123 Ps. 32.29–30, 25, 37, 44, 73.

124 Cummings, *Literary Culture*, pp. 228–9.

125 Pr. III.4–7. Cf. 'Off Cartage he', where 'my pees' hangs in the balance.

126 Pr. III.17–24.

127 Ps. 38.4–5. Zim, *English Metrical Psalms*, pp. 57–8.

128 Twombly, 'Wyatt's Paraphrase', p. 367; Greenblatt, *Renaissance Self-Fashioning*, p. 123. Ps. 38.9–11.

129 Ps. 38.12–15, 27–8, 38. D. M. Friedman, 'The "Thing" in Wyatt's Mind', *EC*, 16 (1966), pp. 377–9.

130 Ps. 38.40–4. See *Wyatt: Poems*, p. 469. R. Southall, *The Courtly Maker: an Essay on the Poetry of Wyatt and his Contemporaries* (Oxford, 1964), pp. 64–5.

131 Ps. 38.62.65. Baron, 'Wyatt's Seven Penitential Psalms', commentary on Psalm 38 and p. 247.

132 Ps. 38.68–70.

133 Pr. IV.9–13.

134 Ps. 51.1–4. I follow the commentaries of Mason and Dr Baron: *Wyatt: Literary Portrait*, pp. 189–211; 'Wyatt's Seven Penitential Psalms'.

135 Ps. 51.13–15.

136 Cummings, *Literary Culture*, pp. 88–95, 230–1.

137 Ps. 51.25–9. See the penetrating discussion of Twombly, who places Wyatt's thought in Reformation context: 'Wyatt's Paraphrase', pp. 369–74.

138 For the resemblance, and the possibility of Luther's influence, see Mason, *Wyatt: Literary Portrait*, pp. 194–5, 209, 211–14. For the tautology of Luther and Wyatt here, see Cummings, *Literary Culture*, pp. 230–1.

139 I am indebted to Chris Stamatakis's brilliant reading: '"Turning the Word"', pp. 108–11. It is not until his paraphrase of the last Penitential Psalm that Aretino is found '*conjugant à la fois justice et miséricorde*': Boillet, *L'Arétin et la Bible*, p. 375.

140 Ps. 51.30, 31–2, 47–9. Baron, 'Wyatt's Seven Penitential Psalms', p. 247.

141 Ps. 51.51–66.

142 Ps. 51.70, 73, 35, 76; Ps. 6.19; Ps. 51.54, 53, 15, 75.

143 Ps. 51.77–9.

144 Pr. V.6, 12–16.

145 Pr. V.18–20.

146 Pr. V.22–4, 25–6.

147 Pr. VI.2; Ps. 102.14–15, 30.

148 Ps. 102.35–6.

149 *Tyndale's New Testament*, p. 214. These probable sources were identified by Baron, 'Wyatt's Seven Penitential Psalms', pp. 300–1. For the evangelion as the 'daily bread of the soul', see *Tyndale's New Testament*, p. 207.

150 Ps. 102.43–4. *Wyatt: Poems*, p. 480; Twombly, 'Wyatt's Paraphrase', pp. 377–9.

151 Ps. 102.48, 67–8, 65, 88–91.

152 *Wyatt: Poems*, p. 481.

153 Pr. VI.15–16.

154 *Tyndale's New Testament*, p. 216. The comparison is drawn by Mason, *Wyatt: Literary Portrait*, pp. 212–14; *Editing Wyatt*, p. 189. Pr. VI.20–4.

155 Ps. 130.1–4, 30–1.

156 Pr. VII.1–8.

157 Mason's understanding of Wyatt's paraphrase and the faith which inspired it is persuasive: *Humanism and Poetry*, pp. 219–20 (the quotation from Tyndale's prologue to St Paul's Epistle to the Romans is at p. 219); *Editing Wyatt*, pp. 178–92.

158 *In librum psalmorum brevis explanatio* (Venice, 1545). This work was placed on the papal index: C. Maddison, *Marcantonio Flaminio: Poet, Humanist and Reformer* (1965), p. 161.

159 Mason, *Humanism and Poetry*, p. 217.

160 'The Prologue to the Epistle of St Paul to the Hebrews', *Tyndale's New Testament*, p. 347.

161 Pr. V.2–3.

162 Ps. 130.7; Pr. VI.8; Ps. 32.55.

163 Ps. 32.30; Ps. 102.35; Pr. VI.5–6.

164 Pr. III.17–24; Pr. VII.4–8.

165 See P. Brown, *Augustine of Hippo* (1968), especially pp. 374–6. Hamm, *The Reformation of Faith*, chs. 4–6. O.-P. Vainio, *Justification and Participation in Christ: the Development of the Lutheran Doctrine of Justification from Luther to the Formula of Concord (1580)* (Leiden and Boston, 2008), chs. 2–3.

166 For a pellucid discussion, see Rex, *Theology of John Fisher*, ch. 7.

167 W. P. Stephens, *The Theology of Huldrych Zwingli* (Oxford, 1986), ch. 7 (especially p. 160). I have been fortunate to read the Oxford doctoral dissertation of Robert Wainwright, 'Covenant and Reformed Identity in England, 1525–1555', and to discuss this concept with him.

168 I am grateful to Robert Wainwright for his elucidation. For the judgement of 'theological mediocrity', see McGrath, *Iustitia Dei*, p. 258. Dr Heale convincingly sets the soteriology of Wyatt's Psalms against the doctrine of the Henrician Church, *Wyatt, Surrey and Early Tudor Poetry*, pp. 165–6, 172–3.

169 Pr. V.10. *Defence; Harley 78*, fo. 10v (*L&L*, p. 197).

170 *Defence; Harley 78*, fo. 10r (*L&L*, p. 195).

171 T. F. Mayer, *Reginald Pole: Prince and Prophet* (Cambridge, 2000), pp. 330–43.

172 D. Fenlon, *Heresy and Obedience in Tridentine Italy: Cardinal Pole and the Counter Reformation* (Cambridge, 1972), p. 280.

173 *Ibid.*, pp. 34, 36, 60–1, 64, 67–8, 107–14, 166–7, 174–94, 200–8; A. Overell, 'Pole's Piety? The Devotional Reading of Reginald Pole and his Friends', *JEH* (forthcoming). I am greatly indebted to Dr Overell for showing me this important article before its publication.

174 Fenlon, *Heresy and Obedience*, pp. 45–68, 131–6; Mayer, *Reginald Pole*, pp. 151–4. For the spirit of reform in Italy, see especially, Overell, *Italian Reform and English Reformations*, pp. 1–39; P. McNair, *Peter Martyr in Italy; an Anatomy of Apostasy* (Oxford, 1967), ch. 1; S. Bowd, *Reform before the Reformation: Vicenzo Querini and the Religious Renaissance in Italy* (Leiden, 2002); D. Cantimori, 'Submission and Conformity: Nicodemism and the expectations of a conciliar solution' in *The Late Italian Renaissance*, ed. E. Cochrane (1970), pp. 226–44.

175 Overell, 'Pole's Piety?'

176 Mayer, *Reginald Pole*, pp. 67–70. Marcantonio Flaminio, *Paraphrasis in duo et triginta psalmos* (Venice, 1538). Maddison, *Marcantonio Flaminio*, pp. 94–5; M. Bottai, '"La Paraphrasis in triginta Psalmos versibus scripta" di Marcantonio Flaminio: un esempio di poesia religiosa del XVI secolo', *Rinascimento*, 40 (2001), pp. 157–70. Michael Throckmorton owned Flaminio's *Paraphrasis*, Savanarola's exposition of Psalm 51 and Campensis' *Enchiridion*: Overell, 'Pole's Piety?'

177 *Pole's Correspondence*, p. 225; Pole to Contarini, 12 May 1539.

178 Mayer, *Reginald Pole*, pp. 112–13.

179 Overell, 'Pole's Piety?'

180 Fenlon, *Heresy and Obedience*, p. 29; Mayer, *Reginald Pole*, p. 123. A. Brundin, *Vittoria Colonna and the Spiritual Poetics of the Italian Reformation* (Aldershot, 2008).

181 *Surrey: Poems*, 31. 10–12. Brigden, 'Henry Howard, Earl of Surrey, and the "Conjured League"', pp. 508–9. P. Tudor-Craig, 'Henry VIII and King David', in *Early Tudor England: Proceedings of the 1987 Harlaxton Symposium*, ed. D. Williams (Woodbridge, 1989), pp. 183–205. Ps. 38.25.

182 Domingo de Soto, *De ratione tegendi et detegendi secretum* (Salamanca, 1541). J.-P. Dedieu, *L'Administration de la foi: L'inquisition de Tolède (XVIe–XVIIIe siècle)* (Madrid, 1992), ch. 6, especially pp. 111–13.

183 In 1584 a French artisan was condemned to six years in the galleys for singing Calvin's 'Psalms of David' in the prison of the Inquisition of Logroño, and another had defended Clément Marot's translation: W. Monter, *Frontiers of Heresy: The Spanish Inquisition from the Basque Lands to Sicily* (Cambridge, 1990), p. 242.

184 Anon., *A Discovery and playne Declaration of sundry subtill practises of the HOLY INQVISITION of Spayne* (1569), sigs. L3r–M1v.

185 *Certayne psalmes chosen out of the psalmes of David, commonle called the. vii. penytentiall psalmes, drawen into englyshe meter by Sir Thomas wyat knyght, wherunto is added a prologe of the auctore before every psalme, very pleasaunt & profitable to the godly reader* (1549). D. R. Carlson, 'Manuscripts after Printing: Affinity, Dissent and Display in the

Texts of Wyatt's Psalms' in *Prestige, Authority and Power in Late Medieval Manuscripts and Texts*, ed. F. Riddy (Woodbridge, 2000), pp. 173–88. A *de luxe* manuscript presentation copy was made, apparently simultaneously: BL, Royal MS 17A xxii.

186 *SP*, viii, p. 517; Wallop to Henry VIII, 26 January 1541, Mélun.

187 *Defence*; *Harley 78*, fo. 10r (*L&L*, pp. 195–6).

188 *Surrey: Poems*, 28. 34–6.

189 *Ibid.*, 30. 9–12.

190 *Index Britanniae Scriptorum: John Bale's Index of British and Other Writers*, ed. R. L. Poole and M. Bateson, intro. C. Brett and J. P. Carley (Woodbridge, 1990), p. 460.

191 D. S. Bailey, *Thomas Becon and the Reformation of the Church of England* (Edinburgh, 1952), ch. 3.

192 Thomas Becon, *The new pollecye of warre* (1542), sigs. B6v–B7r, B7v–C1r.

193 *Original Letters Relative to the English Reformation*, ed. H. Robinson, 2 vols. (Parker Society, Cambridge, 1846), i, pp. 36–7.

16: THE SLIPPER TOPPE OF COURTES ESTATES

1 'The great Macedon': *Egerton*, fo. 85v. *Surrey: Poems*, 31.

2 *Wyatt: Poems*, pp. 485–6.

3 Ps. 38.41–3; Pr. VII.17–21.

4 Pr. VII.27–32.

5 Ps. 143.1–5.

6 *Harley 282*, fo. 92v (*CWTW*, i, letter 20); 7 January 1540, Wyatt to Henry VIII, Paris. *Vindiciae Contra Tyrannos*, ed. G. Garnett (Cambridge, 1994), pp. lii, 183.

7 *Harley 282*, fo. 89 (*CWTW*, i, letter 20); 7 January 1540, Wyatt to Henry VIII, Paris.

8 Constantine, 'Memorial', p. 59.

9 More, *Correspondence*, pp. 509, 537.

10 *Defence*; *Harley 78*, fo. 13v (*L&L*, p. 205).

11 BAV, Vat. Lat. 5826, fos. 70v–71; Vat. Lat 5967, fos. 132v–133 (*LP*, xiv(2). 212; *Epistolarum Reginaldi Poli*, ed. A. M. Querini, 5 vols. (Brescia, 1744–57), ii, pp. 193–4; *Pole's Correspondence*, pp. 242–4); Pole to Contarini, monastery of Montélimar, Carpentras, 22 September 1539.

12 Wyatt's reckoning: Nott, *Wyatt*, pp. 448–50. *Defence*; *Declaration*; *Harley 78*, fos. 14v, 5v (*L&L*, pp. 208, 180).

13 ASPr, CFE, Francia, busta 7; Ferrerio to Cardinal Farnese, 1 July 1539. *LP*, xiv(1). 1137, 1261.

14 R. Graziani, 'Sir Thomas Wyatt at a Cockfight, 1539', *RES*, 27 (1976), pp. 299–303. S. Thurley, *The Royal Palaces of Tudor England* (New Haven and London, 1993), pp. 190–1.

15 *LP*, xiv(1). 1181, 1219; xiv(2). 118, 176, 183.

16 TNA, E 40/12598 (*CAD*, v, A 12598).

17 *Defence*; *Harley 78*, fo. 12v (*L&L*, p. 202).

18 By January 1541 Elizabeth Darrell was expecting Wyatt's child: see above, p. 534. In July 1543 the son of Elizabeth and Thomas Wyatt was named as Henry. But in 1544 and 1546 when Thomas Wyatt the younger, George Acworth and Edward Butler alienated lands to Elizabeth during her lifetime, and to her son after her death, he was called Francis Darrell: *LP*, xviii(1). 981(89); xix(1). 141(77), p. 86; xxi(1). 149(40), p. 78.

19 *CPR, 2 & 3 Philip and Mary*, p. 159.

20 *Letters of Cromwell*, ii, p. 267; *LP*, xiii(2). 1184; xiv(2). 782, p. 341.

21 TNA, SP 1/211, fo. 134 (*LP*, xx(2). 919); William Paget to William Petre, 2 December 1545, Calais.

22 TNA, PCC, Prob 11/26, fo. 50; E. K. Chambers, *Sir Henry Lee: An Elizabethan Portrait* (Oxford, 1936), pp. 27, 304–5; *BRUO*, p. 505.

23 *Egerton*, fo. 73 (*CWTW*, i, letter 2); Wyatt to his son, summer 1537. P. Thomson, *Sir Thomas Wyatt and his Background* (1964), p. 274.

24 For the inheritance of Frances Legh of Calder from Lucy Harper, see *CAD*, v, A 12562. 'Harper, George (1503–58)', *House of Commons*, ii, pp. 302–4; J. Woolfson, 'Morison, Sir Richard, *c.*1510–1556)', *ODNB*.

25 TNA, E 134/35 Eliz/Trin 8; W. Hutchinson, *The History of the County of Cumberland*, 2 vols. (1794), i, p. 592; R. P. Littledale, 'Some Notes on the Patricksons of Ennerdale', *Transactions of the Cumberland and Westmorland Antiquarian and Archaeological Society*, n.s., 26 (1925), pp. 135–7.

26 L.-P. Gachard, *Relations des troubles de Gand sous Charles Quint par un anonyme* (Bruxelles, 1846). I am grateful to Professor Knecht for lending me a copy of this work.

27 *Harley 282*, fo. 157 (*CWTW*, i, letter 18); Wyatt to Henry VIII, 25 December 1539, Paris.

28 R. J. Knecht, 'Charles V's Journey through France, 1539–40' in *Court Festivals of the European Renaissance: Art, Politics and Performance*, ed. J. R. Mulryne and E. Goldring (Aldershot, 2002), pp. 153–70; C. Paillard, 'Le voyage de Charles-Quint en France en 1539–1540', *Révues des questions historiques*, 25 (1879), pp. 506–50; C. Capasso, *Paolo III (1534–1549)*, 2 vols. (Messina, 1924), ii, pp. 1–7.

29 *Estancias y viajes*, pp. 477–9; Knecht, 'Charles V's Journey', p. 159.

30 For the legation, see Capasso, *Paolo III*, ii, pp. 8–16; ASPr, CFE, Francia, busta 7. For Cardinal Farnese's use of the term 'duumvirate'; ASV, Fondo Pio, 56, fo. 220. *Harley 282*, fos. 250v, 121v (*CWTW*, i, letters, 33, 27); Wyatt to Cromwell, 12 April 1540, Ghent; to Henry VIII, 9 March 1540, Ghent.

31 *CSPSp*, viii, *1545–1546*, pp. 605–6. Henry had requested a safe-conduct from the Emperor for Anne to travel to Calais: ASPr, CFE, Francia, busta 7 (*ANG*, 1, p. 494); Ferrerio to Cardinal Farnese, 25 October 1540. A safe-conduct was granted by 5 November: *LP*, xiv(2). 469.

32 *Defence*; *Harley 78*, fo. 14v (*L&L*, p. 208).

33 *Correspondance de Castillon et Marillac*, pp. 143–4 (*LP*, xiv(2). 508).

34 Instructions from the King to 'his trusty and well beloved counsellor, Sir Thomas Wyatt', November 1539: Nott, *Wyatt*, pp. 516–18. *Defence*; *Harley 78*, fo. 14v (*L&L*, p. 208).

35 Wyatt wrote from Paris on the 28th, a letter now lost: *Harley 282*, fo. 133 (*CWTW*, i, letter 15); Wyatt to Henry VIII, 2 December 1539. William Swerder wrote on the 29th of meeting a servant of Cromwell's in Paris: *LP*, xiv(2). 605. For the disparagement of Bonner by Wyatt and his *familia* and by Bishop Gardiner, see above, pp. 392–4, 396–7. Their arrival in Blois was reported by the nuncio in France: ASV, Carte Farnesiane, 8, fo. 8.

36 *Harley 282*, fos. 134–9 (*CWTW*, i, letter 15); Wyatt to Henry VIII, 2 December 1539, Blois. Marguerite, Queen of Navarre, gave an account of this audience to the nuncio, reassuring him that Henry could not reach France in time for the meeting: ASV, Carte Farnesiane, 12, fo. 9. *LP*, xiv(2). 648.

37 *Harley 282*, fos. 143–47v, 104–5 (*CWTW*, i, letters 16, 20); Wyatt to Henry VIII, 12 December 1539, Amboise; 7 January 1540, Paris. For the Duke of Cleves as pretender to Gelderland, see G. Parker, 'The Political World of Charles V' in *Charles V, 1550–1558, and His Time*, ed. H. Soly (1999), pp. 172–3.

38 *Harley 282*, fo. 148 (*CWTW*, i, letter 16); Wyatt to Henry VIII, 12 December 1539, Amboise.

39 *Harley 282*, fos. 139v–140 (*CWTW*, i, letter 15); Wyatt to Henry VIII, 2 December 1539, Blois.

40 *Harley 282*, fos. 155r–v, 121v–122v, 128, 239 (*CWTW*, i, letters 18, 27, 29, 31); Wyatt to Henry VIII, 25 December 1539, Paris; 9 and 14 March 1540, Ghent; Wyatt to Cromwell, 2 April, Ghent. Of his friend Pietro Mocenigo, Wyatt wrote little; nor did Mocenigo mention Wyatt.

41 *Harley 282*, fos. 148v–149 (*CWTW*, i, letter 16); Wyatt to Henry VIII, 12 December 1539, Amboise.

42 ASPr, CFE, Francia, busta 7, Ferrerio to Cardinal Farnese, 13 December 1539, Amboise.

43 ASPr, CFE, Francia, busta 7, Poggio to Pope Paul III, 16 December 1539, Amboise.

44 *Defence*; *Harley 78*, fo. 9v (*L&L*, p. 195).

45 *Harley 282*, fos. 152–3 (*CWTW*, i, letter 17); Wyatt to Henry VIII, 16 December 1539.

46 *LP*, xiv(2). 686 (reports by Edmund Stile and William Honning); *Harley 282*, fos. 151–3v (*CWTW*, i, letter 17); Wyatt to Henry VIII, 16 December 1539. Knecht, 'Charles V's Journey through France', pp. 159–62.

47 See, for example, ASMn, AG, Francia, 639; Giobatista da Gambara to the Duke of Mantua, 7 January 1540, Paris.

48 *Harley 282*, fos. 155–7v (*CWTW*, i, letter 18); Wyatt to Henry VIII, 25 December 1539, Paris.

49 *Harley 282*, fos. 89v, 95v (*CWTW*, i, letter 20); Wyatt to Henry VIII, 7 January 1540, Paris. Branceter told Wyatt that he had been with Pole in Avignon, and had left him in Rome about three months earlier to return to Spain, yet Pole did not return to Rome until Christmas 1539: *Pole's Correspondence*, pp. 246–8.

50 For the story of Wyatt's pursuit of Branceter, see *Harley 282*, fos. 225r–v, 83–98v (*CWTW*, i, letters 19, 20); Wyatt to Henry VIII, [28–30? December 1539], 7 January 1540, Paris. *LP*, xv, pp. iv–viii. Branceter was included in

the massive Act of Attainder of 1539: *LP*, xiv(1). 867 c. 15. *Declaration*; *Defence*; *Harley 78*, fos. 6, 10 (*L&L*, pp. 183, 195). For Welden and Swerder, see *LP* xiii(1). 1193; xiii(2). 25; xiv(2). 605.

51 *Harley 282*, fos. 225v (*CWTW*, i, letter 19); Wyatt to Henry VIII, [28-30?] December 1539; ASMn, AG, Francia, 639; Gambara to the Duke of Mantua, 23 February 1540.

52 For the picaresque life of Branceter, see J. J. Scarisbrick, 'The First Englishman round the Cape of Good Hope?', *BIHR*, 34 (1961), pp. 165–77.

53 *Harley 282*, fos. 99–102v (*CWTW*, i, letter 20); Wyatt to Henry VIII, 7 January 1540, Paris.

54 *Harley 282*, fos. 102v–103v, 105v–106v, 229 (*CWTW*, i, letters 20, 21); Wyatt to Henry VIII, 7 January 1540, Paris; Wyatt to Cromwell, 22 January, Brussels.

55 *SP*, viii, p. 517; Wallop to Henry VIII, 11 February 1541, Paris. Francis remembered the audience taking place in Blois or Amboise, but those audiences in mid-December had been cordial enough.

56 ASV, Carte Farnesiane, 12, fo. 15; Ferrerio to Pope Paul III, 3 January 1540, Paris. ASV, Fondo Pio, 56, fos. 34, 42–8; Cardinal Farnese to Pope Paul III, 1 and 4 January 1540, Paris. Cardauns, *Legationen Farneses und Cervinis*, p. 82.

57 ASV, Fondo Pio, 56, fo. 39; Cardinal Farnese to Pope Paul III, 1 January 1540, Paris.

58 *Estancias y viajes*, pp. 481–2.

59 ASV, Carte Farnesiane, 11, fo. 141r–v; Ferrerio to Pope Paul III, 25 and 27 January 1540. ASPr, CFE, Francia, busta 8; Ferrerio to Pope Paul III, 16 February 1540, Amiens. ASMo, CD, Ambasciatori Francia, 15; Sacrati and Tassone to the Duke of Ferrara, 9 and 20 February 1540, Amiens. *LP*, xv, p. vii; 121, 154–5, 178.

60 *Harley 282*, fos. 116v–117, 231 (*CWTW*, i, letters 22, 23); Wyatt to Henry VIII, and to Cromwell, 3 February 1540, Brussels.

61 For Wyatt's report, see *Harley 282*, fos. 113–17 (*CWTW*, i, letter 22). Charles ventilated reports of the audience: Ribier, i, pp. 496, 499 (*LP*, xv. 169, 189); George de Selve to Montmorency, 6 and 10 February 1540; *Correspondance de Castillon et Marillac*, p. 167. AGR, Papiers Gachard, 643, fo. 309v; Poggio to Cardinal Farnese, 7 February 1540, Brussels. J. Powell, 'Thomas Wyatt and the Emperor's Bad Latin', *NQ*, 49:2 (June 2002), pp. 207–9; 'Puttenham's *Arte of English Poetry* and Thomas Wyatt's Diplomacy', *NQ*, 52:2 (June 2005), pp. 174–6.

62 *Defence*; *Harley 78*, fo. 11v.

63 *Correspondance de Castillon et Marillac*, p. 164; *SP*, viii, pp. 245–52, 276–9; Henry VIII to the Duke of Norfolk; Cromwell to Sir John Wallop, 2 March 1540 (the quotations are at pp. 279, 248, 277).

64 AGR, Papiers Gachard, 643, fo. 310; 644, fos. 15v–16; Poggio to Cardinal Farnese, 7 and 11 February 1540, Brussels.

65 *Estancias y viajes*, p. 483. *Harley 282*, fo. 234 (*CWTW*, i, letter 24); Wyatt to Cromwell, [10] February, 1540, Brussels.

66 *Harley 282*, fos. 253, 119r–v (*CWTW*, i, letters 13, 26); Wyatt to Bonner, 3 March 1539, Toledo; to Henry VIII, 25 February 1540, Brussels. *LP*, xv. 419.

In March Wyatt began to receive letters of advice 'owt off Almayne': *Harley 282*, fo. 126 (*CWTW*, i, letter 28); Wyatt to Henry VIII, 12 March 1540, Ghent. BL, Cotton MS Vitellius B xxi, fos. 194–5 (*LP*, xv. 589); [Dr Udalricus] to Wyatt, 28 April 1540.

67 *Harley 282*, fo. 231 (*CWTW*, i, letter 23); Wyatt to Cromwell, 3 February 1540, Brussels.

68 *Harley 282*, fo. 234 (*CWTW*, i, letter 24); Wyatt to Cromwell, [10] February 1540.

69 *LP*, xiv(1). 233, 247, 248, 249, 257, 264, 308, 321. T. F. Mayer, 'If Martyrs Are Exchanged for Martyrs: the Kidnappings of William Tyndale and Reginald Pole' in *Cardinal Pole in European Context: a* via media *in the Reformation* (Aldershot, 2000), pp. 293–4.

70 *Harley 282*, fo. 232v (*CWTW*, i, letter 25); Wyatt to Cromwell, 14 February 1540, Brussels.

71 ASV, Fondo Pio, 56, fo. 177v; AGR, Papiers Gachard, 644, fo. 35; Cardinal Farnese to Pope Paul III, 5 March 1540, Ghent. In the autumn Pate reported Branceter's journey to Rome: TNA, SP 1/163, fo. 121 (*LP*, xvi. 176).

72 *Harley 282*, fos. 119, 123v, 127, 236v (*CWTW*, i, letters 26, 27, 28, 30); Wyatt to Henry VIII, 25 February 1540, Brussels, 9 and 12 March 1540; Wyatt to Cromwell, [21 March], Ghent. ASF, MP, 4297, fos. 28, 34. J. D. Tracy, *Emperor Charles V, Impresario of War: Campaign Strategy, International Finance, and Domestic Politics* (Cambridge, 2002), pp. 167–8.

73 *Harley 282*, fo. 128 (*CWTW*, i, letter 29); Wyatt to Henry VIII, 14 March 1540, Ghent.

74 ASF, MP, 4297, fo. 29v; Agnolo Niccolini and Giovanni Bandino to the Duke of Florence, 27 February 1540, Ghent; ASMo, CD, Ambasciatori Francia, busta 15 (15 and 22 March 1540).

75 *Harley 282*, fos. 121v, 123, 128v (*CWTW*, i, letters 27, 29); Wyatt to Henry VIII, 9 and 14 March 1540, Ghent.

76 For what follows, see the crucial study: R. McEntegart, *Henry VIII, the League of Schmalkalden, and the English Reformation* (2002), especially pp. 141–202.

77 *Ibid.*, p. 188.

78 *Ibid.*, pp. 177–84, 189–4; D. MacCulloch, *Thomas Cranmer: a Life* (New Haven and London, 1996), pp. 257–8, 261–2.

79 'Account by Ludwig von Baumbach of his journey to England, December 1539–January 1540', *Letters of Cromwell*, i, p. 279. I follow Dr McEntegart's interpretation: *Henry VIII, the League of Schmalkalden*, pp. 191–2.

80 So they were described to Melanchthon: McEntegart, *Henry VIII, the League of Schmalkalden*, p. 185, n. 84.

81 S. Brigden, *London and the Reformation* (Oxford, 1989), pp. 308–18.

82 *LL*, vi, p. 58; Sir John Wallop to Lord Lisle, 31 March 1540.

83 *LL*, v, p. 514. For the religious troubles in Calais and their consequences, see *LL*, v, ch. 12.

84 Bodleian, Jesus College MS 74, fo. 198v.

85 *LL*, v, pp. 412, 432–4, 462–4, 496, 498, 515–17; vi, pp. 40–6.

86 *Ibid.*, v, p. 693; vi, pp. 44, 108.

87 *Ibid.*, v, p. 48.

88 *SP*, viii, p. 166; Wriothesley to Cromwell, 3 March 1539, Brussels.

89 Gregory Botolf's conspiracy is marvellously reconstructed by Miss St C. Byrne: *LL*, vi, pp. 53–6, 74–115, 121–34. The following account confirms, from manuscripts in the Vatican Secret Archive, Miss St C. Byrne's conjectures, and corroborates the testimonies of Botolf and his confederates.

90 *LL*, vi, pp. 126, 132. Edward Corbett placed the departure between Candlemas and Shrovetide (2 to 5 February), a few days too late, but Philip Herbert dated it earlier, to *c.*25 January.

91 ASV, AA Arm. I–XVIII, 6530, fo. 249; Ferrerio to Cardinal Farnese, 31 January 1540. Fondo Pio, 56, fos. 102–4; Cardinal Farnese to Pope Paul III, 2 February 1540, Amiens. Farnese's account of the plot is substantially similar to Philpot's: *LL*, vi, pp. 87–8.

92 *LL*, vi, pp. 87, 88.

93 AGR, Papiers Gachard, 644, fos. 23–4, 25v, 47v; Papal Chancellery to Cardinal Farnese, 27 February, 15 March 1540.

94 *LL*, vi, pp. 76, 126, 245.

95 *Ibid.*, pp. 78, 80, 81.

96 *Ibid.*, pp. 86–8, 121–4; depositions of Clement Philpot.

97 TNA, SP 1/159, fo. 54; *LL*, vi, pp. 92–4, 129–32, 133; depositions of John Browne, Edward Corbett's servant; Philip Herbert's declaration. BL, Cotton MS Galba B x, fo. 103 (*LP*, xv. 449); John Mason to [Cromwell], 2 April 1540, Ghent. Wyatt had been in Ghent since 1 March: *Harley 282*, fo. 121 (*CWTW*, i, letter 27); Wyatt to Henry VIII, 9 March 1540.

98 *LL*, vi, pp. 123, 93–4, 127.

99 TNA, SP 1/159, fo. 55; *LL*, vi, pp. 94, 109.

100 *Declaration*; *Harley 78*, fo. 5v (*L&L*, p. 180).

101 The chronicle of Elis Gruffud: *LL*, vi, p. 103.

102 ASV, Fondo Pio, 56, fo. 224v; Cardinal Farnese to Pope Paul III, 10 April 1540, Ghent.

103 *Harley 282*, fos. 241, 251v (*CWTW*, i, letters 31, 33); Wyatt to Cromwell, 2 and 12 April 1540, Ghent. Lisle's secretary deposed that he thought the letter concerned horses, but this was politic since he was in danger of being charged with concealment of treason: *LL*, vi, pp. 145–6.

104 *Harley 282*, fos. 121v–122v (*CWTW*, i, letter 27); Wyatt to Henry VIII, 9 March 1540, Ghent.

105 *LL*, vi, pp. 95, 98, 104.

106 *Ibid.*, pp. 98–104, 112–15, 167; *LP*, xv. 498. 58 [c. 60].

107 AGR, Papiers Gachard, 644, fos. 146v, 238v, 246v; ASV, Carte Farnesiane, 2, fo. 119; Cervini to Cardinal Farnese, 9 June, 31 August, 9 and 17 September 1540. ASV, AA, Arm. I–VIII, 6533, fos. 188–9; Poggio to Cervini, 19 September 1540. *Pole's Correspondence*, pp. 252–3.

108 *Harley 282*, fos. 126, 128r–v, 244 (*CWTW*, i, letters 28, 29, 32); Wyatt to Henry VIII, 12 and 14 March 1540; Wyatt to Cromwell, 5 April 1540, Ghent.

109 *Harley 282*, fo. 236v (*CWTW*, i, letter 30); Wyatt to Cromwell, 21 March 1540, Ghent.

110 *Harley 282*, fo. 245 (*CWTW*, i, letter 32); Wyatt to Cromwell, 5 April 1540, Ghent.

111 ASV, Fondo Pio, 56, fos. 111, 137, 142; Cardinal Farnese to Pope Paul III, 7 and 13 February 1540, Amiens. ASMn, AG, 639; Giobatista da Gambara to the Duke of Mantua, 11 February 1540.

112 E. Williamson, *Bernardo Tasso* (Roma, 1951), pp. 99–107. AGR, Papiers Gachard, 644, fo. 72v; Poggio to Pope Paul III, 24 March 1540. *CWTW*, i, 16; Wyatt to Henry VIII, 12 December 1539, Amboise. Tasso was not Sanseverino's emissary to Wyatt. He had been sent to Poland to discover the movements of the Turks, and did not leave there until 9 April: *Ven. Dep.*, i, pp. 427–8; Mocenigo *et al.* to the Doge, 26 April 1540, Ghent.

113 *Harley 282*, fo. 245 (*CWTW*, i, letter 32); Wyatt to Cromwell, 5 April 1540, Ghent; *Letters of Cromwell*, ii, pp. 259–60; Cromwell to Ralph Sadler, 7 April 1540.

114 *Declaration; Harley 78*, fo. 5 (*L&L*, p. 180). TNA, SP 1/158, fos. 48r–v, 52r–v; BL, Cotton MS Vitellius B xiv, fo. 264v (*LP*, xv. 358, 369; xiii(2). 847). See above, pp. 377–8.

115 TNA, SP 1/141, fo. 159 (*LP*, xiii(2). 1249); *Harley 282*, fo. 244v (*CWTW*, i, letter 32); Wyatt to Cromwell, 5 April 1540, Ghent.

116 Wyatt was related to John Legh via the Skinners of Reigate: W. B. Robison III, 'The Justices of the Peace in Surrey in National and Gentry Politics, 1483–1570' (unpublished Louisiana State University Ph.D. thesis, 1984), p. 468. Legh was related to Katherine Howard by the marriage of his cousin Joyce to Lord Edmund Howard, Katherine's father: TNA, PCC, Prob. 11/22, fos. 143–4 (will of Dame Isabel Legh). For Katherine, see D. Starkey, *Six Wives: the Queens of Henry VIII* (2003), ch. 73.

117 *Harley 282*, fo. 234v (*CWTW*, i, letter 24); *Letters of Cromwell*, ii, p. 260.

118 AGR, Papiers Gachard, 644, fos. 77v–78; ASV, Fondo Pio, 56, fos. 218r–v, 224; Cardinal Farnese to Pope Paul III, 8 and 10 April 1540, Ghent.

119 *Harley 282*, fos. 247–51v (*CWTW*, i, letter 33); Wyatt to Cromwell, 12 April 1540, Ghent.

120 *Correspondance de Castillon et Marillac*, p. 175; Ribier, i, p. 513 (*LP*, xv. 485–6); Marillac to Francis, and to Montmorency, 10 April 1540. G. R. Elton, 'Thomas Cromwell's Decline and Fall', in *Studies in Tudor and Stuart Politics and Government*, 4 vols. (Cambridge, 1974–92), i, pp. 198–230.

121 *LP*, xv. 481. *SP*, i, pp. 624–5; Sadler to Cromwell, Cromwell to Sadler, [7 April] 1540.

122 *Harley 282*, fos. 130–1v (*CWTW*, i, letter 34); Wyatt to Henry VIII, 16 April 1540, Ghent. The Florentine ambassadors described Wyatt's discomfiture: ASF, MP, 4297, fo. 40.

123 Cardauns, *Legationen Farneses und Cervinis*, pp. 183–4; Cardinal Farnese to Pope Paul III, 20 April 1540, Ghent; ASF, MP, 4297, fos. 48, 79v; Niccolini and Bandino to the Duke of Florence, 27 April and 8 July 1540.

124 Ribier, i, p. 513 (*LP*, xv. 486); *LP*, xv. 541; *Correspondance de Castillon et Marillac*, pp. 179–80.

125 *LP*, xv. 536, 615; BL, Cotton MS Cleopatra E vi, fos. 380–1 (*LP*, xv. 721); *Correspondance de Castillon et Marillac*, pp. 184–7 (the quotation is at p. 187); *LP*, xv. 747.

126 Trinity College, Cambridge, MS R 3.33, fo. 17 (printed in P. Janelle, 'An unpublished poem on Bishop Stephen Gardiner', *BIHR*, 6 (1933), p. 22). For elucidation, see Elton, 'Thomas Cromwell's Decline and Fall', p. 191.

127 AGR, Papiers Gachard, 644, fo. 146r–v; Cervini to Cardinal Farnese, 11 June 1540.

128 *Correspondance de Castillon et Marillac*, pp. 193–4 (*LP*, xv. 804); Marillac to Montmorency, 23 June 1540. *LP*, xv. 498(60). Brigden, *London and the Reformation*, pp. 313–16.

129 *Letters of Cromwell*, ii, pp. 264–7 (the italics are mine).

130 *Ibid.*, pp. 268–76 (the quotations are at pp. 268, 273).

131 *SP*, viii, pp. 349, 355; *Correspondance de Castillon et Marillac*, pp. 189–91.

132 AGR, Papiers Gachard, 644, fos. 150, 154v; Cervini and Poggio to Cardinal Farnese, 14 and 15 June 1540; *LP*, xv. 792.

133 ASV, Carte Farnesiane, 11, fo. 150v; Ferrerio to [Cardinal Farnese], 30 June 1540; *Correspondance de Castillon et Marillac*, p. 188.

134 AGR, Papiers Gachard, 644, fos. 156v–157, 182; Cervini to Cardinal Farnese, 24 June and 11 July 1540, Brussels.

135 *Letters of Cromwell*, ii, p. 262.

136 Ribier, i, p. 519 (*LP*, xv. 548); French ambassador in Venice to Montmorency, 19 April 1540. Capasso, *Paolo III*, ii, p. 32. For the vital role of Henry's foreign political ambitions in Cromwell's fall, see G. W. Bernard, *The King's Reformation: Henry VIII and the Remaking of the English Church* (New Haven and London, 2005), pp. 556–69.

137 *LP*, xv. 877.

138 ASV, Carte Farnesiane, 2, fos. 100v–101; AGR, Papiers Gachard, 644, fo. 181v; Cervini to Cardinal Farnese, 5 and 11 July, Bruges.

139 *Chronicle of Calais*, p. 48; *SP*, viii, pp. 366–7, 375.

140 AGR, Papiers Gachard, 644, fos. 175v–6; Sotheby's, 'Letter Book of Marcello Cervini'; ASV, Fondo Pio, 56, fos. 241, 244; Cervini to Cardinal Farnese and to the nuncios of France and Venice, 3, 4 and 10 July, 1540. Carte Farnesiane, 2, fo. 102; Cervini to [Pope Paul III], 5 July, Bruges. ASMo, CD, Ambasciatori Germania, busta 4; Rossetto to the Duke of Ferrara, 5 July 1540. *Correspondance de Castillon et Marillac*, pp. 197, 199 (*LP*, xv. 847–8).

141 AGR, Papiers Gachard, 644, fo. 184v; Cervini to Cardinal Farnese, 13 July 1540. ASMo, CD, Ambasciatori Germania, 4; Rossetto to the Duke of Ferrara, 5 July 1540, Bruges. *LP*, xv. 877–8, 887; *Chronicle of Calais*, p. 48.

142 ASF, MP, 4297, fo. 79v; Bandino to the Duke of Florence, 8 July 1540. See above, p. 506. *LP*, xvi. 214, 606. For continuing rumours, *CSPSp*, vi(1), *1538–1542*, pp. 282, 285.

143 Sotheby's, 'Letterbook of Marcello Cervini', 5 July 1540.

144 *Correspondance de Castillon et Marillac*, pp. 202–3 (*LP*, xv. 901–2). *SP*, viii, p. 453; Pate to Henry VIII, 18 October 1540. The King's payments attest to the honourable reception of the Prince of Salerno and the 'strangers': *LP*, xvi. 380, pp. 189–92.

145 AGR, Papiers Gachard, 644, fos. 198–9; Cervini to Cardinal Farnese, 23 July 1540, Dordrecht.

146 *Defence*; *Harley* 78, fo. 14v (*L&L*, p. 208); *LP*, xiv(2). 619(49). 32 Hen. VIII c. 77, 75; *LP*, xv. 498, p. 219. For the bitterly contested inheritance of Lord Grey of Codnor, and the dispute over lands in Greys Thurrock, Essex and Hoo, Kent, see *Testamenta Vetusta*, pp. 412–14. TNA, STAC 2/10/56; 2/10/259; 2/17/68; 2/17/395. Wyatt's involvement came initially through his business partnership with George Zouche.

147 BL, Cotton MS Vespasian F xiii, fo. 269 (*CWTW*, i, letter 35).

148 TNA, E 305/2/A55. Dr Nott dated this exchange 14 June 1541: *Wyatt*, pp. 524–6. The signed bill was dated 10 July 1540: *LP*, xv. 942(49). *A Survey of London by John Stow*, ed. C. L. Kingsford, 2 vols. (Oxford, 1908), i, pp. 147–9.

149 *Defence*; *Harley* 78, fo. 13v (*L&L*, p. 205).

150 *Correspondance de Castillon et Marillac*, p. 194 (*LP*, xv. 804); Marillac to Montmorency, 23 June 1540.

151 ASV, Carte Farnesiane, 11, fo. 150v; AGR, Papiers Gachard, 644, fo. 175v; Ferrerio and Cervini to Cardinal Farnese, 30 June and 3 July 1540.

152 *Foxe's Book of Martyrs* (1576 edn.), 11, p. 1759; *Correspondance de Castillon et Marillac*, p. 190 (*LP*, xv. 767); MacCulloch, *Thomas Cranmer*, p. 270.

153 G. Phillips, 'Sadler, Sir Ralph (1507–1587)'; M. A. R. Graves, 'Wriothesley, Thomas, first earl of Southampton (1505–1550)', *ODNB*. *Foxe's Book of Martyrs* (1570 edn.), 8, p. 1361; *Correspondance de Castillon et Marillac*, p. 194 (*LP*, xv. 804); AGR, Papiers Gachard, 644, fo. 157; Cervini to Cardinal Farnese, 24 June 1540.

154 Several accounts exist of Cromwell's scaffold speech: *Foxe's Book of Martyrs* (1563 edn.), 3, p. 602; 'The Chronicle of Anthony Anthony', Bodleian, Fol. Δ 624, facing p. 624. I am grateful to Gary Hill for a copy of his transcript of this chronicle. The version I have followed is found in the commonplace book of Bishop Cox of Ely, which also contains one of Wyatt's verse epistles to John Poyntz: *Parker*, fo. 209. The scaffold speech was printed for circulation, and in September Pole received a copy in Viterbo: *Pole's Correspondence*, p. 254. In later editions of Foxe's *Actes and Monumentes* Cromwell prays in the pure language and spirit of the evangelical faith: for example, *Foxe's Book of Martyrs* (1570 edn.), 8, p. 1361.

155 *Chronicle of King Henry VIII*, pp. 103–4.

156 The phrase is from the poem 'Of the mean and sure estate' in *TM*. This, perhaps a draft of 'Stand who so list' in *Arundel Harington*, is printed in *Wyatt: Poems*, pp. 371–2.

157 *Arundel Harington*, 311. For the most illuminating criticism of this poem, see T. M. Greene, *The Light in Troy: Imitation and Discovery in Renaissance Poetry* (New Haven and London, 1982), pp. 245–6.

158 B. Vickers, 'Leisure and Idleness in the Renaissance: the Ambivalence of Otium', *Renaissance Studies*, 4 (1990), pp. 1–37, 107–54.

17: MYNE UNQUYET MYNDE

1 *Petrarch's Lyric Poems*, 269.

2 *Arundel Harington*, 96. For readings of this sonnet which align it with Cromwell's death, see H. A. Mason, *Sir Thomas Wyatt: A Literary Portrait* (Bristol, 1986), pp. 244–52; S. M. Foley, *Sir Thomas Wyatt*, pp. 39–42. For Professor Foley, it is unambiguously 'the elegy for Cromwell'.

3 J. Kerrigan, 'Wyatt's Selfish Style', *ES*, 34 (1981), pp. 1–3.

4 S. Brigden, 'Henry Howard, Earl of Surrey, and the "Conjured League"', *HJ*, 37 (1994), pp. 529–30.

5 *Quyete of mynde*, sig. C2v. Egerton, fo. 73 (*CWTW*, i, letter 2); Wyatt to his son, summer 1537. 'My mothers maydes', l. 101.

6 *Surrey: Poems*, 28. 1.

7 See B. Vickers, 'Leisure and Idleness in the Renaissance: the Ambivalence of Otium', *Renaissance Studies*, 4 (1990), pp. 1–37, 107–54 (for restlessness as the child of *acedia*, see p. 108; for Petrarch's *De remediis*, pp. 115–17). R. J. Quinones, *The Renaissance Discovery of Time* (Cambridge, Mass., 1972), p. 147. *Quyete of mynde*, A5r.

8 *Egerton*, fo. 73 (*CWTW*, i, letter 2); Wyatt to his son, summer 1537.

9 Vickers, 'Leisure and Idleness', pp. 19–26.

10 'Behold love'; 'Avysing the bright beme'; 'Such vayn thought'; 'My galy charged with forgetfulnes'; 'Yf amours faith': *Egerton*, fos. 4, 22, 38, 21v, 12v.

11 So James Gairdner called him: *LP*, xvi, p. xxv.

12 *LP*, xvi. 379(6).

13 BL, Cotton MS Vespasian F xiii, fo. 269 (*CWTW*, i, letter 35); Wyatt to an unknown lord, summer 1540. *A Survey of London by John Stow*, ed. C. L. Kingsford, 2 vols. (Oxford, 1908), i, pp. 147–9.

14 *Defence*; Harley 78, fo. 7 (*L&L*, p. 187).

15 *Correspondance de Castillon et Marillac*, pp. 239–43 (*LP*, xvi. 238, 269–70); Marillac to Montmorency and Francis I, 5 and 16 November 1540. ASMo, CD, Germania 4; Rossetto to the Duke of Ferrara, 6 and 9 December 1540. For Henry's moves toward the marriage, and the spy sent to urge Chapuys to forward it, see *LP*, xvi. 117, 214.

16 ASV, AA, Arm. I–XVIII, 6533, fos. 198v, 203 (*LP*, xvi. 319); Poggio to Cardinal Farnese, 8 December 1540.

17 TNA, SP 1/163, fo. 219r–v (*LP*, xvi. 258). For the discovery of the letters and the investigation early in October, see TNA, SP 1/163, fo. 56 (*LP*, xvi. 119); *LP*, xvi. 129.

18 TNA, SP 1/164, fo. 12r–v (*LP*, xvi. 294); Wriothesley to the Council in London, 27 November 1540.

19 TNA, SP 1/164, fo. 14 (*LP*, xvi. 295).

20 For Pate's beliefs and career, see D. Fenlon, *Heresy and Obedience in Tridentine Italy: Cardinal Pole and the Counter Reformation* (Cambridge, 1972), pp. 149–60; T.A. Sowerby, 'Richard Pate, the Royal Supremacy and Reformation Diplomacy', *HJ*, 54 (2011), pp. 265–85.

21 TNA, SP 1/164, fo. 57 (*SP*, viii, p. 507). ASV, AA, Arm. I–XVIII, 6533, fo. 209; SS, Germania, 58, fo. 277 (*LP*, xvi. 452); Poggio to Cardinals Farnese and Santa Croce, Worms, 13 January 1541. *Correspondance de Castillon et Marillac*, p. 256 (*LP*, xvi. 446); Montmorency to Marillac, 11 January 1541.

22 *CSPSp*, vi(1), *1538–1542*, p. 307; Chapuys to Mary of Hungary, 4 January 1541.

23 *LP*, xvi. 433, 436, 438, 442, 448, pp. 702, 703. *Correspondance de Castillon et Marillac*, pp. 258, 260 (*LP*, xvi. 449–50); Marillac to Francis I and to Montmorency, 12 January 1541.

24 For the ironic appellation, see *Harley 282*, fo. 227v (*CWTW*, i, letter 11); Wyatt to Cromwell, 2 January 1539. *LP*, xvi, p. 700.

25 *LP*, xvi. 460.

26 *Correspondance de Castillon et Marillac*, p. 262 (*LP*, xvi. 466); Marillac to Francis I, 18 January 1541. *LP*, xvi. 503(11, 12), 580(95).

27 S. Gunn, *Charles Brandon, Duke of Suffolk c.1484–1545* (Oxford, 1988), p. 207; 'Browne, Sir Anthony (*c.*1500–48)'; 'Fitzwilliam, Sir William I (*c.*1490–1542)'; 'Gage, Sir John (1479–1556)'; 'Wingfield, Sir Anthony (by 1488–1552)', *House of Commons*, i, pp. 518–21; ii, pp. 142–5, 179–82; iii, pp. 638–40.

28 *Defence*; *Harley 78*, fo. 12 (*L&L*, p. 201).

29 HHStA, England, Korrespondenz, 8, fo. 6 (*CSPSp*, vi(1), *1538–1542*, p. 308); Chapuys to Mary of Hungary, 17 January 1541.

30 *Correspondance de Castillon et Marillac*, pp. 261–2 (*LP*, xvi. 466); Marillac to Francis I, 18 January 1541.

31 *SP*, viii, pp. 504–6; *LP*, xvi. 1489 (p. 700). HHStA, England, Korrespondenz, 8, fo. 6 (*CSPSp*, vi(1), *1538–1542*, p. 308).

32 *Correspondance de Castillon et Marillac*, pp. 262–3 (*LP*, xvi. 467); Marillac to Montmorency, 18 January 1541.

33 *CSPSp*, vi(1), *1538–1542*, pp. 308–9.

34 *The Lyfe of Sir Thomas Moore, knighte . . . by William Roper*, ed. E. V. Hitchcock (EETS, 197, 1935, repr. 1958), p. 89.

35 For Mason's marriage to Elizabeth Hill, widow, see *Faculty Office Registers*, p. 227. *LP*, xvi. 469.

36 *The Lyfe of Sir Thomas Moore, knighte . . . by William Roper*, p. 84. See also Brigden, 'Henry Howard, Earl of Surrey, and the "Conjured League"', pp. 527, 537.

37 G. Mattingley, *Renaissance Diplomacy* (Boston, 1954), p. 208.

38 *Inventory*, 4477, 3479.

39 *TM*, 92.

40 BL, Cotton MS, Titus B i, fo. 196 (*LP*, xvi. 470). Southwell prepared 'a book' of expenses incurred in shutting down Alington, and a warrant for payment of £53 10s 4½d was issued on 12 March: *LP*, xvi. 611, 1489, p. 704.

41 *Correspondance de Castillon et Marillac*, p. 270 (*LP*, xvi. 534); Marillac to Montmorency, 12 February 1541.

42 *Declaration*; *Harley 78*, fo. 5v (*L&L*, p. 180).

43 *LP*, xvi. 473–4, 1489, pp. 700, 702. *Correspondance de Castillon et Marillac*, pp. 264–5, 269 (*LP*, xvi. 482, 534); Marillac to Francis I and to Montmorency, 25 January and 12 February 1541.

44 AGR, Papiers Gachard, 645, fos. 19–21; Poggio to Cardinal Farnese, 19 February 1541, Nuremberg. For a similar report to Cardinal Santa Croce, see *LP*, xvi. 548. *CSPVen, 1534–1554*, 240; Francesco Contarini to the Signory of Venice, 28 February 1541, Nuremberg.

45 *Correspondance de Castillon et Marillac*, pp. 273–4 (*LP*, xvi. 589–90); Marillac to Francis I and to Montmorency, 3 March 1541. My italics.

46 *CSPSp*, vi(1), *1538–1542*, p. 307; *LP*, xvi. 488, 502, 515–16, 530, 541, 586, 594–5, 597, 599.

47 *Correspondance de Castillon et Marillac*, p. 276 (*LP*, xvi. 606); Marillac to Francis I, 10 March 1541. For Palmer's arrest, see *LP*, xvi. 532, 557, 592, 594, 599, 662. TNA, E 163/10/31.

48 BL, Cotton MS Otho D x, fo. 222v.

49 *Declaration*; *Harley 78*, fos. 5–6v (*L&L*, pp. 178–84). If he wrote to the King, the letters do not survive.

50 *Declaration*; *Harley 78*, fo. 5r–v (*L&L*, pp. 178–80).

51 *Declaration*; *Harley 78*, fo. 5 (*L&L*, pp. 178–9).

52 *Declaration*; *Harley 78*, fos. 5r–v, 6v (*L&L*, pp. 179–80, 184).

53 *Defence*; *Harley 78*, fo. 8v (*L&L*, p. 192).

54 *Defence*; *Harley 78*, fo. 12v (*L&L*, pp. 202–3).

55 *Blage*, fo. 183; see above, p. 275. The irony is Chris Stamatakis's suggestion.

56 For the practical working of this law, see *Spelman's Reports*, ii, especially pp. 103ff. For the conduct of treason trials, see G. R. Elton, *Policy and Police: the Enforcement of the Reformation in the Age of Thomas Cromwell* (Cambridge, 1972), ch. 7.

57 Elton, *Policy and Police*, pp. 317–21.

58 *LP*, xvi. 932.

59 *A Chronicle of England during the Reigns of the Tudors by Charles Wriothesley*, ed. W. D. Hamilton, 2 vols. (Camden Society, new series xi, 1875), i, p. 177; Edward, Lord Herbert of Cherbury, *The Life and Raigne of King Henry the eighth* (1649), p. 565.

60 For the role of the jury, see *Spelman's Reports*, ii, pp. 103–14. For the independence of the judiciary, *ibid.*, ii, pp. 135–7. *Defence*; *Harley 78*, fo. 7 (*L&L*, p. 187).

61 *Defence*; *Harley 78*, fo. 8v (*L&L*, p. 191).

62 For the power of rhetoric to delight in order to move an audience, see B. Vickers, *In Defence of Rhetoric* (Oxford, 1988), pp. 50, 57, 74, 282.

63 For the reception of classical rhetoric in Renaissance England, see Vickers, *In Defence of Rhetoric* and Q. R. D. Skinner, *Reason and Rhetoric in the Philosophy of Hobbes* (Cambridge, 1996), part 1. R. A. Lanham, *A Handlist of Rhetorical Terms: A Guide for Students of English Literature* (Berkeley, Los Angeles, London, 1968) is an invaluable guide to the rhetorical figures and tropes.

64 Quintilian, *Institutio oratoria*, trans. H. E. Butler, 4 vols. (Cambridge, Mass., 1920–2), 8. Pr. 15–16; 8.3.2; Vickers, *In Defence of Rhetoric*, pp. 43, 282, 284, 314.

65 *Defence; Harley 78*, fo. 7r–v (*L&L*, p. 188).

66 Quintilian, *Institutio oratoria*, 8.18–28; Vickers, *In Defence of Rhetoric*, pp. 43–4.

67 *Defence; Harley 78*, fos. 7, 10v (*L&L*, pp. 187, 198).

68 *Defence; Harley 78*, fo. 7v (*L&L*, p. 189).

69 *Defence; Harley 78*, fos. 7r–v, 14 (*L&L*, pp. 188, 206).

70 *Defence; Harley 78*, fos. 7v, 12v (*L&L*, pp. 189, 202).

71 *Defence; Harley 78*, fos. 7v–8 (*L&L*, p. 190).

72 *Defence; Harley 78*, fo. 14 (*L&L*, p. 206). Puttenham, pp. 195, 199–201.

73 *Defence; Harley 78*, fos. 13v, 8v (*L&L*, pp. 204, 192).

74 *Defence; Harley 78*, fo. 7v (*L&L*, p. 189). *Spelman's Reports*, i, pp. 54–5.

75 *Defence; Harley 78*, fo. 7v (*L&L*, p. 189).

76 *Defence; Harley 78*, fo. 9 (*L&L*, p. 194).

77 *Defence; Harley 78*, fo. 9v (*L&L*, p. 195).

78 *Defence; Harley 78*, fo. 10 (*L&L*, pp. 195–6).

79 For the enforcement of the Treason Act, see Elton, *Policy and Police*, pp. 301ff.

80 *Defence; Harley 78*, fo. 10r–v (*L&L*, pp. 196–7).

81 *Defence; Harley 78*, fo.11r–v (*L&L*, pp. 198–9).

82 *Defence; Harley 78*, fos. 11v, 12v (*L&L*, pp. 200, 202).

83 *Defence; Harley 78*, fo. 12r–v (*L&L*, p. 201).

84 *Defence; Harley 78*, fos. 12v, 13v (*L&L*, pp. 202, 205).

85 *Defence; Harley 78*, fo. 14v (*L&L*, p. 208).

86 *Defence; Harley 78*, fo. 12v (*L&L*, p. 202).

87 *Defence; Harley 78*, fo. 15 (*L&L*, p. 209).

88 *SP*, viii, p. 546; Privy Council to Lord William Howard, 26 March 1541.

89 HHStA, England, Korrespondenz, 8, fo. 7v; AGR, Audience, 380, fo. 5v (*CSPSp*, vi(1), *1538–1542*, p. 314); Chapuys to Mary of Hungary, 27 March 1541. *LP*, xvi. 634, 1489, p. 706. *Correspondance de Castillon et Marillac*, p. 281 (*LP*, xvi, 650); Marillac to Francis I, 25 March 1541. The fiat for the pardons of Wyatt and Mason was dated 21 March 1541: *LP*, xvi. 678(41, ii). For another pardon granted at the Queen's behest: *LP*, xvi. 1391(18).

90 *LP*, xii(1). 1225.

91 *The Castell of love, translated out of Spanyshe into Englysshe, by John Bowrchier knyght, lorde Bernes* (1552?), sigs. F6v, H2r–H3r.

92 *LP*, vii. 1655.

93 *SP*, viii, p. 546; Privy Council to Lord William Howard, 26 March 1541. P. Thomson, *Sir Thomas Wyatt and his Background* (Stanford, 1964), p. 73.

94 The King left Greenwich for Dover on 21 March, arrived on the 27th and stayed until the 31st. *Correspondance de Castillon et Marillac*, p. 282 (*LP*, xvi. 650); Marillac to Francis I, 25 March 1541; *CSPSp*, vi(1), *1538–1542*, p. 312; Chapuys to Mary of Hungary, 3 April (but properly 30 or 31 March) 1541. *LP*, xvi. 661, 666, 668, 672, 675, 677(XVII).

95 HHStA, England, Korrespondenz, 8, fo. 7v; AGR, Audience, 380, fo. 5v (*CSPSp*, vi(1), *1538–1542*, p. 314); Chapuys to Mary of Hungary, 27 March 1541.

96 Chapuys confused the niece with the aunt. AGR, Audience, 380, fo. 92 (*CSPSp*, vi(1), *1538–1542*, p. 468); Chapuys to Charles V, 9 February 1542. For the

scandalous romantic history of Elizabeth Brooke and William Parr, Marquess of Northampton, see D. Starkey, *Six Wives: the Queens of Henry VIII* (2003), p. 679; S. James, *Catherine Parr: Henry VIII's Last Love* (Stroud, 2008), pp. 82–4, 123, 133, 287–9; M. Partridge, 'Thomas Hoby's English translation of Castiglione's *Book of the Courtier, HJ*, 50 (2007), pp. 769–86.

97 *CPR, 2 & 3 Philip and Mary*, pp. 57–8. Here Wyatt's will is dated 12 June 33 Henry VIII (1541), but the grant of the reversion of this site was not made until 31 March 1542: *LP*, xvii. 220(98).

98 *LP*, xvi. 1060, 1081–3, 1204; *CSPVen, 1534–1554*, 272, 273, 278, 279.

99 *LP*, xvi. 931–2.

100 *Correspondance de Castillon et Marillac*, pp. 317–18 (*LP*, xvi. 941); Marillac to Francis I, 30 June 1541; *CSPSp*, vi(1), *1538–1542*, pp. 334–5; Chapuys to Mary of Hungary, 2 July 1541.

101 *Spelman's Reports*, i, pp. 228–30; ii, pp. *140, 200*.

102 BL, Sloane MS 4031. C. M. Meale and J. Boffey, 'Gentlewomen's Reading' in *Cambridge History of the Book in Britain*, iii, *1400–1557*, ed. L. Hellinga and J. B. Trapp (Cambridge, 1999), p. 538. The book had once been owned by Lady Carew, who made her will on 21 July 1541: TNA, PCC, Prob. 11/31, fo. 103v. Even the King was 'moved with pity' by the plight of the widows of these young men: *LP*, xvi. 953, 1019.

103 *LP*, xvi. 878(28).

104 *LP*, xvi. 947(31), 1211.

105 *LP*, xvi. 745 (p. 357); TNA, E 305/4/C19, C 20; SP 1/243, fo. 161 (*LP*, *Addenda*, 1500); *CPR, 3 & 4 Philip and Mary*, p. 447.

106 TNA, WARD 2/58/215/7.

107 Hall, fos. 243v–244. *LP*, xvi. 679, 694; *Correspondance de Castillon et Marillac*, pp. 287–8 (*LP*, xvi. 711); Marillac to Francis I, 10 April 1541; *CSPSp*, vi(1), *1538–42*, p. 315; Chapuys to Charles V, 17 April 1541. TNA, SP 1/165, fo. 171v (*LP*, xvi. 808); Southampton and Russell to Henry VIII, 6 May 1541, Calais. The light horsemen came down from the borders of Scotland.

108 Theodore Basille [Thomas Becon], *The new pollecye of warre* (1542), sigs. A2r, B6v.

109 Hall, fos. 243v–244r. TNA, SP 1/165, fos. 171–3 (*LP*, xvi. 808–9); *LP*, xvi. 809, 811, 813; *CSPSp*, vi(1), *1538–1542*, pp. 323–4.

110 *TM*, 16.

111 *Egerton*, fos. 100–1; *Wyatt: Poems*, CLIV. In *Egerton*, this poem is in Wyatt's own hand and revised by him, scribe and editor. For Carthage, see above, pp. 351–4. Professor Tromly writes, however, 'curiously, the content of the poem seems to have nothing to do with Wyatt': 'Surrey's Fidelity to Wyatt in "Wyatt Resteth Here"', *SP*, 77 (1980), p. 377 n. 4.

112 *Blage*, fo. 90v (*Collected Poems of Wyatt*, CXXXI). This is the judgement of Helen Baron: 'The "Blage" Manuscript: the Original Compiler Identified', *English Manuscript Studies*, 1 (1989), p. 101.

113 For the relationship between Wyatt and Surrey, see Thomson, *Thomas Wyatt and his Background*, pp. 72–3; W. A. Sessions, 'Surrey's Wyatt: Autumn 1542 and the

New Poet' in *Rethinking the Henrician Era: Essays on Early Tudor Texts and Contexts*, ed. P. C. Herman (Urbana and Chicago, 1994), pp. 168–92; *Henry Howard, the Poet Earl of Surrey: A Life* (Oxford, 1999), especially ch. 9.

114 *Arundel Harington*, 78; *Blage*, fo. 70. Sessions, *Henry Howard*, pp. 223–7.

115 *Petrarch's Lyric Poems*, 140. For comparisons between Wyatt and Surrey's translations, see Hallett Smith, 'The Art of Sir Thomas Wyatt', *HLQ*, 4 (1946), pp. 333–7; Thomson, *Thomas Wyatt and His Background*, pp. 169–79.

116 *The Whole Works of Roger Ascham*, ed. Dr [J. A.] Giles, 3 vols. (1865), I(i), pp. 35–7. J. P. Carley, 'Blount, Charles, fifth Baron Mountjoy (1516–1544)', *ODNB*. Sessions, *Henry Howard*, pp. 182–3.

117 *Harley 78*, fos. 5–15v, 24r–v, 27–8, 29–30v.

118 *Harley 78*, fos. 18–23.

119 *Harley 282*, fos. 119, 243 (*CWTW*, i, letters 26, 32). 'Blount, Sir Richard (by 1506–64)', *House of Commons*, i, pp. 449–50. TNA, SP 1/245, fos. 108–9v (*LP, Addenda*, 1752); Robert White 'to his right worshipful mistress Mistress Elizabeth Darrell at Montacute this be dd [delivered]'. For Blount in John Legh's service, see TNA, PCC, Prob. 11/48, fos. 281–3v (will of John Legh, knight, 30 April 1563).

120 *House of Commons*, iii, p. 670; *LP*, xvii. 71(24), 1258, fo. 76b.

121 Cicero, *De officiis*, 3.1.1; Vickers, 'Leisure and idleness', p. 7.

122 *TM*, 270. P. Thomson, 'Wyatt's Boethian Ballade', *RES*, 15 (1964).

123 *Quyete of mynde*, sig. C1r.

124 The portraits of Wyatt in Roman pose, after Holbein, are illustrated in R. Strong, 'Holbein's Thomas Wyatt the Younger', *Apollo* (March 2006), pp. 48–56. S. Foister, 'Sixteenth-Century English Portraiture and the Idea of the Classical' in *Albion's Classicism*, ed. L. Gent (New Haven and London, 1995), pp. 163–80.

125 Leland, *Naeniae* (*L&L*, p. 261).

126 *An excellent Epitaffe of Syr Thomas Wyat* (1542).

127 Ps. 102.36.

128 *L&L*, pp. 216–17.

129 J. Hutchins, *The History and Antiquities of the County of Dorset*, 3rd edn., 4 vols. (1861–70), iv, p. 256.

130 This emblem of the rider upon a galloping white horse, which may have been painted by Holbein, has been associated – somewhat tangentially – with Wyatt, partly because of the quasi-Petrarchan inscription, '*E cosi desio me mena* [and so desire leads me]': B. B. Fredericksen, 'E Cosi Desio me mena', *The J. Paul Getty Museum Journal*, 10 (1982), pp. 21–38. *Holbein in England*, ed. S. Foister (2006), 61.

Picture Sources

196 *Map of Westminster and the Court at Whitehall* from the 'Agas' map of London, *c.*1561 © Guildhall Library, City of London

246 *John Poyntz* (coloured chalks with pen and ink on paper) by Hans Holbein the younger (1497/8–1543). The Royal Collection © Her Majesty Queen Elizabeth II/The Bridgeman Art Library

275 *The Bell Tower of the Tower of London.* Detail from 'Agas' map of London, *c.*1561, sheet 10, showing London Bridge, the River Thames and the Tower of London © Guildhall Library, City of London

352 'Off Cartage he' © The British Library Board, Egerton MS 2711, fo. 54v

359 'Madame withouten many wordes' © The British Library Board, Egerton MS 2711, fo. 24v

421 *Auto-da-fé in Valladolid, 1559. Hispanische Inquisition* (engraving). German School. Bibliothèque Nationale, Paris/Giraudon/The Bridgeman Art Library

452 Psalm 51, *Miserere mei domine* © The British Library Board, Egerton MS 2711, fo. 93

523 Wyatt's new mansion at the Crossed Friars. Detail from 'Agas' map of London, *c.*1561, sheet 10, showing London Bridge, the River Thames and the Tower of London © Guildhall Library, City of London

539 Wyatt's *Defence* © The British Library Board, Harley MS 78, fo. 13v

556 *An Allegory of Passion, c.*1532–6 (oil on panel; unframed: 45.4 x 45.4 cm), attributed to Hans Holbein the younger or Circle of Giulio Romano (Giulio Pippi). The J. Paul Getty Museum, Los Angeles

Colour plate sections

I

1 *Thomas Wyatt, c.*1535–7 (coloured chalks with pen and ink on paper) by Hans Holbein the younger (1497/8–1543). The Royal Collection © 2011 Her Majesty Queen Elizabeth II/The Bridgeman Art Library

2 *Katherine of Aragon* (1485–1536) (oil on panel), English School (sixteenth century). Private collection/Photo © Philip Mould, Ltd, London/The Bridgeman Art Library

3 *Anne Boleyn,* 1534 (oil on panel), English School (sixteenth century). Hever Castle, Kent/The Bridgeman Art Library

4 *Sir Henry Wyatt* (*c.*1460–1537) by Hans Holbein the younger (1497/8–1543). Musée du Louvre, Paris/Giraudon/The Bridgeman Art Library

5 Sir Henry Wyatt's jousting standard. College of Arms, MS I. 2, p. 95

6 *Francis I of France* (1494–1547) (oil on oak panel), by François Clouet (*c.*1510–72) (and workshop). Upton House, Warwickshire/NTPL/Upton House (Bearsted Collection)/Angelo Hornak/The Bridgeman Art Library

7 *Charles V (*1500–1558*), Holy Roman Emperor, with his dog,* 1533 (oil on canvas) by Titian (Tiziano Vecellio) (*c.*1488–1576) Prado, Madrid/Giraudon/The Bridgeman Art Library

8 *Andrea Doria* (1468–1560) (oil on panel) by Sebastiano del Piombo (S. Luciani) (*c.*1485–1547). Galleria Doria Pamphilj, Rome/Giraudon/The Bridgeman Art Library

9 *Alfonso I d'Este* (1486–1534) by Dosso Dossi (*c.*1479–1542), Galleria e Museo
   Estense, Modena /The Bridgeman Art Library

10 '*Noli me tangere*' (oil on panel) by Hans Holbein the younger (1497/8–1543). The
   Royal Collection © 2011 Her Majesty Queen Elizabeth II/The Bridgeman Art
   Library

11 *The Tribute Money* (oil on panel) by Titian (Tiziano Vecellio) (*c.*1488–1576)
   Gemäldegalerie Alte Meister, Dresden/© Staatliche Kunstsammlungen Dresden/
   The Bridgeman Art Library

12 *A plan of the harbour and road of Calais*, drawn *c.*1535–40 © The British Library
   Board, Cotton MS Augustus I.ii. 70

13 *Thomas Cromwell*, by Hans Holbein the younger (oak panel), © The Frick
   Collection, New York

14 *Thomas Wriothesley*, *c.*1535, by Hans Holbein the younger. New York,
   Metropolitan Museum of Art. Vellum laid on card. Irregular, cut down, 1 1/8
   x 1 in (28 x 25 mm). The Metropolitan Museum of Art, Rogers Fund, 1925
   (25.205) © 2011. Image copyright The Metropolitan Museum of Art/Art
   Resource/Scala, Florence

II

15 *Pope Paul III (1468–1549) with Alessandro and Ottavio Farnese*, 1545 (oil on canvas)
   by Titian (Tiziano Vecellio) (*c.*1488–1576). Museo e Gallerie Nazionali di
   Capodimonte, Naples/The Bridgeman Art Library

16 *Nicolas Perrenot de Granvelle*, 1548 (oil on canvas) by Titian (Tiziano Vecellio)
   (*c.*1488–1576). Musée du Temps, Besançon/Giraudon/The Bridgeman Art
   Library

17 *Diego Hurtado de Mendoza* (1503–75) by Titian (Tiziano Vecellio) (*c.*1488–1576).
   Palazzo Pitti, Florence/The Bridgeman Art Library

18 *Reginald, Cardinal Pole* (oil on canvas) by Sebastiano del Piombo (S. Luciani)
   (*c.*1485–1547). State Hermitage Museum, St Petersburg/The Bridgeman Art
   Library

19 *Cardinal Juan de Tavera* (oil on canvas) by El Greco (Domenico Theotocopuli)
   (1541–1614). Hospital Tavera, Toledo/The Bridgeman Art Library

20 *Bernardo Tasso* by unknown artist. By kind permission of the Museo dei Tasso e
   della Storia Postale, Camerata Cornello, Italia

21 *Guidobaldo II della Rovere, Duke of Urbino* by Agnolo Bronzino (1503–72). Palazzo
   Pitti, Florence/The Bridgeman Art Library

22 *The Game of Canes, 1539*, by Jan Cornelisz Vermeyen. Private collection.
   Photographic survey, The Courtauld Institute of Art, London

23 *Uriah the Hittite sent to his death*. Tapestry of David and Bathsheba, *c.*1510–15, by
   Flemish School. Musée Nationale de la Renaissance, Ecouen /Peter Willi/The
   Bridgeman Art Library

24 *The Solemn Entrance of Emperor Charles V, Francis I and Cardinal Alessandro Farnese into
   Paris in 1540*, from the 'Sala dei Fasti Farnese', 1557–66 (fresco) by Taddeo
   Zuccaro (1529–66). Villa Farnese, Caprarola/The Bridgeman Art Library

25 *Sir Thomas Wyatt* (*c*.1521–54) by unknown artist © National Portrait Gallery, London

26 *Sir Thomas Wyatt*, *c*.1540, after Hans Holbein the younger © National Portrait Gallery, London

Acknowledgements

Sometimes, pensive in a distant archive or gazing blankly at the wall of my study, I have imagined the mocking laughter of Thomas Wyatt and his friends had they known of my pursuit of them. Wyatt was, and remains, elusive. Coming, one diluvian afternoon, to the Upper Reading Room of the Bodleian, where Wyatt's portrait habitually hung, I discovered in its place plastic sheeting and a bucket; one of his many disappearances as I followed him. My first acknowledgement is to Wyatt himself, for his poetry and his company, and my hope is that I have not traduced him.

This book is my *summa*, but I could never have written it alone. It is a testament to the heroic help and scholarly generosity of many others, and of some in particular. On the first day of a Michaelmas Term – a day which tutors greet with excitement, and dread – I found a letter from someone then unknown to me asking whether I would be interested in his discovery in Florence of a document concerning Wyatt. Would I! The letter was from Jonathan Woolfson, and with his scholarship and his friendship this book began. Since neither of us decipher the document, we summoned the help of Neil McLynn, who did not fail us.

The great munificence of the Leverhulme Trust made this book possible. A Major Research Fellowship gave me the time and freedom to learn languages, to read in new disciplines, to travel. The Trust had reason to expect this work to be completed far sooner, but never pressed. These words and this book are insufficient thanks. I gratefully acknowledge the generosity of the Zilkha Trust of Lincoln College, Oxford, which also funded visits to archives. I record my deep gratitude to the Rector and Fellows of Lincoln College for their support and forbearance, and most of all to the historians, particularly to

Perry Gauci. The benevolence of students who tolerated and encouraged a distracted tutor and superviser has meant a lot.

I thank the following institutions for granting me the privilege of access to their archives and for allowing me to cite manuscripts from their collections: in Belgium, the Archives Générales du Royaume; in England, Christ's, Corpus Christi and Trinity Colleges and the University Library in Cambridge; Doncaster Archives; the Centre of Kentish Studies; the British Library; the College of Arms; London Metropolitan Archives; the National Archives; All Souls College and the Bodleian Library in Oxford; the Borthwick Institute of the University of York; in the Republic of Ireland, Trinity College, Dublin; in Italy, the Archivio di Stato in Florence, Mantua, Modena and Parma; in Spain, the Archivo Histórico Nacional in Madrid and the Archivo General in Simancas; in the United States of America, the Huntington Library in San Marino; and in the Vatican City, the Archivio Segreto and Biblioteca Apostolica. I am grateful to Sotheby's for allowing me to consult manuscripts consigned to them. I have received exemplary help and advice in all the archives and libraries I have visited. Malcolm Underwood of St John's College, Cambridge, revealed Wyatt's absence in the archives there. Isabel Sullivan of the Surrey History Centre and Heather Wolfe of the Folger Shakespeare Library kindly answered queries. My greatest debt is to my home libraries of Oxford – the Bodleian, the Taylorian, the History Faculty Library, and Lincoln College Library, and I particularly thank Fiona Piddock of Lincoln and the staff of the Upper Reading Room Reserve for quotidian kindness. I fondly remember Vera Ryhajlo.

Vilma de Gasperin and the late Clara Florio Cooper, *maestre carissime*, taught me Italian, and the beauties of its grammar. In Rome, Carlo, Giulio and Paolo Casali, Kim Wessling, Sabine Cassola and Sofia Quaroni listened to my Italian (a penance), shared the splendours and secrets of the city, and sang 'Ah, Robin' for me. Even with such perfect instruction, my language skills faltered. Nigel Wilson helped me unfailingly and very often with translations and puzzles. My old friends Tony Woodman and Richard King provided elegant translations from Latin. When I needed help on particular points Adrian Ailes, Gemma Allen, James Carley, Marco Dorigatti, Cecile Fabre, Susan Foister,

James Morwood, Gregory O'Malley, Claudia Nitschke, Edward Nye, Mia Rodriguez-Salgado, Pietro Roversi and Kat and Moussa Sagna very kindly came to my aid. Ioanna Tsakiropoulou photographed a crucial document. I thank Eric Ives for the long loan of microfilms from the Vienna archives, and Robert Knecht for sending me a copy of a scarce document. Tracey Sowerby and Kathryn Murphy generously sent references. David Grummitt and Gina Alexander lent copies of their doctoral theses.

Glyn Redworth initiated me to the mysteries of the great archive at Simancas and showed me the glories of Valladolid. I thank him, and Ben Hazard also. In Simancas, Ciaran O'Scea was my guide to the archives as we worked side by side. Without his help, I might have found nothing there. The search for Wyatt in the archive of the Inquisition in Madrid was all his, and his the discoveries. At the Vatican, I was fortunate to meet Anne Schutte in the Archivio Segreto and to be welcomed to the Biblioteca Apostolica by Timothy Janz.

I pay particular tribute to a constellation who know best the pleasures and pains of following Wyatt: Jason Powell, Chris Stamatakis and Nicola Shulman. Jason Powell's doctoral dissertation was my constant resource, and he read the manuscript of this book with scrupulous care. So did Chris Stamatakis, who has taught me much more than he knows. I thank him for his graceful advice and for making Lincoln's front quadrangle a centre of Wyatt studies. Nicola Shulman offered fortifying friendship, encouragement and commiseration when most needed.

Claire Preston's friendship has sustained me. She saved this book from being a confection of maybes and perhapses, and persuaded me to write about Wyatt's poetry when I quailed. She read the first draft of a manuscript at which I could only squint between my fingers. I am immensely grateful to other friends who read all or part of the manuscript at various stages, and offered valuable criticism and encouragement: Alexandra Gajda, Steven Gunn, Anne Overell, Sandy Sullivan, Robert Wainwright and Blair Worden. Henry Woudhuysen, editing's master, advised me on editorial matters. I thank Roy Foster for telling me of Madame Blavatsky's attachment to Wyatt, and for enlivening conversations along the way.

During my peregrinations, Richard and Vivian King and Catriona Stewart and John Fairley offered sanctuary. Staying with Alan and Mary Gibbins in West Malling, I saw from my window the Abbey which Wyatt claimed. I thank the Earl and Countess of Romney for showing me the paintings which passed down in Wyatt's family, and for generously allowing me to include here the picture of the Papal minotaur. Sir Robert and Lady Worcester kindly entertained me at Allington Castle, Wyatt's home.

My quest for illustrations was aided by the Museo dei Tasso e della Storia Postale in Camerata Cornello, Italy, and by C.L. Stopford Sackville, Charlotte Heyman of the Bridgeman Art Library, Jeremy Smith of London Metropolitan Archive and Jacklyn Burns of the J. Paul Getty Museum.

I owe special thanks to Mike White and Pete Good who cheerfully tolerated my incompetence and saved my manuscript from disappearing into some black hole in cyber space.

Thanks to Catherine Clarke for all her support, and not least for sending this book to Faber and Faber. At this famous publisher of poetry, Wyatt finds a natural home. Paul Keegan, a legendary editor, gave me freedom to write unconstrained, and offered illuminating criticism. I am grateful, too, to Anne Owen for master-minding the production of this book, and for finding me a copy-editor who loves Wyatt's poetry. Eleanor Rees was a wonder, and I thank her for her great sensitivity to this text and its flagging author. Kate Ward's care and vision have made this book more beautiful than I could have imagined.

Despite such great help and from such brilliant quarters, there will be errors enough: all mine, and I apologise for them.

The constant support of my brothers has sustained me. To them I dedicate this book, with love. Lastly, I thank my husband, Jeremy Wormell, with all my heart.

Susan Brigden
Lincoln College, Oxford
March 2012

Index